# THE CASE AGAINST
# THE GLOBAL ECONOMY

# The Case Against the Global Economy

## And for a Turn Toward the Local

EDITED BY

## Jerry Mander
### AND
## Edward Goldsmith

Sierra Club Books ⌇ San Francisco

LIBRARY OF CONGRESS CATALOGING-IN-PUBLICATION DATA

The case against the global economy : and for a turn toward the local / edited by Jerry Mander and Edward Goldsmith.
    p.       cm.
    Includes bibliographical references index.
    ISBN 0-87156-352-5 (cloth : alk. paper)
    1. Economic development — Environmental aspects.   2. Environmental policy — International cooperation.   3. Sustainable development.   4. Environmental economics.   I. Mander, Jerry.
II. Goldsmith, Edward, 1928–   .
HD75.6.c376   1996
363.7 — dc20                                96–20149

Production by Robin Rockey
Cover design by Amy Evans
Book design by David Peattie

# CONTENTS

# ACKNOWLEDGMENTS

We would like to thank several people who have been critically important to this project. Barbara Ras of Sierra Club Books suggested the book in the first place and has been generous with her patience, positive outlook, and useful suggestions. Important editorial advice, ideas, criticism, and some significant rewriting was performed at key stages by Kai Mander and Ernest Callenbach, while Marcella Friel did her normal exemplary high-speed turn on the copyedit. Thanks too to Victor Menotti and our many brilliant colleagues at the International Forum on Globalization, only a few of whose writings could be fit into these pages, unfortunately. Finally, for their exquisitely performed management of the many complex details of this project—from communications to article research, to editorial ideas, to manuscript production—and for their invariable good cheer throughout, we warmly thank Rita Kassai in London and Stephanie Welch in San Francisco.

# NOTES TO THE READER

The chapters compiled for this book were selected by the editors only. As with most anthologies, the chapters offer a wide range of styles and subjects, of different geographical regions, of perspectives from the personal to the technical, and of some partly divergent opinions on a number of issues. We point this out so the reader will understand that none of the individual chapter authors can be held responsible for the ideas expressed by any of the other authors or, for that matter, by the editors. Of course, we assume there exists a fair amount of agreement on most matters among these authors, but if some dissatisfaction is felt, only the editors are to blame. Thank you.

• • •

Each author is profiled briefly at the beginning of his or her article. The editors' biographies are at the end of the book.

• • •

We are not using footnotes in this book. However, the reader will find that most references made to articles, books, or other source materials are listed in the References section or in the Bibliography at the back of the book, which also includes other relevant books and articles. There is also a list of organizations doing effective work on these topics.

March 6, 1996

*Jerry Mander*
SAN FRANCISCO

*Edward Goldsmith*
RICHMOND, ENGLAND

# INTRODUCTION

# I

# FACING THE RISING TIDE

## Jerry Mander

The first goal of this book is to help clarify the form of what is being called the *global economy* and to show how the rush toward globalization is likely to affect our lives. The second goal is to suggest that the process must be brought to a halt as soon as possible, and reversed.

• • •

Economic globalization involves arguably the most fundamental re-design of the planet's political and economic arrangements since at least the Industrial Revolution. Yet the profound implications of these funda-mental changes have barely been exposed to serious public scrutiny or debate. Despite the scale of the global reordering, neither our elected offi-cials nor our educational institutions nor the mass media have made a credible effort to describe what is being formulated or to explain its root philosophies.

The occasional descriptions or predictions about the global economy that *are* found in the media usually come from the leading advocates and beneficiaries of this new order: corporate leaders, their allies in govern-ment, and a newly powerful centralized global trade bureaucracy. The vi-sions they offer us are unfailingly positive, even utopian: Globalization will be a panacea for our ills.

Shockingly enough, the euphoria they express is based on their free-dom to deploy, at a global level — through the new global free trade rules, and through deregulation and economic restructuring regimes — large-scale versions of the economic theories, strategies, and policies that have proven spectacularly unsuccessful over the past several decades wherever they've been applied. In fact, these are the very ideas that have brought us to the grim situation of the moment: the spreading disintegration of the social order and the increase of poverty, landlessness, homelessness, violence, alienation, and, deep within the hearts of many people, extreme anxiety about the future. Equally important, these are the practices that have led us to the near breakdown of the natural world, as evidenced by such symptoms as global climate change, ozone depletion, massive species loss, and near maximum levels of air, soil, and water pollution.

We are now being asked to believe that the development processes that have further impoverished people and devastated the planet will lead to diametrically different and highly beneficial outcomes, if only they can be accelerated and applied everywhere, freely, without restriction; that is, when they are *globalized*.

That's the bad news. The good news is that it is not too late to stop this from happening.

# THE "RISING TIDE"

The recent passage of the Uruguay Round of GATT (the General Agreement on Tariffs and Trade) with its associated WTO (World Trade Organization), was celebrated by the world's political leadership and transnational corporations as a sort of global messianic rebirth. They claim that these new arrangements will bring on a global economic order that can produce a $250 billion expansion of world economic activity in a very short time, with the benefits "trickling down" to us all. The dominant political-economic homily is "the new rising tide will lift all boats."

Indeed, the global economy is new, but less so in form than in scale: the new global rules by which it now operates; the technologically enhanced speedup of global development and commerce that it facilitates; and the abrupt shift in global political power that it introduces. Surely it is also new that the world's democratic countries voted to suppress their own democratically enacted laws in order to conform to the rules of the new central global bureaucracy, as Ralph Nader and Lori Wallach describe in their chapter in this book. Also new is the elimination of most regulatory control over global corporate activity and the liberation of currency from national controls, which lead in turn to what Richard Barnet and John Cavanagh describe as the *casino economy*, ruled by currency speculators.

But the deep ideological principles underlying the global economy are not so new; they are the very principles that have brought us to the social, economic, and environmental impasse we are in. They include the primacy of economic growth; the need for free trade to stimulate the growth;

the unrestricted "free market"; the absence of government regulation; and voracious consumerism combined with an aggressive advocacy of a uniform worldwide development model that faithfully reflects the Western corporate vision and serves corporate interests. The principles also include the idea that all countries — even those whose cultures have been as diverse as, say, Indonesia, Japan, Kenya, Sweden, and Brazil — must sign on to the same global economic model and row their (rising) boats in unison. The net result is *monoculture* — the global homogenization of culture, lifestyle, and level of technological immersion, with the corresponding dismantlement of local traditions and economies. Soon, everyplace will look and feel like everyplace else, with the same restaurants and hotels, the same clothes, the same malls and superstores, and the same streets crowded with cars. There'll be scarcely a reason ever to leave home.

•  •  •

Many elements of this formula have been at work for a long while, with devastating effect, as several of the chapter authors report. And my coeditor, Edward Goldsmith, argues that all of these ideological principles amount to little more than rationalizations for a new kind of corporate colonialism, visited upon poor countries and the poor in rich countries.

But does this system work? Will the promised economic expansion of GATT actually happen? If so, can it sustain itself? Where will the resources — the energy, the wood, the minerals, the water — come from to feed the increased growth? Where will the effluents of the process — the solids and the toxics — be dumped? Who benefits from this? Who will benefit most? Will it be working people who, in the United States at least, seem mainly to be losing jobs to machines and corporate flight? Will it be farmers who, thus far, whether in Asia, Africa, or North America, are being maneuvered off their lands to make way for huge corporate monocultural farming — no longer producing diverse food products for local consumption but coffee and beef for export markets with their declining prices? Will it be city dwellers, now faced with the immigrant waves of newly landless peoples desperate to find, someplace, the rare and poorly paid job? And what of the ecological results? Can ever-increasing consumption be sustained forever? When will the forests be gone? How many cars can be built and bought? How many roads can cover the land? What will become of the animals and the birds — does anyone care about that? Is life better from this? Is all the destruction worth the result? Are we, as individuals, as families, and as communities and nations, made more secure, less anxious, more in control of our destinies? Can we possibly benefit from a system that destroys local and regional governments while handing real power to faceless corporate bureaucracies in Geneva, Tokyo, and Brussels? Will people's needs be better served from this? Is it a good idea or a bad one? Do we want it? If not, how do we reverse the process?

The German economic philosopher Wolfgang Sachs argues in his book *The Development Dictionary* that the only thing worse than the failure of this massive global development experiment would be its success. For even at its optimum performance level, the long-term benefits go only to a tiny minority of people who sit at the hub of the process and to a slightly larger minority that can retain an economic connection to it, while the rest of humanity is left groping for fewer jobs and less land, living in violent societies on a ravaged planet. The only boats that will be lifted are those of the owners and managers of the process; the rest of us will be on the beach, facing the rising tide.

## THE FAILURE OF THE MEDIA

The authors who contributed to this book comment on all the issues raised above: the effects of globalism (Part One), the theories underlying it (Part Two), and the "engines" that drive it (Part Three). In Part Four, they explore alternatives. But it's worth mentioning first of all that it's a failure of our media that a book such as this is even necessary. Our society has been massively launched onto a path to we-know-not-where, and the people who are supposed to shed light on events that affect us have neglected to do so.

From time to time, the mass media do report on some major problem of globalization, but the reporting rarely conveys the connections between the specific crises they describe and the root causes in globalization itself. In the area of environment, for example, we read of changes in global climate and occasionally of their long-term consequences, such as the melting polar ice caps (the *real* rising tide), the expected staggering impacts to agriculture and food supply, or the destruction of habitat. We read too of the ozone layer depletion, the pollution of the oceans, or the wars over resources such as oil and, perhaps soon, water. But few of these matters are linked directly to the imperatives of global economic expansion, the increase of global transport, the overuse of raw materials, or the commodity-intensive life-style that corporations are selling worldwide via the culturally homogenizing technology of television and its parent, advertising. Obfuscation is the net result.

I personally have had some harsh direct experience of this obfuscation.

While working with Public Media Center in the runup to the vote on GATT, my colleagues and I were preparing educational ads about GATT's environmental consequences, particularly its "sabotaging" effect on existing major environmental laws. We collaborated on the project with twenty-five environmental groups who signed the ad, among them the Sierra Club, Public Citizen, Friends of the Earth, and Rainforest Action Network. The groups felt the campaign was important precisely because the media had carried so few stories about environmental opposition to GATT. Instead, news stories tended to lump all opponents together under the single dismissive label of *protectionist*.

One week after our first ad finally appeared in the *New York Times,* a report in *Newsweek* magazine advised its readers that the advertisement was not really from the environmental community at all; it was secretly funded by labor union "protectionists." In outrage, Public Media Center's executive director, Herb Chao Gunther, immediately responded to *Newsweek* and finally got the magazine to run a small corrective notice. But the damage was done. A good opportunity to broaden the public's thinking about economic globalization was undermined.

Other examples of media misunderstanding include the coverage of the Barings Bank debacle of 1995 and the Mexican financial crisis of 1994-95. Rarely has any medium made clear the role that the new global computer networks play in creating the capability for *instantaneous* transfer anywhere on the planet of astounding amounts of money; nor do the media describe the consequences of deregulating financial speculation or the role that the World Bank and the International Monetary Fund (IMF) play in creating the conditions that encouraged such speculation. The Mexican story was carried in the U.S. press as if the United States' "bailout of Mexico" was some kind of do-gooder act on our part; good neighbors coming to the aid of our Mexican friends. In fact, the main people bailed out, as Carlos Heredia and Mary Purcell describe in their chapter, were Wall Street investors who, with the direct complicity of the World Bank and the IMF, largely brought on the crisis in the first place. For middle-class and working-class Mexicans, the bailout was devastating, and that story has yet to be told by the mass media.

For a brief time in early 1996, the media did carry extensive stories about Republican Pat Buchanan and his charge that free trade leads to loss of American jobs. While so reporting, however, most media characterized *all* opposition to free trade as being virtually in a category with belief in a flat earth. And just as the tens of thousands of environmentalists who oppose GATT were dismissed as "protectionists," to be ignored, the press also ignored the important fact that opposition to globalization cuts across all parties, including human rights advocates, small farmers, small businesspeople, advocates of democracy (Nader, et al.) as well as labor and many other categories of people who believe in an equitable, environmentally sustainable society, and who usually occupy a spot on the political spectrum at a great distance from Buchanan's.

Some publications did follow-on stories about "corporate greed" as expressed by the firing of thousands of workers while corporate profits soared and top executive salaries were being raised to unheard levels. Even these stories, however, rarely mentioned the crucial point that the new corporate restructuring is directly hooked to the imperatives of globalization, and that it is happening all over the world. Obfuscation yet again.

In the fall of 1995, the international press carried reports on the paralyzing strike by hundreds of thousands of French railway and other public service workers. Most reports characterized the workers as trying to protect their privileges, benefits, and jobs against government cutbacks. True enough. But the stories left out that the cutbacks were mandated by the rules of Europe's Maastricht "single currency" agreement, itself part of the corporatizing, homogenizing, and globalizing of Europe's economic system to make it compatible and competitive globally.

The media also report daily about the immigration crises, about masses of people trying to cross borders in search of jobs, only to be greeted by xenophobia, violence, and demagoguery in high places. But the role that international trade agreements play in making life impossible for people in their countries of origin is not visible in such reports. The North American Free Trade Agreement (NAFTA), for example, was a virtual knockout blow to the largely self-sufficient, small, corn-farming economy of Mexico's indigenous peoples — as the Zapatista rebels tried to illuminate in 1994 — making indigenous lands vulnerable to corporate buyouts and foreign competition from the United States. Meanwhile, in India, Africa, and South America, similar World Bank development schemes over the past few decades have deliberately displaced whole populations of relatively prosperous peoples, including small-scale self-sufficient farmers, to make way for giant dams and other megadevelopment schemes. The result of such "development" is that millions of small farmers are turned into landless refugees seeking nonexistent urban jobs.

Now and then we see media reports on food shortages, yet rarely is the connection drawn between hunger and the increased control of the world's food supply by a small number of giant (subsidized) corporations, notably Cargill, which effectively determines where food will grow, under which conditions it will grow, and what ultimate price consumers will pay. The food, rather than being eaten by local people who grow it, is now typically shipped thousands of miles (at great environmental cost) to be eaten by the already well fed. Karen Lehman and Al Krebs offer some background on that in their chapter.

Horrible new disease outbreaks are very thoroughly reported with ghoulish relish in the Western press. The part that is omitted, however, is the connection between these outbreaks and the destruction of rain forest and other habitats. As economic expansionism proceeds, previously un-contacted organisms hitch rides on new vectors for new territory, as is ex-plained in the chapter from the Harvard Working Group on New and Resurgent Diseases.

We also read stories about the "last indigenous tribes" in the Amazon, Borneo, Africa, or the Philippines; stories that lament the inevitability that native people, even against their clearly articulated wishes, even against the resistance of arrows and spears, must be drawn into the West-ern economic model to benefit from our development plans. Insufficiently reported are the root causes of this: the demands of economic growth for more water or forest resources; the desperate need for new lands for beef cattle, coffee, or timber plantations; the equally desperate need to convert previously self-sufficient peoples into consumer clones. This is not to men-tion the far deeper need to destroy the "other" for the psychological threat they represent and for their example of viability in an entirely alternative context. *Manifest Destiny*, modernized. These too are part of the globaliza-tion project, the homogenization of conceptual framework, the monocul-turization of peoples and lands, which Helena Norberg-Hodge so artfully describes in the case of Ladakh. The point is further amplified by Martin Khor's eloquent recitation of the effects of economic globalization in the Third World and in the industrial world; and by Maude Barlow and Heather-jane Robertson, who describe the Americanization of Canada's educational system.

As for the role of technology, the powers that be continue to speak of each new generation of technological innovation in the same utopian terms they used to describe each preceding generation, going back to the private automobile, plastics, and "clean nuclear energy," each introduced as panaceas for society. Now we have global computer networks that are said to "empower" communities and individuals, when the exact opposite is the case. The global computer-satellite linkup, besides offering a spec-tacular new tool for financial speculation, empowers the global corpora-tion's ability to keep its thousand-armed global enterprise in constant touch, making instantaneous adjustments at the striking of a key. As we will see later, computer technology may actually be the most centralizing technology ever invented, at least in terms of economic and political power. This much is certain: The global corporation of today could not exist without computers. The technology makes globalization possible by conferring a degree of control beyond anything ever seen before.

Meanwhile, new technologies such as biotechnology bring the development framework to entirely new terrain by enabling the enclosure and commercialization of the internal wilderness of the gene structure, the building blocks of life itself. The invention and patenting of new life forms, from cells to insects to animals to humans, will have profound effects on Third World agriculture, ecology, and human rights as Vandana Shiva and Radha Holla-Bhar and Andrew Kimbrell variously illuminate in Part One.

As for reportage about the corporate conglomerates and transnationals that have become the centers of global power, the determinants of political process, and the unifiers of global consciousness, the media tend to treat corporate figures mainly as subjects of gossip, like glamorous movie stars, athletes, or politicians. *Vanity Fair* and the *New Yorker* take us to their mansions and poolside phones and tell us the real "inside scoop" about their megadeals and mergers, while the *Wall Street Journal* and the *New York Times* speak respectfully in the new language of consolidation — structural engineering, downsizing, and efficiency — without attempting to present such activities within their wider economic, social, and ecological context. In his chapter, Jeremy Rifkin points out that such terminology as presently used to describe corporate activity is euphemistic. *Efficiency* means replacing workers with machines; *competitiveness* means lowering wages to match low-wage foreign competitors; *flattening of the corporate structure* means eliminating middle managers' jobs and effectively spreading well-justified social anxiety from the inner cities to the heart of the suburbs.

The point is this: All of the subjects are treated by the media, government officials, and corporations alike as if they were totally unrelated. This is not helpful to an insecure public that is attempting to grasp what's happening and what might be done about it. The media do not help us to understand that each of these issues — overcrowded cities, unusual new weather patterns, the growth of global poverty, the lowering of wages while stock prices soar, the elimination of local social services, the destruction of wilderness, even the disappearance of songbirds — are the products of the same global policies. They are all of one piece, a fabric of connections that are ecological, social, and political in nature. They are reactions to the world's economic-political restructuring in the name of accelerated global development. This restructuring has been designed by economists and corporations and encouraged by subservient governments; soon it will be made mandatory by international bureaucrats, who are beyond democratic control. All claim that society will benefit from what they are doing. But we don't think so.

· · ·

We are trained to believe that our economic system operates on a rational basis in our behalf and that the people in charge have benevolent motives and know what they are doing. I have doubted that for a while, and on this point the newspapers, inadvertently perhaps, do expose the conflicting realities that come at us like Orwellian econometric doublespeak.

One basic thing is certain. During the past few decades, the gap between rich and poor just about everywhere has been increasing rather than decreasing. A *New York Times* report on April 17, 1995, explained that the period of the United States' most rapid economic growth (the 1960s to the 1990s), which also ushered in the period of rapid corporate and economic deregulation and the most aggressive promotion of "free" trade, also saw a widening gap between rich and poor.

The *Times* quotes the Federal Reserve: "Figures from 1989, the most recent available, show that the wealthiest 1 percent of the U.S. households — with net worth of at least $2.3 million each, own nearly 40 percent of the nation's wealth. Further down the scale, the top 20 percent of Americans — households worth $180,000 or more — have more than 80 percent of the country's wealth, a higher figure than in other industrial nations. Income statistics are similarly skewed."

If this is a rational process, it rationalizes a staggering inequality of benefit. To make matters worse for most people, social services for the poor and the middle class have been assaulted as never before under the same ideological banner of "free market" and "free trade," which produced the skewed figures just mentioned. This dismantling of services within the United States amounts to an internal *structural adjustment* comparable to the infamous World Bank structural adjustment programs that have been imposed on Third World countries ever since the 1980s debt crisis and have produced horrifying social and ecological results. Walden Bello tells us more about those in his chapter. In addition, Alexander Goldsmith points out that the whole world is now being redesigned into a single "free trade zone." England is already advertising globally how its wage levels are decreasing in an effort to encourage foreign investors. The elimination of tariffs, minimum wage laws, and local social services are all symptoms of the same scheme. The goal everywhere is the same: free all economic resources to serve the needs of corporations, not people or the environment.

## FLAWED PARADIGMS

All these problems must be seen as *systemic*. In Part Two of the book and elsewhere (as the subject percolates through every article), we will see that many of the principal paradigms by which this system explains its choices and its behavior are fatally flawed. David Korten summarizes each one briefly, giving us the big picture. Then others take them up in detail. Herman Daly's and Robert Goodland's articles clearly demonstrate the preposterousness of the very idea that, on a finite earth, an economic system based on limitless growth can be supported. A system that feeds on itself cannot keep eating forever.

As for free trade, David Morris and, again, Herman Daly show how the only thing "free" about it is the freedom it provides corporate players to deprive everyone else of their freedoms, including the freedom hitherto enjoyed by democratic nations to protect their domestic economies, their communities, their culture, and their natural environment. The ideology of development itself must also be re-examined. As Wolfgang Sachs argues, development is often the cause of rather than the solution to our problems. And James Goldsmith, at one time one of the world's leading financiers and for most of his life a beneficiary of global economic development, writes about the inevitability that only the transnational corporations and the already super-rich will gain from globalization. Meanwhile, its costs must inevitably be paid by the environment and by the poor — small farmers and workers whose livelihoods depend on the local economies that are being destroyed. But in the end, Goldsmith says, the growth is obviously temporary and unsustainable. Even for the biggest "winners," it will be like "winning at poker on the Titanic."

• • •

Economic philosopher and Greenpeace activist Susan George, together with Fabrizio Sabelli, in their recent book *Faith and Credit* (1994), have argued against the idea popular in some circles that a global conspiracy is at the root of the disastrous direction of global economic policy. At least insofar as concerns the pathetic performance of global institutions such as the World Bank and the International Monetary Fund, George and

Sabelli put the blame more on incompetence, ideology, and a virtually religious belief in the dogmas of Western development. Like religious zealots, as each new development project fails to achieve its highly advertised benefits and causes social and environmental chaos, the global economists simply move on to preparing the ground for yet another disaster, applying the same sad formulas. In their book, George and Sabelli catalog the World Bank's predictions against a performance that has left poor people poorer and destroyed traditional, viable economic arrangements in the name of a fictional development utopia.

Of course we are left to wonder how any bona fide economist, even if trained personally by Milton Friedman, even if blinded by economic zealotry, could believe that benefits would come from the World Bank's Structural Adjustment Program loans (SAPs). These loans are granted only to countries that agree to dismantle their economic and social structures and redesign them according to an imposed free market/free trade ideology.

Walden Bello reports in his chapter on some of the conditions that countries typically have to accept: (1) the removal of protective tariffs, which directly endangers local industry; (2) the removal of rules controlling foreign investment, which ushers in the foreign domination of local industry; (3) the conversion of self-sufficient, small-scale diverse agriculture to corporate export-oriented monocultures, which make it more difficult for local populations to eat; (4) the elimination of price controls but the imposition of wage controls; (5) the drastic reduction in social and health services; (6) the aggressive privatization of government agencies, which renders social services inaccessible to the poor; and (7) the ending of popular "import substitution" programs that encouraged local people toward diverse local production and self-sufficiency.

Ordinary logic suggests that such formulas would only cripple a country's ability to survive, and indeed that has been the result. Countries that accepted these interventions and have now also accepted entry into the WTO (which has similar rules) have seen their own economies crumble and have watched as foreign transnational corporations take dominion over both their economies and their politics.

Why did these countries accept? In many cases, it was less faith than force.

The roots of the trend go back to the infamous Bretton Woods Conference after World War II, as David C. Korten points out in the chapter that follows this one. But a more recent key moment came in 1968, when Robert McNamara became president of the World Bank. Flush from his horrendous performance running the Vietnam War and (according to his own apologetic book, *In Retrospect: The Tragedy and Lessons of Vietnam* [1995]) apparently not feeling so good about himself, McNamara decided he could save his soul by saving the poor via the World Bank. He approached this task with the economist-manager's quantified viewpoint — which doesn't inquire into the people being saved — and the true believer's arrogance. "To this day," he wrote in his book, "I see quantification as a language to add precision to reasoning about the world. I have always believed that the more important the issue the fewer people should be involved in the decision." Confident of his numbers, McNamara pressed Third World countries to accept World Bank conditionalities for loans and to transform their traditional economies to maximize economic specialization and global trade. Countries that did not sign on to the globalization program would be left behind.

McNamara pushed hard, and most countries felt they had little choice but to sign on. No longer "destroying villages to save them," McNamara was destroying whole economies. Today, the countries that went along with him are saddled with silted-up megadams, useless crumbling roads to nowhere, empty high-rise office buildings, ravaged forests and fields, and the overwhelming, unpayable debt to Western bankers that makes up much of the legacy of World Bank policy from McNamara to now. Whatever harms this man caused in Vietnam, he did more during his tenure at the World Bank. Perhaps soon we will see him apologize for that role, as well.

## MECHANISMS OF SELF-DELUSION

In a *London Times* article (Mar. 5, 1994), James Goldsmith is quoted as saying, "What an astounding thing it is to watch a civilization destroy itself because it is unable to re-examine the validity, under totally new circumstances, of an economic ideology." Perhaps it is simply that economists, like other true believers, cannot see outside the framework of their own thinking. This much, at least, is definite: Economists have devised the perfect measurements for gauging their own success and confirming their self-delusions.

Most important among these self-serving illusory measurements are the primary tools now used to judge economic progress: the Gross National Product (GNP) or Gross Domestic Product (GDP). These measure total economic activity — that is, every monetary transaction within a nation-state. By this standard, more economic activity means a healthier economy.

In Part Two, Ted Halstead and Clifford Cobb brilliantly dismantle both GNP and GDP, clearly showing how such negative events as, say, the depletion of natural resources, the construction of more prisons, and the manufacture of bombs are all measures of "health" by current economic theories. Meanwhile, other incomparably more desirable activities, such as unpaid household work, child care, community service, or the production of food to be eaten and artifacts to be used rather than sold via the formal economy are, absurdly, not registered in the statistics at all. They are simply not regarded as indicators of economic health.

To illustrate the point, Edward Goldsmith likes to tell the apocryphal story of two friends who each inherit 10,000-acre tracts of adjoining forestland. Friend Number One decides to do nothing with the forest, leaving it in its pristine state. Friend Number Two sells the trees to McMillan Bloedel Corporation, which cuts them down. He then sells the topsoil and the subsurface mining rights for minerals and coal. When that activity is exhausted, he permits the holes to be filled with low-level toxic waste from a computer chip manufacturer and paves over the place. After that he constructs an industrial complex with a megamall and theme park, multiplex theaters, indoor swimming pools, and wave machines.

Friend Number One is considered odd by the community for permitting such an economic opportunity to go to waste in behalf of trees and birds. He is called idealistic and impractical.

Friend Number Two is considered a pillar of the community for developing the land, employing people, and adding to the GNP. Exceedingly wealthy by now, he puts his millions into high-tech equipment manufacture on the Mexican border and runs for public office. His slogan: "The rising tide will lift all boats." He is elected senator and votes for NAFTA and GATT.

The moral of the tale is clear: In the dominant view, GNP is all that matters. Development is the way. People who act to save nature are mistrusted and marginalized. Such behavior is not beneficial by current economic standards.

Ted Halstead and Clifford Cobb propose an answer for this in their chapter. They have devised a new set of measurements called the Genuine Progress Indicator (GPI), which pulls in all of the social and environmental dimensions of economic activity that are left out of GNP measurements and gives real value to previously unvalued activity that benefits households, community, and the natural world.

· · ·

Whether by conspiratorial design, dogged incompetence, or ideological zealotry, economic globalization obviously brings benefit to certain institutions. Tony Clarke identifies them in the first chapter of Part Three. The unprecedented scale of global corporations and the degree to which they can now consolidate their economic power is instantly apparent in Clarke's opening sentences. He writes that, including the economies of all the nation-states, "forty-seven of the top one hundred economies of the world are actually transnational corporations; 70 percent of global trade is controlled by just five hundred corporations; and a mere 1 percent of the TNCs on this planet own half the stock of foreign direct investment." What is more, the new trade agreements can only greatly accelerate corporate concentration and increase corporate power in relation to nation-states. Indeed, that is one of "free" trade's main purposes.

Among the factors that make this concentration possible are the new technologies of communication: satellite television and global computer capability. The computer-satellite linkup has effectively become the global corporation's nervous system, enabling the diasporous corporate parts to work in synch. Meanwhile, the globalization of television and advertising enables corporations to expand their ideological reach and deliver idealized images of happy Western commodity-intensive life-styles even to places where, until recently, there may not have been roads. Richard Barnet and John Cavanagh offer two chapters on these themes, honing in on the homogenization of global culture (in Part One) and the globalization of money (Part Three).

We also offer two concrete examples of corporate behavior: one by William Greider about the huge political role played by General Electric, and one by Kai Mander and Alex Boston about the "global retailer" Wal-Mart, which is bringing panic to local downtowns and small businesses everywhere, from Iowa to Canada to Japan. Finally, Richard Grossman and Frank Adams, recognizing the futility of corporate reform under present rules, offer a highly original idea about how the rules can be changed. They remind us that corporations owe their original authority and existence to state charters that can be revoked or rewritten, if only we would organize properly to do so. They ask us to imagine new corporate charters (created by initiative processes), that might, for example, forbid corporations to leave a community, to buy other corporations, to take tax deductions for advertising campaigns, to harm others without paying a criminal price, or to pay salaries to top managers that are wildly disproportionate to those paid to line workers.

## THE EBBING TIDE: RELOCALIZATION

Part IV of this book addresses what is invariably the most difficult question regarding these issues: "If we don't do things this way, what do we do?" The answer may be quite simple. Since the direction in which we're heading is sure to fail, we must stop in our tracks and then change direction. If your car is headed for the cliff, first you stop it and back up, then you look at the next road map to follow.

It is critically important to recognize that the course we are on is not something that "we" as citizens have actually chosen. As several chapters (particularly Nader and Wallach's) painfully point out, the democratic process was openly circumvented to create the instruments of globalization. In this anti-democratic rush, the Western "democracies" behaved no better than anyone else; in fact, we were far worse. Since it was our scheme to begin with, we used our economic and military stature to intimidate smaller, more resistant countries into acceptance. The movement toward economic globalization is no expression of democracy, nor is it the kind of "evolutionary" process that its advocates claim it is, like a force of nature. It is simply a scheme people thought up, an economic experiment designed to favor the institutions that promote it. It's been sold to businesses as an answer to the growing problems of the corporate and political elite. But it's the wrong answer, and it's not in the people's or the planet's interest to continue. Although it is still difficult for most people in industrial countries to accept, a better answer than economic globalization is to go in the direction of revitalized, local, diversified, and at least partially self-sufficient smaller economies.

It's also relevant to remember that not too long ago, most of the world was not on the globalization path, nor did it want to be. At this moment, in fact, most people in the world still maintain relatively traditional economies, many are not "poor," and a high percentage of those who *are* poor have been made so by the very policies of free trade that are decried in these pages.

Many of the nonindustrial countries have never really bought the idea that destroying their local economies would somehow improve their lives. In this vein, I am reminded of some comments I heard from Martin Khor, president of the Third World Network, speaking at a PREPCOM Conference in New York, prior to the 1992 United Nations Conference on Environment and Development in Rio. Khor was asked how he could so strongly argue against the big trade agreements. Was he not worried that without an expanded production and consumption base, Third World peoples would be deprived of Western standards of living? His answer, which I am *paraphrasing,* was to this effect: "I think you have it backward. Those who most depend on an expanding economy are not Malaysians or other Third Worlders, but you in the First World. In your world, you no longer have contact with the land, and you don't know how to get along without luxuries. For us, if the whole global trade system collapsed, we might be better off. We have never lost touch with the land; we know how to grow food for our communities, how to make our own clothes, how to develop the fairly simple technologies we need. This is how most of us lived until recently. We wouldn't mind having some of the new technologies you offer, and some kinds of trade are very useful, but if the Western colonial powers and transnational corporations would simply leave us alone, stop exploiting our resources and land so we could again retain their use, we could probably survive quite well. But what would you do?"

In any case, there will not be much choice, ultimately. The globalized economy cannot be made to work for the general benefit. It cannot be maintained. No one can really argue that its fundamental bases — exponential economic growth, economies built for export trade rather than local needs, continued emphasis on commodity accumulation — can be sustained beyond a very short time.

But how *do* we turn in another direction? In the end, of course, this is the task of the hundreds of activist organizations — environmentalists, human rights groups, workers' unions, small businesses, consumer groups, small farmers, and the new economic thinkers, some of whom are featured in this book. We cannot articulate, on their behalf, the campaigns and ideas that they are and will be generating (though we provide a list of organizations at the back of this book for your interest). We are instead going to advance some ideas about the viability of smaller-scale, localized, diversified economies hooked into but not dominated by outside forces. Helena Norberg-Hodge leads off Part Four offering an interesting and extensive list of concrete ideas and proposals for a transitional period away from global economic structures.

Philosopher and farmer Wendell Berry identifies a unique political opportunity of this moment, a natural and clear division between those who favor globalization with its accompanying social, economic, and political arrangements and those who work to promote and protect community and place. In the next chapter, Gandhi scholar Satish Kumar of Schumacher College in England reminds us of some of the still very practical tenets of Gandhian economics, even now applied in many places that emphasize local production for local needs and invariably give preference to the preservation of social structures and the natural environment over purely economic considerations.

David Morris, an expert in the restructuring of urban environments and other communities toward maximum long-term self-sufficiency and sustainability, offers his ideas for appropriate technologies and political structures to help move power to communities and keep it there. Daniel Imhoff adds his description of the growing, new, community-supported agriculture movement, which offers the promise of self-sustainable local economies, and Susan Meeker-Lowry reports on the extraordinary emergence of new local currencies that enable people to separate themselves more easily from the larger economic grid. This may prove a useful means of survival if, in the future, the global economy takes the nosedive that some expect.

Jeannette Armstrong, an Okanagan, then evokes a psychology appropriate to living successfully in community and in harmony with the environment. Kirkpatrick Sale describes the principles that are guiding the popular new bioregional movement, which deliberately organizes itself toward the promotion of local economic and environmental viability, concentrating on local resources and a respect for natural limits.

Mark Ritchie, meanwhile, is an organizer. He speaks directly from his lengthy experience, which dates back to his leadership of the Nestlè infant formula boycott, to point out an evolving trend among organizers to do "cross-border organizing," sure to soon have a far greater role.

The chapters in Part Four may not yet provide a clear road map from here to there, but what is certainly clear, as Edward Goldsmith writes in the final chapter, is that the shift toward a more local direction is mandatory. It is the only way to show promise for sustainability. The present path is, in fact, impossible; it can only lead to negative outcomes. Despite this, many people continue to call it utopianism to speak of changing directions. But it seems clear to me, and to my coeditor in this project, that the charge of utopianism is wrongly directed. What is truly utopian, and perhaps obsessive, is to continue to say that a development model that defies natural limits and economic and social equity can possibly function for long. It's far more practical to explore elsewhere.

# 2

# THE FAILURES
# OF BRETTON WOODS

### David C. Korten

*This chapter is adapted from David C. Korten's keynote address at the 1994 convention of the Environmental Grantmakers Association of America, held at the Mt. Washington Hotel, Bretton Woods, New Hampshire, on the fiftieth anniversary of the famous Bretton Woods conference that created the World Bank, the International Monetary Fund, and, soon after, the General Agreement on Tariffs and Trade (GATT).*

*Korten has emerged as one of the world's clearest critics of the economic philosophies and practices that drive our system. He formerly worked in Asia for the United States Agency for International Development (AID) and the Ford Foundation's development programs. He holds a Ph.D. from Stanford University's Business School and served on the faculty of Harvard University's Business School. He is president of the People-Centered Development Forum in New York, and author of* When Corporations Rule the World *(1995).*

T HE FAME of Bretton Woods and of this hotel dates from July 1944, when the United Nations Monetary and Financial Conference was held here. The world was in the throes of World War II. Mussolini had been overthrown. The Allies had landed at Normandy, but Hitler would last another ten months. War also continued to rage in the Far East, and Japan would not surrender for another thirteen months. The United Nations Charter was still a year away. In that context, the economic leaders who quietly gathered at this hotel were looking beyond the end of the war with hopes for a world united in peace through prosperity. Their specific goal was to create the institutions that would promote that vision.

The Bretton Woods meeting did create new institutions that have shaped and controlled the world's economic activity since that time, but some theorists will say that the plans for these institutions go back still further, to the 1930s and to the U.S. Council on Foreign Relations. A meeting ground for powerful members of the U.S. corporate and foreign policy establishments, the council styled itself as a forum for the airing of opposing views, an incubator of leaders and ideas unified in their vision of a global economy dominated by U.S. corporate interests.

Members of this group assessed early on that, at a minimum, the U.S. national interest required free access to the markets and raw materials of the Western Hemisphere, the Far East, and the British Empire. On July 24, 1941, a council memorandum outlined the concept of a *grand area*: the part of the world that the United States would need to dominate economically and militarily to ensure materials for its industries. The council also called for the creation of worldwide financial institutions for "stabilizing currencies and facilitating programs of capital investment for constructive undertakings in backward and underdeveloped regions." (Sklar 1980) President Franklin D. Roosevelt was duly apprised of the council's views.

Three years later, at the opening session at Bretton Woods, Henry Morgenthau, then U.S. Secretary of the Treasury and president of the conference, read a welcoming message from Roosevelt and gave his own opening speech, which set the tone and spirit of the gathering. Morgenthau envisaged "the creation of a dynamic world economy in which the peoples of every nation will be able to realize their potentialities in peace and enjoy increasingly the fruits of material progress on an earth infinitely blessed with natural riches." He called on participants to embrace the "elementary economic axiom . . . that prosperity has no fixed limits. It is not a finite substance to be diminished by division."

Thus Morgenthau set forth one of several underlying assumptions of the economic paradigm that guided the work of the architects of the Bretton Woods system. Many of these assumptions were reasonably valid, but two of the most important were deeply flawed. The first erroneous assumption is that economic growth and enhanced world trade would benefit everyone. The second is that economic growth would not be constrained by the limits of the planet.

By the end of this historic meeting, the World Bank and the International Monetary Fund (IMF) had been founded, and the groundwork had been laid for what later became GATT. In the intervening years, these institutions have held faithfully to their mandate to promote economic growth and globalization. Through structural adjustment programs (SAPs), the World Bank and the IMF have pressured countries of the South to open their borders and change their economies from self-sufficiency to *export* production. Trade agreements negotiated through GATT have reinforced these actions and opened economies in both North and South to the increasingly free importation of goods and money.

As we look back fifty years later, we can see that the Bretton Woods institutions have indeed met their goals. Economic growth has expanded fivefold. International trade has expanded by roughly twelve times, and foreign direct investment has been expanding at two to three times the rate of trade expansion. Yet, tragically, while these institutions have met their goals, they have failed in their purpose. The world has more poor people today than ever before. We have an accelerating gap between the rich and the poor. Widespread violence is tearing families and communities apart nearly everywhere. And the planet's ecosystems are deteriorating at an alarming rate.

Yet the prevailing wisdom continues to maintain that economic growth offers the answer to poverty, environmental security, and a strong social fabric, and that *economic globalization* — erasing economic borders to allow free flow of goods and money — is the key to such growth. Indeed, the more severe the economic, environmental, and social crises, the stronger the policy commitment to these same prescriptions, even as evidence mounts that they are not working. In fact, there is a growing consensus outside of official circles that they cannot work, for reasons I will explain.

## ECOLOGICAL LIMIT TO GROWTH

As the founder of ecological economics, Herman Daly, regularly reminds us, the human economy is embedded in and dependent on the natural ecosystems of our planet. Until the present moment in human history, however, the scale of our economic activity relative to the scale of the ecosystems has been small enough so that, in both economic theory and practice, we could, up to a point, afford to ignore this fundamental fact.

Now, however, we have crossed a monumental historical threshold. Because of the fivefold economic expansion since 1950 the environmental demands of our economic system have filled up the available environmental space of the planet. In other words, we live in a "full world." [See chapters by Herman Daly and Robert Goodland.]

The first environmental limits that we have confronted and possibly exceeded are not the limits to nonrenewable resource exploitation, as many once anticipated, but rather the limits to renewable resources and to the environment's *sink functions* — its ability to absorb our wastes. These are limits related to the loss of soils, fisheries, forests, and water; to the absorption of $CO_2$ emissions; and to destruction of the ozone layer. We could argue whether a particular limit was hit at noon yesterday or will be passed at midnight tomorrow, but the details are far less important than the basic truth that we have no real option other than to adapt our economic institutions to the reality of a "full world."

The structure and ideology of the existing Bretton Woods system is geared to an ever-continuing expansion of economic output — *economic growth* — and to the integration of national economies into a seamless global economy. The consequence is to intensify competition for already overstressed environmental space. In a "full world," this intensified competition accelerates destruction of the regenerative capacities of the ecosystem on which we and future generations depend; it crowds out all forms of life not needed for immediate human consumption purposes; and it increases competition between rich and poor for control of ecological resources. In a free market — which responds only to money, not needs — the rich win this competition every time. We see it happening all over the world: Hundreds of millions of the financially disenfranchised are displaced as their lands, waters, and fisheries are converted to uses serving the wants of the more affluent.

As long as their resources remain, the demands of the rich can be met — which may explain why so many of the rich see no problem. The poor experience a very different reality, but in a market economy their experience doesn't count.

The market cannot deal with questions relating to the appropriate scale of economic activity. There are no price signals indicating that the poor are going hungry because they have been forced off their lands; nor is there any price signal to tell polluters that too much $CO_2$ is being released into the air, or that toxins should not be dumped into soils or waters. Steeped in market ideology and highly responsive to corporate interests, the Bretton Woods institutions have demonstrated little capacity to give more than lip service either to environmental concerns or to the needs of the poor. Rather, their efforts have *de facto* centered on ensuring that people with money have full access to whatever resources remain — with little regard for the broader consequences.

A new Bretton Woods meeting to update the international system would serve a significant and visionary need — if its participants were to accept that economic growth is no longer a valid public policy priority. Indeed, whether the global economy grows or shrinks is largely irrelevant.

Having crossed the threshold to a full world, the appropriate concern is whether the available planetary resources are being used in ways that: (1) meet the basic needs of all people; (2) maintain biodiversity; and (3) ensure the sustained availability of comparable resource flows to future generations. Our present economic system fails on all three counts.

## ECONOMIC INJUSTICE

In *How Much Is Enough?* (1992), Alan Durning divided the world into three consumption classes: overconsumers, sustainers, and marginals. The overconsumers are the 20 percent of the world's people who consume roughly 80 percent of the world's resources — that is, those of us whose lives are organized around automobiles, airplanes, meat-based diets, and wastefully packaged disposable products. The marginals, also 20 percent of the world's people, live in absolute deprivation.

If we turn to measurements of *income* rather than *consumption,* the figures are even more stark. The United Nations Development Program (UNDP) *Human Development Report* for 1992 introduces the champagne glass as a graphic metaphor for a world of extreme economic injustice. The bowl of the champagne glass represents the abundance enjoyed by the 20 percent of people who live in the world's richest countries and receive 82.7 percent of the world's income. At the bottom of the stem, where the sediment settles, we find the poorest 20 percent of the world's people, who barely survive on 1.4 percent of the total income. The combined incomes of the top 20 percent are nearly sixty times larger than those of the bottom 20 percent. Furthermore, this gap has doubled since 1950, when the top 20 percent enjoyed only thirty times the income of the bottom 20 percent. And the gap continues to grow.

These figures actually understate the true inequality in the world, because they are based on national averages rather than actual individual incomes. If we take into account the very rich people who live in poor countries and the very poor people who live in rich countries, the incomes of the richest 20 percent of the world's people are approximately 150 times those of the poorest 20 percent. That gap is growing as well.

Robert Reich, the U.S. Secretary of Labor in the Clinton administration, explained in his book *The Work of Nations* (1991), that the economic globalization the Bretton Woods institutions have advanced so successfully has served to separate the interests of the wealthy classes from a sense of national interest and thereby from a sense of concern for and obligation to their less fortunate neighbors. A thin segment of the super rich at the very lip of the champagne glass has formed a stateless alliance that defines *global interest* as synonymous with the personal and corporate financial interests of its members.

This separation has been occurring in nearly every country in the world to such an extent that it is no longer meaningful to speak of a world divided into northern and southern nations. The meaningful divide is not geography — it is class.

Whether intended or not, the policies so successfully advanced by the Bretton Woods institutions have inexorably empowered the super rich to lay claim to the world's wealth at the expense of other people, other species, and the viability of the planet's ecosystem.

## FREEING CORPORATIONS FROM CONTROL

The issue is not the market per se. Trying to run an economy without markets is disastrous, as the experience of the Soviet Union demonstrated. However, there is a fundamentally important distinction between markets and free markets.

The struggle between two extremist ideologies has been a central feature of the twentieth century. Communism called for all power to the state. Market capitalism calls for all power to the market — a euphemism for giant corporations. Both ideologies lead to their own distinctive form of tyranny. The secret of Western success in World War II and the early postwar period was not a free market economy; it was the practice of democratic pluralism built on institutional arrangements that sought to maintain balance between the state and the market and to protect the right of an active citizenry to hold both accountable to the public interest.

Contrary to the claims of ideologues who preach a form of corporate libertarianism, markets need governments to function efficiently. It is well established in economic theory and practice that markets allocate resources efficiently only when markets are competitive and when firms pay for the social and environmental impact of their activity — that is, when they *internalize* the costs of their production. This requires that governments set and enforce the rules that make cost internalization happen, and, since successful firms invariably grow larger and more monopolistic, governments regularly step in to break them up and restore competition.

For governments to play the necessary role of balancing market and community interests, governmental power must be equal to market power. If markets are national, then there must be a strong national government. By expanding the boundaries of the market beyond the boundaries of the nation-state through economic globalization, the concentration of market power moves inevitably beyond the reach of government. This has been a most important consequence of both the structural adjustment programs of the World Bank and IMF and the trade agreements negotiated under GATT. As a result, governance decisions are transferred from governments, which at least in theory represent the interests of all citizens, to transnational corporations, which by their nature serve the interests only of their dominant shareholders. Consequently, societies everywhere on the planet are no longer able to address environmental and other needs.

Enormous economic power is being concentrated in the hands of a very few global corporations relieved of constraints to their own growth. Antitrust action to restore market competition by breaking up the concentrations is one of the many casualties of globalization. Indeed, current policy encourages firms to merge into ever more powerful concentrations to strengthen their position in global markets.

The rapid rate at which large corporations are shedding employees has created an impression in some quarters that the firms are losing their power. It is a misleading impression. The Fortune 500 firms shed 4.4 million jobs between 1980 and 1993. During this same period, their sales increased 1.4 times, assets increased 2.3 times, and CEO compensation increased 6.1 times. Of the world's one hundred largest economies, fifty are now corporations, not including banking and financial institutions.

Any industry in which five firms control 50 percent or more of the market is considered by economists to be highly monopolistic. The *Economist* recently reported that five firms control more than 50 percent of the global market in the following industries: consumer durables, automotive, airlines, aerospace, electronic components, electricity and electronics, and steel. Five firms control over 40 percent of the global market in oil, personal computers, and — especially alarming in its consequences for public debate on these very issues — media.

## FORUMS FOR ELITE DOMINATION

It is worth adding here that the forums within which corporate and government elites shape the global policies of the Western world were not limited to Bretton Woods. In May 1954, a powerful group of North American and European leaders also began meeting as an unofficial, low-profile group with no acknowledged membership. Known simply as

Bilderberg, the group played a significant role in advancing the European Union and shaping a consensus among leaders of the Atlantic nations on key issues facing Western-dominated transnational systems. Participants included heads of state, other key politicians, key industrialists and financiers, and an assortment of intellectuals, trade unionists, diplomats, and influential representatives of the press with demonstrated sympathy for establishment views. One Bilderberg insider had observed that "today there are very few figures among governments on both sides of the Atlantic who have not attended at least one of these meetings."

As Japan assumed an increasingly powerful and independent role in the global economy, the need became evident for a forum that included the Japanese and that had a more formal structure than Bilderberg.

In response, the Trilateral Commission was formed in 1973 by David Rockefeller, chair of Chase Manhattan Bank, and Zbigniew Brzezinski, who served as the commission's director/coordinator until 1977 when he became national security advisor to President Jimmy Carter.

The members of the Trilateral Commission include the heads of four of the world's five largest nonbanking transnational corporations; top officials of five of the world's six largest international banks; and heads of major media organizations. U.S. presidents Jimmy Carter, George Bush, and Bill Clinton were all members of the Trilateral Commission, as was Thomas Foley, former speaker of the House of Representatives. Many key members of the Carter administration were both Bilderberg and Trilateral Commission members. Many of President Clinton's cabinet and other appointments are former members of the Trilateral Commission.

Both Bilderberg and the Trilateral Commission have provided forums in which top executives from the world's leading corporations meet regularly, informally, and privately with top national political figures and opinion leaders to seek consensus on immediate and longer-range problems facing the most powerful members of the Western Alliance.

To some extent, the meetings help maintain "stability" in global policies, but they also deprive the public of meaningful participation and choice — as some participants explicitly intend. Particularly significant about these groups is their bipartisan political membership. Certainly, the participation of both George Bush and Bill Clinton in the Trilateral Commission makes it easier to understand the seamless transition from the Republican Bush administration to the Democratic Clinton administration with regard to U.S. commitment to pass GATT and NAFTA. Clinton's leadership in advancing what many progressives saw as a Bush agenda won him high marks from his colleagues on the Trilateral Commission.

## INSTRUMENTS OF CONTROL

Corporations have enormous political power, and they are actively using it to reshape the rules of the market in their own favor. The GATT has now become one of the corporations' most powerful tools for reshaping the market. Under the new GATT agreement, a World Trade Organization, the WTO, has been created with far-reaching powers to provide corporations the legal protection they feel they need to continue expanding their far-flung operations without the responsibility to serve any interest other than their own bottom line. [See chapter by Ralph Nader and Lori Wallach.]

The WTO will hear disputes brought against the national or local laws of any country that another member country considers to be a trade barrier. Secret panels made up of three unelected trade experts will hear the disputes, and their rulings can be overturned only by a unanimous vote of the member countries. In general, any health, safety, or environmental standard that exceeds international standards set by industry representatives is likely to be considered a trade barrier, unless the offending government can prove that the standard has a valid scientific basis.

As powerful as the large corporations are, they themselves function increasingly as agents of a global financial system that has become the world's most powerful governance institution. The power in this system lies within a small group of private financial institutions that have only one objective: to make money in massive quantities. A seamless electronic web allows anyone with proper access codes and a personal computer to conduct instantaneous trade involving billions of dollars on any of the world's financial markets. The world of finance itself has become a gigantic computer game. In this game the smart money does not waste itself on long-term, high-quality commitments to productive enterprises engaged in producing real wealth to meet real needs of real people. Rather, it seeks short-term returns from speculation in erratic markets and from simultaneous trades in multiple markets to profit from minute price variations. In this game the short-term is measured in microseconds, the long-term in days. The environmental, social, and even economic consequences of financial decisions involving more than a trillion dollars a day are invisible to those who make them.

Joel Kurtzman, former business editor of the *New York Times* and currently editor of the *Harvard Business Review,* estimates that for every $1 circulating in the productive economy today, $20 to $50 circulates in the world of pure finance. Since these transactions take place through unmonitored international computer networks, no one knows how much is really involved. The $1 trillion that changes hands each day in the world's international currency markets is itself twenty to thirty times the amount required to cover daily trade in actual goods and services. If the world's most powerful governments act in concert to stabilize exchange rates in these same markets, the best they can manage is a measly $14 billion a day — little more than pocket change compared to the amounts mobilized by speculators and arbitrageurs. [See chapter on electronic money by Richard Barnet and John Cavanagh.]

The corporations that invest in *real* assets (as opposed to ephemeral financial assets), are forced by the resulting pressures to restructure their operations in order to maximize immediate short-term returns to share-holders. One way to do this is by downsizing, streamlining, and automating their operations, using the most advanced technologies to eliminate hundreds of thousands of jobs. The result is jobless economic growth. Contemporary economies simply cannot create jobs faster than technology and dysfunctional economic systems can shed them. In nearly every country in the world there is now a labor surplus, and those lucky enough to have jobs are increasingly members of a contingent work force without either security or benefits. The resulting fear and insecurity make the jobs-versus-environment issue a crippling barrier to essential environmental action.

Another way to increase corporate profits is to externalize the cost of the firm's operations on the community, pitting localities against one another in a standards-lowering competition to offer subsidies, tax holidays, and freedom from environmental and employment standards. Similarly, workers are pitted against one another in a struggle for survival that pushes wages down to the lowest common denominator. This is the true meaning of *global competitiveness* — competition among localities. Large corporations, by contrast, minimize their competition through mergers and strategic alliances.

Any corporation that does not play this game to its limit is likely to become a takeover target by a corporate raider who will buy out the company and profit by taking the actions that the previous management — perhaps in a fit of social conscience and loyalty to workers and community — failed to take. The reconstruction of the global economic system makes it almost impossible for even highly socially conscious and committed managers to operate a corporation responsibly in the public interest.

• • •

We are caught in a terrible dilemma. We have reached a point in history where we must rethink the very nature and meaning of human progress;

yet the vision and decisions that emerged some fifty years ago catalyzed events that have transformed the governance processes of societies everywhere such that the necessary changes in thought and structure seem very difficult to achieve. It has happened so quickly that few among us even realize what has happened. The real issues are seldom discussed in a media dependent on corporate advertising.

Nonetheless, the fact is that sustainability in a growth-dependent globalized economy is what Herman Daly calls an impossibility theorem. What is the alternative? Among those of us who are devoting significant attention to this question, the answer is the opposite of globalization. It lies in promoting greater economic localization — breaking economic activities down into smaller, more manageable pieces that link the people who make decisions in ways both positive and negative. It means rooting capital to a place and distributing its control among as many people as possible.

Powerful interests stand resolutely in the way of achieving such a reversal of current trends. The biggest barrier, however, is the limited extent of public discussion on the subject. The starting point must be to get the issues on the table and bring them into the mainstream policy debates in a way that books like this may help to achieve.

# PART I

# THE MULTIPLE IMPACTS
# OF GLOBALIZATION

*The shift toward "a global economy" brings with it major changes in nearly every aspect of our personal and public lives. Each of the following chapters focuses on different but overlapping aspects of that change: from the impacts on democracy and power, to the effects on employment, community, farms, and food; on public health and the preservation of cultural and biological diversity; and on the remaining wilderness places. The consequences vary regionally, as between the Third World and the Western world, but everywhere the impact is very great.*

# 3

# THE PRESSURE TO
# MODERNIZE AND GLOBALIZE

## Helena Norberg-Hodge

*For thirty years, on three continents, Swedish philosopher, teacher, and activist Helena Norberg-Hodge has been fighting the excesses of today's economic development models, particularly their effects on traditional societies and local culture. She was the first foreigner accepted to make her home in the Himalayan province of Ladakh (Kashmir). There, over three decades, she learned the native language and helped people study and resist the hidden perils and culturally destructive effects of modernization. Meanwhile in Europe, she was a leading campaigner in the Norwegian vote opposing entry into the European Economic Community, and is now codirector of the International Forum on Globalization-Europe. In the United States, her organization, the International Society for Ecology and Culture, runs educational campaigns on globalization issues. She is the author of* Ancient Futures: Learning from Ladakh *(1991), and coauthor of* From the Ground Up *(1993).*

L ADAKH IS a high-altitude desert on the Tibetan Plateau in northernmost India. To all outward appearances, it is a wild and inhospitable place. In summer the land is parched and dry; in winter it is frozen solid by a fierce, unrelenting cold. Harsh and barren, Ladakh's land forms have often been described as a "moonscape."

Almost nothing grows wild — not the smallest shrub, hardly a blade of grass. Even time seems to stand still, suspended on the thin air. Yet here, in one of the highest, driest, and coldest inhabited places on Earth, the Ladakhis have for a thousand years not only survived but prospered. Out of barren desert they have carved verdant oases — terraced fields of barley, wheat, apples, apricots, and vegetables, irrigated with glacial meltwater brought many miles through stone-lined channels. Using little more than stone-age technologies and the scant resources at hand, the Ladakhis established a remarkably rich culture, one that met not only their material wants but their psychological and spiritual needs as well.

Until 1962, Ladakh, or "Little Tibet," remained almost totally isolated from the forces of modernization. In that year, however, in response to the conflict in Tibet, the Indian Army built a road to link the region with the rest of the country. With the road came not only new consumer items and a government bureaucracy but, as I shall show, a first misleading impression of the world outside. Then, in 1975, the region was opened up to foreign tourists, and the process of "development" began in earnest.

Based on my ability to speak the language fluently from my first year in Ladakh, and based on almost two decades of close contact with the Ladakhi people, I have been able to observe almost as an insider the effect of these changes on the Ladakhis' perception of themselves. Within the space of little more than a decade, feelings of pride gave way to what can best be described as a cultural inferiority complex. In the modern sector today, most young Ladakhis — the teenage boys in particular — are ashamed of their cultural roots and desperate to appear modern.

## TOURISM

When tourism first began in Ladakh, it was as though people from another planet suddenly descended on the region. Looking at the modern world from something of a Ladakhi perspective, I became aware of how much more successful our culture looks from the outside than we experience it on the inside.

Each day many tourists would spend as much as $100 — an amount roughly equivalent to someone spending $50,000 per day in America. In the traditional subsistence economy, money played a minor role and was used primarily for luxuries — jewelry, silver, and gold. Basic needs — food, clothing, and shelter — were provided for without money. The labor one needed was free of charge, part of an intricate web of human relationships.

Ladakhis did not realize that money meant something very different for the foreigners; that back home they needed it to survive; that food, clothing, and shelter all cost money — a lot of money. Compared to these strangers, the Ladakhis suddenly felt poor.

This new attitude contrasted dramatically with the Ladakhis' earlier self-confidence. In 1975, I was shown around the remote village of Hemis Shukpachan by a young Ladakhi named Tsewang. It seemed to me that all the houses we saw were especially large and beautiful. I asked Tsewang to show me the houses where the poor people lived. Tsewang looked perplexed a moment, then responded, "We don't have any poor people here."

Eight years later I overheard Tsewang talking to some tourists. "If you could only help us Ladakhis," he was saying, "we're so poor."

Besides giving the illusion that all Westerners are multimillionaires, tourism and Western media images also help perpetuate another myth about modern life — that we never work. It looks as though our technologies do the work for us. In industrial society today, we actually spend more hours working than people in rural, agrarian economies, but that is not how it looks to the Ladakhis. For them, work is physical work: ploughing, walking, carrying things. A person sitting behind the wheel of a car or pushing buttons on a typewriter doesn't appear to be working.

## MEDIA IMAGES

Development has brought not only tourism but also Western and Indian films and, more recently, television. Together they provide overwhelming images of luxury and power. There are countless tools, magical gadgets, and machines — machines to take pictures, machines to tell the time, machines to make fire, to travel from one place to another, to talk with someone far away. Machines can do everything; it's no wonder the tourists look so clean and have such soft, white hands.

Media images focus on the rich, the beautiful, and the mobile, whose lives are endless action and glamour. For young Ladakhis, the picture is irresistible. It is an overwhelmingly exciting version of an urban American Dream, with an emphasis on speed, youthfulness, super-cleanliness, beauty, fashion, and competitiveness. "Progress" is also stressed: Humans dominate nature, while technological change is embraced at all costs.

In contrast to these utopian images from another culture, village life seems primitive, silly, and inefficient. The one-dimensional view of modern life becomes a slap in the face. Young Ladakhis — whose parents ask them to choose a way of life that involves working in the fields and getting their hands dirty for very little or no money — feel ashamed of their own culture. Traditional Ladakh seems absurd compared with the world of the tourists and film heroes.

This same pattern is being repeated in rural areas all over the South, where millions of young people believe contemporary Western culture to be far superior to their own. This is not surprising: looking as they do from the outside, all they can see is the material side of the modern world — the side in which Western culture excels. They cannot so readily see the social or psychological dimensions: the stress, the loneliness, the fear of growing old. Nor can they see environmental decay, inflation, or unemployment. This leads young Ladakhis to develop feelings of inferiority, to reject their own culture wholesale, and at the same time to eagerly embrace the global monoculture. They rush after the sunglasses, walkmans, and blue jeans — not because they find those jeans more attractive or comfortable but because they are symbols of modern life.

Modern symbols have also contributed to an increase in aggression in Ladakh. Young boys now see violence glamorized on the screen. From Western-style films, they can easily get the impression that if they want to be modern, they should smoke one cigarette after another, get a fast car, and race through the countryside shooting people left and right.

## WESTERN-STYLE EDUCATION

No one can deny the value of real education — the widening and enrichment of knowledge. But today in the Third World, education has become something quite different. It isolates children from their culture and from nature, training them instead to become narrow specialists in a Westernized urban environment. This process has been particularly striking in Ladakh, where modern schooling acts almost as a blindfold, preventing children from seeing the very context in which they live. They leave school unable to use their own resources, unable to function in their own world.

With the exception of religious training in the monasteries, Ladakh's traditional culture had no separate process called education. Education was the product of a person's intimate relationship with the community and the ecosystem. Children learned from grandparents, family, and friends and from the natural world.

Helping with the sowing, for instance, they would learn that on one side of the village it was a little warmer, on the other side a little colder. From their own experience children would come to distinguish different strains of barley and the specific growing conditions each strain preferred. They learned how to recognize and use even the tiniest wild plant, and how to pick out a particular animal on a faraway mountain slope. They learned about connection, process, and change, about the intricate web of fluctuating relationships in the natural world around them.

For generation after generation, Ladakhis grew up learning how to provide themselves with clothing and shelter: how to make shoes out of yak skin and robes from the wool of sheep; how to build houses out of mud and stone. Education was location-specific and nurtured an intimate relationship with the living world. It gave children an intuitive awareness that allowed them, as they grew older, to use resources in an effective and sustainable way.

None of that knowledge is provided in the modern school. Children are trained to become specialists in a technological rather than an ecological society. School is a place to forget traditional skills and, worse, to look down on them.

Western education first came to Ladakhi villages in the 1970s. Today there are about two hundred schools. The basic curriculum is a poor imitation of that taught in other parts of India, which itself is an imitation of British education. There is almost nothing Ladakhi about it.

Once, while visiting a classroom in Leh, the capital, I saw a drawing in a textbook of a child's bedroom that could have been in London or New York. It showed a pile of neatly folded handkerchiefs on a four-poster bed and gave instructions as to which drawer of the vanity unit to keep them in. Many other schoolbooks were equally absurd and inappropriate. For homework in one class, pupils were supposed to figure out the angle of incidence that the Leaning Tower of Pisa makes with the ground. Another time they were struggling with an English translation of *The Iliad.*

Most of the skills Ladakhi children learn in school will never be of real use to them. In essence, they receive an inferior version of an education appropriate for a New Yorker, a Parisian, or a Berliner. They learn from books written by people who have never set foot in Ladakh, who know nothing about growing barley at 12,000 feet or about making houses out of sun-dried bricks.

This situation is not unique to Ladakh. In every corner of the world today, the process called *education* is based on the same assumptions and the same Eurocentric model. The focus is on faraway facts and figures, on "universal" knowledge. The books propagate information that is believed to be appropriate for the entire planet. But since the only knowledge that can be universally applicable is far removed from specific ecosystems and cultures, what children learn is essentially synthetic, divorced from its living context. If they go on to higher education, they may learn about building houses, but these "houses" will be the universal boxes of concrete and steel. So too, if they study agriculture, they will learn about industrial farming: chemical fertilizers and pesticides; large machinery and hybrid seeds. The Western educational system is making us all poorer by teaching people around the world to use the same global resources, ignoring those that the environment naturally provides. In this way, Western-style education creates artificial scarcity and induces competition.

In Ladakh and elsewhere, modern education not only ignores local resources but, worse still, robs children of their self-esteem. Everything in school promotes the Western model and, as a direct consequence, makes children think of themselves and their traditions as inferior.

Western-style education pulls people away from agriculture and into the city, where they become dependent on the money economy. Traditionally there was no such thing as unemployment. But in the modern sector there is now intense competition for a very limited number of paying jobs, principally in the government. As a result, unemployment is already a serious problem.

Modern education has brought some obvious benefits, such as improvement in the literacy rate. It has also enabled the Ladakhis to be more informed about the forces at play in the world outside. In so doing, however, it has divided Ladakhis from each other and the land and put them on the lowest rung of the global economic ladder.

## LOCAL ECONOMY VERSUS GLOBAL ECONOMY

When I first came to Ladakh the Western macroeconomy had not yet arrived, and the local economy was still rooted in its own soils. Producers and consumers were closely linked in a community-based economy. Two decades of development in Ladakh, however, have led to a number of fundamental changes, the most important of which is perhaps the new dependence on food and energy from thousands of miles away.

The path toward globalization depends upon continuous government investments. It requires the buildup of a large-scale industrial infrastructure that includes roads, mass communications facilities, energy installations, and schools for specialized education. Among other things, this heavily subsidized infrastructure allows goods produced on a large scale and transported long distances to be sold at artificially low prices — in many cases at lower prices than goods produced locally. In Ladakh, the Indian government is not only paying for roads, schools, and energy installations but is also bringing in subsidized food from India's breadbasket, the Punjab. Ladakh's local economy — which has provided enough food for its people for two thousand years — is now being invaded by produce from industrial farms located on the other side of the Himalayas. The food arriving in lorries by the ton is cheaper in the local bazaar than food grown a five-minute walk away. For many Ladakhis, it is no longer worthwhile to continue farming.

In Ladakh this same process affects not just food but a whole range of goods, from clothes to household utensils to building materials. Imports from distant parts of India can often be produced and distributed at lower prices than goods produced locally — again, because of a heavily subsidized industrial infrastructure. The end result of the long-distance transport of subsidized goods is that Ladakh's local economy is being steadily dismantled, and with it goes the local community that was once tied together by bonds of interdependence.

Conventional economists, of course, would dismiss these negative impacts, which cannot be quantified as easily as the monetary transactions that are the goal of economic development. They would also say that regions such as the Punjab enjoy a "comparative advantage" over Ladakh in food production, and it therefore makes economic sense for the Punjab to specialize in growing food, while Ladakh specializes in some other product, and that each trade with the other. But when distantly produced goods are heavily subsidized, often in hidden ways, one cannot really talk about comparative advantage or, for that matter, "free markets," "open competition in the setting of prices," or any of the other principles by which economists and planners rationalize the changes they advocate. In fact, one should instead talk about the unfair advantage that industrial producers enjoy, thanks to a heavily subsidized infrastructure geared toward large-scale, centralized production.

In the past, individual Ladakhis had real power, since political and economic units were small, and each person was able to deal directly with the other members of the community. Today, "development" is hooking people into ever-larger political and economic units. In political terms, each Ladakhi has become one of a national economy of eight hundred million, and, as part of the global economy, one of about six billion.

In the traditional economy, everyone knew they had to depend directly on family, friends, and neighbors. But in the new economic system, political and economic interactions take a detour via an anonymous bureaucracy. The fabric of local interdependence is disintegrating as the distance between people increases. So too are traditional levels of tolerance and cooperation. This is particularly true in the villages near Leh, where disputes and acrimony within close-knit communities and even families have dramatically increased in the last few years. I have even seen heated arguments over the allocation of irrigation water, a procedure that had previously been managed smoothly within a cooperative framework.

As mutual aid is replaced by dependence on faraway forces, people begin to feel powerless to make decisions over their own lives. At all levels, passivity, even apathy, is setting in; people are abdicating personal responsibility. In the traditional village, for example, repairing irrigation canals was a task shared by the whole community. As soon as a channel developed a leak, groups of people would start shoveling away to patch it up. Now people see this work as the government's responsibility and will let a channel go on leaking until the job is done for them. The more the government does for the villagers, the less the villagers feel inclined to help themselves.

In the process, Ladakhis are starting to change their perception of the past. In my early days in Ladakh, people would tell me there had never been hunger. I kept hearing the expression *tungbos zabos*: "enough to drink, enough to eat." Now, particularly in the modern sector, people can be heard saying, "Development is essential; in the past we couldn't manage, we didn't have enough."

The cultural centralization that occurs through the media is also contributing both to this passivity and to a growing insecurity. Traditionally, village life included lots of dancing, singing, and theater. People of all ages joined in. In a group sitting around a fire, even toddlers would dance, with the help of older siblings or friends. Everyone knew how to sing, to act, to play music. Now that the radio has come to Ladakh, people do not need to sing their own songs or tell their own stories. Instead, they can sit and listen to the *best* singer, the *best* storyteller. As a result, people become inhibited and self-conscious. They are no longer comparing themselves to neighbors and friends, who are real people — some better at singing but perhaps not so good at dancing — and they never feel themselves to be as good as the stars on the radio. Community ties are also broken when people sit passively listening to the very best rather than making music or dancing together.

## ARTIFICIAL NEEDS

Before the changes brought by tourism and modernization, the Ladakhis were self-sufficient, both psychologically and materially. There was no desire for the sort of development that later came to be seen as a "need." Time and again, when I asked people about the changes that were coming, they showed no great interest in being modernized; sometimes they were even suspicious. In remote areas, when a road was about to be built, people felt, at best, ambivalent about the prospect. The same was true of electricity. I remember distinctly how, in 1975, people in Stagmo village laughed about the fuss that was being made to bring electric lights to neighboring villages. They thought it was a joke that so much effort and money was spent on what they took to be a ludicrous gain: "Is it worth all that bother just to have that thing dangling from your ceiling?"

More recently, when I returned to the same village to meet the council, the first thing they said to me was, "Why do you bother to come to our backward village where we live in the dark?" They said it jokingly, but it was obvious they were ashamed of the fact they did not have electricity.

Before people's sense of self-respect and self-worth had been shaken, they did not need electricity to prove they were civilized. But within a short period the forces of development so undermined people's self-esteem that not only electricity but Punjabi rice and plastic have become needs. I have seen people proudly wear wristwatches they cannot read and for which they have no use. And as the desire to appear modern grows, people are rejecting their own culture. Even the traditional foods are no longer a source of pride. Now when I'm a guest in a village, people apologize if they serve the traditional roasted barley, *ngamphe,* instead of instant noodles.

Surprisingly, perhaps, modernization in Ladakh is also leading to a loss of individuality. As people become self-conscious and insecure, they feel pressure to conform, to live up to the idealized images — to the American Dream. By contrast, in the traditional village, where everyone wears the same clothes and looks the same to the casual observer, there seems to be more freedom to relax, and villagers can be who they really are. As part of a close-knit community, people feel secure enough to be themselves.

## A PEOPLE DIVIDED

Perhaps the most tragic of all the changes I have observed in Ladakh is the vicious circle in which individual insecurity contributes to a weakening of family and community ties, which in turn further shakes individual self-esteem. Consumerism plays a central role in this whole process, since emotional insecurity generates hunger for material status symbols. The need for recognition and acceptance fuels the drive to acquire possessions that will presumably make you somebody. Ultimately, this is a far more important motivating force than a fascination for the things themselves.

It is heartbreaking to see people buying things to be admired, respected, and ultimately loved, when in fact the effect is almost inevitably the opposite. The individual with the new shiny car is set apart, and this furthers the need to be accepted. A cycle is set in motion in which people become more and more divided from themselves and from one another.

I've seen people divided from one another in many ways. A gap is developing between young and old, male and female, rich and poor, Buddhist and Muslim. The newly created division between the modern, educated expert and the illiterate, "backward" farmer is perhaps the biggest of all. Modernized inhabitants of Leh have more in common with someone from Delhi or Calcutta than they do with their own relatives who have remained on the land, and they tend to look down on anyone less modern. Some children living in the modern sector are now so distanced from their parents and grandparents that they don't even speak the same language. Educated in Urdu and English, they are losing mastery of their native tongue.

Around the world, another consequence of development is that the men leave their families in the rural sector to earn money in the modern economy. The men become part of the technologically based life outside the home and are seen as the only productive members of society. In Ladakh, the roles of male and female are becoming increasingly polarized as their work becomes more differentiated.

Women become invisible shadows. They do not earn money for their work, so they are no longer seen as "productive." Their work is not included as part of the Gross National Product. In government statistics, the 10 percent or so of Ladakhis who work in the modern sector are listed according to their occupations; the other 90 percent — housewives and traditional farmers — are lumped together as nonworkers. Farmers and women are coming to be viewed as inferior, and they themselves are developing feelings of insecurity and inadequacy.

Over the years I have seen the strong, outgoing women of Ladakh being replaced by a new generation — women who are unsure of themselves and extremely concerned with their appearance. Traditionally, the way a woman looked was important, but her capabilities — including tolerance and social skills — were much more appreciated.

Despite their new dominant role, men also clearly suffer as a result of the breakdown of family and community ties. Among other things, they are deprived of contact with children. When men are young, the new macho image prevents them from showing any affection, while in later life as fathers, their work keeps them away from home.

# BREAKING THE BONDS
# BETWEEN YOUNG AND OLD

In the traditional culture, children benefited not only from continuous contact with both mother and father but also from a way of life in which different age groups constantly interacted. It was quite natural for older children to feel a sense of responsibility for the younger ones. A younger child in turn looked up to the older ones with respect and admiration and sought to be like them. Growing up was a natural, noncompetitive learning process.

Now children are split into different age groups at school. This sort of leveling has a very destructive effect: By artificially creating social units in which everyone is the same age, the ability of children to help and to learn from each other is greatly reduced. Instead, conditions for competition are automatically created, because each child is put under pressure to be just as good as the next one. In a group of ten children of quite different ages, there will naturally be much more cooperation than in a group of ten twelve-year-olds.

The division into different age groups is not limited to school. Now there is a tendency to spend time exclusively with one's peers. As a result, a mutual intolerance between young and old has emerged. Young children nowadays have less and less contact with their grandparents, who often remain behind in the village. Living with many traditional families over the years, I have witnessed the depth of the bond between children and their grandparents. It is clearly a natural relationship that has a very different dimension from that between parent and child. To sever this connection is a profound tragedy.

Similar pressures contribute to the breakdown of the traditional family. The Western model of the nuclear family is now seen as the norm, and Ladakhis are beginning to feel ashamed about their traditional practice of polyandry, one of the cultural controls on population growth. As young people reject the old family structure in favor of monogamy, the population is rising significantly. At the same time, monastic life is losing its status, and the number of celibate monks and nuns is decreasing. This too contributes to population increase.

## VIOLENCE

Interestingly, a number of Ladakhis have linked the rise in birth rates to the advent of modern democracy. "Power is a question of votes" is a current slogan, meaning that in the modern sector, the larger your group, the greater your access to power. Competition for jobs and political representation within the new centralized structures is increasingly dividing Ladakhis. Ethnic and religious differences have taken on a political dimension, causing bitterness and envy on a scale hitherto unknown.

This new rivalry is one of the most painful divisions that I have seen in Ladakh. Ironically, it has grown in proportion to the decline of traditional religious devotion. When I first arrived, I was struck by the mutual respect and cooperation between Buddhists and Muslims. But within the last few years, growing competition has actually culminated in violence. Earlier there had been individual cases of friction, but the first time I noticed any signs of group tension was in 1986, when I heard Ladakhi friends starting to define people according to whether they were Buddhist or Muslim. In the following years, there were signs here and there that all was not well, but no one was prepared for what happened in the summer of 1989, when fighting suddenly broke out between the two groups. There were major disturbances in Leh bazaar, four people were shot dead by police, and much of Ladakh was placed under curfew.

Since then, open confrontation has died down, but mistrust and prejudice on both sides continue to mar relations. For a people unaccustomed to violence and discord, this has been a traumatic experience. One Muslim woman could have been speaking for all Ladakhis when she tearfully told me, "These events have torn my family apart. Some of them are Buddhists, some are Muslims, and now they are not even speaking to each other."

The immediate cause of the disturbances was the growing perception among the Buddhists that the Muslim-dominated state government was discriminating against them in favor of the local Muslim population. The Muslims for their part were becoming anxious that as a minority group they had to defend their interests in the face of political assertiveness by the Buddhist majority.

However, the underlying reasons for the violence are much more far-reaching. What is happening in Ladakh is not an isolated phenomenon. The tensions between the Muslims of Kashmir and the Hindu-dominated central government in Delhi; between the Hindus and the Buddhist government in Bhutan; and between the Buddhists and the Hindu government in Nepal, along with countless similar disturbances around the world, are, I believe, all connected to the same underlying cause: The intensely centralizing force of the present global development model is pulling diverse peoples from rural areas into large urban centers and placing power and decision making in the hands of a few. In these centers, job opportunities are scarce, community ties are broken, and competition increases dramatically. In particular, young men who have been educated for jobs in the modern sector find themselves engaged in a competitive struggle for survival. In this situation, any religious or ethnic differences quite naturally become exaggerated and distorted. In addition, the group in power inevitably tends to favor its own kind, while the rest often suffer discrimination.

Most people believe that ethnic conflict is an inevitable consequence of differing cultural and religious traditions. In the South, there is an awareness that modernization is exacerbating tensions; but people generally conclude that this is a temporary phase on the road to "progress," a phase that will only end once development has erased cultural differences and created a totally secular society. On the other hand, Westerners attribute overt religious and ethnic strife to the liberating influence of democracy. Conflict, they assume, always smoldered beneath the surface, and only government repression kept it from bursting into flames.

It is easy to understand why people lay the blame at the feet of tradition rather than modernity. Certainly, ethnic friction is a phenomenon that predates colonialism, modernization, and globalization. But after nearly two decades of firsthand experience on the Indian subcontinent, I am convinced that "development" not only exacerbates tensions but actually creates them. As I have pointed out, development causes artificial scarcity, which inevitably leads to greater competition. Just as importantly, it puts pressure on people to conform to a standard Western ideal — blond, blue-eyed, "beautiful," and "rich" — that is impossibly out of reach.

Striving for such an ideal means rejecting one's own culture and roots — in effect, denying one's own identity. The inevitable result is alienation, resentment and anger. I am convinced that much of the violence and fundamentalism in the world today is a product of this process. In the industrialized world we are becoming increasingly aware of the impact of glamorous media and advertising images on individual self-esteem: problems that range from eating disorders such as anorexia and bulimia to violence over high-priced and "prestigious" sneakers and other articles of clothing. In the South, where the gulf between reality and the Western ideal is so much wider, the psychological impacts are that much more severe.

## COMPARING THE OLD WITH THE NEW

There were many real problems in the traditional society, and development does bring some real improvements. However, when one examines the fundamentally important relationships — to the land, to other people, and to oneself — development takes on a different light. Viewed from this perspective, the differences between the old and the new become stark and disturbing. It becomes clear that the traditional nature-based society, with all its flaws and limitations, was more sustainable, both socially and environmentally. It was the result of a dialogue between human beings and their surroundings, a continuing coevolution that meant that, during two thousand years of trial and error, the culture kept changing. Ladakh's traditional Buddhist worldview emphasized change, but that change occurred within a framework of compassion and a profound understanding of the interconnectedness of all phenomena.

The old culture reflected fundamental human needs while respecting natural limits. And it worked. It worked for nature, and it worked for people. The various connecting relationships in the traditional system were mutually reinforcing and encouraged harmony and stability. Most importantly, having seen my friends change so dramatically, I have no doubt that the bonds and responsibilities of the traditional society, far from being a burden, offered a profound sense of security, which seems to be a prerequisite for inner peace and contentment. I am convinced that people were significantly happier before development and globalism than they are today. The people were cared for, and the environment was well sustained — which criteria for judging a society could be more important?

By comparison, the new Ladakh scores very poorly when judged by these criteria. The modern culture is producing environmental problems that, if unchecked, will lead to irreversible decline; and it is producing social problems that will inevitably lead to the breakdown of community and the undermining of personal identity.

# 4

# GLOBAL ECONOMY
# AND THE THIRD WORLD

## Martin Khor

*When confronted with growing joblessness, Americans and Europeans often blame competition from low-wage Third World countries, or the influx of immigrants from those countries. In fact, it is more directly the new round of economic colonialism that is the culprit, as it sets into motion the kinds of changes that cause the immigration and also have dire effects on the poorest countries themselves — countries whose economies have fallen under the control of foreign corporations and whose resources are raided and shipped north to the wealthiest industrial nations. The new trade rules leave Third World countries with little ability to resist or protect themselves, or to seek alternative economic strategies. In this chapter, Martin Khor presents a summary review of the negative impacts on the environment and social structures.*

*Formerly a professor of political economy, Khor is now president of the Third World Network in Penang, Malaysia, one of the world's leading voices of opposition to the present globalization pattern, with offices in Asia, Africa, and South America. He has been research director of the Consumer's Association of Penang and vice president of Friends of the Earth-Malaysia. He is editor of* Third World Resurgence *magazine and author of* Malaysian Economy: Structures and Dependence *(1983).*

BEFORE COLONIAL rule and the infusion of Western systems, people in the Third World lived in relatively self-sufficient communities, planted rice and other staple crops, fished and hunted for other food, and satisfied housing, clothing, and other needs through home production or small-scale industries that made use of local resources and indigenous skills. The modes of production and style of life were largely in harmony with the natural environment.

Colonial rule — accompanied by the imposition of new economic systems, new crops, the industrial exploitation of minerals, and participation in the global market (with Third World resources being exported and Western industrial products imported) — changed the social and economic structures of Third World societies. The new structures, consumption styles, and technological systems became so ingrained in Third World economies that even after the attainment of political independence, the importation of Western values, products, technologies, and capital continued and expanded. Third World countries grew more and more dependent upon global trading and financial and investment systems, with transnational corporations setting up trading and production bases in the Third World and selling products there. With the aid of infrastructure programs funded by industrial governments, multilateral institutions such as the World Bank, and transnational banks, Third World governments were loaned billions of dollars to finance expensive infrastructure projects and to import highly capital-intensive technologies. They were also supported by foundations, research institutions, and scientists in the industrialized countries that carried out research on new agricultural technologies that would "modernize" the Third World — that is, that would create conditions whereby the Third World would become dependent on the transnational companies for technology and inputs.

To finance the import of modern technology and inputs, Third World countries were forced to export even more goods, mainly natural resources such as timber, oil, and other minerals, and export crops that consumed a larger and larger portion of the total agricultural land area. Economically, financially, and technologically, Third World countries were sucked deeper and deeper into the whirlpool of the world economic system and consequently lost or are losing their indigenous skills, their capacity for self-reliance, their confidence, and, in many cases, the very resource base on which their survival depends. But the Western world's economic and technological systems are themselves facing a crisis. The Third World is now hitched onto these systems, over which they have very little control. The survival and viability of most Third World societies will thus be put to the test in the next few decades. Even now, there are numerous examples of how the Western system has caused the degradation of the environment and the deterioration of human health in the Third World.

# IMPORT OF HAZARDOUS TECHNOLOGIES
# AND PRODUCTS

Many transnational companies have shifted their production operations to the Third World, where safety and environmental regulations are either very lax or nonexistent. Some corporations are also concentrating their sales efforts on the markets of the Third World, where they can sell lower-quality products or products that are outright toxic and thus banned in the industrialized countries.

As a result, Third World people are now exposed to extremely toxic or dangerous technologies that could potentially cause great harm. The Bhopal gas tragedy, in which six thousand lives were lost and another two hundred thousand people suffered disabilities, is the most outstanding example to date of what can happen when a Western transnational company adopts industrial safety standards far below acceptable levels ,in its home country. There are hundreds of other substandard industrial plants sold to the Third World or relocated there by transnationals to escape health and pollution standards in their home countries. The Batoon nuclear plant in the Philippines is one such example.

Hazardous products are also being pushed on the Third World in increasing volume. There are many examples of these: pharmaceutical drugs, contraceptives, and pesticides banned years ago in Europe, America, or Japan but sold by companies of these same countries to the Third World; cigarettes with a far higher tar and nicotine content than in the rich countries; and, most recently, milk products contaminated with high radioactivity resulting from the Chernobyl nuclear disaster. The health effects on Third World peoples are horrendous. For example, it is estimated that forty thousand people in the Third World die from pesticide poisoning each year. Moreover, millions of babies have died of malnutrition or illness from diluted or contaminated baby formula pushed by transnational companies that persuaded mothers to give up breast feeding on the argument that infant formula is a superior form of nourishment.

The hazardous technologies and products imported from the industrialized countries often displace indigenous technologies and products that may be more appropriate to meet the production and consumption needs of the Third World. Labor-intensive technologies that provide employment for the community and are in harmony with the environment (traditional fishing methods, for instance) are replaced with capital-intensive modern technologies that in many instances are ecologically destructive. Appropriate products or processes (such as breast feeding) are replaced by modern products that are thrust upon the people through high-powered advertising, sales promotions, and pricing policy. The Third World is thus losing many of its indigenous skills, technologies, and products, which are unable to survive the onslaught of the modern world.


## THE GREEN REVOLUTION

The modern industrial system has changed the face of Third World agriculture. In many Third World societies, under the new plantation system, much of the lands formerly planted with traditional food crops have been converted into cash-crop production for export. If export prices are high, the incomes obtained could be higher for export-crop farmers; but when prices fall, as they have in recent years, the farmers are not able to buy enough food with their incomes, and also many agricultural workers lose their jobs.

The so-called Green Revolution is a package program that makes it possible to grow more than one crop per year through the introduction of high-yielding seed varieties (especially of rice), high doses of chemical fertilizers and pesticides, agricultural machinery, and irrigation. While its stated purpose was to increase food supply, the entire Green Revolution was little more than a market expansion program of the U.S. chemical industry, largely paid for by U.S. aid programs. In many areas where this "revolution" was implemented there was an initial rise in production because more than a single crop could be produced in a year. But the corresponding rise in farmers' incomes was soon offest by the increasing costs of imported chemical inputs and machinery. High-input agriculture favored richer farmers who could afford to pay for the chemicals, and drove out poorer farmers who could not. The pesticides exacted a heavy toll in thousands of poisoning cases. In addition, the high-yielding crop varieties are very susceptible to pest attacks as insects become resistant to the pesticides. Yields in some areas have dropped. Meanwhile, thousands of indigenous rice varieties that had withstood generations of pest attacks have been abandoned and are now only preserved in research laboratories, most of which are controlled by international agencies and corporations in rich countries. Third World farmers and governments will increasingly be at the mercy of the transnational food companies and research institutions that have collected and patented the seeds and germ plasm originating in the Third World itself. [See chapter by Vandana Shiva and Radha Holla-Bhar.]

# BIOTECHNOLOGY: THE LATEST WEAPON

Although it is still relatively new, the application of biotechnology to agriculture has already had severely detrimental impacts on Third World economies. A few examples will illustrate this point.

Fructose produced by biotechnology has captured over 10 percent of the world sugar market and caused sugar prices to fall, throwing tens of thousands of sugar workers in the Third World out of work. Seventy thousand farmers in Madagascar growing vanilla were ruined when a Texas firm produced vanilla in biotech labs. [See chapter by Jeremy Rifkin.] In 1986, the Sudan lost its export market for gum arabic when a New York company discovered a process for producing gum.

It is now estimated that biotechnology can find substitutes for $14 billion worth of Third World commodities now exported to the rich countries. This will dramatically reduce the Third World's income.

# MODERN FISHING DESTROYS
# FISHERY RESOURCES

In many Third World countries, fish is the main source of animal protein, and fishing was once a major economic activity. In traditional fishing, the nets and traps were simple, and ecological principles were adhered to: The mesh size of the nets was large enough to avoid trapping small fish, the breeding grounds were not disturbed, and fish stocks could multiply. Fishing required hard work and tremendous human skill, passed on through generations. Boats and nets were usually made from local materials, and the whole community was involved in fishing, fish preservation, mending nets, the making of boats, and so on.

Then modern trawl fishing was introduced, in many cases funded by aid programs. (In Malaysia, for instance, it was introduced through a German aid program.) There was an explosive increase in the number of trawlers, usually owned by nonfishing businessmen and operated by wage-earning crews. This led to gross overfishing, and much of the fish caught by trawlers was not used for human consumption but sold to factories as feed-meal for animals. The criterion in trawl fishing was maximum catch for maximum immediate revenue. The mesh size is usually small so that even small fish could be netted and sold, and crews used destructive gear that scraped the bottom of the seabed and disturbed breeding grounds. As a result, there was a decrease in fish stocks in many parts of the Third World for both traditional and trawl fishermen.

Meanwhile, riverine fishery resources have also been destroyed by industrial toxic effluents, which kill off fish life and poison villagers' water supplies. In the rice ponds, where farmers used to catch freshwater fish to supplement their diet, the pesticides introduced by the Green Revolution have also killed off fish life. Thus the livelihoods of millions of small-scale fishermen in the Third World have been threatened, while an important source of protein for the general population has been depleted. In Malaysia, where fish used to be abundant and considered a poor man's meat, the depletion of marine life has caused seafood to become one of the most expensive items on restaurant menus, seriously reducing poor people's access to fish protein.

## LOGGING OF TROPICAL FORESTS

Another fast-disappearing Third World resource is the tropical forest. Traditionally, forests were inhabited by indigenous peoples practicing *swidden agriculture*, which, contrary to modern propaganda, was an ecologically sound agricultural system that caused minimal soil erosion in the hilly tropical terrain and endured for millennia. Massive logging activities have threatened this system, as trees are chopped down by transnational corporations for log export to the industrialized countries or for conversion of primary forest to cattle-grazing land for the U.S. hamburger industry. Between 1900 and 1965, half the forest area in developing countries was cleared, and since 1965 the destruction has further accelerated. Many millions of acres are destroyed or seriously degraded each year, and by the end of this century little primary forest will be left.

The massive deforestation has myriad ecological and social consequences: the loss of land rights and way of life (or even life itself) for millions of tribal peoples throughout the Third World; massive soil erosion due to the removal of tree cover, thus causing the loss of invaluable topsoil; much-reduced intake of rainwater in catchment areas, as the loss of tree cover increases water runoff to rivers; extensive flooding in downstream rural and urban areas, caused by excessive silting of river systems; not to mention its contribution to climatic change.

## MODERN INDUSTRIAL PLANTS
## AND ENERGY MEGAPROJECTS

The introduction of Western consumer goods, industrial plants, and energy megaprojects has also greatly contributed to the loss of well-being in the Third World.

The indigenous, small-scale industries of the Third World produced simple goods that satisfied the basic needs of the majority of people. The technology employed to manufacture these goods was also simple and labor-intensive. Many of these indigenous industries have been displaced by the entry of modern products that, when heavily promoted through advertising, became glamorized, rendering the local products low in status by comparison. With modern products capturing high market shares, modern capital-intensive industries (usually foreign-owned) set up their bases in Third World countries and displace the traditional, locally owned industries.

But many Third World countries were not content simply with modern consumer-goods industries. They also copied the cities of the industrial nations and set up large infrastructure and industrial projects: steel mills, cement plants, vast highways, big bridges, and super-tall buildings. The political leaders and elites of the Third World feel their countries need to have all this in order to appear "developed," just like the industrial countries.

Huge amounts of energy are required by modern industrial plants and infrastructure, hence the need for the megaprojects in the energy sector — particularly large hydroelectric dams and nuclear power stations. Each such project has its problems: The huge dams require the flooding of large tracts of forest and agricultural land, causing the displacement of many thousands of people living there. In any case, the dams do not last for long due to siltation, so they are usually not viable financially. Their costs far outweigh their benefits. There are also health effects, as ecological changes associated with dams and irrigation canals spread schistosomiasis (carried by snails), malaria, and other waterborne diseases. Finally, there is the possibility of a major tragedy should the dam burst, as has occurred in India and elsewhere.

In the case of nuclear power plants, those sold to the Third World do not have the same quality and safety standards as those installed in industrialized countries, where there is stricter quality control and greater technical expertise. If a power plant installed in a Third World country is found unsafe, the government has a dilemma: stop its operation and incur a huge loss or continue using it but run the risk of a tragic accident. In the Philippines, Westinghouse Corporation built a nuclear power plant for $2 billion, but there were so many doubts about its safety that the Aquino government decided to "mothball" it. Even when a nuclear power plant is declared safe enough to start operating, there is the difficulty of disposing of its radioactive waste.

These huge industrial, infrastructural, and energy projects often cost hundreds of millions or billions of U.S. dollars. The projects are invariably marketed by transnational corporations that stand to gain huge sums in sales and profits per approved project. Financing is arranged by the World Bank, by transnational commercial banks, or by First World governments, usually under aid programs. Such projects are rarely appropriate for genuine development, since they end up underutilized, grossly inefficient, or too dangerous to use. Absorbing so much investment funding, they deprive communities of much-needed finance for genuine development projects while leading the borrowing Third World nations into the external debt trap. Finally, they cause widespread disruption and displacement of poor communities, especially indigenous peoples, who by the hundreds of thousands have to be "resettled" as their forests and lands are flooded out by dams.

## THE DRAIN OF RESOURCES
## FROM SOUTH TO NORTH

In this way, via their powerful technological capacity and their domination of the new global systems of trade and finance, the industrial countries have rapidly sucked out forest, mineral, and metal resources from the Third World and used its land and labor resources to produce the raw materials that feed the machinery of industrialism. It is worth reminding readers that the industrial nations — approximately one-fifth of the world's population — use up four-fifths of the world's resources, mostly for making luxury products. The Third World, by contrast, with three-quarters of the world's population, uses only 20 percent of the world's resources. Since incomes are also unequally distributed within Third World nations, a large part of these resources are used to make or import the same luxury products as are enjoyed in the industrial nations and to import capital-intensive technologies required to produce such elite consumer goods. Thus, only a small portion of the world's resources serves the basic needs of the poor majority in the Third World, who sink deeper into the trough of poverty and destitution. This is the ultimate environmental and social tragedy of our age.

Worse yet, the very processes of extracting Third World resources result in environmental disasters such as massive soil erosion and desertification, pollution of water supplies, and poisonings from toxic substances and industrial accidents. The resource base on which communities have traditionally relied for both production and home needs has been rapidly eroded. Soils required for food production become infertile; forests that are home to indigenous peoples are logged; water from the rivers and wells are clogged up with silt and toxic industrial effluents.

The transfer of resources from South to North takes place through many channels. First, there is the transfer of physical resources. For example, only 20 percent of the world's industrial wood comes from tropical forests, but more than half of that is exported to the richest nations. The developed countries produce and keep 80 percent of the world's industrial wood but also import much of the rest of the world's timber harvest as well. Most of it is used for furniture, high-class joinery, housing, packing material, even matchsticks. Thus the wood that is exported to First World countries mainly for luxury use is lost to Third World peoples, who now have difficulty getting wood for essential uses such as making houses, furniture, and boats.

Second, there is a transfer of financial resources in that the prices of Third World commodities (often obtained at a terrible environmental cost) are low and declining even more. Between $60 and $100 billion per year were lost to Third World countries in 1985 and 1986 alone due to the fall in commodity prices. In human terms, this means drastic cuts in living standards, massive retrenchments of workers, and big reductions in government budgets in many Third World countries.

Third, many of the "development projects" that lead to the loss of resources are financed by foreign loans. It is rare for these projects to generate sufficient returns to enable repayment of debt, so debt repayments are ultimately met by the already impoverished Third World citizens.

## THE NEW GATT

This deteriorating situation has been exacerbated by the passage of the Uruguay Round of GATT. The United States and other developed countries have expanded the powers of GATT (which formerly dealt only with the regulation of trade in goods) to include service industries. The major areas included are banking, insurance, information and communications, the media, and professional services such as law, medicine, tourism, accounting, and advertising.

It is now possible to predict that because of the new rules of GATT, many of the service industries in the Third World will come under the direct control of the transnational service corporations within a few years. This means that the last sectors in the Third World that are still controlled by national corporations will be taken over by northern transnationals. In terms of manufacturing and agriculture, many Third World countries are already controlled by transnational corporations, either through investments or through dependence upon products from the global market.

Now the multinational service corporations are able to set up in the Third World and are not only given the freedom to trade and invest there but also to benefit from what is referred to as *national treatment*, which means that a transnational company must be given the same terms as those accorded to a national or local company. Some Third World countries formerly restricted the participation of foreign banks in the economy by, for instance, giving a limited number of licenses to foreign banks or by allowing foreign banks to participate only in certain kinds of banking. [See chapter on electronic money by Richard Barnet and John Cavanagh.] Foreign banks may be prohibited from setting up branches in small towns so that local banks will have more of the deposit business. Now, under GATT, foreign banks are given total freedom and will be treated just like local companies. We are thus going to see the marginalization of local banks, local financial services, and professional services. It may even mean that media companies in the United States or Australia may be given the freedom to set up television and print media companies in the Third World and thereby actually control the cultures of Third World countries.

GATT will also drastically affect people's health. The commercial health care industry and the insurance companies of the Northern countries are launching a very big drive to commercialize health care services in the Third World. Health insurance companies, in conjunction with the private sector (the big hospital establishments of the North), are beginning to buy up hospitals and accelerate the commercialization of health care in the Third World, thus making it unavailable to the vast bulk of its population.

Third World countries may believe that if they give way to the developed countries in areas such as services, investments, and intellectual property rights, they may benefit in other areas. For instance, they may be given better access to the markets of the industrialized countries through lower tariffs. But this may be an illusion. The industrialized countries have violated similar bargains with Third World countries in the past, and Third World complaints may be given especially short shrift by the World Trade Organization.

Under the new conditions for trade and investments, neither the Third World nor the United States will have the authority to establish environmental, occupational health, or other safety regulations, some of which will be considered to be against the principles of free trade and free investment. For instance, Indonesia recently proposed to ban the export of rattan, which is a very important forest product. Rattan is getting ever scarcer, and the government wanted to retain rattan in Indonesia for domestic use. This of course was welcomed by environmentalists, who do not want to see the depletion of forest resources. Immediately, however, the United States and the European Community criticized the Indonesian government on the grounds that the export ban was against the principle of fair trade. They accused the Indonesian government of taking protectionist steps and threatened retaliation against its exports.

Under GATT rules, a government can theoretically propose to ban international trade in toxic wastes or in products that are banned in countries where they are produced because they are considered dangerous, such as pesticides, drugs, and so on. But when some Third World governments actually tried to put trade in toxic wastes onto the agenda of GATT, it was resisted by the developed countries.

## AN ALTERNATIVE VISION

The analyses just given clearly show that a radical reshaping of the international economic and financial order must occur so that economic power, wealth, and income are more equitably distributed and so that the developed world will be forced to lower its irrationally high consumption levels. If this is done, the level of industrial technology will be scaled down, and there will be less need for the tremendous waste of energy, raw materials, and resources that now go toward the production of superfluous goods simply to maintain "effective demand" and to keep the monstrous economic machine going. If appropriate technology is appropriate for the Third World, it is even more essential as a substitute for the environmentally and socially obsolete high technology in the developed world.

But it is almost impossible to hope that the developed world will do this voluntarily. It will have to be forced to do so, either by a new unity of the Third World in the spirit of OPEC in the 1970s and early 1980s or by the economic or physical collapse of the world economic system.

In the Third World, there should also be a redistribution of wealth, resources, and income, so that farmers have their own land to till and thus do not have to look for employment in timber camps or on transnational company estates. This will enable a redistribution of priorities away from luxury-oriented industries and projects and toward the production of basic goods and services. If the poor are allocated more resources, the demand for the production of such basic goods and services would increase. With people given the basic facilities to fend for themselves, at least in terms of food crop production, housing, and health facilities, Third World governments can reduce their countries' dependence on the world market.

Thus there could be a progressive reduction in the unecological exploitation of resources. With increasing self-reliance based on income redistribution and the resurgence of indigenous agriculture and industry, the Third World could also afford to be tough with transnationals; it would be able to insist that those invited adhere to other health and safety standards that now prevail in the industrial countries. It would be able to reject the kinds of products, technologies, industries, and projects that are inappropriate for need-oriented, ecologically sustainable development.

In development planning, the principles of such ecologically sustainable development should be adopted: minimizing the use of nonrenewable resources; developing alternative renewable resources; and creating technologies, practices, and products that are durable and safe, and satisfy real needs.

` In searching for the new environmental and social order we should realize that it is in the Third World that the new ecologically sound societies will be born. Within each Third World nation there are still large areas where communities earn their livelihoods in ways that are consistent with the preservation of their culture and of their natural environment. Such communities have nearly disappeared in the developed world. We need to recognize and rediscover the technological and cultural wisdom of our indigenous systems of agriculture, industry, shelter, water and sanitation, and medicine.

By this I do not mean here the unquestioning acceptance of everything traditional in a romantic belief in a past Golden Age. For instance, exploitative feudal or slave social systems also made life more difficult in the past. But many indigenous technologies, skills, and processes are still part and parcel of Third World life and are appropriate for sustainable development and harmony with nature and the community. These indigenous scientific systems have to be accorded their proper recognition. They must be saved from being swallowed up by modernization.

Third World governments and peoples in the developed world have first to reject their obsession with modern technologies, which absorb a bigger and bigger share of investment funds for projects such as giant hydrodams, nuclear plants, and heavy industries that serve luxury needs.

We need to devise and fight for the adoption of appropriate, ecologically sound, and socially equitable policies to satisfy our needs for such necessities as water, health, food, education, and information. We need appropriate technologies and even more so the correct prioritizing of what types of consumer products to produce; we can't accept appropriate technology producing inappropriate products. Products and technologies need to be safe to handle and use; they need to fulfill basic human needs and should not degrade or deplete the natural environment. Perhaps the most difficult aspect of this fight is the need to deprogram Third World peoples away from the modern culture that has penetrated our societies, so that life-styles, personal motivations, and status structures can be delinked from the system of industrialism and its corresponding creation of culture.

• • •

The creation and establishment of a new economic and social order, based on environmentally sound principles, to fulfill human rights and human needs is not such an easy task, as we know too well. It may even be an impossible task, a challenge that cynics and even good-hearted folks in their quiet moments may feel will end in defeat. Nevertheless, it is the greatest challenge in the world today, for it is tackling the issue of the survival of the human species and of Earth itself. It is a challenge that we in the Third World readily accept. We hope that together with our friends in the developed countries we will grow in strength to pursue the many paths toward a just and sustainable social and ecological order.

# 5

# HOMOGENIZATION
# OF EDUCATION

## Maude Barlow and Heather-jane Robertson

*Before Canada joined the Canada-U.S. Free Trade Agreement and NAFTA,
citizens' groups waged a tremendous opposition campaign not only on environmental and economic grounds but also on the basis of the resultant Americanization of Canadian culture, entertainment, and education. Maude Barlow
and her organization, The Council of Canadians, were the leaders of that bat-
tle. Here, Barlow joins Canadian education writer Heather-jane Robertson in
describing the effects of NAFTA, particularly on Canadian education.*

*Robertson is director of professional development for the Canadian Teachers
Federation, a member of the Canadian Centre for Policy Alternatives, and a
frequent commentator for the Canadian Broadcast Corporation. Barlow and
Robertson are coauthors of* Class Warfare: The Assault on Canada's Schools
*(1994), and Barlow is author of* Parcel of Rogues *(1991), a bestseller, and*
Take Back the Nation *(1991, with Bruce Campbell).*

*D*URING THE last decade, Canada has fundamentally realigned its
orientation from east-west to north-south, in essence becoming part
of a new borderless North American economy. The resulting harmonization can be seen everywhere.

Big business' interest in our schools is symbolic of the Americanization
of Canadian education, which in turn is part of the current major transformation of Canadian economic, social, and cultural life. It comes as no
surprise to anyone who has witnessed the transformation of the workplace and the street. Canada is now experiencing an unprecedented, cor-
porate-led assault on the sense of collective responsibility upon which our
country was founded.

All Canadian institutions are now under intense pressure to operate as if they were businesses. The corporate model, based on head-to-head competition and survival of the fittest, has become the prototype for all government and, more recently, educational institutions. As the United States and Canada effectively merge, Canada finds itself adopting American-style individualism, unabashed entrepreneurialism, and a culture of competitiveness.

## CONTINENTAL DRIFT

In the wake of NAFTA, virtually all control over foreign investment in Canada has been removed, and thousands of Canadian enterprises have been taken over by American and other transnationals, which often shut down production and convert the Canadian branch office to a warehouse or marketing division. North American corporations, whether Canadian-based or not, now see Canada as another "state," about the market size of California.

Wal-Mart, the world's largest retailer and America's third-largest corporation, has invaded the Canadian market with a vengeance, swallowing Woolco stores in one gulp. Deregulation in the telecommunications industry has opened the door to the invasion of U.S. firms; as many as eighty companies, including AT&T and all its major American competitors, have set up shop to lease phone circuits at deep discounts, bringing to Canada the same consumer chaos and industry layoffs that characterize the deregulated U.S. system of a decade ago.

The Canadian tax structure is also being adapted to the reality of a continental, indeed global, economy in which capital can move across national borders as if they don't exist. The federal government is contracting out many operations formerly handled by the public service sector, and competition for these contracts must now be open to American companies. One of the last acts of the Mulroney government was to award the contract to computerize the entire delivery system of Family Allowance, Canada Pension, and Old Age Pension checks to a Texas-based transnational formerly owned by Ross Perot.

Canadian culture takes up less air and screen time than ever. Protections — postal rates for Canadian magazines, film distribution, tax credits for Canadian films, legislation to keep Canadian book publishing companies in Canadian control — are being eliminated steadily.

Canada no longer has an energy policy to protect our supplies of natural gas and oil. The labeling of water as a "tradeable commodity" under the terms of NAFTA sets the stage for massive water-diversion projects to the thirsty U.S. midwest, California, and Mexico. An acre of Canadian forest is being clearcut every twelve seconds (Brazil cuts one acre every nine seconds), mostly by foreign-based transnationals.

Our constitutionally mandated transfer payments to less-advantaged regions of the country are being diminished, thus ensuring a future of great regional disparity resembling that of our southern neighbors. Universal coverage in all social programs, except health care, is history. Our system of unemployment insurance is being fundamentally reorganized to conform to the system in the United States, where relatively few citizens are entitled to it. Even health care is under severe strain, and some provinces are openly setting the stage for a user-fee system.

Most provinces have broken collective bargaining agreements, even those whose governments have traditional ties to labor. Like the United States, Canada is developing an entrenched underclass, and our middle class is under assault. Increasingly, we are adopting the American definition of welfare as charity for those unable to make it in a system that goes unquestioned and moving away from our traditional view of welfare as protection for the community as a whole. We are becoming a harsher people — less compassionate about the unemployed, less responsible to one another.

Given all the sweeping changes to Canada's structures and values and the unprecedented continentalization that has occurred in so short a time, it is not reasonable to suppose that Canadian education can escape the pressures to "harmonize" with the U.S. system of education.

## FREE TRADE IN EDUCATION

The Canada-U.S. Free Trade Agreement and its successor, the North American Free Trade Agreement, have been sold fraudulently to the Canadian people as mere processes to liberalize trade and solve cross-border disputes. In fact, they establish a whole new framework of social and economic policy for the Americas and create an alternative, nonelected continental governing structure that has as much influence on education as on every other sector.

In their book *Pandora's Box* (1993), John Calvert, of the Canadian Union of Public Employees, and Larry Kuehn, of the British Columbia Teachers' Federation, warn that: "NAFTA, like the Canada-U.S. Free Trade Agreement before it, treats many of our social institutions, including education, as service commodities that must be opened up to the competitive pressures of the marketplace. The assumption that educational services can — indeed should — be treated as economic commodities constitutes a fundamental break with our Canadian traditions and presents a clear and present danger to the educational programs that we cherish."

Here's how NAFTA poses this danger: First, the agreement opens up Canada's services, including many public sector and educational services, to U.S. companies for competition in our market and for government contracts. Although the deal technically allows governments to run public education systems, they must do so within the rules set out in the sections dealing with services. This is the catch: NAFTA gives U.S. companies what are called *national treatment rights*. This means that Canadian governments must treat U.S. companies as if they were Canadian and cannot give preference to domestic companies. The rule also applies to provincial governments and contracts. In other words, governments cannot favor Canadian companies, even if they believe that in culture, broadcasting, and educational services, a Canadian perspective is crucial.

Second, Canadian governments can no longer require that companies bidding on Canadian contracts maintain a presence in the country. As Calvert and Kuehn point out, U.S. companies can carry out work or services in Canada without having any investment in the country, without providing any employment, and without even having an office in Canada. This means that public licensing and regulation of educational service providers could be carried out in a manner that does not favor Canadian firms. What will that mean to Canadian standards and content?

Third, NAFTA extends what are called *procurement rights* to American companies, enabling them to bid on public and government contracts. Under this provision, for example, the Canadian government could not reverse a contract with an American transnational to process and deliver Canada's social security checks.

For provincial, state, and local governments, procurement rights do not begin right away, but the process for establishing them does. The intention of opening up other levels of government to transnational bids is quite explicit.

NAFTA negotiators argued that the concerns raised by educators and others were exaggerated, because the agreement allows for some exemptions to the rights just mentioned; that is, a province can opt to exclude certain current public practices from a NAFTA challenge. But there are so many qualifications to the exemption that it is almost meaningless.

Several provincial governments are already rapidly privatizing many educational and other public services and functions. The conservative government in Alberta is perhaps the most radical in its privatization drive. And should future Alberta governments, of whatever political persuasion, want to reverse the privatization steps, the new rules of NAFTA will not allow it.

• • •

The economic "harmonization" of the continent will forever change the nature of education in Canada. It will become more privatized, much closer to the American system, and more commercial in its operations, allowing business big and small to move into this once-restricted sector. As jobs become scarcer and the competition for them more fierce, and as education comes to be viewed as a competitive advantage, education as a business is attracting more corporations and entrepreneurs.

Only 25 percent of educational book publishers in Canada are now Canadian. Under NAFTA, transnationals can now develop educational products for a pan–North American market. Because of their size, American firms will have a market advantage and will be able, under NAFTA, to lower their costs by operating their data processing in low-wage Mexico. Like other U.S.-based corporations, they now view Canada as part of a single North American market and will be impatient to erase any inconsistencies in the systems.

With high-tech telecommunications, one might operate a college, trade, or language school from Florida, say, for all of North America without employing a single Canadian or Mexican and not all that many Americans. The information highway will make it possible for teaching to be done electronically. Thus, a private American corporation could win and fulfill a provincial contract to provide teaching materials or advise on cost-cutting without leaving the head office, wherever that may be. (Several provinces have already hired U.S. management consultants to advise on cutting health care costs.)

As long as educational services are performed by the public sector, they can be kept in Canada; but once a service is privatized, it must be governed by NAFTA rules of "national treatment" and cannot be returned to the public sphere without financial compensation to private interests that were making money in that area or might one day. For instance, the government of British Columbia decided several years ago to contract out the preparation of twelfth-grade provincial examinations. When the contract with the local firm expires, it will have to be opened to competing firms from all over the continent. The Department of Education will have a difficult time arguing that cultural concerns should keep the contract in British Columbia. Under NAFTA, such action could be challenged as a barrier to free trade.

In 1992, the Ottawa Separate School Board hired Texas-based Energy Education Ltd., at a cost of $17,000 a month, to advise it on energy conservation and to design a curriculum for the students on how to implement the project. The board also hired a $50,000-per-year "energy educator." Angry school trustees charged that the company was being paid to "turn off the lightbulbs" and rightly pointed out that Canadian companies, including Ontario provincial government consultants, could do the job for much less money. It was a disgrace, they argued, to allow private American consultants to design student curriculum when the board was laying off teachers. Should their concerns result in a resolution to hire a Canadian company when the contract comes up for renewal, however, the board would be in violation of NAFTA.

At present, contracting extends to support services such as cleaning, food services, school-bus transportation, building maintenance, computer services, and consulting. Eventually, U.S. firms will be able to bid on government educational purchases of computers, supplies, and teaching aids. American fast-food chains, such as Wendy's and Pizza Hut, have already obtained contracts to provide cafeteria services to many U.S. schools and universities and now have the right to bid in Canada.

The current debate in Canadian schools about YNN, the for-profit youth education and news network, will seem a mere skirmish when its American competitors expand into Canada. NAFTA and GATT establish an international framework to protect the private investments of telecommunications firms while opening public systems to privatization.

As Calvert and Kuehn state, "The fact that a communications system is the vehicle through which a nation speaks to itself, or that a telecommunications system has cultural and other non-economic functions, is simply ignored."

When the deregulated information highway becomes a reality and is dominated by transnational phone, cable, and retail giants, and when non-Canadian companies are guaranteed national treatment in Canada, there will be no way to prevent the mass marketing of American for-profit "educational services" once the precedent has been set by YNN. Nor will there be a way to force the services to offer Canadian content — after all, the companies will not even have to have an office in Canada.

Another crucial set of corporate rights contained in both NAFTA and GATT that have wide implications for education is intellectual property rights. Large transnationals, which hold the vast majority of the world's patents, have been attempting for years to enshrine ownership and control of technology and knowledge in international law. The complex ethical and legal question of who owns the fruits of learning is a long-standing issue. In Canada, a compromise position of public and private rights has characterized our legal framework. Knowledge was viewed as a common heritage to be used for the public good, but public access had to be balanced with the rights of the inventor or creator.

The new system, however, skews the balance away from the public interest. The intellectual property provisions of NAFTA and GATT treat knowledge as a commodity and as the exclusive property of the company that takes a patent or holds a copyright on it. That this knowledge may be the consolidation of years, maybe hundreds of years, of collective research, by many individuals or even communities, is irrelevant. The large pharmaceutical, publishing, telecommunications, computer, agribusiness, and other corporations specializing in leading-edge technologies stand to gain worldwide monopoly rights.

This has serious implications for education and for access to the technology that carries it. The trade agreements cover interactive computer and audiovisual learning devices, out-of-country cable and satellite transmission of educational programs, and learning aids. These rights will give transnational education-service companies the power to extract royalties from our public education system that will go to private interests outside of Canada.

## UNIVERSITIES FIRST

To speculate on the implications for our schools, we should examine our universities, which are already moving down this road. Canada's universities and colleges, like our schools, have a different history than their American counterparts. They were created as public institutions accountable to the public through the government. The United States favors private institutions financed both by foundation and corporate wealth and by governments; even the U.S. public system, set up to serve less-affluent students, has now been forced to chase private sources. The distinction between public and private has blurred.

In Canada, cash-strapped universities are now also turning to business for sponsorship, as governments cut back on funding. This is creating serious ethical questions about who owns the results of research done on their premises and which research gets done. Universities have the researchers and scientists; corporations have the money.

In "Universities for Sale," an article from *This Magazine* (September 1991), journalist John Harris says, "Knowledge that was free, open and for the benefit of society is now proprietary, confidential and for the benefit of business. Educators who once jealously guarded their autonomy now negotiate curriculum planning with corporate sponsors. . . . Professors who once taught are now on company payrolls churning out marketable research in the campus lab, while universities pay the cut-rate fee for replacement teaching assistants. . . . University presidents, once the intellectual leaders of their institutions, are now accomplished bagmen."

In exchange for free merchandise, universities offer exclusive access to students for corporate sponsors. A professor's ability to attract private investment is now often more important than academic qualifications or teaching ability. Provincial and federal funding to postsecondary institutions is also increasingly tied to commercial considerations. The federal government is giving research grants to individual faculty members whose projects have commercial viability while cutting general transfer payments. Funding-agency mandates now state clearly that grant money should directly benefit business.

Universities now have CEOs, business-liaison officers, and corporate advisers. Fund-raising campaigns are increasingly, of necessity, the highest priority of the administration, the board of governors, and the faculty; and in more and more universities, the arts and humanities, considered "soft" largely because they do not attract corporate sponsorship, are being phased out. Companies footing the bill for the departments that survive increasingly consider the results of research to be their own.

A department will often consider the number of patents it has registered to be more important than the number or quality of its faculty members' publications. Some are establishing their own foundations and companies to license their research for patents in cooperation with the private sector. Many universities now have an intellectual-property office that seeks private enterprise partners.

A convergence of academic and corporate heavyweights has formalized these interlocking interests in the Corporate–Higher Education Forum (CHEF), a national coalition of university presidents and corporate CEOs designed to merge goals and activities. Modeled on the American Business Higher Education Forum, the Canadian group promotes corporate-university interaction by placing members on one another's governing bodies. Like its American counterpart, the forum campaigns against government regulation of postsecondary education and for closer business-university ties. It actually advocates maintaining government underfunding of education so that free-market forces will pick up the difference and increase universities' dependence on corporate funding.

The forum advocates that "activist corporations" set up their own development offices to negotiate deals with universities as part of their business strategy.

Harris describes a discovery in chemical-pollution control in a lab at the University of Waterloo. There are no cheers, no rush to make the university's achievement public or to share it with colleagues. The business interest that funded the project keeps it quiet until patents are secured. Next to be determined are royalty shares for faculty, jobs for grad students, and marketing plans. Thus, a discovery with significant potential for the environment is now in the hands of a private transnational, out of Canadian control, safe from being used for the public good.

## CONTINENTAL EDUCATION
## SUPERSTRUCTURE

As postsecondary education in Canada becomes more like that of the United States, the next logical step is to create North American educational institutions that "harmonize" standards, training, and certification for education professionals. It is, of course, highly desirable to establish models of educational cooperation across the continent and globally, but it is essential to examine the motivation behind the projects now underway and the form they are taking.

To see what the future of continental education would look like, we must examine the makeup and history of the U.S.-based Business Higher Education Forum (BHEF) and the CHEF (mentioned earlier), the corporate lobby groups behind the education project. The BHEF links representatives of the corporate Who's Who — Ford, AT&T, Pfizer, Eastman Kodak, Johnson & Johnson, Rockwell, Heinz, General Electric, and others — with university presidents in a sustained campaign against government regulations, environmental protection, health and safety laws, and equitable income distribution. BHEF includes many of the same corporate players appointed to former president Bush's New American Schools Development Corporation, established to funnel corporate funds into for-profit elementary schools, and to spearhead the privatization of American schools.

The Canadian CHEF, like the BHEF, is made up of the CEOs of many major corporations, including Imperial Oil, Spar Aerospace, Xerox, IBM, Alcan, and Du Pont, all sponsors of free trade agreements. It has close ties to the Business Council on National Issues (BCNI), which is calling for higher university and college tuition fees, the replacement of provincial transfer payments with direct grants to students to enable them to choose public or private institutions, and government cutbacks to post-secondary education. The BCNI was the most influential lobby group behind the Mulroney government's economic and social policies — privatization, the destruction of universal social programs, massive deregulation, and the disciplining of the workforce through unemployment and competition for jobs. Key players in these groups are represented at the conferences and meetings being held across the continent.

A series of tri-national conferences — in Racine, Wisconsin; Guadalajara, Mexico; and Vancouver, British Columbia — brought together senior North American educational officials and university administrators to facilitate the creation of an "academic common market in North America." Notably absent among the delegates were teachers' organizations, faculty associations, and unions.

The United States Information Agency describes the purpose of the conferences: to "promote a North American approach to the development of higher education programs and projects." The Vancouver meeting, in September 1993, called for a North American distance education and research network; a trilateral electronic information highway "to be easily accessible by the academic community, business, and government foundations"; a North American corporate higher education council comprising senior representatives of the corporate and higher-education communities of the three countries "to act as advocates . . . for further partnering in the realization of mutually agreed objectives"; and a consortium of North American businesses for trilateral research, development, and training to "secure private sector funding, through the membership of individual corporate citizens of the three countries, to be used to implement research and training initiatives of value to both the corporate and higher education communities."

Canada's participation in the group is coordinated by the Department of Foreign Affairs, signaling that a convergence of purpose is being sought between higher education and the free market model of continental trade and economic development. In other words, the government is collaborating in turning over the future of higher education in North America to the corporate forces behind NAFTA and to their aim of commercialization and privatization of our universities.

Recently, the governments of Mexico and the United States have been meeting to discuss ways to coordinate their primary and secondary education programs. They are focusing on shared curriculum reforms, teacher exchanges, and the redesign of teacher education. These meetings signal negotiations under another provision of NAFTA that is of concern. The agreement establishes a process for the "harmonization" of professional standards of teachers across the continent. It calls for the "development of mutually acceptable professional standards and criteria" including "conduct and ethics, professional development and re-certification and scope of practice"(NAFTA, Annex 1210). The Canadian institutions responsible for teacher standards must provide recommendations to a commission set up under the agreement; the commission will review the recommendations from Canada and from the other countries and develop for adoption common standards "within a mutually agreed period."

The intention to override Canadian authority in education isn't even being denied. Trade minister Michael Wilson responded to teachers' concern over certification in May 1993: "Professional services rank as one of the more important components of cross-border trade in services. . . . There is every logic to seeing that trade agreements covering cross-border services address matters of licensing and accreditation."

Standards for educators vary widely on the continent and reflect the cultural and societal values of each country. The "harmonization" of these standards, particularly if driven by an economic agenda, would seriously invade the countries' political and educational sovereignty. Under the new process, which Canada is legally obligated to enter, an unelected trinational commission will have more power over professional standards than the federal government has been given in our constitution.

The "harmonization" of the continent to conform to corporate models is well underway. The process will give Canadians who rarely question the purpose or nature of our schools an opportunity to confront the ideological nature of the attack on public schools and to understand the crucial role education plays in the political life of a nation. The conscious recognition of the role of foreign corporations in the transformation of Canada may provoke the question, How will a Canadian public system, serving our needs and transmitting our culture and social commitment, survive?

To remodel a society, it is essential to influence the hearts and minds of the young. At its most basic level, the assault on Canada's education system is an attack on the history, culture, and values of the nation itself.

# 6

# HOMOGENIZATION OF GLOBAL CULTURE

### Richard Barnet and John Cavanagh

*An intrinsic part of the process of economic globalization is the rapid homogenization of global culture. In this chapter, Richard Barnet and John Cavanagh look particularly at the role the entertainment industry plays in that process. As Western transnational corporations are given full access to all other countries of the world, the cultural transmissions conveyed in Western television, film, fashion, and music ride right in with them, overpowering local media. The effect is to diminish the viability of traditional local cultures and tastes and to accelerate the standardization of markets within the Western conceptual framework.*

*Richard Barnet was cofounder of the Institute for Policy Studies, Washington, D.C., and John Cavanagh is now codirector of IPS and head of its Working Group on the World Economy. Barnet is coauthor of* Global Reach *(1974), and his articles have appeared in the* New Yorker, Harper's, *and the* New York Times. *Cavanagh is coauthor of seven books on development issues, including* Plundering Paradise *(1993, with Robin Broad) and* Global Dreams: Imperial Corporations and the New World Order *(1994, with Barnet).*

SATELLITES, CABLES, walkmans, videocassette recorders, CDs, and other marvels of entertainment technology have created the arteries through which modern entertainment conglomerates are homogenizing global culture. With the toppling of the Berlin Wall and the embrace of free market ideologies in former and current communist countries, literally the entire planet is being wired into music, movies, news, television programs, and other cultural products that originate primarily in the film

and recording studios of the United States. The impact of this homogenization on the rich cultural diversity of communities all around the world
is immense, and its contours are beginning to emerge.

Unlike American automobiles, television sets, and machine tools,
American cultural products are sweeping the globe. Reruns of "Dallas"
and the "Bill Cosby Show" fill the television screens on every continent.
The 1990 fairy-tale hit *Pretty Woman* became the all-time best-selling film
in Sweden and Israel within weeks of its release. Disneyland is now a
global empire; its Japanese incarnation outside Tokyo draws three hundred thousand visitors a week, and Euro Disneyland, a theme park on the
outskirts of Paris occupying a space one-fifth the size of the city itself,
hoped to draw more tourists than the Eiffel Tower, Sistine Chapel, British
Museum, and the Swiss Alps combined.

When the Berlin Wall came down in late 1989, East German families
flocked to West Berlin to taste the fruits of capitalism; what they wanted
most were oranges and pop-music records. In Rio, school kids adorn their
workbooks with pictures of Michael Jackson. In Kashmir, teenagers hum
Beatles songs. All over the world, people are listening to pop music and
watching videos that offer excitement, and a feeling of connectedness to a
larger world. Most of the consumers of these global cultural products are
young.

As governments, families, and tribal structures are thrown into crisis
by the sweeping changes of late twentieth-century society, pop artists have
emerged as global authority figures. Thanks to the microphone and the
camera, a few megastars can communicate the appearance of power and
strong commitment at great distance. Unlike parents, mullahs, chiefs, bureaucrats, and politicians, they ask little of their fans except that they
enjoy themselves and keep buying. On the few occasions when rock stars
call upon their worldwide audiences for personal contributions — for rain
forests, famine relief, AIDS, or political prisoners — the global outpouring
is astounding.

Global entertainment companies are pinning their hopes on the two-
fifths of the world's population who are under the age of twenty. The
competition to hook millions of new fans at increasingly early ages is intense. Sony has expanded into the children's market with its "My First
Sony" line of toylike radios, its new Sony Kids' Music label, and an expanding children's library of videos.

The most spectacular technological development of the 1980s for expanding the reach of global entertainment was MTV. By the beginning of
1993, MTV programming was beamed daily to 210 million households in
seventy-one countries. The cable network, which began in August 1981,

claims to have 39 million viewers in Europe and well over 50 million in the United States. It has already spun off a second network called VH-1. Viacom, the parent company, also has a channel aimed at children called Nickleodeon. (In the early 1990s, Nickleodeon's hit attraction was the "Ren & Stimpy Show," a cartoon saga of a hyperactive Chihuahua and a cat that spits up hair balls.)

The owner of this global network of networks is Sumner Redstone, a Boston multibillionaire who made a fortune in movie theaters. Although his name is unknown to the general public, he has become one of the most influential educators of young people in the world. As MTV was announcing plans to extend its worldwide home entertainment networks to China, Korea, and Taiwan and to launch "Ren & Stimpy" in Europe, Redstone was celebrating the arrival of the global child. "Just as teenagers are the same all over the world, children are the same all over the world," he declared.

Although hundreds of millions of children and teenagers around the world are listening to the same music and watching the same films and videos, globally distributed entertainment products are not creating a positive new global consciousness — other than a widely shared passion for more global goods and vicarious experience. The exotic imagery of music videos offers their consumers the illusion of being connected to cultural currents sweeping across the world, but this has little to do with the creation of a new global identification with the welfare of the whole human species and with the planet itself, as consciousness philosophers, from Kant to McLuhan, had hoped for and predicted. So far, *commodity consciousness* is the only awareness that has been stimulated. The spread of commercially produced popular music, most of it conceived in the United States, is speeding up as once-formidable ideological barriers come down. The collapse of communism makes it easier to export music, film, and video to Eastern Europe, the former Soviet Union, and China. But integrating vast reaches of the world into a global story-and-song market is not a simple task. In 1990, Rudi Gassner was president of BMG International and in direct charge of Bertelsmann's music business. "Our priority," he stated, is "signing acts on a worldwide basis exclusive to BMG for worldwide exploitation." Months before the reunification of Germany was completed, Bertelsmann had hired someone to head its sales force for what had been the German Democratic Republic, where, Gassner says, he is counting on picking up an additional 15 million customers. "Our next target group," he wrote in an internal newsletter for BMG management in 1990, "includes Hungary, Czechoslovakia, and to a certain extent, Poland." But he anticipated "enormous problems for us because of the currency constraints. . . . We will not make money immediately; we will not be able to take money out. But I feel that long term we should be there and be one of the first, if not the first . . . for political and strategic reasons."

The strongest remaining ideological barrier to American music, television, and film is Islamic fundamentalism. In the Khomeini era in Iran American cultural products were the supreme symbols of satanic decadence. The more fanatical Iranian and Saudi authorities became in their attempts to purify their traditional cultures, the more people were drawn to forbidden music and films. Underground video clubs sprang up all over Iran, and crowds came to watch tapes of the latest American network programs and, of course, X-rated films. Pirated Michael Jackson videotapes were available for $50, and underground discos flourished. The Islamic Guards regularly raided all these activities, but in recent years there have been a few signs of liberalization. The technologies of penetration are so powerful that the industry is planning for the day when Iran will rejoin the global market in music and film.

The biggest growth potential for pop music is in Latin America and Asia. (Africa is almost never mentioned.) BMG Ariola Discos operates in Brazil and has 55 percent of the market. About 80 percent of the records sold are by local artists. A country with a yearly inflation rate of 1,800 percent is not an easy place in which to to do business, and when the rate suddenly drops to zero it is no easier; one has to assume that next year it will again be closer to 1,800 percent. But despite Brazil's political and economic difficulties, BMG remains bullish. Today only 50 million of Brazil's 150 million people buy records. But in a few years, Gassner predicts, "another half will be active economically, doubling our market potential."

Musicians, social critics, and politicians in poor countries of Asia, Africa, and Latin America worry that the massive penetration of transnational sound will not only foreclose employment opportunities for local artists but will doom the traditional music of their local culture. "My fear is that in another 10 or 15 years' time what with all the cassettes that find their way into the remotest village, and with none of their own music available, people will get conditioned to this cheap kind of music." This remark by a Sri Lankan musician typifies the anxiety felt throughout the nonindustrialized world — that industrial musical products will sweep away hundreds, perhaps thousands of years of traditional music. "However small a nation we are, we still have our own way of singing, accompanying, intonating, making movements, and so on. We can make a small but distinctive contribution to world culture. But we could lose it."

In the 1980s the environmental movement began to popularize the important idea that biological diversity is a precious global resource, that the disappearance of snail darters, gorgeous tropical birds, and African beetles impoverishes the earth and possibly threatens the survival of the human species. The cultural-environmental movement has no powerful organizations promoting its message, but it has a large, unorganized global constituency. The feeling that world culture will be degraded if diversity is lost is widely shared among artists, cultural conservatives, and nationalists. Yet these concerns are overwhelmed by the sheer power of global popular culture, which threatens local cultural traditions and the traditional communities from which they spring.

The impact of the global music industry on the character of local music has been significant. The Indian pop star Babydoll Alisha sings Madonna songs in a Hindi rendering. Tunisian artists now routinely use synthesizers to accompany the traditional bagpipes at live concerts. The need for financing for expensive electronic instruments and the dependence on access to electricity is changing local music cultures. In Trinidad, the introduction of multichannel recording has transformed the employment prospects of the famous steel bands. It used to be that a hundred musicians would crowd into someone's backyard, all with tuned oil drums, and two microphones would pick it all up to make local tapes. Now, as Roger Wallis of the Swedish Broadcasting Corporation, and Krister Malm, director of the Music Museum in Stockholm, report, a few of the best musicians are brought into a studio, and they now "record all the various parts on different channels on the tape recorder at different times. The final mix . . . might be technically perfect, but it no longer represents the collective communication of 100 musicians and their audiences."

The globalization of the music market and the technology of multiple-channel recording have made it possible to create fresh sounds from all over the world. Everything from *zouk, rhi,* and *jit* from Africa to *salsa* from the Caribbean islands to the chants of India known as *bhangra* are mixed with a variety of American pop genres to produce a blend that is promoted around the world as "world beat." *Lambada,* promoted by French entrepreneurs as the dance craze of Brazil, is Bolivian in origin. A recorded version of this music performed by mostly Senegalese musicians became a global hit. Paul Simon used South African singers and songs for his hit album *Graceland,* but he wrote his own words, and the political message was diluted.

Local musicians are of course excited by the audiences, fame, and money that the international record companies can provide, but some are concerned that their rich cultural traditions are being mined and skimmed to make an international product. The companies, though much agitated about protecting their own intellectual property from pirates, feel no compunction about uprooting the music of indigenous peoples from its native soil and treating it as a free commodity.

To be sure, painters and composers have often borrowed many different artistic traditions. Picasso's use of African images and Dvorak's renderings of folk dances in sophisticated works of chamber music are examples. But there is a line between tapping into an exotic musical tradition and stealing uncopyrighted songs, and sometimes the line is crossed.

The spectacular growth of global commercial entertainment has inspired myriad explanations. The role of technology clearly has been important. The wiring of the world through global transmission of pictures, talk, and music by satellite greatly accelerated the spread of a global market for movies, videos, and television programs. The VCR turned homes, bars, daycare centers, buses, waiting rooms, and nursing homes into a global chain of movie theaters. On the remote island of Siquijor in the Philippines, the inhabitants still gather at "The Hangout" to eat *halo-halo* (chopped ice, corn flakes, fruit, and beans) and watch *Rambo* on videotape. In Colombia, long-distance buses keep their all-night movie fans on the edge of their seats (and the others grumpily awake) with *Robocop*. Hours once written off as commercially irrelevant were suddenly transformed into marketable time; insomniacs, housebound invalids, children with enough disposable income to rent a film, and couch potatoes of every variety could thrust a videocassette into their VCR at any time of the day or night. Old television programs and movies bounce off satellites or travel by cable into homes, schools, and prisons around the world, achieving a certain immortality previously denied to most cultural products. Not many dead poets, pundits, or even departed best-selling novelists last long on the shelf, but, thanks to videotape and the near-universal hunger for American movies, music, and television programs, dead rock stars and movie actors go on forever.

One persuasive explanation is that it fills the vacuum left by the pervasive collapse of traditional family life, the atrophying of civic life, and the loss of faith in politics that appears to be a worldwide trend. Others, such as Helena Norberg-Hodge, argue that the entertainment industry also causes the collapse of these traditions. Popular culture acts as a sponge to soak up spare time and energy that in earlier times might well have been devoted to nurturing and instructing children or to participating in political, religious, civic, or community activities or to crafts, reading, and continuing self-education. Such pursuits may sound a bit old-fashioned today, although political theory still rests on the assumption that these activities are central to the functioning of a democratic society. Yet increasingly, vicarious experience via film, video, and music is a substitute for civic life and community. As it becomes harder for young people in many parts of the world to carve out satisfying roles, the rush of commercial sounds and images offers escape.

In the United States, global cultural products may outrage local sensibilities, but at least they are mostly made in the USA. In Latin America and parts of Asia, American films and television programs dominate the airways. It costs next to nothing to air an old Hollywood B film or a rerun of "I Love Lucy" or "Mr. Ed." Even less antique programs such as "Dallas" or "L.A. Law" are much less expensive to run than local programs with local talent, and the American product is likely to draw a bigger audience. Of the four thousand films shown on Brazilian television, according to the Brazilian film producer Luis Carlos Barreto, 99 percent are from rich countries, mostly from Hollywood. Television is the most powerful force for mass education in most poor countries. Cultural nationalists in Latin America and in pockets of Asia are enraged that the most influential teachers of the next generation are Hollywood film studios and global advertising agencies. But recent trends all over the world — advances in intrusive technologies, privatization, deregulation, and commercialization of electronic media — are making it increasingly difficult for families and teachers to compete with the global media for the attention of the next generation.

# 7

# GLOBAL TRADE
# AND THE ENVIRONMENT

## Edward Goldsmith

*Expanded economic growth and global development cannot be achieved with-out an immense overuse of resources, a fierce assault on remaining species of flora and fauna, the creation of toxic wastelands (and seas), and the degrada-tion of the planet's natural ability to function in a healthy way. The idea, pro-moted in corporate circles, that first we must make countries wealthy through development and then take care of the environment is high cynicism, since de-velopment does not produce wealth, save for a few people; the wealth that is produced is rarely spent on environmental programs; and anyway, by the time the theoretical wealth is generated, life will be unlivable.*

$B$ Y NOW it should be clear that our environment is becoming ever less capable of sustaining the growing impact of our economic activities. Everywhere our forests are overlogged, our agricultural lands over-cropped, our grasslands overgrazed, our wetlands overdrained, our groundwaters overtapped, our seas overfished, and nearly all our terres-trial and marine environment is overpolluted with chemical and radioac-tive poisons. Worse still, our atmospheric environment is becoming ever less capable of absorbing either the ozone-depleting gases or the green-house gases generated by these activities without creating new climatic conditions to which human beings cannot indefinitely adapt.

In such conditions, there can only be one way of maintaining the hab-itability of our planet, and that is to set out methodically to *reduce* the im-pact. Unfortunately, the overriding goal of just about every government in the world is to maximize this impact through economic globalization. Increased trade is seen to be the most effective way of increasing economic development, which we equate with progress and which is believed to provide a means of creating a material and technological paradise on Earth that will methodically eliminate all the problems that have confronted us thus far.

Unfortunately, economic development itself, by its very nature, *increases* the environmental impact of our economic activities. This point is well illustrated by the terrible environmental destruction that has occurred in Taiwan and South Korea, the two principal newly industrialized countries that in the last decades, following the World Bank's dictates to permit heavy interventions by foreign transnational corporations, have achieved the most stunning rates of economic growth. The bank holds them up as models for all Third World countries to emulate.

## THE CASE OF TAIWAN

In the case of Taiwan, as Walden Bello and Stephanie Rosenfeld have carefully documented in their book *Dragons in Distress* (1990), forests have been cleared to accommodate industrial and residential developments and to provide space on plantations for fast-growing conifers. The virgin broadleaf forests that once covered the entire eastern coast have now been almost completely destroyed. The vast network of roads built to open up the forests to logging, agriculture, and development have caused serious soil erosion, especially in the mountain areas, where whole slopes of bare soil have slid away.

Following "free trade" principles, efforts to maximize agricultural production for export-oriented plantations have led to the tripling of fertilizer use between 1952 and 1980, which has led to soil acidification, zinc losses, and decline in soil fertility, with water pollution and fertilizer runoff contaminating groundwater — the main source of drinking water for many Taiwanese. The use of pesticides has also increased massively, and it is a major source of contamination of Taiwan's surface waters and groundwaters. Because of deregulation, pesticide sale is subject to no effective government controls. The food produced is so contaminated with pesticides that, according to the sociologist Michael Hsiao, "many farmers don't eat what they sell on the market. They grow another crop without using pesticides, and that is what they consume."

A substantial number of Taiwan's ninety thousand factories have been located in the countryside, on rice fields along waterways and near private residences. In order to maximize competitiveness, factory owners disregard whatever waste-disposal regulations exist and simply dump much of the waste into the nearest waterway. Not surprisingly, 20 percent of farmland, according to the government itself, is now polluted by industrial wastewater. Nor is it surprising that 30 percent of the rice grown in Taiwan is contaminated with heavy metals, including mercury, arsenic, and cadmium. Human waste, of which only about 1 percent receive even primary treatment, is flushed into rivers, providing nutrients for the unchecked growth of weeds, which use up the available oxygen and kill off the fish life. This also explains why Taiwan now has the world's highest incidence of hepatitis. Agricultural and industrial poisons and human waste have now severely polluted the lower reaches of nearly every one of Taiwan's major rivers, many of which are little more than flowing cesspools, devoid of fish. In Hou Jin, a small town near the city of Kaohsiung, forty years of pollution by the Taiwan Petroleum Company has not only made the water unfit to drink but actually combustible.

The shrimp-farming industry has achieved a fantastic growth rate, with prawn production increasing forty-five times in just ten years. Shrimp farmers, however, have themselves become deprived of the fresh water they need because of the buildup of toxic chemical wastes in rivers and wells from upstream industries. As a result, the mass deaths of prawns and fish have become a regular occurrence.

Air pollution has also increased massively, reaching levels that are double those judged harmful in the United States. The incidence of asthma has quadrupled since 1985, and cancer has now become the leading cause of death in Taiwan, its incidence having doubled since 1965. Even if the annual rate of economic growth in Taiwan were cut to 6.5 percent, stresses on Taiwan's already degraded environment would double in a decade — a horrifying thought.

Theoretically, once Taiwan has achieved a certain level of GNP, it might afford to install technological equipment to mitigate the destructiveness of the development process. However, with the advent of the global economy, competitiveness has become the order of the day. This has meant the elimination rather than the application of regulations, including environmental regulations, that increase costs to industry. In fact, not even the rich countries can now afford environmental controls, as the new GATT rules reflect.

# THE CREATION OF CONSUMER CULTURES

Creating a global economy means seeking to *generalize* this destructive process, which means transforming the vast mass of still largely self-sufficient people living in the rural areas of the Third World into consumers of capital-intensive goods and services, mainly those provided by the transnational corporations (TNCs) (Menotti 1995).

For this to be possible, the cultural patterns that still imbue most Third World cultures and that commit them to their largely self-sufficient life-styles must be ruthlessly destroyed and supplanted by the culture and values of Western mass-consumer society. To this end, Western advertising firms, equipped with the latest global communication technologies, are already exporting the gospel of consumerism to the most distant areas of the Third World. Their purpose is to export the socially and environmentally devastating and utterly nonsustainable Western life-style to the five billion or so people who have not yet entirely adopted it. Of course, only the appetite for this life-style can be exported — the life-style itself only an insignificant minority will ever enjoy, and even then for but a brief period of time, for the whole enterprise is ecologically doomed.

The biosphere is incapable of sustaining all six billion of us at the consumption levels of the North. Indeed, the destruction that the global environment has suffered in the last fifty years, since global economic development has actually got under way, is certainly greater than all the destruction we have caused since the beginning of our tenancy on this planet. Our planet cannot possibly sustain a repetition of the last fifty years, let alone a similar period of still greater environmental destruction, without becoming incapable of sustaining complex forms of life.

To bring all Third World countries to the consumption level of the United States by the year 2060 would require 4 percent economic growth per year. The annual world output, however, and in effect the annual impact of our economic activities on the environment, would be 16 times what it is today — which is not even remotely conceivable. Nonetheless, America's Big Three automakers soon hope to finalize deals in China, with the hope of bringing automobiles to each person who now rides a bicycle or simply walks (Menotti 1995). The extra carbon dioxide emissions from several hundred million more automobiles would make nonsense of the tentative prognostics of the United Nations Intergovernmental Panel on Climate Change and lead to a massive escalation in global warming. If every Chinese were to have a refrigerator as well, which is an official goal of the Chinese government, emissions of CFCs and HCFCs would make nonsense of the Montreal protocol to cut down on emissions of ozone-depleting substances.


## THE EMPHASIS ON EXPORT

One of the principles of economic globalization and "free trade" is that countries should specialize in producing and exporting a few commodities that they produce particularly well and import almost everything else from other countries.

A very considerable portion of the world's most basic commodities is already produced for export — 33 percent in the case of all plywood, 84 percent of coffee, 38 percent of fish, 47 percent of bauxite and alumina, 40 percent of iron ore, and 46 percent of crude oil (French 1993).

Since globalization has advanced, timber has also now become an export crop. In Malaysia, more than half the trees that are felled for timber are exported. This brings in one and a half billion dollars a year in foreign exchange but at a terrible environmental cost. Around 1945, Peninsula Malaysia was 70 to 80 percent forested. Today the trees are mostly gone. The result is escalating soil erosion, the fall of the water table in many areas, and a general increase in droughts and floods. The Malaysian states of Sarawak and Sabah are being stripped so rapidly by TNCs that in a few years all but the most inaccessible forests will be destroyed, and the culture and life-style of the local tribal people annihilated as well.

As country after country is logged out, the loggers simply move elsewhere. In Southeast Asia loggers move to New Guinea, Laos, Myanmar, and Cambodia, the last countries that are still forested — and, significantly, those that have remained outside the orbit of the world trading system. At the current rate of forest destruction, these countries will be deforested within the next decade. Already, Mitsubishi and Weyerhauser are moving into Siberia — the last major unlogged forest area on the planet.

Measures to control logging are unlikely. In most Southeast Asian countries, for instance, the politicians and their families own the concessions, and the transnational logging companies they deal with are too powerful to control (Marshall 1990). Only a collapse of the world economy is likely to save the remaining loggable forests.

Somalia has become increasingly dependent on exports of sheep, goats, and cattle, which have grown at least tenfold, and of camels, which have increased twentyfold since 1955. This has contributed to "a breakdown of the traditional, ecologically sensitive, nomadic system of livestock rearing

— leading to overgrazing, soil erosion, and the degradation of range lands, all of which will diminish the ability of the land to provide sustenance for the Somali people" (French 1993). Internal warfare and gangsterism has been one result.

Tobacco is another crop grown for export worldwide, accounting for 1.5 percent of total agricultural export. In the case of Malawi it represents 55 percent of the country's foreign exchange earnings. Robert Goodland (1984) notes that "tobacco depletes soil nutrients at a much higher rate than most other crops, thus rapidly decreasing the life of the soil." But the heaviest environmental cost of tobacco production lies in the sheer volume of wood needed to fuel tobacco-curing barns. Every year, the world loses some 12,000 square kilometers of forest (some experts estimate 50,000 square kilometers), which are cut down, with 55 cubic meters of cut wood burnt for every ton of tobacco cured (Goldsmith and Hildyard 1990).

Coffee is also largely a high-export crop, and its production causes the most serious environmental degradation. As Georg Borgstrom (1967) writes: "The almost predatory exploitations by the coffee planters have ruined a considerable proportion of Brazil's soils."

The same can be said of peanut plantations in French West Africa. Indeed it has been estimated that "after only two successive years of peanut growing, there is a loss of thirty percent of the soil's organic matter and sixty per cent of the colloidal humus. In two successive years of peanut planting, the second year's yield will be from twenty to forty per cent lower than the first" (Franke and Chasin 1981).

What the export-oriented logging industry is doing to our forests and the livestock-rearing schemes and intensive plantations are doing to our land, the high-tech fishing industry, itself dependent on exports — with 38 percent of fish caught worldwide exported — is doing to the seas. Today, nine of the world's seventeen major fishing grounds are in decline, and four are already "fished out" commercially (Wilkes 1995). Total catches in the Northwest Atlantic have fallen by almost one-third during the last twenty years. In 1992, the great cod fisheries of the Grand Banks off Newfoundland in Canada were closed indefinitely, and in Europe mackerel stocks in the North Sea have decreased by fiftyfold since the 1960s.

As fish stocks are depleted in the North, the fleets are now congregating in the south, but the volume of fish exported from developing nations has increased by nearly four times since 1975, and southern fisheries are already under stress (French 1993). The predictable result is the depletion of Third World fisheries too, with the most drastic consequences for local fishing communities.

The expansion of many export-oriented industries gives rise to a whole range of adverse environmental consequences affecting most aspects of peoples' lives. An obvious case in point is the intensive prawn-farming industry that has been expanding rapidly not only in Taiwan but throughout Asia and some parts of the Americas and Africa.

To accommodate prawn farms, about half of the world's mangrove forests have already been cut down. In Ecuador 120,000 hectares of mangroves have been destroyed for this purpose. In Thailand the figure is 100,000 hectares. The consequences of mangrove destruction are catastrophic for local fishing communities, as many fish species necessarily spend the early part of their life cycle among the mangroves.

Another environmental consequence of prawn farms is a reduction in the availability of fresh water for irrigation in nearby rice paddies, the reason being that prawn farms require large amounts of a fresh water–sea water mix in order to produce the brackish water that the prawns require. In the Philippines the overextraction of groundwater for prawn farms in Negros Occidental "has caused shallow wells, orchards and ricelands to dry up, land to subside and salt water to intrude from the sea" (Wilkes 1995).

Because shrimps are carnivorous and feed on fishmeal, prawn farming has also further increased the pressure on world fish supplies. By 1991, 15 percent of world fishmeal supply was consumed by prawn farms. This has seriously reduced the supply of inexpensive locally available fish, such as sardines, for local consumption.

As more and more land is required for the cultivation of export crops, the food needs of rural peoples must be met by production from an ever-shrinking land base. Worse, it is always the good land that is devoted to export crops — land that lends itself to intensive, large-scale mass production. Production for export always has priority since it offers what governments are keenest to obtain: foreign exchange. The rural population is thus increasingly confined to often forested but nevertheless rocky and infertile lands, or steep slopes that are very vulnerable to erosion and totally unsuited to agriculture. These areas are rapidly stripped of their forest cover, ploughed up, and degraded. This has occurred, and continues to occur, just about everywhere in the Third World.

An example is provided by the rapid growth of the soya bean cultivation in Brazil — now the second largest soya bean exporter after the United States. One of the results of such growth has been the forced migration of vast numbers of peasants from their lands in the southern state of Rio Grande do Sul and into Amazonia, in particular to the states of Rondonia and Para, where they have cleared vast areas of forest to provide the land from which they must now derive their sustenance. The land, which is largely lateritic, is totally unsuitable to agriculture and after a few years becomes so degraded that it is no longer of any use. This forces the peasants to clear more forest, which provides them with land for another few years — a process that could theoretically continue until all available forest has been destroyed.

I recently toured the province of Kwa Zulu Natal, in the company of South Africa's leading conservationist, Ian Player, who for a long time was director of Natal's national parks. He showed me that most of the good agricultural land had been converted into plantations producing cash crops, in particular sugar cane and eucalyptus, largely for export. The "tribal lands" to which the bulk of the Zulu population has been consigned occupy rocky and infertile slopes that are eroding fast. The various tribal groups are desperately seeking more land. They know that they cannot obtain access to the plantations, because the lands provide foreign exchange, so they are lodging claims for much of the land that at present forms part of the national parks. In the meantime, because of the deforestation required to accommodate the plantations and the subsistence agriculture in the tribal lands — and also because sugar cane and eucalyptus are highly water-intensive crops (sugar cane being ten times more so than wheat for instance) — the local rivers have dried up and only flow during the rainy season. We flew over one dried-up river bed after another, where in Ian Player's youth there were magnificent rivers with clean water and abundant fish life.

## INCREASED TRANSPORT

So far we have only considered the local effects of extractive export industries, such as logging, ranching, fishing, and prawn farming. But the produce of such industries and that of mining minerals, oil, coal, natural gas, and manufactured goods, must be transported to the countries that import them. With the development of the global economy the volume of such produce and the distances over which it must be transported increase significantly.

Already in 1991, four billion tons of freight were exported by ship worldwide, and this required 8.1 exajoules of energy, which is as much as was used by the entire economies of Brazil and Turkey combined. Seventy million tons of freight that year were sent by plane, and this used 0.6 exajoules, which is equal to the total annual energy use of the Philippines (French 1993).

A European Union task force calculated that the creation of the single market in Europe in 1993 would greatly increase cross-border traffic with a consequent increase in air pollution and noise by 30 to 50 percent. With the growth in trade between North America and Mexico, cross-border trucking has doubled since 1990, and this is even before trade barriers were reduced between the two countries. The U.S. government predicted that after the signature of the North American Free Trade Agreement (NAFTA), cross-border trucking would increase nearly sevenfold. The ratification of the GATT Uruguay Round can only increase the worldwide transport of goods even more dramatically — which means that a vast number of new highways, airports, harbors, and warehouses must be built, which in itself can only cause serious environmental destruction.

The trans-Amazonian highway, for instance, which is designed to supply Asian markets with more timber and minerals, is ripping through one of the most richly forested areas of the tropics. Like previous World Bank–funded highways carved through primary forests (such as the notorious Polonoereste Project, which catalyzed the deforestation of Rondonia and the annihilation of most of its tribal groups), the trans-Amazonian will fragment habitat and open up previously inaccessible lands to loggers, miners, ranchers, and settlers.

In its aim to expand and accelerate the transport of goods along the Río de la Plata, the Hidrovia project of the MercoSur countries will dry out Brazil's Pantanal (the world's largest wetland, which contains the highest diversity of mammals), while worsening flooding downstream. The building of more ports, essential for exporting and importing goods, destroys coastal habitats by demolishing wetlands and mangrove forests, increasing chemical spillage, and dredging the bottoms of bays and lagoons. The increased transport itself will give rise to even more environmental devastation, considering the pollution caused by the extra combustion of fossil fuels — particularly the effect of increased $CO_2$ emissions on global warming — and the accidents during transport that lead to oil and chemical spills. Indeed, if the environmental costs of increased transport were properly internalized, much of world trade would be revealed as uneconomic, and we would return to a more localized, less environmentally destructive trading system (Menotti 1995).

## INCREASED COMPETITION

A European Community (EC) report has seriously questioned the effectiveness of current environmental regulations in protecting our environment as the impact on it continues to grow. The report points out that there has already been a 13 percent increase in the generation of municipal wastes between 1986 and 1991, a 35 percent increase in the EC's water withdrawal rate between 1970 and 1985, and a 63 percent increase in fertilizer use between 1986 and 1991. The report predicts that if current growth rates continue, carbon dioxide emissions will increase by 20 percent by the year 2010, rendering unapplicable the EU countries' commitment to stabilize them by the year 2000.

Clearly then, these regulations must be seriously strengthened. However, in the free-for-all of the global economy no country can strengthen environmental regulations that increase corporate costs without putting itself at a "comparative disadvantage" vis-à-vis its competitors — and running afoul of GATT.

The push for a global carbon tax illustrates the problem. The European Union (EU) and Japan both proposed adopting an international tax on fossil fuels as a first step in a campaign to reduce carbon dioxide emissions. In the United States, however, the Clinton administration decided that it could not get such a tax through Congress; it was called "electorally impossible." So the EU and Japan dropped the idea. Fossil fuel use and carbon dioxide emissions thereby remain almost entirely out of control (Menotti 1995).

In other words, responsible producers who seek to minimize environmental impacts must compete against those who do not and are thereby "more competitive." This, among other things, endangers — indeed condemns — the world's remaining ecologically sustainable economic activities.

An important example is the dilemma of Amazonia's rubber tappers, who extract latex from the rubber trees scattered throughout much of the Amazonian forests in a perfectly sustainable manner. They will encounter increasing difficulty in competing with rubber grown on Asian plantations that have been created by clearing entire tropical forests. They will especially feel pressure from transnational tire companies with plants in Brazil — such as Michelin and Goodyear — as tariffs on natural rubber imports are due to be eliminated in the next decade (Menotti 1995).

Also, in order to increase competitiveness, corporations are increasingly undertaking cost-cutting measures that include reducing, often drastically, the number of their employees. This can significantly increase environmental accidents. A case in point is the Exxon *Valdez* disaster, which would probably not have occurred if Exxon had not eliminated eighty thousand jobs, including reducing the crews of its supertankers by one-third (Hawken 1993). In addition, before the days of "competitiveness," the supertanker would normally have navigated in a safe but slow shipping lane. Instead, it moved to a much faster though more dangerous lane, passing through ice floes from the Columbia glacier. The Bhopal disaster also probably would not have occurred if Union Carbide had not indulged in cost-cutting measures at the risk of safety (Hultgren 1995).

# DEREGULATION

Until recently, corporations were limited in their efforts to cut costs by a host of national regulations that protected the interests of labor, the unemployed, the poor, and, of course, the environment. To the hard-nosed businessman, these regulations were bureaucratic red tape, serving only to increase costs and reduce competitiveness and profit. Pressure has mounted everywhere to get rid of these regulations as quickly as possible. The term used to achieve this short-sighted goal is *deregulation,* and it has recently become the order of the day. When George Bush was vice president, he headed the Reagan administration's Task Force on Regulatory Relief, which, according to Public Citizen's Congress Watch, was involved in thwarting workers' safety regulations, obstructing consumer product safety controls, rolling back highway safety initiatives, and weakening environmental protection. In 1989, during the Bush administration, the work was taken over by Vice President Quayle's Council on Competitiveness. The council was active in opening up for development half of the United States' protected wetlands while tabling over a hundred amendments to the EPA's implementation proposals for the 1990 Clear Air Act.

Whatever deregulation could not be achieved within countries has now been neatly achieved by the new GATT and WTO agreements and through the creation of "free trade zones."

There are now some two hundred free trade zones in the Third World, usually situated near key communication centers. Foreign industries are enticed to establish themselves in these zones by being freed from any effective labor or environmental controls. In such areas, deregulation has been systematic and complete, and environmental devastation has occurred on a literally horrific scale. As Alexander Goldsmith argues in his chapter, the ratification of GATT effectively transforms the whole world into one vast free trade zone.

•  •  •

Further instances of the environmental consequences of increased competitiveness and deregulation are found in those Third World countries that in the last ten years have been subject to brutal International Monetary Fund (IMF) and World Bank structural adjustment programs.

For example, Costa Rica was subjected to nine IMF and World Bank structural adjustment programs between 1980 and 1989. The massive expansion of the banana industry and of heavily subsidized cattle ranching greatly facilitated the increase of exports. But the expansion took place at the cost of self-sufficient small-scale agriculture and of the country's forest cover, which dropped from 50 percent in 1970 to 37 percent in 1987 and still further since. Increasing banana production has also been directly destructive to the environment. Huge amounts of chemical fertilizers and pesticides have been used, which are washed into the rivers and end up in the sea, severely damaging coral reefs. Ninety percent of such reefs have been annihilated in some areas.

By signing the GATT Uruguay Round Agreement, our politicians are effectively subjecting the entire world to one vast structural adjustment program, which ruthlessly subordinates all environmental, social, and indeed moral considerations to the overriding goal of maximizing trade. The environmental consequences can only be grave.

• • •

More effective than deregulation carried out by national governments within their own country is a process that we can call *cross deregulation* — deregulation that is conveniently imposed on countries by their own trading partners under the GATT Uruguay Round Agreement. For example, the EU's April 1994 *Report on U.S. Barriers to Trade and Investment* suggests that the commissioners should seek to overturn a large number of Californian and U.S. federal environmental laws that it felt can successfully be classified as GATT illegal trade barriers. These include California's Safe Drinking Water and Toxic Enforcement Act (Proposition 65), which requires warning labels on products containing known carcinogenic substances. Among the U.S. federal laws targeted by the EU are the "gas guzzler" law and other laws that aim to encourage the production of smaller, more fuel-efficient cars. [For a more extensive list of the laws threatened by GATT challenges, see chapter by Ralph Nader and Lori Wallach.]

It has been estimated by the U.S. chief negotiator at one of the preparatory meetings for the Rio environmental conference that 80 percent of America's environmental legislation could be challenged in this way, and most of it could be declared illegal before WTO panels.

Meanwhile, the United States and other countries can also obligingly challenge European Union environmental laws, resulting in a process whereby countries deregulate each other to the benefit of TNCs.

# THE "STANDARDS" OF FREE TRADE

It is important to realize that the new free trade agreements were designed and promoted by associations of businesses for whom environmental regulations are no more than costs that interfere with profits and therefore must be minimized.

From the very start of the negotiations that led to the signing of these treaties, the environmental issue has been avoided altogether whenever possible. As Canadian Greenpeace activist Steven Shrybman reports (1990), the Canadian government actually sought to justify this omission in the case of the Canada-U.S. agreement on the grounds that "it is a commercial accord between the world's two largest trading partners. It is not an environmental agreement," and "the environment is not therefore a subject for negotiation; nor are environmental matters included in the text of the agreement." Shrybman goes on: "This is an astonishing statement, in view of the fact that the agreement explicitly deals with such issues as energy, agriculture, forest management, food safety and pesticide regulations, matters that could not bear more directly on the environment."

Nor is it surprising that the very word *environment* appears nowhere in the mandate of GATT. Neither is it mentioned in the constitution of the World Trade Organization, save in a cursory manner in the preamble.

Public pressure has, of course, forced the bureaucrats to take some notice of environmental issues, and there is even talk of "greening the GATT." But, whatever the rhetoric, environmental standards that will increase costs to industry are summarily rejected. Thus in 1971 the GATT secretariat stated that it was inadmissible to raise tariffs so as to take into account pollution abatement costs. In 1972 it refused to accept "the polluter pays principle," even though it had been adopted by the Organization for Economic Cooperation and Development (OECD) Council that same year.

It is thereby not surprising that the international standards for food safety set by the Codex Alimentarius (a little-known U.N. agency that now fixes international food safety standards) are not designed to influence countries to increase their pitifully lax environmental standards but, on the contrary, to reduce them. Thus 42 percent of the Codex standards for pesticides are lower than EPA and FDA standards. Fifty times more DDT, for instance, may be used on or left in residual amounts on peaches and bananas, and thirty three times more DDT may be applied on broccoli.

In the interests of the international harmonization of standards, the

EPA and FDA standards will almost certainly be challenged. They are too high, but if they were lower, they would not be challenged, for, as Ralph Nader puts it, "the international standards provide a ceiling but not a floor" for environmental and health protection (testimony before the House Small Business Committee, April 26, 1994). Governments might theoretically set standards that are higher than the WTO standards, but only if the standards can avoid being classified as nontariff barriers to trade and hence as GATT-illegal. This is extremely difficult.

The global economy we are creating can therefore only massively increase environmental destruction — not only by increasing its impact on an environment that cannot sustain the present impact but also by eliminating regulations designed to contain this impact, and which necessarily increase corporate costs.

Clearly, there is no way of protecting our environment within the context of a global "free trade" economy committed to continued economic growth and hence to increasing the harmful impact of our activities on an already fragile environment.

We must reverse our course. As Tim Lang and Colin Hines recommend in their book, *The New Protectionism* (1994), we must seek to emphasize local production for local consumption, reduce global trade, and ensure strong environmental standards at all times. There is no evidence that trade or economic development are of any great value to humanity. World trade has increased by twelve times since 1950 and economic growth has increased fivefold, yet during this period there has been an unprecedented increase in poverty, unemployment, social disintegration, and environmental destruction. The environment, on the other hand, is our greatest wealth, and to kill it, as the TNCs are methodically doing, is an act of unparalleled criminality. What is more, it can only be in their own very short-term interests to do so, for, as their leaders should realize, there can be no trade and no economic development on a dead planet.

# 8

# GATT, NAFTA, AND THE SUBVERSION OF THE DEMOCRATIC PROCESS

Ralph Nader and Lori Wallach

*Ralph Nader has repeatedly been rated in national polls as "the most respected person in America," and he has surely been the single most effective voice in the United States on behalf of consumers, democracy, and the environment over the past three decades. He and his colleague Lori Wallach were among the first American activists to recognize clearly the unique dangers and vast scope of NAFTA, GATT, and the entire globalization agenda. In this chapter, they focus on the undemocratic manner in which the agreements were created, sold, and passed and, should they continue to exist, their crushing effects on worldwide democracy. Ralph Nader is the founder of Public Citizen, and Lori Wallach is a public interest lawyer who is director of Public Citizen's Global Trade Watch.*

*I*N THE FALL OF 1994, just prior to the vote by the Congress on the Uruguay Round of GATT, the vote that would establish the World Trade Organization, we offered a $10,000 donation to the charity of choice of any congressperson who could do the following: (1) sign an affidavit stating that he or she had read the five-hundred-page agreement and (2) successfully answer ten simple questions about its contents.

Not one member of congress accepted.

Here our country was on the brink of a vote that would have corrosive effects on the supremacy of our domestic democratic procedures, including the right of federal, state, and local governments to establish our laws, and on the ability of the United States of America to maintain some control over the powers of transnational corporations. This vote would essentially decide whether half a century of laws protecting the safety of consumers, workers, and the environment could be expanded or even sustained into the future, and not one member of Congress could state that he or she had read the text.

The text is several hundred pages long, complicated, and duplicitous. However, if legislators are vested with the responsibility to legislate, they should have read what they were voting on.

Finally, after the scheduled fall vote on GATT was postponed until December 1994, one senator, Colorado Republican Hank Brown, stepped forward and accepted the challenge. He read the text, signed the affidavit, and, with the media watching in the Senate Foreign Relations Committee room, answered all ten questions correctly.

He then held a news conference stating that he had planned to vote *in favor* of GATT, but after reading the text of the agreement, he was aghast. Even though he described himself as a supporter of "free trade" and had voted for NAFTA in 1993, he could not support GATT because of its elimination of even the most basic due process guarantees.

On December 1, 1994, Congress approved GATT in the House 235 to 200 and in the Senate 68 to 32 *without knowing what was in it*. Here is a summary report on some of the details that the Congress missed and on the consequences of their uninformed vote.

## THE MECHANICS OF POWER

When they approved the far-reaching, powerful World Trade Organization and smaller international trade agreements such as NAFTA, the U.S. Congress, like legislatures of other nations, left much of the United States' capacity to protect its citizens subject to the WTO's autocratic regimes and accepted harsh legal limitations on what domestic policies the country may pursue. Approval of these agreements has institutionalized a global economic and political situation that places every government in a virtual hostage situation, at the mercy of a global financial and commercial system run by empowered corporations. This new system is not designed to promote the health and well-being of human beings but to enhance the power of the world's largest corporations and financial institutions.

Under the new system, many decisions that affect billions of people are no longer to be made by local and national governments but instead, if challenged by any WTO Member nation, would be deferred to a group of unelected bureaucrats sitting behind closed doors in Geneva. The bureaucrats can decide whether or not people in California can prevent the destruction of their last virgin forests or determine if carcinogenic pesticides can be banned from their food; or whether European countries have the right to ban the use of dangerous biotech hormones in meat. Moreover, once these secret tribunals issue their edicts, no external appeals are possible; worldwide conformity is required. A country must make its laws conform or else face perpetual trade sanctions.

At risk is the very basis of democracy and accountable decision making that is the necessary undergirding of any citizen struggle for sustainable, adequate living standards and health, safety, and environmental protections. The decline of democratic institutions in favor of deepening multinational corporate power has taken place in Western nations over the past several decades; but the establishment of the World Trade Organization (WTO) marks a landmark formalization, strengthening, and politicalization of this formerly ad hoc system.

Best described as *corporate globalization*, the new economic model establishes supranational limitations on any nation's legal and practical ability to subordinate commercial activity to the nation's goals. The objective is to overrule democratic decision making on matters as intimate as food safety or conservation of land, water, and other resources.

One cannot open a newspaper today without facing myriad examples of the problems this system spawns: lowering standards of living for most people in the developed and developing world; growing unemployment worldwide; endemic business criminality and the collapse of associated legal order; environmental degradation and natural resource shortages; growing political chaos and a global sense of despair about the future.

Conspiratorial meetings have not been necessary to fuel the push for globalization. Corporate interests share a common, perverse outlook: The globe is viewed only as a common market with a labor and capital pool. From the corporate perspective, a good new system eliminates barriers to trade on a global scale, whereas from any *other* perspective, such barriers — that is, any nation's laws that foster economic well-being, democratic processes, worker and citizen health and safety, and sustainable use of resources — are seen as valued safeguards on unfettered, harmful business activity. From a corporate perspective, the diversity that is a blessing of democracy is *itself* the major barrier.

On rare occasions, promoters of the economic globalization agenda have been frank about their intentions. "Governments should interfere in the conduct of trade as little as possible," said Peter Sutherland, then director general of GATT, in a March 3, 1994, speech in New York City.

The *Wall Street Journal* was more direct. After the agreement was signed, the *Journal* editorialized that GATT "represents another stake in the heart of the idea that governments can direct economies. The main purpose of GATT is to get governments out of the way so that companies can cross jurisdictions (i.e., national boundaries) with relative ease. It seems to be dawning on people . . . that government is simply too slow and clumsy to manage trade." Should it be corporations, then?

What makes such statements especially alarming is that what is being characterized as "trade" these days includes the workings of a large portion of each nation's economic and *political* structures. GATT and other trade agreements have moved beyond the traditional roles of setting quotas and tariffs and are instituting new and unprecedented controls over investment flows, innovations, public assets, and democratic governance. Undermining national and local laws and erasing economic boundaries via capital mobility and "free trade" have caused the likes of Monsanto, Pfizer, Citicorp, General Motors, Cargill, Shell, and other corporations to rejoice. But the prospect of global commerce without democratic controls suggests impending disaster for everyone else in the world.

As economist Herman Daly warned in his January 1994 "Farewell Lecture to the World Bank," the push to eliminate the nation-state's capacity to regulate commerce "is to wound fatally the major unit of community capable of carrying out any policies for the common good . . . Cosmopolitan globalism weakens national boundaries and the power of national and subnational communities, while strengthening the relative power of transnational corporations."

The philosophy allegedly behind the globalization agenda is that maximizing global economic liberalization will result in broadly based economic and social benefits. However, anyone who believes that corporate economic globalization has any purpose other than to maximize short-term profit need only consider the case of U.S.-China economic relations. In 1994, the Clinton administration ended the historical linkage between favorable trade status and a country's human rights record. However, in early 1995, when there was a threat to property rights, McDonald's lease, and Mickey Mouse's royalties, China was threatened with a billion dollars of trade restrictions. This threat resulted in Chinese government policy changes to enforce intellectual property rights.

GATT and NAFTA do not target for elimination all "fetters" on commerce. Rather, the agreements promote the elimination of restrictions that protect people but increase protection for corporate interests. For instance, the regulation of commerce to protect environmental, health, or other social goals is strictly limited, and labor rights, including prohibitions on child labor, were entirely left out as inappropriate limitations on global commerce. On the other hand, the protection of corporate property rights (such as intellectual property) received expanded monopoly power. The right to invest capital in any country without local restrictions or conditions was also strengthened.

## Targeting Democratic Laws

The world community founded GATT after World War II as an international contract that set rules for world trade. At present, more than one-hundred nations responsible for more than four-fifths of world trade belong to it. In its first forty years of existence, GATT concerned itself primarily with tariffs, quotas, and related matters. Periodically, the GATT signatories, called "contracting parties," would meet and negotiate tariff and quota rules for trade in products. Things changed, however, when the GATT Uruguay Round negotiations began in 1986.

The Uruguay Round puts into place comprehensive international rules about which policy objectives so-called independent countries are permitted to pursue and which means a country might use to obtain even GATT-legal objectives. In other words, GATT placed controls over national democracies. In the United States, congressional and presidential approval of GATT and NAFTA gave the agreements the status of U.S. federal law. Thus, GATT and NAFTA rules trump U.S. state and local laws as a matter of U.S. constitutional jurisprudence. As one memo leaked out of the Pennsylvania House of Representatives warned: "GATT will require the federal government to get a state law overturned if the WTO ruled that the state law violated the GATT."

Under WTO rules, for example, certain *objectives* are forbidden to all domestic legislatures, including the U.S. Congress, the state legislatures, and county and city councils. These *objectives* include providing any significant subsidies to promote energy conservation, sustainable farming practices, or environmentally sensitive technologies. Laws with *mixed goals*, such as provisions of the U.S. Clean Air Act that implement the international ozone agreement (which bans the import and sale of products made with ozone-depleting production methods), conflict with the WTO's requirements. In addition, the WTO trumps provisions in pre-existing international agreements, including environmental treaties that conflict with trade rules.

Further, the *means* used to implement even these *objectives* that the WTO allows must be the "least trade restrictive," regardless of whether these are politically feasible. Thus, for instance, policies banning the export of raw logs, adopted in many countries to slow the cutting of forests, would be threatened. Till now, such laws have been the *only* politically viable options to save forests in certain countries, for they provided lumber processing jobs for people who could no longer be loggers. Unfortunately, such export bans are seen as highly "trade restrictive."

Third, most government procurement must meet GATT rules. One such rule is that all corporations must be given *national treatment*, meaning that they must be treated the same way whether local or foreign. In the past the use of tax dollars through government purchases of goods and services has always been considered a key governmental policy tool. Procurement rules advanced economic development in poor regions, promoted certain businesses, and furthered policies such as recycling or alternative energy development. Local preferences also put tax dollars back into communities. But under the recent procurement rules, with few exceptions, governments must allow equal treatment of domestic and international companies for providing government goods and services.

Finally, to limit a vast array of national, state, and local environmental, health, consumer, and worker safety standards, the Uruguay Round expanded coverage of *nontariff barriers* — that is, any measure that is not a tariff but inhibits certain trade. However, what the WTO (and NAFTA) view as nontariff barriers, most Americans see as basic environmental and health protections. Any national, state, or local standard that provides more protection than does a specified industry-shaped international standard must pass a gauntlet of WTO tests to avoid being labeled an illegal trade barrier.

Any WTO Member may challenge any U.S. law as an illegal trade barrier before a WTO tribunal in Geneva. The tribunal has the power to approve sanctions against countries that refuse to remove laws that are deemed GATT-illegal. Such decisions are made by officials of other countries and by lobbies that have no accountability requirements.

The concept of nontariff barriers being illegal gives corporate interests a powerful tool to undermine safety, health, or environmental regulations they do not like. For example, right now, pesticide manufacturers and wine importers are using GATT and NAFTA to claim that the United States cannot institute a planned ban of the carcinogenic fungicide Folpet on food residues.

• • •

There is no mystery as to which U.S. laws other countries consider to be nontariff trade barriers. The European Union, Japan, and Canada publish annual reports describing the U.S. laws they view as illegal trade barriers. Here is a recent sampling of targeted U.S. laws: the Delaney Clause, which prohibits carcinogenic food additives; the Nuclear Non-Proliferation Act; the asbestos ban; driftnet fishing and whaling restrictions; the Consumer Nutrition and Education Labeling Act; state recycling laws; and limitations on lead in consumer products.

The U.S. Corporate Average Fuel Economy (CAFE) standards and gas-guzzler taxes were challenged in 1994 under the old GATT and ruled to be partially in violation. U.S. laws designed to protect dolphins have twice been challenged under the old GATT rules. Venezuela has already submitted a formal challenge against the reformulated gas rules of the U.S. Clean Air Act under the WTO. Laws of other nations — such as Canadian cigarette packaging requirements, Thai cigarette sales limitations, Danish bottle recycling laws, and Canadian reforestation requirements — have also been formally challenged as nontariff barriers under existing free trade agreements or threatened with future challenges under the Uruguay Round rules. There are other laws to be challenged: the U.S., Filipino, and Malaysian bans on raw log export; European bans on smokeless tobacco; laws controlling the capture of animals for fur using brutal steel-jaw leg-hold traps; and laws preventing import of beef tainted with growth hormones. These trade actions have resulted in getting some of these initiatives withdrawn, delayed, or weakened.

It's a very neat arrangement. European corporations target U.S. laws they do not like. U.S. corporations target European laws they do not like. Then European and U.S. corporations attack Japanese laws and vice versa — the process can go on until all laws protecting people and their environment have either been reversed or replaced by weaker laws that do not interfere with the immediate interests of the corporations. Thus, the U.S. government threatens the European ban on Bovine Growth Hormone in its meats (a consumer protection that European citizens want) and threatens to challenge Europe's ban on the sales of furs caught with inhumane steel leg-hold traps. Meanwhile, Europe challenges our fuel-consumption standards and threatens our food labeling laws. Corporations are poised to win at both ends, while citizens and democracy lose.

Most Americans, including members of the U.S. Congress, probably find this unbelievable. After all, most people would suppose that the United States could impose whatever standards it wants on products that will enter our marketplace and be consumed in this country without being second-guessed by anonymous trade bureaucrats. But in approving GATT and NAFTA, the United States has surrendered such laws to the secret judgment of trade bureaucrats.

## The Process: Undemocratic from Beginning to End

From start to finish, all elements of the negotiation, adoption, and implementation of the recent globalized "free trade" agreements were designed to foreclose citizen participation.

*Negotiations.* Trade negotiations invariably have taken place behind closed doors between unelected and largely unaccountable government agents who mainly represent business interests.

Secrecy enveloped the GATT negotiating process itself. Through a variety of stops and starts in the eight years of Uruguay Round negotiations, small cliques of major nations regularly retreated to "green rooms" to make deals that were then forced, on a take-it-or-tough-luck basis, on other GATT signatory countries as "consensus" positions. The conclusion of the Uruguay Round was held hostage as U.S. and European negotiators retreated for a year of private talks, while one hundred other nations waited for the outcome on agriculture. The U.S.-EU negotiations extended grain-export subsidies that promoted the dumping of grain on other nations, putting large numbers of small farmers out of business. Narrowly tailored to suit U.S. and European agribusiness, the conclusions reached at these secret meetings were then announced as the outcome of global agriculture negotiations.

Corporate lobbyists have exerted tremendous influence over the negotiations. The business coalition calling itself the Intellectual Property Committee — whose members include Pfizer, IBM, Du Pont, and General Electric — bragged in its literature that its "close association with the U.S. Trade Representative and [the Department of] Commerce has permitted the IPC to shape the U.S. proposals and negotiating positions." Meanwhile, citizen organizations have not had the resources to post lobbyists in Geneva or coordinate global lobbying campaigns.

As if the advantage in resources were not enough, the corporate lobbying function has been institutionalized in the United States in a set of official trade advisory committees. In 1974, Richard Nixon, a president renowned for his disdain for democracy, proposed *fast track*, a uniquely antidemocratic procedure that requires Congress to vote yes or no on an entire trade agreement and the changes it requires of U.S. law, with no amendments permitted. Congress is required to conduct such a vote within sixty to ninety days of the president's submission of the agreement and its implementing legislation, and debate is limited to twenty hours. As part of the fast-track procedure, Nixon proposed a system of private sector trade advisory groups appointed by the president with extraordinary access to and influence on the negotiating process.

During the recent Uruguay Round negotiations, the advisory committees were composed of over eight hundred business executives and consultants (with limited labor representation), five representatives from the few environmental groups that were supportive or neutral on NAFTA, and no consumer rights or health representatives. Under intense pressure to provide more public participation, the Clinton administration started the Trade and Environment Policy Advisory Committee, appointing equal numbers of corporate and citizen representatives. But the trade advisory committees on timber, chemicals, and other key environmental and consumer interests have exclusively business representatives.

Meetings of the advisory groups are closed to the public, with representatives required to obtain a security clearance from the government after a background check. All documents are considered confidential.

• • •

Once a trade agreement is completed, any person who wants to figure out what the agreement says faces a herculean task.

The first difficulty is to obtain a copy of the actual text. When then-President Bush announced that he had come to a final NAFTA deal with Mexico and Canada in August 1992, he gave an optimistic spin to the agreement. But the actual text was not made available to the American people at his news conference or any other time. An unofficial text appeared a month later, but the official 752-page text, priced at $41, was not available until after Bush left office in 1993.

The second difficulty is that the agreements are unnecessarily complex. Only those with an expansive knowledge of GATT-ese or NAFTA-ese can comprehend what the texts mean for their jobs, food, or environment.

Third, in many countries, the GATT text was simply not available at all. Although the Uruguay Round negotiations were completed in December 1993, by October 1994 (months after the agreement was to have been approved in most countries) it still had not been translated into Japanese for the Japanese Diet or for the public. Translations of the text became available only a few days before it was approved — unread — by the Diet. Many governments around the world failed to translate the agreement into their languages at all but approved it anyway.

This difficulty in obtaining and understanding the actual agreements was no accident; it reflected a purposeful effort by globalization proponents to conceal the agreements' terms and effects from the public, the news media, and even the parliamentary bodies that approved it. The agreements' promoters preferred that citizens only read a sanitized summary suitably interpreted by the agreements' promoters. In their view, it is anathema that citizens should be informed of international commerce and investment issues, never mind actually having a say in their approval.

*"Approval."* Most legislators worldwide had little idea of what they were approving because they relied on the propaganda of their negotiators rather than independent analysis. Even though the WTO has an agenda rivaling that of the United Nations, it was set up with little public or parliamentary debate. It was little more than rubber-stamped by the very elected officials whose democratic powers it was designed to usurp.

Despite unified opposition by U.S. citizens' organizations — including every environmental and labor group and major family farm, consumer, religious, and civil rights organization — and even though U.S. public opinion polls showed majority opposition to the very concept of the WTO, the U.S. Congress approved the Uruguay Round, just as under similar conditions it had passed NAFTA.

Such perversions of democracy were repeated in many nations. In the Philippines, the Catholic Church had joined the official GATT opposition, along with a broad array of civic groups. Despite this and despite anti-GATT street riots, the Filipino Senate ultimately approved the deal.

In Spain, public opposition had forced the government to keep the vote off the parliamentary agenda. However, on Christmas Eve, without public notice, a rump session of Parliament approved the deal.

In Belgium, police dragged citizen protestors out of the parliament building so the deal could be rubber-stamped.

In India, powerful public opposition forced Parliament to eliminate provisions in the Indian bill that implements the WTO. They specifically eliminated the WTO's hated intellectual property rules. Thus, the Indian parliament only approved a portion of the WTO text rather than fully agreeing to become a WTO Member and abide by all of the WTO rules. However, the Indian prime minister then reinstated the intellectual property provisions by executive decree, making India a full WTO Member despite Parliament's opposition. Six months after that, the Indian parliament vetoed the prime minister's action. The prime minister is seeking another way to sidestep the workings of the democratically elected legislature. [See chapter by Vandana Shiva and Radha Holla-Bhar.]

## WTO: GLOBAL ENFORCER

The WTO, the new "governing" structure, was crafted at the end of the Uruguay Round negotiations to organize and enforce this new system of limits on every nation's laws and policies. The new global agency was not in the original plans for the Uruguay Round when its terms of reference were agreed upon in 1986. The WTO was hatched to provide a global executive branch that would judge a country's compliance with the rules, enforce the rules with sanctions, and provide the legislative capacity to expand the rules in the future.

The WTO gives the trade rules both a permanent organizational structure (powers that GATT did not have) and the kind of "legal personality" enjoyed by the U.N., the World Bank, and the I.M.F. The binding provisions that define the WTO's functions and scope do not incorporate *any* environmental, health, labor, or human rights considerations. Moreover, there is nothing in the institutional principles of the WTO to inject any procedural safeguards of openness, participation, or accountability. The WTO provides no mechanism for nongovernmental organizations to participate in its activities and, in several key provisions, requires that documents and proceedings remain confidential.

• • •

The WTO "dispute resolution system" is the mechanism that enforces WTO control over democratic governance. Disputes are not decided by democratically elected officials or their appointees but by secret tribunals of foreign-trade bureaucrats from a preset roster. Only national government representatives are allowed to participate in the dispute resolution process. State and local government representatives (such as a state attorney general), citizens, and the press are locked out.

For U.S. citizens, the notion of delegating "judicial" review to forums that do not have the procedural safeguards of the U.S. federal and state judicial systems is troubling. Trade dispute panels, whether in the WTO, NAFTA, or 1988 Canada-U.S. Free Trade Agreement, share highly problematic traits:

- Tribunals have no guarantee of impartiality or economic disinterest of decisionmakers.

- There is no required disclosure of potential conflicts of interest. (In a recent timber dispute under the Canada-U.S. Free Trade Agreement, two of the five members of the panel were attorneys from firms representing Canadian lumber interests directly affected by the case.)

- All documents, transcripts, and proceedings are secret.

- No media and no citizens can sit in and observe the proceedings. And there is no outside appeal or review available.

The WTO text lists qualifications for dispute tribunal members that ensures they will represent only a *trade uber alles* perspective. The qualifications primarily include experience in a country's trade delegation or experience as a lawyer on a past trade dispute. Such qualifications produce panelists with a uniformly pro-trade perspective.

There is no mechanism to expose such panelists to any alternative perspectives or expert opinions on environmental, health, labor, consumer, or human rights issues. The WTO tribunal rules also forbid identification of panelists who have supported particular positions and conclusions, adding an additional layer of secrecy and lack of accountability.

Ironically, the only specific procedural requirement for WTO tribunals is that they be conducted in *secret*. Unlike complaints, briefs, and affidavits in the U.S. court system, documents presented to the WTO tribunals are kept confidential. Thus it is only as a result of a Public Citizen lawsuit that the U.S. Trade Representative (USTR) must finally release the U.S. submissions to the GATT panels. Even so, these submissions are censored by USTR officials in order to conceal the arguments of the other party. Documents from other parties in the dispute are *still* not available. So, if a state law were to be challenged, governors or state attorney generals would only have access to those documents or proceedings that the federal government chose to make available.

## THE OLD RULES AND THE NEW

A comparison of the rules of the old GATT and the recently established WTO reveals much about the intentions of the people who created the system. At nearly every turn, with nearly every rule, the clear intention is to diminish if not eliminate the democratic process, not only in the internal operations of the GATT bureaucracy and the WTO but also among Member nations. The new rules clearly favor the largest, most developed, and most powerful nations. Here are some examples of those rules:

• Unlike the old rules of GATT, the new WTO requires that all members agree to be bound by all the Uruguay Round accords. The old GATT rules did not require this all-or-nothing standard. From a trade perspective, this rule seems a good idea because it eliminates free riders — countries that do not accept certain provisions but benefit from other countries' compliance. But from the point of view of democracy, the rule forces many countries, usually small ones, to accept trade in areas that might be undesirable in the long run. Their choice is to agree or to forfeit participation in the world trade system. Such all-or-nothing international laws are very rare, because they pose choices incompatible with national sovereignties.

• When countries join the WTO, they authorize the WTO to conduct ongoing negotiations on WTO provisions; many may never be submitted for approval by any elected legislatures. Only a simple majority vote is required to initiate these WTO negotiations; under the old GATT that vote had to be unanimous. Thus the new rules lead to a higher potential for coercion of small nations by larger ones.

• Perhaps the most ominous change is this one: WTO rules and restrictions are now enforceable as regards all existing federal, state, and local laws, and future laws too. As the text says, "Each Member shall ensure the conformity of its laws, regulations and administrative procedures with its obligations as provided in the annexed agreement." So, U.S. law and the laws of every other nation must "conform" to the WTO and each other. Perhaps with this provision in mind, the Clinton administration announced that all *future* U.S. environmental proposals would be put through trade reviews that ensured their compliance with U.S. trade obligations. In effect, the administration voluntarily sacrificed U.S. sovereignty.

• Under yet another WTO provision, a law of a Member nation can be challenged if "the attainment of any objective (of the WTO) is being impeded" by the existence of the law. The vagueness of this provision makes it possible to "smuggle" into the WTO's grasp many national laws that would seem to be free of any implications for trade.

• One additional point of difference concerns the WTO's attack on its Members' democratic and sovereign decision making: Under the old GATT rules, there had to be unanimous approval of all GATT's contracting parties before trade sanctions were imposed on a GATT nation by the other nations. Under the new WTO rules, the determinations by WTO tribunals become automatically binding. This holds unless *all Member countries vote to stop the decision within ninety days.* This is another case where antidemocratic procedural rules determine much of the outcome; the obvious result is that few, if any, tribunal decisions would ever be voted down unanimously. This requirement of consensus to stop the action of an international institution rather than to authorize it is uniquely empowering for the WTO; it means its bureaucratic decisions will be honored and feared, thus further intimidating any resistant strains among nations. Under the old GATT, the opposite rule applied: Decisions were not adopted unless all countries agreed; any single country had the right to block a GATT ruling and thus maintain greater autonomy.

Thus the Bush administration was able to freeze an old GATT tribunal ruling against the Marine Mammal Protection Act, which prevented the import of Mexican tuna caught in a manner that also killed dolphins. A GATT tribunal called that an illegal trade barrier, but Bush, under massive public pressure, was able to veto the ruling by the requirement of unanimity. The new WTO removes all countries' veto power and effectively their ability to maintain laws that protect people or the environment from WTO challenge.

• • •

As mentioned above, the WTO rules require that Members' *future* laws also comply with WTO rules. So WTO Member countries are now required, when promulgating new federal, state, or local laws, to take into account whether or not the new law will conform with WTO rules. Thus the WTO has a chilling effect on policies that are now being written and *re*written with the fear of a future WTO challenge in mind. In some cases, such as a 1994 child labor law proposed in the U.S. Senate, conflict with the WTO was a primary weapon used to squash the bill's progress. To avoid the time and expense of later having to defend a law against a WTO charge, countries can use regulatory discretion, annual budgets, or legislative reauthorization to alter democratically achieved laws to meet WTO rules.

Another example of the WTO's effect occurred in the 1995 New York State budget. Buried in the voluminous state legislation was a list of laws *to be eliminated* because they conflicted with the rules of the WTO. The list included a tropical timber procurement ban, a law requiring that state contractors only purchase from Northern Ireland companies that maintain certain human rights standards (called the MacBride Principles), and a small preference for New York-produced food. Luckily, an enterprising reporter discovered the provisions. The embarrassing revelations and the outrage they generated ultimately forced New York Governor Pataki to withdraw the provisions — at least for the moment. However, such stealth rollbacks of democratically supported policies undoubtedly lurk in other state-level proposals, and the provisions could be tucked into some other bulky state legislation later.

• • •

As a legal matter, the WTO's rules and powerful enforcement mechanism promote downward harmonization of wages, environmental,

worker, and health standards and the undermining of democratic procedures and policies. However, in practice, the race to the bottom set off by
the WTO is even more devastating than the sum of the WTO's provisions. Both NAFTA and GATT have actual provisions requiring harmonization of environmental, safety, food, and other standards. For instance,
under NAFTA, the trucking industry is working through a land transportation harmonization committee to get an increase in truck weights
and lengths for all North American trucks. Such a move would lower
U.S. safety standards through the back door.

By giving up the right to make investment in a country conditional on
certain standards or the entry of products into domestic markets conditional on compliance with national rules, countries have eliminated whatever leverage they had on corporate behavior. U.S. corporations long ago
learned how to pit states against each other in "a race to the bottom" to
profit from whichever state would offer the most miserable wages, the
most lax pollution standards, and the lowest taxes. Now, via NAFTA and
GATT, multinational corporations can play this game at the global level.
After all, externalizing environmental and social costs is one way to boost
corporate profits. Paying child laborers slave wages in some countries may
increase a U.S. firm's bottom line. It is a tragic lure that has its winners
and losers determined before it even gets underway: Workers, consumers,
and communities in all the countries lose, short-term profits soar, and the
corporation "wins."

Under the WTO, the race to the bottom is not only in standard of living, environmental, and health safeguards but in democracy itself. Enact-
ment of the free trade deals virtually guarantees that democratic efforts to
make corporations pay their fair share of taxes, provide their employers a
decent standard of living, or limit their pollution of the air, water, and
land will be met with the refrain, "You can't burden us like that. If you
do, we won't be able to compete. We'll have to close down and move to a
country that offers us a more hospitable climate." This message is extremely powerful — communities already devastated by plant closures
and a declining manufacturing base are desperate not to lose more jobs.
They know all too well that threats of this sort are often carried out.

## STOPPING GLOBALIZATION

One of the clearest lessons that emerges from a study of industrialized societies is that highly centralized commerce is environmentally and democratically unsound. Some international trade is useful and productive,

while other global trading favors corporate advantages over those of workers, consumers, and the environment.

But societies need to focus their attention on fostering community-oriented production. Such smaller-scale operations are more flexible and adaptable to local needs and environmentally sustainable production methods. They are also more easily subjected to democratic control, less likely to threaten to shift their operations abroad, and more likely to perceive their interests as overlapping with community interests.

Similarly, allocating power to reachable governmental bodies tends to increase citizen power. Concentrating power in international organizations, as the trade pacts do, tends to remove critical decisions from citizen control. You can talk to your city council representative but not to some faceless international trade bureaucrat in Geneva, Switzerland.

If a foreign country's simple cry of "nontariff trade barrier" can jeopardize local or state laws, if a country must pay a bribe in trade sanctions to maintain its own laws, if a company claims that the burden of citizen safeguards are so great that it will pick up stakes and move elsewhere, then global living standards will continue to spiral downward.

In the United States, where most wages are at their lowest level in real terms since President Johnson initiated the war on poverty in 1964, a major swath of the American population is working harder to earn less. Polling continues to show a growing "anxious" class. A sense of despair and loss of control is at least part of the explanation for the tumultuous electoral behavior of the past two U.S. federal elections. This new anxious class is politicized and looking for answers.

We must make the clear connection between our local problems and the multinational corporate drive for economic and political globalization. If we don't, then others will blame these increasing problems on other causes. "It's the immigrants!" "It's the welfare system!" "It's greedy farmers or workers!" Allowing the camouflage of the real causes of these multifaceted problems means that citizens are divided against each other to the benefit of the corporate agenda.

We now face a race against time: How will citizens reverse the devastating globalization agenda while democratic options and institutions are still available? The degree of suppression and subterfuge necessary to continue to globalize will be hard to maintain in the presence of *any* democratic oversight. To obtain this oversight and to actually reverse NAFTA, GATT, and the push to globalization will require a revitalized citizenry here and abroad. There will be no dearth of provocations.

# 9

# NEW TECHNOLOGY
# AND THE END OF JOBS

## Jeremy Rifkin

*Jeremy Rifkin is a unique combination of dedicated activist, best-selling au-
thor, and leading philosopher on the social and environmental impacts of new
technologies. Here he describes the relationship between economic globalization, the new computer technologies that accompany it (particularly automation), and the dire future of workers in all segments of economic activity, an
abbreviated version of the themes in his brilliant new book,* The End of Work
*(1995). Rifkin is also known for his crusade against the excesses of biotechnol-
ogy. His many books include* Biosphere Politics *(1991),* Declaration of a
Heretic *(1985), and* Algeny *(1983). He is president of the Foundation on
Economic Trends in Washington, D.C.*

A TECHNOLOGICAL REVOLUTION is fast replacing human beings with
machines in virtually every sector and industry in the global economy.
Already, millions of workers have been permanently eliminated from the
economic process, and whole work categories have largely or totally disappeared. Global unemployment has now reached its highest level since
the Great Depression of the 1930s. Worldwide, more than eight hundred
million human beings are now unemployed or underemployed. And that
figure is likely to rise sharply between now and the turn of the century.

Corporate leaders and mainstream economists tell us that the rising
unemployment figures represent short-term "adjustments" to powerful
market-driven forces that are speeding the global economy in a new direction. They hold out the promise of an exciting new world of high-tech
automated production, booming global commerce, and unprecedented

material abundance. But millions of working people remain skeptical. In the United States, *Fortune* magazine (Sept. 20, 1992) found that corporations are eliminating more than two million jobs annually. While some new jobs are being created in the U.S. economy, they are in the low-paying sectors and are usually temporary.

This same pattern is occurring throughout the industrialized world. Even developing nations are facing increasing "technological unemployment" as transnational companies build state-of-the art, high-tech production facilities, and shed millions of low-wage laborers who can no longer compete with the cost efficiency, quality control, and speed of delivery achieved by automated manufacturing.

Current surveys show that fewer than 5 percent of companies around the world have even begun the transition to the new machine culture. This means that massive unemployment of a kind never before experienced is all but inevitable in the coming decades. Reflecting on the significance of the transition taking place, the distinguished Nobel laureate economist Wassily Leontief (1983) warned that, with the introduction of increasingly sophisticated computers, "the role of humans as the most important factor of production is bound to diminish in the same way that the role of horses in agricultural production was first diminished and then eliminated by the introduction of tractors."

In all three key employment sectors — agriculture, manufacturing, and services — machines are quickly replacing human labor and promise an economy of near-automated production by the mid decades of the twenty-first century.

## NO MORE FARMERS

The high-technology revolution is not normally associated with farming. Yet some of the most impressive advances in automation are occurring in agriculture. New breakthroughs in the information and life sciences threaten to end much of outdoor farming by the middle decades of the coming century. The technological changes in food production are leading to a world without farmers, with untold consequences for the 2.4 billion people who still rely on the land for their survival.

The mechanical, biological, and chemical revolutions in American agriculture over the past one hundred years put millions of farm laborers out of work and transformed the country from a largely agricultural society to an urban industrial nation. In 1850, 60 percent of the working population was employed in agriculture. Today, less than 2.7 percent of the workforce is engaged directly in farming. There are currently more than nine million persons living under the poverty line in depressed rural areas across the United States — all casualties of the great strides in farm technology that have made the United States the number-one food producer in the world and American agriculture the envy of every nation.

Although the farm population is less than three million, it sustains a food industry employing more than twenty million. In our highly industrialized urban culture, most people would probably be surprised to learn that the food and fiber industry is the single largest industry in the United States. More than 20 percent of the GNP and 22 percent of the workforce is dependent on crops grown on America's agricultural lands and animals raised on feed lots and in factory farms.

The decline in the number of farms is likely to accelerate in the coming years. Advances in agricultural software and robotics will lead to higher yields and fewer workers. A new generation of sophisticated computer-driven robots may soon replace many of the remaining tasks on the land, potentially transforming the modern farm into an automated outdoor factory. Israel's farmers are already well along the way to advanced robotized farming. Concerned over the potential security risks involved in employing Palestinian migrant labor, the Israelis turned to the Institute for Agricultural Engineering to help develop mechanical farm laborers. In a growing number of kibbutzes, it is not unusual to see self-guided machines traveling on tracks laid out between rows of plants, spraying pesticides on crops.

The Israelis are also experimenting with a robotic melon picker (ROMPER) that uses special sensors to determine whether a crop is ripe to pick. The introduction of ROMPER and other automated machinery will dramatically affect the economic prospects of the more than thirty thousand Palestinians employed during harvesting season. In the United States, Purdue University scientists say they expect to see ROMPER in use "in every Indiana county by the end of the decade." Similar robots are being developed with artificial intelligence to plow and seed fields, feed dairy cows, even shear live sheep. Researchers predict that the fully automated factory farm is less than twenty years away.

New gene-splicing technologies, which change the way plants and animals are produced, are greatly increasing the output of animals and plants and threatening the livelihood of thousands of farmers. To eliminate the cost of insecticides and the labor required to monitor and spray crops, scientists are engineering pest-resistant genes directly into the genetic structure of plants.

Genetic engineering is also being used to increase productivity and reduce labor requirements in animal husbandry. Bovine Growth Hormone (BGH) is a naturally occurring hormone that stimulates the production of milk in cows. Scientists have successfully isolated the key growth-stimulating gene and cloned industrial portions in the laboratory. The genetically engineered growth hormone is then injected back into the cow, forcing the animal to produce between 10 and 20 percent more milk. A study conducted several years ago predicted that within three years of the introduction of BGH into the marketplace, nearly one-third of all remaining U.S. dairy farmers may be forced out of business because of overproduction, falling prices, and dwindling consumer demand.

Scientists have succeeded in producing genetically engineered pigs that are 30 percent more efficient and brought to market seven weeks earlier than normal pigs. A faster production schedule will mean less labor is required to produce a pound of flesh. In 1993, researchers at the University of Wisconsin announced a successful attempt to increase the productivity of brooding hens by deleting the gene that codes for the protein Prolactin. The new genetically engineered hens no longer sit on their eggs as long. They also produce more eggs.

The merging of the computer revolution and the biotechnology revolution into a single technological complex foreshadows a new era of food production — one divorced from land, climate, and changing seasons, long the conditioning agents of agricultural output. In the coming half-century, traditional agriculture is likely to wane, a victim of technological forces that are fast replacing outdoor farming with manipulation of molecules in the laboratory.

Chemical companies are already investing heavily in indoor tissue-culture production in the hope of removing farming from the soil by the early decades of the twenty-first century. Recently, two U.S.-based biotechnology firms announced they had successfully produced vanilla from laboratory-grown plant-cell cultures. Vanilla is the most popular flavor in America. One-third of all the ice cream sold in the United States is vanilla. Vanilla, however, is expensive to produce because it has to be hand-pollinated and requires special attention in the harvesting and curing process. Now, the new gene-splicing technologies allow researchers to produce commercial volumes of vanilla in laboratory vats, eliminating the bean, the plant, the soil, the cultivation, the harvest — and the farmer. While natural vanilla sells on the world market for about $1,200 per pound, Escagenetics, a California biotechnology company, says it can sell its genetically engineered version for less than $25 per pound.

Over 98 percent of the world's vanilla crop is grown in the island countries of Madagascar, Reunion, and Comoros. For these tiny islands in the

Indian Ocean, the indoor production of vanilla is likely to mean economic catastrophe. The export of vanilla beans accounts for more than 10 percent of the total annual export earnings of Madagascar. In Comoros, vanilla represents two-thirds of the country's export earnings. According to the Rural Advancement Fund International, more than one hundred thousand farmers in the three vanilla-producing countries are expected to lose their livelihood over the next several decades.

Vanilla is only the beginning. The global market for food flavors is hovering near $3 billion per year and is expected to grow at an annual rate of 30 percent or more. According to a Dutch study, nearly ten million sugar farmers in the Third World may face a loss of livelihood as laboratory-produced sweeteners begin invading the world markets in the next several years. In addition, scientists have successfully grown orange and lemon vesicles from tissue culture, and some industry analysts believe that the day is not far off when orange juice will be grown in vats, eliminating the need for planting orange groves.

Martin H. Rogoff and Stephen L. Rawlins, biologists and former research administrators with the Department of Agriculture, envision a food-production system in which fields would be planted only with biomass perennial crops. Using enzymes, the crops would be harvested and converted to sugar solution. The solution would then be piped to urban factories and used as a nutrient source to produce large quantities of pulp from tissue cultures. The pulp would then be reconstituted and fabricated into different shapes and textures to mimic the forms associated with traditionally grown crops. Rawlins says that the new factories would be highly automated and require few workers.

The era of whole-commodities food production is likely to decline in the decades ahead as chemical, pharmaceutical, and biotech companies increasingly substitute tissue-culture production, significantly lowering the price of food products on world markets. The economic impact on farmers could be catastrophic. Many Third World nations rely on the sale of one or two key export crops. Tissue-culture substitution could mean the near collapse of national economies, unprecedented unemployment, and default on international loans, which in turn could lead to the destabilization of commercial banking and to bank failures in the industrialized nations.

Hundreds of millions of farmers across the globe face the prospect of being permanently excluded from the economic process. Their marginalization could lead to global-scale social upheaval and social and political reorganization along radically new lines in the coming century.

## NO MORE FACTORY WORKERS

The specter of the world's farmers being made redundant and irrelevant by the computer and biotechnology revolutions is deeply troubling. Even more unsettling, the manufacturing and service sectors, which have traditionally absorbed displaced rural workers, are undergoing their own technological revolution, shedding millions of jobs to make room for "re-engineered," highly automated work environments. Transnational corporations are entering a new era of fast communications, lean-production practices, and "just-in-time" marketing and distribution operations that rely increasingly on a new generation of robotic workers. Much of the human workforce is being left behind and will likely never cross over into the new high-tech global economy.

From the very beginning of the Industrial Revolution, machines and inanimate forms of energy were used to boost production and reduce the amount of labor required to make a product. Today, the new information and communication technologies are making possible far more sophisticated continuous-process manufacturing. Some of the most dramatic breakthroughs in re-engineering and technology displacement are occurring in the automotive industry. The world's largest manufacturing activity, auto manufacturers produce more than fifty million new vehicles each year. The automobile and its related industrial enterprises generate one out of every twelve manufacturing jobs in the United States and are serviced by more than fifty thousand satellite suppliers.

Industry experts predict that by the late 1990s, Japanese-owned factories will be able to produce a finished automobile in fewer than eight hours. The shortening of production time means that fewer workers are required on the line. Kenichi Ohmae, a leading Japanese management consultant, notes that Japan's nine automakers employ fewer than 600,000 workers to produce more than twelve million cars a year. Detroit automakers employ more than 2.5 million workers to produce the same number of vehicles.

Following Japan's lead, U.S. automakers are beginning to re-engineer their own operations in the hope of increasing productivity, reducing labor rolls, and improving on their market share and profit margin. In 1993, General Motors president John F. Smith, Jr. announced plans to implement changes in production practices that could eliminate as many as ninety thousand auto jobs, or one-third of its workforce, by the late 1990s. These new cuts come on top of the two hundred fifty thousand jobs GM had already shed since 1978. Other global automakers are also re-engineering their operations and eliminating thousands of workers. By 1995, industry analysts predict that German automakers could eliminate as many as one in seven jobs — this in a country where 10 percent of the entire industrial workforce is either in the automotive industry or services it.

As the new generation of "smart" robots, armed with greater intelligence and flexibility, make their way to the market, automakers are far more likely to substitute them for workers, because robots are more cost-effective. It is estimated that each robot replaces four jobs in the economy and, if in constant use twenty-four hours a day, will pay for itself in little over one year. In 1991, according to the International Federation of Robotics, the world's robot population stood at six hundred thirty thousand. That number is expected to rise dramatically in the coming decades as machines become far more intelligent, versatile, and flexible.

The steel industry's fortunes are so closely related to those of the automobile industry that it is not surprising to see the same sweeping changes in organization and production taking place in the steel business. By the 1890s, the United States was the leader in steel production. Today, that competitive edge has been seriously eroded, in large part due to U.S. companies' failure to keep up with Japanese steel manufacturers, which have transformed steel making to a highly automated continuous operation. Nippon Steel's new $400 million cold-rolling mill near Gary, Indiana — a joint venture with Inland Steel — is run by a small team of technicians and has reduced the production cycle of some items from twelve days to one hour.

The increasing automation of steel production has left thousands of blue-collar workers jobless. In 1980, United States Steel, the largest integrated steel company in the United States, employed one hundred twenty thousand workers. By 1990, it was producing roughly the same output using only twenty thousand. These numbers are projected to fall even more dramatically in the next ten to twenty years as even more advanced computerized operations are introduced into the manufacturing process.

The highly automated manufacturing methods are being combined with radical restructuring of the management hierarchy to bring steel making into the area of lean production. Japanese companies, with joint ventures in the United States, have re-engineered traditional plant operations, restructured management hierarchies, and slashed job classifications to improve efficiency. According to the International Labor Organization (ILO), finished steel output from 1974 to 1989 dropped only 6 percent in the Organization for Economic Cooperation and Development (OECD) countries, while employment fell by more than 50 percent. More than one million jobs were lost in the steel industry in OECD nations during this fifteen-year period. "In up to 90 percent of the cases," says the ILO, "the basic explanation for the reduction in employment is therefore not changes in the level of output but improvement in productivity" (van Liemt 1993).

In industry after industry, companies are replacing human labor with machinery and in the process changing the nature of industrial production. One of the industries most affected by re-engineering and the new information-based technologies is rubber. Since the 1980s, tire companies around the world have been restructuring their operations by introducing work teams, flattening the organizational hierarchy, reducing job classifications, instituting job-retraining programs, and investing in new equipment to automate the production processes.

Less than five years after the Japanese-owned Bridgestone acquired a Firestone facility in La Vergne, Tennessee, the production increased from 16,400 to 82,175 tires per month, while the production of tires with blemishes declined by 86 percent. Goodyear claims a similar success story. Goodyear earned a record $352 million in 1992 on sales of $11.8 billion. The company is producing 30 percent more tires than in 1988 with twenty-four thousand fewer employees.

The mining industries, like agriculture, have been undergoing a steady process of technology displacement since 1925, when 588,000 men, nearly 1.3 percent of the nation's entire workforce, mined 520 million tons of coal. In 1982, fewer than 208,000 men and women produced more than 774 million tons of coal. With the use of advanced computer technology, faster excavation and transportation equipment, improved blasting technologies, and new processing methods, mining companies have been able to increase output at an average annual rate of 3 percent since 1970. The Bureau of Labor Statistics forecasts a yearly decline in employment of 1.8 percent through the year 2005. By the first decade of the coming century, a labor force 24 percent smaller than present will produce all of the coal to meet both domestic and overseas demand.

Not surprisingly, some of the most significant strides in re-engineering and automation have occurred in the electronics industry. General Electric, a world leader in electronic manufacturing, has reduced worldwide employment from 400,000 in 1981 to less than 230,000 in 1993, while tripling its sales. In the household appliance industry, new labor and time-saving technologies are eliminating jobs at every stage of the production process. By the year 2005, a mere 93,500 workers — fewer than half the number employed in 1973 — will be producing the nation's total output of home appliances.

In recent years, even the labor-intensive textile industry has begun to catch up with other manufacturing industries by introducing lean-production practices and advanced computer automation systems. The goal is to introduce flexible manufacturing and just-in-time delivery so that orders can be "tailor-made" to consumer demand. The new technologies are beginning to make garment manufacturing in the industrial nations cost-competitive with firms operating in low-wage countries. As more and more of the manufacturing process bends to re-engineering and automation, even Third World exporters such as China and India will be forced to shift from current labor-intensive manufacturing processes to cheaper and faster methods of mechanized production.

## THE LAST SERVICE WORKER

While the industrial worker is being phased out of the economic process, many economists and elected officials continue to hold out hope that the service sector and white-collar work will absorb the millions of unemployed laborers in search of work. These hopes are likely to be dashed. Automation and re-engineering are also replacing human labor across a wide swath of service-related fields. The new "thinking machines" are capable of performing, at greater speeds, many of the mental tasks now performed by human beings.

A *Wall Street Journal* front-page story warned that a historic shift was occurring in the service sector, with growing numbers of workers being permanently replaced by the new information technologies. According to the *Journal*, "Much of the huge U.S. service sector seems to be on the verge of an upheaval similar to that which hit farming and manufacturing, where employment plunged for years while production increased steadily. . . . Technological advances are now so rapid that companies can shed far more workers than they need to hire to implement the technology or support expanding sales"(Rigdon 1994).

Anderson Consulting Company, one of the world's largest corporate restructuring firms, estimates that in just one service industry, commercial banking and thrift institutions — re-engineering will mean a loss of 30 to 40 percent of jobs by 2002 — nearly seven hundred thousand jobs altogether. Many banks are using voice-mail systems for customer service calls, greatly reducing the amount of time representatives have to spend answering inquiries. Automatic teller machines have become ubiquitous in U.S. cities and suburbs, significantly reducing the number of human tellers. Between 1983 and 1993, banks eliminated 179,000 human tellers, or 37 percent of their workforce. By the year 2000, upwards of 90 percent of banking customers will use automated teller machines.

In *The Future Impact of Automation on Workers* (1983), economists Wassily Leontief and Faye Duchin describe the improved efficiency of automated tellers: "A human teller can handle up to 200 transactions a day, works 30 hours a week, gets a salary anywhere from $8,000 to $20,000 a year plus fringe benefits, gets coffee breaks, a vacation and sick time. . . . In contrast, an automated teller can handle 2,000 transactions a day, works 168 hours a week, costs about $22,000 a year to run, and doesn't take coffee breaks or vacations."

The insurance industry is also making a quick transition into the high-tech era. Mutual Benefit Life (MBL) was among the first of the nation's giant insurance companies to re-engineer its operations. MBL did away with the slow, cumbersome, multilayered system of processing applications and installed a single (human) case manager. Armed with a new computer-based workstation and programmed with an "expert system" to help answer questions, the case manager can now process an application in less than four hours. The average turnaround for an application has been reduced from nearly twenty-two days to only two to five days. This allows MBL to eliminate one hundred field office staff while processing twice the volume of applications as before.

The transformation of the traditional office from a paper-handling to an electronic-processing operation will greatly increase the productivity of businesses and eliminate millions of clerical workers by the end of the decade. The nation's secretaries are among the first casualties of the electronic office revolution. The number of secretaries has steadily declined as personal computers, electronic mail, and fax machines replace manual typewriters, paper files, and routine correspondence. Leontief and Duchin estimate that the conversion from paper handling to electronic processing will save offices 45 percent of all secretarial time and between 25 percent and 75 percent of all office-related activity. Receptionists are also being reduced in number as new automated computer systems can answer calls, record messages, and even hunt down the party being phoned.

The intelligent machine is steadily moving up the office hierarchy, subsuming not only routine clerical tasks but even work traditionally performed by management. High-tech computerized hiring systems have been installed in hundreds of companies to screen job applications. Field tests have shown the systems to be at least as skilled as human personnel in making evaluations and quicker in processing applications.

Dramatic gains in productivity have led to the elimination of jobs in virtually every area of the telephone industry. Recent technological innovations, including fiber-optic cable, digital switching systems, satellite communications, and office automation have kept the telephone industry's output per employee increasing at nearly 5.9 percent per year. Between 1981 and 1988 alone, employment declined by 179,800. AT&T announced that it is replacing more than six thousand long-distance operators with computerized voice-recognition technology. Over the next several years, AT&T expects to replace more than half of its long-distance operators with the voice-recognition technology, which is able to distinguish key words and respond to callers' requests. The new silicon operators are the latest in a string of technological advances that have allowed AT&T to handle 50 percent more calls with 40 percent fewer workers in recent years. The number of workers employed in central office repair is expected to decline by more than 20 percent by the year 2000.

Equally dramatic developments are taking place in the U.S. Postal Service. In 1991, Postmaster General Anthony Frank announced the replacement of more than forty-seven thousand workers by 1995 with automated machines capable of sight recognition. The new silicon sorters can read street addresses on letters and cards and automatically sort them faster than postal workers, who often spend up to four hours a day hand-sorting mail for their routes.

While the office is being revolutionized by intelligent machines, so too is every other area of the service economy. The changes have been dramatic in the wholesale and retail sectors. Wholesalers, like middle management, are becoming increasingly redundant in the age of instant electronic communication. Retailers such as Wal-Mart are now bypassing wholesalers altogether, preferring to deal directly with manufacturers. Using computerized monitoring and scanning equipment at the point of sale, retailers can transmit shipping orders directly to manufacturers' warehouses by way of electronic data interchange. At the other end, automated warehouses staffed by computer-driven robots and remote-controlled delivery vehicles fill orders in a matter of minutes without the assistance of human physical labor. Since 1989, the wholesale sector has dropped more than a quarter-million jobs. By early in the next century most wholesaling, as we have come to know it, will have been eliminated.

Retail establishments are also quickly re-engineering their operations wherever possible, introducing intelligent machines to improve productivity and reduce labor costs. In most retail outlets, the use of electronic bar codes and scanners at the point of sale has greatly increased the efficiency of cashiers. According to a survey prepared by the Bureau of Labor

Statistics, the new electronic scanning equipment "permits a 30 percent increase in ringing speed and possible overall 10 to 15 percent reduction in unit labor requirements for cashiers and baggers." Some retailers hope to eliminate cashiers altogether by using new electronic technology that allows the customer to insert his or her credit card in a slot on the shelf holding the desired product. Cashiers are currently the third-largest clerical group after secretaries and bookkeepers, with nearly 1.5 million employed in the United States alone.

The retail sector has long acted as an unemployment sponge, absorbing countless numbers of displaced blue-collar workers let go by the automation of manufacturing industries. Now, with retail industries undergoing their own automation revolution, the question becomes one of where all the workers will go. Many economists look to the food service industry to rescue the workers cast adrift by the technological innovations in other sectors. Even here, though, employment is sluggish, suggesting hard times ahead for the unskilled and semiskilled service workers. In many restaurants, computer systems allow the waiters to transmit orders electronically, avoiding unnecessary trips back to the kitchen. The same electronic transmission can be used by the computer to prepare a check for the customer and alert the store manager or suppliers to replenish the stocks being depleted. A new state-of the-art cooking method, which allows food to be cooked in large centralized commissaries, reduces labor costs by 20 percent in most restaurants. Some fast-food drive-through restaurants are beginning to replace human order takers with touch-sensitive screens that list the items on the menu. Drive-through restaurants have become so highly automated and efficient that six to eight employees can serve as many customers at peak hours of operation as 20 employees working in a sit-down restaurant.

Electronic shipping of products will likely mean the loss of tens of thousands of jobs in the warehousing, shipping, and transportation industries in the coming years. In May 1993, IBM and Blockbuster Video announced a new joint venture that will provide made-to-order audio compact discs, video games, and videocassettes through Blockbuster's thirty-five hundred retail outlets. The store will bypass the warehouses, shippers, truckers, and loading docks and transport products electronically to the customer by way of the information highway. Each store will have a kiosk where customers can order selections by touching a computer screen. The information will be transmitted to a central computer that will make an electronic copy of the item required and transmit it back to the store within minutes. Machines in the store will copy the electronic information into recordings, CDs, and cassettes. Color laser printers in the kiosk will reproduce the jacket pictures with the same clarity and resolution as exists on pre-existing stock. Other retailers are expected to follow Blockbuster's lead.

Electronic shipping is only a small part of the revolutionary changes taking place in retailing. Electronic shopping is also quickly penetrating the retail market, threatening the jobs of tens of thousands of sales clerks, managers, stock personnel, maintenance crews, security guards, and others who make up the retail employment complex. Many industry analysts are convinced that electronic home shopping will take over more and more of the nation's $1-trillion-per-year retail market. A *Forbes* article called the new revolution in retailing "a serious threat to the country's traditional retail industry and to the nineteen million people it employs" (Morgenson 1993).

Intelligent machines are already invading a range of professional disciplines and even encroaching on education and the arts, long considered immune to the pressures of mechanization. Doctors, lawyers, accountants, business consultants, scientists, architects, and others regularly use specifically designed information technologies to assist them in their professional endeavors. The nation's 152,000 librarians are growing increasingly concerned over electronic data systems that are able to search, retrieve, and electronically transmit books and articles over the information highways in a fraction of the time spent performing the same task with human labor. Data networks can provide abstracts from thousands of journals and books within a matter of minutes. Even the art of book writing itself is falling victim to intelligent machines. According to a *New York Times* report by Steve Lohr (July 2, 1993), a writer named Scott Finch used software equipped with artificial intelligence to pump out nearly three-quarters of the prose of a torrid potboiler entitled *Just This Once*, which Finch then "published" on-line.

Although novelists may have little to fear in the short run, musicians have every reason to be alarmed by the new generation of high-tech synthesizing machines that are fast redefining the way music is made. Piano sales have dropped by one-third to one-half in recent years, while digital keyboards, or synthesizers, have increased in sales by 30 percent or more in the same period. A synthesizer reduces musical sound to digitized form. Once digitized, the sounds can be stored and, when needed, combined with other digitized sounds to create an entire symphony orchestra. In a process called *sampling*, the computer might record a single note or a combination of notes by great musicians that can be rearranged into wholly different performances that were never performed by the artist. Vince Di Bari, former vice president of the Los Angeles local of the

American Federation of Musicians, estimates that recording jobs for human musicians have dropped off by 35 percent or more because of synthesizers. Many musicians compare their circumstances with those of auto workers replaced by automation in Detroit.

Even more troubling than synthesized music is the new technology of *morphing*, which allows movie and television producers to isolate, digitize, and store every visual expression, movement, and sound of an actor and then reprogram them in virtually any new combination, effectively creating new roles and performances for the artist. Nick de Martino, head of the American Film Institute's computer lab, says that the new computer technologies make it possible to eliminate soundstages, sets, and even actors and replace them with *synthespians*, which are "created from libraries of gestures and expressions housed in a computer bank." Already, Humphrey Bogart, Louis Armstrong, Cary Grant, and Gene Kelly have been digitized and put back to work in new television commercials. According to *Forbes ASAP*, live actors and entertainers are going to be increasingly competing for parts against both their digitized past images and those of actors long deceased (Cringely 1992).

• • •

The rapid elimination of work opportunities resulting from technical innovation and corporate globalization is causing men and women everywhere to be worried about their future. The young are beginning to vent their frustration and rage in increasingly antisocial behavior. Older workers, caught between a prosperous past and a bleak future, seem resigned, feeling increasingly trapped by social forces over which they have little or no control. In Europe, fear over rising unemployment is leading to widespread social unrest and the emergence of neofascist political movements. In Japan, rising concern over unemployment is forcing the major political parties to address the jobs issue for the first time in decades. Throughout the world there is a sense of momentous change taking place — change so vast in scale that we are barely able to fathom its ultimate impact.

# 10

# CONTROL OF THE WORLD'S FOOD SUPPLY

## Karen Lehman and Al Krebs

*There is surely no more important consequence of "free trade" and the new rules of economic globalization than its effects on food production and distribution. Small farmers are rapidly disappearing, poor countries are getting hungrier, and pesticide-intensive monocrop production is increasing. Meanwhile, small farmers are now squeezed between the corporate monopolies that control seeds and fertilizers, and the ones that the farmer must sell to at an unsatisfactory price. Often it's the same TNC at both ends.*

*This report is by Karen Lehman, research director of the Institute for Agriculture and Trade Policy in Minneapolis, and by Al Krebs, director of the Corporate Agribusiness Project in Washington, D.C., and author of* The Corporate Reapers: The Book of Agribusiness *(1992).*

WELCOME TO the global economy — it's on your dinner plate. In a Mexican mountain village, the corn may be home-grown and home-ground, the chicken in the soup fed on scraps in the yard, and the wild greens gathered from the fields nearby — but the cheese in the *quesadilla* could come from a U.S. commodity program. In the United States, an entire meal could be brought to you by the Philip Morris tobacco company under the misleading brand names of Sungold Dairies, Tombstone Pizza, Lender's Bagel Bakery, and Kraft Macaroni and Cheese.

How is it possible, we might ask, that ten cents of every dollar spent on food in the United States winds up in Philip Morris' coffers? Or that food travels an average of two thousand miles before it lands on our plates? Or that there are so few farmers left in the United States that the government is considering removing "farming" as a category on the census? Or that five thousand pigs can spend their entire lives under a single roof in what amounts to a pig factory and never see the light of day before they are led to slaughter? Or that U.S. and European food is so cheap it is replacing the native diets of peoples in Africa, Asia, and Latin America, destroying native agriculture systems, and accelerating urban migration?

The answers lie in the policies that governments throughout the world have promoted both domestically and internationally. Intentionally or inadvertently, they have strengthened the stranglehold corporate agribusiness has on our food system.

## FOOD IN A GLOBAL ECONOMY

Establishing a secure supply of food, both in quality and safety, has been a primary goal of humankind since the dawn of our species. Its availability, quality, and price are matters of life and death, and the cultures it nourishes and its moral and religious significance make it history's "staff of life."

The global economy poses threats to food security in several important ways. First, people who eat food are separated from the farms that produce it by great distances — economic, political, and physical. Second, the rules of the global economy place the world's food supply under the control of multinational corporations that have no allegiance to countries or their citizens. As a result, family-farm agriculture and the rural communities that depend on it are destroyed. Finally, the global economy threatens the biological wealth of the planet.

• • •

Imagine a system in which a single company sells seed to the farmer, operates the local grain elevator, owns the railroad and the port facility, buys the grain from the farmer, and sells the grain to itself to be processed into food. That's the system we have now in grain production in the United States and, increasingly, around the world. By eliminating tariffs and making many forms of public support to farmers "illegal," GATT will further increase the control exerted by corporations over all the different stages of the food production process. Under such conditions farmers are completely at the mercy of the corporation, which, in effect, sets the price at which they buy the imports and sell the produce.

Corporate agribusiness manufactures and markets over 95 percent of the food in the United States. As other countries in the world emulate the

U.S. model, agribusiness is gaining ground throughout the globe. Multinational corporations have relatively easy access to credit, tax advantages, and rapidly expandable production modes. There are three single overriding corporate objectives upon which corporate agribusiness is based and upon which it thrives: (1) substituting capital for efficiency and technology for labor; (2) standardizing the food supply; and (3) creating synthetic food. In pursuing each of these objectives, corporate agribusiness has sought first to diminish the role of family farmers in the production of our food. Second, it has sought to relegate the farm community to a small and select group of economically and politically impotent raw material producers serving a nationwide food manufacturing system. Such a system can be controlled from afar by a select number of giant corporations and economically powerful individuals.

Between January 1 and January 31, 1995, while most Americans were still figuring out how to break their New Year's resolutions, Philip Morris merged Kraft and General Foods into Kraft Foods; Ralston Purina sold Continental Baking Company to Interstate Bakeries Corporation, the nation's largest bread maker; Perdue Farms, the nation's fourth-largest poultry producer, acquired Showell Farms Inc., the nation's tenth-largest poultry producer; and Grand Metropolitan proposed to acquire Pet, Inc. The brand names are all that's left of the small companies that became huge conglomerates through mergers and acquisitions.

Nor is the concentration of agribusiness isolated from the rest of the economy. Wells Fargo Bank, the second-largest bank in California, is among the top six shareholders of five major agriculture-related corporations: Tyson, Archer Daniel Midland, ConAgra, Monsanto, and Philip Morris. The largest bank in California, Bank of America, is the nation's largest agricultural lender.

This accelerated concentration of the food industry has as much impact on the political process as it does on the dinner table. U.S. agribusiness companies such as Cargill, the world's largest grain-trading company, had a disproportionate role shaping the rules in the GATT framework. President Nixon's first trade advisor was William Pearce, a vice president of Cargill. Another Cargill alum, Daniel Amstutz, drafted the U.S. agriculture proposal for GATT for President Reagan.

# EXPORTS, IMPORTS, AND THE FAMILY FARM

Those who promote the global economy say that the rules for trade should be based on *comparative advantage*. In its simplest form, the logic of comparative advantage dictates that countries should buy low and sell high regardless of a product's importance to the local culture and economy. Thus, if Mexico can buy corn more cheaply elsewhere than it can be raised domestically, it should abandon domestic corn production, buy corn elsewhere, and sell products such as tomatoes to countries that can't produce them as economically. Such reasoning is at the root of international trade agreements such as GATT and NAFTA.

At first, this looks good on the plate, because, theoretically, food would be cheaper for all of the world's consumers. However, there are two primary problems with the pursuit of markets based on comparative advantage. First, it leads countries to depend on foreign food suppliers — and international trading companies. Second, countries will implement policies that are destructive to their own citizens to maintain their comparative advantage in a given market.

In times of war and in times of famine, the lack of domestic production for domestic consumption in food-importing countries has had disastrous consequences when food-producing nations suddenly designate their production for their own populations, at the expense of those who have become accustomed to constant supplies. In 1973, for example, the United States decided to restrict exports of soybeans because of a drought-related shortage in the States. This created problems for European farmers who were using U.S. soybeans in their animal feed and made meat more expensive at European dinner tables. Europe learned its lesson and became more aggressive in local cereal production to ensure a constant supply.

Furthermore, international trade's dependence on multinational corporations poses a threat to food security. Two companies, Cargill and Continental, shared 50 percent of U.S. grain exports in 1994. This is important to the rest of the world, given that, in the same year, the United States exported 36 percent of the wheat traded worldwide; 64 percent of the corn, barley, sorghum, and oats; 40 percent of the soybeans; 17 percent of the rice; and 33 percent of the cotton. By controlling the flow of these volumes of agricultural products, the companies are capable of manipulating prices and supplies throughout the globe. When farmers have attempted to bypass the companies and market their grain directly to foreign countries, as the American Agriculture Movement did in the late 1970s, the companies can retaliate, as Cargill did in 1984 by importing one million bushels of Argentine wheat. This degree of monopoly control has serious long-term implications. These huge companies now have the power to shift comparative advantage simply by their decisions on where to build warehouse, transport, and processing facilities. Our food system is very close to being totally managed — without citizen involvement.

Governments, too, pursue strategies to improve their comparative advantage with effects that can be disastrous for the domestic population. For example, the United States, in its efforts to maintain its dominance as the world's most important supplier of grains such as wheat and corn, has driven prices below the cost of production to increase exports — a policy that has devastated farmers in both the United States and developing countries. Between 1987 and 1992, 38,500 farms per year were eliminated, and the country's newspapers were filled with stories of suicide, spouse abuse, bankruptcy, and farmers applying for food stamps.

Other countries, unable to compete with this low-priced grain, tried in some cases to protect their farmers by imposing tariffs or quotas on the cheap grain. This is the poor country's form of agricultural subsidy. By making imported grain more expensive with a tariff or tax, the government makes domestically produced grain more competitive in local markets.

Mexico is a case in point. Until Carlos Salinas de Gortari became president in 1988, Mexico attempted to protect its corn production system from artificially cheap U.S. corn. Corn is the Mexican food staple and is produced by 2.5 million small farmers, mostly of indigenous decent. Half of the land under cultivation in Mexico is dedicated to corn, which is as important culturally as it is economically. NAFTA's Congressional Budget Office Report on Agriculture stated that Mexico's corn program had been a "de facto rural employment and anti-poverty program." But to ensure the passage of NAFTA, Mexico promulgated a series of reforms in the agriculture sector, including the breakup of the cooperative farms (*ejidos*) and signed away its right to protect corn in NAFTA. As a result, economists predicted that as few as seven hundred thousand and as many as ten million farmers could be displaced during the decade after NAFTA took effect. This is a pattern repeating itself all over the world, creating problems of overpopulation in the Third World's megacities, where rural people migrate to seek nonexistent jobs.

The world's governments could change global trade policy to favor domestic food security over comparative advantage marketing. But that would require controlling corporate behavior to a degree most governments have lacked the courage to do. Countries, with a few notable exceptions, don't generally engage in trade. Corporations do. The countries' role in the process is to set the rules by which corporations conduct their business. Unfortunately, they have structured the rules to benefit multinationals at the expense of domestic food systems.

## THE DEATH OF THE FAMILY FARM

Already, agriculture statistics read like tombstones for family farmers and tabloid headlines for agribusiness corporations:

- Since 1945, the number of farms has declined by two-thirds in the United States, while the area in farmland acres has remained about the same (Peterson, USDA, 1993).

- In 1994, three packers controlled the slaughter of over 80 percent of the beef in the United States (Feder, *N.Y. Times*, 1995).

- In 1994, 73 percent of all U.S. farms accounted for 9 percent of the annual total cash farm commodity and food sales, while 2 percent of the farms accounted for 50 percent of the total sales.

- The average farm-operator household in 1990 earned 14 percent of its income from the farm and the rest from off-farm employment. In that same year, 22 percent of U.S. farm-operator households had incomes below the official poverty threshold, twice the rate of all U.S. families.

Implicit in these statistics are stories of corporate concentration, the foreclosure of family farms that have been in families for generations, and the reduction of real choice and quality on U.S. dinner tables.

The numbers also chronicle the deaths of rural communities, where family farm dollars paid to equipment dealers, grocery stores, and gas stations recirculated through the local economy four times. With the family farms went many rural community businesses, and the main streets across the upper Midwest in the United States are full of abandoned store fronts and empty schools.

Some startling figures developed by Dr. Stewart Smith, a senior economist for the Congressional Joint Economic Committee, vividly illustrate how agriculture has shifted from a system based on farmers to one based on agribusiness. In a study released in October 1992, he examined the economic activity of agribusiness's three basic economic sectors: farming, inputs (seeds, fertilizers, herbicides, pesticides), and marketing.

Viewing the economic activity within agribusiness sector by sector, he found that farming suffered a shocking descent from 41 percent in 1910 to 9 percent in 1990, while the input sector rose from 15 percent to 24 percent and the marketing sector climbed from 44 percent to 67 percent over the past eighty-year period.

Equally shocking was the fact that while the value of the marketing sector in real dollars increased from \$35 billion to \$216 billion and the input sector went from \$13 billion to \$58 billion, farming shrank from \$24 billion to \$23 billion.

U.S. agriculture has been transformed from a one-time integral sector of the nation's economy to a dependent labor arrangement in which family farmers are merely providers of raw materials for a giant food manufacturing industry that substitutes technology for labor and capital for efficiency. As countries around the world seek to replicate the U.S. agriculture system, similar dynamics are being integrated into their farm sectors.

During the postwar boom of the 1950s and 1960s, there was ample employment in urban areas for the many American farmers who left the land. This is not the case today, and the hemorrhaging from the countryside continues not only in the United States but in Canada, France, Mexico, Japan, and Somalia. Many urban problems are the results of bad agriculture policy, and the global economy, if anything, is exacerbating them.

Unless the decline of family farms and rural communities is reversed, our increasingly urban societies will be entirely dependent on multinational corporations that will someday own the farm land and hire "farm managers" to work it.

## THREATS TO BIOLOGICAL DIVERSITY

The global economy has another impact on the food that will be produced in the future. For the first time, multinational corporations are within reach of controlling the planet's genetic wealth through a global legal framework established under the World Trade Organization. Companies can patent living organisms and the genetic information that determines their nature and development.

For centuries, seeds moved freely across the continents on the wind, in birds' bellies, in traders' caravans, conquerors' pockets, and immigrants' knapsacks. They were available to all, the sole property of none, the common heritage of the planet Earth.

The common misunderstanding about the world's food seeds is that they are naturally occurring. But behind every food crop seed there is a long line of farmers who literally created them through a process the Mende people of Sierra Leone call *hungoo*, meaning innovation or invention. Just as the yucca moth and the yucca cactus have evolved together, so have the world's people and its grains.

Early on, the forerunners of agribusiness disrupted this relationship when they transplanted bananas and sugarcane from Asia and coffee from Africa to Latin America and produced them in heavily policed plantations for export to European countries. The French outlawed the export of indigo seed from Antigua, and the Dutch destroyed all of the nutmeg and clove trees in the Molucca Islands after they had established their own plantations. By separating the seed from its cultural root, the colonizers changed it forever from the living symbol of a community's history into a commodity.

The United States is known as the breadbasket of the world — yet of the food and industrial crops so abundantly harvested each fall, only one, the sunflower, is native to this continent. All fifteen U.S. food crops worth $1 billion or more depend on genetic material from other countries: corn, potatoes, tomatoes, and cotton from Latin America; rice and sugarcane from Indochina; soybeans and oranges from China; wheat, barley, grapes, and apples from West Central Asia.

In the early 1960s, the United States passed a law granting plant breeders the rights to patent seeds, thus preventing others from selling the same variety. Corporations made billions of dollars on seeds developed in U.S. labs from germ plasm that farmers in other lands had carefully bred over generations. With the passage of GATT, farmers all over the world will be forced to adhere to U.S.-style law and pay royalties to companies that hold patents on the genetic material they or their ancestors helped to shape.

This new form of genetic piracy has an interesting name — *intellectual property rights* — defined as the rights to protection of innovation. Intellectual property rights would only be recognized when they generated profit, which occurs when a worker pulls a gene out of a seed in a Boston laboratory, but not when a Mende farmer saves some seeds and rejects others. Intellectual property rights are also only respected when the innovation is capable of industrial application. Pioneer Hi-Bred can be protected when it mass-produces seed varieties, but the Indian farmer who collects and saves seeds for next year's planting cannot.

This means that innovation that took place in communities over centuries, or even innovation in plant varieties that takes place in the present in a communal fashion, is not eligible for protection. As more power is concentrated in the hands of the corporate gene manipulators, the genetic diversity that has been tended by farmers in millions of fields around the world is lost.

On October 2, 1993, five hundred thousand Indian farmers demonstrated against GATT and vowed to protect their right to produce and protect their own seeds. They created a charter of farmers' rights, especially the right to conserve, reproduce, and modify seed and plant material. They speak for the rest of the farmers of the world who want to continue their partnership of *hungoo* with the vegetable kingdom. Resistance to the piracy of the earth's diversity could ensure that for future generations, seeds will continue to be the fruit of our common heritage and not the exclusive property of the gene splicers. [See chapter by Vandana Shiva and Radha Holla-Bhar.]

## REROOTING THE LOCAL ECONOMY

Actions like those taken by the Indian farmers to challenge the hegemony of global corporations are one important response to the destruction of local economy and culture. In addition, people in countries all over the world are challenging the practices of *export dumping*, in which food is sold at prices lower than production costs, thus driving small farmers off the land and into the slums throughout the Third World.

There are other approaches, however, that don't involve challenges to the global institutions themselves but instead regenerate local food systems. These approaches will be different in every community, in every region, and in this diversity lies their strength. Peasants in a Mexican mountain village can continue to grow corn, and urban dwellers in the United States can make connections directly with farmers who grow their food without the aid of a multinational corporation. Replacing corporate products with local produce on the dinner plate is a small first step in relocalizing the economy.

# 11

# BIOCOLONIZATION

*The Patenting of Life*
*and the Global Market in Body Parts*

Andrew Kimbrell

*Promoted as a panacea for solving the problems of disease and food supply,*
*biotechnology has made its entry into one of the last great uncommercialized*
*wilderness areas: the genetic structure of living organisms, from plants to hu-*
*mans. In this chapter, Andrew Kimbrell, who has successfully brought many of*
*this era's landmark legal actions against corporate excess in the area of biotech-*
*nology, describes the latest instrument of global control, the patenting of life*
*forms, as a potent neocolonizing technique.*

*Kimbrell is an activist attorney in Washington, D.C., founder and president*
*of the International Center for Technology Assessment and the Jacques Ellul*
*Society. He is former program director of the Foundation on Economic Trends.*
*Kimbrell is author of* The Human Body Shop *(1993) and* The Masculine
Mystique *(1995).*

BIOTECHNOLOGY EXTENDS humanity's reach over the forces of nature as no technology in history has ever done. Bioengineers are now
manipulating life forms in much the same way as the engineers of the Industrial Revolution were able to separate, collect, utilize, and exploit inanimate materials. Just as previous generations manipulated plastics and
metals into the machines and products of the Industrial Age, we are now
manipulating and indeed transferring living materials into the new commodities of the global age of biotechnology.

With current technology, it is becoming possible to snip, insert, recom-
bine, edit, and program genetic material, the very blueprint of life. Using

these techniques, the new life-engineers are rearranging the genetic structures of the living world, crossing and intermixing species at will to create
thousands of novel microbes, plants, and animals. Recent examples include pigs engineered with human growth genes to increase their size;
tomatoes engineered with flounder genes to resist cold temperatures;
salmon with cattle growth genes spliced in to increase their size; tobacco
plants engineered with the fluorescent gene of fireflies to make them glow
at night; and laboratory mice encoded with the AIDS virus as part of their
permanent genetic makeup.

Biotechnologists are also able to screen for and isolate valuable genetic
material from virtually any living organism. They then can clone industrial amounts of valuable DNA, hormones, enzymes, and other biochemicals. Recent advances even allow the cloning of innumerable "xerox"
copies of whole organisms, including higher mammals.

With these new capabilities, genetic engineering represents the ultimate tool in the manipulation of life forms. For the first time, scientists
have the potential of becoming the architects of life itself, the initiators of
an ersatz technological evolution designed to create new species of microbes, plants, and animals that are more profitable to enterprises involved in agriculture, industry, biomass energy production, and research.

The raw material for this new enterprise is genetic resources. Just as
the powers of the Industrial Age colonized the world in search of minerals and fossil fuels, the biocolonizers are now in search of new biological
materials that can be transformed into profitable products through genetic engineering.

The new bio-prospectors know where to find the biodiversity they
need. According to the World Resources Institute, more than half the
world's plant and animal species live in the rain forests of the Third
World — *and nowhere else on Earth*. The nonindustrialized world's coastal
regions add millions more species to those already available to the new engineers of life. The Third World is now witnessing a "gene rush," as governments and multinational corporations aggressively scour forests and
coasts in search of the new genetic gold. The human body is not immune
from the reaches of the bio-prospectors. Organ and fetal transplantation,
reproductive technology, and genetic manipulation of blood and cells
have made body parts, including blood, organs, cells, and genes, extremely valuable. The collection and sale of human parts is becoming a
major worldwide industry.

Many predict that the twenty-first century will become the age of
biotechnology. Biocolonizing companies and governments know that the
economic and political entities that control the genetic resources of the

planet may well exercise decisive power over the world economy in coming decades. However, the new drive for international hegemony in the engineering and marketing of life represents an extraordinary threat to the earth's fragile ecosystems and to those living in them. Moreover, embarking on the long journey in which corporations and governments eventually become the brokers of the blueprints of life raises some of the most disturbing and important questions ever to face humanity: Do scientists and corporations have the right to alter the genetic code of life forms at will? Should we alter the genetic structure of the entire living kingdom in the name of utility or profit? Is there a limit to the number or type of human genes that should be allowed to be engineered into other animals? Should the genetic integrity of the biotic community be preserved? Is there something sacred about life, or should life forms, including the human body and its parts, be viewed simply as commodities in the new bio-tech marketplace? Is the genetic makeup of all living things the common heritage of all, or can it be appropriated by corporations and governments?

The companies, governments, and scientists at the forefront of the biorevolution — goaded by scientific curiosity or profit — have avoided virtually any discussion of the extraordinary implications of their actions. Further, the so-called "bioethicists" employed by various government and educational institutions appear incapable of saying no to any advance in the manipulation and sale of life. They seem intent on seeing the unthinkable become the debatable, the debatable become the justifiable, and the justifiable become the routine. While virtually all polls show that the international public is opposed to much of biotechnology and biocolonization, this has not yet led to a major biodemocracy movement that demands public participation and decision making in these issues. Without such a movement, the international biotechnology revolution, with all of its unprecedented environmental and ethical implications, will remain totally uncontrolled.

## MONOPOLY ON LIFE FORMS

The age of biocolonization was "officially" launched in 1980. That year witnessed a little-noted U.S. Supreme Court decision, *Diamond* v. *Chakrabarty*. This unheralded case will eventually be seen as one of the most important and infamous legal decisions of the century.

The case began in 1971, when Indian microbiologist Ananda Mohan Chakrabarty, an employee of General Electric (GE), developed a type of bacteria that could digest oil. GE quickly applied to the U.S. Patent and Trademark Office (PTO) for a patent on Chakrabarty's genetically engineered oil-eating bacteria. After several years of review, the PTO rejected the GE patent application under the traditional legal doctrine that life forms ("products of nature") are not patentable.

Eventually, the case was appealed to the Supreme Court. GE and other corporations argued before the court that life forms were simply chemical products that could be patented just like any other "manufacture." A small number of public interest groups argued against the patenting of the microbe on the grounds that "to justify patenting living organisms, those who seek such patents must argue that life has no 'vital' or sacred property . . . and that once this is accomplished, all living material will be reduced to arrangements of chemicals, or 'mere compositions of matter.' " Opponents also reasoned that with patent profits as fuel, the accelerated drive to commercialize engineered life would eliminate all chance of objective public education and participation in the policy decisions involved.

Most expected the Supreme Court to support the PTO and to reject the GE patent. However, in June 1980, the Supreme Court handed down its surprise opinion. By a five-to-four margin, the court decided that Chakrabarty was to be granted his patent. *The highest court in the United States had decided that life was patentable.* The court dismissed the vision of a "parade of horribles" suggested by those who thought that the decision would lead to the engineering and patenting of higher life forms; it stated that the issue was not whether there was a "relevant distinction (in patentability) between living and inanimate things" but whether living products could be seen as "human-made inventions."

The next decade was to show that both patenting proponents and opponents were correct. Patenting did provide the economic trigger for a lucrative biotechnology industry, as GE had hoped. However, it also produced the "gruesome parade of horribles" feared by many and showed how inevitable was the slippery slope from the genetic engineering and patenting of microbes to that of plants, animals, and, finally, human genes, cells, and tissues.


# THE END OF NATURE

Some called it the mouse that roared. Others called it the end of nature. On April 12, 1988, the PTO issued the first patent on a living animal (to Harvard Professor Philip Leder and Timothy A. Stewart of San Francisco) for their creation of a transgenic mouse containing a variety of genes derived from other species, including chickens and humans. The foreign genes were engineered into the mouse's permanent germline in order to predispose it to developing cancer, making it a better research animal on which to test the virulence of various carcinogens. While the media dubbed the patented animal the "Harvard mouse," it should really have been called the "DuPont mouse," since that company financed the Harvard research and now holds the license for its manufacture.

However, Du Pont got a lot more than just a genetically engineered mouse from the PTO. The patent licensed to DuPont is extraordinarily broad, embracing any animals of any species, be they mice, rats, cats, or chimpanzees that are engineered to contain a variety of cancer-causing genes. The patent may well be among the broadest ever granted so far.

Eight other altered animal species, including mice, rabbits, and nematodes, have been patented. Currently, well over two hundred genetically engineered animals, including genetically manipulated fish, cows, sheep, and pigs, are standing in line to be patented by a variety of researchers and corporations.

The Patent and Trademark Office's decision to patent genetically altered animals was a direct result of the misguided *Chakrabarty* decision by the Supreme Court. In 1985, five years after the court's historic decision, the PTO ruled that *Chakrabarty* could be extended to apply to the patenting of genetically engineered plants, seeds, and plant tissue. Thus the entire plant kingdom was opened up to patent protection. Then on April 7, 1987, the PTO issued a ruling specifically extending the *Chakrabarty* decision to include all "multicellular living organisms, including animals." The radical new patenting policy suddenly transformed a Supreme Court decision on patenting microbes into one allowing the patenting of all life forms on Earth including animals. Under the ruling, a patented animal's legal status is no different from that of other manufactures such as automobiles or tennis balls.

It is doubtful that the PTO was prepared for the controversy it stirred up by issuing its edict permitting animal patenting. Editorials across the country lambasted the new policy. Bioethicist Robert Nelson saw it as "a staggering decision. . . . Once you start patenting life," he asked, "is there no stopping it?"

The revolutionary 1987 ruling on the patenting of animals did appear to have a silver lining: It *excluded* human beings from patentability. The restriction on patenting human beings was based on the Thirteenth Amendment of the Constitution, the antislavery amendment, which prohibits ownership of a human being. Unfortunately, there were several major loopholes. For one, under the PTO's 1987 ruling, embryos and fetuses are patentable and so, apparently, is the patenting of discrete human organs, tissues, cells, and genes.

The first human materials to be patented were *cell lines* — a sample of cells grown through artificial laboratory cultivation. Soon after the *Chakrabarty* decision, researchers began to file applications to patent cell lines that were valuable for the study of biological processes and that could test the effects of chemicals and pharmaceuticals on human cells. Cell lines were just the beginning. On October 29, 1991, the PTO granted patent rights to a *naturally occurring* part of the human body. Systemix Inc., of Palo Alto, California, was given corporate control of human bone marrow *stem cells* — the progenitors of all types of cells in the blood. What makes the patent remarkable (and legally suspect) is that the patented cells had not been manipulated, engineered, or altered in any way. The PTO had never before allowed a patent on an unaltered part of the human body. Under the patent, any researcher who wishes to use human stem cells in the search for cures for disease will have to come to a licensing agreement with Systemix. Systemix now has a monopoly on human stem cells. Peter Quesenberry, medical affairs vice chair of the Leukemia Society of America, has pointed out how outlandish it is "to believe you can patent a stem cell. Where do you draw the line?" he asks. "Can you patent a hand?" Author and ethicist Thomas Murray adds, "[Systemix has] invaded the commons of the body and claimed a piece of it for themselves."

The Patent and Trademark Office has also allowed the patenting of several human genes, and there are now scores of patent applications pending on thousands of them, including the recently discovered gene purportedly responsible for some forms of breast cancer. The granting of patents on human genes to government agencies and private corporations creates a unique and profoundly disturbing scenario. The entire human *genome* — the tens of thousands of genes that are our most intimate common heritage — will be owned by a handful of companies and governments. We are faced with the privatization of our genetic heritage — the corporate enclosure of our genetic commons.

Many are concerned that the patenting of genes and cells will eventually allow for the patenting of the entire human body. Derek Wood, head of the biotechnology patent office in London comments, "This is clearly an area that is going to prove a pretty horrendous problem in the future. The difficulty is in deciding where to draw the line between [patenting] genetic material and human beings per se."

The European Patent Office (EPO) has already received patent applications that would allow the patenting of women who have been genetically engineered to produce valuable human proteins in their mammary glands. The patent, jointly filed by the Baylor College of Medicine and Grenada Biosciences of Texas, was carefully crafted to include all female mammals — including humans — under its coverage. Brian Lucas, a British patent attorney who represented Baylor College, has stated that the application was designed to include women because "someone, somewhere may decide that humans are patentable."

As cells, genes, animals, and plants are now engineered and patented, most of the "gruesome parade of horribles" predicted by the those opposing the 1980 *Chakrabarty* decision have become realities in dizzying rapidity.

## TRANSGENIC ANIMALS AND PLANTS

Pig number 6707 was meant to be "super": super fast growing, super big, super meat quality. It was supposed to be a technological breakthrough in animal husbandry, among the first of a series of high-tech animals that would revolutionize agriculture and food production. Researchers at the United States Department of Agriculture (USDA) implanted the human gene governing growth into the pig while it was still an embryo. The idea was to have the human growth gene become part of the pig's genetic code and thus create an animal that, with the aid of the new gene, would grow far larger than any before.

To the surprise of the bioengineers, the human genetic material that they had injected into the animal altered its metabolism in an unpredictable and unfortunate way. Transgenic pig number 6707 was in fact a tragicomic creation, a "super cripple." Excessively hairy, riddled with arthritis, and cross-eyed, the pig rarely even stood up, the wretched product of a science without ethics.

Despite such setbacks, researchers around the globe are creating thousands of transgenic creations like number 6707. They have inserted over two dozen different human genes into various fish, rodents, and mammals. Livestock containing human genes have become commonplace at research installations in the United States. Carp, catfish, and trout have been engineered with numbers of genes from humans, cattle, and rats to boost growth and reproduction. Researchers have used cell-fusion techniques to create *geeps*, astonishing sheep-goat combinations with the faces and horns of goats and the bodies of sheep. Chickens have been engineered so that they no longer contain the genetic trait for brooding, in order to make them more efficient egg producers.

Genetic engineers in the United States and Canada have also begun to successfully clone higher mammals. Although glitches have occurred, biotechnologists now feel they can alter animals to be more efficient sources of food and then clone unlimited copies of their patented "perfect" lamb, pig, or cow.

• • •

Besides food animals, the U.S. government and several corporations are also patenting and field testing numerous food plants with unique genetic combinations. Among these new creations are cantaloupe and yellow squash containing genes from bacteria and viruses, potatoes with chicken and wax moth genes, tomatoes with flounder and tobacco genes, corn with firefly genes, and rice with pea genes. The vast majority of the plants are genetically altered to increase their shelf life or improve their appearance; virtually none of the genetic changes are designed to improve nutritional values.

As with the creation of genetically engineered animals, there is good reason to be concerned about the new genetically engineered plants. Of immediate urgency is the threat of biological pollution. When hundreds (and soon thousands) of novel, genetically engineered plants are taken out of the laboratory and introduced into the environment, ecological havoc could result. Scientists compare the risk of releasing genetically engineered organisms into the environment with that of introducing exotic organisms into the North American habitats. Although most of these organisms have adapted to our ecosystem, several, such as chestnut blight, kudzu vine, Dutch elm disease, and the gypsy moth, have been catastrophically destructive. In one survey, one hundred top U.S. environmental scientists warned that "genetic engineering's imprudent or careless use . . . could lead to devastating damage to the ecology of the planet."

There are also potential human health problems. In May 1992, the U.S. Food and Drug Administration (FDA) approved the use of genetically engineered Bovine Growth Hormone (BGH) in cows to increase milk production. The animal drug produced by Monsanto not only has devastating health impacts on dairy cows but also creates milk that has significantly higher levels of hormones and antibiotics. This milk is being sold, unlabeled, in countries around the globe, including the United States, Mexico, Russia, and India. There are also significant concerns about consumption of a genetically engineered, FDA-approved tomato produced by Calgene that contains an antibiotic-resistant gene that might confer resistance to common antibiotics used to treat children.

The increased creation, patenting, and use of genetically engineered plants and animals could also have a devastating impact on small farmers throughout the world. Only large, highly capitalized farms are likely to survive the increased overhead costs of growing and raising these patented organisms and the consequent price fluctuations caused by greater amounts of produce flooding the market. Moreover, new techniques in cloning tissue of various plants could eliminate outdoor farming of certain crops altogether. As noted by one economist, "Biotechnology will likely become dominant in the coming decades and will drive activities from the farm to the nonfarm sector at an increasing rate. . . . Full-time farming as we know it will cease to exist."

The controversy over genetically engineered animals and plants will certainly grow in the coming years, especially as more genetically engineered foods enter the global marketplace. Questions will continue to be raised about the unprecedented risks these organisms pose for human health and the environment, and society will increasingly confront the profound ethical concern over the appropriateness of unlimited cross-species genetic transfers and the patenting of life.

One powerful new community of resistance was announced on May 18, 1995. Nearly two hundred religious leaders announced their opposition to the patenting of animals and human materials. The unprecedented coalition included many Catholic bishops, along with leaders of most of the Protestant denominations and representatives of Jewish, Muslim, Buddhist, and Hindu groups. The published statement of the coalition of religious leaders was clear: "We believe that humans and animals are creations of God, not humans, and as such should not be patentable as human inventions." Southern Baptist leader Richard Land summed up the outrage of many religious leaders when he stated, "This [patenting] is not a slippery slope. This is a drop into the abyss. . . . We are seeing the ultimate commercial reduction of the very nature of human life and animal life."

Nevertheless, many in the science community and in the media remain undaunted in their support of the alteration and patenting of life. Over several years, the *New York Times* has several times singled out patenting opponents for editorial criticism. In a lead editorial entitled "Life, Industrialized," the *Times* succinctly stated a shockingly reductionist view of life perfectly suited to the new age of biocolonization: "Life is special, and humans even more so, but biological machines are still machines that now can be altered, cloned and patented. The consequences will be profound but taken a step at a time can be managed."

## GLOBAL MARKET IN BODY PARTS

The biotechnologists and the new marketeers of life are not only after the Third World's microbes, plants, and animals — they are also attempting to expropriate the body parts of people around the world. Techniques such as blood transfusions, plasmapheresis, and organ transplantation have saved countless lives, but despite their benefits, these advances pose serious risks, especially to the peoples of the Third World.

Blood, organs, reproductive substances, small amounts of human tissues, even genes and cells have suddenly become valuable. The new medical technologies have created a demand in body parts that vastly exceeds supply, and the trade in human parts and elements has rapidly become a worldwide industry, a boom market in the human body. Responding to public pressure, many First World nations have restricted the sale of human parts. This has sent body-part entrepreneurs to the Third World for their bioprofiteering.

Blood transfusion was the first major biological technology to be used successfully in medicine. In recent times, as transfusion technology became more sophisticated, major pharmaceutical and bio-tech corporations began relying on the blood of Third World people for their profits. Grisly reports began to emerge of the new "vampirism" occurring in South America and Asia as blood centers opened up to buy the blood of the poor. One well-publicized instance involved Anastasio Somoza, the brutal dictator whose family occupied the Nicaraguan presidency for nearly half a century. In the 1970s, Somoza opened a blood collection center in Managua called *Plasmaferesis*. The center bought blood from the poor and undernourished and forced political prisoners to donate blood. Remarkably, the center was licensed by the U.S. FDA, and the plasma collected was sold primarily to the United States and Western Europe. Each year over one hundred thousand "donations" were collected, two-thirds of which were sold for export. The center, like so many throughout the Third World, was virtually unregulated.

While the international blood trade was eventually halted in Nicaragua, similar centers continue to operate in countries throughout the Third World. The United States and Western Europe remain the main beneficiaries of the blood industry. By the end of the 1980s, the United States had become the world's leading dealer in blood plasma products. One commentator called the United States "the OPEC of blood."

Transfusion technology was the first advancement that led to the international marketing of body parts. But then, in the 1980s, organ transplantation came of age. Thanks to better surgical techniques, greater understanding of the body's immune system, and the development of effective drugs to combat rejection, survival rates for those undergoing transplantations improved dramatically. With each new success, the numbers of organ transplantations in the United States and Europe skyrocketed. Since 1982, the yearly number of heart transplants in the United States has increased twenty times; the number of liver transplants forty times. Tens of billions of dollars are spent on this worldwide technology. The new and urgent demand for new organs, combined with the prohibition of organ sales in many Western countries such as the United States, Great Britain, and Germany, has resulted in a growing international market for human organs. Each year, tens of thousands of organs are being bought and sold in India, Eastern Europe, the Soviet Union, and Egypt and other African countries. Several international organ procurement businesses have been initiated. In many poor countries donors sell the irreplacable to buy food and shelter and to pay off debts. Currently, kidneys in Egypt sell for $10,000 to $15,000. In India, the going rate for a kidney from a live donor is $1,500; for a cornea, $4,000; for a patch of skin, $50. In many countries it is routine to see renal patients pay for newspaper advertisements offering living donors up to $4,300 for the organ.

In India, a recent survey found that a majority of paid donors are poor laborers for whom the price paid for an organ could be more than they could save in a lifetime. One donor who set up a modest tea shop with the money paid for his kidney commented, "I am even prepared to sell one of my eyes or even a hand for a price." In many places, the practice among the poor is, if they have two kidneys or two eyes, one is for sale.

In 1991, the World Health Organization (WHO) reported that organ selling in the Third World had reached "alarming proportions." "It is a burning issue for us," said one WHO official, "and we are trying to decide how to deal with it." In 1987, a conference of European health ministers called organ sales in the world's poorest countries "one of the greatest risks man has ever run: that of giving a value to his body, a price to his life."

## GENE RUSH

While blood and organs are being colonized, the human body element of greatest future potential value is the gene. Throughout the world, scientists are using screening techniques to locate and identify genes that may be of enormous value in curing disease or in imparting desirable cosmetic, physical, or mental traits (high IQ, blond hair, slimness). The discovery and patenting of any such gene would bring unprecedented profits. In the United States alone, the government has launched a $3 billion dollar Human Genome Project, which is attempting to compile a complete map of human genes and their attributes. Japan, Canada, and Germany have

similar initiatives, and a growing horde of private companies are also involved in mapping and sequencing the human genome in the hope of dis-
covering genes of value.

In 1990, scientists in North America and Europe launched a new initiative in the international hunt for new genes. They announced a global
campaign to take blood, skin tissue, and hair samples from hundreds of
"endangered" and unique human communities throughout the world.
The initiative is called the Human Genome Diversity Project (HGDP).
The HGDP's initial five-year effort to collect human DNA samples from
a minimum of 400 indigenous communities has an estimated cost of between $23 to $35 million. The project was initially funded by the U.S. National Science Foundation (NSF). Out of a larger group of 722 targeted
communities, the project will select between 400 and 600. Blood samples
from twenty-five unrelated individuals per population will be studied and
used to create "transformed" cell lines of each population. In addition, an-
thropologists expect to collect blood, saliva, and hair samples from at least
ten times as many individuals in the same and neighboring populations.
All the cell lines and samples will be stored at the American Type Culture
Collection in Rockville, Maryland, and will be available for patenting and
commercial exploitation.

Particularly targeted in this process are the world's indigenous peoples.
The case of the Guaymi is instructive. The Guaymi are an indigenous
people of Panama, direct descendants of various Central American Indian
groups, who now find themselves in the center of the controversy over international biocolonization.

In recent years, epidemiologists have been aware that there is a high
prevalence of a virus known as HTLV-II in the Guaymi. HTLV-II infection has been loosely associated with incidence of hairy-cell leukemia, but
comparatively little is known about the virus' disease associations and
transmission routes. Researchers wasted little time in exploiting the
apparent genetic predisposition of Guaymis to the virus. U.S. scientists
descended on the Guaymis and took their blood for analysis. Of special
interest was the blood sample obtained in early 1990 from a twenty-six-
year-old Guaymi woman, a mother of two who had contracted leukemia
(but eventually survived).

The researchers claimed that they had "oral consent" from the woman
to obtain and utilize her blood in any way they saw fit. However, they do
not describe how this consent could have lived up to the requirement of
"informed consent." How, for example, could the researchers have adequately explained to the young mother that they were going to use sophisticated biotechnology techniques to analyze her blood and cultivate a cell

line from her sample — one that might produce profitable patented pharmaceuticals for transnational corporations? Nor do they detail how they could have explained to the Guaymi woman that they were going to apply for international patent ownership on the cell line created from her body fluids. But that is what the U.S. researchers did. In November 1991, on behalf of the Department of Commerce, an international patent application was filed on the cell line cultivated from the blood of the Guaymi mother. Scientist Jonathan Kaplan of the Centers for Disease Control is listed on the patent application as an "inventor" of the Guaymi women's cell line. He states that he filed the patent application because "the government encourages scientists to patent anything of interest."

Revelation of the patent's existence shocked the Guaymi people. Isidro Acosta, president of the Guaymi General Congress, stated, "It's fundamentally immoral, contrary to the Guaymi view of nature and our place in it. To patent human material . . . to take human DNA and patent its products . . . that violates the integrity of life itself and our deepest sense of morality."

Thanks to an international alarm sounded by the Rural Advancement Foundation International (RAFI) and the fact that the patent had not resulted in any commercial application, the Department of Commerce abandoned the Guaymi application in November 1993. However, numerous patent claims on cell lines of indigenous peoples, including those from communities in Papua New Guinea and the Solomon Islands are still pending.

Leaders in both the religious and indigenous communities have condemned the Human Genome Diversity Project. Methodist Bishop Kenneth Carder called the effort to colonize the genes of indigenous people "genetic slavery. . . . Instead of whole persons being marched in shackles to the market block, human cell-lines and gene sequences are labeled, patented and sold to the highest bidders."

Yet recently, new international treaties such as GATT and the Convention on Biological Diversity further legally codify the right of gene hunters to seize and patent the bodies and resources of indigenous peoples and restrict the ability of governments to control or regulate the process.

• • •

Humans are not the only target of the biocolonizers. Corporations have also begun scouring the globe for valuable animals and plants and then lining up for patents on the newly discovered or engineered life forms. In one remarkable example, several northern corporations, including W. R. Grace, have been granted over fifty U.S. patents on the neem tree of India.

For thousands of years, the tree's bark and leaves have been used as a natural pesticide, a treatment for disease, and a dentifrice. Companies learning of these traditional uses have appropriated and patented not only the tree but the indigenous knowledge about the tree's many uses. [See chapter by Vandana Shiva and Radha Holla-Bhar.]

The patenting of indigenous animals, plants, and microbes is inherently unjust and inequitable, not to mention immoral. Despite the immeasurable contribution that Third World indigenous knowledge and biodiversity have made to the wealth of the industrialized countries, corporations, governments, and aid agencies of the North continue to create legal and political frameworks that lead to a bizarre scenario: The Third World has to buy back what it originally produced. When northern corporations patent important Southern agricultural and medicinal plants, the patent often prevents millions of farmers and other peoples throughout the globe from freely using the seeds and plants they have relied on for millennia.

## CONCLUSION: A NEW BIODEMOCRACY

On March 1, 1995, after six years of debate, the European Parliament (EP) rejected a European Union directive that would have allowed the patenting of virtually all life forms. The historic vote was a significant blow to life patenting in Europe and represents a surprise victory for "biodemocracy" and for ethics over profit. The action of the EP in rejecting life patents reflects the growing opposition that culminated in numerous street demonstrations in Brussels prior to the vote. For years, polls in Europe have shown overwhelming opposition to life patenting, especially animal and human materials patenting.

The U.S. Congress has taken no action against the engineering or patenting of life. However, polls of Americans show a high resistance to biotechnology. A 1992 USDA survey showed that 90 percent of those polled opposed the insertion of human genes into animals; 75 percent opposed the insertion of animal genes into plants; 60 percent opposed the insertion of foreign genes into animals; and over fifty percent felt that using biotechnology to change animals was "morally wrong."

About 80 percent felt that the public should have a greater voice in biotechnology decisions, believing that "citizens have too little to say about whether or not biotechnology should be used." This is a clear statement in favor of a new *biodemocracy*.

Biodemocracy requires that nation-states follow the example of the

European Parliament and reject the patenting of life in all forms. It also requires governments and transnational corporations to stop biocolonizing the earth's genetic resources. In addition, biodemocracy requires the immediate cessation both of the Human Genome Diversity Project and similar initiatives and of the sordid international trafficking in blood and human organs. Finally, biodemocracy would lead to a moratorium on the engineering of the permanent genetic code of plants and animals. This work is potentially catastrophic for the environment and is profoundly unethical. Clearly, a mass movement for biodemocracy is needed if the international drive toward the engineering and patenting of life is to be halted. Biodemocracy involves respecting the collective will both to restrict biotechnology and to ban the patenting of life. It also involves the key ethical insight that all life forms have intrinsic value and genetic integrity and cannot be used as raw material for new commodities on the global market.

# 12

# PIRACY BY PATENT

*The Case of the Neem Tree*

Vandana Shiva and Radha Holla-Bhar

*Vandana Shiva is a physicist and philosopher of science. She is also an indefatigable activist, having played a key role in the famous Chipko movement to save the Himalayan forests. She is now director of the Research Foundation for Science, Technology and Natural Resource Policy in Dehradun, India, and is the science and environment adviser of the Third World Network. Her books include* Monoculture of the Mind *(1993),* Biotechnology and the Environment *(1993), and* Staying Alive: Women, Ecology and Development *(1989). In 1993, Shiva was awarded the Right Livelihood Award.*

*Radha Holla-Bhar is a researcher at the Research Foundation for Science, Technology and Natural Resource Policy. One of the many campaigns of this institute is to oppose patenting of life forms, particularly the wild plants and crops to which rural people of India have always had free access and that may now only be available to those who can afford to pay royalties to such companies as Cargill and W. R. Grace.*

UNTIL VERY recently in India, biodiversity was something held entirely in common by local communities of people. Resources and knowledge about forest or agricultural properties were freely shared. Whether it was seeds of the farm or plants of the forest, all were clearly understood to be part of the cultural, spiritual, and biological commons.

The idea that the commons could be divided up, purchased, and owned by individuals or companies for their own commercial purposes was unknown to Indian farmers until the early 1960s, when certain international conventions established "plant breeder's rights." These new "rights" allowed commercial plant breeders to take traditional indigenous varieties of seed, for example, "improve" them (often by very minor alterations of genetic structure), and then patent and commercialize them, eventually selling back the patented seeds to the communities that first provided them freely.

The new rules were based on the new idea that biodiversity, by now existing mainly in the countries of the South, should be the "common heritage" of all humanity. This globalization of the South's biodiversity commons was a windfall for northern corporations, which began a race to patent and privatize as much of this natural commons as possible, without ever paying royalties to the original breeders and farmers — the local communities and indigenous people — who gathered all the knowledge about them. By the 1970s, strong protests were developing.

As G. S. Nijar and Chee Yoke Ling wrote in *Third World Resurgence* (January 1992), "Developing countries objected to the inherent unfairness in having to give their genetic resource materials freely when these were being used for developing biological materials which were then subject to property rights. The common heritage of mankind, taken freely from the South, was now returned as a commodity at a price."

However, the industrialized northern countries argued that the technologically altered materials were not part of the common heritage of humankind, thus creating a huge double standard. They argued that the materials, created and developed from generations of innovation in the South by farmers, were common heritage, thus allowing northern corporations free access, but the benefits derived from this common heritage were corporate property and should be protected by patent.

The issue came to crisis during the GATT negotiations, when the United States and other northern countries imposed their new rules of Trade-Related Intellectual Property Rights (TRIPS), which forced all countries to honor the northern interpretation of patent rights. The northern countries argued that when southern farmers' attempted to retain free use of their own seeds, developed by them over thousands of years, it was a form of piracy, but the pirate's hat clearly belongs on the other head.

For example, the United States argues that its corporations lose $202 million a year in royalty payments for agricultural chemicals and $2.5 billion in pharmaceuticals from Third World countries such as India that have not recognized patents for intellectual property. But an analysis by the Rural Advancement Fund International (RAFI) of Canada has shown that if the long history of plant-breeding work of indigenous

Third World farmers over thousands of years were properly taken into account, along with the discovery and care of plants with pharmaceutical properties, the piracy accusation would be sharply reversed. The United States would rightfully owe the Third World's farmers $302 million annually for royalties on farmers' seeds that the United States now uses and $5.1 billion for pharmaceuticals now in U.S. drug stores.

Indian farmers understand the issue exquisitely well. They staged repeated mass demonstrations against the GATT Uruguay Round agreement. In 1993, about a half-million farmers converged upon Bangalore to voice their fears about the GATT legislation, fully aware of the direct threat that it posed to their livelihoods.

In particular, many of them began to understand that the new GATT institutionalizes the international "harmonization" of property rights legislation and global monopoly ownership of life forms along the lines of U.S. law.

Before GATT, Indian law excluded the private ownership of patent rights and biological materials. This helped ensure that entitlements to food and nutrition remained as broad-based as possible. But with GATT, there is tremendous pressure to change. The inclusion of these living resources in frameworks of private ownership of patents will threaten our rights to survival as a country and as a people. Sovereignty in the matter of patent law is essential because it is a matter of survival, especially for the economically weaker sections of our society that have no purchasing power and can be protected only through the public interest.

## THEFT OF THE NEEM TREE

As part of their demonstration, thousands of the protesting Indian farmers carried twigs or branches cut from the neem tree, abundantly found throughout the drier areas of India.

Of all the plants that have proved useful to humanity, a few are distinguished by astonishing versatility. The coconut palm is one; bamboo is another. In the more arid areas of India, this distinction is held by a hardy, fast-growing evergreen of up to 20 meters in height — *Azadirachta indica*, commonly known as the neem tree.

The neem's many virtues are to a large degree attributable to its chemical constituents. From its roots to its spreading crown, the tree contains a number of potent compounds, particularly a chemical noted for its astringency that makes it useful in many fields:

- *Medicine*. Neem is mentioned in many ancient texts, and traditional Indian medical authorities place it at the pinnacle of their pharmacopoeia. The bark, leaves, flowers, seeds, and fruit pulp are used to treat a wide range of diseases and complaints, from leprosy and diabetes to ulcers, skin disorders, and constipation.

- *Toiletries*. Neem twigs are used by millions of Indians as an antiseptic tooth brush. Its oil is used in the preparation of toothpaste and soap.

- *Contraception*. Neem oil is known to be a potent spermicide and is considered to be 100 percent effective when applied intravaginally before intercourse. Intriguingly, it is also taken internally by ascetics who wish to abate their sexual desire.

- *Timber*. Besides being hard and fast-growing, its chemical resistance to termites makes neem a useful construction material.

- *Fuel*. Neem oil is used as lamp oil, while the fruit pulp is useful in the production of methane.

- *Agriculture*. The *Upavanavinod*, an ancient Sanskrit treatise dealing with forestry and agriculture, cites neem as a cure for ailing soils, plants, and livestock. Neem cake, the residue from the seeds after oil extraction, is fed to livestock and poultry, while its leaves increase soil fertility. Most importantly, neem is a potent insecticide, effective against locusts, brown plant-hoppers, nematodes, mosquito larvae, Colorado beetles, and boll weevils.

These properties, and others, known to Indians for millennia, have given the tree its Sanskrit name, *sarva roga nivarini*, "the curer of all ailments," or, in the Muslim tradition, *shajar-e-mubarak*, "the blessed tree." Access to its various products has been free or cheap: there are some fourteen million neem trees in India, and the age-old village techniques for extracting the seed oil and pesticidal emulsions do not require expensive equipment. A large number of different medicinal compounds based upon the neem are commonly available.

Since 1925, there has been considerable research into the properties of neem carried out by over twenty Indian scientific institutes ranging from the Indian Agricultural Research Institute and the Malaria Research Center to the Tata Energy Research Institute and the Khadi and Village Industries Commission (KVIC). Much of this research was fostered by Gandhian movements, such as the Boycott of Foreign Goods movement, which encouraged the development and manufacture of local Indian products, including pesticides, medicines, and cosmetics. These have come on the market in recent years, some of them produced in the small-scale sector under Indian law. Until recently, such agricultural and medicinal products were not patentable.

## W. R. GRACE DISCOVERS NEEM

For centuries, the Western world ignored the neem tree and its properties. The practices of Indian peasants and doctors were not deemed worthy of attention by the majority of British, French, and Portuguese colonists. In the last few years, however, growing opposition to chemical products in the West, in particular to pesticides, has led to a sudden new interest in the pharmaceutical properties of neem.

In 1971, U.S. timber importer Robert Larson observed the tree's usefulness in India and began importing neem seed to his company headquarters in Wisconsin. Over the next decade, he conducted safety and performance tests upon a pesticidal neem extract called Margosan-O and in 1985 received clearance for the product from the U.S. Environmental Protection Agency (EPA). Three years later, he sold the patent for the product to the multinational chemical corporation, W. R. Grace and Co.

Since 1985, over a dozen U.S. patents have been taken out by U.S. and Japanese firms on formulae for stable neem-based solutions and emulsions and even for a neem-based toothpaste. At least four of these are owned by W. R. Grace; three are owned by another U.S. company, the Native Plant Institute; and two by the Japanese Terumo Corporation.

Having garnered their patents and with the prospect of a license from the EPA, Grace set about manufacturing and commercializing the product by establishing a base in India. The company approached several Indian manufacturers with proposals to buy up their technology or convince them to stop producing their value-added pharmaceutical products and instead to supply Grace with raw material.

In many cases, Grace met with a rebuff. M. N. Sukhatme, director of Herringer Bright Chemicals Pvt. Ltd., which manufactures the neem-based insecticide Indiara, was put under pressure by Grace to sell the technology for a storage-stable neem extract that does not require heating or any chemical change. Sukhatme refused their offers, stating, "I am not interested to commercialize the product," (M. N. Sukhatme, personal communication).

But Grace eventually managed to arrange a joint venture with a firm called P. J. Margot Pvt. Ltd. The companies are now setting up a plant in

India that will process neem seed for export to the United States. Initially, the plant will process 20 tons of seed per day. They are also setting up a network of neem seed suppliers, to ensure a constant supply of seed and a reliable price.

Grace is likely to be followed by other patent-holding companies. A *Science* magazine article ("The Wonders of the Neem Tree, Jan. 17, 1992), stated that the U.S. National Research Council (NRC) published a report designed to "open up the Western world's corporations to the seemingly endless variety of products the tree might offer." According to one of the members of the NRC panel, "In this day and age, when we're not very happy about synthetic pesticides, [neem] has great appeal."

The appeal is blatantly commercial. The U.S. pesticides market is worth about $2 billion annually. At the moment, biopesticides such as pyrethrin, together with their synthetic mimics, constitute about $450 million, but that figure is expected to rise to over $800 million by 1998.

## PLAGIARISM OR INNOVATION?

Grace's aggressive interest in Indian neem production provoked a chorus of objections from Indian scientists, farmers, and political activists, who assert that multinational companies have no right to expropriate the fruit of centuries of indigenous experimentation and several decades of Indian scientific research. This has stimulated a bitter intercontinental debate about the ethics of intellectual property and patent rights.

In April 1993, a Congressional Research Service (CRS) report to the U.S. Congress titled, "Biotechnology, Indigenous Peoples, and Intellectual Property Rights," set out some of the arguments used to justify patenting and its corresponding market control: "Azadirachtin itself is a natural product found in the seeds of the neem tree and it is its significant active component. There is no patent on it, perhaps because everyone recognizes it as a product of nature. But . . . a synthetic form of a naturally occurring compound may be patentable, because the synthetic form is not technically a product of nature, and the process by which the compound is synthesized may be patentable." However, neither azadirachtin, a relatively complex chemical, nor any of the other active principles of the neem tree have yet been synthesized in laboratories. The existing patents apply only to methods of extracting the natural chemical in the form of an emulsion or solution — methods that are simply an extension of the traditional processes used for millennia for making neem-based products. The biologically active polar chemicals can be extracted using technology already available to villages in developing countries, says Eugene Shulz, chair of the NRC panel. "Villagers smash 'em [the seeds] up, soak [them] in cold water overnight, scoop the emulsion off the top and throw it on the crops" (*Science*, Jan. 17, 1992).

In a letter to Professor Nanjundaswamy, convener of the Karnataka Rajya Raitha Sangha farmers' organization, W. R. Grace's justification for patents therefore pivots on the claim that these modernized extraction processes constitute a genuine innovation over traditional extraction processes, used for millenia: "Although traditional knowledge inspired the research and development that led to these patented compositions and processes, they were considered sufficiently novel and different from the original product of nature and the traditional method of use to be patentable. . . . Azadirachtin which was being destroyed during conventional processing of Neem Oil/Neem Cake is being additionally extracted in the form of Water Soluble Neem Extract and hence it is an add-on rather than a substitute to the current neem industry in India."

In short, these corporate processes are supposedly novel advances on Indian techniques. However, this novelty exists mainly in the context of the ignorance of the West. Over the two thousand years that neem-based biopesticides and medicines have been used in India, many complex processes were developed to make them available for specific use, though the active ingredients were not given Latinized scientific names. In fact, the widespread common knowledge and common use of neem was one of the primary reasons given by the Indian Central Insecticide Board for not registering neem products under the Insecticides Act of 1968. The board argued that neem materials had been in extensive use in India for various purposes since time immemorial, without any known deleterious effects. The U.S. EPA, on the other hand, does not accept the validity of traditional knowledge and has imposed a full series of safety tests upon Margosan-O.

The allegation that azedirachtin was being destroyed during traditional processes is inaccurate. The extracts were subject to degradation over time, but this was not a problem, since farmers make such extracts to use when they need them. The problem of stabilization only arose when it needed to be packaged and transported for a long time to be marketed commercially.

Moreover, stabilization and other advances attributed to modern laboratory technology had already been developed by Indian scientists in the 1960s and 1970s, well before U.S. and Japanese companies expressed an interest. In a conversation with Dr. Vandana Shiva, Dr. R. P. Singh of the Indian Agricultural Research Institute asserted, "Margosan-O is a simple ethanolic extract of neem seed kernel. In the late sixties we discovered the potency of not only ethanolic extract but also other extracts of neem. . . . Work on the neem as pesticide originated from the division as early as 1962. Extraction techniques were also developed for a couple of years. The azadirachtin-rich dust was developed by me."

The reluctance of Indian scientists to patent their inventions, thus leaving their work vulnerable to piracy, may in part derive from a recognition that the bulk of the work had already been accomplished by generations of anonymous experimenters. This debt has yet to be acknowledged by the U.S. patentees and their apologists. The April 1993 CRS report claims that "the method of scattering ground neem seeds as a pesticide would not be a patentable process, because this process . . . would be deemed obvious." Such a statement betrays either lamentable misjudgment or a racist dismissal of indigenous knowledge. The discovery of neem's pesticidal properties and of the means to process it was by no means "obvious" but evolved through extended systematic knowledge development in non-Western cultures. In comparison to this first nonobvious leap of knowledge, the subsequent minor derivatives are quite "obvious" indeed.

## FROM WASTE TO WEALTH

W. R. Grace and P. J. Margo also claim in the letter to Professor Nanjundaswamy that their project benefits the Indian economy. It does so, they say, by "providing employment opportunities at the local level and higher remuneration to the farmers as the price of Neem Seeds has gone up in recent times because value is being added to it during the process. Over the last 20 years the price of the neem seed has gone up from Rs.300 a ton to current levels of Rs.3000–4000 a ton."

The increase in the price of neem seeds has turned an often free resource into an exorbitantly priced one, with the local user now competing for the seed with an industry that is supplying wealthy consumers in the North. As the local farmer cannot afford the price that industry can, the diversion of the seed as raw material from the community to industry will ultimately establish a regime in which a handful of companies holding patents will control all access and all production processes related to neem as raw material.

P. J. Margo claims in the letter to Professor Nanjundaswamy that this is "a classic case of converting waste to wealth and beneficial to the Indian farmer and its economy." This statement is in turn a classic example of the assumption that local use of a product does not create wealth but waste and that wealth is created only when corporations commercialize the resources used by local communities.

There is a growing awareness throughout India that the commoditization of neem will result in its expropriation by multinational companies. On August 15, 1995, on Indian Independence Day, farmers in the state of Karnataka rallied outside the offices of the district collector in each district to challenge the demands for "intellectual property rights" of multinationals companies such as W. R. Grace. The farmers carried neem branches as a symbol of collective indigenous knowledge.

Their campaign has been supported by many noted Indian scientists. Dr. R. P. Singh expressed to the authors his "whole [hearted] support [for the] campaign against the globalization of neem." Dr. B. N. Dhawan, emeritus scientist at the Central Drug Research Institute, maintains, "It is really unfortunate that the benefits of all this work should go to an individual or to a company. I sincerely hope that . . . the neem will continue to remain available for use by people all over the world without paying a high price to a company." Dr. V. P. Sharma, director of the Malaria Research Institute, agrees: "We have discovered the repellent action of the neem oil. . . . There is no question of anybody else in India or outside taking a priority or patent on this aspect of neem oil. I would like this discovery to be used as widely as possible to prevent nuisance from insect pests of public health importance and in the prevention of the disease transmitted by them."

## GLOBAL TRIPS

The movement that has crystallized around the issue of neem patents represents a direct challenge to the attempt, in the Uruguay Round of GATT, to impose upon Third World countries the patent regime known as Trade Related Intellectual Property (TRIPS), which already obtains in the North. Before now, it was accepted internationally that different countries have different needs and priorities; each country is allowed to formulate its own patent laws, and the patents granted by or registered in the country are applicable only there. However, developed nations, particularly the United States, accuse Third World countries of engaging in "unfair trade practices" if they fail to adopt stringent patent laws. As part of such accusations, the industrialized nations claim to have lost millions of dollars due to "piracy" by the Third World.

Under the new GATT agreement, all this will change. Universalization of the TRIPS regime under GATT means that national laws that protect domestic innovation and manufacture will have to be altered to conform with the more stringent patent laws of developed countries, where the maximization of profits is the cornerstone of culture.

Neem is by no means the only living organism that has become subject to a patent. Scientists are traveling the globe to secure prior rights on potentially patentable organisms. Here is an excerpt from a recent report on this issue by Canada's Rural Advancement Foundation (RAFI), giving several examples of corporate piracy of life:

### African Soapberry

Another plant that, like neem, has been at the center of attention is the African Soapberry of endod (*Phytdacca dodecandra*). Its properties as an insecticidal soap, a fish intoxicant and a spermicidal contraceptive have long been known to Africans, but in 1964, the Ethiopian Dr. Aklilu Lemma reported to the Tropical Products Institute in Britain that it killed the water-snails that are the only vector of the disease, bilharzia. He was subsequently alarmed to find out that in his absence the Institute patented an extraction process without consulting him or crediting him. Northern companies are not interested in endod as a preventative for bilharzia in the Third World (which is the province of Baylucide, an expensive and mutagenic German chemical molluscicide), but for use in toxically sensitive situations in the North — in particular, to kill zebra mussel which clog North American water pipes and disrupt U.S. fisheries. Patenting endod means that the people of Ethiopia and other African countries will receive no royalties and may eventually be deprived of the free use of the plant, as it will be needed for the commercial production of molluscicide for the U.S.

### Cotton

Patents on life forms can be very wide-ranging. A subsidiary of W. R. Grace, Agracetus Inc., has taken out U.S. patents which cover all genetically engineered cotton varieties until 2008, and has the patent pending in Europe, Brazil, China and India. The patents cover methods of inserting genes into cotton using both bacteria and "gene gun" technology. Agracetus' vice-president of finance, Russel Smestad, claims: "All transgenic cotton products, regardless of which engineering technique is used, will have to be commercially licensed through us before they can enter the marketplace." The patent has provoked a chorus of objections from scientists and breeders. Dr. Jerry Quisenberry of the U.S. Department of Agriculture commented: "Public research on cotton, at least at the molecular level, will have to come to a screeching halt. . . . What's to say the same thing won't happen for other commodities?"

## Patent Banks

U.S. multinationals such as Pfizer, Bristol Meyers, and Merck now hold several hundred patents on life forms, many housed in the American Type Culture Collection (ATCC) in Rockville, Maryland, where there are some 60,000 patented or potentially patentable organisms. The collection holds potentially commercial micro-organisms such as yeasts, algae, bacteria, and viruses — for example, U.S. Patent No. 4,925,663, owned by the University of Florida, is a Brazilian fungus known to be fatal to fire ants, which cause billions of dollars in damage to U.S. crops. Many of the samples stored in ATCC involve tissue or cell lines scraped from living humans or exhumed bodies. These include World Patent No. WO 9208784, or "human t-lymphotropic virus type 2 from Guaymi Indians in Panama." This patent is claimed by the U.S. Department of Commerce which has demanded global acquiescence to the patenting of life forms.

For Third World countries, all of these corporate monopolies over neem and also other life forms will have numerous negative consequences. Firstly, it will undermine our cultural and ethical fabric that supports our agriculture. We have viewed fundamental life processes as sacred, not as commodities to be bought and sold on the market. The sacred cow will give way to patented and cloned livestock. (According to U.S. patent law, the offspring of patented livestock would also be subject to royalty charges throughout the seventeen to twenty-two years of patent protections, so that farmers will be made to pay royalties each time a calf is born.) And seeds, which have been traditionally treated as sacred gifts from Earth exchanged freely between farmers, will become patented commodities that Third World farmers will have to buy. Hans Lenders, secretary general of the world seed houses and their breeders, has actually proposed to abolish farmers' rights to save seed. He says, "Even though it has been a tradition in most countries that a farmer can save seed from his own crop, it is, under the changing circumstances, not equitable that a farmer can use this seed and grow a commercial crop out of it without payment of royalty. . . . [T]he seed industry will have to fight hard for a better kind of protection."

The corporate demand to change a common heritage into a commodity and to treat profits generated through this transformation as a property right will bring ethical, cultural, and economic harm to Third World farmers. The Third World farmer has a three-fold relationship with the corporations that demand a monopoly of life forms and life processes. Firstly, the farmer is a *supplier* of germ plasm to TNCs. Secondly, the farmer is a *competitor* in terms of innovation and rights to genetic resources. Finally, the Third World farmer is a *consumer* of the technological and industrial products of TNCs. Patent protection displaces farmers as competitors, transforms them into suppliers of free raw materials, and makes them totally dependent on industrial supplies for vital inputs such as seeds. Above all, the frantic cry for patent protection in corporate agriculture is really for protection *from* farmers, who are the original breeders and developers of biological resources in agriculture. The corporations argue that patent protection is essential for innovation — but only for innovation that brings profits to corporate businesses. Farmers have carried out innovations over centuries, and public institutions have carried out innovations over decades without any property rights or patent protection.

## NEW IDEA: COLLECTIVE PATENTING

The unfortunate logic of patenting is that if you can't beat patentees, you may have to join them. India's traditional absence of property rights on biological organisms and medicinal and agricultural products has offered no protection against the outsiders such as W. R. Grace, who put an international patent upon them. Particularly vulnerable are those farmers whose seed stock, animal breeding stock, and natural pesticides may gradually become the intellectual property of national or multinational companies; they will lose their independence and be forced to pay high prices for products that they could formerly provide for themselves.

For this reason a new alliance of farmers and scientists has embarked upon the formulation of an alternative form of intellectual property, the *collective patent* — called *samuhik gyan sanad,* or collective intellectual property rights (CIPRs). The patents invest the right to benefit commercially from traditional knowledge in the community that developed it. The collective patent recognizes knowledge as a social product subject to local common rights, rather than an element adrift in a limbo of free global access until the first commercial venture snatches it up. Any com-

pany purloining local knowledge and local resources is engaging in intellectual piracy, and the farmers' organizations see it as their right to punish
such violators. Hence, farmers are demanding that disputes between
multinational companies and Third World farmers be settled through
village organizations rather than in GATT panels.

To many observers in the North, long alienated from their environment, the debate about intellectual property rights may seem somewhat
ethereal and detached from the mechanics of everyday life. To farmers in
India, however, it represents an expropriation of their immediate surroundings and an attack on their way of life. By targeting the village
neem tree, W. R. Grace's U.S. patents have brought the issue of TRIPS
home to Indian peasants. In so doing, farmers have made the versatile,
sturdy, "blessed tree" and "curer of all ailments" a standard of resistance
to the creeping power of global capital.

## AFTERWORD

In June 1995, the Upper House of the Indian Parliament (*Rajya Sabha*)
forced the government to defer indefinitely a "patent amendment" bill the
government had proposed. That government bill would have brought
India into "compliance" with GATT and the WTO's new rules concerning intellectual property rights.

The deferment of the patent bill created an unprecedented situation.
The legislature of the largest democracy in the world has gone in one direction, while the central government feels it must alter its nation's laws to
conform to the WTO.

As this chapter goes to press (February 1996), *India's laws still do not
permit product patents in pharmaceuticals and agriculture*. The indigenous
farmers of India, through their protest activities about neem and other
seeds, deserve full credit for this remarkable development.

• • •

Another recent development: On June 9, 1995, a section of the European
Parliament registered strong support for India's parliamentary refusal to
grant pharmaceutical product patents and registered a "legal opposition"
in the European Patent Office to W. R. Grace's request for a fungicide
based on the extraction of neem oil. This gives hope that the movement is
spreading.

Whether the Indian Parliament will hold the line in the long run, or whether the Indian government can find ways to circumvent the Parliament and the farmers, remains to be seen. But Indian refusal to comply thus far with the WTO has the potential for creating a grave crisis for an organization not accustomed to such democratic challenges.

# 13

# GLOBALIZATION, DEVELOPMENT, AND THE SPREAD OF DISEASE

The Harvard Working Group
on New and Resurgent Diseases

*The authors of this chapter have worked together since 1991 and are authors of*
Diseases in Evolution: Global Changes and Emergence of Infectious
Diseases *(1994, edited by Mary E. Wilson, Richard Levins, and Andrew
Spielman). In this chapter they explore how globalization and environmental
destruction from development projects are accelerating the spread of disease.
The members of the Harvard Working Group on New and Resurgent Diseases
are: Tamara Awerbuch, who is a biomathematician; Uwe Brinkmann, an international health epidemiologist; Irina Eckardt, a philosopher of science; Paul
Epstein, a medical practitioner; Tim Ford, an environmental microbiologist;
Richard Levins, an ecologist; Najwa Makhoul, a sociologist of science; Chris-
tina Albuquerque de Possas, a social scientist; Charles Puccia, a systems ecologist; Andrew Spielman, a public health entomologist; and Mary E. Wilson, a
specialist in clinical infectious disease.*

$T$HE CHANGING patterns in the global economy are driven by economic considerations — profits, trade balances, debt, investment
opportunities. Their impacts on health are *side effects*, inadvertent consequences of activities undertaken for other reasons. The major economic
strategies — privatization, export agriculture, deregulation, rapid growth,
free trade — have altered the epidemiology of our species through multiple pathways:

1. Changed land use, including deforestation, irrigation, monoculture, and urbanization, all of which cause a loss of biodiversity

2. Widespread malnutrition, as the gap between rich and poor is widened; loss of publicly provided health care

3. Resource depletion and chemical pollution of land and sea

4. Migration to escape political turmoil and to seek economic opportunity

5. Increased, uncontrolled use of chemical therapies — drugs, vaccines, and pesticides — which turns health care itself into a commodity

These changes effect health by many pathways. The loss of biodiversity means fewer natural predators are available to control disease vectors; people move into new regions with unfamiliar pathogens; *eutrophication* of coastal waters (from runoff of sewage and fertilizer) allows plankton blooms to increase bacteria and viruses. We have to look at the details of each particular situation and then step back and squint to see the whole pattern.

The general result has been that exposure to pathogenic microorganisms has increased, while human resistance to them has been undermined. Old diseases have come back, new diseases have appeared, and the public health system has been caught unprepared.

• • •

It has been a quarter-century since W. H. Stewart, then surgeon general of the United States, told the U.S. Congress that "the time has come to close the book on infectious disease." With tuberculosis, polio, and other killer infections on the decline throughout the industrialized world, Stewart and many other public health officials were confident that, thanks to improved hygiene and the development of new drugs and vaccines, the "war" against infectious disease was all but won — at least in the West. As one prominent biologist, John Cairns, would write in *Cancer, Science and Society* in 1975, "During the last 150 years, the Western world has virtually eliminated death due to infectious disease."

At the time, such a claim did not seem wholly unjustified. Yet today infectious diseases remain the leading causes of death in the world, killing more people than heart disease or cancer, while the incidence of these infections, which were once deemed to be under control, are increasing.

In 1993, according to the World Health Organization (WHO), 16.4 million persons died of infectious diseases. In the United States, the incidence of tuberculosis (TB), which had been declining steadily since 1882, rose by 18 percent between 1985 and 1992.

Worldwide, in 1991, eight million new TB cases were reported. One-third of the world's population is now estimated to be carrying the infection. While the TB infection is dormant in most of these people, the spread of the human immunodeficiency virus (HIV), which destroys the immune cells that keep the TB bacterium under control in the body, is expected to cause many of them to succumb to the disease. With several strains of the bacterium now resistant to all anti-TB drugs, the WHO admits that the disease "is out of control in many parts of the world."

Diphtheria has re-emerged as a major killer of adults in the former Soviet Union; the number of cases more than doubled between 1985 and 1992 in Russia alone. Plague has resurfaced in India, while malaria has returned to regions from which it had supposedly been eliminated and is spreading to previously unaffected areas. Cholera, for the first time in almost a century, has re-emerged as a major killer in Latin America.

Epidemics of dengue fever, a viral infection transmitted primarily by the *Aedes aegypti* mosquito, have swept parts of Venezuela, Brazil, India, and Australia for the first time ever. WHO officials, quoted in the *New Scientist,* warn that dengue "is spreading . . . throughout the globe, affecting tens of millions [of people] annually." Cases of the more severe forms of the disease, dengue hemorrhagic fever and dengue shock syndrome, are skyrocketing: Between 1986 and 1990, an annual average of 267,692 cases were reported, as compared with an average of 29,803 cases in previous years. Yellow fever is also on the increase. The first documentation of extensive yellow fever in western Kenya occurred between 1992 and 1993. Suddenly, the euphoric proclamations of freedom from infection seem, at best, premature; at worst, dangerously hubristic.


## DISEASE TURNOVER

Few scientists now predict the total elimination of infectious disease and maintain instead that the pattern of infection will be one of "disease turnover." Within mainstream science, medical practitioners generally hold that mutations in viruses and other microbes are responsible for such turnover — new diseases emerging as evolutionary pressures cause pathogens to move from animals to humans or to convert from innocuous forms into lethal ones.

A growing number of researchers, doctors, and public health officials, however, are beginning to question this view. Many viruses do indeed show high mutation rates; and viral variation per se undoubtedly plays a role in causing some diseases, such as influenza, to persist. But to focus solely on the evolution of pathogens is to overlook changes to the genetic makeup of pathogens — whether micro-organisms, such as bacteria or viruses, or larger organisms, such as protozoa, fungi, and worms — and neglects many other factors that contribute to the emergence of disease.

The way in which pathogens spread from host to host is one of these factors. To facilitate such transmissions, many pathogens require an accomplice, called a *vector*, which is often an insect. The insect bites an animal infected with the pathogen and ingests some of its blood. When the insect feeds again, it deposits in the subsequent host's tissues pathogens derived from the first host.

Certain "reservoir hosts" may also perpetuate the pathogen. Rodents, for instance, may harbor a microbe without apparent symptoms, while also supporting the fleas, ticks, or other ectoparasites that serve as the vehicle for transmission. The degree of contact between reservoir, vector, and pathogen largely determines the prevalence of infection. Whether or not a potential host succumbs to the disease, however, depends on its general health and nutrition and on its genetic disposition.

## PATHWAYS FOR DISEASE

In fact, virtually all pathogens that are regarded as "new" agents of disease have generally resulted not from pathogen changes but from social and environmental changes that have enabled the pathogens to gain access to new host populations or to become more virulent in immunocompromised hosts. Marburg and yellow fever viruses, for example, originally were infections of monkeys; Rift Valley fever was an inherited infection of mosquitoes; and hanta virus was maintained in rodent populations. These pathogens transferred to humans because human activity created the opportunity for them to do so.

In the case of yellow fever, humans serve as hosts for the pathogen mainly when forests are being cleared, and people come into contact with the mosquitoes that normally live in the canopy along with the monkey reservoir. Humans represent a literal "dead-end host" for this pathogen, since each epidemic rapidly exhausts the reservoir of potential susceptible hosts.

The complex interaction of events that can result in the emergence of a new disease is well illustrated by Oropouche fever, a nonfatal disease that causes severe headaches, muscle pains, and, occasionally, meningitis. Frequent epidemics of the disease have occurred in Brazil, where hundreds of thousands of people have been affected. The first outbreaks followed the building of a highway in the early 1950s from Belem on the coast to the capital, Brasilia, in Amazonia. Soon after construction of the highway, researchers isolated the Oropouche virus in the blood of highway workers and discovered that it was the same as that found in the blood of a sloth on the side of the Belem-Brasilia highway. Writer Ann Gibbons recorded in *Science* magazine in 1993 that the connection between the virus, the sloth, and the epidemic took nineteen years of epidemiological detective work: "By 1980 researchers had the answer: in that year, they isolated the virus from biting midges (*Culicoides paraensis*), which proved to be the missing link. The forest-dwelling midges, it seems, had gone through a population explosion when the settlers started clearing the forest and planting cacao for chocolate. After the farmers harvested their cacao beans, they discarded the hulls in piles that were an ideal breeding ground for the midge which spread the virus to humans along the Amazon roads."

Viewed from this perspective, the etiology of Brazil's Oropouche epidemics cannot be traced to a single cause. Rather, the fever resulted from a complex dialectic between a pathogen and its environment, where human activity — the colonization of the Amazon region, the cultivation of cacao, and subsequent environmental changes that encouraged the proliferation of *Culicoides* and their interaction with humans — created the opportunity for Oropouche to become a disease in humans. Attempts to explain Oropouche through a narrow focus on viral evolution are thus highly misleading, especially because they render invisible the role that specific economic and social forces played in creating the epidemic.

What is true for Oropouche is true for numerous other diseases. Most bacteria are not human pathogens; most arthropods are not disease vectors; and most mammals are not a source of human disease. If they emerge as agents of disease, it is often because of environmental change from human activity. In continent after continent, country after country, both old and modern technologies and ways of living have created new niches for pathogens. As economies become increasingly globalized, environments degraded, and growing sections of society impoverished, the pace of this change increases.

## GLOBAL MICROBIAL TRAFFIC

Increased travel and trade have greatly increased the opportunities for pathogens and vectors to spread to new areas. This problem is not a new one — yellow fever and its principal vector, the *Aedes aegypti* mosquito, probably spread from Africa to the Americas via the slave trade — but the rapidity with which goods and people now move around the globe has augmented the likelihood of "microbial traffic."

Modern transportation has cut travel time to almost anywhere in the world to a few days at most, less than the average incubation period of many pathogens. Travel time, therefore, presents a less significant barrier to the spread of disease than it once did. In Christopher Columbus's time, for example, crossing the Atlantic Ocean was slow compared to the progression of, say, the smallpox virus. Since all carriers of smallpox manifest symptoms of the disease, any infected traveler would have either become sick and died or recovered before reaching the New World. As a result, smallpox did not reach the Americas until several decades after Columbus's voyage. Today, travelers routinely arrive home with diseases they have picked up abroad: In the United States, virtually all of the 1,173 cases of malaria reported in 1991 were contracted overseas.

The concern, however, is not simply with sporadic cases of travelers being struck down with tropical illnesses. The large-scale movement of goods and people around the globe increases the probability of vectors (often insects) and nonhuman carriers of disease being introduced — frequently with fatal results — into areas where neither previously existed. The reintroduction of cholera to South America in the 1990s, for example, is thought to have resulted from a freighter discharging ballast water from China into Peruvian coastal waters. The water carried the cholera vibrio, which flourished in algal blooms enriched with nitrogen and phosphorous from sewage and fertilizers. Algae are filtered and eaten by molluscs, crustaceans, and fish that are, in turn, eaten by people. Once it entered Latin America, the infection spread rapidly, encouraged by rapid urbanization and IMF– and World Bank–imposed cutbacks in sanitation and public health programs. As of December 1994, millions of Latin Americans had become ill, while thousands had died. Numbers can only be estimated, as reported cases are thought to be only a fraction of those infected.

Likewise, though as yet with less drastic consequences, the Asian tiger mosquito, a potential vector for dengue fever virus and other viruses, was recently introduced into the United States in a shipment of rubber tires imported from Asia. The mosquito is now established in at least eighteen states and has similarly been introduced to Brazil and parts of Africa through the trade in tires.

Current development policies have also contributed considerably to the spread of disease by undermining local livelihoods and forcing people to migrate in search of work. The resurgence of malaria, for example, has been greatly exacerbated not only by the building of irrigation schemes, which create drainage problems that increase the opportunities for vector mosquitoes to breed, but also by migrant workers bringing the pathogen into areas where it previously did not exist. Nonimmune migrants entering endemic areas may fuel another kind of outbreak. Political and economic oppression has exacerbated the problem, as more and more people are forced to move both within countries and between them. The net effect is that diseases once limited to small regions of the globe are no longer confined.

The increase in yellow fever has generated the fear that in Africa the disease will be carried from savannah areas and forest fringes, where it is currently confined, to the continent's major cities, where the mosquito vector is plentiful, but the virus as yet is absent. Migration of people from rural to urban areas, spurred by current development policies, could bring the virus to the vector and thus spur an urban epidemic. Similarly, in Latin America, public health officials fear that the stage is set for a major outbreak of yellow fever: As in Africa, the risk is that urban mosquitoes will pick up the virus from rural migrants seeking work in the cities. Air travel could then spread the infection still further afield to countries such as the United States, where the competent mosquito vector is now firmly established in the southeast of the country. According to the U.S. Institute of Medicine, a future yellow fever outbreak in New Orleans alone could cause ten thousand to die within ninety days, and one hundred thousand more to become ill. Jim Le Duc, a virologist and epidemiologist working for the WHO, warns in *New Scientist* about the spread of yellow fever that "we could be in for a major worldwide catastrophe."

## ALTERED ECOSYSTEMS

The emergence of new diseases has been greatly assisted by environmental degradation. Importation into a new location does not ensure that a pathogen will take hold there. In fact, most introductions do not result in colonization because the species does not find a hospitable niche and dies. To colonize new terrain, the intruding pathogen must find a suitable environment and a receptive host population.

In general, colonization is easiest in regions of low biological diversity, where the intruder faces less competition from native species. Oceanic islands are notoriously vulnerable to colonization; they have been devastated by colonization of rats, goats, or weeds, because the few native species could not compete. Also vulnerable are habitats that have been disturbed by natural events or human activity, which eliminate predators and competitors and create opportunities for new species to take up residence.

For example, the spread in much of the northeastern United States of Lyme disease, which causes symptoms ranging from a distinctive rash to meningitis and acute and chronic arthritis, is related to several human activities that have dramatically altered the region's ecology. Forest clearance during previous centuries to make way for agriculture eliminated deer and their predators from the area. The forests eventually returned during the 1900s, as did the deer — but not the deer's predators. The deer tick, carrier of the Lyme disease infection, was able to spread unimpeded throughout the deer population. At the same time, many more homes were built in forested sites, leading to greater numbers of people being bitten by infected ticks that had acquired their infection from local rodents — and Lyme disease emerged as a major epidemic. The disease is now the most common vector-borne disease in the United States, with all fifty states now affected and over forty thousand cases reported to the U.S. Centers for Disease Control since 1982.

Infrastructure development, poverty, and pollution have also combined to create new niches for pathogens. Sewage and fertilizer pouring into marine ecosystems, the overharvesting of fish and shellfish, the loss of wetlands, and myriad climatic changes have conspired to cause massive algal blooms in coastal areas worldwide, providing a rich environment for diverse communities of micro-organisms. The sea-surface temperatures in these environments are frequently high, encouraging a shift toward more toxic forms of pathogens, possibly by increasing their rates of mutation and reproduction. Among the new species that have been identified in these algal blooms is a new variant of the cholera vibrio called *V. cholerae 0139*. Antibodies that recognize other known variants of cholera do not recognize this new variant, which is now present in at least ten Asian nations. Many fear that this environmentally hardy, new form of disease could easily become the agent of a worldwide cholera epidemic.

On land, piles of used rubber tires around the edges of rapidly growing cities collect water in which the mosquito *Aedes aegypti*, a vector for dengue fever and yellow fever, reproduces. Irrigation ditches, borrow pits, construction sites, poorly drained water sumps, and puddled river bottoms may all serve as breeding sites for the mosquitoes that carry malaria. The pathogens carried by the mosquitoes can feed in these new habitats without being diverted to other animals, who are less successful in shuttling the pathogen to human hosts. In this manner, whole new niches have been created beyond the original geographic and ecological range of the vectors.

Moreover, as the environment of affluent areas becomes increasingly "engineered" — through, for example, the impoundment, treatment, and distribution of water and the design of closed buildings in which air recirculates — organisms that can survive in disinfected and "hygienic" environments prosper.

Diseases such as legionellosis, cryptosporidiosis (four hundred thousand infected in Milwaukee, Wisconsin, in March 1993), and "sick-building syndrome" are the result. Likewise, multiple-occupancy institutions such as prisons, nursing homes, and hospitals, where residents are particularly susceptible to infection, have been sites for the transmission of tuberculosis and other antibiotic-resistant infections.

## CLIMATE CHANGE

In addition, there is now widespread concern about the potential effects of climate change on disease. Changes in global temperatures would carry with them changes in wind and precipitation patterns, ocean currents, humidity, soil composition, and vegetation. All of these affect human activity and movement, vector redistribution, and new breeding sites for disease. In Zimbabwe and western Mozambique, periods of drought, associated with the El Niño effect, have regularly led to major infestations of rats, which serve as carriers for a number of pathogens. In India and Colombia, a warmer climate is believed to be responsible for proliferation of *Aedes aegypti* mosquitoes at altitudes above 2,000 meters; previously they were limited by temperature to altitudes below 1,000 meters.

Climatic disruption in the form of floods and drought may also trigger new diseases. In late 1993, for example, a mysterious illness emerged in the Four Corners region of the United States (the area that encompasses southeastern Utah, southwestern Colorado, northwestern New Mexico, and northeastern Arizona). A thirty-seven-year-old farmer who worked in the area sought medical help when an illness he had had for six days took a turn for the worse. At first, the farmer experienced "flu-like" symptoms, including fever, nausea, and vomiting, which progressed to coughing and shortness of breath. An X-ray showed fluid in both of the farmer's lungs. After twelve hours, he developed acute respiratory distress and died. Several weeks and several cases later, scientists at the Centers for Disease Control in Atlanta linked the mysterious disease to a new strain of hanta virus, one of a group of viruses that have been associated with hemorrhagic fevers and kidney disease in Europe and Asia but that had not previously been known to cause disease in North America. Studies at the University of New Mexico linked the emergence of the disease to a sudden increase of deer-mice, which are carriers of the hanta virus, following the end of a six-year drought in the spring of 1992. Heavy rains deluged the area, producing an abundance of piñon nuts and grasshoppers — food for mice. Deer-mice flourished, but the drought had eliminated virtually all of their predators. Between May 1992 and May 1993, the numbers of deer-mice increased tenfold and did not decline until October 1993, at which point the epidemic came to an end. As of February 1995, 102 cases of hanta virus pulmonary syndrome had been reported in twenty-one states, mostly clustered in the Southwest. Fifty-two percent were fatal.

## VULNERABILITY

Finally, the spread of a human pathogen requires a vulnerable human population. The vulnerability of a group of people to a pathogen depends not only on how contagious the pathogen is and how quickly it is transmitted, but also on the population's immunity as a whole. In this equation, all social and environmental changes are potentially reflected epidemiologically, since conditions can affect the opposing processes of contagion and recovery, acquisition and loss of immunity.

The degree of contagion, for example, depends on the number of pathogens that leave an infected individual, through, say, sneezing or coughing, and enter the environment. It also depends on the number that survive in that environment and gain contact with and ultimately infect other people. Each of these steps is complex and combines biological and social factors that are not constant. Also, no two people are equally susceptible to infection. A person's general state of health is as much determined by social, nutritional, age, and gender factors as by genetics; and the condition of their immune system may be critical. Personal habits such as smoking, unsafe sexual activity, alcohol consumption, and food availability and preferences can also contribute to a person's susceptibility to a particular disease, as do social and economic factors.

Communicability may depend on factors ranging from housing conditions to the availability of food to the extent of exposure to pollutants and are in turn skewed by the differential impacts of class, gender, race, and ethnicity. In the United States, African American and Native American communities tend to be more exposed to environmental pollutants than more affluent communities. The rise of TB primarily affects poor inner-city communities. The poverty of those marginalized by the development process leaves them without adequate nutrition, shelter, or access to basic health provisions and thus more vulnerable to disease.

In addition, aging populations, the increased numbers of people with damaged immune systems, and the spread of AIDS have provided susceptible hosts for a wide range of infectious diseases that would otherwise be easily repelled by the host's immune system. In a susceptible population, the diseases are more likely to reach epidemic proportions.

## CONFRONTING COMPLEXITY

Disease cannot be understood (let alone countered) in isolation from the social, ecological, epidemiological, and evolutionary contexts in which it emerges and spreads. Indeed, if one lesson has emerged from the spectacular failure of Western medicine to eradicate certain diseases, it is that diseases cannot be reduced to a single cause or explained within a prevailing linear scientific method: Complexity is their hallmark. The network of factors that lead to disease is so complex that the conventional classification of diseases as infectious, environmental, psychosomatic, auto-immune, genetic, and degenerative is probably applicable only to a few diseases where one factor overwhelms all others.

Such complexity has still to be embraced by many of the most powerful institutions governing health policy. The failure of the WHO to implement successfully its extended program of immunization (EPI) against its six target diseases has been blamed not on a failure of approach but on a failure of administration. Now that EPI has been replaced by the Children's Vaccine Initiative (CVI), funded by the Rockefeller Foundation and the World Bank, the WHO is concentrating its efforts on developing "supervaccines." Short-sighted focus on technological objectives such as these does little to address the multiple causes of disease; nor does it help create new social and ecological conditions that would help minimize their incidence. And as economic globalization continues to bring with it such increased emphases on large-scale, quick-fix technological solutions, we may merely be repeating the errors of the past and removing ourselves still further from the needed social and ecological changes that would truly benefit human health everywhere on the planet.

# 14

## THE WINNERS
## AND THE LOSERS

### James Goldsmith

*After a phenomenally successful career in business and finance, James Goldsmith withdrew from business in 1990 to devote his time to campaigning on environmental issues and on the negative consequences of economic globalization. In 1994 he cofounded a new political movement in France, L'Autre Europe, which campaigned against the Maastricht Treaty and GATT, and he was elected a member of the European Parliament. His 1994 book, The Trap, from which the following chapter was adapted, was a number one best-seller in France. He has since written a followup, The Response (1995), which argues against GATT and global free trade.*

*E*very society in the modern world is confronting serious problems that have no simple, universal solutions but that do have a common root. Science, technology, and the economy have been treated by modern societies as ends in themselves rather than important tools to enhance well-being. The increase in scientific knowledge, the development of new technologies, and economic growth are pursued as if they — and not well-being — should be the objectives of human effort. The social stability of many cultures and sometimes entire cultures themselves are sacrificed in the pursuit of these goals. I believe that this inversion of values is the cause of many of our ills.

Industrial societies need economic prosperity, but I do not accept that economic growth is the principal measure of the success of nations. Look at the United States and Great Britain. The United States has achieved the greatest economic growth and the greatest material prosperity known to history. During the past fifty years its Gross National Product (GNP) has more than quadrupled, adjusted for inflation. Yet U.S. society is in serious social crisis. In Great Britain there has also been a surge of material prosperity during the past fifty years. Its GNP has more than tripled in real terms. So according to conventional modern criteria, both these nations have succeeded beyond their grandest dreams. Nonetheless, both nations are profoundly troubled.

## THE EFFECTS OF FREE TRADE

Global free trade has become a sacred principle of modern economic theory, a sort of moral dogma. That is why it is so difficult to persuade politicians and economists to reassess its effects on a world economy that has changed radically. I believe that GATT and the theories on which it is based are flawed and that, as they become implemented, they will impoverish and destabilize the industrialized world while at the same time cruelly ravaging the Third World.

The principal theoretician of free trade was David Ricardo, a British economist of the early nineteenth century. He believed in two interrelated concepts: specialization and comparative advantage. According to Ricardo, each nation should specialize in those activities in which it excels, so that it can have the greatest advantage relative to other countries. Thus, a nation should narrow its focus of activity, abandoning certain industries and developing those in which it has the largest comparative advantage. As a result, international trade would grow, as nations export their surpluses and import the products that they no longer manufacture. Efficiency and productivity would increase, and prosperity would be enhanced.

But these ideas are not valid in today's world. During the past few years, four billion people have suddenly entered the world economy. They include the populations of China, India, Vietnam, Bangladesh, and the countries of the former Soviet Union, among others. These populations are growing fast. They are forecast to expand to over 6.5 billion in thirty-five years. These nations have very high levels of unemployment, and those people who do find jobs offer their labor for a tiny fraction of the pay earned by workers in the developed world.

Until recently, these four billion people were separated from our economy by their political systems, usually communist or socialist, and by a lack of technology and capital. Today all that has changed. Their political systems have been transformed, technology can be transferred instantaneously anywhere in the world on a microchip, and capital is free to be invested wherever the anticipated yields are highest.

The principle of global free trade is that anything can be manufactured anywhere in the world and sold anywhere else. Our economies, therefore, will be subjected to a completely new type of competition. For example, take two enterprises, one in the developed world and one in Vietnam. Both make the identical product destined to be sold in the same market, say France or the United States; both can use identical technology; both have access to the same pool of international capital. The only difference between the two is that the Vietnamese enterprise can employ forty-seven people for the cost of only one French person. You do not have to be a genius to understand what will happen in such a case.

In most developed nations, an average manufacturing company pays its employees, including social costs, an amount equal to 25 to 30 percent of sales. If such a company decides to keep only its head office and sales force in its home country while transferring its production to a low-cost area, it will save about 20 percent of sales volume. Thus, a company with sales of $500 million will increase its pretax profits by up to $100 million every year. If, on the other hand, it decides to maintain its production at home, the enterprise will be unable to compete with low-cost imports and will perish.

It must surely be a mistake to adopt an economic policy that makes you rich if you eliminate your national workforce and transfer production abroad and that bankrupts you if you continue to employ your own people.

High-tech industries can survive and prosper under these circumstances because they are highly automated and therefore employ few people. Labor is a minor item in the overall cost of the products they make. But obviously, the fact that they employ few people means that they are incapable of employing very many. As soon as they need to employ a reasonable number, they will be forced to move offshore. For example, IBM is moving its disk-drive business from the United States and Western Europe to low labor-cost countries. According to the *Wall Street Journal*, IBM plans to establish this new site with an undetermined Asian partner and use non-IBM employees so that it will be easier to move to an even lower-cost region when warranted. Moving from higher-cost regions to Asia cuts in half the cost of assembling a disk drive. Mr. Zschau of IBM "admitted that the moves will put IBM on only even footing with its competitors." ("IBM Is Overhauling Disk Drive Business, Cutting Jobs, Shifting Production to Asia." *Wall Street Journal.* August 5, 1993.)

Proponents of global free trade constantly say that exporting high-tech products such as high-speed trains, airplanes, and satellites will create jobs on a large scale. Alas, this is not true. The recent $2.1 billion contract selling high-speed French trains to South Korea has resulted in the maintenance, for four years, of only 800 jobs in France — 535 for the main supplier and 265 for the subcontractors. Much of the work is carried out in Korea by Asian companies using Asian labor. What is more, following the transfer of technology to South Korea, in a few years' time Asia will be able to buy high-speed trains directly from South Korea and bypass France. As for planes and satellites, the numbers employed in this industry in France have fallen steadily. Over the five years from 1987 to 1992, they have declined from 123,000 to 111,000 and are forecast to fall to 102,000 in the short term.

One of the big mistakes that we make is that when we talk about balancing trade we think exclusively in monetary terms. If we export $1 billion worth of goods and import products of the same value, we conclude that our overseas trade is in balance. The value of our exports is equal to that of our imports. But this is a superficial analysis and leads to wrong conclusions. The products that we export must necessarily be those that use only a minor amount of labor. If they don't, they would be unable to compete with products manufactured in low labor-cost countries. The number of people employed annually to produce $1 billion worth of high-tech products in the developed nations could be under one thousand. But the number of people employed in the low-cost areas to manufacture the goods that we import would amount to tens of thousands of people, because these are not high-tech products but ones produced with traditional levels of employment. So, our trade might be in balance in monetary terms, but if we look beyond the monetary figures we find that the employment value of the products is terribly out of balance. That is how we export jobs and import unemployment.

Even the service industries will be subjected to substantial transfers of employment to low-cost areas. Today, through satellites, employees can remain in constant contact with offices in distant lands. This means that companies employing large back offices can close them and shift employment to any other part of the world. Swissair, for example, has recently transferred a significant part of its accounts department to India.

Exchange rates also have a substantial impact on the power to compete. When Ricardo calculated comparative advantage, he did so in money terms. If a product costs $X$ French francs in France and $Y$ dollars in the States, all one needs to do is to convert dollars into francs at the going rate of exchange, and it will be clear where the advantage lies. In other words, in Ricardo's formula, the nation that produces the cheaper product is the nation that has the comparative advantage.

But this calculation can be brutally and suddenly transformed by a devaluation or a revaluation of one of the currencies. In 1981, one U.S. dollar was worth 4.25 French francs; by 1985, the dollar had risen sharply and was worth 10 French francs; by 1992, it had fallen again and was worth only 4.80 French francs. Yet, according to Ricardo, each nation is supposed to specialize in those products in which it has a comparative advantage. If you followed this reasoning, industries that would have been concentrated in the United States in 1981 would have had to be abandoned in 1985, the reason being that comparative advantage would have disappeared purely for monetary reasons. Then as the dollar fell again in 1992, the theory would require that you recreate the industry in the United States. All that is obvious nonsense. No one should sacrifice and recreate industries merely to be in rhythm with fluctuations in exchange rates.

Those who believe in global free trade contend that consumers will benefit from being able to buy less-expensive imported products manufactured with low-cost labor. But consumers are not just people who buy products; they are the same people who earn a living by working and who pay taxes. As consumers they may be able to buy certain products cheaper, although when Nike moved its manufacturing from the United States to Asia, shoe prices did not drop. Instead, profit margins rose. But the real cost of apparently cheaper goods will be that people will lose their jobs, get paid less for their work, and have to face higher taxes to cover the social cost of increased unemployment. Consumers are also citizens, many of whom live in towns. As unemployment rises and poverty increases, towns and cities will grow even more unstable. So the benefits of cheap imported products will be heavily outweighed by the social and economic costs they bring with them.

According to figures published by the U.S. Department of Labor, since 1973 real hourly and weekly earnings have already dropped by an average of 16.4 percent, and that was before the Uruguay Round of GATT. If four billion people enter the workforce and offer their work at a fraction of the price paid to people in the developed world, it is obvious that such a massive increase in supply will reduce the value of labor. Also, organized labor will lose practically all its negotiating power. When trade unions ask for concessions, the answer will be, "If you put too much pressure on us, we will move offshore where we can get much cheaper labor that does not seek job protection, long holidays, and all the other items that you want to negotiate."

Under a system of global free trade, the losers will, of course, be those people who become unemployed as a result of production being moved to low-cost areas. They will also be those who lose their jobs because their companies do not move offshore and are not able to compete with cheap imported products. Finally, there will be those whose earning capacity is reduced as value-added is shifted away from labor.

The winners will be those who can benefit from an almost inexhaustible supply of very cheap labor. They will be the companies who move their production offshore to low-cost areas, the companies who will benefit from paying lower salaries at home, those who have capital to invest where labor is cheapest, and who, as a result, will receive larger dividends. But they will be like the winners of a poker game on the *Titanic*. The wounds inflicted on their societies will be too deep, and brutal consequences will follow.

Thus it is the poor in the rich countries who will subsidize the rich in the poor countries.

Some argue that developed nations have a moral responsibility to open their markets to the Third World. Let me respond by quoting from a report by Herman Daly and Robert Goodland, published by the World Bank: "If by wise policy or blind luck, a country has managed to control its population growth, provide social insurance, high wages, reasonable working hours, and other benefits to its working class (that is, most of its citizens), should it allow these benefits to be competed down to the world average by unregulated trade? This leveling of wages will be overwhelmingly downward due to the vast number and rapid growth rate of underemployed populations in the world. Northern laborers will get poorer, while Southern laborers will stay much the same."

## MASS MIGRATIONS OF THE POOR

But the application of GATT will also cause a great tragedy in the Third World. Modern economists believe that an efficient agriculture produces the maximum amount of food for the minimum cost, using the least number of people. That is bad economics. When you intensify the methods of agriculture and substantially reduce the number of people employed on the land, those who become redundant are forced into the cities. Everywhere in the world, one sees those terrible slums made up of people who have been uprooted from the land. But, of course, the hurt is deeper. Throughout the Third World, families are broken, the countryside is deserted, and social stability is destroyed. This is how the slums in Brazil, known as *favelas,* came into existence.

It is estimated that there are still 3.1 billion people in the world who live from the land. If GATT manages to impose worldwide the sort of "productivity" achieved by the intensive agriculture of nations such as Australia, then it is easy to calculate that about two billion of these people will become redundant. Some of these GATT refugees will move to urban slums, but a large number of them will be forced into mass migration. Today, as we contemplate these issues, there is great concern about the two million refugees who have been forced to flee the tragic events in Rwanda. GATT will create mass migrations of refugees on a scale a thousand times greater. We will have profoundly and tragically destabilized the world's population.

There is a misconception that Third World nations themselves support global free trade. It should be remembered that one of the characteristics of developing countries is that a small handful of people control the overwhelming majority of their nation's resources. These people own most of their nation's industrial, commercial, and financial enterprises and who assemble the cheap labor that is used to manufacture products for the developed world.

We must distinguish, therefore, between the populations on the one hand and their ruling elites on the other. It is the elites who are in favor of global free trade; it is they who will be enriched. In India there have been demonstrations of up to one million people opposing the destruction of their rural communities, their culture, and their traditions. In the Philippines, several hundred thousand farmers protested against GATT because it would destroy their system of agriculture.

The employment problem in Europe and elsewhere is not solely because of GATT. Other problems must be treated forcefully. But even if the treatment is successful, it would not solve the problems created by global free trade. Imagine that we were able to reduce at a stroke social charges and taxation so as to diminish the cost of labor by a full 33 percent. All that would mean is that instead of being able to employ forty-seven Vietnamese or forty-seven Filipinos for the price of one French worker, you could employ only thirty-one.

In any case, we must remember the example of France, where, over the past twenty years, spectacular growth in GNP has been surpassed by an even more spectacular rise in unemployment. This has taken place while Europe has progressively opened its market to international free trade. How can we accept a system that increases unemployment from 420,000 to 5.1 million during a period in which the economy has grown by 80 percent?

We are not talking about normal competition between nations. The four billion people who are joining the world economy have been part of a wholly different society — indeed, a different world. It is absurd to believe that suddenly we can create a common market with countries such as China without massive changes leading to consequences that we cannot anticipate.

It is not possible to repeat our "successes" in enriching countries such as Taiwan, Hong Kong, South Korea, and Singapore for several reasons. The combined population of those countries is about 75 million people, so the scale of the problem is quite different. The United States might be able to achieve a similar success with Mexico, and, progressively, Western Europe could accommodate Eastern Europe. But attempting to integrate four billion people at once is blind utopianism.

In any case, countries such as Taiwan and Hong Kong have been beneficiaries of the Cold War. During that period, one or other of the superpowers sought to bring every part of the world into its camp. If one failed to fill the void, the other succeeded. That is why very favorable economic treatment was granted by the West to South Korea after the Korean War, and to Taiwan, Singapore, and Hong Kong while China was considered a major communist threat. Special economic concessions combined with their cheap and skilled labor made them successful. Over the past thirty years, the balance of trade between these countries and the West has resulted in a transfer of tens of billions of dollars from us to them. The West has been hemorrhaging jobs and capital so as to help make them rich.

• • •

We must reject the concept of global free trade and replace it with regional free trade. That does not mean closing off the regions from trading with the rest of the world. It means allowing each region to decide whether and when to enter into bilateral agreements with other regions for mutual economic benefit. We must not simply open our markets to any and every product regardless of whether it benefits our economy, destroys our employment, or destabilizes our society.

Freedom of movement of capital should be maintained. If a Japanese or a European company wishes to sell its products in North America, it should invest in America. It should bring its capital and its technology, build factories in America, employ American people, and become a corporate citizen of America. The same is true for American and Japanese firms wishing to sell their products in Europe.

GATT makes it almost imperative for enterprises in the developed world to close down their production, eliminate their employees, and move their factories to low-cost labor areas. I am suggesting the reverse: To gain access to our markets, foreign corporations would have to build factories, employ our people, and contribute to our economies. It is the difference between life and death.

## DIVERSIFICATION, NOT SPECIALIZATION

We must also reject the concept of specialization. We need the contrary, a diversified economy, for only such an economy will allow our populations to participate fully in our society.

Specialization inevitably leads to chronic unemployment and to lower wages. Growth in GNP has not solved this problem. Usually it creates part-time, lower-paid jobs. That has been the trend in the developed world during the past decades. In addition to the large corporations, we need a society based on a multitude of small and medium-sized businesses and crafts workers covering a wide range of activities, and we need a decentralized economy. We must encourage local activity rather than urban centralization. Everything must be done to return life and vigor to the small towns and villages throughout our nations.

It is extraordinary to read economists commenting on the state of the nation. They believe that the profits of large corporations and the level of the stock market are reliable guides to the health of society and the economy. A truly healthy economy does not exclude from active life a substantial proportion of its citizens.

We seem to have forgotten the purpose of the economy. The present British government is proud of the fact that labor costs less in Britain than in other European countries. But it does not yet understand that in a system of global free trade its competitors will no longer be in Europe but in the countries that supply labor at an even lower cost. Compared to those countries, Britain's labor will remain uncompetitive, no matter how deeply the British government decides to impoverish its people. In the great days of the United States, Henry Ford stated that he wanted to pay high wages to his employees so that they could become his customers and buy his cars. Today, we are proud of the fact that we pay low wages. We have forgotten that the economy is a tool to serve the needs of society, not a tool to be used at society's expense.

# PART II

# PANACEAS THAT FAILED

*In the worldview in which we have all been trained, economic growth, also called "economic development" when applied to the Third World, is the central panacea for our problems. In such a view, free markets and free trade are essential tools for maximizing growth and development, since they both strive for business activity that is unfettered by regulations on environment or health or workers' rights, by tariffs, by protection of local businesses, or by democratic governance itself. If trade worldwide can be freed from all this, then a single global economy can be created that unifies all nations and peoples in the same activity under corporate guidance, supposedly leading to global prosperity.*

*So effectively have these notions been promoted by corporate economists, bankers, and the world's politicians that they are no longer contested in establishment circles. But these advocates of free trade and development use economic measurements, such as GNP, to convince themselves of their success when it is obvious that, in human, environmental, and economic terms, they — and we — have a disaster on our hands.*

*In Part Two, the authors methodically demonstrate that each of the "panaceas" such as free trade, economic growth, development, structural adjustment, and technological innovation are actually the source of, rather than the solution to, our problems. Whatever benefits they provide are temporary and accrue mainly to the transnational corporations that promote them.*

# 15

# THE MYTHIC VICTORY OF MARKET CAPITALISM

## David C. Korten

*Among the least challenged of conventional wisdoms is the idea that the globalization of market capitalism will solve all economic and social problems. David C. Korten opens that premise to serious question and also argues that the original ideas of Adam Smith have been distorted beyond recognition by right-wing economic idealogues.*

*A*s THE Soviet empire was being dismantled in 1989, free market capitalism declared a global victory. With Marxist ideology wholly discredited, the state in decline as a significant institution, and economic globalization erasing national borders, many concluded that the full forces of the market could now be unleashed to focus human attention exclusively on the production and consumption of endless material wealth. The long path of human evolution was reaching its ultimate conclusion — the victory of a universal, consumer society.

Of course, much of the world remained a long way from universal peace and prosperity, even within free market capitalism's own borders, but this did little to moderate the claims to victory. Nor did the fact that it is no more accurate to attribute the West's economic and political triumph to the unfettered marketplace than it is to blame the Soviet Union's failure on an activist state.

The much-touted victory is little more than a myth propagated to legitimize an extremist ideology. Contrary to the carefully cultivated public perceptions, the West did not prosper in the post–World War II period by rejecting the state in favor of the market. In fact, it prospered by rejecting ideological extremism in favor of *democratic pluralism* — a system of governance based on a pragmatic, nonideological, institutional balance among the forces of government, market, and civil society.

## IDEOLOGICAL EXTREMISM:
## SOCIALIST AND CAPITALIST

Most of us who live in Western societies associate extremist ideology with the discredited ideas of Socialists and Marxists. For us, economic ideology died when the economies of Eastern Europe and the former Soviet Union collapsed, and their governments embraced free markets.

Marxist socialism did indeed die an ignoble death. Ironically, its passing has given new life to its counterpart, the equally extremist ideology of *economic liberalism* — otherwise known as free market capitalism.

The defining doctrine of economic liberalism will be familiar to anyone conversant with the language of contemporary economic discourse. The following are among its most basic tenets.

- Sustained *economic growth* as measured by Gross National Product is the foundation of human progress and is essential to alleviate poverty and protect the environment.

- *Free markets*, free from governmental interference or regulation, result in the most efficient and socially optimal allocation of resources.

- *Economic globalization* — moving toward a single integrated world market in which goods and capital flow freely across national borders — spurs competition, increases economic efficiency and growth, and is generally beneficial to everyone.

- Localities achieve economic success by abandoning goals of self-sufficiency and aspiring to become *internationally competitive* in providing conditions that attract outside investors.

These tenets have become so deeply embedded within our institutions and popular culture that they are accepted by most people without question, much as the faithful take for granted the basic doctrines of their religious faith. To question them openly has become virtual heresy and invokes the risk of professional censure and career damage in most institutions of business, government, and academia.

There is also little examination of the more fundamental — often implicit, sometimes explicit — assumptions on which the doctrine of economic liberalism rests:

- Humans are motivated by self-interest, expressed primarily through the quest for financial gain.

- The action that yields the greatest financial return to the individual or firm is the one that is most beneficial to society.

- Competitive behavior is more rational for the individual and the firm and more beneficial to society than cooperative behavior.

- Human progress is best measured by increases in the value of what the members of society consume, and those who consume the most contribute the most to that progress.

The moral perversity of economic liberalism is perhaps most evident in what it views as *economic success* in a world in which more than a billion people live in absolute deprivation, go to bed hungry each night, and live without the minimum of adequate shelter and clothing. The publications that most aggressively advocate the economic liberalist ideology — such as *Fortune, Business Week, Forbes,* the *Wall Street Journal,* and the *Economist* — rarely, if ever, praise an economy for its progress toward eliminating absolute deprivation. Rather, they measure an economy's performance by the number of millionaires and billionaires it produces; they evaluate the competence of managers by the cool dispassion with which they fire tens of thousands of employees; they gauge the success of individuals by how many millions of dollars they acquire in a year; and they judge companies as successful according to the global reach of their power and their monopolistic domination of the markets in which they operate.

## ADAM SMITH BETRAYED

Proponents of economic liberalism — that is, free market capitalism — like to suggest that theirs is an economic system created for the purpose of satisfying the economic needs not of monopolies but of all people. In this regard, they invoke as their chief theorist Adam Smith and his book *The Wealth of Nations.* First published in 1776, *The Wealth of Nations* presented a radical critique of government and state protection of business monopolies. Smith demonstrated the ways in which state support and protectionism tended to distort the self-corrective mechanisms of a *com-*

*petitive market that comprised small buyers and sellers.* What today's economic liberalists fail to report is that the economic system they are now creating in Smith's name bears a far greater resemblance to the monopolistic market system he condemned than it does to the theoretical competitive market system he hypothesized would result in an optimal allocation of a society's resources.

Adam Smith's ideal was a market that comprised solely small buyers and sellers, each too small to influence the market price of the commodities exchanged. Thus, Smith's concept of a competitive market was one in which there were no large businesses with monopolistic market powers. He started from the premise that each product has its *natural price*, which included the average or "natural rates of wages, profit, and rent, at the time and place in which they commonly prevail."

The natural price, according to Smith, is exactly what the item is worth. The natural price may, however, differ from the *market price*, the price at which it is actually sold. The market price is set by the interplay of supply and demand.

Over the longer term, if excess supply leads to market prices being consistently bid down below the natural price, the weaker or more adventuresome producers will be induced to shift their capital to another enterprise that offers a more favorable relationship between natural and market prices. Similarly, if continued deficiencies result in persistent unearned profits by keeping the market price above the natural price, more producers will be enticed to enter the market, and supplies will be increased until prices fall to their natural level. Thus by the working of the wondrous "invisible hand" of the competitive market, over time the market price will approximate the natural price — producing a satisfactory outcome for both buyers and sellers and an optimal outcome for society in terms of the allocation of its resources. The items people need and want are produced and exchanged in a manner that is fair to both sellers and buyers while maintaining a constant pressure to keep prices in line with natural cost. All highly socially desirable outcomes.

This gives a very specific meaning to the term *market competition*. It is a process by which the market adjusts prices to a level that will "clear" the market in the short term and harmonize the market price and the natural price over the long term. The process assumes that all buyers and sellers are small, that there is no advertising or promotional cost or product differentiation, and that the attention of producers is on selling their goods at the best possible price, rather than driving other producers out of the market to capture their market share.

Smith was opposed to any kind of monopoly power, which he defined as the power of a seller to maintain a price for an indefinite time above its natural price. In this regard, he specifically opposed monopoly power resulting from the successful protection of trade secrets, many of which in our present-day world fall into the category of intellectual property rights.

Adam Smith also assumed that investors have a natural preference for selling close to home. In other words, *Adam Smith assumed that capital would be rooted in a particular place.* Furthermore, he clearly considered this assumption to be fundamental to his theory that the invisible hand of the market translates the pursuit of self-interest into optimal public benefit.

The circumstance that Adam Smith believed induced the individual to invest locally was the inability to supervise capital when employed far from home. In an age of instant communications by phone, fax, and computer and twenty-four hour air travel to anywhere in the world, that circumstance no longer endures. However, it is still desirable for a community to hold its investments locally. The prosperity of a community depends on what it produces with the resources available to it. That requires local investment that provides local jobs, produces goods for local consumption, and builds a local tax base. When local investment is locally owned, it also means that the social and environmental costs associated with an investment are more likely to be visible to and to some extent shared by investors and their neighbors. To the extent that costs are externalized, the local people who are forced to bear them know who the investor is and are more likely to have personal access to that person.

Indeed, the local ownership of capital is so fundamental to the argument that free markets produce a socially optimal use of resources that when economists build the computer simulations they use to demonstrate the benefits of international trade, they commonly include in the program the assumption that capital may be converted to produce a different product when trade barriers are removed, but it will still remain rooted in place. Such an assumption is in complete defiance of reality.

Adam Smith also believed that, for the market to function efficiently, those who own the assets must be directly involved in their management. This conclusion was based on the observation that owners exercise greater diligence in ensuring the most efficient use of assets than do managers who do not have an ownership stake. Of course, in Smith's preferred world of small artisans and shop keepers, ownership and management were almost always in the same hands. He would surely be shocked by a world in which the management of most corporate assets is not only distinct from ownership but commonly separated from the real owners by a layer of mutual funds and pension trust managers in an arrangement under which the real owners seldom know in which companies their funds are invested, let alone what those companies do or whether their management is diligent.

Adam Smith was most definitely not an advocate of gigantic corporations, detached from commitment to any place, funded through capital markets that separate the management of capital from its actual ownership. The liberal economic model, which Smith's name is invoked to legitimize, is in fact much like the model he opposed as inefficient and contrary to the public interest.

## SELF-INTERESTED EXTREMISM

The deregulation of markets and the move toward global economic integration has provided rich financial rewards to those at the pinnacles of financial power and has widened the gap between the market's winners and losers, rich and poor. Thus, it is not surprising that the ideological vision of economic liberalism commands such a strong following among those whose fortunes it has favored — top managers of major corporations, most heads of state, mainstream economists, and commercial media — in addition to those who simply harbor an inherent dislike of government.

Reminiscent of Marxist ideologues now passed from the scene, advocates of economic liberalism regularly proclaim the inevitability of the historical forces advancing their cause. They assert that globalization and the triumph of the free market are inevitable and that those who oppose it will be swept aside by the rising tides and had best get on board to reap the benefits that are available only to the faithful.

The extremist quality of their position is revealed in the stark choices they pose. They would have us believe the only choice available is between a "free" market unencumbered by government restraint and a centrally planned, state-controlled, Soviet-style economy in which the state sets every price, has a direct role in every transaction, and leaves people standing in long lines to get a loaf of bread. Similarly, it is implied that we must either throw open national borders to "free" trade so that goods and capital can cross unimpeded, or erect impenetrable walls that cut us off from the rest of the world and deprive us of the benefits of participating in international commerce. In other words, if you are not a *free* trader, then you are a protectionist.

In defiance of history and logic, economic liberalism's worldview permits no possibility of supporting a market economy without supporting the *free* market or favoring trade without advocating free trade. In its extremist manifestations, economic liberalism seeks to paint its opponents into an equally extremist corner and denies the possibility of a middle ground — even though that middle ground has been the very strength of the Western democracies.

Contrary to what ideological extremists would have us believe, there is a third model for the design of the governance systems by which priorities for allocating a nation's economic resources are set and implemented. This model is called democratic pluralism.

## PLURALISM VERSUS EXTREMISM

The 1920s were a period that closely approximated the free market ideal of economic liberalism. In the United States, financial interests had virtual free rein, having gained control of the agencies intended to regulate them. A highly leveraged stock market was driven ever upward by speculative fervor. Large corporations merged freely into ever larger and more monopolistic ones. Ownership of the nation's assets became concentrated in ever fewer hands.

The financial crash in 1929 brought a sweeping political change and a trend toward greater government involvement in economic affairs, in ensuring public welfare, and in protecting the rights of people against the power of money. A social safety net was put into place. Programs of public employment were implemented. Monopolies were broken up through aggressive antitrust action. The regulation of business and money markets was significantly strengthened.

World War II brought governments into an even more central and politically accepted role in managing economic affairs. They placed controls on consumption, coordinated industrial output, and decided how national resources would be allocated in support of the war effort. A combination of a highly progressive tax system to finance the war effort, full employment at good wages, and a strong social safety net brought about a massive shift in wealth distribution in the direction of greater equity. In 1929 there had been twenty thousand millionaires in the United States and two billionaires. By 1944 there were only thirteen thousand millionaires and no billionaires. The share of total wealth held by the top .5 percent of U.S. households fell from a high of 32.4 percent in 1929 to 19.3 percent in 1949. It was a great victory for the expanding middle class and for those among the working classes who rose to join its ranks.

In the post–World War II years, the United States had a strong, dynamic, and reasonably competitive domestic market sector. At the same time, government was also strong, and the interests of working people were represented by strong labor unions. A relatively egalitarian income distribution created an enormous mass market that in turn drove aggressive industrial expansion. While the specifics differed, these basic patterns prevailed in most of the Western industrial nations. Indeed, many of the European nations styled themselves as social democracies during this period. Some became deeply involved in the public ownership and management of nationalized industries but always within the framework of a market economy.

Democratic pluralism is fundamental to the very concept of democracy. It was in full bloom in the decades that followed World War II in the Western industrial democracies, and the citizens of the countries that embraced it prospered.

In contrast, the Soviet system employed an ideological extremism so strongly antimarket that the market was virtually eliminated, except for an underground black market economy. Since the same ideology eliminated the governance role of civil society, the state emerged as totally dominant and unaccountable. Lacking the pluralistic balance among the institutions of state, market, and civil society essential to democracy and a healthy economy, the Soviet economy became nonadaptive to new opportunities, unresponsive to popular needs, and inefficient in the use of resources. The consequent suffering of the Soviet people was not a consequence of an activist state. It was the consequence of an extremist ideology that excluded everything except the state.

The Western triumph was not a victory for the free market. Certainly the Western industrial nations had market economies and private ownership of capital, but the free market functioned within a framework of democratic pluralism. Their market economies were hardly *free* in the sense in which economic liberalists define the free market. The Western triumph was a victory for democratic pluralism. However, by the time the Soviet Union and its Eastern European empire actually collapsed, the economic liberalists had in an aggressive campaign to dismantle the institutional framework of democratic pluralism already well in place. They seized the opportunity of the moment and quickly claimed the victory on behalf of their cause.

What economic liberalists seem not to recognize is the irony that a modern economic system based on the ideology of free market capitalism is destined to self-destruct for many of the same reasons that the Marxist economy collapsed in Eastern Europe and the former Soviet Union:

- Both lead to the concentration of economic power in unaccountable, centralizing institutions — the state in the case of Marxism and the transnational corporation in the case of capitalism — which invites and rewards the abuse of power.

- Both create economic systems that destroy the living systems of the earth in the name of economic progress.

- Both produce a disempowering dependence on megainstitutions that erodes the social capital that supports the efficient function of markets, governments, and society.

- Both take a narrow economistic view of human needs that erodes the sense of spiritual connection to the earth and the community of life essential to maintaining the moral fabric of the society.

An economic system can remain viable over time only so long as society establishes mechanisms to counter the abuses of either state or market power and the consequent erosion of the society's natural, social, and moral capital. Democratic pluralism isn't a perfect answer to the governance problem, but it seems the best we have yet discovered in our imperfect world.

The practice of democratic pluralism maintains a dynamic tension among the forces of the market, government, and civil society to balance the often competing societal needs for essential order, the efficient production of goods and services, the accountability of power, the protection of human freedom, and continuing institutional innovation. This balance finds expression in the regulated market, not the free market, and in trade policies that link national economies to one another within a framework of rules that maintains domestic competition and favors domestic enterprises employing local workers, meeting local standards, paying local taxes, and functioning within a well-developed system of democratic governance. Foreign competition is not excluded. It simply does not share the preferred status of locally owned businesses that are rooted in place and serve the community in many ways that imported goods and footloose investors cannot.

• • •

Democratic pluralism was the framework that guided the post–World War II economic boom of Western nations and resulted in the broad sharing of development benefits throughout their societies. It was also the framework for survival against the failed socialist system. To say that "free market capitalism" was victorious is to deny history and perpetrate an illusion that will lead us to massive social, environmental, and economic failure.

# 16

# SUSTAINABLE GROWTH?
# NO THANK YOU.

## Herman E. Daly

*For the last twenty-five years, Herman E. Daly has been one of the pioneer critics questioning the validity of conventional economics. Even more remarkably, he did much of his most important criticism while maintaining his position as senior economist in the Environmental Department of the World Bank, which he left in 1994. Dr. Daly has been a professor of economics at Louisiana State University and is now professor of ecological economics at the University of Maryland. He is coauthor, with philosopher and theologian John B. Cobb, Jr., of the book that is arguably the seminal critique of modern economics,* For the Common Good *(1994).*

*In this chapter, Daly confirms that sustainable economic growth is simply no longer a serious option. Nor is development,* as the term is normally used *(involving the increased "throughput" of resources). What Daly believes is possible and desirable is purely qualitative "development" that enhances people's lives without increased throughput and hence without increasing the impact on the natural environment.*

*I*MPOSSIBILITY STATEMENTS are the very foundation of science. In science, many things are impossible: traveling faster than the speed of light; creating or destroying matter-energy; building a perpetual motion machine, and so on. By respecting impossibility theorems we avoid wasting resources on projects that are bound to fail. Economists should therefore be very interested in impossibility theorems, especially the one I demonstrate in this chapter: Namely, that it is impossible for the world economy to grow its way out of poverty and environmental degradation. In other words, *sustainable growth is impossible.*

In its physical dimensions, the economy is an open subsystem of the earth's ecosystem, which is finite, nongrowing, and materially closed. As the economic subsystem grows, it incorporates an ever greater proportion of the total ecosystem into itself and must reach a limit at 100 percent, if not before. Therefore its growth is not sustainable. The term *sustainable growth* when applied to the economy is a bad oxymoron — self-contradictory as prose and unevocative as poetry.

Economists will complain that growth in GNP is a mixture of quantitative and qualitative increase and therefore not strictly subject to physical laws. They have a point. Quantitative and qualitative changes are very different and so best kept separate and called by the different names already provided in the dictionary. To *grow* means "to increase naturally in size by the addition of material through assimilation or accretion." To *develop* means "to expand or realize the potentials of; to bring gradually to a fuller, greater, or better state." When something grows it gets bigger. When something develops it gets different. The earth's ecosystem develops (evolves) but does not grow. Its subsystem, the economy, must eventually stop growing but can continue to develop.

The term *sustainable development* therefore makes sense for the economy but only if understood as *development without growth* — qualitative improvement of a physical economic base that is maintained in a steady state by a throughput of matter-energy that is within the regenerative and assimilative capacities of the ecosystem. Currently, the term *sustainable development* is used as a synonym for the oxymoronic *sustainable growth*. It must be saved from this perdition.

It is very difficult politically to admit that growth, with its almost religious connotations of ultimate goodness, must be limited. But it is precisely the nonsustainability of growth that gives urgency to the concept of sustainable development. The earth will not tolerate the doubling of even one grain of wheat sixty-four times, yet in the past two centuries we have developed a culture dependent on exponential growth for its economic stability. Sustainable development is a cultural adaptation made by society as it becomes aware of the emerging necessity of nongrowth. Even "green growth" is not sustainable. There is a limit to the population of trees the earth can support, just as there is a limit to the populations of humans and of automobiles. To delude ourselves into believing that growth is still possible and desirable if only we label it *sustainable* or color it *green* will just delay the inevitable transition and make it more painful.

If the economy cannot grow forever, then by how much can it grow? Can it grow by enough to give everyone in the world a standard of per capita resource use equal to that of the average American? That would turn out to be a factor of seven, a figure that is neatly bracketed by the Brundtland Commission (The United Nations' Commission on Environment and Development [UNCED], headed by Mrs. Gro Brundtland) in its call for the expansion of the world economy by a factor of five to ten. The problem is that even expansion by a factor of four is impossible if Vitousek and others (1986) are correct in their calculation that the human economy currently preempts one-fourth of the global net primary product (NPP) of photosynthesis. We cannot go beyond 100 percent, and it is unlikely that we will increase NPP, since historical tendency up to now is for economic growth to reduce global photosynthesis. Since land-based ecosystems are the more relevant, and we preempt 40 percent of land-based NPP, even the factor of four is an overestimate.

Also, reaching 100 percent is unrealistic, since we are incapable of bringing under direct human management all the species that make up the ecosystems upon which we depend. Furthermore, it is ridiculous to urge the preservation of biodiversity without being willing to halt the economic growth that requires human takeover of all places in the sun now occupied by other species.

If growth up to the factor of five to ten recommended by the Brundtland Commission is impossible, then what about just sustaining the present scale — that is, what about zero net growth? Every day we read about stress-induced feedbacks from the ecosystem to the economy, such as greenhouse buildup, ozone layer depletion, acid rain, and so on, which constitute evidence that even the present scale is unsustainable.

How then can people keep on talking about "sustainable growth" when (1) the present scale of the economy shows clear signs of unsustainability, (2) multiplying that scale by a factor of five to ten, as recommended by the Brundtland Commission, would move us from unsustainability to imminent collapse, and (3) the concept itself is logically self-contradictory in a finite, nongrowing ecosystem? Yet *sustainable growth* is the buzzword of our time. Occasionally it becomes truly ludicrous, as when writers gravely speak of "sustainable growth in the rate of increase of economic activity." Not only must we grow forever, we must accelerate forever! This is hollow political verbiage, totally disconnected from reality.

The important question is the one that the Brundtland Commission leads up to but does not really face: How far can we alleviate poverty by development without growth? I suspect that the answer will be a significant amount, but less than half. If the five- to tenfold expansion is really going to be for the sake of the poor, then it will have to consist of things needed by the poor — food, clothing, shelter — not information services. Basic goods have an irreducible physical dimension, and their expansion will require growth rather than development, although development via improved efficiency will help. In other words, the reduction in resource content per dollar of GNP observed in some rich countries in recent years cannot be heralded as severing the link between economic expansion and the environment, as some have claimed. Sustainable development must be development without growth — but with population control and wealth redistribution — if it is to be a serious attack on poverty.

In the minds of many people, *growth* has become synonymous with increase in wealth. They say that we must have growth to be rich enough to afford the cost of cleaning up and curing poverty. That all problems are easier to solve if we are richer is not in dispute. What is at issue is whether growth at the present margin really makes us richer. There is evidence that in the United States growth now makes us poorer by increasing costs faster than it increases benefits. In other words, we appear to have grown beyond the optimal scale.

The concept of an optimal scale of the aggregate economy relative to the ecosystem is totally absent from current macroeconomic theory. The aggregate economy is assumed to grow forever. Microeconomics, which is almost entirely devoted to establishing the optimal scale of each micro level activity by equating costs and benefits at the margin, has neglected to inquire if there is not also an optimal scale for the aggregate of all micro activities. A given scale (the product of population times per capita resource use) constitutes a given load on the environment and can consist of many people each consuming little or fewer people each consuming correspondingly more.

An economy in sustainable development adapts and improves in knowledge, organization, technical efficiency, and wisdom; it does this without assimilating or accreting an ever greater percentage of the matter-energy of the ecosystem into itself but rather stops at a scale at which the remaining ecosystem can continue to function and renew itself year after year. The nongrowing economy is not static — it is being continually maintained and renewed as a steady-state subsystem of the environment.

Which policies are implied by the goal of sustainable development as here defined? Both optimists and pessimists should be able to agree on the following policy: Strive to hold throughput at present levels (or reduced, truly sustainable levels) by taxing resource extraction, especially energy, very heavily. Seek to raise most public revenue from such resource severance taxes and compensate (achieve revenue neutrality) by reducing the income tax, especially on the lower end of the income distribution, perhaps even financing a negative income tax at the very low end.

At the project level there are some additional policy guidelines for sustainable development. Renewable resources should be exploited in a manner such that: (1) harvesting rates do not exceed regeneration rates and (2) waste emissions do not exceed the renewable assimilative capacity of the local environment. Nonrenewable resources should be depleted at a rate equal to the rate of creation of renewable substitutes. Projects based on exploitation of nonrenewable resources should be paired with projects that develop renewable substitutes. The net rents from the nonrenewable extraction should be separated into an income component and a capital liquidation component. The capital component would be invested each year in building up a renewable substitute. The separation is made such that by the time the nonrenewable is exhausted, the substitute renewable asset will have been built up by investment and natural growth to the point where its sustainable yield is equal to the income component. The income component will have thereby become perpetual, thus justifying the name *income*, which is by definition the maximum available for consumption while maintaining capital intact.

However, before these operational steps toward sustainable development can get a fair hearing, we must first take the conceptual and political step of abandoning the thought-stopping slogan of *sustainable growth*.

# 17

# THE NEED FOR NEW
# MEASUREMENTS OF PROGRESS

Ted Halstead and Clifford Cobb

*Ted Halstead and Clifford Cobb are among the leaders of a new wave of young economists who challenge many of the economic premises that are presently employed to measure economic performance. In this chapter they make a blistering critique of Gross National Product (GNP) for measuring the wrong things and leading to the wrong conclusions and wrong policies.*

*Halstead is founder and executive director of Redefining Progress, the new San Francisco–based organization that studies and reports upon public policy in economic matters. Clifford Cobb is research director of the same organization. He was recently appointed as a nonvoting member of President Clinton's Council on Sustainable Development, and was the principal researcher for the ground-breaking book by Herman E. Daly and John B. Cobb, Jr., For the Common Good (1994). Clifford Cobb's own books include The Green National Product (1994, with John B. Cobb, Jr.) and Responsive Schools, Renewed Communities (1992). Cobb and Halstead were coauthors (with Jonathan Rowe) of the controversial 1995 Atlantic magazine cover story, "If the Economy Is Up, Why Is America Down?"*

$F$OUR TIMES a year, the U.S. Commerce Department releases the latest figures for Gross Domestic Product (GDP), and a liturgy of obfuscation ensues. Obedient newscasters repeat the figures with deadpan solemnity. Politicians race to microphones to take credit or assign blame while proclaiming they know how to expand the GDP faster than their opponents. Throughout this ritual, it is simply assumed that the GDP is synonymous with progress; that it is an adequate and accurate measure of national well-being.

The strange thing is that the economists who first devised the GDP in the 1930s never intended it for this role. It was an emergency measure designed for a specific purpose; only bureaucratic inertia combined with entrenched economic interests have kept it alive for a half a century. It should not be a mystery why multinational corporations prefer a form of accounting that measure's society's "well-being" solely by the amount of "services" and goods it produces and pays for and that hides real social and ecological costs and ignores the value of unpaid work done in family and community. The mystery is why the press and public interest community have not exposed the GDP as the statistical deception it actually is.

## BOOM FOR WHOM?

The startling gap between the economy portrayed by conventional economic indicators and the economy Americans actually experience has become one of the basic facts of American politics.

To hear economists tell it, life in America has never been better. The GDP — their standard gauge of progress — has continued an upward climb for the last fifty years. Through early 1995, newspapers were marveling at the most recent period of "economic growth." Things were so good, the experts said, that the Federal Reserve Board was striving to dampen the flames, lest the riotous good times get out of hand.

Most Americans could only scratch their heads and wonder what economy these experts were talking about. They were not experiencing this supposed boom in their own lives. To the contrary, they were working longer hours, making less, seeing more opulence at the top, worrying more about crime and social conditions, and generally feeling more strained and anxious.

"Paradox of '94: Gloomy Voters in Good Times" the *New York Times* proclaimed on the front page (Wilkerson 1994). "Boom for Whom?" asked the cover of *Time* magazine (October 24, 1994). This puzzlement among respectable opinion makers was epitomized by Federal Reserve Chairman Alan Greenspan. In a speech to a business audience, Greenspan heralded what he saw as the solid evidence of economic strength, yet he said, "There seemingly, inexplicably, remains an extraordinarily deep-rooted foreboding about the outlook" (Pender 1994).

The media talked about this public gloom as a kind of vague psychological disorder. After all, the experts had pronounced the economy booming, so the problem must be with the voters. The Clinton administration treated those voters with condescension, as children going through the pains of adjustment to the wondrous new global economy it was help-ing to bring about. President Clinton actually sent his economic advisors on the road to convince Americans that their experience was wrong and that the indicators were right.

Through all this, virtually no one in the media thought to ask the basic question: How do these experts define "good times" in the first place? Had the question been asked, voter unrest would not have seemed such a paradox. Put simply, the American economy has changed fundamentally over the last fifty years — often to the disadvantage of most Americans — but the way the experts measure economic health and progress has not. The GDP had major flaws when it was first developed during the De-pression and World War II. Now it is almost totally out of synch with the economy that Americans actually experience.

The GDP reflects the desire of the major forces in our economy to rig national accounting systems to keep social and environmental destruction out of sight and therefore out of mind. It perpetuates the illusion that progress and national well-being should be judged according to only one standard: the volume of production and consumption.

The use of GDP as a measure of "progress" is perverse. It not only masks the breakdown of families and communities and the depletion of the natural environment; it actually makes this breakdown — as reflected, for example, in such things as car crashes, divorces, and new prison con-struction — appear as economic gain. It denies what people intuitively know — that just because more money is changing hands does not mean that life is getting better.

## BREADLINE ECONOMICS

The first versions of the Gross Domestic Product were devised in the De-pression. The GDP eventually served as a guide to Keynesian economic management and came close to its present form amidst the massive pro-duction effort of World War II. The circumstances that spawned it were ones in which sheer output was the overriding concern. With the bread-lines and idle factories of the Depression, few could be concerned about such matters as the possible impacts of production upon habitats and com-munities. Then, the war pushed the nation into an output frenzy. The whole purpose was destruction anyway, so the destructive side effects of the expanding industrial machine could easily get lost in the shuffle.

Moreover, economists did not regard such questions as their concern to begin with. Rather, in the revealing term of the profession, such massive social and environmental effects were considered *externalities* — external to the concerns of economists, though not to people generally. Thus the GDP reflected not just the crisis of the times but the narrow premises of the economists who guided the response.

The GDP is the statistical distillation of the worldview of conventional economics. It is basically a measure of total output, and it assumes that everything produced is good by definition. It is a balance sheet with no cost side of the ledger; it does not differentiate between costs and benefits, between productive and destructive activities, or between sustainable and unsustainable ones. It is a calculating machine that adds but does not subtract. It treats everything that happens in the market as gain for humanity while ignoring everything that happens outside the realm of monetized exchange, regardless of its importance to well-being.

To do otherwise, economists generally say, would be to make "value judgments." But refusing to make such judgments is of course a judgment in itself. Economic thinking implicitly assumes that the value of nature's "capital" is zero, and that the value of work done within the family and community settings is also zero. In fact, this calculus precludes even the possibility of any negative costs to growth, which is precisely where the collision of worldviews between economists and ordinary people arises — people are directly experiencing the very costs of modern life that economists deny.

As is obvious to most people outside the economics profession, much of the most important production in the economy happens off the books, where economists (and the GDP) can't see it. Partly, this is the nonmonetized exchange that happens in family and community settings — the care of parents for children, for example, and of neighbors in keeping their neighborhoods clean and safe. Similarly, nature does real work in supplying clean air and water and materials such as wood and oil. To deplete or degrade these natural resources involves real costs, but such costs don't factor into formula.

## MAJOR DISTORTIONS OF GDP

The GDP distorts reality in a multitude of ways. Here's a short list, which doesn't even include the numerous estimates and imputations that make the GDP suspect even on its own terms.

- *The GDP takes no account of the depletion of natural resources.* When a timber company harvests an ancient redwood forest, for example, the

GDP rises by the market value of the wood. But it takes no account of the economic, environmental, and social costs involved in the loss of the forest.

*In accounting terms, the GDP treats the extraction of natural resources as income, rather than the depletion of an asset, which it is.* Even the former president of the World Bank, Barber Conable, has admitted the absurdity of this. "GDP figures . . . are generally used without the caveat that they represent an income that cannot be sustained," Conable said. "Current calculations ignore the degradation of the natural resource base and view the sales of nonrenewable resources entirely as income."

- *The GDP likewise counts family breakdown and disease as economic boons.* Divorce means lawyer bills, moving costs, and two households where one existed before — all these show up as growth in the GDP. Similarly, the rapidly growing medical industry — much of which arises from the health hazards and life-style that are the fruit of "progress" — is also reckoned as economic advance. By this standard, the nation's economic hero is a terminal cancer patient who has just gone through a bitterly contested divorce. Few citizens add more to the GDP.

- *The GDP completely ignores transactions that are not conducted through money.* The most productive part of an economy — and probably the most important, especially in developing countries — is the informal exchanges in which no money changes hands. Generally speaking, for example, parents care for children much better than daycare does. Yet the GDP treats these functions as having no value whatsoever. It does, however, count the police, prisons, social workers, and so on that result from the breakdown of the nonmonetized social realm.

  In this fashion, much of what economists call growth and the GDP records as growth is really just the shifting of functions from the nonmarket economy of household and community, where economists can't see them, to the market, where they can. The garden plot becomes the supermarket, home sewing of clothes becomes the sweatshop; parenting becomes childcare; visits on the side porch become the entertainment economy and psychiatry. Up and down the line, the things people used to do freely for and with one another turn into products and services. The market grows by cannibalizing the family and community realms that nurture and sustain it.

- *The GDP takes no account of income distribution.* Just because total output goes up does not mean everyone's life is better. Over the last twenty years, the GDP in the United States rose by 55 percent, adjusted for inflation. Yet real wages dropped by 14 percent, while the top 5 percent of households enjoyed an income boost of almost 20 percent. Such figures call to mind the adage about the man six feet tall who drowns in the stream that averages three feet deep. The GDP works that way too.

• *The GDP ignores the drawbacks of living on foreign assets.* Much as the United States has been borrowing resources from nature, it has also been borrowing money from foreign lenders. Although this enables us to consume more for a while, the debts eventually have to be repaid, and our nation becomes less self-sufficient in the process. Yet the GDP takes no account of this accumulating debt. Once again, as the country's well-being diminishes, our national books spin reality around by 180 degrees and create the illusion that things are getting better and better.

## A MORE HONEST BALANCE SHEET: GPI

We would like to suggest an alternative to the GDP, which we have named the Genuine Progress Indicator, or GPI. Our goal in developing it was to determine whether the "growth" measured by the GDP is actually translating into national well-being and to demonstrate that more accurate measurements of progress are possible. Basically, we broadened the accounting lens by looking at some twenty aspects of economic life that the GDP either ignores totally or else includes, perversely, on the plus side. In so doing, we began to construct a cost side to the growth ledger from 1950 to the present.

We took many factors into account in developing the Genuine Progress Indicator:

• *Resource depletion.* A sustainable economy is one that doesn't rob from our children and grandchildren but instead draws from the resource base no more than can be sustained over the long haul. Accordingly, the new GPI measures the consumption and depletion of resources, wetlands, farmland, and minerals (including oil) as a current cost, which is weighed against the short-term economic gain from this depletion.

• *Pollution.* The GPI subtracts the costs of air and water pollution as measured by actual damage to human health and environment.

• *Long-term environmental damage.* Greenhouse warming and the disposal of nuclear wastes are two long-range costs of nonrenewable energy use that do not show up in conventional economic accounts. The depletion of the ozone layer from the use of chloroflourocarbons is another enduring environmental problem. Nonrenewable energy consumption and the use of ozone-depleting chemicals are treated as costs by the GPI.

- *Housework and nonmarket transactions.* Much of the most important work in a society is what we do for ourselves within our own homes, extended families, and communities: childcare, cooking, cleaning, home repairs, and similar tasks. These are ignored in official figures such as the GDP, but the GPI includes the value of the time spent on these activities.

- *Changes in leisure time.* As a nation grows richer, people should be able to choose between more work and more leisure time. Things have not worked out that way, however. For many reasons, people have had to work longer and longer just to stay even. The GPI treats an increase in leisure as a benefit and a decrease in leisure as a cost.

- *Unemployment and underemployment.* Although some people in our society are overworked, there are many others who are unable to find a job or to work as many hours as they need. The GPI counts the value of the hours of chronic unemployment or underemployment as a cost.

- *Income distribution.* The GPI rises when the poor receive a larger share of national income and falls when their share decreases.

- *Lifespan of consumer durables and infrastructure.* The GDP greatly distorts the real benefits of the economy by counting only the money people spend on products without regard to the length of service they get in return. This has implications both for the family pocketbook and for the drain on the earth's resources. For instance, when you buy an appliance, the GDP records the price in the year of purchase as an economic advance, but it ignores how long the commodity lasts. By contrast, the GPI treats money spent to buy capital items as a benefit. This applies both to private capital items and to public infrastructure.

- *Defensive expenditures.* Funds spent to maintain a given level of service without increasing the amount of service received are treated as "defensive expenditures" (that is, costs) in the GPI. For example, the amount of money spent on commuting, the medical and material costs of automobile accidents, and the money that households are forced to spend on personal pollution-control devices such as water filters are defensive expenditures that the GPI subtracts from the GDP.

- *Sustainable investments.* If a nation allows its capital stock to decline, or if it finances its investments out of borrowed capital rather than savings, it is living beyond its means. The GPI measures net additions to the capital stock as a positive contribution to sustainable well-being and treats money borrowed from other countries as reductions in national self-sufficiency and sustainability. If borrowed money is used for investment purposes, the negative effects of borrowing are neutralized by the positive effects of investment. But if the borrowed money is used only to finance consumption, the GPI declines.

• • •

Our calculations are conservative. For example, we could include only those items for which statistics are available going back to 1950 — not an easy task, since the federal data-gathering process is driven largely by the existing GDP. Nevertheless, even this preliminary inventory of costs produces a new picture of the economy and one with very large implications. Judging by the GDP, you'd think that life has gotten progressively better from the early 1950s to the present, with only some minor dips along the way. The GPI, by contrast, suggests a gradual increase in national well-being until the early 1970s, and then a gradual decline since then.

If the mood of the electorate is any barometer at all, then it would appear that the GPI is a more accurate accounting of the economy that Americans experience. Certainly, the United States has produced vast amounts of stuff over the last twenty-five years. But whether life has gotten correspondingly better in the process is questionable, at best.

The GPI is a warning that our economy is locked into a course that is imposing large unreckoned costs on our present and future. It demonstrates that much of what the nation now considers *economic growth*, as measured by the GDP, is really just an attempt at any of three things: (1) fixing blunders from the past; (2) borrowing resources from the future; or (3) transferring functions from the traditional realm of family and community to that of the market.

The GPI implicitly challenges the very premise of the global economic model embodied in NAFTA and GATT both present and future — namely, that growth as presently defined is necessarily a boon for all. The GPI strongly suggests that, to the contrary, the costs of current modes of economic activity have begun to outweigh the benefits.

## IMPACT ON THE SOUTH

If the use of the GDP as a measure of progress has been bad for industrialized countries, it has been absolutely devastating for the developing nations of the South. For decades, the United States has used GDP-based models as the primary rationale for foisting the northern version of economics and development upon the South. The GDP is also the template for the lending policies and draconian structural adjustment policies of the World Bank and the IMF.

The disastrous impacts of the GDP accounting model on the South arises in part from the very nature of southern economies; that is, much of the South's production occurs in the informal sector of community and household exchange. In the South, much more than in the North, a large portion of production still resides in the household sector — and in particular with women. Women grow and prepare food, make and mend clothing, and frequently carry a heavier part of the workload than their male counterparts. Yet their work goes unrecognized in the national ledgers. Subsistence agriculture in particular provides the sustenance for many families in the South. Yet the GDP hides its value behind a smokescreen of statistical lassitude. As a result, northern countries can claim to be boosting the economies of the southern ones with their development schemes when they are actually uprooting the traditional patterns of production that maintain stability and social cohesion. This results in huge capital-intensive projects that undermine local cultures and economic self-sufficiency.

On top of that has been the blatant political manipulation of accounting protocols on behalf of multinational corporations and against the southern interest. A recent insidious example has been the shift from GNP to GDP. In the mid 1980s, international agencies made a quiet change from the old Gross National Product (GNP) to the new Gross Domestic Product (GDP) as the indicator of economic progress. What appeared a mere technical adjustment was in fact a fundamental shift that exaggerated the contributions of multinational corporations.

Under the old GNP, the profits of multinationals were attributed to the nation in which the corporation was based. If Goodyear, say, owned a factory in Indonesia, the profits generated in Indonesia were included in the United States' GNP. Now such profits are included in Indonesia's GDP, even if those profits eventually come back to roost in the States.

For the United States, with its enormous economy, this change doesn't make much difference. But for developing countries the new accounting rule caused a major shift. Suddenly, multinationals seemed an unqualified boon. The bookkeeping maneuver made it appear that southern countries were growing in wealth and well-being when actually the multinationals were simply walking off with their resources for the benefit of northern investors. The old GNP was itself a perverse measure of progress. Now, transmogrified into the GDP, it has become an even greater statistical cover-up for the social and ecological costs of globalization.

# WHAT NEXT?

A business that counted debts as assets and costs as income would think it was booming — for a while. But sooner or later the bills would come due, and that's what's happening now with the United States and other industrialized countries. For decades they have hidden their social and ecological breakdown and wanton borrowing from the future behind an accounting methodology that counted all this as gain. The GDP portrays as good many of the things that Americans experience as bad, from the breakdown of the family to traffic and noise to the fouling of the air and water. If anyone wonders why America's economic policies keep digging us into a deeper hole, the place to begin is here.

Better accounting alone will not bring better policies, just as crime statistics alone do not stop crime. Yet such data do help build an awareness of crime and help to define the issue that the political arena has to address.

Similarly, economic change is not likely to come until the nation produces an honest set of books that enables people to see the consequences of current policies more clearly than they can now. As recently as a few years ago, this seemed a remote possibility. But today it seems much less so. The gap between economic indicators and life experience is getting too large to ignore. The politics of the issue are changing as social conservatives join environmentalists in questioning whether economic growth and globalization actually lead to a better country and a better life.

Perhaps most important, there are now alternatives to the GDP. In the past, critics have had little to offer besides criticism. Now they can demonstrate the dishonesty of current accounting practices with concrete alternatives. New measures, such as the Genuine Progress Indicator, which take into account a host of factors ignored by the GDP, expose the GDP as a statistical facade maintained by proponents of the global economy to hide the real impact of their policies upon families and communities, upon our natural habitat, and upon the generations to come.

# 18

# GROWTH HAS REACHED
# ITS LIMIT

Robert Goodland

*Robert Goodland is an ecologist who has done a lot of his work in Brazil. For many years, he directed the Carey Arboretum in Millbrook, New York, and then joined the World Bank, where he is now environment adviser to the Environment Department. He has written a number of key books, including* Environmental Management of Tropical Agriculture *(1984, with Catherine Watson). He has also written innumerable reports in conjunction with Herman Daly that attempt to bring World Bank policies into line with the principles of ecological economics, especially the ecological limits to growth: the limits to resources and to* sinks, *that is, places to dump our wastes.*

To GAUGE the prospects of sustainability on our planet requires a single formula — population times per capita resource consumption. This is the scale of the human economic subsystem with respect to the global ecosystem on which it depends and of which it is a part. The global ecosystem — that is, the natural world — is the source of all material inputs feeding the economic subsystem and the sink for all its wastes. Population times per capita resource consumption is the total flow — *throughput* — of resources from the ecosystem to the economic subsystem, then back to the ecosystem as waste.

The global ecosystem's source and sink functions have limited capacity to support the economic subsystem. The imperative, therefore, is to keep the size of the global economy sustainable within the capacity of the ecosystem. It took all of human history to grow to the $60 billion–scale economy of 1900. Today, the world economy grows by this amount every two years. Unchecked, today's $20 trillion global economy may be five times larger only one generation or so hence.

In this chapter, I argue that we have reached the limits to throughput growth and that it is futile to insist that such growth can still alleviate poverty in the world today. We thus need to devise other strategies, such as qualitative development. Many local thresholds have been broached because of population pressures and poverty; global thresholds are being broached by industrial countries' overconsumption.

## LOCALIZED LIMITS TO GLOBAL LIMITS

The signs are clear that we have already fouled our nest. There is hardly a place on this earth where traces of the human economy are absent: From the center of Antarctica to Mount Everest, human wastes are evident and increasing. It is impossible to find even a tiny sample of ocean water with no sign of the twenty billion tons of human wastes added annually. Polychlorinated biphenyls (PCBs) and other persistent toxic chemicals such as DDT and heavy metal compounds have already accumulated throughout the marine ecosystem. One-fifth of the world's population breathes air more poisonous than World Health Organization (WHO) standards recommend, and an entire generation of Mexico City children may be mentally stunted by lead poisoning.

Since the Club of Rome's 1972 "Limits of Growth" report, the constraints on growth have shifted from source limits to sink limits. Source limits are more open to substitution and are more localized. Since then, awareness of the need to limit throughput growth has increased. Some limits, such as the chlorofluorocarbon (CFC) phaseout under the Montreal Convention, are tractable and are being tackled partly, at least; other limits are less tractable, such as the massive human appropriation of biomass (discussed later in detail). The key limit is the sink constraint of fossil energy use. To remain within it, the rate of transition to renewables, including solar energy, must parallel the rate of the transition to sustainability. As for new technologies, they have hardly started to focus on input reduction and even less on sink management, which suggests the need for improvements.

Landfill sites are becoming harder to find; garbage is shipped thousands of miles from industrial states to developing countries in search of unfilled sinks. It has so far proved impossible for the U.S. Nuclear Regulatory Commission to rent a nuclear waste site anywhere for less than $100 million per annum. Germany's Kraft-Werk Union (a company) signed an agreement with China in July 1987 to bury nuclear waste in Mongolia's Gobi Desert. These facts prove that landfill sites and toxic dumps — two types of sinks — are increasingly hard to find and hence that sustainability limits are near.

## First Evidence of Limits:
## Human Biomass Appropriation

The best evidence that there is an absolute limit is the calculation by Vitousek and others in *Bioscience* (1986) that the human economy — directly or indirectly — uses about 40 percent of the net primary product of terrestrial photosynthesis today. (This figure drops to 25 percent if the oceans and other aquatic ecosystems are included.) And desertification, urban encroachment onto agricultural land, blacktopping, soil erosion, and pollution are increasing. This means that with a mere doubling of the world's population (in, say, thirty-five years) we will use 80 percent, and 100 percent shortly thereafter. As Herman Daly points out, 100 percent appropriation is impossible ecologically and highly undesirable socially. The world will go from "half empty" to "full" in one doubling period, irrespective of the sink being filled or the source being consumed.

## Second Evidence of Limits:
## Climate Change

The evidence of atmospheric carbon dioxide accumulation is pervasive. It is geographically extensive, and unimaginably expensive to cure if allowed to worsen. In addition, the consequences are unambiguously negative. There may be a few exceptions, such as plants growing faster in carbon dioxide–enriched laboratories, where water and nutrients are not limiting. In the real world, however, it seems more likely that crop belts will not shift with changing climate, nor will crops grow faster if other factors such as suitable soils and water are limited. The prodigious North American breadbasket's climate may indeed shift north, but this does not mean the breadbasket will follow, because the rich prairie soils will stay put, and Canadian boreal soils and muskeg are very infertile.

Another indicator that limits have been exceeded is global climate change. The year 1990 was the warmest in more than a century of record keeping. Seven of the hottest years on record all occurred in the last eleven years. The 1980s were 1°F warmer than the 1880s, while 1990 was 1.25°F warmer. These changes contrast alarmingly with the preindustrial constancy in which the earth's temperature did not vary more than 2 to 4°F in the last ten thousand years. Humanity's entire social and cultural infrastructure over the last seven thousand years has evolved entirely within a global climate that never deviated more than 2°F from today's climate.

It is too soon to be absolutely certain that global "greenhouse" climate change has begun; normal climatic variability is too great for such a conclusion. But all the evidence suggests that global climate change may well be underway, that $CO_2$ accumulation started a century ago and that it is worsening fast. Scientists are now in near universal agreement that such warming will occur, although differences remain on the rates. The U.S. National Academy of Science has warned that global warming may well be the most pressing international issue of the next century. A dwindling minority of scientists remain agnostic, but the dispute concerns policy responses much more than predictions.

The scale of today's fossil fuel–based human economy seems to be the dominant cause of greenhouse gas accumulation. The carbon dioxide released from burning coal, oil, and natural gas — the biggest contribution to climate change — is accumulating fast in the atmosphere. Today's 5.3 billion people annually burn the equivalent of more than one ton of coal each.

The next significant contributor to climate change is all the other pollutants released by the economy that exceed the biosphere's absorptive capacity: methane, CFCs, and nitrous oxide. Relative to carbon dioxide, these three pollutants are many times more damaging, although the total amount emitted is much less than fossil fuels. Today, the cost shouldered by polluters for using atmospheric sink capacity for $CO_2$ disposal is zero, although the real cost may be astronomical.

The costs of rejecting the greenhouse hypothesis if it proves to be true are vastly greater than the costs of accepting the hypothesis if it is false. By the time the evidence is irrefutable, it is sure to be too late to avert unacceptable costs: such as the influx of millions of refugees from low-lying coastal areas (55 percent of the world's population lives on coasts or estuaries); damage to ports and coastal cities; increase in storm frequency and intensity; and, worst of all, damage to agriculture. Moreover, steps to abate climate change may save money, not cost it, when the benefit from lower fuel bills is taken into consideration. The greenhouse threat is more than sufficient to justify action now, even if only as insurance. The only question now is, How much insurance to buy?

Admittedly, great uncertainty prevails. But uncertainty cuts both ways; busines-as-usual or wait-and-see attitudes are thus imprudent, if not foolhardy. Underestimation of greenhouse or ozone shield risks is just as likely as overestimation. Recent studies suggest that underestimation may be the case. In May 1991, the EPA increased by twentyfold their estimates of UV-related cancer deaths, and the earth's ability to absorb methane was estimated downward by 25 percent in June 1991. In the face of uncertainty about global environmental health, prudence should be paramount.

The relevant component here is the tight relationship between carbon released and the scale of the economy. Global carbon emissions have increased annually since the Industrial Revolution; now they are increasing at nearly 4 percent per annum. If energy use parallels economic activity, then the carbon emissions that go with energy use are an index of the scale of the economy. Fossil fuels account for 78 percent of all U.S. energy consumed.

There is tremendous scope for reducing the energy intensity of industry and of the economy in general; that is why reductions in carbon emissions are possible without reducing standards of living. Decoupling economic growth from energy throughput appears substantially achievable: Witness the 81 percent increase in Japan's output since 1973 using the same amount of energy, or the United States' near 39 percent increase in GNP since 1973, with only a modest increase in energy use. This means energy efficiency increased by almost 26 percent.

Sweden — cold, gloomy, industrialized, and very energy efficient — is the best example of how profitable it is to reduce $CO_2$. The Swedish State Power Board found that doubling electric efficiency and phasing out nuclear power, which supplies 50 percent of the country's electricity, actually reduces $CO_2$ emissions by 34 percent while lowering consumers' electricity bills by U.S. $1 billion per year. Other, less energy-efficient nations should be able to do even better. Reducing energy intensity is possible in all industrial economies and in the larger developing economies, such as China, Brazil, and India. Increasing energy use without increasing $CO_2$ means primarily hastening the overdue transition to renewables: biomass, solar, hydro, and wind.

The other major source of carbon emissions — deforestation — also parallels the scale of the economy. With economic growth, people develop more land and diminish the wilderness.

Climate change is a compelling indication that limits have been exceeded because it is globally pervasive rather than limited to the atmosphere of the region where the $CO_2$ is generated. In comparison, acid rain, which affects large numbers of lakes in the United States, Canada, and Scandinavia while causing a $30 billion loss of forests in Europe, is more regional in character.

The nearly seven billion tons of carbon released each year by human activity (from fossil fuels and deforestation) accumulate in the atmosphere, which suggests that the ecosystem's carbon-absorption sinks have been exceeded. Carbon accumulation appears to be irreversible on any relevant time frame, hence it is of major concern for future generations. The removal of carbon dioxide by liquefying it or chemically scrubbing it from the stacks might double the cost of electricity. Optimistically, new technology may reduce this cost, but it will still seriously affect industry and the consumer alike.

## Third Evidence of Limits:
## Rupture of the Ozone Shield

It is difficult to imagine more compelling evidence that human activity has already damaged our life-support systems than the cosmic holes in the ozone shield. The damage that CFCs would cause to the ozone layer was predicted as far back as 1974 by Sherwood Rowland and Mario Molina. But when the damage was first detected — in 1985 in Antarctica — disbelief was so great that the data were rejected as coming from faulty sensors. A new series of tests and a search of hitherto undigested computer printouts confirmed that not only did the hole exist in 1985 but that it had appeared each spring since 1979. The world had failed to detect a vast hole that threatened human life and food production and that was more extensive than the United States and taller than Mount Everest. All subsequent tests have proved that the global ozone layer is thinning far faster than any model predicted.

Ultraviolet B radiation let through the impaired ozone shield intensifies skin cancers. The world seems set for one billion additional skin cancers, many of them fatal, among people alive today. An equally serious human health effect is the depression of our immune systems, which will increase our vulnerability to an array of infectious diseases and parasites. In addition, as the shield weakens, crop yields and marine fisheries decline. But the gravest effect may be the possibility of upsetting normal balances in natural vegetation. *Keystone species* — those upon which many others depend for survival — may decrease, leading to accelerating extinctions and a widespread reduction in environmental services.

The one million or so tons of CFCs annually dumped into the biosphere take about ten years to waft up to the ozone layer, where they destroy the ozone over a half-life of 100 to 150 years. The tonnage of CFCs and other ozone-depleting gases already released into the atmosphere is increasing damage to the ozone shield. Today's damage, although serious, only reflects the relatively low levels of CFCs released in the early 1980s. If

CFC emissions completely ceased today — which they have not, despite the Montreal Protocols — the world will still be condemned to ten years of increased damage, which would then gradually return to pre-damage levels over the next century.

Clearly, the global ecosystem's sink capacity to absorb CFC pollution has been vastly exceeded. Humankind is headed for damaged and diminished environmental services, human health, and food production. This is truly a global problem since 85 percent of all CFCs are released in the industrialized North, but the main "hole" in the ozone layer, which is now as big as North America, has occurred in Antarctica 20 kilometers up in the sky, showing the global scale of the damage.

## Fourth Evidence of Limits:
## Land Degradation

Decreased productivity caused by accelerating soil erosion, salination, and desertification is one of the many topics that must be included here. The phenomenon is not new; land that degraded thousands of years ago in the valley of the Tigris and Euphrates rivers or on the Greek Islands remains unproductive today. But the increased scale of such degradation is important, because practically all food for human consumption comes from land rather than aquatic or ocean systems. As 35 percent of the earth's land is already degraded, and since this figure is increasing and largely irreversible on any time scale of interest to society, such degradation is but further evidence that we have exceeded the regenerative capacity of the earth's agricultural land.

Pimentel and others (1987) found soil erosion to be serious in most of the world's agricultural areas and concluded that this problem is worsening as more and more marginal land is brought into production. Soil loss rates, generally ranging from 10 to 100 tons per hectare, exceed soil formation rates by at least ten times. Present agricultural practices are leading to erosion, salination, or waterlogging, to a point where 6 million hectares are abandoned every year.

The degradation of the world's agricultural land can only raise food prices and exacerbate income inequality, at a time when one billion people are already malnourished. At the same time, about one-third of the population of developing countries is now faced with a serious fuelwood shortage. Crop residues and dung are diverted from agriculture for use as fuel, which further intensifies land degradation and leads to more malnutrition and poverty.

## Fifth Evidence of Limits:
## Diminishing Biodiversity

The scale of the human economy is now such that the wilderness areas that sustain much of the world's remaining biological diversity are shrinking fast. The rates of wildlife habitat takeover and of species extinctions are the fastest they have ever been in recorded history, and they are accelerating. Tropical forests, the world's richest species habitats, have already been 55 percent destroyed, and the current rate exceeds 168,000 square kilometers per year. As the total number of species extant is not yet known even to the nearest order of magnitude (estimates range from five million to thirty million or more), it is impossible to determine precise extinction rates. However, conservative estimates put the rate at more than 5,000 species each year. This is about ten thousand times as fast as prehuman extinction rates. Less conservative estimates put the rate at 150,000 species per year. Ecosystems have built-in redundancy, but no one knows how far this process can go before it causes serious ecological catastrophes, which must lead to further poverty and misery.

# POPULATION

The Brundtland Commission Report (April 1987) was realistic on the subject of population. One-fourth of the world's population can no longer afford a healthy diet. Birthweight is declining in some places. Poverty stimulates population growth. Direct poverty alleviation is essential; to do nothing about it is clearly unacceptable. William MacNeill (1989) states it plainly: "Reducing rates of population growth is an essential condition for achieving sustainability."

Stabilizing population is more important in industrial countries than in developing countries, since the former overconsume and hence overpollute and are thereby responsible for the greatest increase in the impact of human activities on the already overtaxed environment. The richest 20 percent of the world consume over 70 percent of the world's commercial energy. Thirteen countries have already reached a fertility rate required in order to achieve zero population growth, so it is not utopian to expect others to follow. The population growth-rate of developing countries of course must also be reduced very dramatically. Their population is now 77 percent of the world's total, and they are responsible for 90 percent of the world's annual population growth.

The poor must be helped and will justifiably demand to reach at least minimally acceptable living standards by obtaining access to the remaining natural resource base. When industrial nations switch from input growth to qualitative development, more resources and environmental functions will be available for the poor in the South.

It is in the interests of both developing countries and the world as a whole that developing countries not follow the fossil fuel model. It is thus in the interest of industrial countries to subsidize alternative sources of energy. This is an important task for the World Bank; this is also the view of Dr. Qu Wenhu of the Academica Sinica, who points out that if a billion Chinese each require an automobile, sustainable development becomes impossible. Today, developing countries account for 17 percent of world commercial energy, but if unchecked, this figure would almost double by the year 2020 (OTA 1991).

Merely meeting the unmet demand for family planning would help enormously. Educating girls and providing them with employment opportunities and credit for productive purposes are probably even more effective. A full 25 percent of U.S. births and a much larger number of developing-country births are to unpartnered mothers who are largely unable to care for their children as well as are two-parent families. Most of these births are unwanted, which also tends to reduce the care bestowed on children. Certainly, international development agencies should assist high-population-growth countries in their family planning programs.

## GROWTH VERSUS DEVELOPMENT

The adverse impact of the economy on the biosphere and the exhaustion of the earth's regenerative and assimilative capacities can only mean that economic growth will increase the overexploitation of our already highly overtaxed environment.

However, opinions differ. MacNeill, director of United Nation's Commission on Environment and Development (UNCED), claims "a minimum of 3 percent annual per capita income growth is needed to reach sustainability during the first part of the next century," and this would need higher growth in national income, given population trends. The Dutch ecological economist Roefie Hueting disagrees in "The Brundtland Report: A Matter of Conflicting Goals" (1990). He believes that to achieve sustainability what we need least is an increase in national income. In his view, sustainability can only be achieved by stabilizing quantitative throughput growth and replacing it with qualitative development. If the impact of our activities on the environment can be measured by population times per capita resource use (as described earlier), then both must be seriously reduced.

The Brundtland Commission Report is excellent on three of the four necessary conditions. First is producing more with less through conservation, energy efficiency, technological improvements, and recycling. Japan excels in this regard, producing 81 percent more real output than it did in 1973 using the same amount of energy. Second is reducing the population explosion. Third is the redistribution of goods and wealth from overconsumers to the poor. Brundtland was probably being politically astute in leaving fuzzy the fourth necessary condition: the transition from economic growth to qualitative development, holding the scale of the economy consistent with the regenerative and assimilative capacities of global life-support systems. In several places, the Brundtland report hints at this.

In qualitative, sustainable development, production replaces depreciated assets, and births replace deaths, so that stocks of wealth and people are continually renewed and even improved. A developing economy is one in which the well-being of the (stable) population steadily improves, whereas an economy that merely increases throughput is only getting bigger, exceeding limits, and damaging the self-repairing capacity of the planet.

Our leaders must recognize that growth has reached its limits and decide to reduce further expansion in the scale of the economy. In doing this, they must prevent hardship in this tremendous transition for poor countries. But only raising the bottom without lowering the top will not bring about sustainability (Haavelmo 1990).

## CONCLUSION

When economies evolve from agrarian to industrial to more service-oriented, then smokestack throughput growth may be upgraded to growth that has a lower impact on sources and sinks: Coal and steel are replaced by fiber optics and electronics, for example. We must accelerate production modes that are less throughput-intensive. We must also accelerate technical improvements in resource productivity and thus fulfill Brundtland's maxim of "producing more with less." Presumably, this is what the Brundtland Commission and subsequent follow-up authors label "growth of a different kind." Vigorous promotion of this trend will indeed help the transition to sustainability and indeed is probably essential. It is also largely true that conservation and efficiency improvements and recycling are profitable and will become much more so the instant environmental externalities (such as carbon dioxide emissions) are internalized.

But it will be insufficient for three reasons. First, all growth, even Brundtland's unspecified new type of growth, consumes resources and produces wastes. Now that we have reached the limits of the ecosystem's regenerative and assimilative capacities, throughput growth exceeding such limits will not herald sustainability. Second, the size of the service sector relative to the production of goods has limits. Third, even many service-oriented industries, such as tourism, universities, and hospitals, are fairly throughput-intensive.

To conclude on an optimistic note, however: OECD found in 1984 that environmental expenditures are good for the economy and good for employment. Money is available; thus it is not finance capital shortage that is the limit to expenditure but shortages of both natural capital and political will in the industrialized world (Brown 1988).

Today, many nations spend less on environment, health, education, and welfare than they do on arms, which now annually total $1 trillion. Global security is increasingly prejudiced by source and sink constraints as recent natural resource wars have shown: examples include the 1974 "cod" war between the United Kingdom and Iceland, the 1969 "football" war between the overpopulated El Salvador and Honduras, and the 1991 Gulf War. It is only when the damage to global life-support systems is perceived as a more serious security risk than military conflict that governments will realize that the achievement of true sustainability must be their overriding priority.

# 19

# FREE TRADE
## *The Great Destroyer*

***

### David Morris

*David Morris has been one of the most widely quoted critics of the new free trade agreements, arguing his case on the grounds of environmental harm and the devastating effects upon local communities. Morris is director and vice president of the Institute for Local Self-Reliance (ISLR) in Minneapolis, a research and educational organization that provides technical assistance and information on environmentally sustainable economic practices. ISLR works with citizen groups, governments, and businesses to develop policies that extract maximum economic value from resources drawn and used locally.*

F REE TRADE is the religion of our age. With its heaven as the global economy, free trade comes complete with comprehensive analytical and philosophical underpinnings. Higher mathematics are used in stating its theorems. But in the final analysis, free trade is less an economic strategy than a moral doctrine. Although it pretends to be value-free, it is fundamentally value-driven. It assumes that the highest good is to shop. It assumes that mobility and change are synonymous with progress. The transport of capital, materials, goods, and people takes precedence over the autonomy, the sovereignty, and, indeed, the culture of local communities. Rather than promoting and sustaining the social relationships that create a vibrant community, the free trade theology relies on a narrow definition of efficiency to guide our conduct.

## THE POSTULATES OF FREE TRADE

For most of us, after a generation of brain washing about its supposed benefits, the tenets of free trade appear almost self-evident:

- Competition spurs innovation, raises productivity, and lowers prices.

- The division of labor allows specialization, which raises productivity and lowers prices.

- The larger the production unit, the greater the division of labor and specialization, and thus the greater the benefits.

The adoration of bigness permeates all political persuasions. The Treasury Department proposes creating five to ten giant U.S. banks. "If we are going to be competitive in a globalized financial services world, we are going to have to change our views on the size of American institutions," it declares. The vice chair of Citicorp warns us against "preserving the heartwarming idea that 14,000 banks are wonderful for our country." The liberal *Harper's* magazine agrees: "True, farms have gotten bigger, as has nearly every other type of economic enterprise. They have done so in order to take advantage of the economies of scale offered by modern production techniques." Democratic presidential adviser Lester Thurow criticizes antitrust laws as an "old Democratic conception [that] is simply out of date." He argues that even IBM, with $50 billion in sales, is not big enough for the global marketplace. "Big companies do sometimes crush small companies," Thurow concedes, "but far better that small American companies be crushed by big American companies than that they be crushed by foreign companies." The magazine *In These Times,* which once called itself an independent socialist weekly, concluded, "Japanese steel companies have been able to outcompete American steel companies partly by building larger plants."

The infatuation with large-scale systems leads logically to the next postulate of free trade: the need for global markets. Anything that sets up barriers to ever-wider markets reduces the possibility of specialization and thus raises costs, making us less competitive.

The last pillar of free trade is the law of comparative advantage, which comes in two forms: absolute and relative. Absolute comparative advantage is easier to understand: Differences in climate and natural resources suggest that Guatemala should raise bananas and Minnesota should raise walleyed pike. Thus, by specializing in what they grow best, each region enjoys comparative advantage in that particular crop. Relative compara-

tive advantage is a less intuitive but ultimately more powerful concept. As
the nineteenth-century British economist David Ricardo, the architect of
free trade economics, explained: "Two men can both make shoes and hats
and one is superior to the other in both employments; but in making hats
he can only exceed his competitor by one-fifth or 20 percent, and in making shoes he can exceed him by one-third or 33 percent. Will it not be for
the interest of both that the superior man should employ himself exclusively in making shoes and the inferior man in making hats?"

Thus, even if one community can make every product more efficiently
than another, it should specialize only in those items it produces most efficiently, in relative terms, and trade for others. Each community, and ultimately each nation, should specialize in what it does best.

What are the implications of these tenets of free trade? That communities and nations abandon self-reliance and embrace dependence. That
we abandon our capacity to produce many items and concentrate only on
a few. That we import what we need and export what we produce.

Bigger is better. Competition is superior to cooperation. Material self-
interest drives humanity. Dependence is better than independence. These
are the pillars of free trade. In sum, we make a trade. We give up sovereignty over our affairs in return for a promise of more jobs, more goods,
and a higher standard of living.

• • •

The economic arguments in favor of free trade are powerful. Yet for most
of us it is not the soundness of its theory but the widely promoted idea that
free trade is an inevitable development of our market system that makes
us believers. We believe that economies, like natural organisms, evolve
from the simple to the complex.

From the Dark Ages, to city-states, to nation-states, to the planetary
economy, and, soon, to space manufacturing, history has systematically
unfolded. Free trade supporters believe that trying to hold back economic
evolution is like trying to hold back natural evolution. The suggestion
that we choose another developmental path is viewed, at best, as an attempt to reverse history and, at worst, as an unnatural and even sinful act.

This kind of historical determinism has corollaries. We not only move
from simple to complex economies. We move from integrated economies
to segregated ones, separating the producer from the consumer, the
farmer from the kitchen, the power plant from the appliance, the dump
site from the garbage can, the banker from the depositor, and, inevitably,
the government from the citizenry. In the process of development we sep-

arate authority and responsibility — those who make the decisions are not those who are affected by the decisions.

Just as *Homo sapiens* is taken to be nature's highest achievement, so the multinational and supranational corporation becomes our most highly evolved economic animal. The planetary economy demands planetary institutions. The nation-state itself begins to disappear, both as an object of our affection and identification and as a major actor in world affairs.

The planetary economy merges and submerges nations. Yoshitaka Sajima, vice president of Mitsui and Company USA, asserts, "The U.S. and Japan are not just trading with each other anymore — they've become a part of each other." Lamar Alexander, former Republican Governor of Tennessee, agreed with Sajima's statement when he declared that the goal of his economic development strategy was "to get the Tennessee economy integrated with the Japanese economy."

In Europe, the Common Market has grown from six countries in the 1950s to ten in the 1970s to sixteen today, and barriers between these nations are rapidly being abolished. Increasingly, there are neither Italian nor French nor German companies, only European supracorporations. The U.S., Canadian, and Mexican governments formed NAFTA to merge the countries of the North American continent economically.

Promotion of exports is now widely accepted as the foundation for a successful economic development program. Whether for a tiny country such as Singapore or a huge country such as the United States, exports are seen as essential to a nation's economic health.

Globalism commands our attention and our resources. Our principal task, we are told, is to nurture, extend, and manage emerging global systems. Trade talks are on the top of everybody's agenda, from Yeltsin to Clinton. Political leaders strive to devise stable systems for global financial markets and exchange rates. The best and the brightest of this generation use their ingenuity to establish the global financial and regulatory rules that will enable the greatest uninterrupted flow of resources among nations.

The emphasis on globalism rearranges our loyalties and loosens our neighborly ties. "The new order eschews loyalty to workers, products, corporate structure, businesses, factories, communities, even the nation," the *New York Times* announces. Martin S. Davis, chair of Gulf and Western, declares, "All such allegiances are viewed as expendable under the new rules. You cannot be emotionally bound to any particular asset."

We are now all assets.

Jettisoning loyalties isn't easy, but that is the price we believe we must pay to receive the benefits of the global village. Every community must achieve the lowest possible production cost, even when that means breaking whatever remains of its social contract and long-standing traditions.

The revised version of the American Dream is articulated by Stanley J. Mihelick, executive vice president for production at Goodyear: "Until we get real wage levels down much closer to those of the Brazils and Koreas, we cannot pass along productivity gains to wages and still be competitive."

Wage raises, environmental protection, national health insurance, and liability lawsuits — anything that raises the cost of production and makes a corporation less competitive — threatens our economy. We must abandon the good life to sustain the economy. We are in a global struggle for survival. We are hooked on free trade.

## THE DOCTRINE FALTERS

At this very moment in history, when the doctrines of free trade and globalism are so dominant, the absurdities of globalism are becoming more evident. Consider the case of the toothpick and the chopstick.

A few years ago I was eating at a St. Paul, Minnesota, restaurant. After lunch, I picked up a toothpick wrapped in plastic. On the plastic was printed the word *Japan*. Japan has little wood and no oil; nevertheless, it has become efficient enough in our global economy to bring little pieces of wood and barrels of oil to Japan, wrap the one in the other, and send the manufactured product to Minnesota. This toothpick may have traveled 50,000 miles. But never fear, we are now retaliating in kind. A Hibbing, Minnesota, factory now produces one billion disposable chopsticks a year for sale in Japan. In my mind's eye, I see two ships passing one another in the northern Pacific. One carries little pieces of Minnesota wood bound for Japan; the other carries little pieces of Japanese wood bound for Minnesota. Such is the logic of free trade.

Nowhere is the absurdity of free trade more evident than in the grim plight of the Third World. Developing nations were encouraged to borrow money to build an economic infrastructure in order to specialize in what they do best (comparative advantage, once again) and thereby expand their export capacity. To repay the debts, Third World countries must increase their exports.

One result of these arrangements has been a dramatic shift in food production from internal consumption to export. Take the case of Brazil. Brazilian per capita production of basic foodstuffs (rice, black beans, manioc, and potatoes) fell 13 percent from 1977 to 1984. Per capita output of exportable foodstuffs (soybeans, oranges, cotton, peanuts, and tobacco) jumped 15 percent. Today, although some 50 percent of Brazil suffers malnutrition, one leading Brazilian agronomist still calls export promotion "a matter of national survival." In the global village, a nation survives by starving its people.

• • •

What about the purported benefits of free trade, such as higher standards of living?

It depends on whose standards of living are being considered. Inequality between and, in most cases, within countries has increased. Two centuries of trade has exacerbated disparities in world living standards. According to economist Paul Bairoch, per capita GNP in 1750 was approximately the same in the developed countries as in the underdeveloped ones. In 1930, the ratio was about 4 to 1 in favor of the developed nations. Today it is 8 to 1.

Inequality is both a cause and an effect of globalism. Inequality within one country exacerbates globalism because it reduces the number of people with sufficient purchasing power; consequently, a producer must sell to wealthy people in many countries to achieve the scale of production necessary to produce goods at a relatively low cost. Inequality is an effect of globalism because export industries employ few workers, who earn disproportionately higher wages than their compatriots, and because developed countries tend to take out more capital from Third World countries than they invest in them.

Free trade was supposed to improve our standard of living. Yet even in the United States, the most developed of all nations, we find that living standards have been declining since 1980. More dramatically, according to several surveys, in 1988 U.S. workers worked almost half a day longer for lower real wages than they did in 1970. We who work in the United States have less leisure time in the 1990s than we had in the 1790s.

## A NEW WAY OF THINKING

It is time to re-examine the validity of the doctrine of free trade and its creation, the planetary economy. To do so, we must begin by speaking of values. Human beings may be acquisitive and competitive, but we are also loving and cooperative. Several studies have found that the voluntary, unpaid economy may be as large and as productive as the paid economy.

There is no question that we have converted more and more human relationships into commercial transactions, but there is a great deal of question as to whether this was a necessary or beneficial development.

We should not confuse change with progress. Bertrand Russell once described change as inevitable and progress as problematic. Change is scientific. Progress is ethical. We must decide which values we hold most dear and then design an economic system that reinforces those values.

## REASSESSING FREE TRADE'S ASSUMPTIONS

If price is to guide our buying, selling, and investing, then price should tell us something about efficiency. We might measure efficiency in terms of natural resources used in making products and the lack of waste produced in converting raw material into a consumer or industrial product. Traditionally, we have measured efficiency in human terms; that is, by measuring the amount of labor-hours spent in making a product.

But price is actually no measure of real efficiency. In fact, price is no reliable measure of anything. In the planetary economy, the prices of raw materials, labor, capital, transportation, and waste disposal are all heavily subsidized. For example, wage-rate inequities among comparably skilled workforces can be as disparate as 30 to 1. This disparity overwhelms even the most productive worker. An American worker might produce twice as much per hour as a Mexican worker but is paid ten times as much.

In Taiwan, for example, strikes are illegal. In South Korea, unions cannot be organized without government permission. Many developing nations have no minimum wage, maximum hours, or environmental legislation. As economist Howard Wachtel notes, "Differences in product cost that are due to totalitarian political institutions or restrictions on economic rights reflect no natural or entrepreneurial advantage. Free trade has nothing to do with incomparable political economic institutions that protect individual rights in one country and deny them in another."

The price of goods in developed countries is also highly dependent on subsidies. For example, we in the United States decided early on that government should build the transportation systems of the country. The public, directly or indirectly, built our railroads, canals, ports, highways, and airports.

Heavy trucks do not pay taxes sufficient to cover the damage they do to roads. California farmers buy water at as little as 5 percent of the going market rate; the other 95 percent is funded by huge direct subsidies to corporate farmers. In the United States, society as a whole picks up the costs of agricultural pollution. Having intervened in the production process in all these ways, we then discover it is cheaper to raise produce near the point of sale.

Prices don't provide accurate signals within nations; they are not the same as cost. *Price* is what an individual pays; *cost* is what the community as a whole pays. Most economic programs in the industrial world result in an enormous disparity between the price of a product or service to an individual and the cost of that same product or service to the society as a whole.

When a U.S. utility company wanted to send electricity across someone's property, and that individual declined the honor, the private utility received governmental authority to seize the land needed. This is exactly what happened in western Minnesota in the late 1970s. Since larger power plants produced electricity more cheaply than smaller ones, it was therefore in the "public interest" to erect these power lines. If landowners' refusal to sell had been respected, the price of electricity would be higher today, but it would reflect the cost of that power more accurately.

Because the benefit of unrestricted air transportation takes precedence over any damage to public health and sanity, communities no longer have the authority to regulate flights and noise. As a consequence, airplanes awaken us or our children in the middle of the night. By one survey, some four million people in the United States suffer physical damage due to airport noise. If communities were given the authority to control noise levels by planes, as they already control noise levels from radios and motorcycles, the price of a plane ticket would increase significantly. Its price would be more aligned with its actual cost to society.

It is often hard to quantify social costs, but this doesn't mean they are insignificant. Remember urban renewal? In the 1950s and 1960s inner-city neighborhoods were leveled to assemble sufficient land area to rebuild our downtowns. Skyscrapers and shopping malls arose; the property tax base expanded; and we considered it a job well done. Later, sociologists, economists, and planners discovered that the seedy areas we destroyed were not fragmented, violence-prone slums but more often cohesive ethnic communities where generations had grown up and worked and where children went to school and played. If we were to put a dollar figure on the destruction of homes, the pain of broken lives, and the expense of relocation and re-creation of community life, we might find that the city as a whole actually lost money in the urban renewal process. If we had used a full-cost accounting system, we might never have undertaken urban renewal.

Our refusal to understand and count the social costs of certain kinds of development has caused suffering in rural and urban areas alike. In 1944, Walter Goldschmidt, working under contract with the Department of Agriculture, compared the economic and social characteristics of two rural California communities that were alike in all respects, except one. Dinuba was surrounded by family farms; Arvin by corporate farms. Goldschmidt found that Dinuba was more stable, had a higher standard of living, more small businesses, higher retail sales, better schools and other community facilities, and a higher degree of citizen participation in local affairs. The USDA invoked a clause in Goldschmidt's contract forbidding him to discuss his finding. The study was not made public for almost thirty years. Meanwhile, the USDA continued to promote research that rapidly transformed the Dinubas of our country into Arvins. The farm crisis we now suffer is a consequence of this process.

How should we deal with the price-versus-cost dilemma as a society? Ways do exist by which we can protect our life-style from encroachment by the global economy, achieve important social and economic goals, and pay about the same price for our goods and services. In some cases we might have to pay more, but we should remember that higher prices may be offset by the decline in overall costs. Consider the proposed Save the Family Farm legislation drafted by farmers and introduced in Congress several years ago by Iowa Senator Tom Harkin. It proposed that farmers limit production of farm goods nationwide at the same time as the nation establishes a minimum price for farm goods that is sufficient to cover operating and capital costs and provides farm families with an adequate living. The law's sponsors estimate that such a program would increase the retail cost of agricultural products by 3 to 5 percent, but the increase would be more than offset by dramatically reduced public tax expenditures spent on farm subsidies. And this doesn't take into consideration the cost benefits of a stable rural America: fewer people leaving farms that have been in their families for generations; less influx of jobless rural immigrants into already economically depressed urban areas; and fewer expenditures for medical bills, food stamps, and welfare.

Economists like to talk about externalities. The costs of job dislocation, rising family violence, community breakdown, environmental damage, and cultural collapse are all considered "external." External to what, one might ask?

The theory of comparative advantage itself is fast losing its credibility. Time was when technology spread slowly. Three hundred years ago in northern Italy, stealing or disclosing the secrets of silk-spinning machinery was a crime punishable by death. At the beginning of the Industrial Revolution, Britain protected its supremacy in textile manufacturing by banning both the export of machines and the emigration of men who knew how to build and run them. A young British apprentice, Samuel Slater, brought the Industrial Revolution to the United States by memorizing the design of the spinning frame and migrating here in 1789.

Today, technology transfer is simple. According to Dataquest, a market research firm, it takes only three weeks after a new U.S.-made product is introduced before it is copied, manufactured, and shipped back to the U.S. from Asia. So much for comparative advantage.

## THE EFFICIENCIES OF SMALL SCALE

This brings us to the issue of scale. There is no question that when I move production out of my basement and into a factory, the cost per item produced declines dramatically. But when the factory increases its output a hundredfold, production costs no longer decline proportionately. The vast majority of the cost decreases are captured at fairly modest production levels.

In agriculture, for example, the USDA studied the efficiency of farms and concluded, "Above about $40–50,000 in gross sales — the size that is at the bottom of the end of medium sized sales category — there are no greater efficiencies of scale." Another USDA report agreed: "Medium sized family farms are as efficient as the large farms."

Harvard Professor Joseph Bain's pioneering investigations in the 1950s found that plants far smaller than originally believed can be economically competitive. Further, it was found that the factory could be significantly reduced in size without requiring major price increases for its products. In other words, we might be able to produce shoes for a region rather than for a nation at about the same price per shoe. If we withdrew government subsidies to the transportation system, then locally produced and marketed shoes might actually be less expensive than those brought in from abroad.

Modern technology makes smaller production plants possible. For instance, traditional float glass plants produce 550 to 600 tons of glass daily, at an annual cost of $100 million. With only a $40 to 50 million investment, new miniplants can produce about 250 tons per day for a regional market at the same cost per ton as the large plants.

The advent of programmable machine tools may accelerate this tendency. In 1980, industrial engineers developed machine tools that could be programmed to reproduce a variety of shapes so that now a typical Japanese machine tool can make almost one hundred different parts from an individual block of material. What does this mean? Erich Bloch, director of the National Science Foundation, believes manufacturing "will be so flexible that it will be able to make the first copy of a product for little more than the cost of the thousandth." "So the ideal location for the factory of the future," says Patrick A. Toole, vice president for manufacturing at IBM, "is in the market where the products are consumed."

# CONCLUSION

When we abandon our ability to produce for ourselves, when we separate authority from responsibility, when those affected by our decisions are not those who make the decisions, when the cost and the benefit of production or development processes are not part of the same equation, when price and cost are no longer in harmony, we jeopardize our security and our future.

You may argue that free trade is not the sole cause of all our ills. Agreed. But free trade as it is preached today nurtures and reinforces many of our worst problems. It is an ideological package that promotes ruinous policies. And, most tragically, as we move further down the road to giantism, globalism, and dependence, we make it harder and harder to back up and take another path. If we lose our skills, our productive base, our culture, our traditions, our natural resources; if we erode the bonds of personal and familial responsibility, it becomes ever more difficult to recreate community. It is very, very hard to put Humpty Dumpty back together again.

Which means we must act now. The unimpeded mobility of capital, labor, goods, and raw materials is not the highest social good. We need to challenge the postulates of free trade head on, to propose a different philosophy, to embrace a different strategy. There is another way. To make it the dominant way, we must change the rules; indeed, we must challenge our own behavior. And to do that requires not only that we challenge the emptiness of free trade but that we promote a new idea: economics as if community matters.

## 20

# FREE TRADE
### *The Perils of Deregulation*

## Herman E. Daly

*Prior to the ratification of NAFTA and GATT, one of the few major criticisms published in any American journal was this one, originally published in* Scientific American *magazine. Dr. Daly convincingly shows why free trade cannot be a panacea for our ills. Quite the opposite, free trade must cause immense ecological and economic harm.*

No POLICY prescription commands greater consensus among economists than that of free trade based on international specialization according to comparative advantage. Free trade has long been presumed good unless proved otherwise. That presumption is the cornerstone of the General Agreement on Tariffs and Trade (GATT) and the North American Free Trade Agreement (NAFTA). The tenets of the Uruguay Round of negotiations strengthen GATT's basic commitment to free trade and economic globalization.

Yet that presumption should be reversed. The default position should favor domestic production for domestic markets. When convenient, balanced international trade should be used, but it should not be allowed to govern a country's affairs at the risk of environmental and social disaster. The domestic economy should be the dog, and international trade its tail. GATT seeks to tie all the dogs' tails together so tightly that the international knot would wag the separate national dogs.

The wiser course was well expressed in the overlooked words of John Maynard Keynes: "I sympathize, therefore, with those who would maximize economic entanglement between nations. Ideas, knowledge, art, hospitality, travel — these are the things which should of their nature be international. But let goods be homespun whenever it is reasonably and conveniently possible; and, above all, let finance be primarily national." Contrary to Keynes, the defenders of the Uruguay Round of changes to GATT not only want to downplay "homespun goods," they also want finance and all other services to become primarily international.

• • •

Economists and environmentalists are sometimes represented as being, respectively, for and against free trade, but that polarization does the argument a disservice. The real debate is over which kinds of regulations are to be instituted and which goals are legitimate. The free traders seek to maximize profits and production without regard for considerations that represent the hidden social and environmental costs. They argue that when growth has made people wealthy enough, they will have the funds to clean up the damage done by growth. Conversely, environmentalists and some economists, myself among them, suspect that growth is increasing environmental costs faster than benefits from production, thereby making us poorer, not richer.

A more accurate name than the persuasive label *free trade* — because who can be opposed to freedom? — is *deregulated international commerce*. Deregulation is not always a good policy: Recall the recent experience of the U.S. deregulation of the savings and loan institutions. As one who formerly taught the doctrine of free trade to college students, I have some sympathy for the free traders' view. Nevertheless, my major concern about my profession today is that our disciplinary preference for logically beautiful results over factually grounded policies has reached such fanatical proportions that we economists have become dangerous to the earth and its inhabitants.

The free trade position is grounded in the logic of comparative advantage, first explicitly formulated by the early nineteenth-century British economist David Ricardo. He observed that countries with different technologies, customs, and resources will incur different costs when they make the same products. One country may find it comparatively less costly to mine coal than to grow wheat, but in another country the opposite may be true. If nations specialize in the products for which they have a comparative advantage and trade freely to obtain others, everyone benefits.

The problem is not the logic of this argument. It is the relevance of Ricardo's critical but often forgotten assumption that factors of production (especially capital) are internationally immobile. In today's world, where billions of dollars can be transferred between nations at the speed of light, that essential condition is not met. Moreover, free traders encourage such foreign investment as a development strategy. In short, the free traders are using an argument that hinges on the impermeability of national boundaries to capital to support a policy aimed at making those same boundaries increasingly permeable to both capital and goods!

That fact alone invalidates the assumptions that international trade will inevitably benefit all its partners. Furthermore, for trade to be mutually beneficial, the gains must not be offset by higher liabilities. After specialization, nations are no longer free not to trade, and that loss of independence can be a liability. Also, the cost of transporting goods internationally must not cancel out the profits. Transport costs are energy-intensive. Today, however, the cost of energy is frequently subsidized by governments through investment tax credits, federally subsidized research, and military expenditures that ensure access to petroleum. The environmental costs of fossil-fuel burning also do not factor into the price of gasoline. To the extent that energy is subsidized, then, so too is trade. The full cost of energy, stripped of these obscuring subsidies, would therefore reduce the initial gains from long-distance trade, whether international or interregional.

• • •

Free trade can also introduce new inefficiencies. Contrary to the implications of comparative advantage, more than half of all international trade involves the simultaneous import and export of essentially the same goods. For example, Americans import Danish sugar cookies, and Danes import American sugar cookies. Exchanging recipes would surely be more efficient; it would also be more in accord with Keynes' dictum that knowledge should be international and goods homespun (or, in this case, home-baked).

Another important but seldom mentioned corollary of specialization is the reduction in the range of occupational choices. Uruguay has a clear comparative advantage in raising cattle and sheep. If it adhered strictly to the rule of specialization and trade, it would afford its citizens only the choice of being either cowboys or shepherds. Yet Uruguayans feel a need for their own legal, financial, medical, insurance, and educational services, in addition to basic agriculture and industry. That diversity entails some loss of efficiency, but it is necessary for community and nationhood.

Uruguay is enriched by having a symphony orchestra of its own, even though it would be cost-effective to import better symphony concerts in exchange for wool, mutton, beef, and leather. Individuals, too, must count the broader range of choices as a welfare gain: Even those who are cowboys and shepherds are surely enriched by contact with countrymen who are not *vaqueros* or *pastores*. My point is that the community dimension of welfare is completely overlooked in the simplistic argument that if specialization and trade increase the per capita availability of commodities, they must be good.

Let us assume that even after those liabilities are subtracted from the gross returns on trade, positive net gains still exist. They must still offset deeper, more fundamental problems. The arguments for free trade run afoul of the three basic goals of all economic policies: the efficient *allocation* of resources, the fair *distribution* of resources, and the maintenance of a sustainable *scale* of resource use. The first two are traditional goals of neoclassical economics. The third has only recently been recognized and is associated with the viewpoint of ecological, or steady-state, economics. It means that the input of raw materials and energy to an economy and the output of waste materials and heat must be within the regenerative and absorptive capacities of the ecosystem.

In neoclassical economics, the efficient allocation of resources depends on the counting and internalization of all costs. Costs are *internalized* if they are directly paid by those entities responsible for them — as when, for example, a manufacturer pays for the disposal of its factory wastes and raises its prices to cover that expense. Costs are *externalized* if they are paid by someone else — as when the public suffers extra disease, stench, and nuisance from uncollected wastes. Counting all costs is the very basis of efficiency.

Economists rightly urge nations to follow a domestic program of internalizing costs into prices. They also wrongly urge nations to trade freely with other countries that do not internalize their costs (and consequently have lower prices). If a nation tries to follow both those policies, the conflict is clear: Free competition between different cost-internalizing regimes is utterly unfair.

International trade increases competition, and competition reduces costs. But competition can reduce costs in two ways: by increasing efficiency or by lowering standards. A firm can save money by lowering standards for pollution control, worker safety, wages, health care, and so on — all choices that externalize some of its costs. Profit-maximizing firms in competition always have an incentive to externalize their costs to the degree that they can get away with it.

For precisely that reason, nations maintain large legal, administrative, and auditing structures that bar reductions in the social and environmental standards of domestic industries. There are no analogous international bodies of law and administration; there are only national laws, which differ widely. Consequently, free international trade encourages industries to shift their production activities to the countries that have the lowest standards of cost internalization — hardly a move toward global efficiency.

• • •

Attaining cheapness by ignoring real costs is a sin against efficiency. Even GATT recognizes that requiring citizens of one country to compete against foreign prison labor would be carrying standards-lowering competition too far. GATT therefore allows the imposition of restrictions on such trade. Yet it makes no similar exception for child labor, for insured risky labor, or for subsistence-wage labor.

The most practical solution is to permit nations that internalize costs to levy compensating tariffs on trade with nations that do not. *Protectionism* — shielding an inefficient industry against more efficient foreign competitors — is a dirty word among economists. That is very different, however, from protecting an efficient national policy of full-cost pricing from standards-lowering international competition.

Such tariffs are also not without precedent. Free traders generally praise the fairness of "anti-dumping" tariffs that discourage countries from trading goods at prices below their production costs. The only real difference is the decision to include the costs of environmental damage and community welfare in that reckoning.

This tariff policy does not imply the imposition of one country's environmental preferences or moral judgments on another country. Each country should set the rules of cost internalization in its own market. Whoever sells in a nation's market should play by that nation's rules or pay a tariff sufficient to remove the competitive advantage of lower standards. For instance, under the Marine Mammal Protection Act, all tuna sold in the United States (whether by U.S. or Mexican fishermen) must count the cost of limiting the kill of dolphin associated with catching that tuna. Tuna sold in the Mexican market (whether by U.S. of Mexican fishermen) need not include that cost. No standards are being imposed through "environmental imperialism"; paying the costs of a nation's environmental standards is merely the price of admission to its market.

Indeed, free trade could be accused of reverse environmental imperialism. When firms produce under the most permissive standards and sell their product elsewhere without penalty, they press on countries with higher standards to lower them. In effect, unrestricted trade imposes lower standards.

Unrestricted international trade also raises problems of resource distribution. In the world of comparative advantage described by Ricardo, a nation's capital stays at home, and only goods are traded. If firms are free to relocate their capital internationally to wherever their production costs would be lowest, then the favored countries have not merely a comparative advantage but an absolute advantage. Capital will drain out of one country and into another, perhaps making what H. Ross Perot called "a giant sucking sound" as jobs and wealth move within it. This specialization will increase world production, but without any assurance that all the participating countries will benefit.

When the capital flows abroad, the opportunity for new domestic employment diminishes, which drives down the price for domestic labor. Even if free trade and capital mobility raise wages in low-wage countries (and that tendency is thwarted by overpopulation and rapid population growth), they do so at the expense of labor in the high-wage countries. They thereby increase income inequality there. Most citizens are wage earners. In the United States, 80 percent of the labor force is classified as "nonsupervisory employees." Their real wages have fallen 17 percent between 1973 and 1990, in significant part because of trade liberalization.

Nor does labor in low-wage countries necessarily gain from free trade. It is likely that NAFTA will ruin Mexican peasants when "inexpensive" U.S. corn (subsidized by depleting topsoil, aquifers, oil wells, and federal treasury) can be freely imported. Displaced peasants will bid down wages. Their land will be bought cheaply by agribusinesses to produce fancy vegetables and cut flowers for the U.S. market. Ironically, Mexico helps to keep U.S. corn "inexpensive" by exporting its own vanishing reserves of oil and genetic crop variants, which the United States needs to sustain its corn monoculture.

Neoclassical economists admit that overpopulation can spill over from one country to another in the form of cheap labor. They acknowledge that fact as an argument against free immigration. Yet capital can migrate toward abundant labor more easily than labor can move toward capital. The legitimate case for restrictions on labor immigration is therefore easily extended to restrictions on capital emigration.

●  ●  ●

When confronted with such problems, neoclassical economics often answer that growth will solve them. The allocation problem of standards-lowering competition, they say, will be dealt with by universally "harmonizing" all standards upward. The distribution problem of falling wages in high-wage countries would only be temporary; the economists believe that growth will eventually raise wages worldwide to the former high-wage level and beyond.

Yet the goal of a sustainable scale of total resource use forces us to ask, What will happen if the entire population of the earth consumes resources at the rate of high-wage countries? Neoclassical economists generally ignore this question or give the facile response that there are no limits.

The steady-state economic paradigm suggests a different answer. The regenerative and assimilative capacities of the biosphere cannot support even the current levels of resource consumption, much less the manifold increase required to generalize the higher standards worldwide. Still less can the ecosystem afford an ever-growing population that is striving to consume more per capita. As a species, we already preempt about 40 percent of the land-based primary product of photosynthesis for human purposes. What happens to biodiversity if we double the human population, as we are projected to do over the next thirty to fifty years?

These limits put a brake on the ability of growth to wash away the problems of misallocation and maldistribution. In fact, free trade becomes a recipe for hastening the speed with which competition lowers standards for efficiency, distributive equity, and ecological sustainability.

Notwithstanding those enormous problems, the appeal of bigger free trade blocs for corporations is obvious. The broader the free trade area, the less answerable a large and footloose corporation will be to any local or even national community. Spatial separation of the places that suffer the costs and enjoy the benefits becomes more feasible. The corporation will be able to buy labor in the low-wage markets. The larger the market, the longer a corporation will be able to avoid the logic of Henry Ford, who realized that he had to pay his workers enough for them to buy his cars. That is why transnational corporations like free trade and why workers and environmentalists do not.

• • •

In the view of steady-state economics, the economy is one open sub-system in a finite, nongrowing, and materially closed ecosystem. An *open system* takes matter and energy from the environment as raw materials and returns them as waste. A *closed system* is one in which matter constantly circulates internally, while only energy flows through. Whatever enters a system as input and exits as output is called *throughput*. Just as an organism survives by consuming nutrients and excreting wastes, so too an economy must to some degree both deplete and pollute the environment. A steady-state economy is one whose throughput remains constant at a level that neither depletes the environment beyond its regenerative capacity nor pollutes it beyond its absorptive capacity.

Most neoclassical economic analyses today rest on the assumption that the economy is the total system and nature is the subsystem. The economy is an isolated system involving only a circular flow of exchange value between firms and households. Neither matter nor energy enters or exits this system. The economy's growth is therefore unconstrained. Nature may be finite, but it is seen as just one sector of the economy, for which other sectors can substitute without limiting overall growth.

Although this vision of circular flow is useful for analyzing exchanges between producers and consumers, it is actively misleading for studying *scale* — the size of the economy relative to the environment. It is as if a biologist's vision of an animal contained a circulatory system but not a digestive tract or lungs. Such a beast would be independent of its environment, and its size would not matter. If it could move, it would be a perpetual motion machine.

Long ago, the world was relatively empty of human beings and their belongings (human-made capital) and relatively full of other species and their habitats (natural capital). Years of economic growth have changed that basic pattern. If human-made and natural capital were good substitutes for one another, then natural capital could be totally replaced. The two are complementary, however, which means that the short supply of one imposes limits. What good are fishing boats without populations of fish? Or sawmills without forests? Once the number of fish that could be sold at market was primarily limited by the number of boats that could be built and staffed; now it is limited by the number of fish in the sea.

As long as the scale of human economy was very small relative to the ecosystem, no apparent sacrifice was involved in increasing it. The scale of the economy is now such that painless growth is no longer reasonable. If we see the economy as a subsystem of a finite, nongrowing ecosystem, then there must be a maximal scale for its throughput of matter and energy. More important, there must also be an optimal scale. Economic growth beyond that optimum would increase the environmental costs faster than it would the production benefits, thereby ushering in an antieconomic phase that impoverished rather than enriched.

One can find disturbing evidence that we have already passed that point and, like Alice in *Through the Looking Glass*, the faster we run, the farther behind we fall. Thus the correlation between gross national product (GNP) and the index of sustainable economic welfare (which is based on personal consumption and adjusted for depletion of natural capital and other factors) has taken a negative turn in the United States.

Like our planet, the economy may continue forever to develop qualitatively, but it cannot grow indefinitely and must eventually settle into a steady state in its physical dimensions. That condition need not be miserable, however. We economists need to make the elementary distinction between *growth* (a quantitative increase in size resulting from the accretion or assimilation of materials) and *development* (the qualitative evolution to a fuller, better, or different state). Quantitative and qualitative changes follow different laws; conflating the two, as we currently do in the GNP, has led to much confusion.

Development without growth is sustainable development. An economy that is steady in scale may still continue to develop a greater capacity to satisfy human wants by increasing the efficiency of its resource use, by improving social institutions, and by clarifying its ethical priorities — but not by increasing the resource throughput.

• • •

In the light of the growth-versus-development distinction, let us return to the issue of international trade and consider two questions: What is the likely effect of free trade on growth? What is the likely effect of free trade on development?

Free trade is likely to stimulate the growth of throughput. It allows a country in effect to exceed its domestic regenerative and absorptive limits by "importing" those capacities from other countries. True, a country "exporting" some of its carrying capacity in return for imported products might have increased its throughput even more if it had made the products domestically. Overall, nevertheless, trade does postpone the day when countries must face up to living within their natural regenerative and absorptive capacities. That some countries still have excess carrying capacity is more indicative of a shortfall in their desired domestic growth than of any conscious decision to reserve that capacity for export.

By spatially separating the costs and benefits of environmental exploitation, international trade makes them harder to compare. It thereby increases the tendency for economies to overshoot their optimum scale. Furthermore, it forces countries to face tightening environmental constraints more simultaneously and less sequentially than would otherwise be the case. They have less opportunity to learn from one another's experiences with controlling throughput and less control over their local environment.

The standard arguments for free trade based on comparative advantage also depend on static promotions of efficiency. In other words, free trade in toxic wastes promote static efficiency by allowing the disposal of wastes wherever it costs less, according to today's prices and technologies. A more dynamic efficiency would be served by outlawing the export of toxins. That step would internalize the disposal costs of toxins to their place of origin — to both the firm that generated them and the nation under whose laws the firm operated. This policy creates an incentive to find technically superior ways of dealing with toxins or of redesigning processes to avoid their production in the first place.

All these allocative, distributional, and scale problems stemming from free trade ought to reverse the traditional default position favoring it. Measures to integrate national economies further should now be treated as a bad idea unless proved otherwise in specific cases. As Ronald Findley of Columbia University characterized it, comparative advantage may well be the "deepest and most beautiful result in all of economics." Nevertheless, in a full world of internationally mobile capital, our adherence to it for policy direction is a recipe for national disintegration.

# 21

# NEO-DEVELOPMENT
## *"Global Ecological Management"*

### Wolfgang Sachs

*Wolfgang Sachs has been active in the German and Italian Green movements and was coeditor of the journal* Development, *published in Rome. He later became visiting professor at Pennsylvania State University, where he worked closely with Ivan Illich on a course that reconsidered technology in its philosophical, social, and ecological context. Sachs then became a fellow of the Institute for Cultural Studies at Essen, Germany, and is now a fellow of the Wüppertal Institute in Wüppertal.*

*Sachs is the author of* For Love of the Automobile: Looking Back into the History of our Desires *(1992), and editor of two superlative books,* Global Ecology — A New Arena of Political Conflict *(1993) and* The Development Dictionary *(1992).*

*In this chapter, Sachs explains that the need to preserve what remains of our natural environment is being used as a means to justify further economic aggression by pretending that development can be sustainable. Sachs argues that the very term* sustainable development *calls for the conservation of development, not the conservation of nature.*

EPOCHS GENERALLY define themselves slowly, but the development era opened at a specific date and hour. On January 20, 1949, it was President Harry Truman who, in his inauguration speech before Congress, drew the attention of his audience to conditions in poorer countries, and defined them for the first time as "underdeveloped areas." Suddenly, a seemingly indelible concept was established, cramming the immeasurable diversity of the South into one single category: the underdeveloped. That Truman coined a new term was not a matter of accident but the precise expression of a worldview: For him, all the peoples of the world were moving along the same track — some faster, some slower, but all in the same direction. The northern countries, in particular the United States, were running ahead, while he saw the rest of the world — with its absurdly low per capita income — lagging far behind. An image that the economic societies of the North had increasingly acquired about themselves was the one the United States projected upon the rest of the world: A country's degree of civilization is indicated by the level of its production. Starting from that premise, Truman conceived of the world as an economic arena where nations compete for a better position on the GNP scale. No matter which ideals inspired Kikuyus, Peruvians, or Filipinos, Truman recognized them only as stragglers whose historical task was to participate in the development race and catch up with the lead runners. Consequently, it was the objective of development policy to bring all nations into the arena and enable them to run in the race.

Turning the South's societies into economic competitors not only required the injection of capital and the transfer of technology but a cultural transformation, for many "old ways" of living turned out to be "obstacles to development." The ideals and mental habits, patterns of work and modes of knowing, webs of loyalties and rules of governance in which the South's peoples were steeped were usually at odds with the ethos of an economic society. In the attempt to overcome these barriers to growth, the traditional social fabric was often dissected and reassembled according to the textbook models of macroeconomy. To be sure, "development" had many effects, but one of its most insidious was the dissolution of cultures that were not built around a frenzy of accumulation. The South was thus precipitated into a transformation that had long been going on in the North: the gradual subordination of ever more aspects of social life under the rule of the economy. In fact, whenever development experts set their sights on a country, they fell victim to a particular myopia: They did not see a society that *has* an economy but a society that *is* an economy. As a result, they ended up revamping all kinds of institutions, such as work, schools, or the law, in the service of productivity and degrading the indigenous style of doing things in the process. But the shift to a predominantly economic society involves a considerable cost: It undermines a society's capacity to secure well-being without joining unconditionally the economic race. The unfettered hegemony of Western productivism has made it more and more impossible to take exit roads from the global racetrack; thus, the maneuvering space for countries in times of uncertainty is dangerously limited.

After forty years of development, the state of global affairs is dismal.

The gap between frontrunners and stragglers has not been bridged; on the contrary, it has widened beyond a point where it could ever conceivably be closed. The aspiration of catching up has ended in a blunder of planetary proportions. The figures speak for themselves: During the 1980s, the contribution of developing countries (where two-thirds of humanity live) to the world's GNP shrank to 15 percent, while the share of the industrial countries, with 20 percent of the world population, rose to 80 percent.

Admittedly, closer examination reveals that the picture is far from homogenous, but neither the Southeast Asian showcases nor the oil-producing countries change the result that the development race has ended in disarray. The truth of this is more sharply highlighted if the destiny of large majorities of people within most Southern countries is considered; they live today in greater hardship and misery than at the time of decolonization. The best one can say is that development has created a global middle-class with cars, bank accounts, and career aspirations. It is made up of the majority in the North and small elites in the South, and its size roughly equals that 8 percent of the world population that owns a car. The internal rivalries of that class make a lot of noise in world politics, condemning to silence the overwhelming majority of the world's people. At the end of development, the question of justice looms larger than ever.

A further result of the development era has come dramatically to the fore in recent years. It has become evident that the race track leads in the wrong direction. While Truman could still presume that the North was at the head of social evolution, this premise of superiority has today been fully and finally shattered by the ecological predicament. For instance, much of the glorious rise in productivity is fueled by a gigantic through-put of fossil energy, which requires mining the earth on the one side and covering it with waste on the other. By now, however, the global economy has outgrown the earth's capacity to serve as mine and dumping ground. If all countries followed the industrial example, five or six planets would be needed to serve as "sources" for the inputs and "sinks" for the waste of economic growth. Economic expansion has already come up against its biophysical limits; recognizing the earth's finiteness is a fatal blow to the idea of development as envisaged by Truman.

## AMBIGUOUS CLAIMS FOR JUSTICE

The United Nations Conference on Environment and Development (UNCED) in June 1992 unfolded against this background of forty years

of postwar history. As the title of the conference implies, any consideration of global ecology has to respond both to the crisis of justice and the
crisis of nature. While the northern countries' professed main concern
was about nature, the South managed to highlight the question of justice.
In fact, during the debates leading up to UNCED, attentive spectators
wondered if they had not seen it all before. Slogans that had animated the
1970s discussions on the "New International Economic Order" kept
creeping back to the forefront. Suddenly, calls for better terms of trade,
debt relief, entry to northern markets, technology transfer, and aid, aid,
and more aid drowned the environmentalist discussion. The South,
deeply hurt by the breakdown of development illusions, launched demands for further rounds of development. Already, in the June 1991 Beijing Ministerial Declaration on Environment and Development, of the
Group of 77, the point was made clearly and bluntly: "Environmental
problems cannot be dealt with separately; they must be linked to the
development process, bringing the environmental concerns in line with
the imperatives of economic growth and development. In this context,
the right to development for the developing countries must be fully
recognized."

Since the North expects environmentally good behavior worldwide,
the South, grasping this opportunity, discovered environmental concessions as diplomatic weapons.

The spotlight was thus largely focused on the North's willingness to
come up with $125 billion of yearly assistance to fulfill its long overdue
promise of allocating 0.7 percent of its GNP to development aid, to provide clean technologies, or to allow access to bioindustrial patents. But in
using the language of development, the South appears to keep believing
that the North shows the way to the rest of the world. As a consequence,
the South seems incapable of escaping the North's cultural hegemony; for
development without hegemony is like a race without a direction. Apart
from all the economic pressures, adherence to development puts the
South, culturally and politically, in a position of structural weakness, leading to the absurd situation in which the North can present itself as the
benevolent provider of solutions to the ecological crisis.

The fact that "development," the race without a finishing line, remains
uncontested allows the North to continue the relentless pursuit of over-
development and economic power, since the idea of societies that settle for
their accomplished stage of technical capacity becomes unthinkable.
Indeed, limits to road building, to high-speed transport, to economic concentration, to the production of chemicals, to large-scale cattle ranching,
and so on, were not even considered at the 1992 Earth Summit in Rio.

The unholy alliance between development enthusiasts in the South and growth fatalists in the North, however, works not only against the environment but also against greater justice in the world. For in most countries, while development has benefited rather small minorities, it has done so at the expense of large parts of the population. During the development era, growth was expected to abolish poverty; instead it led to social polarization. In many cases, communities that guaranteed sustenance have been torn apart in the attempt to build a modern economy. Southern elites, however, often justify their unmitigated pursuit of development by ritual reference to the persistence of poverty, cultivating the worn-out dogma that growth is the antidote to poverty. In fact, both ecology and poverty call for limits to development. Without such a change in perspective, the struggle for redistribution of power and resources between North and South, which is inevitably renewed in facing environmental constraints, can be only what it was in the 1970s: a quarrel within the global middle class on how to divide the cake.

## EARTH'S FINITUDE
## AS A MANAGEMENT PROBLEM

*Development* is, above all, a way of thinking. Whatever the item on the agenda in the postwar era, the assumptions of development — like the universal road, the superiority of economics, the mechanical feasibility of change — tacitly shaped the definition of the problem, highlighted certain solutions, and consigned others to oblivion.

*Sustainable development*, which UNCED enthroned as the reigning new concept of the 1990s, emasculates the environmental challenge by - insinuating the validity of developmentalist assumptions, even when confronted with a drastically different historical situation. In Rachel Carson's *Silent Spring*, the book that gave rise to the environmental movement in 1962, development was understood to inflict injuries on people and nature. Since the "World Conservation Strategy" in 1980 and later the Brundtland Report, development has come to be seen as the therapy for the injuries caused by development. What accounts for this shift?

Firstly, in the 1970s, under the impact of the oil crisis, governments began to realize that continued growth depended not only on capital formation or skilled labor, but also on the long-term availablity of natural resources. Foods for the insatiable growth machine, such as oil, timber, minerals, soils, and genetic material seemed on the decline; concern grew about the prospects of long-term growth. This was a decisive change in perspective: Not the health of nature but the continuous health of development became the center of concern. In 1992, the World Bank summed up the new consensus in a laconic phrase from the *World Development Report* (1992): "What is sustainable? Sustainable development is development that lasts."

Even bearing in mind a very loose definition of development, the anthropocentric bias of the statement is clear. It is not the preservation of nature's dignity that is on the international agenda but the preservation of human-centered utilitarianism to posterity. Needless to say, the naturalist and biocentric currents of present-day environmentalism have been cut out by this conceptual operation. With "development" back in the saddle, the view of nature changes. The question now becomes, which of nature's "services" are indispensable for further development, and to what extent? Or the other way around: Which "services" of nature are dispensable or can be replaced by, for example, new materials or genetic engineering? In other words, nature turns into a variable, albeit a critical one, in sustaining development. It comes as no surprise, therefore, that *natural capital* has already become a fashionable notion among ecological economists.

Secondly, a new generation of postindustrial technologies suggested that growth was not invariably linked to the squandering of ever more resources, as in the time of smokestack economies, but could be pursued through less resource-intensive means. While in the past, innovations were aimed largely at increased productivity of labor, it now appeared possible that technical and organizational intelligence could concentrate on increasing the productivity of nature. In short, growth could be delinked from a rising consumption of energy and materials. In the eyes of developmentalists, the "limits to growth" did not call for abandoning the race but for changing the running technique. After "no development without sustainability" had spread, "no sustainability without development" also gained recognition.

Thirdly, environmental degradation has been discovered to be a worldwide condition of poverty. Poverty is now exemplified by people who search desperately for firewood, find themselves trapped by encroaching deserts, are driven from their soils and forests, or are forced to endure dreadfully unsanitary conditions. Once the lack of natural development is identified as a cause of poverty, it follows neatly that development agencies, since they are in the business of "eliminating poverty," have to diversify into programs for the environment. But people who are dependent upon nature for their survival have no choice other than to pursue the last remaining fragments of its bounty. As the decline of nature is also a consequence of poverty, the poor of the world suddenly enter the stage as agents of environmental destruction.

The persistence of "development," the newly found potentials for less resource-intensive growth paths, and the discovery of humanity in general as the enemy of nature — these notions were the conceptual ingredients for the type of thinking that received diplomatic blessings at UNCED. In the other words, the world is to be saved by more and better managerialism. The message, which is ritually repeated by many politicians, industrialists, and scientists who have recently decided to slip on a green coat, goes as follows: Nothing should be done (the dogmatic version) or can be done (the fatalist version) to change the direction the world's economies are taking. Problems along the way can be solved, if the challenge for better and more sophisticated management is taken up. As a result, ecology, once a call for new public virtues, has now become a call for new executive skills. In short, alternatives to development are blackballed, but alternatives within development are welcome.

Nevertheless, it was an achievement for UNCED to have delivered the call for environmental tools from a global rostrum, an opening that will give a boost to environmental engineering worldwide. But the price for this achievement is the subordination of environmentalism to managerialism. For the task of global ecology can be understood in two ways: It is either a technocratic effort to keep development afloat against the drift of plunder and pollution, or it is a cultural effort to shake off the hegemony of aging Western values and gradually retire from the development race. These two ways may not always be exclusive in detail, but they differ deeply in perspective. In the first case, the paramount task becomes the management of the biophysical limits to development. All powers of foresight have to be mustered in order to steer development along the edge of the abyss, continuously surveying, testing, and maneuvering the biophysical limits. In the second case, the challenge consists in designing cultural and political limits to development. Unfortunately, too many "global ecologists" — implicitly or explicitly — favor the first choice: global management.

## BARGAINING FOR THE REST OF NATURE

Since time immemorial, humanity defended itself against nature. Now nature must defend itself against humanity. In particular danger are the "global commons": the Antarctic, the ocean beds, and the tropical forests.

Many species are threatened by the voracious growth of demand for new inputs, while Earth's atmosphere is overburdened with the residues growth leaves behind. For that reason, the 1980s saw the rise of a global environmental consciousness, expressed by many voices, all deploring the threats to the earth's biosphere and the burdens being passed on to the generations to come. The collective duty to preserve the common heritage of humankind was invoked, and caring for the earth became an imperative that agitated spirits worldwide. Respect for the integrity of nature independent of its value for humans, along with proper regard for the rights of humanity, demanded that the global commons be protected.

International environmental diplomacy, however, is about something else. The rhetoric, which ornaments conferences and conventions, ritually calls for a new global ethic, but the reality at the negotiating tables suggests a different logic. There, for the most part, one sees diplomats engaged in the familiar game of accumulating advantages for their countries, eager to outmaneuver their opponents, shrewdly tailoring environmental concerns to the interests dictated by their nation's economic position. Their parameters of action are bounded by the need to extend their nation's space for "development"; therefore in their hands environmental concerns turn into bargaining chips in the struggle of interests. In that respect, the thrust of UNCED's negotiations was no different from the thrust of previous negotiations about the Law of the Sea, the Antarctic, or the Montreal protocol on the reduction of CFCs. Upcoming negotiations on climate, animal protection, or biodiversity are hardly likely to be different.

The novelty of the Earth Summit in Rio, if there was one, lay not in commitments to a collective stewardship of nature but rather in international recognition of the scarcity of natural resources for development. The fragility of nature came into focus, because the services she offers as source and sink for economic growth have become depleted or saturated; after centuries of availability, nature can no longer be counted upon as a silent collaborator in the process of "technical civilization." In other words, environmental diplomacy has recognized that nature is finite as a mine for resources and a container for waste. Given that development is intrinsically open ended, the logic underlying international negotiations is pretty straightforward. First, limits are to be identified at a level that permits the maximum use of nature as mine and container, right up to the critical threshold beyond which ecological decline would rapidly accelerate. This is where scientists gain supremacy, since such limits can only be identified on the basis of "scientific evidence." Second, each country's proper share in the utilization of the source or sink in question should be defined. Here diplomacy finds a new arena, and the old means of power, persuasion and bribery come in handy in order to maximize one's own country's share. Finally, mechanisms have to be designed to secure all parties' compliance with the norms stated by the treaty — an effort that calls for international monitoring and enforcement institutions. Far from "protecting the earth," environmental diplomacy that works within a developmentalist frame cannot but concentrate its efforts on rationing what is left of nature. To normalize — rather than eliminate — global overuse and pollution of nature will be the unintended effect.

Four major lines of conflict cut through the landscape of international environmental diplomacy: (1) rights to further exploitation of nature; (2) rights to pollution; (3) rights to compensation; and (4) overall conflict over responsibility. In the UNCED discussions on the biodiversity convention, for example, the rights to further exploitation of nature held center stage. Who is entitled to have access to the world's dwindling genetic resources? Can nation-states exert their sovereignty over them, or are they to be regarded as "global commons"? Who is allowed to profit from the use of genetic diversity? Countries rich in biomass but poor in industrial power were thus counterposed against countries rich in industrial power but poor in biomass. Similar issues arise with respect to tropical timber, the mining of ocean beds, or wild animals. At the climate convention, on the other hand, diplomatic efforts were aimed at optimizing pollution rights over various periods of time. Oil-producing countries were not happy about ceilings for carbon dioxide emissions, while small-island states, understandably, hoped for the toughest limits possible. Moreover, the more economies depend on a cheap fuel base — the United States in the forefront, followed by the large, newly industrialized countries — the less the respective representatives of those countries were inclined to be strong on $CO_2$. Europe and Japan, on the other hand, could afford to urge stricter limits. In both cases, claims to compensation were voiced by an insistent chorus. How much compensation for retrospective development can the South demand? Who carries the losses incurred by a restrained exploitation of nature? Who should foot the bill for transferring clean technologies? Obviously, here the South was on the offensive, led by countries with potentially large middle classes, while the North found itself on the defensive. In all these matters, however, the conflict over responsibilities loomed large; and again, the North was under pressure. After all, didn't the industrialized countries fell their own forests to feed development? Haven't they in the past used the entire world as the hinterland for their industrialization? With regard to greenhouse gases, is it appropriate or even justifiable to lump together methane emissions from India's rice fields with $CO_2$ emissions from U.S. car exhausts? In sum, a new class of conflicts has thrown diplomatic routines into disarray.

## EFFICIENCY AND SUFFICIENCY

Twenty years ago, *limits to growth* was the watchword of the environmental movement worldwide; today the buzzword of international ecology experts is *global change*. The messages implied are clearly different. *Limits to growth* calls on *homo industrialis* to reconsider its project and to abide by nature's laws. *Global change*, however, puts humankind in the driver's seat and urges it to master nature's complexities with greater self-control. While the first formula sounds threatening, the second has an optimistic ring: It believes in a rebirth of *homo faber* and, on a more prosaic level, lends itself to the belief that the powers of the modern economy — product innovation, technological progress, market regulation, science-based planning — will show the way out of the ecological predicament.

The cure for all environmental ills is called the *efficiency revolution*. It focuses on reducing the throughput of energy and materials in the economic system by means of new technology and planning. Be it for the lightbulb or the car, for the design of power plants or transport systems, the aim is to produce innovations that minimize the use of nature for each unit of output. Under this prescription, the economy will supposedly gain in fitness by keeping to a diet that eliminates the overweight in slag and dross. "More with less" is the motto for this new round in the old game. Optimizing input, not maximizing output, as in the postwar era, is the order of the day. One already sees economists and engineers taking a renewed pleasure in their trade by puzzling out the minimum input for each unit of output. The hope that accompanies this strategic turnabout is again concisely stated by the World Bank in the *World Development Report* (1992): "Efficiency reforms help reduce pollution while raising a country's economic output."

But the past course of economic history — in the East, West, and South, though with considerable variations — suggests that there is little room for efficiency strategies in earlier phases of growth, whereas such strategies seem to work best — and are affordable — when applied after a certain level of growth has been attained. Since in the South the politics of selective growth would be a much more powerful way to limit the demand for resources, to transfer wholesale the efficiency revolution there makes sense only if the South is expected to follow the North's path of development.

Even for the North, skepticism is in order. Those who hail the rising information and service society as environment-friendly often overlook the fact that these sectors can grow only on top of the industrial sector and in close symbiosis with it. The size of the service sector in relation to production has its limits, just as the dependence on resources can be considerable for such sectors as tourism, hospitals, or data processing. Even commodities without any nature content, such as patents, blueprints, or money, derive their value from the command over a resource base that they provide. More specifically, gains in environmental efficiency often consist in substituting high technology for energy and materials — a process that presupposes the presence of a resource-intensive economy. In short, the efficiency potential that lies in well-tuned engines, biotechnological processes, recycling technologies, or systems thinking is indigenous to the northern economies. But the efficiency strategy obviously plays into the North's hands: this way, the North can again offer the South a new selection of tools for economic progress at a price that will be scarcely different from that paid in the decades of technology transfer.

Environmentalists who rest their hopes on efficient resource management concentrate social imagination on the revision of means rather than on the revision of goals. An increase in resource efficiency alone leads to nothing unless it goes hand-in-hand with an intelligent restraint of growth. Instead of focusing on how many supermarkets or how many bathrooms are enough, the focus is on how all these — and more — can be obtained with a lower input of resources. If, however, the dynamics of growth are not slowed down, the achievements of rationalization will soon be eaten up by the next round of growth. Consider the example of the fuel-efficient car. Today's vehicle engines are definitely more efficient and low-polluting than in the past; yet the relentless growth in the number of cars and miles driven has canceled out those gains. Efficiency without sufficiency is counterproductive; the latter must define the boundaries of the former.

However, the random-development creed impedes any serious public debate on the moderation of growth. Under its shadow, any society that decided not to exceed certain levels of commodity intensity, technical performance, or speed appears to be backward. As a result, the consideration of *zero options* — that is, choosing not to do something that is technically possible — is made into a taboo in the official discussion on global ecology.

# THE HEGEMONY OF GLOBALISM

*Sustainable development* can mean many things to many people, but nevertheless contains a core message: Keep the volume of human extraction and emission in balance with the regenerative capacities of nature. That sounds reasonable enough, but it conceals a conflict that has yet to win public attention, even though fundamental issues are at stake. Sustainability, yes, but at which level? At the level of a village community, a country, or an entire planet? Until the 1980s, environmentalists were usually concerned with the local or the national space; ideas such as "eco-development" and "self-reliance" had aimed to increase the economic and political independence of a place by reconnecting ecological resource flows. But in subsequent years, environmentalists began to look at things from a much more elevated vantage point: They adopted the astronaut's view, taking in the entire globe at one glance. Today's ecology is in the business of saving nothing less than the planet. That suggestive globe, suspended in the dark universe, delicately furnished with clouds, oceans, and continents, has become the object of science, planning, and politics.

Modesty hardly seems to be the hallmark of such thinking. The September 1989 special issue of *Scientific American*, with the programmatic title "Managing Planet Earth," sets the tone: "It is as a global species that we are transforming our planet. It is only as a global species — pooling our knowledge, coordinating our actions, and sharing what the planet has to offer — that we may have any prospect for managing the planet's transformation along the pathways of sustainable development. Self-conscious, intelligent management of the earth is one of the great challenges facing humanity as it approaches the 21st century."

Perceiving the earth as an object of environmental management is, on the cognitive level, certainly an outcome of space travel, which revolutionized human perception by turning the planet into a visible object. But there are also political, scientific, and technological perspectives. Politically, it was only in the 1980s that acid rain, the ozone hole, and the greenhouse effect drove home the message that industrial pollution affects the entire globe across all borders.

Only a few years ago, invoking the wholeness of the globe meant something else. Environmentalists waved around the picture of the earth taken from outer space in order to remind the public of the majestic finiteness of the earth and to spread the insight that there is in the end no escape from the consequences of human action. While they appealed to the reality of the finite planet, and invited people to embrace humility, a new tribe of global ecocrats is ready to act upon the newly emerged reality of the planet by imagining that they can preside over the world. Research on the biosphere is rapidly becoming big science. Spurred by a number of international programs, "planetary science," including satellite observation, deep-sea expeditions, and worldwide data processing, are being institutionalized in many countries.

With this trend, sustainability is increasingly regarded as a challenge for global management. The new experts set out to identify the planetary balance between human extractions and emissions on the one side and the regenerative capacities of nature on the other, mapping and monitoring, measuring and calculating resource flows and bio-geochemical cycles around the globe.

The implicit agenda of this endeavor is eventually to be able to moderate the planetary system and supervise species diversity, fishing grounds, tree-felling rates, energy flows, and material cycles. The management of resource budgets thus becomes a matter of world politics.

Satellite pictures scanning the globe's vegetative cover, computer graphs running interacting curves through time, threshold levels held up as worldwide norms are the language of global ecology. It constructs a reality that contains mountains of data but no people. The data do not explain why Tuaregs are driven to exhaust their water-holes or why Germans are so obsessed with high speed on freeways; they do not point out who owns the timber shipped from the Amazon or which industry flourishes because of a polluted Mediterranean Sea; and they are mute about the significance of forest trees for Indian tribals or what water means in an Arab country. In short, they provide a knowledge that is faceless and placeless, an abstraction that carries considerable cost: It consigns the realities of culture, power, and virtue to oblivion. It offers data but no context; it shows diagrams but no actors; it gives calculations but no notions of morality; it seeks stability but disregards beauty. Indeed, the global vantage point requires ironing out all the differences and disregarding all the circumstances; rarely has the gulf between the observers and the observed been greater than between satellite-based forestry and the *seringueiro* in the Brazilian jungle. It is inevitable that the claims of global management are in conflict with the aspirations for cultural rights, democracy, and self-determination. Indeed, it is easy for an ecocracy that acts in the name of "one earth" to become a threat to local communities and their life-styles. After all, has there ever, in the history of colonialism, been a more powerful motive for streamlining the world than the call to save the planet?

Yet the North faces a problem, for the bid for global management has been triggered by a new historical constellation. Ever since Columbus arrived in Santo Domingo, the North has largely remained unaffected by the tragic consequences that followed his expansion overseas; others have borne the burden of sickness, exploitation, and ecological destruction. Now this historical tide is about to turn; for the first time, the northern countries themselves are exposed to the bitter result of westernizing the world. Immigration, population pressure, tribalism with mega-arms, and, above all, the environmental consequences of worldwide industrialization threaten to destabilize the northern way of life. The rational planning of the planet becomes a matter of northern security.

The celebrated control of (Western) man over nature leaves much to be desired. Science and technology successfully transform nature on a vast scale, but so far with unpleasant and unpredictable consequences. In fact, only if these consequences were under control would it be possible to speak of having accomplished domination over nature. It is here that technocratic environmentalism comes in. The obvious task is to prepare for regulating the global transformation of nature in an optimal fashion. In that light, *Scientific American* (Sept. 1989) can elevate the following questions posed by William C. Clark to key issues for future decision making: "Two central questions must be addressed: What kind of planet do we want? What kind of planet can we get? . . . How much species diversity should be maintained in the world? Should the size or the growth rate of the human population be curtailed? How much climate change is acceptable?"

If there are no limits to growth, there surely seem to be no limits to hubris.

## 22

# DEVELOPMENT AS COLONIALISM

Edward Goldsmith

*The massive efforts to develop the Third World in the years since World War II were not motivated by purely philanthropic considerations but by the need to bring the Third World into the orbit of the Western trading system in order to create an ever-expanding market for our goods and services and a source of cheap labor and raw materials for our industries. This has also been the goal of colonialism especially during its last phase, which started in the 1870s. For that reason, there is a striking continuity between the colonial era and the era of development, both in the methods used to achieve their common goal and in the social and ecological consequences of applying them.*

$I$T IS CUSTOMARY to trace the origin of the idea of development to a statement made by President Harry Truman in 1949. [See chapter by Wolfgang Sachs.] Truman may have formulated the idea in a new way, but it is an old idea, and the path along which it is leading the countries of the Third World is a well-trodden one.

As François Partant, the French banker-turned-archcritic of development, has put it (1982), "The developed nations have discovered for themselves a new mission — to help the Third World advance along the road to development . . . which is nothing more than the road on which the West has guided the rest of humanity for several centuries."

The thesis of this chapter is that Partant was right. *Development* is just a new word for what Marxists called *imperialism* and what we can loosely refer to as *colonialism* — a more familiar and less loaded term.

A quick look at the situation in the Third World today undoubtedly reveals the disquieting continuity between the colonial era and the era of development. There has been no attempt by the governments of the newly independent countries to re-draw their frontiers. No attempt has been made to restore precolonial cultural patterns. With regards to the key issue of land use, the colonial pattern has also been maintained. As Randall Baker notes (1984), "Essentially the story is one of continuity." And the peasants, who, as Erich Jacoby writes (1983), "identified the struggle for national independence with the fight for land," never recovered their land. "National independence simply led to its take-over by a new brand of colonialists."

If development and colonialism (at least, in its last phase from the 1870s onward) are the same process under a different name, it is largely because they share the same goal. This goal was explicitly stated by its main promoters. For instance, the infamous English businessman and colonialist Cecil Rhodes (who named Rhodesia [now Zimbabwe] after himself), once frankly declared that "we must find new lands from which we can easily obtain raw materials and at the same time exploit the cheap slave labor that is available from the natives of the colonies. The colonies would also provide a dumping ground for the surplus goods produced in our factories." (Similar sentiments were expressed openly during the late 1800s by Lord Lugard, the English governor of Nigeria, and by former French president Jules Ferry.)

But many countries in Asia and elsewhere were simply not willing to allow Western powers access to their markets or to the cheap labor and raw materials required. Nor were they willing to allow corporations to operate on their territory and undertake large-scale development projects such as road building and mining.

In Asia, a small number of states were eventually bullied into complying with Western demands. Thus, in 1855, Siam signed a treaty with Britain as did Annam with France in 1862. However, China was not interested, and two wars had to be fought before it could be persuaded to open its ports to British and French trade. Japan also refused, and only the threat of an American naval bombardment persuaded its government to open its ports to Western trade.

By 1880, European powers had obtained access to the markets of most of Asia's coastal regions, having negotiated special conditions for expatriate residents, such as greater freedom of activity within the countries concerned and the right to build railways and set up enterprises inland.

However, just as is the case today, commercial interests continued to demand and often obtain ever more comprehensive concessions, creating ever more favorable conditions for European corporations.

Throughout the nonindustrial world, formal annexation was resorted to only if economic conditions could no longer be enforced, usually when a new nationalist or populist government came to power. As D. K. Fieldhouse put it (1989), "colonialism was not a preference but a last resort."

D. C. Platt, another student of nineteenth-century colonialism, adds that colonialism was necessary "to establish a legal framework in which capitalist relations could operate." If no new colonies were created in Latin America in the late nineteenth century, it is largely because a legal system that "was sufficiently stable for trade to continue was already in existence." This was not so in Africa, where the only way to create the requisite conditions was by establishing colonial control (Platt 1976).

Slowly, as traditional society disintegrated under the impact of colonialism and the spread of Western values, and as the subsistence economy was replaced by the market economy on which the exploding urban population grew increasingly dependent, the task of maintaining the optimum conditions for Western trade and penetration became correspondingly easier. As a result, says Fieldhouse, by the mid twentieth century, "European merchants and investors could operate satisfactorily within the political framework provided by most reconstructed indigenous states as their predecessors would have preferred to operate a century earlier but without facing those problems which had once made formal empire a necessary expedient" (Fieldhouse 1984).

In other words, formal colonialism came to an end not because the colonial powers had decided to forego the economic advantages it provided but because, in the new conditions, these could now be obtained by more politically acceptable and more effective methods.

This was probably clear to the foreign policy professionals and heads of large corporations that began meeting in Washington, D.C., in 1939 under the aegis of the U.S. Council on Foreign Relations to discuss how the postwar, postcolonialist world economy could best be shaped in order to satisfy American commercial interests — discussions that eventually led to the notorious Bretton Woods conference of 1944. [See chapter on Bretton Woods by David Korten.]

Economic development was the means for achieving this goal, and it was by promoting free trade that development could be maximized. Free trade is seen to involve competition on "a level playing field," and nothing could seem more fair. However, when the strong confront the weak on a level playing field the result is a foregone conclusion, as it was at Bretton

Woods. At the time of that conference, in the twilight of World War II, the United States totally dominated the world politico-economic scene; the European industrial powers had been ruined by the war, their economies lying in tatters; and Japan had been conquered and humiliated.

We must not forget that a century earlier, it was Britain that was preaching free trade to the rest of the world and for the same reasons. At that time, she effectively dominated the world economy. Not only was one-fourth of the world's terrestrial surface under her direct imperial control, not only did her navy control the seas, but the city of London was the world's financial center and was alone capable of financing the industrial expansion that free trade would make possible. Besides, according to Eric Hobsbawm, Britain already produced about two-thirds of the world's coal, perhaps about half its iron, five-sevenths of its steel, half of its factory-produced cotton cloth, 40 percent (in value) of its hardware, and a little less than one-third of its manufactures. Labor in Britain was also cheap and plentiful, for the population had more than tripled since the beginning of the Industrial Revolution and had accumulated in the cities while there was little social regulation to protect the rights of the workers.

In such conditions, Britain was far more "competitive" than her rivals, and free trade was clearly the right vehicle for achieving her commercial goals. As George Lichtheim, another well-known student of imperialism, puts it (1971), "A country whose industries could undersell those of its competitors was favorably placed to preach the universal adoption of free trade, and so it did — to the detriment of those among its rivals who lacked the wit or the power to set up protective barriers behind which they could themselves industrialize at a pace that suited them."

As a result, between 1860 and 1873, Britain succeeded in creating something not too far removed from what Hobsbawm refers to as "an all embracing world system of virtually unrestricted flows of capital, labor and goods," though nowhere near the scale on which it is being achieved today with the signature of the GATT Uruguay Round Agreement. Only the United States remained systematically protectionist, though it slowly began to reduce its duties in 1832, continuing to 1860, and again between 1861 and 1865 during the Civil War.

By the 1870s Britain was already losing her competitive edge over her rivals. Partly as a result, British exports declined considerably at the end of the century. At the same time, between the 1870s and 1890s there were prolonged economic depressions, also weakening the belief in free trade. Tariffs were raised in most European countries, especially in the 1890s, though not in Belgium, the Netherlands, or Britain. Companies now found their existing markets reduced by these factors and started looking abroad, toward the markets of Africa, Asia, Latin America, and the Pacific, which, with the development of faster and more capacious steamships, had become much more accessible. As Fieldhouse (1984) notes, if free trade did not work, the answer was to take over those countries where goods could be sold at a profit without having to worry about competition from more efficient European countries. There followed a veritable scramble for colonies. In 1878, 67 percent of the world's terrestrial area had been colonized by Europeans. By 1914 the figure had risen to 84.4 percent.

## SETTING UP INDIGENOUS ELITES

The most effective means of opening up markets is undoubtedly to set up a westernized elite hooked on economic development, which it is willing to promote regardless of adverse effects on the vast majority of its fellow citizens. This has now been very effectively achieved, and, as a result, the interests of Third World governments today, as François Partant says, are "largely antagonistic to those of the bulk of their countrymen." The Third World elites are in fact our representatives in the countries they dominate, probably to the same extent as were the colonial administrators that they have supplanted.

The need to create such an elite was of course well-known to the western powers during the colonial era. During the debate in British political circles after the 1857 Indian Mutiny, the main question at issue was whether an anglicized elite favorable to British commercial interests could be created in time to prevent further uprisings. If not, it was generally conceded, formal occupation would have to be maintained indefinitely (Fieldhouse 1984).

Of course, the elite must be suitably armed if it is to impose economic development on the rest of the population, since development must lead to the expropriation and eventual impoverishment of most people. Today, this is one of the main objects of our so-called aid programs, some two-thirds of U.S. aid taking the form of "security assistance." This includes military training, arms, and cash transfers to governments that are regarded as defending American interests.

Even food aid provided by the U.S. is security-related. It falls into two categories: Title 1 and Title 2. Most of it is in the former category and consists of low-interest loans to Third World governments, "which use their money to buy U.S. food and then sell it on the open market, keeping the proceeds." Such food aid is thus "little more than another transfer of funds to governments considered strategically important" (Danaher 1988). Title 2 food aid can also help make countries increasingly dependent on American aid for their very sustenance. U.S. politicians have openly stated that food must be used as a political weapon. A special issue of the *Ecologist* ("Whose Common Future?" Nov.–Dec., 1993) quoted Vice President Hubert Humphrey as saying that, "If you are looking for a way to get people to lean on you and to be dependent on you, in terms of their co-operation with you, it seems to me that food-dependence would be terrific."

Most of the governments that have received security aid are military dictatorships such as those in Nicaragua, El Salvador, Chile, Argentina, Uruguay, and Peru in the sixties and seventies. These countries faced no external threats. It was not to defend themselves against a potential foreign invader that all this security aid was required but to impose economic development on people who had already been impoverished by it and whom it could only still further impoverish.

Of course when a government unfavorable to Western commercial interests somehow succeeds in coming to power, Western governments will go to any ends to remove it from office. Thus in 1954, the United States organized the military overthrow of the government of Guatemala that had nationalized U. S.-owned banana plantations, and it did the same to the government of José Goulart in Brazil in the 1960s. Goulart had sought to impose a limit to the amount of money foreign corporations could take out of the country. Worse still, he initiated a land-reform program that would have taken back control of the country's mineral resources from Western transnational corporations. He also gave workers a pay raise, thereby increasing the cost of labor to the transnationals, in defiance of IMF instructions. As a result of Goulart's actions, aid was immediately cut off, and an alliance of the CIA, U.S. investors, and Brazil's landowning elite engineered a coup d'état that brought a military junta to power. The military reversed Goulart's reforms and reintroduced precisely those conditions that best satisfied U.S. commercial interests.

During the colonial era, the colonial powers constantly sent in troops to protect compliant regimes against popular revolts. Both France and Britain, for instance, participated in the suppression of the populist Tai Ping rebellion in China and later in the xenophobic Boxer Rebellion. Britain also sent troops to help the Khedive Ismail put down a nationalist revolt in Egypt.

The Western powers still do not hesitate to do this if there is no other way of achieving their goals. Thus, when President Mba, the dictator of Gabon, was threatened by a military coup, French paratroopers immediately flew in to restore him to power, while the coup leaders were imprisoned despite wide-spread popular demonstrations. Significantly, the paratroopers remained to protect Mba's successor, President Bongo, whom Pierre Pean regards as "the choice of a powerful group of Frenchmen whose influence in Gabon continued after Independence" against any further threats to him and hence to French commercial interests. Neither the United Kingdom nor the United States has been any less scrupulous in this respect (Colchester 1993).

## KILLING THE DOMESTIC ECONOMY

If the role of the colonies was to provide a market for the produce of the colonial countries and a source of cheap labor and raw materials for their industries, then it could not at the same time provide a market for local produce and a source of labor and raw materials for its own productive enterprises.

In effect, the colonial powers were committed to destroying the domestic economy of the countries they had colonized. This was explicitly admitted by a delegate to the French Association of Industry and Agriculture in March 1899. For him, the aim of the colonial power must be "to discourage in advance any signs of industrial development in our colonies, to oblige our overseas possessions to look exclusively to the mother country for manufactured products and to fulfill, by force if necessary, their natural function, that of a market reserved by right to the mother country's industry" (Dumont, quoted by Colchester 1993). The favorite method was to tax whatever the colonials particularly liked to consume. In Vietnam it was salt, opium, and alcohol, and a minimum level of consumption was set for each region, village leaders being rewarded for exceeding their quotas. In the Sudan it was crops, animals, houses, and households that were singled out for taxation. Of course, there is no way in which local people could meet their tax obligations save by agreeing to work in the mines and plantations or by growing cash crops for sale to the colonial masters.

At the same time, every effort was made to destroy indigenous crafts, particularly in the production of textiles. In this way the British destroyed the textile industry in India, which had been the very lifeblood of the village economy throughout the country. In French West Africa in 1905, special levies were imposed on all goods that did not come from France or a region under French control; this forced up the price of local products and ruined local artisans and traders.

Economic development after World War II, on the other hand, was theoretically supposed to help the colonies build up their domestic economies, but such development by its very nature could not occur. At the very start the colonies were forced to reorient their production toward exports — what is more, toward an exceedingly small range of exports. A typical example is sugar. Under World Bank influence, vast areas of land in the Third World were converted to sugarcane cultivation, without any consideration for whether a market for sugar existed abroad. In fact, the United States has continued to apply very strict quotas on sugar imports while continuing to countenance the production of corn syrup and the increasing use of artificial sweeteners, while the European Union persisted in subsidizing sugar beet production among its member states. However, none of these considerations have prevented the World Bank from encouraging the production of ever more sugar for export. Cynics might maintain that this was the object of the operation in the first place since, after all, it was implicitly at least part of the World Bank's original brief to encourage the production of cheap resources for the Western market.

At the same time, Third World countries that have sought to diversify their production have immediately been accused of practicing *import substitution* — a heinous crime in the eyes of today's economists, especially those who are influential within the Bretton Woods institutions. Indeed, import substitution is precisely what Third World countries must promise not to undertake if they hope to obtain a structural adjustment loan. Not surprisingly, as Walden Bello notes in his book *Dark Victory* (1994), when a country is subjected to a structural adjustment program, its commodity exports tend to rise, but not necessarily its GNP, because of the inevitable contraction of its domestic economy.

When Third World countries have nevertheless succeeded in developing a modest domestic economy, the World Bank and IMF, in league with U.S. government officials and transnational corporations, have set out systematically to destroy it, a process that could not be better documented, in the case of the Philippines, than by Walden Bello and his colleagues in their book *Development Debacle: The World Bank in the Philippines* (1982). This book, based on eight hundred leaked World Bank documents, shows how that institution, in league with the CIA and other U.S. agencies, set out purposefully to destroy the domestic economy of the Philippines so as to create those conditions that best favored TNC interests. Achieving this goal, Bello and his colleagues point out, first meant sacrificing the peasantry and transforming it into a rural proletariat. The standard of living of the working class had to be reduced since, as a Bank spokesman said at the time, "wage restraint" is required to encourage "the growth of employment and investment." Meanwhile, the local middle class that depended for its very existence on the domestic economy had to be annihilated to make way for a new cosmopolitan middle class dependent on the TNCs and the global economy.

Clearly, such a drastic social and economic transformation of an already partly developed country could not be achieved by a democratic government. This explains why it was decided to provide dictator Ferdinand Marcos with the funding he required to build up an army capable of imposing such a program by force. As Marcos himself put it at the time,"Only an authoritarian system will be able to carry forth the mass consent and to exercise the authority necessary to implement new values, measures and sacrifices" (Bello and others 1982). In essence, this is what he did. Martial law was declared by Marcos, and the people were bludgeoned into accepting the transformation of their society, economy, and natural environment.

## LENDING MONEY

Lending large sums of money to the compliant elite of a nonindustrial country is the most effective method of controlling it and thereby obtaining access to its market and natural resources. However, if the borrowing government is to be capable of repaying the money borrowed or of paying interest, it must be invested in enterprises that are competitive on the international market, for interest payments must be paid in foreign exchange, usually U.S. dollars. Unfortunately, this is extremely unlikely to occur. To begin with, up to 20 percent of the loan funds are likely to be skimmed off in the form of kickbacks to various politicians and officials. Some of the money will be spent on useless consumer products, mainly luxury goods for the elite; much will be spent on infrastructural projects that will not generate in a direct return for a very long time, if at all; and more will go to armaments to enable the government to put down uprisings by the victims of the development process. So the countries that borrow large sums of money must inevitably fall into unrepayable debt. Once in debt, they inevitably become hooked on further and further borrowing rather than cutting down on expenditure and thus fall under the power of the lending countries. At this point the latter, through the IMF, can institutionalize their control over the debtor country through structural adjustment programs (SAPs) that, in effect, take over its economy to ensure that interest payments are regularly met. This arrangement leaves the borrowing country as a de facto colony.

This technique of informal colonialist control is by no means new. It was often resorted to during the colonial era, as in Tunisia and Egypt in the mid 1800s. In the case of Tunisia, a lot of money was lent to the bey of Tunis to build up an army so as to loosen his ties with Turkey, not a particularly profitable investment — and, of course it did not take long before the bey was unable to pay interest on the loan. Much of the money borrowed was in the form of bonds, and most of the bondholders were French. The latter viewed the situation with considerable alarm and appealed to the French Foreign Office for help, which was granted. The bey's economy was subjected to financial supervision, "a technique frequently used by the British and French governments in Latin America" just as it still is today (Fieldhouse 1984).

A joint Franco-Tunisian commission was set up in 1869 for such supervision and the conditions it imposed were draconian to say the least. It had the right to collect and distribute the state's revenues so as to ensure the shareholders' precedence over any other debtors. (Significantly, President Clinton imposed a similar deal on the Mexican government in 1995 as a condition for lending it the billions of dollars required to bail out its Wall Street creditors.)

From 1869 onward, Tunisian "public finance and therefore effectively government were now under alien control" (Fieldhouse 1984). Tunisia had been reduced to the status of an informal colony. To pay interest on the loans, the bey had to increase taxes, which gave rise to a popular protest movement. To secure control and protect its interests, France finally annexed Tunisia in 1881.

The course of events in Egypt was similar. It is summed up very neatly by Harry Magdoff (1978). "Egypt's loss of sovereignty" he writes "resembled somewhat the same process in Tunisia: easy credit extended by Europeans, bankruptcy, increasing control by foreign-debt commissioners, mulcting of the peasants to raise revenue for servicing the debt, growing independence movements, and finally military conquest by a foreign power."

During the era of development, we have perfected the technique of lending money to Third World countries as a means of controlling them. Much of it now goes euphemistically under the name *development aid*. To justify aid, "poverty" in the Third World is made out to be but a symptom of the latter's "underdevelopment," and development is thereby offered as an automatic cure. However, Third World countries are also seen to be seriously hampered in their development efforts because they lack the requisite capital and technical knowledge — precisely, as Cheryl Payer notes (1991), "what the Western corporative system is capable of providing." She quotes Galbraith, who puts it, "Having the vaccine we have invented smallpox."

There is no reason to believe that borrowing money from abroad, even at concessionary rates, is a means of achieving economic success, let alone of eliminating poverty. Nor should we believe that the money borrowed can be paid off by increasing exports. The countries that are held up as models for Third World countries to emulate are the newly industrialized countries (NICS) South Korea, Taiwan, Singapore, and Hong Kong. Neither Singapore nor Hong Kong, as Payer notes, borrowed any significant amount of money for their development. Taiwan borrowed a little in the early days but managed to resist U.S. pressure to overspend and borrow more extensively. South Korea is the only country to have borrowed fairly extensively. Payer argues that if South Korea succeeded in exporting its way out of what debts it had where others failed is largely because it resisted World Bank and IMF pressures to open up its markets. Imports and capital controls were also maintained, as they previously had been by Japan. Clearly, some capital is required for development, but, as Payer notes, "the truly scarce commodity in the world today is not capital, it is markets."

Aid is a particularly good instrument for opening up markets, because much of the aid is officially tied to purchasing goods from donor countries. In the same way that colonies were once forced to buy their manufactured goods from the country that had colonized them, aid recipients must spend much of the money that is supposed to relieve their poverty and malnutrition on irrelevant manufactured goods that are produced by the donor countries. If they dare refuse, they are immediately brought to heel by the simple expedient of threatening to cut off the aid on which they become increasingly dependent.

Thus, a few years ago the British government threatened to cut off aid to the government of India if it did not go ahead with its plan to buy twenty-one large helicopters, costing £60 million, from a British corporation called Westland — an effort, it is encouraging to note, that was bitterly opposed by responsible elements within Britain's Overseas Development Agency (ODA). This is but a more sophisticated method of achieving what Britain achieved in the previous century when it went to war with China to force that country to buy opium from British merchants in India.

In general terms, aid cannot be of use to the poor of the Third World for the critical reason that they necessarily depend on the local economy for their sustenance, and the local economy does not require the vast highways and large dams, or, for that matter, the hybrid seeds, fertilizers, and pesticides of the green revolution any more than it does the fleet of helicopters that the British government imposed on India. These are only of use to the global economy, which can only expand at the expense of the local economy, whose environment it degrades, whose communities it destroys, and whose resources (land, forests, water, and labor) it systematically appropriates for its own use.

## THE NEW CORPORATE COLONIALISM

After the debt crisis of the early eighties there was very little private investment into the Third World, and the new money provided by the multinational development banks served above all to enable debtor countries to continue paying interest on loans contracted with the private banks.

In the last few years, all this has changed. Private investment in the Third World has increased by leaps and bounds, and it now stands at something like $200 billion a year — about half that money represents long-term investments; the other half represents short-term speculative funds. This amount dwarfs the World Bank's until-now determinant contribution of about $23 billion per year and has triggered off stock-exchange booms in the so-called "emergent markets," though admittedly these have been interspersed with crashes such as the one that occurred in Mexico in 1994–95. [See chapter by Carlos Heredia and Mary Purcell.]

This massive increase in private investment has occurred partly because of the mismatch between the vast sums of U.S. money seeking investment opportunities and the availability of such outlets in the industrialized world. Also, conditions have now been created worldwide that could not be more favorable to TNC interests. Not only have they been provided throughout the world with an abundant unskilled labor force, but also with highly skilled technical and managerial staff at an insignificant fraction of what they would cost in the industrial world. TNCs also now have access to whatever finance they require and to the latest computer-based technology and management methods.

Furthermore, as a result of GATT, Third World countries are under obligation to accept all investments from abroad; give "national treatment" to any foreign corporation that establishes itself within its borders, whether it is involved in agriculture, mining, manufacturing, or the service industries; eliminate tariffs and import quotas on all goods, including agricultural produce; and abolish nontariff barriers, such as regulations to protect labor, health, or the environment, that might conceivably increase corporate costs.

Conditions more favorable to the immediate interests of TNCs could scarcely be imagined. Many of these conditions were imposed during GATT negotiations by the American delegation and by the delegations of other industrial powers who presumably believed the vast bulk of the TNCs were and always would be located in such countries.

However, it seems more and more that this may change. Even strong national governments are no longer able to exert any sort of control over TNCs. If a country passes a law that TNCs regard as a hindrance to their further expansion, they merely threaten to leave and establish themselves elsewhere, which, under the new conditions, they can do at the drop of a hat. Indeed, TNCs are now free to scour the globe and establish themselves wherever labor is the cheapest, environmental laws are the laxest, fiscal regimes are the least onerous, and subsidies are the most generous. They need no longer be swayed by sentimental attachment to any nation-state.

Already Volvo, one of the leading Swedish corporations, is now Swedish in name only, having transferred nearly all of its operations abroad. What, we might ask, is to prevent GM or IBM from becoming German or Chinese, or from merely shifting their headquarters from one country to another as and when it becomes advantageous for them to do so? And what is to prevent them from becoming even larger, more powerful, and less controllable than they already are?

Consider that a *monopoly* is usually defined as a situation in which more than 40 percent of the market for a particular commodity is controlled by fewer than four or five corporations. This is already the case for most of the commodities traded on the world market today and will only become more pronounced as there is no way in which a national government can impose antitrust legislation on stateless TNCs. Nor can the WTO, which they control, be counted on to do so.

As a few giant TNCs consolidate their respective control in the worldwide sale of a particular commodity, so is it likely to become ever less advantageous for them to compete with each other. Competition mainly reduces profit margins; cooperation, on the other hand, enables them to increase their hold over governments and to deal with the inevitable opposition from populist and nationalist movements and others who might seek to restrict their power and influence.

Already, TNCs are resorting to more and more vertical integration, thereby controlling virtually every step in the economic process in their respective fields, from the mining of minerals, to the construction of the factories, to the production of goods: their storage, their shipping to subsidiaries in other countries, and their wholesaling and retailing to local consumers. In this way, TNCs are effectively insulating themselves from market forces and ensuring that it is they themselves, rather than competition from their rivals, that determine, at each step, the prices that are to be charged (Hultgren 1995).

Already, between 20 percent and 30 percent of world trade is between TNCs and their subsidiaries. Rather than being real trade, this is but a facet of corporate central planning on a global scale. For Paul Ekins, the British ecological economist, TNCs are becoming "giant areas of bureaucratic planning in an otherwise market economy." He sees a "fundamental similarity between giant corporations and state enterprises. Both use hierarchical command structures to allocate resources within their organizational boundaries rather than the competitive market."

What, we might ask, is to prevent 50 percent, 60 percent, or even 80 percent of world trade from eventually occurring within such "organizational boundaries?" At present, very little, and as we move relentlessly in this direction, so may we be entering a new era of global corporate central planning, one that will be geared to a new type of colonialism: global corporate colonialism.

The new colonial powers have neither responsibility for, nor accountability to anybody but their shareholders. They are little more than machines geared to the single goal of increasing their immediate profitability. What is more, TNCs will now have the power to force national governments to defend corporate interests whenever such interests are in conflict with those of the people whose interest the governments have been elected to protect.

The new corporate colonialism is thus likely to be more cynical and more ruthless than anything we have seen so far. It is likely to dispossess, impoverish, and marginalize more people, destroy more cultures, and cause more environmental devastation than either the colonialism of old or the development of the last fifty years. The only question is, How long can it last? In my opinion, a few years perhaps, or a decade at most, for an economy of a sort that creates misery on such a scale is both aberrant and necessarily short-lived.

# 23

# SEEDS OF EXPLOITATION
## *Free Trade Zones in the Global Economy*

### Alexander Goldsmith

*The subject of "free trade zones," also referred to as "export processing zones," is of particular relevance to our subject, since they illustrate the social, ecological, and human consequences of almost total deregulation, which we now seek to achieve globally as a means of maximizing world trade.*

*Alexander Goldsmith studied anthropology at Jesus College, Cambridge. He went into journalism, specializing in environmental issues, and became the editor of the* Geographical Magazine, *which is produced in conjunction with the Royal Geographic Society. He has recently accepted the post of editor of a journal to be published by the newly created Forum for the Future.*

$F$REE TRADE zones (FTZs), also known as export processing zones, were first created in the early 1970s, officially as a means of attracting foreign investment to "undeveloped" regions. In the words of Sri Lanka's President Jayewardene, when he created the Katunayake FTZ in 1978, "Foreign investment in our country will help us acquire higher technology, develop new export markets and generate employment."

*Free trade zones* are regions that have been fiscally or juridically redefined by their "host country" to give them a comparative advantage over neighboring regions and countries in luring transnational corporate activity. Most FTZs share the following characteristics: lax social, environmental, and employment regulations; a ready source of cheap labor; and fiscal and financial incentives that can take a huge variety of forms, although they generally consist of the lifting of customs duties, the removal of foreign exchange controls, tax holidays, and free land or reduced rents.

By 1986, there were 116 FTZs in forty different countries. About 48 percent of them were located in Latin America and the Caribbean, and 42 percent were in Asia. At that time, the total direct employment in FTZs exceeded one million. Sizes of FTZs vary enormously: Some employ over thirty thousand people; others as few as one hundred.

FTZs attract labor-intensive work such as textile and clothing manufacture and the assembly of electronic goods. Nearly 50 percent of the total labor force in the FTZs of Asia are engaged in the electronics industry.

The workforce is mostly composed of unmarried women between the ages of seventeen and twenty-three. In Mexican FTZs, these women account for about 50 percent of the workforce. They are the preferred workers, as their wages tend to be lower (often less than $1 per day), and they are considered better suited to repetitive tasks that require nimble fingers.

Mexico's *maquiladoras* are some of the best-documented FTZs. They consist mainly of U.S.-owned factories that import U.S. materials for assembly and re-export. It is too early to say what effect NAFTA will have on these industries; however, at NAFTA's birth, the *maquiladoras* numbered more than twenty-one hundred and represented Mexico's second-largest source of foreign exchange after oil, earning the country $3 billion in 1989. They quadrupled in number after 1982, employing a half-million Mexicans and accounting for 20 percent of Mexico's manufacturing industry. Prior to NAFTA, no Mexican duties were charged on the imports, and U.S. duties were levied only on the value added.

The *maquiladoras* are characterized by providing poor living and working conditions and strong restrictions on union activities. Health and safety regulations are routinely ignored. A 1993 random examination of twelve U.S.-owned plants showed that not one was in compliance with Mexican environmental law. An Arizona-based environmental group, the Border Ecology Project, found that *maquiladoras* are unable to account for 95 percent of the waste they generated between 1969 and 1989. The average productive work life of a worker is ten years. Employee turnover is nearly 180 percent annually, in spite of the lack of alternative forms of employment.

*Maquiladoras* import most of their raw materials from the United States and are supposed to return waste there for disposal, but, according to the EPA, a tiny percentage is actually returned. The EPA's Mexican counterpart, Sedesol, estimated that while half of the twenty-one hundred plants generate hazardous waste, only 307 have obtained official licenses.

The U.S. National Toxics Campaign has detected high levels of pollutants outside the plants, including drainage water containing xylene, an industrial solvent, at concentrations 6,000 times the U.S. drinking water standard. Tests carried out by an EPA-certified laboratory reveal levels of xylene up to 50,000 times what is allowed in the United States, and of methylene chloride up to 215,000 times the U.S. standard.

Pollution-related health problems have been the inevitable result. In Brownsville, Texas, between 1990 and 1992, thirty babies were born with anencephaly, a fatal birth condition in which the brain fails to develop and is filled with liquid. This is four times the U.S. national average. During the same period in Matamoros, on the Mexican side of the border, fifty-three cases were recorded. In March 1993, twenty-seven Brownsville families filed a lawsuit against eighty-eight different *maquillas* in Matamoros. They claimed that an airborne cocktail of solvents, acids, and heavy metals, blown over the Rio Grande by prevailing winds, was responsible for the high incidence of children with spina bifida and anencephaly. Among those accused were companies twinned with such international household names as General Motors, Union Carbide, Fisher Price, and Zenith Electronics. All of them deny responsibility.

Also in Matamoros, social workers identified 110 children who shared certain deformity symptoms: mongoloid features and a range of physical and mental defects. The worst-affected boys have only one testicle, and the girls have only partially developed vaginas. All seventy-six mothers had worked while pregnant at Mallory Capacitors, a *maquilla* that produces electronic components. Workers there, almost entirely young women, said they had handled highly toxic polychlorinated biphenyls without proper safety equipment or clothing.

Clearly, then, part of the "incentive" package that a government offers to companies when it creates FTZs is the right to despoil the environment, the right to flout basic standards of social welfare, and the right to poison workers. These, along with attractive financial and fiscal incentives, form an integral part of the "subsidy" offered by a government to attract industry to its territory. As David C. Korten writes in his book *When Corporations Rule the World* (1995), "Mexican workers, including children, have become world class competitors by sacrificing their health, lives and futures to subsidize the profits of investors."

In that sense, when a government sets up an FTZ it renounces its sovereignty over the area involved. The role of FTZs in the global economy is similar to that of *tax havens,* which provide boltholes for capital that are beyond the purview of government. FTZs provide locales where such capital can be invested.

In *Global Dreams* (1994), Richard J. Barnet and John Cavanagh note,

Leaders of nation states are losing much of the control over their own territory they once had. More and more, they must conform to the demands of the outside world because the outsiders are already inside the gates. Business enterprises that routinely operate across borders are linking far-flung pieces of territory into a new world economy that bypasses all sorts of established political arrangements and conventions. Tax laws intended for another age, traditional ways to control capital flows and interest rates, full employment policies, and old approaches to resource development and environmental protection are becoming obsolete, unenforceable or irrelevant.

The complex interplay between trade, territory, and sovereignty can be well-discerned in Southeast Asia's *growth triangles*. These are quasi-FTZs whose operations bring together regions from different nation-states. One of these is the Singapore-Batam-Johor growth triangle, which seeks to establish a synergistic relationship between three politically divided but geographically adjacent regions.

It was Singapore's deputy prime minister who first proposed a growth triangle in 1989. According to William Mellor, senior writer for *Asia, Inc.* magazine, Singapore was running short on land and labor but possessed high-tech skills, financial muscle, and excellent international transport links. Batam Island, only 20 kilometers from Singapore, had been given "freeport" status by Indonesia in 1978 in its attempt to compete with Singapore. Batam could supply plenty of land, fresh water, and a cheap labor force, courtesy of Indonesia's Transmigration Program. On the mainland, connected to Singapore by road and rail, was Malaysia's Johor State, which equally had plentiful land and a large skilled and semiskilled labor force.

The triangle was established in spite of considerable suspicion on the part of the nations involved. Malaysia was worried that Johor would grow closer to Singapore than to its federal government. Indonesia was concerned that it was being exploited by Singapore. But business pressures made it inevitable. Mellor quotes Noordin Sopiee from the Kuala Lumpur–based Institute of Strategic and International Studies: "Nationalism and national governments will remain very important. But business is going to flow according to its own rules — like water."

The Singapore-Batam-Johor growth triangle is only one of several developing in Southeast Asia. Of course, many of these make good sense, insofar as they represent a renewal of links between regions whose historical trade and cultural relations were fractured by the colonial and postcolonial era. But at the same time they represent new configurations of exploitation that are subject to few controls. And, needless to say, in regions that still possess relatively unexploited natural resources, the environment is as important a part of the equation as cheap labor, investment capital, and tax breaks.

FTZs also affect the global economy through the straightforward mechanism of competition. By offering lower production costs through the elimination of basic standards, FTZs take work away from regions in which those standards are maintained. Kumar Rupesinghe, author of a report on the Katunayake FTZ in Sri Lanka, has written that the project "destabilized certain sections of the domestic industrial sector." A 1980 World Bank report on Sri Lanka stated with diplomatic caution that "some of the exports by foreign garment firms may have been at the expense of potential exports by Sri Lankan firms."

The phenomenon of free trade zones is no longer limited to "developing" nations. In an effort to adapt to the competitive environment engendered by the creation of FTZs, the same variables are being manipulated in different places and on different scales in the industrialized countries. In the United States, towns, counties, and even states fall over themselves in an effort to attract corporations to their respective areas, regardless of the social and ecological costs. In *When Corporations Rule the World* (1995), David C. Korten cites the case of Moore County in South Carolina:

> It benefited handsomely when large manufacturers fled the union-ized industrial regions of the Northeastern United States in the 1960s and 1970s, lured south by promises of tax breaks, lax environmental regulations and compliant labor. Not only did Moore County offer attractive tax breaks to prospective investors, it worked with them to provide publicly financed facilities tailored to their individual needs. When Proctor Silex expanded its local plant, Moore County floated a $5.5 million bond to finance the necessary sewer and water hookups — even though nearby residents were without tap water and other basic public services. Then in 1990, NACCO Industries, the parent company of Proctor Silex, decided to move its assembly lines to Mexico, eliminating the jobs of 800 workers and leaving behind drums of toxic waste and the public debts the county incurred on the company's behalf.

Equally, whole countries are no longer immune to using similar techniques, as demonstrated by the deregulatory frenzy initiated by President Reagan. The Quayle Council on Competitiveness was the direct successor of Reagan's Task Force on Regulatory Relief, which was chaired by then Vice President George Bush. According to Nancy Waltzman of Public Citizen's Congress Watch, these groups succeeded in "thwarting worker safety regulations, obstructing consumer product safety controls, rolling back highway safety initiatives, and weakening environmental protection."

The United Kingdom has its own deregulatory program. Initiated in 1993, the task force overseeing the process made 605 different recommendations. The majority of these affected the Department of the Environment. They included measures relaxing regulations in such fields as health and safety, biotechnology, advertising in sensitive areas, hedgerow preservation, and energy efficiency in buildings.

A brochure produced by the state-owned Invest in Britain Bureau trumpets Britain's numerous advantages for multinational companies looking for a home. It boasts of a "pro-business environment" and highlights "liberal and undemanding labor regulations," "labor costs significantly below other European countries," "no exchange controls on repatriated profits," and a "commitment to reduce the burdens on business." To hammer home the point, the brochure goes into detail: "The UK has the least onerous labor regulations in Europe, with few restrictions on working hours, overtime, and holidays. Many companies setting up in the UK have negotiated single union agreements. However, there is no legal requirement to recognize a trade union. Many industries operate shift work, and twenty-four hour, seven days-a-week production for both men and women." Also, "no new laws or regulations," it says, "may be introduced without ascertaining and minimizing the costs to business." The UK is thus already well on the way to becoming a national FTZ — with the usual consequences.

Now with ratification of GATT, free trade zones have moved beyond specific locales and begun to encompass the entire globe. Under the rules by which countries (serving their corporations) can initiate challenges to other countries' trading practices or their environmental or consumer laws, an alarming process of *mutual deregulation* is underway. European corporate interests, among others, can now effectively deregulate U.S. corporate interests via external challenges, while Americans can do likewise to Europeans and to others. By this friendly arrangement, corporations are effectively collaborating in transforming the entire world into a free trade zone with all the opportunities to operate without controls that were formerly limited to Sri Lanka, small zones of Mexico, and elsewhere. How far this global process will advance before a public reaction sets in remains to be seen.

# 24

# STRUCTURAL ADJUSTMENT AND THE POLARIZATION OF MEXICAN SOCIETY

Carlos Heredia and Mary Purcell

*One of the greatest frauds perpetrated on the American and Mexican peoples was to persuade them that the 1994 $50 billion economic "bailout" of Mexico by U.S. taxpayers was done as a neighborly act to help the people of Mexico. In fact, it only bailed out the Wall Street speculators and the World Bank theorists who had imposed devastating economic "adjustments" on Mexico that failed to deliver their promised benefits and led directly to the infamous peso crisis.*

*Carlos Heredia and Mary Purcell, economists with Equipo Pueblo (the People's Team), work with grass-roots organizations to advance economic democracy. They had firsthand experience of the effects of the Bank's development programs upon the middle class and working poor in Mexico and coauthored the report published by The Development Gap, "The Polarization of Mexican Society: A Grassroots View of World Bank Economic Adjustment Policies" (1994), from which this chapter is adapted.*

*Heredia was deputy director of international economics with the Mexican Ministry of Finance until 1988. He is now director of international programs with Equipo Pueblo and is on the executive committee of the Mexican Action Network on Free Trade. Mary Purcell is a visiting fellow at Equipo Pueblo. She previously worked in Washington, D.C., with the "50 Years Is Enough" campaign.*

IN JANUARY 1994, the North American Free Trade Agreement (NAFTA) came into effect. Three months later, Mexico was admitted to the Organization for Economic Cooperation and Development, the twenty-five-member club of industrialized nations. Emboldened by these developments, the World Bank and the International Monetary Fund (IMF) claimed "victory" for Mexico's economic program. Mexico became the shining example of how structural adjustment programs (SAPs) can benefit a country's economy. Before 1994 came to a close, the emptiness of this claim was clearly apparent: The Mexican economy virtually collapsed. In December of 1994, after years of maintaining an overvalued currency, the Mexican government was forced to allow the peso to float. Within three weeks there was a 40 percent devaluation, touching off a crisis in international financial markets and an even more serious structural crisis in Mexico.

Following the devaluation, both the World Bank and the IMF continued to insist that "the fundamentals" of Mexico's economic program were sound. They are wrong: Mexico's economic adjustment program is fatally flawed and unsustainable, and it will produce even greater crises in the future.

There are three critical factors behind the failure of Mexico's economic program: (1) the absence of an income-generating strategy for the poor and working class; (2) the lack of productive capacity to provide the basis for growth; and (3) the absence of a democratic system by which Mexicans can participate in national debate and decision making about the future of their country.

A look at the structural adjustment policies implemented over the past twelve years illustrates the inability of such policies to produce sustainable, equitable development. The grim realities of structural adjustment for most of Mexico's population — reduced wages and income, increased consumer prices, reduced social services, and growing poverty and desperation — have been evident for years. But Mexico is not exceptional. Everywhere that these policies are applied, the results are similar. Not surprisingly, a growing number of people are urging a major shift in economic policy toward a strategy that puts people first.

• • •

Mexico's declaration of a temporary moratorium on its foreign debt in August 1982 ushered in a new era of economic policy. Faced with the threat of excommunication from international capital and trade, the government discarded the inward-looking import-substitution industrialization model of development, which had been in place since the 1940s, and replaced it with an export-oriented economic model.

Since 1982, Mexico has followed an economic policy that was forged along the lines of a classical "structural adjustment" program in conjunction with the World Bank and the IMF. Today, in spite of the fact that the program allowed a drastic reduction in inflation and stimulated an unprecedented flow of foreign investment, poverty continues to increase, wealth is evermore concentrated, and the foreign debt is growing at an unprecedented pace.

Throughout this process, Mexico's authoritarian single-party political system managed to keep discontent under control by negotiation, co-optation, patronage, and outright repression, as it has always done during its sixty-five-year rule. However, in recent years economic hardships for most of the population and the loss of confidence in the political system have led to increasingly frequent outbreaks of social discontent. A series of events in 1994, including the declaration of war by the Zapatista Army of National Liberation (EZLN) and the assassination of presidential candidate Luis Donaldo Colosio, illustrate the inability of Mexico's political system to deal with the extreme economic polarization it has helped to create. This social instability, in turn, will help to determine Mexico's economic future.

## STRUCTURAL ADJUSTMENT IN MEXICO

Desperate for foreign exchange following the eruption of the debt crisis in 1979, Mexico signed agreements with the IMF and the World Bank that, in effect, provided access to foreign currency in exchange for the implementation of a program of strict fiscal discipline and economic adjustment.

Since 1982, the Mexican government has implemented virtually all of the adjustment policies promoted by the World Bank and the IMF: a reduction in public expenditures (including those on social services); the elimination of subsidies; the restriction of credit; the privatization of most state enterprises; trade liberalization; tax reform; devaluation; the removal of barriers to foreign investment; and the introduction of "competitive" wages.

For the first five years (from 1982 to 1987), drastic austerity measures, a far-reaching trade liberalization program, and the privatization of some state enterprises failed to bring about any positive results. During that time, Mexico experienced a severe recession, very high inflation rates, and a growing financial deficit.

In 1988, a critical political component was added to the adjustment program. Each year, the government has had to negotiate with the business sector and official labor and peasant organizations and sign a stabilization "pact" designed to control prices and wages (and thus inflation).

The pact has been modified and renewed each year to reflect the government's changing economic priorities.

The pact has been the backbone of the program since 1988. Party control of labor unions and peasant associations ensured the official "stamp of approval" each year, which in turn has helped to generate investor confidence. The pact always restricts wage increases more than price increases and thus leads to the continual decline in workers' purchasing power. The 1995 pact, renegotiated following the peso crisis in December 1994, restricts wage increases to 7 percent, while inflation is expected to exceed 20 percent. During these negotiations, however, official labor leaders gave clear signals that their patience for such antiworker policies is wearing thin.

## HAVE ADJUSTMENT PROGRAMS
## ACHIEVED THEIR GOALS?

According to the World Bank, the purpose of a structural adjustment program is to restore "sustainable" economic growth and make lasting progress in alleviating poverty. If these are truly the goals of adjustment, the record shows it has not worked. In Mexico (a supposed model of adjustment) the average rate of economic growth was ∅ percent during the de la Madrid administration (1982 to 1988) and only 2.2 percent — barely above the rate of population growth — during the Salinas administration (1988 to 1994).

Between 1988 and 1992, the adjustment program was successful at reining in inflation and balancing the budget. However, this was achieved at the expense of the poor and working class and the poor in general, who have seen their standard of living fall over the past decade as wealth has become more concentrated. At the same time, huge imbalances in the external sector raise serious questions about the sustainability of the program, even in the short term. The fact that a promise of $53 billion in international capital from U.S. public sources was needed to avert a financial disaster in 1995 illustrates the inability of the "free market" to provide for sustainable development on its own.

A look at the impact of adjustment in four sectors — the public sector, trade, the finance sector, and the labor market — shows mixed results in accomplishing short-term policy objectives. It is apparent, however, that even when short-term objectives are achieved, the reforms do not contribute to the two supposedly important goals of structural adjustment: economic growth and poverty alleviation. Consequently, it is time for the international financial institutions to drastically alter the policy prescriptions of structural adjustment programs.

## Public Sector Reform

One of the first adjustment policies implemented was a drastic reduction in public spending. In general, the international financial institutions recommend the cutting of "nonproductive" spending so as not to affect output or revenues. This implies cuts in social spending. The federal budget for social development (health, education, transportation, and so on) fell sharply between 1982 and 1988; although it gradually increased in the following years, in 1993 it was still below 1980 levels. In the early nineties, the World Bank pointed to these overall increases as evidence that the hardest part of adjustment was over and argued that now the poor would see the fruits of their sacrifice. Then came the December 1994 crisis, which was followed by commitments to cut an additional $5 billion in government spending in 1995. Whatever brief hopes Mexicans had for improved social services were eliminated overnight. Of course, the poor who rely on these services will be hardest hit by such cuts.

During the 1980s, the health budget as a percentage of overall public spending fell from 4.7 percent to 2.7 percent. Even the World Bank (1990) has acknowledged that the Mexican government "may be under-spending on health care."

There are signs that cutbacks in health services during the eighties reversed certain positive trends in previous decades. For example, between 1980 and 1992, infant deaths due to nutritional deficiencies almost tripled to rates higher than those in the 1970s. The overall decline in the quality and extent of public services has driven those who can afford it to seek private health care. Given the fact that about one-half of all Mexicans live in poverty, reliance on a private health care system must exclude most of the population. Still, the World Bank (1990) argues that Mexico must look for alternative sources of health care financing, "including the possibility of privatizing health sector activities such as curative services."

The United Nations recommends that developing countries spend 8 percent of their GDP on education. Between 1982 and 1990, overall public spending on education in Mexico declined almost 21 percent, from 5.5 percent of GDP in 1982 to 2.5 percent in 1990. Mexico spends approximately $45 per person per year on educational programs (the United States spends $1,400). In 1982, teachers earned 3.5 times the minimum wage, but by 1990 they earned only 1.5 times the minimum wage. (The real minimum wage was cut in half during this period.) There is concern among education officials that the economic crisis is forcing many children (especially those in secondary school) to drop out. Paralleling a similar phenomenon in the health sector, government cutbacks in education funding have coincided with an increase in the number of private schools, which threatens Mexico's long-standing desire to make education more accessible to all income groups.

The privatization process, one of the most ambitious ever carried out and for which Mexico has been applauded by the World Bank, began in 1982. By mid 1994 there was little left to sell off: The number of state-owned enterprises declined during that period from 1,155 to fewer than 150. The 1995 peso crisis prompted calls to privatize the remaining state enterprises, including parts of the national oil (PEMEX) and electric (CFE) companies and the country's railroads and ports. The fact that the constitution states that certain key sectors, such as railroads and telecommunications, must be owned by the state was but a minor obstacle. The Senate simply voted to change the constitution, as it has done countless times; indeed, there were over thirty NAFTA and adjustment-related constitutional amendments during the Salinas administration alone.

The privatization of state companies has earned the Mexican government over $26 billion in revenues, but has also led to a greater concentration of wealth and an increase in private monopolies, as the World Bank itself freely admits.

## Trade Reform and External Balance

According to the World Bank, trade liberalization was the centerpiece of the adjustment program. The World Bank gave Mexico $1 billion to support the reduction of tariff and nontariff barriers, simplify the tariff structure, and eliminate subsidies on import-competing industries.

In 1986, in the midst of the trade liberalization program, Mexico became a signatory of the General Agreement on Tariffs and Trade (GATT). The abrupt liberalization of trade resulted in an enormous trade deficit ($23 billion in 1993). The December 1994 peso devaluation made it clear that Mexico could no longer afford imports financed by borrowing from abroad and sustained through an overvalued currency.

Trade liberalization was somewhat successful in increasing and diversifying exports and in raising export revenues from nonpetroleum industries. However, imports continued to outpace the growth of exports. Small and medium-sized Mexican businesses (which employ 80 percent of Mexican workers) simply could not compete with international competitors. Many of these companies have now gone out of business or have been transformed into retailers of U.S.-manufactured goods. Many former entrepreneurs have turned to speculation as a means of earning their living. As one Mexican businessman put it, "If you own a business that is worth 100 pesos, and you need to invest another 100 to make it competitive, you may decide that the prospect of facing very tough competition from Southeast Asian or American producers is not as inviting as quick, high yields in the stock exchange or the money market." This incentive structure is at the heart of the failure of the economic program in Mexico.

Signing NAFTA has had similar effects. One year afterward, unemployment rates were on the rise, and small and medium-sized factories were closing down. The 1995 crisis of the peso and the massive bailout has totally shattered NAFTA's promise of prosperity for everyone.

Despite government attempts to underplay the seriousness of Mexico's foreign debt, debt-service payments continue to be a serious burden on the economy, since resources that would otherwise be allocated to development are instead sent abroad. Between 1982 and 1989, approximately $15 billion per year was paid out to service the debt. Meanwhile, the overall foreign debt rose from $86.23 billion in 1982 to over $140 billion in 1994, while the 1995 "bailout" package could increase Mexico's outstanding debt to around $180 billion.

There is growing concern that Mexico will be forced to suspend some of its debt payments, as $58 billion worth of debt will mature in 1995 alone. Meanwhile, Mexican consumers have seen interest rates on their mortgages, car payments, and credit cards skyrocket in the wake of the devaluation. Only two months after the peso crisis occurred, the banking system was on the verge of bankruptcy, with irrecoverable loans making up more than 30 percent of its portfolio. The banks responded by rescheduling debts over longer periods of time and at higher interest rates, which simply means postponing the inevitable defaults.

Still more critical was the maintenance until the last moment of an unjustifiably high exchange rate for the peso. After massive devaluations and exchange-rate fluctuations in the early eighties, there was relative exchange-rate stability between 1987 and 1994 because the government sought to control prices by holding down the real exchange rate. The Mexican government was able to sustain this overvaluation until March 1994 by increasing a U.S. swap loan facility from $1 billion to $6 billion, maintaining a fairly high level of reserves at the Bank of Mexico, and applying very high real interest rates. But, as the U.S. Federal Reserve hiked up interest rates, investors in emerging markets took their money out of Mexico in search of higher yields in the United States. By mid 1994, the current account deficit had become unmanageable, but President Salinas still refused to devalue the peso for fear that it would hurt his political party, the PRI, in the August 21 presidential elections and hamper his own bid to head the World Trade Organization (WTO). As a result, the new Zedillo administration was forced in 1994 to let the peso float, making a 40 percent devaluation inevitable about three weeks later (to prevent the further hemorrhage of foreign capital).

## Financial Sector Reforms

For decades the Mexican financial system included sectoral development banks to fund projects undertaken by low-income sectors of the population. Under the financial-sector reforms of the structural adjustment programs, virtually all credit is channeled through commercial banks at commercial rates, drastically reducing credit subsidies. Total credit has been restricted, and priority is given to producers with export potential. However, the government is faced with another dilemma: Interest rates cannot be reduced because this would encourage capital flight, but high interest rates lead to economic stagnation, which in turn leads to reduced investment. Some low-income sectors are eligible for no-interest credits from the National Solidarity Program (PRONASOL), but the amount of credit is so low that it leaves producers seriously short of funds.

There has been an extreme concentration of financial assets in Mexico. Commercial banks, brokerage houses, investment banks, currency-exchange houses, and other financial institutions have merged into newly formed "financial groups." Two of these groups, Accival-Banamex and Vamsa-Bancomer, account for one-half of all financial assets. Approximately 180,000 individual accounts (out of 25 million) command 80 percent of total assets in the financial system. The financial groups are concentrating on the more profitable corporate banking operations rather than expanding services to the average consumer. But the magic of the market also failed here: In 1990 the banking system was reprivatized, and in 1995 the Mexican government was forced to create a special trust to bail out ailing banks.

In the area of investment, the government has sought to attract foreign capital to make up for a low level of domestic savings and investment. Accumulated direct foreign investment increased threefold between 1981 and 1991. However, most capital inflows in recent years have taken the form of portfolio investments — buying into existing assets — rather than funding productive activity. This has resulted in low job creation and growth rates. In addition, short-term speculative investment makes Mexico extremely vulnerable to the whims of foreign governments and private investors, who can pull their money out with the touch of a button.

## Labor Market Reforms

A decline in real wages is usually made a de facto condition of adjustment, presumably to avoid an increase in unemployment. In addition, the World Bank recommends the elimination of labor-market institutions and regulations that "restrict the mobility of labor," such as large severance payments and nonwage benefits. Private-sector leaders continue to try to make the labor force even more "flexible" and attractive to foreign investors by giving them the right to employ people on hourly wages and to reduce nonwage benefits yet further.

As for salaries, the World Bank and the IMF argue that a temporary reduction in real wages can help offset an SAP's negative effects on employment. However, in spite of a steep and persistent decline in real wages during the eighties, there have still been massive layoffs and a high level of unemployment.

At the end of 1994, the minimum wage in Mexico was about fifteen new pesos ($4.40) per day. In dollar terms it fell to $3.15 per day in the weeks following the January 1995 peso devaluation. According to a study by researchers at the Faculty of Economics of the National Autonomous University of Mexico (UNAM), from the initiation of the pact in December 1987 until May 1, 1994, the minimum wage had increased 136 percent, while the cost of the Basket of Basic Goods had gone up 371 percent. Meanwhile, wage labor as a percentage of GDP fell from 36 percent to 22 percent during the eighties, while that of capital rose from 54 percent to 62 percent (Oswald 1991).

The Clinton administration campaigned for NAFTA arguing that in Mexico there were over 80 million potential consumers for American exports. The truth is, however, that the Mexican middle-class consists of fewer than 8 million of Mexico's 90 million people, and only they have the incomes that can enable them to purchase American products on any scale.

In a 1991 study, the Mexican Labor Congress (CT) indicated that, out of an economically active population of 34 million, 15 percent were openly unemployed, while over 40 percent — some 14 million people — were underemployed. In the meantime, the government has never ceased to understate the seriousness of the unemployment problem, claiming unemployment in 1993 was only 2.9 percent. These figures were reached by questionable methods of calculation and failed to take into account both the rural unemployed and the large number of jobless people who eke out a living in the rapidly expanding informal economy, which, according to the National Institute of Statistics, Geography and Information Systems (INEGI), currently employs about one-third of the active labor force.

Overall, massive layoffs and lower growth rates in domestic investment have meant reduced employment opportunities. According to a study by Bancomer, Mexico's second-largest commercial bank, in 1993 alone 600,000 jobs were lost in the manufacturing sector. Between 1988 and 1992, only 583,208 new jobs were created, in spite of the fact that over one million workers enter the labor force each year.

According to the United Nations' Economic Commission for Latin America and the Caribbean (ECLAC), there is now an inverse relationship between investment and employment in Mexico. While the former has increased by 9 percent over the last three years, the creation of new jobs has gone down. With the automation and computerization of Mexican industry, this new trend can only accelerate.

# IMPACTS ON POVERTY
# AND INCOME DISTRIBUTION

## Poverty

Although statistics on changes in poverty rates vary, several studies indicate that poverty has increased under structural adjustment. According to one such study, commissioned by the government poverty-alleviation program PRONASOL in 1992 and reported in *La Jornada* (Sept. 6, 1992), about one-half of all Mexicans (42 million) were living in poverty in 1990, with 18 million living in conditions of extreme poverty. As the study stated, "Economic growth is not sufficient to eradicate poverty and extreme poverty. Even when it accelerates, it doesn't succeed in absorbing the entire labor force, and sectors of the population remain marginalized from commercial production and, therefore, unable to access the market. If the poverty figures are frightening, their consequences should be even more frightening. Malnutrition has become the normal condition of society."

## Income Distribution

Since 1982, privatization and deregulation have contributed to a steep concentration of income and wealth. In what analysts term a "trickle-up" process, there has been in Mexico a massive transfer of resources from the salaried population to owners of capital and from public control to (a few) private hands. Over the past decade, the already large gap between the rich and the poor has widened. The richest 20 percent of the population received 54.2 percent of national income in 1992, compared to 48.4 percent in 1984, while the income of the poorest 20 percent fell from 5 percent in 1984 to 4.3 percent of national income in 1992.

To illustrate the extreme concentration of wealth and income, during the Salinas administration the number of billionaires in Mexico rose from two to twenty-four, while about 20 percent of the population — seventeen million people — subsisted on incomes of less than $350 per person per year. The assets of one of the richest men in Mexico actually total more than the annual income of the poorest seventeen million people combined.

## IMPACTS ON THE ENVIRONMENT

Mexico is one of the world's thirteen "megadiversity" areas that together account for about 60 percent of the planet's species. It ranks fourth in the world in the total number of species that inhabit it. However, this great biological wealth is being rapidly eroded. The country had serious environmental problems long before structural adjustment began. Under adjustment, however, the reduction in funding for environmental protection, partly explained by the adoption of an economic model that does not realize the true value of natural resources, has further threatened Mexico's natural environment. Decades of industrialization without environmental protection stimulated agricultural policies that have encouraged the large-scale export of natural resources. Subsidies for large-scale cattle ranching caused deforestation and soil erosion, which have taken their toll on the Mexican environment. Equally serious are air and water pollution, water shortages, and growing inventories of toxic waste.

As part of the fiscal discipline required by adjustment, the budget for SEDUE, the environmental protection agency, has been reduced 60 percent in real terms between 1986 and 1989. Although it was increased in the following years, it is still far from what is required to run an effective environmental monitoring agency.

Proponents of NAFTA claim that the agreement will make Mexico a richer country, which in turn will create the financial resources to clean up the environment and prevent further degradation of the natural resource base. An increased budget will mean better oversight and enforcement, because more personnel can be trained and hired to ensure that the law is observed. However, the *maquiladora* workers who have to drink water from polluted sources, the Tarahumara Indians whose forest lands have been destroyed by lumber companies, the coastal fishermen faced with a reduction of fish stocks resulting from PEMEX's oil drilling, and the millions of Mexico City residents whose health has been impaired by air pollution see little hope for a solution to their problems.

## CONCLUSIONS

Adjustment in Mexico was undertaken too quickly and drastically. The program has not been modified in response to the social, economic, and environmental problems that have emerged. And now the government refuses to alter its course for fear of losing the confidence of major economic actors.

What has been lacking throughout the structural adjustment process in Mexico is a social and economic policy that truly puts people first. Both the Mexican government and the multilateral development banks have supported an economic policy that is more concerned with subsidizing creditor commercial banks than with addressing the people's needs. There remains a pressing need to strike a balance between efficiency on the one hand and social justice on the other, in order to promote the well-being of society as a whole.

The very principle of adjustment needs to be reconsidered if it is to encourage sustainable development. A new approach would include income-generating strategies for the poor, low-interest credit for small- and medium-scale producers, and a role for the state in planning and providing basic services to the population.

Mexico is just one of many cases worldwide where adjustment and the free market have not only failed to alleviate poverty — as their proponents insisted they would — but have further polarized the country, economically and politically. World Bank and IMF officials continue to insist that the beneficial effect of adjustment on poverty will take time, but, after more than a decade of adjustment in Mexico, there is still no light at the end of the tunnel. The time has come to acknowledge that the structural adjustment model has failed and to develop a new set of strategies.

# 25

# STRUCTURAL ADJUSTMENT PROGRAMS
## *"Success" for Whom?*

### Walden Bello

*Walden Bello is a Philippine activist, scholar, and writer. He obtained his Ph.D. degree in sociology from Princeton University in 1975, and he has taught at the University of California at Berkeley and, presently, at the University of the Philippines. During the Marcos dictatorship, Bello worked in Washington, D.C., as a lobbyist advocating democratic rights in the Philippines. Until recently, Bello was executive director of the San Francisco–based Institute for Food and Development Policy, also known as Food First.*

*Bello's books include* Dragons in Distress *(1990, with Stephanie Rosenfeld), a book that documents the terrible social and ecological costs that the newly industrialized countries have incurred as by-products of their much-publicized economic "success," and* Development Debacle: The World Bank in the Philippines, *(1982, with David Kinley and Elaine Elison). Bello's latest book,* Dark Victory *(1994, with Shea Cunningham and Bill Rau), is a critique of structural adjustment programs.*

I N THE last years of the McNamara era, structural adjustment loans (SALs) began to be provided to debtor countries. The immediate objective was to rescue northern banks that had become overextended in the Third World; the longer-term objective was to further integrate southern countries into the North-dominated world economy. To accomplish these twin goals, the World Bank and the International Monetary Fund (IMF) became the linchpin of a strategy that involved providing compliant Third World debtors with billions of dollars in quick-disbursing SALs or "standby loans" that would then be transferred as interest payments to the private banks. But to receive SALs, the southern governments had to agree to undergo structural adjustment programs (SAPs), which were ostensibly designed to make their economies more efficient and better capable of sustained growth.

The conditions usually attached to SALs included:

- Removing restrictions on foreign investments in local industry, banks, and other financial services. No longer could local industry or banks be favored or protected against giant foreign intervention.

- Reorienting the economy toward exports in order to earn the foreign exchange required for servicing the debt and to become correspondingly more dependent on the global economy. The effect was to reduce self-sufficiency and diverse local production in favor of single-product manufacture or single-crop agriculture.

- Reducing wages or wage increases to make exports more "competitive." Radically reducing government spending, including spending on health, education, and welfare combined with wage reduction, would control inflation and ensure that all available money would be channeled into increasing production for export. But the few social services that remained were gutted.

- Cutting tariffs, quotas, and other restrictions on imports, to grease the way for global integration.

- Devaluing the local currency against hard currencies such as the U.S. dollar in order to make exports still more competitive.

- Privatizing state enterprises, thereby providing further access for foreign capital.

- Undertaking a deregulation program to free export-oriented corporations from government controls that protect labor, the environment, and natural resources, thereby cutting costs and further increasing export competitiveness. (This had the secondary effect of forcing down wages and standards in other countries — including industrialized countries — to maintain their competitiveness.)

Since structural adjustment programs covered so many dimensions of economic policy, agreeing to an SAL virtually meant turning over a country's economic control to the World Bank and the IMF.

# THE GLOBALIZATION OF "ADJUSTMENT"

Initially, few governments felt eager to receive SALs. But the eruption of the Third World debt crisis in mid 1982 provided a grand opportunity to further the Reaganite agenda of re-subordinating the South via structural adjustment schemes. As more and more Third World countries ran into ever greater difficulties in servicing the huge loans made to them by northern banks in the 1970s, the United States government via the Bretton Woods institutions took advantage of "this period of financial strain to insist that debtor countries remove the government from the economy as the price of getting credit" (Sheahan 1992).

In accordance with guidelines set by the U.S. Treasury Department, the U.S. private banks invariably made (and continue to make) World Bank consent a prerequisite for debt rescheduling. Predictably, the World Bank's seal of approval and its cash, which debtor countries desperately needed to make interest payments to the private banks, came dearly. As one Treasury official involved in the debt negotiations with Mexico put it, "Only countries that commit to market-oriented economic reform will get the [World Bank's] help" (Miller 1991).

Debtor countries had no choice but to capitulate. By the beginning of 1986, twelve of the fifteen countries designated by then Secretary of the Treasury James Baker as top-priority debtors — including Brazil, Mexico, Argentina, and the Philippines — had agreed to SAPs. From 3 percent of total World Bank lending in 1981, structural adjustment credits rose to 25 percent in 1986. By the end of 1992, about 267 SALs had been approved.

Thirteen years after the World Bank's first SAP was introduced, the bank declared structural adjustment a success. In its publication "Global Economic Prospects and the Developing Countries" (1993), the bank asserted that developing countries face brighter prospects that can be attributed mainly to the widespread economic reforms, notably privatization, greater openness to trade, reduction of fiscal deficits, and commercial debt overhangs. This was, needless to say, a minority opinion.

A number of comprehensive studies, including one conducted by the IMF itself, admits that SALs did not achieve their overt goal of stimulating growth. Comparing countries that underwent stabilization and adjustment programs with those that did not over the period 1973 to 1988, IMF economist Mohsin Khan found that economic growth was higher in the latter than in the former.

Focusing on the African experience in the 1980s, UNICEF economist Eva Jespersen assessed a sample of twenty-four countries that were subjected to structural adjustment programs, on three counts: the rate of capital accumulation, the share of manufacturing in Gross Domestic Product (GDP), and the growth of exports (Cornia and others 1992). The data showed that capital accumulation slowed in twenty countries; the share of manufacturing in GDP stagnated in eighteen countries; exports fell in thirteen countries; and the increases experienced in eleven countries did not compensate for the increase in imports.

## EXPLAINING STAGNATION

Why such a dismal record? The problem, according to Massachusetts Institute of Technology economist Lance Taylor and his associates, is that the World Bank and the IMF misdiagnosed the problem. The main barrier to growth in the pre-SAL period was not that Third World economies had been insufficiently integrated into the global economy, as the IMF and the World Bank insisted, but above all that they had been subjected to two great shocks: the OPEC oil price rise in the 1970s and the debt crisis in the early 1980s (Fanelli 1992). Using the bank's own data, Taylor and his associates found that the much-derided prior strategy called *import substitution* had been effective at fostering productivity. (Import substitution policies emphasized local production for local consumption and thereby promoted diverse production and national self-sufficiency, especially in the area of key goods and services. This was the common practice in Latin America from 1960 to 1973.) After the 1982 debt crisis, on the other hand, private investment fell dramatically in developing countries, while the money made available by multinational development banks was mainly designated to repay old debts. At the same time, there was a massive outflow of resources to the industrial countries that could otherwise have gone to domestic local investment.

Taylor and his associates, along with other academic critics of structural adjustment programs, have also stressed the way SAPs trigger a range of adverse consequences that cannot be predicted on the basis of IMF and World Bank theories but that must seem inevitable to anyone with a common-sense view of economics.

By reducing government spending, cutting wages, and literally destroying the domestic economy in order to build up a new export-oriented economy, a structural adjustment program must necessarily lead to an overall economic contraction and cause increased unemployment. Even in such conditions, the programs prevent the state from stepping in to reverse the decline in private investment. The absence of intervention further accentuates all these trends and creates a vicious cycle of stagnation and decline rather than growth, rising employment, and rising investment, as World Bank theory originally predicted.

To further promote exports, when devaluation and the lifting of price controls on imports are added to this policy of monetary and fiscal austerity, the economy has to contract still further. This must raise the local costs of both imported capital and the raw materials and components used in local assembly plants. For instance, letting the market determine fertilizer prices has led in many countries to reduced applications, lower yields, and reduced investment in agriculture.

At the same time, rising exports of the small range of crops (such as sugar, palm oil, and bananas) that the World Bank encourages developing countries to produce (regardless of a market need) have led to a continuous fall in prices and thus often to reduced foreign earnings. Much of the earnings are in any case used for servicing debt rather than for productive domestic investment.

## CHILE: AN ECONOMIC LABORATORY

The sharp disparity between the expected and the actual results of a structural adjustment program is illustrated by the case of Chile in the 1980s. Chile is probably the country with the longest-running structural adjustment program in the world, one that began immediately after General Augusto Pinochet's 1973 bloody coup against the democratically elected government of President Salvador Allende. Adjustment took a particularly radical form in Chile, as Chilean economists trained at the University of Chicago sought to transform, vis-à-vis the new government's dictatorial powers, an economy dependent on heavy state intervention into a free market paradise. All the standard paraphernalia of structural adjustment programs were called into play and applied with ideological fervor.

By the end of the 1980s, Chile's economy had indeed been transformed:

- Some six hundred state enterprises had been sold off, with fewer than fifty remaining in state hands.

- Chile had gone from being one of the most protected to one of the least protected of Latin America economies, with all quantitative restrictions on trade abolished and tariffs set at a single flat rate of 10 percent on all items.

- Foreign investors had achieved a strong presence in the economy as part owners of former state enterprises in strategic sectors such as steel, telecommunications, and airlines.

- The radical deregulation of the domestic financial market had been accomplished.

- The economy had become substantially more integrated into the international economy, with total trade amounting to 57.4 percent of GDP in 1990 compared to 35 percent in 1970.

The World Bank and the IMF had been central to this transformation, and they were proud of the results of their policies. But were they really a success? It depends on the criterion one wishes to apply. If success is to be measured by the effects on Chile's external accounts, then structural adjustment has had dubious results. Chile's external debt rose to $19 billion in 1991, which was 49 percent of GNP, with close to 9 percent of GDP flowing out of the country to service it. In reality the situation was much worse, since a significant portion of the debt that is in fixed-interest bonds had been exchanged for ordinary shares (equity holdings) in strategic sectors of the Chilean economy via "debt-equity swaps."

If sustained growth is regarded as the key measure of success for structural adjustment, then Chile could hardly be considered successful. As Ricardo Ffrench-Davis and Oscar Muñoz point out, the growth in GDP during the Pinochet years (1974 to 1989) averaged only 2.6 percent per year as opposed to 4 percent from 1950 to 1961 and 4.6 percent from 1961 to 1971, the period before structural adjustment programs had been applied. The result of the adjustment was even more dismal when viewed in terms of growth per capita GDP: This had averaged 1.1 percent in the 1970s and only 0.9 percent in the 1980s (Inter-American Development Bank 1992).

These results are even more disappointing when one considers that in order to achieve them, free market policies plunged Chile into two major depressions in one decade: first in 1974–75, when GDP fell by 12 percent, then again in 1982–83, when it dropped by 15 percent. As Lance Taylor and his associates noted in their report for the U.N. Conference on Trade and Development, "the [Chilean] economy reeled through a 12-year sequence of disastrous experiments amply supported by the Bank and the Fund" (Fanelli 1992).

The reasons for the failure of the World Bank's and IMF's restructuring of the Chilean economy are clear. The combination of a lower rate of investment with draconian trade liberalization caused the manufacturing sector to lose ground, declining from an average of 26 percent of GDP in the late 1960s to an average of 20 percent in the late 1980s. Indeed, from 1979 to 1981, manufacturing shrank in absolute terms, and it was not until 1988 that gross profits in industry surpassed the level that had been attained in 1974. On the other hand, export-oriented enterprises involved in forestry, fishing, agriculture, and mining greatly expanded. However, this led among other things to serious environmental problems: The logging of vast tracts of ancient alerce forests, the massive growth of agricultural monocropping and of large-scale intensive fish-farming, the building of huge dams on wild rivers, and the replacement of natural forests with plantations of fast-growing exotics all drastically increased soil erosion, desertification, and the pollution of rivers and estuaries while causing a massive reduction in biological diversity.

In addition, the transformed Chilean economy, with its extreme dependence on exports of primary and processed goods and its shrinking manufacturing base, was by the late 1980s far less stable than it had been before the Pinochet era.

However, the social impact of the radical free market policy may have been the least tolerable of all the consequences of structural adjustment. When the debt crisis broke out in 1983, the government (and hence the taxpayers) absorbed the massive debts ($3.5 billion, or nearly 20 percent of GDP) that had been incurred by private institutions whose owners and managers, rather than being penalized for their incompetence and irresponsibility, were allowed to carry on as before.

Also, in order to raise the money to pay for these losses, public spending was severely cut back, wages were frozen, and the Chilean peso was drastically devalued, correspondingly reducing the standard of living of the poor. Indeed the contraction of domestic expenditure that led to a 15 percent drop in GDP put over 30 percent of the work force out of work in a single year, with unemployment remaining at 25 percent for three years. The 50 percent devaluation of the peso in real terms caused the purchasing power of the workforce to fall by nearly 20 percent. At the same time, in contrast to the huge sums paid to subsidize the private institutions, benefits made available to the newly unemployed were minimal and were actually paid to less than half of those who should have received them.

Not surprisingly, between 1980 and 1990, the proportion of families below "the line of destitution" had risen from 12 to 15 percent and of those living below the poverty line (but above the line of destitution) from 24 to 26 percent. This meant that at the end of the Pinochet era, some 40 percent, or 5.2 million people out of 13 million, were now classified as poor in a country that had once boasted a large middle class. Increased poverty also meant increased hunger and malnutrition; indeed for 40 percent of the population, the daily caloric intake dropped from 2,019 in 1970 to 1,751 in 1980 to 1,629 in 1990 — well below international minimums for human nutrition.

Structural adjustment in Chile had a similar effect on income distribution. The share of the national income going to the poorest 50 percent of the population declined from 20.4 percent to 16.8 percent, while the share going to the richest 10 percent rose from 36.5 percent to 46.8 percent.

To all these costs must be added the replacement of a popular democratic government by a military dictatorship, which, as in the Philippines, was probably required in order to impose such a socially disruptive program of economic transformation. Indeed, a study for the Organization for European Cooperation and Development (OECD), having asserted that the costs of the Chilean adjustment were "among the largest in Latin America," actually asked whether "this type of adjustment [could] have been feasible under a democratic regime" (Meller 1992).

• • •

The experience of Chile in the 1980s is by no means unique in this respect. [See chapter by Carlos Heredia and Mary Purcell.] During that period, except in East Asia and in some areas of South Asia, most countries in the South experienced stagnation or sharp reversals in growth, escalating poverty, and increasing inequality both within and between countries.

With per capita income stagnant in the South and rising by 2.4 percent per year in the North during 1980s, the gap between living standards in the North and the South widened, with the average income in the North reaching U.S. $12,510, or eighteen times the average in the South.

Especially ravaged during the decade were the regions that were most severely subjected to structural adjustment. In Latin America, the force of adjustment programs struck with special fury, "largely cancelling out the progress of the 1960s and 1970s" (Iglesias 1992). The number of people living in poverty rose from 130 million in 1980 to 180 million at the beginning of the 1990s. In a decade of negative growth, income inequalities — already among the worst in the world — worsened. As Enrique Iglesias, president of the Inter-American Development Bank, reports (1992), "the bulk of the costs of adjustment fell disproportionately on the middle and low-income groups, while the top 5 percent of the population retained or, in some cases, even increased its standard of living."

With hunger and malnutrition on the rise, tuberculosis and cholera — diseases that were once thought to be banished by modern medicine — returned with a vengeance throughout the continent, with cholera claiming at least thirteen hundred in Peru alone in 1991.

Sub-Saharan Africa has been even more devastated than Latin America, with total debt in 1994 amounting to 110 percent of GNP, compared to 35 percent for all developing countries. Cut off from significant capital flows except for aid, battered by plunging commodity prices, wracked by famine and civil war, and squeezed by structural adjustment programs, Africa's per capita income declined by 2.2 percent per annum in the 1980s. By the end of the decade it had plunged to the same level as at the time of independence in the early 1960s. Some 200 million of the region's 690 million people are now classified as poor, and even the least pessimistic World Bank projection sees the number of poor rising by 50 percent to reach 300 million by the year 2000.

## ADJUSTMENT: THE OUTCOME

Judged by its ostensible objectives — resolving the debt problems of Third World economies and bringing about renewed and sustained growth while reducing poverty and unemployment — structural adjustment has been a resounding failure.

Judged by its concealed underlying strategic goals, however, it has been a resounding success. From Argentina to Ghana, state participation in the economy has been drastically curtailed; government enterprises are passing into private hands; protectionist barriers on northern imports have been eliminated wholesale; restrictions on foreign investments have been lifted; and export-first policies have been implemented with quasi-religious zeal. As a result, debtor countries have, on the whole, been able to pay interest on the loans contracted to northern banks, and, most important of all, they have become more tightly integrated into the capitalist world market and thereby made increasingly dependent for their sustenance on the northern powers and the transnational corporations that effectively control them.

# PART III

# ENGINES OF GLOBALIZATION

*We have looked at the disastrous social and environmental consequences of economic globalization, and we have considered the theories that attempt to justify the present global development project, finding them flawed, impractical, and counterproductive. In rational societies, such utter failure would have led governments to reconsider both the processes and the ideas on which their economic practices are based. Instead, governments are seeking to intensify globalization. The reason governments don't turn away from this path is because democracy and the public interest have little role in these decisions. The system is really guided by economic theorists and political leaders heavily backed by transnational corporate interests with much to gain. For corporations, the overwhelming drive is constantly to expand their resource bases and their markets to create globally homogenized consumerist life-styles. Those goals are directly served by the free trade, deregulation, and privatization agendas of the global economy.*

*In modern times, another little-noted factor is the emergence of technologies that enable and encourage corporations to operate on a scale, at a speed, and with a degree of global control that was formerly unthinkable. Given such technologies, corporations also need to maintain organizational structures that are geographically compatible with their new capabilities, or they fall behind their competitors. So the corporations drive the machine, but the machine also drives them.*

*The net effect is a coevolution of corporate form and technological form to achieve an unprecedented global reach (let's call it* dominance) *that is far more efficient than ever before; efficient, that is, from a corporate viewpoint.*

*This part of the book takes a close look at corporations as the prime engines of globalization. It examines the extent of their global reach, some examples of their antisocial behavior, their symbiotic relationship with the new communications technologies, the legal systems by which they live, and finally suggests what we might do about it.*

# 26

# MECHANISMS OF
# CORPORATE RULE

## Tony Clarke

*In this comprehensive overview, Canadian scholar and activist Tony Clarke surveys the growing power of the transnational corporations. No longer ordinary players on the international scene, corporations have achieved effective global governance by virtue of their control of economic processes, of financial markets, of the new global trade bureaucracy, of the media, and, increasingly, of education.*

*Clarke brings to bear on this issue more than two decades of experience in social activism and leadership. After receiving his Ph.D. degree in social ethics and professional ministry from the University of Chicago in 1974, he became director of the Social Affairs Department of the Canadian Conference of Catholic Bishops and later chair of the Justice and Peace Commission of the Canadian Council of Churches. From 1987 to 1993, he led Action Canada Network, a coalition of labor and social groups that fought to prevent Canada's adherence to the Canada-U.S. Free Trade Agreement and NAFTA. Clarke is also chair of the Corporations Committee of the International Forum on Globalization. His books include* Behind the Mitre: The Moral Leadership Crisis in the Canadian Catholic Church *(1995) and* Witness to Justice *(1979, with Theresa Clarke).*

$I$N THEIR famous book, *Global Reach* (1974), Richard Barnet and Ronald Mueller state this: "The men who run global corporations are the first in history with the organization, technology, money, and ideology to make a credible try at managing the world as an integrated economic unit."

In the twenty-odd years since these words were penned, transnational corporations (TNCs) have consolidated their power and control over the world. Today, forty-seven of the top one hundred economies in the world are actually transnational corporations; 70 percent of global trade is controlled by just five hundred corporations; and a mere 1 percent of the TNCs on this planet own half the total stock of foreign direct investment. At the same time, the new free market and free trade regimes (such as GATT and NAFTA) have created global conditions in which TNCs and banks can move their capital, technology, goods, and services freely throughout the world, unfettered by the regulations of nation-states or democratically elected governments.

In effect, what has taken place is a massive shift in power, out of the hands of nation-states and democratic governments and into the hands of TNCs and banks. It is now the TNCs that effectively govern the lives of the vast majority of the people on Earth; yet these new world realities are seldom reflected in the strategies of citizen movements for democratic social change. All too often, strategies are aimed primarily at changing government policies, while the real power being exercised by TNCs behind the scenes is rarely challenged, let alone dismantled. When the operations of TNCs do become a prime target for citizen action campaigns, there is a tendency to employ a rather piecemeal approach to what is a deeply systemic problem.

As we approach the twenty-first century, it is imperative that social movements in both the North and the South develop a new politics for challenging the dominant global rule of transnational enterprises.

The following overview examines some of the salient ingredients of the new powers that now give corporations effective control over the lives of peoples and nations in this age of globalization and then offers some suggestions as to changing the situation.

● ● ●

Over the past three decades, as David C. Korten points out, the world's leading business and governmental elites have been gathering on a regular basis in elite forums, such as the Council on Foreign Relations, and the Trilateral Commission, to develop a consensus on an agenda for globalization.

Behind closed doors, these leaders have been able to agree on certain common approaches, which include global economic integration; the "harmonization" of various trade, tax, and regulatory measures; and an economic philosophy that should guide all nations, combined with political strategies to achieve such changes. With passage of the new free trade agreements to augment the Bretton Woods agreement and to establish the

World Trade Organization (WTO), this unelected and unaccountable global elite has effectively seized important instruments of governance in the three dominant regions of the world.

Regardless of their nominal home bases, Japanese, North American, and European corporations have increasingly become stateless, juggling multiple national identities and loyalties to achieve their global competitive interests. No matter where they operate in the world, these transnational conglomerates can use their overseas subsidiaries, joint ventures, licensing agreements, and strategic alliances to assume foreign identities whenever it suits their purposes. In so doing, they develop chameleon-like abilities to change their identities to resemble insiders wherever they are operating. As one CEO put it, "When we go to Brussels, we're member states of the EEC and when we go to Washington we're an American company too." Whenever they need to, they will wrap themselves up in the national flag of choice to get support for tax breaks, research subsidies, or governmental representation in negotiations affecting their marketing plans. Through this process, stateless corporations are effectively transforming nation-states to suit their interests.

## THE CORPORATE-STATE ALLIANCE

In most of the industrialized countries, business councils composed of the CEOs of the largest corporations and banks have formed new corporate-state alliances. In the United States, for example, the Business Round-table's two hundred members include the heads of forty-two of the fifty largest Fortune 500 corporations, seven of the eight largest U.S. commercial banks, seven of the ten largest insurance companies, five of the seven largest retail chains, seven of the eight largest transportation companies, and nine of the eleven largest utility companies. In Canada, the Business Council on National Issues has organized itself into a shadow cabinet of the federal government, with CEOs heading up task forces on major public policy issues. Once a policy consensus is reached among the principal TNCs, massive lobbying and advertising campaigns are mounted around key policy issues. Armed with a network of policy research institutes and public relations firms, these business coalitions mobilize facts, policy positions, expert analysis, and opinion polls and organize citizen-front groups for their campaigns to change national governments and their policies. By campaigning for debt elimination, privatization, and deregulation, business coalitions have effectively dismantled many of the powers and tools of national governments.

The fundamental purposes of the new free trade deals (such as GATT

and NAFTA) are to enable TNCs and banks to act unhindered by national laws and constitutions. As Carla Hills, chief U.S. negotiator for
both NAFTA and GATT, put it, "We want corporations to be able to
make investments overseas without being required to take a local partner,
to export a given percentage of their output, to use local parts, or to meet a
dozen other restrictions." As a result, the "national treatment" clauses in
NAFTA and GATT guarantee that foreign investors have the same
rights and freedoms as domestic firms. The investment codes in the new
free trade regimes ensure that various regulations of nation-states are
removed, including foreign investment requirements, export quotas,
local procurement, job content, and technology specifications. Through
this new kind of constitutional protection, the rights of TNCs take precedence over the rights of citizens in their respective nation-states. In addition, the legislative authority of GATT and NAFTA supersedes the
legislation of participating nation-states when matters of conflict arise.

The creation of a globalized consumer culture is another key element
of the new corporate tyranny. The transnationals want to be able to sell
their products with the same basic advertising design in Bangkok and
Santiago as in Paris, Tokyo, New York, or London. The prime example is
the way Coca-Cola has become a global symbol transcending all national
and cultural boundaries. Through television images and satellite communications, a homogenous set of perspectives, tastes, and desires can be
transmitted to all corners of the globe to create a worldwide culture of
corporate-friendly consumers. It is now estimated that transnationals
spend well over half as much money in advertising as the nations of the
world combined spend on public education. In turn, all this corporate advertising tends to forge a connection in peoples' mind-sets between private interests (that of the TNCs) and the public interest. As a result, a
global monoculture is emerging, which not only disregards local tastes
and cultural differences but threatens to serve as a form of social control
over the attitudes, expectations, and behavior of people all over the world.

•  •  •

The two main Bretton Woods institutions, the World Bank and the International Monetary Fund (IMF), have become principal tools by which the
new global managers maintain corporate control over nations and peoples, especially in countries of the South. Both the bank and the fund are
directly linked to the transnational financial sector vis-à-vis the borrowing
and lending ends of their operations. Loan agreements are routinely negotiated in secret between banking and government officials who, for the
most part, are not accountable to the people on whose behalf they are

obligating the national treasury to foreign lenders. The bank and the fund must be regarded, as one observer puts it, "as governance institutions, exercising power through [their] financial leverage to legislate entire legal regimens and even to alter the constitutional structure of borrowing nations." The officials of these organizations often have the power to "rewrite a country's trade policy, fiscal policies, civil service requirements, labor laws, health care arrangements, environmental regulations, energy policy, resettlement requirements, procurement rules, and budgetary policy."

In the 1980s, the World Bank and the IMF used debt renegotiations as a club to force the developing nations into implementing structural adjustment programs (SAPs) in their economies. Each SAP package called for sweeping economic and social changes designed to channel the country's resources and productivity into debt repayments and to enhance transnational competition. The SAP measures included large-scale deregulation, privatization, currency devaluation, social spending cuts, lower corporate taxes, expansion of the export of natural resources and agricultural products, and removal of foreign investment restrictions. In order to obtain the foreign exchange to service their massive debts, developing countries were compelled to become export-oriented economies, selling off their natural resources and agricultural commodities on global markets while rapidly increasing their dependency on the imports of goods and services. In effect, the SAPs have become instruments for the recolonization of many developing countries in the South in the interests of TNCs and banks. [See chapters by Edward Goldsmith and Walden Bello.]

The new World Trade Organization established by the Uruguay Round of GATT is designed, in effect, to serve as a global governing body for transnational corporate interests. The WTO will have both legislative and judicial powers and a mandate to eliminate all barriers to international investment and competition. Under the WTO, a group of unelected trade representatives will act as a global parliament with the power to override economic and social policy decisions of nation-states and democratic legislatures around the world. At the same time, the world's major TNCs will have a powerful role to play in the new WTO through direct linkages with the trade representatives of participating countries. In the case of the United States, for example, members of the Advisory Committee for Trade Policy and Negotiations include such corporate giants as IBM, AT&T, Bethlehem Steel, Time Warner, Corning, Bank of America, American Express, Scott Paper, Dow Chemical, Boeing, Eastman Kodak, Mobil Oil, Amoco, Pfizer, Hewlett-Packard, Weyerhauser, and General Motors — all of which are members of the Business Roundtable.

## SYSTEMS OF CORPORATE RULE

The sections that follow describe some of the ways that global systems have been effectively usurped by transnational corporations and banks.

### Global Finance

The globalization of finance markets has been nothing short of revolutionary. The days when national authorities could stabilize financial markets through banking regulations, reserve requirements, deposit insurance, limits on interest rates, and the separation of commercial and investment banking are all but gone. In country after country there has been a massive deregulation of finance and mergers between commercial and investment banking. In addition, TNCs are now bypassing banks altogether and issuing their own commercial paper. Information technology has transformed global banking to the point where $2 trillion is transferred every day around the world. Electronic transfer systems make more than 150,000 international transactions in a single day. The speed and frequency of these transactions — from Malaysia to Toronto to New York to Miami to the Cayman Islands to the Bahamas to Switzerland — makes the money trail difficult to trace, let alone regulate. But this deregulated, global finance market has become fragile and unstable to the point where a financial shock in one country (such as Mexico) can dramatically upset financial markets in other countries before national authorities have a chance to intervene. Unless radically new regulatory measures are introduced, the fiscal policies of national governments will not only be dictated but also threatened by a volatile global finance system. [See chapter on the casino economy by Richard Barnet and John Cavanagh.]

### Global Industrial Production

As the auto, electronics, textile, and clothing industries have outgrown their home countries and shifted their production and supplier operations off-shore to independent contractors, the "global factory," coupled with a radically new international division of labor, has emerged. With the globalization of production networks, transnational manufacturing firms can quickly move their operations around the world, in search of cheap labor, more profitable investment opportunities, and freedom from the demands of unionized workers. In the auto industry, Ford and GM have forged strategic alliances with Mazda and Toyota to produce for each others' markets, while in other industries, companies such as Nike and Schwinn have begun to shift from manufacturing to designing, merchandising, and distributing. The new global factory has resulted in a dramatic loss of manufacturing jobs in the industrial North (the United States, Japan, and Europe) as manufacturing companies move their production to low-wage, tax-free countries in the South. Increasingly, workers around the world find themselves lumped together in the same global labor pool to the point where exploitation in Guatemala, Malaysia, or China is felt as wage competition by workers in London, New York, or Montreal. While the staggering wage gap between workers in the North and the South has begun to narrow, there is a very real danger that the forces of global competition will drag workers everywhere down to the lowest common wage standards.

## Global Product Distribution

In *Global Dreams* (1994), Richard Barnet and John Cavanagh describe the global supermarket that is transforming agricultural production throughout the world while undercutting the capacity of nations to meet the basic food needs of their populations. Transnational food corporations are demanding an end to the system of agricultural subsidies, regulation, and protection that has maintained a relatively cheap food policy in the industrial North. At the same time, poor countries in the South that were once self-sufficient in food but are now desperate for foreign exchange to pay down their debts are forced to turn over valuable agricultural lands to transnational agribusinesses and to convert to cash-crop production while importing food products to feed their own peoples. "Export or die," is the message, but "export *and* die" is the reality. The introduction of biotech production methods — laboratory-produced vanilla, bioengineered celery, freeze-resistant flowers and tomatoes, and Bovine Growth Hormone for cows, combined with long-distance food transportation — pose further threats not only to the livelihood of traditional farmers in poor countries but also to the quality and safety of food products in general. Meanwhile, the giant food corporations — General Foods, Kraft, Pillsbury, Philip Morris, Del Monte, President's Choice, Procter and Gamble, Pepsico, and others — have merged their operations and expanded their marketing strategies on a global basis. National authorities are also finding it increasingly difficult to maintain adequate food inspection at the border, especially for the massive imports of fruits and vegetables, thereby requiring expanded use of ozone-depleting chemical fumigants such as methyl bromide.

The corporate dream of turning the whole world into a global shopping paradise is also near at hand. Not only have Coca-Cola and Marlboro become universally recognized brand names through massive corporate advertising, but global retailers such as Procter and Gamble, Philip Morris, RJR Nabisco, Kellogg, General Motors, Sears, Unilever, Pepsico, Nestlè, and McDonalds have been spending billions of advertising and promotion dollars each year to create a steadily expanding global market based on mass consumption. The strategy is to sell the same things in the same way everywhere with little or no regard for local customs, tastes, or cultural or religious differences. Giant retailers such as Wal-Mart have led the way with development of a chain of superstores designed to sell the largest range of retail consumer goods (food, clothing, hardware, furniture, pharmaceuticals, and so on) in cities and towns throughout North America. Using a variety of tactics ranging from low-wage part-time employment, misleading advertising, predatory pricing, competition law violations, and coercive sourcing from suppliers, Wal-Mart has managed to force local merchants out of business and, in some cases, create ghost towns. Now the most aggressive giant retailer in the world, Wal-Mart has plans to expand its operations into parts of Latin America, Europe, and Asia. [See chapter by Kai Mander and Alex Boston.]

## Resource Control

Transnational resource giants such as Exxon, Mitsubishi, Texas Gulf, Shell, Rio Tinto Zinc, and Alcan and a host of energy, mining, forestry, and hydro corporations have expanded their operations to the four corners of the earth, posing serious threats to the environment by causing massive oil spills, reversing river flows, flooding huge land tracts, depleting vast forest areas, eliminating fish stocks, and destroying vegetation and wildlife. The only thing new about this is the new atmosphere of deregulation in areas such as environmental protection. The resource and energy codes built into NAFTA and GATT are designed to accelerate the rapid development and export of natural resources. Moreover, "the export or die" demands of the IMF mean that poor countries with resource-based economies have no choice but to open their doors to transnational resource companies without regulation or environmental protection. Rapid exports not only accelerate the depletion of nonrenewable resources but greatly intensify the global demand for supplies of fresh water that are now being targeted by TNCs. Add to this the persistent destruction of the last rain forests plus the continuous dumping of hazardous wastes into the ecosystem by companies such as Union Carbide, Dow Chemical, and Du Pont. It leaves little wonder why the world is on the verge of an ecological holocaust.

## Banking, Insurance, Education

Transnational corporations are also rapidly taking control of basic services such as health care and education, which have been the public responsibility of governments in most countries. Through a series of vertical and horizontal mergers, a system of large-scale health care corporations is emerging. In the United States, the major drug companies such as Eli Lily are merging with health insurance industries such as PCS for the takeover of hospitals, pharmacies, free-standing clinics, nursing homes, and doctors' practices. The world's largest profit-oriented hospital companies, Columbia and Health Trust, have merged to form a giant health care corporation with sales exceeding that of Eastman Kodak or American Express. In a deregulated global economy, these new health care giants are poised to swallow up pieces of the public health care system in countries such as Canada, where there is enormous pressure to privatize. At the same time, TNCs are also invading the education system. In the United States, organizations such as the Business Higher Education Forum and the New American Schools Development Corporation (which funnels corporate finances into profit-oriented elementary schools) are composed of TNCs such as AT&T, Ford, Eastman Kodak, Pfizer, General Electric, Heinz, and many others. Companies that sport household brand names such as Coca-Cola, Pepsi, McDonalds, Burger King, and Procter and Gamble are also directly involved in developing curricula for schools along with advertising promotions to help kids grow up corporate.

## Patenting of Life Forms

While government regulations over TNCs are being dismantled in countries all over the world, the monopoly rights of the transnationals over information and technology are now internationally protected under the intellectual property rights components of GATT. Moreover, the international patent right protection has been extended to genetic materials, including seeds and natural medicines. The patenting of life forms allows

TNCs to secure widespread control over genetically engineered organisms, from micro-organisms to plants and animals. Worse still, transnationals are now able to obtain monopoly rights over genetic research, plus any products derived from that research, concerning an entire species. The W. R. Grace Corporation, for example, through its subsidiary Agracetus Inc., has secured a U.S. patent on all genetically engineered or "transgenic" cotton varieties (1992) and a European patent on all transgenic soybeans (1994). In addition, it has applications pending in other countries including India, China, and Brazil, to take control of 60 percent of the world's cotton crop. Under these conditions, farmers who traditionally save seed from one harvest to replant for the next crop find themselves in violation of international patent law. Unless they pay a royalty to the TNC that owns the patented seed, farmers around the world are now prohibited from growing their own seed stocks. Furthermore, there are moves to have these global monopoly rights and patent protection laws extended to include the cloning of human embryos. [See chapters by Andrew Kimbrell and by Vandana Shiva and Radha Holla-Bhar.]

## Cultural Cloning

Armed with satellite communications, global entertainment corporations are selling their pop music cultural products all over the world. The target audience of this global entertainment industry is the two-fifths of the world's population who are under the age of twenty. The biggest technological leap in the global entertainment industry came with MTV in the 1980s. By 1993, MTV programs were reaching 210 million households in seventy-one countries throughout the world. Bertelsman's pop music empire presently dominates youth markets throughout Europe, North America, and Latin America and is now moving into Asia. Sony, Philips, and Matsushita have also been expanding into these markets.

Increasingly, the big six global entertainment corporations are focusing their energies on opening up markets in Latin America and Asia, where the greatest growth potential exists. But this expansion is also being challenged as a new form of cultural imperialism. For the poor countries of Asia, Africa, and Latin America the big six's penetration of transnational sound will choke off traditional music of the local culture and restrict employment opportunities for local artists. At the same time, the global entertainment industry will increasingly generate a homogenized culture that reflects Western corporate values and priorities. [See chapter on homogenization of global culture by Richard Barnet and John Cavanagh.]

## NEW BASES FOR SOCIAL ACTION

The best hope for countering growing corporate domination lies in the building of social movements in which people reclaim their sovereign rights over TNCs and banks.

Most people now feel that they have lost control over their economic, social, and ecological future. This is not only true among the poor majority in the South, following the damage done by massive SAPs, but increasingly among the majority of working, middle-class peoples in the North. For many, the dream of securing a full-time job, a relatively stable and crime-free community, or a clean environment with a bright future for their children has been shattered. In this climate, the politics of fear and insecurity have become rampant in most of our countries, expressing themselves sometimes as ethnic violence or, more recently, as right-wing citizen militias.

Underlying the politics of fear and insecurity is the fundamental question of democracy itself. These conditions, in turn, could create new political opportunities for building social movements to re-establish democratic control.

### Popular Sovereignty

In the building of social movements today, emphasis must be placed on the notion of popular sovereignty as a common base for action. Throughout this century alone, peoples all over the world have fought for the recognition of fundamental democratic and human rights — the right to adequate food, clothing, and shelter; the right to employment, education, and health care; the right to a clean environment, social equality, and public services — and the right to self-determination and participation in the decisions that affect these rights. Together, these basic communal rights, which constitute the core of popular sovereignty, have been codified and enshrined in the Universal Declaration of Human Rights, the International Covenant on Economic, Social, and Cultural Rights, and the International Covenant on Civil and Political Rights.

The emergence of the corporate state, however, wherein the reins of democratic governance have been taken over by corporations and banks, has completely disfigured and distorted the responsibilities of the national governments. The moral and political obligations of nation-states to intervene in the market economy have been eliminated in order to ensure that the entire national system — economic, fiscal, social, cultural, environmental, political — functions for the purpose of providing a profitable climate for transnational investment and competition in the new global economy. As the politics of insecurity unfold, however, a brand of right-wing nationalism is likely to arise with new forms of protectionism against immigration and cheap imports for the major TNCs — in other words, protectionism for the powerful. In this climate, social movements must focus their energies on resisting the corporate state and the rise of the new right-wing nationalism. Peoples' energies need to be mobilized around a new social vision of the nation-state in an age of global interdependence, where governments reclaim the power and tools necessary to exercise democratic control over TNCs and banks. In effect, the nation-state must be retooled to serve the people's rights to determine their economic, social, and ecological future. But this new nationalism must be simultaneously carried out in concert with social movements in other countries that are engaged in similar struggles.

## Citizens' Manifesto

In order to build social movements in both North and South that are committed to re-establishing democratic control, a common platform and agenda need to be developed. This could take the form of a common manifesto for citizens of the world, which would include (1) a declaration of the fundamental rights of people to determine their own economic, social, and ecological future; (2) the sovereign rights of peoples over TNCs and banks; (3) the demand that TNCs meet certain basic economic, social, and environmental conditions; (4) the insistence that governments develop and enact new regulatory measures for exercising democratic control over TNCs; and (5) the responsibility of social movements to take whatever forms of action are needed to ensure that peoples' basic rights are upheld and that democratic control over TNCs is maintained. The core of this citizens manifesto would be the spirit and practice of popular sovereignty. Its primary purpose would be to provide social movements in both the North and the South with a common platform for action in dismantling the corporate state and challenging the operations of TNCs at local, regional, national, and international levels.

# 27

# THE RULES OF
# CORPORATE BEHAVIOR

## Jerry Mander

*The main factors that determine corporate behavior have far less to do with the people who work inside the corporate structure than they do with the corporate structure itself. The people inside corporations are simply following the legal and "ethical" standards of corporate form. Profit comes first; growth is a close second; amorality — not morality — comes third; and there are quite a few more. To ask corporations to behave better by making growth and profit a lower priority or to act foremost in the interests of local communities, the environment, or the workers is like asking armies to give up guns. Managers who might personally like to develop more pro-social or pro-environment policies are constrained; they cannot give such factors higher priority than the bottom line, or they may find themselves out of work. This chapter describes some of the inherent rules that govern corporate behavior.*

$I$N THE PREVIOUS chapter, Tony Clarke described in exquisite detail the global role corporations now play. Myriad other chapters in this book describe specific negative behaviors by corporations: factory closings and export of jobs; toxic dumpings; genetic piracy; terrible environmental destruction; and the abandonment of communities for "free trade zones," where environmental and social laws are lax. But one important issue remains: Why do they behave this way?

Most people tend to see corporate behavior as merely reflecting *human greed*, and the problems with corporations as stemming strictly from the makeup of the people within the corporate structure — people who are inevitably irresponsible, dishonest, overly ambitious, or otherwise so self-interested as to eschew moral, ethical, social, and environmental values.

To see corporate behavior as rooted in the people who work within them is far too narrow a view, and, in the end, excuses corporations from their ultimate responsibilities, for it puts the blame on individuals. In fact, the basic problems with corporations are structural, and inherent in the forms and rules by which they are compelled to operate. The corporation is not as subject to human control as most people believe it is; rather, it is a largely autonomous technical structure that behaves by a system of logic uniquely well-suited to its primary functions: to make profit, to give birth and impetus to new products and technologies, to expand its reach and powers, and to spread the consumer life-style around the globe. If all the problems of corporations could be traced to the personnel involved, they could be solved by changing the personnel. Unfortunately, all employees are obligated to behave in accordance with corporate form and corporate law. If someone attempted to revolt against them, the corporation would simply throw the person out and replace her or him with someone who would play by the rules. Form determines content. Corporations are machines.

## CORPORATE CONSCIOUSNESS

The failure to grasp the nature and inevitabilities of corporate structure has left our society far too unconscious and passive to corporate desires and has helped corporations increase their global influence, power, and freedom from accountability. More than any other institution (including government), corporations dominate our conceptions of how life should be lived. Corporate ideology, corporate priorities, corporate styles of behavior, corporate value systems, and corporate modes of organization have become synonymous with "our way of life." *Corporate culture* has become the virtual definition of American life, to be defended at all costs, even militarily. Now that global trade agreements have removed most obstacles to corporate invasion of all the countries of the world, and with the power of U.S. media globally dominant, U.S. corporate culture will soon be ubiquitous.

If you switch on your radio, flip on the television, or open your newspaper, corporations speak to you. They do it through public relations and through advertising. U.S. corporations spend more than $150 billion yearly on advertising, which is far more than is spent on all secondary education in this country. In some ways, corporate advertising is the dominant educational institution in our country, surely in the realm of life-style.

According to *Advertising Age*, about 75 percent of commercial network television time is paid for by the hundred largest corporations in the country. Many people do not react to this statistic as being important. But consider that there are presently 450,000 corporations in the United States and some 250 million people with extremely diverse viewpoints about life-style, politics, and personal and national priorities. Yet, only one hundred corporations get to decide what will appear on television and what will not. These corporations do not overtly announce their refusal to finance programs that contain views disconsonant with their own; their control is far more subtle. When television producers think about which programs to produce, they have to subordinate other considerations to the need to sell the programs to corporate backers. An effective censorship results.

While one hundred corporations pay for 75 percent of commercial broadcast time and thereby dominate the commercial channels, they now also pay for more than 50 percent of public television. During the Reagan years, federal support for noncommercial television was virtually eliminated, leaving a void that public television filled by appealing to corporations. In 1995, the Gingrich-led Congress threatened to remove the remainder of public support, leaving the field entirely to corporations. As corporate influence grows in "public" television, so do the visibility and length of the corporate commercial tags before and after the shows they sponsor. Whereas public television once featured such modest messages as, "This program has been brought to you through a grant by Exxon," now we see the Exxon logo, followed by an added advertising phrase or two and an audio slogan. Recently, several so-called "noncommercial" TV stations, such as PBS affiliate KQED-TV in San Francisco, have announced that they will accept commercials. This, of course, was the original intention of defunding them, from Reagan to Gingrich.

The average U.S. viewer already watches 22,000 commercials every year. Twenty-two thousand times, corporations place images in our brains to suggest that there is something great about buying commodities. Some commercials advertise cars; others advertise drugs — but all commercials agree that you should buy *something* and that human life is most satisfying when inundated with commodities. Between commercials there are programs, also created by corporations, that espouse values consistent with the ads.

Corporations are also the major providers of educational materials for U.S. schools and, as Maude Barlow and Heather-jane Robertson point out in their chapter, in Canada and other countries, too. Some of the largest corporations are now providing books, tapes, films, and computer programs free of charge to public and private schools, as a "public service" in these budget-conscious times. They get a lot of praise for these contributions. Oil and chemical companies have been particularly generous in providing materials to help explain nature to young people. The materials portray nature as a valuable resource for human use and celebrate concepts such as "managing nature" through chemicals, pesticides, and large-scale agribusiness. Thus, a generation of American youngsters is trained to regard nature in a way that coincides with corporate objectives.

This same ideological training via television is inevitably becoming the norm all over the world. It is a further expression of the way corporations create the ideal conditions for their own expansion.

## CORPORATE SHAME

I keep awaiting the day when the president of a Fortune 500 company expresses shame for a corporate transgression against the public or the environment. The statement would go something like this: "On behalf of my company, its management, and its shareholders, I wish to express our grief concerning injuries suffered by people living downstream from our factory, along the Green River. We are ashamed to admit that over the years, our poisonous wastes have found their way into the river, putting the community in peril. We will do anything to relieve the suffering we have caused. We are also concerned that safe storage for such potent chemicals now seems impossible, and so henceforth we will use our facilities only for safer forms of manufacturing. Under no circumstances will we give thought to abandoning this community or its workers."

No such statements are made for several reasons. No manager of a publicly held company could *ever* place community welfare above corporate interest. An individual executive might personally wish to do so, but such a gesture could subject the company to seriously damaging lawsuits by victims. It could also open management to lawsuits from its shareholders. Corporate law holds that management of publicly held companies must act primarily in the economic interests of shareholders. So managers are actually legally *obligated* to *ignore* community welfare issues (such as worker health and satisfaction and environmental concerns) if those needs interfere with profitability. And corporate managers must deny that corporate acts have any negative impact if that impact might translate into costly damage suits that reduce profits.

As a result, we have witnessed countless cases in which companies deny any responsibility for corporate acts that caused death, injury, or illness. We have heard cigarette company executives lie, with great transparency, about the products' harmful effects. We have heard the same from manufacturers of pesticides, chemicals, asbestos materials, and birth-control technologies.

In instances such as these, withholding information means that people — perhaps tens of thousands of people — become sick. Some people die. In other contexts, murder charges would be in order.

## CORPORATE SCHIZOPHRENIA

That murder charges are not levied against corporations, and that corporations do not express shame at their own actions, is a direct result of the peculiar nature of corporate form, its split personality. Though human beings work inside corporations, a corporation itself is not a person (except in the legal sense) and does not have feelings. A corporation is not even a thing. It may have offices and/or a factory where it may manufacture products, but a corporation does not have any physical existence or form — no *corporality*. So when conditions in a community or country become unfavorable — safety standards become too rigid, or workers are not submissive — a corporation can dematerialize and rematerialize in another town or country. This tendency is dramatically accelerated under the new free trade regimes.

If a corporation is not a person or thing, what is it? It is basically a *concept* that is given a name, and a legal existence, on paper. Though there is no such actual creature, our laws recognize the corporation as an entity. So does the population. We think of corporations as having concrete form, but their true existence is only on paper and in our minds.

Even more curious than a corporation's ephemeral quality is the way our laws give this nonexistent entity a great many rights similar to those given to human beings. The law calls corporations *fictitious persons*, with the right to buy and sell property or to sue in court for injuries, slander, and libel. And *corporate speech* — advertising, public relations — is protected under the First Amendment to the Constitution governing freedom of speech. This latter right has been extended to corporations despite the fact that when the Bill of Rights was written in 1792, corporations as we now know them did not exist. (The First Amendment was originally intended to protect *personal* speech in a century when the media consisted only of single news sheets, handbills, and books. The net result of expanding First Amendment protection to corporate speech is that $150 billion worth of advertising from a relative handful of sources gets to dominate public perception, free from nearly all government attempts at regulation.)

Though corporations enjoy many "human" rights, they have not been required to abide by human responsibilities. Even in cases of negligence causing death or injury, the state cannot jail or execute the corporation. In rare instances, individuals within a corporation can be prosecuted if they perpetrate acts that they know cause injury. And a corporation may be fined or ordered to alter practices, but its structure is never altered — its "life" is never threatened. Unlike human beings, corporations do not die a natural death. A corporation usually outlives the human beings who have been a part of it, even those who own it. A corporation actually has the possibility of immortality.

Lacking the sort of physical, organic reality that characterizes human existence, this entity, this concept, this collection of paperwork called a *corporation* is not capable of feelings such as shame or remorse. Instead, corporations behave according to their own unique system of standards, rules, forms, and objectives, enshrined in state charters and confirmed through our legal structures.

## THE INHERENT RULES
## OF CORPORATE BEHAVIOR

The most basic rule of corporate operation is that it must show a profit over time. Among publicly held companies there is a second basic rule: It must expand and grow, since growth is the standard by which the stock market judges a company. All other values are secondary: the welfare of the community, the happiness of workers, the health of the planet, and even the general prosperity.

So human beings within the corporate structure, whatever their personal morals and feelings, are prevented from operating on their own standards. Like the assembly-line workers who must operate at the speed of the machine, corporate employees are strapped onto the apparatus of the corporation and forced to operate by its rules.

In this sense, a corporation is essentially a machine, a technological structure, an organization that follows its own principles and its own morality. In such a structure, human morality is anomalous. Because of this double standard — one for real human beings and another for fictitious persons such as corporations — we sometimes see bizarre behavior from executives who, though presumably knowing what is right and moral, behave in a contrary fashion.

For example, in 1986, Union Carbide's chemical plant in Bhopal, India, accidentally released methyl isocyanate into the air, injuring some 200,000 people and killing more than 6,000. Soon after the accident, the chair of the board of Union Carbide, Warren M. Anderson, was so upset at what happened he informed the media that he would spend the rest of his life attempting to correct the problems his company had caused and to make amends. Only one year later, however, Mr. Anderson was quoted in *Business Week* as saying that he had "overreacted," and was now prepared to lead the company in its legal fight *against* paying damages and reparations. What happened? Very simply, Mr. Anderson at first reacted as a human being. Later he realized (and perhaps was pressed to realize) that this reaction was inappropriate for a chair of the board of a company whose obligations are not to the poor victims of Bhopal but to shareholders; that is, to its profit picture. If Mr. Anderson had persisted in expressing his personal feelings or acknowledging the company's culpability, he certainly would have been fired.

Clearly, human beings within corporations are seriously constrained in their ability to act out of their personal sense of right and wrong. And yet, I have mentioned only two of the rules that serve to constrain this influence: the profit imperative and the need for growth. The following list is an attempt to articulate some of the obligatory rules by which corporations operate. Taken together, they help reveal why corporations behave as they do today and how they have come to dominate their environment and the human beings within it.

## ELEVEN RULES OF CORPORATE BEHAVIOR

### 1. The Profit Imperative

This is the ultimate measure of corporate decisions. It takes precedence over community well-being, worker health, public health, peace, environmental preservation, or national security. Corporations will even find ways of trading with national "enemies" — Libya, Iran, Cuba — though public policy may abhor it. The profit imperative and the growth imperative are the most fundamental corporate drives; together they represent the corporation's instinct to live.

## 2. The Growth Imperative

Corporations live or die by whether they can sustain growth. Growth determines relationships to investors, to the stock market, to banks, and to public perception. The growth imperative also fuels the corporate desire to find and develop scarce resources in obscure parts of the world.

This effect is now clearly visible, as the world's few remaining pristine places are sacrificed to corporate production. The peoples who inhabit these resource-rich regions are similarly pressured to give up their traditional ways and climb onto the production-consumption wheel. Corporate planners consciously attempt to bring "less developed societies into the modern world" in order to create both infrastructures for development and a cadre of new workers and consumers. Corporations claim they do this for altruistic reasons — to raise the living standard — but corporations have no altruism.

Theoretically, *privately held corporations* — those owned by individuals or families — do not have any intrinsic imperative to expand. In practice however, the behavior is usually the same. There are economies of scale and usually increased profits from growth. Privately held giants such as Bechtel Corporation have shown no propensity to moderate growth; their behavior, in fact, shows quite the opposite. And even among smaller privately held companies — "green" companies with "enlightened" management — resistance to growth is difficult. Banks will resist funding companies that limit their growth. And even internally, middle managers and staff tend to see their opportunities for the future diminished. Corporate "culture" abhors limiting goals and profits.

## 3. Competition and Aggression

On the one hand, corporations require a high degree of cooperation within management. On the other hand, they place every person in management in fierce competition with each other. Anyone interested in a corporate career must hone his or her abilities to seize the moment, to gain an edge over another company or over a colleague within the company. As an employee, you are expected to be a part of the "team" — you must aggressively push to win against the other corporations — but you also must be ready to climb over your own colleagues.

## 4. Amorality

Not being human, not having feelings, corporations do not have morals or altruistic goals. So decisions that may be antithetical to community goals or environmental health are made without misgivings. In fact, corporate executives tend to praise nonemotionality as a basis for "objective" decisions.

Corporations, however, seek to hide their amorality and attempt to act as if they were altruistic. Lately, U.S. industry has made a concerted effort to seem concerned with contemporary social issues such as environmental cleanups, community arts, or drug rehabilitation programs. Corporations' efforts to exhibit social responsibility occur precisely because they are innately *not* responsible to the public. They have little interest in community goals except the ones that serve their purposes.

For example, corporations have taken to advertising about how they work to clean the environment. A company that installs offshore oil rigs will run ads that show fish thriving under the rigs. Logging companies known for their clear-cutting practices will run millions of dollars' worth of ads about their tree farms, as if they were interested in renewable resources when they are not.

In fact, it is a fair rule of thumb that corporations will tend to advertise the very qualities they do not have in order to allay a negative public perception. When corporations say "we care," it is almost always in response to the widespread perception that they do not care. And they don't. How could they? Corporations do not have feelings or morals. All their acts are in service to profit.

## 5. Hierarchy

Corporate law requires that corporations be structured into classes of superiors and subordinates within a centralized pyramidal structure: chairman, directors, CEO, vice presidents, division managers, and so on. The efficiency of this hierarchical form, which also characterizes the military, the government, and most institutions in our society, is rarely questioned. (Lately, there has been some focus on new Japanese-style "flat" structures, but these function only at levels below top management and do not set overall corporate policy.)

These pervasive, hierarchical forms make it seem natural to us that we have all been placed within a pecking order. Some jobs are better than others; some life-styles are better than others; some neighborhoods, some races, some kinds of knowledge. Men over women. Westerners over non-Westerners. Humans over nature. Most Americans barely realize that effective, nonhierarchical modes of organization exist on the planet and have been successful for millennia.

## 6. Quantification, Linearity, and Segmentation

Corporations require that subjective information be translated into objective form, that is, into numbers. This excludes from the decision-making process all values that cannot be quantified in such a way. The subjective or spiritual aspects of forests, for example, cannot be quantified and so do not enter corporate equations. Forests are evaluated as "board feet." Production elements that pose a danger to public health or welfare — pollution, toxic waste, carcinogens — are translated to value-free objective concepts such as "cost-benefit ratio" or "trade-off." Auto manufacturers evaluating the safety level of certain production standards calculate the number of probable accidents and deaths at each level of the standard. This number is then compared with the cost of insurance payments and lawsuits from dead drivers' families. A number is also assigned to the public relations problem, and a balance is sought.

The drive toward objectification enters every aspect of corporate activity. For example, on the production end, great effort is made, through time-and-motion studies, to measure each fragment of every process performed by a worker. The goal is to segment tasks sufficiently for them to be eventually automated, and workers eliminated altogether. Where the task is not automated, it is reduced to its simplest repetitive form. As a result, workers become subject to intense comparisons with other workers. If they survive on the job, the repetitive task leaves them horribly bored and without a sense of participating in corporate goals. They feel like mere cogs in the machine, and they are.

## 7. Dehumanization

Just as the environment and the community are objectified by corporations, and all the decisions are measured against public relations or profit standards, so is the employee objectified and dehumanized.

Corporations make a conscious effort to depersonalize. The recent introduction of computer surveillance technology into business operations, especially in measuring and supervising the performance of office workers, has made this dehumanization task simpler and more thorough. Now, every keystroke and every word of every worker can be counted by a central computer that compares each individual's performance against others and against corporate standards. Those people found to be too slow or inconsistent, or who take too many breaks, are simpler to find and to discipline or dismiss.

As for management employees, though not subject to quite the same indignities, they nonetheless must practice a style of decision making that "does not let feelings get in the way." This applies as much to firing employees as it does to dealing with the consequences of corporate behavior in the environment or the community.

## 8. Exploitation

All corporate profit is obtained by a simple formula: Profit equals the difference between the amount paid to an employee and the economic value of the employee's output. It also equals the difference between the amount paid for raw materials used in production (including processing costs) and the ultimate sales price of the processed raw materials. Karl Marx was right: A worker is not compensated for the full value of his or her labor; neither is the raw material supplier. The owners of capital skim off part of the value as profit. Profit is based on underpayment.

Capitalists argue that this is a fair deal, since both workers and the people who mine or farm the resources (usually in Third World environments) get paid something. But the arrangement is inherently imbalanced. The owner of the capital — the corporation or the bank — always obtains additional benefit. While the worker earns a wage, the owner of the capital receives the benefit of the worker's labor plus the surplus profit the worker produces, which is then reinvested to produce yet more surplus. This even applies to the rare cases where workers are very highly paid, as with professional athletes and entertainers. In those cases, the corporations pay high wages because the workers will generate more income (and thus more profit) for the corporations. So the formula remains intact: Profit is based on paying less than actual value for workers and resources.

## 9. Ephemerality and Mobility

Corporations exist beyond time and space. As we have seen, they are legal creations that exist only on paper. They do not die a natural death; they outlive their own creators. And, especially under the new rules of global trade, they have no commitment to locality, employees, or neighbors. This makes the modern global corporation entirely different from the bakers or grocers of previous years who survived by cultivating relationships with their neighbors, their customers. Having no morality, no commitment to place, and no physical nature (a factory someplace, while being a physical entity, is not the corporation), a corporation can relocate all of its operations to another place at the first sign of inconvenience: demanding employees, too high taxes, restrictive environmental laws. The traditional ideal of community engagement is antithetical to corporate behavior.

## 10. Opposition to Nature

Though some individuals who work for corporations may personally love nature, corporations themselves and corporate societies are intrinsically committed to intervening in, altering, and transforming the natural world. For corporations engaged in commodity manufacturing, profit comes from transmogrifying raw materials into salable forms. Metals from the ground are converted into cars. Trees are converted into boards and then into houses, furniture, and paper products. Oil is converted into energy. In all such activity, a piece of nature is taken from where it belongs and processed into a new form. In rare instances, elements of nature can be renewed, or trees can be replanted, but even in such cases they do not return to their original forms. So all manufacturing activity depends upon intervention in and reorganization of nature. After natural resources are used up in one part of the globe, the corporation moves on to another part.

This transformation of nature occurs in all societies where manufacturing takes place. But in capitalist corporate societies, and especially in a global economy, the process is accelerated because capitalist societies and corporations must grow. Extracting resources from nature everywhere on Earth and reprocessing them at an ever-quickening pace is intrinsic to corporate existence. Meanwhile, the consumption end of the cycle is also accelerated — corporations have an intrinsic interest in convincing people that commodities bring satisfaction. Modes of fulfillment that are based on self-sufficiency — inner satisfaction, contentment in nature or in relationships, satisfaction with one's material possessions — are subversive to corporate goals. The net effect is the corporate ravaging of nature.

## 11. Homogenization

U.S. rhetoric claims that commodity society delivers greater choice and diversity than other societies. *Choice* in this context means product choice, choice in the marketplace: many brands to choose from and diverse features on otherwise identical products (such as flashing lights on toasters). Actually, corporations have a stake in all of us living our lives in a similar manner, achieving our pleasures from the things that we buy. While it is true that different corporations seek different segments of the market — elderly people, let's say, or organic food buyers — all corporations share an identical economic, cultural, and social vision and seek to accelerate the social and individual acceptance of that vision.

Life-styles and economic systems that emphasize sharing commodities and labor, that do not encourage commodity accumulation, or that celebrate nonmaterial values, are not good for business. People living collectively, for example, sharing expensive hard goods such as washing machines, cars, and appliances — or worse, getting along without them — are outrageous to corporate commodity society. The nuclear family is a far better idea for maintaining corporate commodity society: Each family lives alone in a single-family home and has all the same machines as every other family on the block. Recently, the singles phenomenon has proved even more productive than the nuclear family, since each person duplicates the consumption of every other person.

As for Native societies, which celebrate an utterly nonmaterial relationship to life, the planet, and the spirit and whose life-styles are completely antithetical to corporate ideology, they are regarded as inferior and unenlightened. Backward. We are told they envy the choices we have. To the degree Native societies continue to exist, they represent a threat to the homogenization of worldwide markets and culture. Corporate society works hard to retrain such people in attitudes and values appropriate to corporate goals. But in the nonindustrial parts of the world, where corporations are just arriving, the ideological retraining process is just getting under way. Satellite communications technology, which brings Western television and advertising, is combined with a technical infrastructure to speed up the pace of development. Most of this activity is funded by the World Bank and the International Monetary Fund along with agencies such as U.S. AID, the Inter-American Bank, and the Asian-American Bank, all of which serve multinational corporate enterprise.

As for the ultimate goal? In the book *Trilateralism* (1980), editor Holly Sklar quotes the president of Nabisco Corporation: "One world of homogenous consumption . . . [I am] looking forward to the day when Arabs and Americans, Latins and Scandinavians will be munching Ritz crackers as enthusiastically as they already drink Coke or brush their teeth with Colgate."

## FORM IS CONTENT

The most important aspect of these rules is the degree to which they are inherent in corporate structure. Corporations are inherently bold, aggressive, and competitive. Though they exist in a society that claims to operate by moral principles, they are structurally amoral. It is inevitable that they will dehumanize the larger society as well. They are disloyal to workers, including their own managers. If community goals conflict with corporate goals, then corporations are similarly disloyal to the communities they may have been a part of for many years. It is inherent in corporate activity that they seek to drive all consciousness into one-dimensional channels. They must attempt to dominate alternative cultures and effectively clone the world population into a form more to their liking. Corporations do not care about nations; they live beyond national boundaries. They are intrinsically committed to destroying nature. And they have an inexorable, unabatable, voracious need to grow and expand. In dominating other cultures, in digging up the earth, corporations blindly follow the codes that have been built into them. It is as if such codes were part of their genetic programming. [See also chapter by Richard L. Grossman and Frank T. Adams, who discuss the role of state charters and court decisions in confirming the rules of corporate activity.]

Articulating these principles of corporate form now gives us a picture we should have had a long time ago. Now that we see the inherent direction of corporate activity, we must abandon the assumption that the form of the corporate structure is neutral. Given the rules of corporate operation, to ask corporate executives to behave in a morally defensible manner is absurd. Corporations and the people within them are not subject to appeals toward moral behavior. They are following a system of logic and rules that leads them inexorably toward dominant behavior. Form is content.

# 28

# "CITIZEN" GE

## William Greider

*When we evaluate corporations as political players, we tend to think of their political donations. Here, William Greider uses the example of General Electric to illustrate that corporations operate in a far more comprehensive way, attempting to rewrite laws, control public agencies, create new institutions favorable to their purposes, and undertake long-term public education — from grade schools to mass media advertising — to sell concepts and policies that serve corporate conceptual frameworks for "future generations."*

*William Greider writes on politics for* Rolling Stone *magazine and is former assistant managing editor of the* Washington Post. *His books include* Who Will Tell the People? *(1992), and* Secrets of the Temple *(1987).*

CORPORATIONS, by their nature, do not function as democratic organizations, yet it is they who have stepped into the vacuum created by failed political institutions and taken up the daily work of politics. Their tremendous financial resources, the diversity of their interests, their squads of talented professionals — all these assets and some others are now relentlessly focused on the politics of governing. The reality can be adequately demonstrated by describing the politics of one outstanding example among many — an especially skillful political organization known as the General Electric Company. Like many other major companies, "Citizen GE" is active in everyday politics despite its anomalous status as an ex-convict.

Phillip A. Lacovara, a former Watergate prosecutor and the top litigator in a Washington law firm, joined GE for the chance, he said, to be "involved in major policy and issues." As GE's chief of litigation, Lacovara expected to write friend-of-the-court briefs on such diverse matters as the

First Amendment and securities law, government contracts and corporate responsibility. "GE recognizes that as a major economic entity it has the stature and responsibility to form opinions," he explained.

One of Lacovara's first projects at GE was to try to head off the new corporate sentencing guidelines being prepared for the federal courts — guidelines intended to stiffen the consequences for corporations that break the law. General Electric has more than a theoretical interest in this policy question, since the company itself has been convicted of a series of crimes in recent years, including defrauding the federal government. The legal standards for corporate criminality, Lacovara argued, "should be narrowed substantially."

Companies cannot be held responsible for the transgression of far-flung employees, Lacovara argued in comments he filed with the U.S. Sentencing Commission. Instead of stiffer penalties for corporate violators, Lacovara suggested that federal prosecutors ought to offer special rewards to companies that cooperate with the government — lenient fines and forgiveness — in order to encourage what he called the "good corporate citizen."

When the Justice Department endorsed a draft of the more severe sentencing guidelines in the spring of 1989, the GE lawyers took their complaint to the White House. An associate of Lacovara's warned the president's legal counsel that the proposed guidelines were "a corporate death sentence." George Bush's lawyer made some phone calls. The Justice Department backed off and withdrew its endorsement ("Preliminary Comments of General Electric Company on the U.S. Sentencing Commission's Proposed Organizational Sanctions," Sept. 11, 1989).

As this episode suggests, there are no longer any distinct boundary lines between law, politics, and corporate management. In the modern milieu of governing, these are all the same subject. General Electric recognizes this reality more astutely than most and, as GE General Counsel Ben Heineman explained to the *American Lawyer*, GE was beefing up its legal department to take "an aggressive, offensive look at the problems in the company." GE's lawyers, Heineman said, would track not just litigation but also new legislation and regulation, alongside the company's lobbyists. "Preventing litigation is one thing," Heineman said. "But how do you calculate [the benefit] if you change a regulation or work something out with Congress?"

•  •  •

GE is the United States' second-largest plastics manufacturer and, therefore, keenly interested in environmental law enforcement. But then it also manufactures pollution-control systems. Its medical diagnostic equipment leads the world market — as do GE circuit breakers, industrial turbines, electric motors, and aircraft engines. The company is intensely engaged in trade policy and the emerging global economy.

GE is a stockbroker, since it owns the Kidder Peabody brokerage. GE is also a major bank, since its financial subsidiary, GE Capital, has $91 billion in assets — equivalent in size to the fourth-largest U.S. commercial bank. General Electric is also a media giant, since it owns the NBC network and NBC's seven local television stations and has footholds in television broadcasting in three other countries. It purchased Financial News Network and closed it down in order to eliminate competition for its own cable venture, the Consumer News/Business Channel.

For all these reasons, General Electric is a conglomerate that, in addition to its productive, profit-making activities, also functions as a ubiquitous political organization. With great sophistication and tenacity, GE represents its own interests in the political arena, as one would expect. But that is not what makes it so influential.

General Electric also tries to act like a mediating institution, speaking on behalf of others. Like many other companies, GE claims to represent various groups of other citizens in politics: workers, consumers, shareholders, even other businesses and the well-being of Americans at large. GE has the resources to develop and promote new political ideas and to organize public opinion around its political agenda. It has the capacity to advise and intervene and sometimes veto. It has the power to punish political opponents. It also has the sophistication to lend its good name to worthy causes, such as the Urban League, that are only remotely related to the company's profits.

In Washington, GE has a permanent team of two dozen lobbyists with a large support staff, but, as the need arises, it regularly hires outside lawyers and lobbyists for targeted assignments.

Like other companies, GE finances the politicians in both parties. During the 1988 election cycle, GE political action committees (PACs) contributed $595,000 to congressional campaigns. One year, the company also paid $47,000 directly to senators and representatives to listen to these public officials give speeches (the speakers, it turns out, were mostly members of the armed services and defense appropriations committees). The second-ranking lobbyist in GE's Washington office, Robert W. Barrio, is a leading "money guy" for congressional Democrats and always willing to get on the phone and canvass the lobbying community for money.

GE is also a social philanthropist. Its tax-exempt foundations gave away $18.8 million in 1989, mostly to colleges and school systems, including major commitments to scholarships for the poor and racial minorities. Like any other good citizen, GE donates to United Way and other local community projects. Alongside the company's 1989 earnings of $3.9 billion, GE's sense of charity does not seem too immoderate.

But the corporation's philanthropy also serves its own political objectives in direct ways. GE's tax-exempt contributions went, for instance, to lobbyist Charles Walker's American Council for Capital Formation (an "educational" front group that campaigns against the corporate income tax and for a national sales tax), the Institute for International Economics (a think tank that promotes the multinational corporate line on trade and economic policy), and Americans for Generational Equity (an issues front that campaigns for cuts in entitlement programs such as Social Security). GE gives substantially to the major policy think tanks that promote the conservative business perspective — the Brookings Institution and American Enterprise Institute — though not to zealously right-wing outfits such as the Heritage Foundation.

GE is also directly active in political education and propaganda. It sponsors the *McLaughlin Group*, a right-wing television talk show that is popular among political devotees for its quick, abusive style of discourse. GE is a leading member in the Business Roundtable, which disseminates the political agenda of Fortune 500 corporations. GE also enters dozens of trade associations and a continuous galaxy of temporary joint ventures such as the Superfund Coalition, formed to prepare public opinion to accept business objectives.

The Committee on the Present Danger, founded with defense-industry financing in 1976, created the propaganda base for the huge defense buildup of the 1980s. The Center for Economic Progress and Employment, despite its public-spirited title, is a front group formed by GE, Union Carbide, Ford, and other manufacturers to weaken the product-liability laws. The center financed a lengthy study attacking liability lawsuits and, for added authority, arranged to have the Brookings Institution publish it.

General Electric also fosters a positive political image directly through its own advertising — soft-focused television spots that portray GE as an admirable citizen. According to INFACT, the Boston group leading a boycott of GE products, the company tripled its image advertising to $26.8 million a year after it came under attack in the mid 1980s as a producer of nuclear weapons. The increased self-promotion also coincided, however, with GE's embarrassing criminal indictment for cheating the government on defense contracts.

What difference does all this propaganda make in terms of political action? Market research suggests that, while corporate propaganda may not do so much to reduce the public's collective distrust of business generally, individual companies can dilute the hostility directed at them.

GE accumulates power by pretending to serve as a mediating institution. The company lobbies expertly to enhance its own sales and profit, but General Electric routinely invokes millions of other citizens as the ultimate beneficiaries of its politics. When GE is threatened in Washington, it claims to be defending broader constituencies from injury. But when GE defines its policy objectives, it does not bother to consult the people it ostensibly represents. GE accepts no obligation to those for whom it claims to be speaking.

General Electric has 177 plants in the United States (plus 103 others in twenty-three foreign countries), which automatically provides a broad and varied platform of economic interests, including workers, whom it can plausibly claim to represent. Some 243,000 Americans make their living working for GE. Approximately 506,000 Americans are stockholders. About three hundred retailers, from Montgomery Ward to Levitz furniture, use credit-card systems run by GE capital. The GE-owned NBC network has two hundred affiliate stations. GE's jet-engine assembly plants in Evendale, Ohio, and Lynn, Massachusetts, make the engines for two dozen different kinds of military aircraft.

In other words, the potential span of political interests that a corporation presumes to represent can be made to look much larger than the company itself. GE's political voice multiplies itself and intersects with millions of others — people who may or may not actually agree with its political objectives. GE mobilizes allies and its local cadres — workers, managers, customers, suppliers — when they do agree. If they don't, it simply dismisses their input and merely invokes their names.

Defense issues, argued out in public on the esoteric plane of grand military strategy or weapons technology, are lobbied in private on an earthier stratum: How many jobs in my district or state are attached to this bomber or tank?

When General Electric speaks for its shareholders' interest in maximized profits, its approach necessarily becomes more oblique, since politicians are not likely to be terribly excited by the narrow goal of boosting stock values. The company's profit objective is, therefore, reformulated as a question of broad national economic policy — how to stimulate the economic growth from which the multitudes will presumably benefit.

According to GE, this goal can be achieved by cutting its taxes. Reginald H. Jones, Jack Welch's predecessor as CEO, was a much more visible political player in Washington, relentlessly selling his arguments for corporate tax relief. Jones "seemed to spend his life at the Senate Finance Committee, lobbying for tax breaks and with some success," said Robert McIntyre of Citizens for Tax Justice. "Jones was literally at every single Finance Committee hearing I ever went to. His line was the same old bullshit about how we have to increase American competitiveness and all you need to do to increase American competitiveness is reduce GE's taxes."

As it turned out, General Electric was possibly the biggest single winner in Ronald Reagan's celebrated tax cuts. It had corporate profits of $6.5 billion between 1981 and 1983 and, astonishingly, received a tax rebate of $283 million from the federal government. Its tax burden went from $330 million a year to minus $90 million a year — money the government now owed GE. By rough estimate, the 1981 tax legislation yielded as much as $1.3 billion for General Electric over several years and probably much more in the long run.

GE's windfall did not, however, create any new jobs for U.S. workers. On the contrary, the company was drastically shrinking its U.S. workforce — eliminating nearly fifty thousand people from its payroll through layoffs, attrition, and the sell-off of subsidiaries. The tax windfall, however, did help GE finance its aggressive campaign of corporate acquisitions, as it bought such important companies as Utah Construction, RCA, and NBC.

The same pattern was pervasive in U.S. business. After the generous tax cuts of 1981, capital investment by U.S. corporations accelerated, but not in the United States. The new investments were primarily made in foreign countries. U.S. taxpayers, in other words, were unwittingly subsidizing the globalization of their own industrial structure.

The distinctive quality in General Electric's politics is not its behind-the-scenes deal making or the skillful ways in which it amplifies its own interests of workers, small business, or consumers. These are the standard approaches employed by corporate political organizations of every kind.

What sets GE apart from most other companies is the seriousness with which it claims to represent people in the society whose lives are not visibly connected to the fate of General Electric — especially society's losers. These include children and poor people, disadvantaged racial minorities, and even ex-workers, the tens of thousands who lost their jobs at General Electric during the 1980s. In various ways, as GE's leaders have figured out, this claimed concern is good for the company.

GE Senior Vice President Frank Doyle has testified eloquently, for instance, on behalf of greater federal funding for Head Start and early childhood education programs, invoking an economic rationale for the company's social concern. "A competitive America — let alone a compassionate America — will need every trained mind and every pair of skilled hands," Doyle declared. "But the appalling fact is that one in five of our teenage children and younger live in poverty" (Doyle 1990).

GE cares about these children, Doyle explained, because if they are not trained for high-skill work in the global economy, they will become future costs to the society in terms of welfare and crime.

While the rhetoric sounds public-spirited and compassionate — even bleeding heart for tough-minded business executives — General Electric's social concern serves its own long-term political interests. It provides a shield against hostile political action and deflects political attention from the company's own controversial behavior in the U.S. economy. Above all, it defines the economic debate in the terms that are most congenial to GE's own future.

Like other major multinational corporations, GE wants maximum freedom to do as it chooses in the global economy — shifting production and jobs wherever it seems most profitable. And it wants minimal responsibility for the economic consequences that follow for the U.S. workforce — the steady loss of high-wage industrial jobs. The company's "social concern" is, thus, quite shallow: It cares about educating little children but accepts no responsibility for the effects their economic dislocations have on adult workers and their communities.

GE and other important corporate voices, including the Business Roundtable, instead argue that the simple remedy for job losses and the downward mobility of industrial workers is more education and better training. This analysis conveniently shifts the blame from corporations to the educational system and the workers themselves. But it requires the corporations to make a highly dubious claim: that America is facing a shortage of skilled workers.

Labor economists from the Economic Policy Institute examined the corporate claim of an impending "skills shortage" and declared it a hoax. The corporate political objective, they concluded, is to divert attention from the real labor problems — the proliferation of low-wage jobs and the declining value of industrial wages generally.

Doyle's assertion of skilled-labor shortages, in fact, comes from a company that abandoned fifty U.S. plants and shrank its overall workforce, foreign and domestic, by roughly one-fourth during the last decade. The forty-six thousand American workers let go by GE since 1981 were not mainly janitors or unskilled laborers or low-level clerks. They were people with premium wages — machinists and electricians, engineers and white-collar managers. Union leaders bitterly dubbed GE's CEO "Neutron Jack" because, like the so-called neutron bomb, Jack Welch eliminates the people and leaves the buildings standing.

Welch's strategy, widely admired in business and financial circles, is to create what he calls *a boundaryless company* — a corporation that "will recognize no distinctions between 'domestic' and 'foreign' operations." In practice, his restructurings compelled GE unions to negotiate wage contracts that were really job-shrinking agreements with provisions for severance pay and early retirement.

A politically active corporation such as General Electric operates like a modern version of the "political machine," with some of the same qualities of the old political machines that used to dominate U.S. cities. Except, of course, there is not just one urban corporate "machine" operating in U.S. politics but hundreds of them.

Unlike a party organization, however, a company such as GE does not develop its political agenda by consulting its cadres or the constituencies for whom it speaks, not even the shareholders. Most of the old local party organizations, notwithstanding their negative qualities, did give ordinary people a connecting point to government and sometimes a genuine venue for speaking to power. Political decisions are closely held in the corporate machine, not unlike the worst of the big-city political circles. The dependent constituencies are reduced to a passive role resembling that of ward heelers, with not much choice except to follow the dictates of the organization. For these political machines, there are no elections.

Above all, the formidable, ubiquitous presence of corporate political organizations persuades many citizens to retreat from the contest. That may be the gravest damage of all. Faced with this assembled power, many people accept their own perceived impotence and defer. They assume that the hard work of democracy — debating public issues, contesting elections, helping to organize their own lives — is work that belongs to others.

The price for this default is enormous in terms of government decision making. When the corporate perspective defines the outlines of debate, it shrinks the nation's political values to the amoral arithmetic of the bottom line. The rich and complicated fabric of U.S. life — and the limitless political imagination of its citizens — is reduced to sterile calculations of cost-benefit analyses. Competing political aspirations, whether for equitable taxation or environmental protection or affordable housing, are judged according to a narrow question: Is it good for the machine?

• • •

These facts add up to a daunting challenge for democracy — how to come to terms with the institutional reality of corporate power without disrupting anyone's elementary rights. The guarantees of free speech and open debate, after all, extend to agents of concentrated economic power as much as anyone else. The solution does not lie in curtailing democratic *rights* for certain parties — even though corporations are not people in any but a legal sense. It involves applying the *obligations* of citizenship to corporations as forcefully as they are applied to individuals.

Corporations claim to be "citizens" of the republic, not simply for propaganda or good public relations but in the actual legal sense of claiming constitutional rights and protections. Whatever legal theories may eventually evolve around this question, the political implications are profound. If corporations are citizens, then other citizens — the living, breathing kind — necessarily become less important to the process of self-government.

A corporation, because it is an "artificial person," has inherent capacities that mortal citizens do not possess. For one thing, it can live forever. For another, a corporation, unlike people, can exist in many places at once. Or it can alter its identity — chop off its arms or legs and transform itself into an utterly different "person." Or it can sell itself to new owners, including owners who are not themselves from the United States. Are these foreigners now empowered as U.S. "citizens" by virtue of owning a "U.S. corporation"?

Above all, a corporation by its nature possesses political resources that very few individual citizens can ever hope to accumulate. Thus, if corporations are to be regarded as citizens, they are equipped to hold the front rank in U.S. politics, and nearly everyone else will inevitably become citizens of the second class.

But the corporate claim to citizenship raises a crucial contradiction: When corporations commit crimes, they do not wish to be treated as people but as "artificial legal entities" that cannot be held personally accountable for their misdeeds. When individual citizens are convicted of a felony, they automatically lose their political rights — the right to vote, the right to hold office — and sometimes their personal freedom as well. More broadly, ex-convicts are not normally invited to testify before congressional hearings or to advise the White House on important policies.

When corporations are convicted of crimes, they lose none of their diverse abilities to act in politics. Corporations are "citizens" who regularly offend the law — both in the criminal sense and in the civil terms of flouting regulatory statutes. Yet their formidable influence on political decisions goes forward undiminished, along with the substantial financial rewards they harvest from government.

This contradiction is not a narrow complaint against a handful of corporate rogues. It applies generally to many (though not all) of the nation's leading corporations — Fortune 500 names that are regularly listed as "defendants" for criminal activity or civil complaints. Reforming the permissiveness and nonenforcement of modern laws cannot possibly be accomplished without addressing the ambiguous terms by which corporations presume to be citizens.

General Electric, for instance, is certainly not the worst "corporate citizen" in the land, but the company has accumulated an impressive rap sheet in recent years. Understandably, GE does not depict this side of its character in its engaging corporate-image commercials.

After a fourteen-week trial in 1990, a jury in Philadelphia convicted GE of criminal fraud for cheating the Army on a $254 million contract for battlefield computers. Rather than appeal, GE paid $16.1 million in criminal and civil fines, including $11.7 million to settle government complaints that it had padded its bids on two hundred other military and space contracts. In Cincinnati, GE agreed to pay the government $3.5 million to settle five civil lawsuits alleging contractor fraud at the Evendale, Ohio, jet-engine plant. A machinist at Evendale came forward and accused company managers of altering nine thousand daily labor vouchers to inflate its Pentagon billings for military jet engines.

Given this record, one begins to grasp why GE wants the best lawyers it can find, especially lawyers familiar with Washington. GE has cheated the Army, Navy, and Air Force. A defense contractor such as GE is sometimes "suspended" from doing business with the Pentagon, but, in GE's case, the disbarment is always lifted in time for the next round of contracts. GE has been convicted of offending the law in numerous other areas, including bribery, employment discrimination, insider trading, and price fixing.

General Electric is implicated in a harrowing list of places ruined by pollution. Four of GE's factories were on the EPA's list of the most dangerous industrial sources of toxic air pollution. The company has been identified as responsible for contributing to the damage at forty-seven Superfund sites. In Alabama, General Electric (and Monsanto) settled out of court when the state sued it for dumping PCBs in the Coosa River. In New York, a 40-mile stretch of the Hudson River above Albany was polluted in the same way; GE has been arguing with state officials for fifteen years over the multimillion-dollar cleanup for the river. Meanwhile, GE agreed with New York authorities to spend $20 million restoring the groundwater at its Waterford, New York, plant contaminated with benzene, trichloroethylene, vinyl chloride, and other toxics. In New Hampshire and Massachusetts, GE and forty-eight other companies settled for

$33.1 million for illegally dumping toxics at four sites. In Ohio, GE was part of a $13.5 million cleanup agreement for a chemical dump site in the Cincinnati suburbs. And so on.

The basic question is, What exactly produces this repetition of injurious or illegal behavior by corporations? It is not properly blamed on the ethical failings of company managers, who, as indiviuals, are presumably as moral as anyone else in the society. The core cause is the corporation's own values — an ethic of efficiency that creates the cost-cutting imperative that drives every manager's behavior. A plant manager can never escape from this imperative, regardless of his or her personal values.

The power of this cost-cutting imperative was dramatically illustrated in a case in which General Electric was accused of concealing design flaws in a giant nuclear-containment vessel it sold to the Washington Public Power Supply Systems. WPPSS was forced to spend hundreds of millions on repairs to make the plant safe, and it sued GE for contract fraud. The presiding judge cited internal company documents that made it clear GE had identified the potential dangers early on but chose to do nothing. "General Electric knew these problems should be examined but decided to adopt only an analytical approach," Judge Alan A. McDonald declared, "because the full-scale tests required . . . would be — I am quoting from the documents — 'very expensive'" (Roy 1990).

How might U.S. corporations be compelled to accept their obligations to law and society in a more reliable manner? And why is it that corporations, while regularly abusing public law and trust, are allowed to continue functioning as the preeminent citizens in U.S. politics? For ordinary citizens, the law has elaborated thorough answers to those questions — people who are criminals are barred from formal politics. For corporate criminals, the law is forgiving.

The two questions could be answered together if meaningful sanctions and penalties are developed that will punish lawless corporations in the only language that an "artificial legal person" understands: profit and loss. The corporation must know that repeatedly offending the law puts it at risk of losing real value — not only the financial privileges of government contracts or tax preferences but also the political privileges of appearing in the public arena as an advocate for itself and others.

Criminal prosecution of companies, though somewhat increased in recent years, is still quite rare — especially for major corporations that have the legal capacity to negotiate away their troubles with the law. In 1988, for instance, there were only 475 federal criminal cases brought against companies — and 85 percent of those involved very small businesses with fewer than fifty employees and sales of less than $1 million. Criminal prosecution of individuals can be therapeutic, especially in pollution cases, but sending the managers to jail will not necessarily change the behavior of a recidivist corporation.

In the interest of equity, law and legal doctrine must fashion methods for altering corporate behavior: sanctions that reverse the incentives inside corporations by raising the bottom-line cost of lawlessness. Any company, to be sure, may on rare occasions be unwittingly implicated in an offense. For the repeat offender, however, a system of graduated penalties ought to extract real losses. Because it is not a real person, a corporation cannot be sent to prison, but its freedom can be taken away in other ways.

The basic principles of accountability could be incorporated in many different kinds of statutes — especially the tax code — with evidentiary thresholds that are less demanding than criminal law. [See chapter by Richard L. Grossman and Frank T. Adams.] A company that accumulates repeated civil offenses against the environment or public health could be treated in a law as an antisocial organization that has lost its usual privileges. The tax code, for instance, provides a long list of allowances, exceptions, and preferences that feed tens of billions into corporate balance sheets. When Congress enacts such tax benefits, it could stipulate that no corporation will be eligible for the money if it has violated laws and regulations during the preceding years. This would be harsh medicine, indeed. Why should law-abiding taxpayers subsidize the lawless ones?

Addressing the legal obligations of corporations leads to broader questions about corporate social obligations. Why, for example, should companies receive tax credits for their research and development when they are simultaneously shrinking their U.S. employment? Why should government pick up the tab for cleaning up social problems that were generated by private employers who failed to observe minimal social obligations to their workers and communities? The questions lead in the direction of establishing in law a social context for corporations — legal obligations such as parental leave and other worker benefits that involve using the government's authority rather than spending the taxpayer's money. As it stands now, in the name of fostering prosperity, U.S. workers and taxpayers are helping to finance enterprises that do not reciprocate the loyalty.

# 29

# WAL-MART
## *Global Retailer*

## Kai Mander and Alex Boston

*Part of the expression of cultural diversity among regions and countries is the manner in which local economies operate in everyday life. Japan, for example, a country usually seen as an economic monolith, has nonetheless maintained the character of its neighborhoods by protecting small, family-owned stores against giant foreign retailers. With GATT, that will change. As Kai Mander and Alex Boston demonstrate, giant retailers such as Wal-Mart are already exerting terrible economic pressure on U.S. and Canadian small towns, effectively turning downtowns into ghost towns by substituting gigantic malls that are nearly identical everywhere. Now Wal-Mart is turning to foreign markets.*

*Kai Mander is former director of communications for the Institute for Agriculture and Trade Policy and former editor of* Trade News Bulletin. *He also worked for the Advocacy Institute in Washington, D.C. Alex Boston is director of research and communications at the Council of Canadians, Ottawa.*

THE U.S. RETAIL giant Wal-Mart, with its capital, power, and infrastructure, exemplifies the kind of corporation equipped for success in the global economy. Wal-Mart operates more than twenty-seven hundred warehouse-size retail outlets across the United States, Canada, and Mexico. Already the largest American retailer, by the year 2000 it may be the largest American corporation. Despite making phenomenal profits — $2.68 billion in 1993 — Wal-Mart continues to expand at a frenetic pace, opening a new store somewhere in North America every three days. With three discount clubs already operating in Hong Kong and ten new outlets in Argentina and Brazil, company officials are exploring possibilities for

Wal-Marts around the world. Ultimately, Wal-Mart hopes to become the first global retailer, with stores in every nation offering products at prices below local competitors.

Has Wal-Mart set an unrealistic goal for itself? Hardly. The new trade and investment rules established in the Uruguay Round of GATT and enforced by the new World Trade Organization give Wal-Mart a freer hand as it scouts the globe for the most lucrative countries in which to manufacture and/or retail its products. Such nations are generally those least "encumbered" by labor unions, health and safety standards, minimum wage laws, strict environmental standards, and restrictions on investment. Shrewd manufacturing, mass purchasing, and an automated inventory and distribution system that eliminates the middle man made Wal-Mart a dominant force in North America and will help Wal-Mart achieve its global dreams. The result may be that the small, diverse, family-run neighborhood stores, which are the economic and cultural backbone of communities throughout Asia, Europe, and South America, will soon give way to the mighty, homogenizing global retailer.

# MR. SAM'S CLUB

Until his death in 1992, Sam Walton, founder of Wal-Mart, was unfailingly portrayed by the media as a folksy, kind-hearted embodiment of the American Dream. He was lauded for his humility and his shunning of excess. Walton spent his final years piloting his plane around the continent visiting the stores he owned but had never seen. On the day a store was told that Walton planned to visit, palpable excitement and euphoria filled the air. When he showed up, Mr. Sam — as he was called by everyone from the store manager to the stock worker — was treated almost like a benevolent cult leader.

On these visits, Mr. Sam cheered his employees on and extolled the virtues of team work and company pride. He instilled in them the sense that their hard work would enrich them personally, with financial rewards to follow. He projected an image of an ordinary man made good. In reality, Mr. Sam was in the business of driving small shops out of business across the continent and paying most of his workers minimum wage, while he amassed a fortune of $23.5 billion.

According to Wal-Mart's public relations, its success stems from a philosophy of superb service, a wide assortment of quality merchandise, and the lowest possible prices. When it seeks the necessary permits to establish a new store, Wal-Mart portrays itself as a friendly addition to a local community. It contends that a new giant superstore will provide good jobs and sorely needed income to a regional economy and that local consumers will benefit from Wal-Mart's low prices. But study after study confirms what hundreds of American towns learned the hard way: Wal-Mart leads to a net loss of jobs, decreased income for the community, and a decline of central shopping areas. Even Wal-Mart's vaunted low prices are exaggerated.

## FROM DOWNTOWN TO GHOST TOWN

When a normal retail business opens in a small town, it tries to integrate into the existing economic base of the area. It usually locates in a pre-existing commercial section, hoping to become a stopping point on a shopper's list. In order to succeed, the owner, who probably lives nearby, makes the new shop's prices and hours of operation consistent with others in the area. The new shop then attempts to establish a distinctive charm and atmosphere all its own, along with a unique mix of products, to attract business without going beyond the social norms of the community. Such a shop becomes a welcome part of the town.

In contrast, Wal-Mart does not join communities so much as it attempts to take them over. It ignores a town's capacity to absorb another retailer and instead aims to steal customers away from the shops they frequent. Typically, Wal-Mart locates on the outskirts of town and sets prices below cost to draw customers away from the commercial center. It offers 2-for-1 deals, loss leaders, category killers, anything that will attract customers. From automotive supplies to clothing to pharmaceuticals to kitchenware, Wal-Mart moves sector by sector to undercut its competitors.

Big enough to sustain losses for a long time, Wal-Mart keeps prices low as long as it must. Soon, the lure of one-stop shopping and cheap prices are too much for local consumers already watching their budgets. Every time a shopper saves 40 cents on a tube of toothpaste at Wal-Mart, a local shop loses a sale. The piggy banks of small shop owners are depleted, and local businesses start disappearing from the formerly lively town. According to an Iowa State University study quoted in *Wal-Mart Watch* (December 1994), five years after the opening of a new Wal-Mart, stores within a 20-mile radius suffer an average 19 percent loss in retail sales. Journalist Maria Gilardin reports that in Anamosa, Iowa, a JC Penney, two men's clothing stores, a shoe store, a children's clothing store, a drug store, a hardware store, and a dime store closed shortly after a Wal-Mart opened. Soon the busy downtowns and surrounding neighborhoods resemble ghost towns.

Wal-Mart officials contend that when a new Wal-Mart opens, sales of nearby businesses increase. The Iowa State study confirmed that spillover traffic resulting from new Wal-Mart stores did increase the sales of adjacent businesses selling goods and services that were not available at Wal-Mart. However, many of these owners and employees now fear for their livelihoods as Wal-Mart stores expand the goods and services offered. More and more Wal-Mart stores sell groceries and pharmaceuticals, using the corporation's tremendous buying power, efficient distribution system, and low labor costs to gain competitive advantages. Wal-Mart stores are also increasingly providing sit-down meals to shoppers. The company recently equipped over one hundred of its Canadian stores with McDonald's restaurants.

Wal-Mart plans to increase the number of stores offering a wider range of goods through its Super Centers. The Super Centers are open twenty-four hours and feature bakeries, delis, and in-store cafés. Some offer other services such as dry cleaning, eye care, banking, tax preparation, and photo processing. Currently, Wal-Mart has only 143 of the much larger Super Centers, compared to 2,133 Wal-Marts, 438 Sam's Clubs, and 75 Bud's Discount Stores. But the Super Centers represent the future of Wal-Mart. According to Betsy Reithemeyer, public relations coordinator for Wal-Mart stores, the number of Super Centers will continue to increase, probably doubling in 1995.

With carte blanche to continue expanding and utilizing cutthroat pricing tactics, many analysts expect Wal-Mart's sales to increase from approximately $82.5 billion in 1994 to $125 billion by the year 2000. By then, some predict Wal-Mart will account for 20 cents of every dollar spent on general merchandise, apparel, and furniture in the United States.

## PAYCHECKS FROM WAL-MART

Wal-Mart employs more people than the Big Three automakers combined. Company spokespeople proudly claim that in some parts of the United States a Wal-Mart exists for every thirty-five thousand people, providing needed jobs to local economies. Contrary to company statements, however, the entry of Wal-Mart does not provide a net increase in a region's jobs. In fact, some studies have shown that for every job created by Wal-Mart, as many as 1.5 jobs are lost.

The jobs Wal-Mart does provide are at the bottom end of the economic scale. Notorious for wringing the most work out of its employees for the least pay, Wal-Mart rarely pays workers more than the minimum wage. The average annual income for a full-time worker at Wal-Mart in the United States, even with a well-publicized profit-sharing plan, hovers around $12,000 — well below the poverty line. Most "associates," as the company calls its employees, are given only part-time work so that the company can avoid paying the benefits full-time workers must receive. In addition, "associates" have very little job security, real health benefits, or meaningful pensions.

For this pittance, Wal-Mart demands complete and unquestioning loyalty from its sales clerks. They have to pass drug tests and, until recently, had to submit to lie detector tests. Wal-Mart even prohibits dating among employees. Workers are expected to work long and irregular hours for no additional pay — "free hours" as they're called. Unbelievably, many stores require their employees to start each day with a company cheer like, "Give me a *W*. Give me an *A*. Give me an *L*" and so on. According to Maria Gilardin, some stores have even cheered, "Stack it deep/sell it cheap/watch it fly/hear those downtown merchants cry!"

When he was seventeen years old, Nathan Hoff worked at the Fergus Falls, Minnesota, Wal-Mart for a summer: "Sam Walton was considered to be a god at Wal-Mart. On the first day of training the new employees were shown a thirty-minute video on the life of Sam Walton and the growing of the Wal-Mart corporation. It told about the first Wal-Drug, I think it was called, and how it eventually grew into Wal-Mart. It sort of felt like a cult working there. If you weren't friendly to everyone who set foot in the store you were regarded as a bad person. Everybody took things so seriously. It wasn't an enjoyable experience."

Given Wal-Mart's labor abuses, organized labor should be having a field day with Wal-Mart. But Wal-Mart's fanatically antiunion stance has succeeded in keeping unions out of all its stores in the United States. It has had similar success in Canada, where it hopes to have almost two hundred Wal-Marts by 1997. In its recent purchase of Canada's Woolco retail chain, its refusal to buy the seven Woolcos that were unionized put one thousand Canadians out of work. Many of the remaining Woolco staff were forced to accept lower wages or lose their jobs. Wal-Mart converted Woolco auto-repair shops to more profitable oil and lube operations and cut mechanics' wages in half. It fired 500 well-paid Woolco warehouse workers then charitably offered to rehire them at near minimum wage. Wal-Mart told 750 former Woolco supervisors they could keep their $28,000-per-year salaries only if they worked an extra twelve hours per week in addition to their regular forty. In the province of Québec, Wal-

Mart forced workers, many of whom spoke only French, to sign new contracts written only in English. On the one-year anniversary of Wal-Mart's announced takeover of Canadian Woolcos, it laid off 2,700 workers.

In Mexico, where the government has encouraged foreign investment by offering extremely lax enforcement of labor laws, Wal-Mart has opened eleven Super Centers and twenty-two Sam's Clubs since 1991, employing 6,900 people. Wal-Mart's commitment to Mexico, however, only goes so far. Within days of the peso devaluation in December 1994, Wal-Mart held back trucks of goods headed for Mexican stores and laid off 250 people at its Laredo, Texas, warehouse. Layoffs of Mexican employees were certain to follow.

Wal-Mart's retail employees are treated far better than the child and prison laborers in Asia who manufacture many of Wal-Mart's garments. The television program *Dateline NBC* ran an exposé on the appalling conditions in garment sweatshops of Bangladesh, where nine- to twelve-year-old boys and girls worked long into the night and were paid as little as five cents an hour. NBC also carried scenes from factories in China, where false labels were sewn into Wal-Mart clothes to indicate they were made in countries other than China, which is well-known for its use of forced prison labor. Back in the United States, NBC found most of these Asian garments in bins sporting glossy, bold "Made in America" signs.

When Wal-Mart decided to enter Canada, it launched a massive public relations and advertising campaign to convince weary Canadians that the stores were Canadian as maple sugar and hockey. "Wal-Mart Canada is a Canadian company, managed by Canadians and staffed with Canadian Associates" proclaimed full-page newspaper ads. Wal-Mart Canada President Bruce West assured Canadians of Wal-Mart's commitment to creating Canadian jobs and supporting Canadian manufacturers. But upon Wal-Mart's arrival, the Canadian government dropped its requirement that subsidiaries of foreign-based transnationals release their yearly financial audits, leaving the public with no way of knowing how much money Wal-Mart reinvested in Canada, where products were purchased, or how much of its profits were diverted back to the United States.

## LOSS OF COMMUNITY INCOME

Wal-Mart's economic impact on communities goes beyond the number of employees it fires or hires. Wal-Mart tends to locate outside established commercial districts, often on valuable farm land. By doing so, Wal-Mart avoids paying high property taxes and often forces the county to extend services to that area. A DuPage County, Illinois, study found that the increased cost of roads, water and sewage, security, telephone, and other services for these peripheral locations exceeded the sales and property tax revenues generated by the new stores.

Furthermore, as surrounding businesses buckle under Wal-Mart's formidable competition, regional income declines, and the community's tax base erodes, along with the funds needed to maintain adequate municipal services.

University of Massachusetts researchers found that a dollar spent on a locally owned business has four to five times the economic spin-off of a dollar spent at Wal-Mart (*Wal-Mart Watch,* Dec. 1994). Traditional businesses inevitably funnel their profits back into the community one way or another. However, each Wal-Mart store sends its profits back to the head office in Bentonville, Arkansas, removing from the community money that was formerly deposited in local banks or invested in local projects. Under NAFTA and GATT, Wal-Mart and other corporations can "repatriate" money from around the world.

Local media outlets have become increasingly vocal in their criticism of Wal-Mart. They have found that after an initial promotional blitz surrounding a Wal-Mart opening, their advertising revenue actually declines as Wal-Mart begins to dominate the area. The newspaper industry's disenchantment with Wal-Mart was even displayed in a series of *Doonesbury* comic strips depicting Wal-Mart as a threat to small businesses. In an attempt to recapture the favor of the media, Wal-Mart CEO David Glass told a gathering of newspaper business writers and editors that the company would probably increase advertising.

Wal-Mart tries to get maximum mileage from the little bit of charity it provides to a community. In contrast to most independent businesses, which often contribute as much as 5 percent of profit to local causes, Wal-Mart's donations from local stores amount to a mere 0.0004 percent of sales, according to researchers in Lake Placid, New York. In the United States, this translates into about $4,000 per year per store. Much of the charity provided by the Wal-Mart Foundation comes in the form of matched employee donations. For every bit the employees take out of their own meager earnings, the foundation provides an equal amount, but usually receives the full credit.

As for long-term community commitment, there is none from Wal-Mart. It has so many stores, it can close and relocate at any time it feels its profits in one area are not high enough. With its new focus on the giant Super Centers, Wal-Mart is shutting down many of its older stores so as to attract customers throughout a region. Some small towns have been double losers. First they lost their Main Street stores and saw downtown turn into a ghost town. Then they lost Wal-Mart. As a result, the community lost its tax base, and residents were forced to drive as far as thirty miles to do their shopping.

Even Wal-Mart's notoriously low prices have come into question. A U.S. advertising association recently forced Wal-Mart to stop using the slogan, "Always the low price, always" because it was misleading. Researchers have found that Wal-Mart puts its fifteen-hundred or so lowest-priced items at the front of the store. These are everyday products such as toothpaste and toilet paper of which people tend to know the price. Deeper into the store are the approximately eighty thousand high-profit items. As the local competition decreases, all of Wal-Mart's prices begin to climb.

## HOLDING WAL-MART BACK

In his autobiography, *Sam Walton: Made in America* (1992), Walton wrote, "If some community, for whatever reason, doesn't want us in there, we aren't interested in going in and creating a fuss."

Thousands of people across North America are taking steps to show the global giant it is unwelcome in their community. In the past two years, citizens of small towns in Massachusetts, New Hampshire, and Maine rejected new Wal-Mart stores in their areas. People have joined together in Oregon, Colorado, Iowa, Florida, Pennsylvania, Maryland, New York, Connecticut, Rhode Island, and elsewhere in hopes of fending off new Wal-Marts. Vermont — the only state without a Wal-Mart — told the retail giant it could come in only if it set up in existing downtowns and agreed to a long list of demands regarding the size and operations of the store. Puerto Rico rejected a Wal-Mart because of its likely effect on small and medium-sized businesses. An Ontario town developed a tough official plan outlining the type of development envisioned for the community. Only if Wal-Mart conforms to the guidelines will it be allowed to establish in the area.

Unions, manufacturers, small businesses, and municipal governments have filed lawsuits against Wal-Mart for a variety of reasons. Several churches and a garment workers' union won a case forcing Wal-Mart to stop violating legislation promoting the hiring of minorities and women. In 1993, an Arkansas circuit court found Wal-Mart guilty of selling merchandise below cost to drive smaller stores out of business and awarded almost $300,000 to three small pharmacies. In January 1995, the Arkansas

Supreme Court overturned the lower court ruling by a 4–3 vote. The court acknowledged that Wal-Mart sold some items below cost to entice customers, but said the pricing policies were not intended to injure competitors. Nonetheless, small businesses are forging ahead with similar lawsuits in twenty states.

The many battles with community groups led *U.S. News and World Report* to state recently that Wal-Mart looks "less and less like a juggernaut." But more needs to be done. Of course, Wal-Mart is just one of the many giant corporations putting its greed before the needs of people. However, unlike some of the faceless corporations poised to dominate the new global economy, Wal-Mart invades our communities directly and is thus familiar to most consumers. Stopping Wal-Mart offers people a concrete opportunity to act locally to fight globalization. Once we realize that Wal-Mart's bigness makes it our enemy instead of our ally, perhaps all transnational corporations will be thought of differently, and citizens and communities will begin reining in the elite powers that have overstepped our boundaries.

As a small first step to combating such corporations, we turn once again to the immortal words of Sam Walton: "There is only one boss. The customer. And he can fire everybody in the company, from the chairman on down, simply by spending his money somewhere else."

Words to live by.

# 30

# TECHNOLOGIES
# OF GLOBALIZATION

Jerry Mander

*Earlier chapters in this book presented evidence of the multiple harms caused by biotechnology, robotics, global computer networks, global television, the production and dumping of toxics, and of industrial expansion. We also read about the negative effects of export-oriented pesticide-intensive agriculture, and long-distance commodity transport. All of these technologies and processes are intrinsic aspects of a globalized economy.*

*Given the evidence, however, we still hesitate to draw conclusions about the political drift of modern technologies. We cling to the idea that technologies are "neutral," just as we like to think of science as "value free"; that it is only a matter of access. This chapter argues that the very idea that technology is neutral is itself not neutral, as it leads to passivity to technology's onrush and unconsciousness about its role in the globalization process. Energy technologies, automobiles, television, and computers are examined further in this light.*

*I*T IS COMMONPLACE nowadays to hear new technologies described as "revolutionary," but rarely do we learn whether the revolution is rightwing or left. This is especially true of the most dominant technologies and those with the greatest impact. Automobiles, television, and computers, for example, have so enveloped society that we scarcely remember a world before they existed. Society accepts the onrush of these technologies with alarming passivity, and without any systematic consideration of the social and political changes they bring. Indeed, despite calling the technologies revolutionary, we rarely acknowledge they have any political implications, such as the way they accelerate the globalization process. The great technology critic Langdon Winner has written that "all artifacts have politics," meaning that each technology has predictable social, political, and environmental outcomes. He says "The most interesting puzzle of our times is that we so willingly sleepwalk through the process for reconstituting the conditions of human existence. . . . In the technical realm we repeatedly enter into a series of social contracts, the terms of which are revealed only after the signing" (Winner 1986).

Two decades earlier, Marshall McLuhan made surely one of the most important and importantly misunderstood comments of the century when he said "the medium is the message" (1964). He meant that the most significant aspects of technology lie not in their apparent content (the transportation that a car provides or the news program that the television supplies) but in the systemic changes that they catalyze. The questions we need to learn to ask are such as these: How does the technology change work, family life, leisure, art? How does it alter our experience of everyday life? How does it change our concepts of self, community, politics, nature, time, distance? How does it influence how we learn, what we know, and what we are capable of knowing? What are its implications for human health and disease, and the environment? How does it reorganize power arrangements in society? For instance, does it centralize power or decentralize it? Does it serve to homogenize cultures or, on the contrary, to maintain diversity? Who gains and who loses?

Why hasn't our society developed a process of articulating and evaluating the totality of the effects caused by technology and then voting upon them before they become so pervasive that they become extremely difficult to dislodge? Indeed, certain technological inventions change society far more dramatically than any of the political figures we vote for do. Our total immersion in computers, for example, has and will continue to revolutionize our experience of life far more than whether our president is Republican or Democrat. But there is no congressional vote on this; there are no popular referenda. Even in this most democratic of societies, we have no process for decision-making about technology and little practice in evaluating it. We have only the market to make our decisions for us, and that process is profoundly skewed, as we will see.

How did things get this way? There are dozens of possible explanations, but I will only cite three main points.

The first has to do with the information climate about technology. It is a melancholy fact that in our society the first waves of descriptions about new technologies invariably come from the corporations and scientists who invent and market these technologies and who have much to gain by our accepting a positive view. Their descriptions are invariably optimistic, even utopian, and are supported by hundreds of millions of dollars in advertising and public relations: "The 'Green Revolution' will solve global hunger." "Nuclear power will solve the world's energy problems and provide clean, safe, cheap, inexhaustible energy." "Television will unify global consciousness and bring peace and understanding everywhere." "The microcomputer revolution will bring all the information in the world to every person merely by striking of a key."

One could find similarly optimistic statements for every new technology that comes along. The sources of such statements have nothing to gain from our learning of the possible negative consequences of these new commodities, so we are left with a constant stream of *best-case scenarios* and virtually no countervailing voice. As we have discovered, however, many manufacturers and industries — including nuclear, chemical, auto, cigarette, and tobacco — have been aware of serious negative potentialities of their technologies, but chose not to share these with the public and often to hide them even from investigative inquiry.

Over the century since the Industrial Revolution, wave after wave of techno-utopian visions have so immersed us in positive expectation that they have solidified into a paradigm that new technology is virtually synonymous with the general advancement of society. It is only long after a technology has entered into general production and may have gained an important role in everyday life that we begin to perceive its adverse effect upon humans or nature. Even then, the proposed solutions usually consist of creating new generations of technology designed to fix the problems of the old. Thus the wave rolls on to the next technical generation.

A second factor explaining our utter passivity to technology is that, when we do attempt to analyze the virtues of a particular technology we do so in personal terms. The car drives us where we need to go in relative comfort and convenience. The rifle brings down the animal at 300 feet. The television is often entertaining and informative. The airplane shrinks the globe; we can be anywhere on Earth in hours. The computer edits, stores data, hooks us to other like-minded people, speeds up our work, and permits us to "publish" our viewpoints to a potentially vast audience. On such observations are based our feeling that these technologies are useful, and indeed they are. In fact, all technology is useful or entertaining, or else we'd have no interest in it in the first place. But to base our ultimate conclusions about technology mainly on our personal experience leaves out the social, political, and ecological dimensions; in other words, it overlooks the effects outside of ourselves. What else do guns do? What are the other consequences of high-speed travel? Is a smaller world better? Who else benefits from global computer networks?

In our individualistic society, we are not practiced in making judgments beyond our personal experience, but it is just that practice — seeking the systemic or holistic effects — that will help us evaluate the positive and negative aspects of specific technologies. The question then is not how or whether technology benefits us but who benefits most, and what does it cause to happen outside ourselves?

This brings us to the third and I think most important reason for our passivity about technology — the blinding notion that technologies are neutral, that the only thing that matters about them is who has access to their controls, that they have no intrinsic qualities that inevitably produce certain ecological or political outcomes. It may be one of the most important survival skills of our times to break with this idea. Every technology has a predetermined political drift, and it is critical that we perceive that and make our judgments and adjustments accordingly.

To help clarify this point, I'll use two familiar examples of energy technologies: nuclear power and solar power. Both of these technologies will light the lamps in your house and run the refrigerator, the television, and the computer. But there the similarities end.

## INTRINSIC BIAS IN ENERGY TECHNOLOGIES

When a society decides to use nuclear power, it commits itself to many additional outcomes besides the delivery of the energy itself. To build and operate nuclear power plants requires a large, highly technical, and very well-financed infrastructure. It's not something that people in your neighborhood could get together and decide to do. It can only be done by huge, centralized institutions. Without such institutions, nuclear power could not exist.

Nuclear power also depends upon substantial military protection against possible terrorist attacks, or thefts of dangerous ingredients. And nuclear energy produces a terrifying waste product, some of which needs to be stored safely someplace for as long as 250,000 years — a technical task that is still not solved — requiring techno-scientific-military care and protection for all that time, something no society could guarantee. This also preempts many choices that might otherwise be available for future generations. For example, what if, a few centuries down the road, a society wishes to re-establish agrarianism and low-impact technology as its primary modi operandi? This may seem unlikely right now, but nonetheless, such a society would be greatly inhibited from making that choice, as it would still have to monitor the dangerous wastes from centuries earlier and maintain a technical capability for doing it. So, nuclear power today predetermines much about the form of future society.

Solar power, on the other hand, has entirely different intrinsic characteristics. The technology is so simple and inexpensive that my sons and I and a few friends could probably install solar units on most of the houses in our neighborhood, without backing from any centralized financial interests. We would require no military to protect the units; there would be very negligible dangerous waste product; and the technology would not predetermine the shape of any future society.

So it would be fair to say that nuclear power is an appropriate technology for an industrialized, mass society such as ours, organized around large central military and financial systems. Solar power is more appropriate for societies made up of small communities, catering to local markets, with very low environmental impact.

What is important to note is that the significant features of each of these rival technologies are *intrinsic* to them. They don't depend upon who runs them or who owns them. If the authors in this book — universally benevolent people — were somehow put in charge of the world's nuclear power plants, we would surely have to run them in more or less the same way as they are presently being run, albeit perhaps with a higher degree of caution. But all of the major implications of nuclear power — financial, military, and environmental — would remain, because they are determined by the technology itself. So it is truly preposterous to argue that either of these technologies is neutral, when both are intrinsically predisposed to produce dramatically divergent outcomes.

That kind of comparative *systemic* technological analysis should have occurred long before our society made any of its choices about which energy technologies to employ. Other energy sources such as coal, gas, oil, and biomass, should also have been included in such a comprehensive comparison, long before corporate marketing interests were able to exert their persuasive influence. In the end, the question becomes, What kind of technology relates to what kind of society?

In fact, a far more comprehensive analysis than that should be performed before any technology is so fully integrated into society that it becomes impossible to extricate. Consider the case of the automobile.

## REFERENDUM ON THE AUTO

What would have happened if a *systemic* analysis of the automobile had been offered to the public at the time of its invention? It's not as if most of the negative effects were not known ahead of time, for businesses spend enormous sums researching both the market potential of their product and the possible downside disasters; businesses don't like surprises. Indeed, an excellent study of the level of awareness of certain technologies' impacts at the time of their invention can be found in the "Retrospective Technology Assessment" reports financed by the National Science Foundation, managed by the Massachusetts Institute of Technology.

When Henry Ford and others first promoted the automobile before the turn of the century, the technology was described, as usual, solely in "best-case" terms. Automobiles would bring a "revolutionary" new era of personal freedom and democracy in the form of private transportation that was fast, clean (no mud or horse manure), and independent. But what if people had been told that the car would bring with it the modern concrete city? Or that the car would contribute to cancer-causing air pollution, to noise, to solid waste problems, and to the rapid depletion of the world's resources? What if the public had been made aware that a nation (and now a globe) of private car owners would require the paving of virtually the entire landscape, at public cost, so that eventually automobile sounds would be heard even in areas of deep wilderness? What if it had been reported that for production efficiency the private car would likely be manufactured by a small number of giant corporations that would acquire tremendous economic and political power? That these corporations would create a new mode of mass production — the assembly line — which in turn would cause worker alienation, physical injury, drug abuse, and alcoholism? That these corporations might conspire to eliminate other means of popular transportation, including trains? That the automobile would facilitate suburban growth with its intolerable impact on landscapes? What if there had been an appreciation of the psychological results of the privatization of travel and the modern experience of isolation? What if we had known that thirty thousand people would die annually in car accidents? What if the public had been forewarned of the unprecedented need for oil that the private car would create, and that horrible wars would be fought over oil supplies? What if the public had realized that automobiles and roads would redesign even the most exotic societies into forms and behavior very much like ours? That cities such as Bangkok and Kathmandu would increasingly feel like Manhattan at rush hour?

Would a public informed of such outcomes have decided to proceed with developing the private automobile? Would the public have still thought it a good thing?

I really cannot guess whether a public so well informed and given the chance to vote would have voted against cars. Perhaps not. But the public was not so informed. There was never a meaningful debate; never a vote of any kind, save for the very recent votes on certain highway construction projects, as a few communities awake from their somnambulism. So four generations since its introduction, this single technology has drastically transformed our towns and cities; the way we live, think and relate; and indeed, the very essence of our societies, all to accommodate the car.

If such a debate about the automobile had occurred in the public realm, the knowledge thus shared would certainly have changed the level of acceptance for the private car and the kinds of restructuring undertaken to accommodate it. There surely would have been sufficient concern about pavement, pollution, wars, and resource use that we would doubtless have given more support to public transport, and we surely would not have seen quite the proliferation of private cars and public roads. Some countries and locales might have prohibited private cars completely and thereby retained their indigenous social, cultural, biological, and geographical characteristics.

## TV: THE CLONING OF CULTURES

Several contributors to this book have described aspects of the globalization and homogenization of values, culture, and consciousness that cultural exports of Western films, fashion, music, and television have introduced. [See chapters by Helena Norberg-Hodge and by Richard Barnet and John Cavanagh.] With the new trade agreements effectively suppressing the remaining ability of individual nations to resist such cultural invasions, the process of cultural cloning is accelerating, but it has been advancing for some while.

Because of the advent of satellite television in the 1970s and 1980s, more than 75 percent of the global population now has access to daily television reception. People living in remote parts of Borneo, or in the Himalayas, or in the tundras of Siberia are watching nearly identical programs, mostly produced by Western corporate interests, all of it expressing Western values and imagery, instigating enormous cultural change.

I had the chance to observe this process up close during a visit to the Mackenzie River Valley of the Northwest Territories of Canada in the mid 1980s. I was invited there by the Native Women's Association, which expressed deep concern about the sudden changes caused by the recent introduction of satellite television into their communities.

The Mackenzie Valley stretches south from the Arctic Circle and runs

1,500 miles to the Great Slave Lake. If you're not familiar with the area, let me remind you of the Russian nuclear satellite that fell from orbit some years ago. It was feared it would fall on Paris or New York or Tokyo, so there was a great relief when it fell on what was described in the press as "an icy unpopulated wasteland."

To call this area unpopulated only confirms how invisible Native people are to the mass media because it is actually populated by twenty-six communities of Dene Indians and Inuit (Eskimo) peoples — about twenty thousand people in all — who have lived there successfully for four thousand years. To this day they speak twenty-two native tongues, mostly as a first language. In many of these places, the traditional economy of hunting, ice fishing, and dog sled travel has survived, largely because the Canadian government had little interest in the area. But when oil was discovered in the 1960s, oil workers were needed, and the government decided it was time that the Natives be turned into Canadians.

Television is the normal instrument of choice for such cultural conversion. The government offered each of the twenty-six communities free satellite dishes and television sets; most communities accepted, but not all.

The Native Women's Association was concerned about some of the obvious early effects that television was having in their communities, and they were holding workshops on the subject. When I arrived in Yellowknife, the capital city of the Northwest Territories (population then 9,000; the only town with paved streets and cars) the weather was 40 degrees below zero. The women who greeted me told me they were at first pleased about television. Dene and Inuit communities are often hundreds of miles from each other, without any connecting roads. Communications between these places was difficult: dog team, radio, and airplane. "Until recently it didn't matter," I was told by the Dene Nation communications director, Cindy Gilday. "Most of the communities have been self-sufficient for centuries, but now the government is changing things so fast, it's important for people to know what's going on."

Television had seemed a logical advance in communications, but it had not lived up to its potential. As with most indigenous and Third World locales where television is just arriving, the programs are not produced locally, but come mostly from the United States or other Western countries. Sixty percent of the programs in the NWT were from the United States, including "Dallas," "Edge of Night," "Happy Days," and "The Six Million Dollar Man" (and, lately, CNN). Gilday said:

> There's only one hour per week of local shows, and rarely does that have anything to do with Native people, though we're the majority

population here. . . . We can already see that TV has had a devastating effect, especially in the villages out in the bush. People are sitting in their log houses, alongside their frozen lakes with dog teams tied up outside, watching a bunch of white people in Dallas standing around their swimming pools, drinking martinis, and plotting to destroy each other or steal from each other or get their partners' wives into bed. Then after that comes a show about a man turning into a machine. . . .

The effect has been to glamorize behaviors and values that are poisonous to life up here. Our traditions have a lot to do with survival. Community cooperation, sharing, and nonmaterialism are the only ways that people can live here. But TV always presents values opposite to those.

Many of the women I met were schoolteachers, and they said that when television came to the villages they saw an immediate change. The children immediately lost interest in the Native language; they wanted only to learn Canadian English. Now the children want all kinds of new things like cars; yet most of the communities have no roads. They don't want to learn how to fish on the ice or go hunting anymore. "But worst of all is what it's doing to the relations between the young and the old," I was told by the women. "TV makes it seem like the young people are all that's important, and the old have nothing to say. And yet in our cultures, the old people are the ones who tell the stories and teach the kids how to be Indians."

Most important of all, the women said, was that TV had put a stop to storytelling. It used to be that the old people would sit each evening in the corner of the house, telling the children ancient stories about life in the North. Through that process, the elders had been the windows through which the younger generation could see their own past and traditions; it was how the children could sense their own Indian roots. It was also an educational system teaching how to survive in such a harsh place. The women were horrified that the process was being interrupted by television. They saw it as the death of their culture. Gilday told me,

You have to realize that most people still live in one- or two-room houses. The TV is going all the time, and the little kids and the old people are all sitting around together watching it. They're watching something totally alien, and they're not hearing the stories anymore; they don't want to be Indians now. They hate being Indians.

They want to be Canadians and Americans. . . . It's so crazy and so awful. Nobody ever told us that all this would be coming in with TV. It's like some kind of invasion from outer space or something. First it was the government coming in here, then those oil companies, and now it's TV.

With satellite television now bringing "Dallas," "The Edge of Night," and "The Oprah Winfrey Show" to 75 percent of the world population, the process just described in the Mackenzie Valley is happening globally. Television technology is clearly the most efficient instrument ever invented for global cultural cloning, and it is the pathbreaker for what follows: cars; paved roads; Western franchise foods; economies converted from self-sufficiency to corporate export; frantic and stressful life-styles; loss of traditional skills; immersion in computers, walkmans, and CD ROMs, and so on. As the process advances, the development maw envelopes the resources that were once under the control of indigenous societies, and all distinctive places on Earth lose their uniqueness, their cultures, and, some say, their souls.

Of course, some readers may wonder about the real harm in all this. One can certainly argue that the benefits of modernization are well worth the sacrifice, even when the sacrifice is not apparent at the time of the change and comes as a shocking surprise. In fact, it is the ultimate rationalization for the entire Western development ethic that the sacrifice of cultural and biological diversity is worth what is gained, even if every place on Earth begins to look like Bakersfield, California. That viewpoint notwithstanding, we should become exquisitely aware of the nature of the bargain and give ourselves the freedom and the opportunity to conclude that, on balance, it may be a losing proposition for everyone.

Television is one technology that does live up to the promises proposed by its inventors: It produces a unified global consciousness. But is that good?

## THE COMPUTER REVOLUTION

The computer revolution is an odd kind of revolution, because every corner of society, including those that normally disagree fiercely with each other on most issues, is in agreement on this one: They all think it's good. The engineers and the artists; the Al Gores and the Newt Gingriches; corporations and their anticorporate counterparts; conservatives and liberals

—all are dazzled by images of computer-driven utopias, though it's possible they have slightly different utopias in mind.

Most of my own friends and colleagues share this utopian expectation. My writer friends wonder how it is even possible to write books without a computer, though several writers in history — from Shakespeare to Hemingway to Atwood to Illich — are known to have done it. Even now, there are those who write books by longhand (Edward Goldsmith and Wendell Berry among them). And there is the impressive fact that four hundred thousand generations of human beings got through their days without computers. It has been done.

"That is not the point," my friends say. They argue that I fail to appreciate how "empowering" computers can be (a popular way of describing them these days) and how they can help us organize against the corporate juggernaut. Computers bring real power back to the individual, and the cybernet helps us build new alliances with like-minded radicals sitting at their terminals, using e-mail and web pages to spread news and mobilize battles. By such analyses, computers seem clearly to be in service of "progressive," democratizing, decentralizing tendencies.

The more esoteric among my colleagues like to invoke the views of influential *Wired* magazine editor Kevin Kelly, who has described a new "revolutionary" political structure that he feels microcomputation has wrought. "The correct symbol of today is no longer the atom," he says, "it's the net." The political center has been wiped out, and a revolutionary structure has replaced it. This is leading in turn to a new decentralized worldview that "elevates the power of the small player" and promotes heterogeneity. It also leads to a new kind of pure democracy and an "incipient technospiritualism" (Kelly 1994).

Kelly is right on the "technospiritualism" point, though frankly I prefer the old kind of spiritualism that requires no mediation through machines. As for the main idea that the old political center has been eliminated and that our new net or web politics brings us computer-enhanced democracy run through cyberspace, let me ask: Should we call it *virtual democracy*? I think so, because someone forgot to tell the transnational corporations in Tokyo, New York, Brussels, or Geneva that the real power was no longer in the center. Judging by the evidence of the preceding pages, centralized corporate and political power is accelerating more rapidly than ever, and the computer has had a critically important role in this. As Richard Barnet and John Cavanagh point out in the next chapter, on the casino economy, the giant financial institutions of today could not exist at their present scale if there were no computers. Computers are their global nervous systems;

their way of keeping track of their billions of moving parts, keeping them synchronized and moving in the same direction for central purposes. Richard Sclove of the Loka Institute put it this way:

> The emerging technical infrastructure makes possible a new level of deepening, widening and acceleration in global economic integration. Multinational corporations are decentralizing operations and jobs around the world, but at the same time, they are intensifying their centralized control over these decentralized operations.... [political leaders] cannot risk alienating the international financial community. This is doubtless why President Clinton, who refused to stand firmly for anything else in his first year as president, was willing to go to the mat for the passage of GATT and NAFTA. So for all the hype in the media about how the new technologies will enhance democracy, what we are getting is not individual empowerment but a new empowerment for multinational corporations and banks, with respect to workers, consumers, and political systems (Sclove 1994).

What kind of revolution, then, do we have here? To continue to use terms such as *empowerment* for on-line individual and democratic organizing is to deeply misunderstand real versus *virtual* political power. Computers may help individuals feel powerful or competent, and surely they are useful in many ways. But they do nothing to alter the rapid global centralization of power that is now underway; quite the opposite. In fact, it is my opinion that computer technology may be the single most important instrument ever invented for the acceleration of centralized power. While we sit at our PCs editing our copy, sending our e-mail, and expressing our cyberfreedoms, the transnational corporations are using their global networks, fed by far greater resources. They are able to achieve not only information exchange but concrete results that express themselves in downed forests, massive infrastructural development, destruction of rural and farming societies, displacement of millions of people, and domination of governments. In a symbiotic embrace with other technologies of rapid economic development, they operate on a scale and at a speed that makes our own level of cyberempowerment pathetic by comparison. Speaking in traditional political terms, the new telecommunications technologies assist the corporate, centralized, industrialized enterprise (the "right"?) far more efficiently than the decentralized, local, community-based interests (the "left"?), which suffer a net loss.

So much for elevating "the power of the small player."

• • •

I have been describing a few macro effects of computers. It is relevant to at least mention a few other dimensions: the role computer production plays in creating the toxic crises of the industrial world and the Third World; the role of computer-based surveillance technologies in corporations to measure and objectify worker performance; and the manner in which microcomputation has sped up and amplified the power of the military technologies of the advanced industrialized nations. This was already obvious in the infamous "launch-on-warning" phenomenon of the old Cold War and the "smart bombs" of the hotter and more recent U.S.-Iraq war, where mass killing by automated bombs left human beings (save for those at the receiving end) free of dirty-handed engagement in the killing process.

Then there is the simple dimension of *speed*. E. F. Schumacher told us that small is beautiful, but one could also make the case that *slow* is beautiful, especially in preserving the natural world. Computers speed up communications exchanges over long distance, a quality that is most advantageous to the large centralized institutions we have been describing in this book. Of course, it also offers a speedup for resistance movements, but that speedup is mainly to keep pace with the high-speed activity of corporations.

Has there been a net gain? In political terms, I think not. In environmental terms, surely not. To ensure the survival of nature, everything, especially development and especially people, must slow down and synchronize with the more subtle and slower rhythms of the natural world. In our cyber-walkman-airplane-fax-phone-satellite world, we are so enclosed within a high-speed technical reality that the values and concerns of nature tend to become opaque to our consciousness.

• • •

Portland State University professor of education C. A. Bowers has been focusing on the way computer usage affects the basic ecological and political values of the people who use them. Bowers makes the case that the advance of computers is contributing to a loss of ecological sensitivity and understanding, since the very process of using computers, particularly educating through computers, effectively excludes an entire set of ideas and experiences that heretofore had been the building blocks for a developing connection with the earth. Bowers opposes the use of computers in primary and secondary education, saying that they change the way children's minds process information and affect not only what they know but what they are capable of knowing — that is, computers alter the pathways of children's cognition. Newly immersed in data-based forms of knowledge and limited to information transmissible in digital form, our culture is sacrificing the subtle, contextual, and memory-based knowledge gleaned from living in a nature-based culture, meaningful interactive learning with other humans, and an ecologically-based value system (Bowers 1993).

So, by accepting computers so completely for schools, says Bowers, our society also accepts a massive cultural transformation, leaving human beings altered in predictable ways. McLuhan said that we turn into the technologies that we use. And so, says Bowers, the more we use the computer and the more it is used globally, the stronger its culturally homogenizing effects and the greater likelihood that our new globalized digital culture will be less concerned about the disappearance of nature.

Bowers points out that many activists who *oppose* globalization still feel that computer communications can have a positive result, enabling us to communicate globally and thus organize resistance in behalf of biological and cultural diversity. Bowers argues that wiring the world together and accelerating cybercommunications between New York, and people living in grass houses in Southeast Asia, and the far northern tundras will not help preserve cultural diversity and autonomy. When everyone is sitting at their computer terminals all over the planet, this will be an expression of uniformity, not diversity; uniformity of experience, conceptual framework, categories of knowledge, content of knowledge, and worldview. The melancholy result: *monoculture.*

Richard Sclove adds this final political point:

> People are using telecommunications to establish [virtual] social bonds that are completely unrelated to territorial relations or face-to-face acquaintance. I might now have a lively social life with people in Amsterdam but not a clue about what's going on with my neighbor next door. Spending one's life on-line, with little direct experience of the natural world — without sensuous knowing — debases our willingness to act with responsibility toward the environment. . . . The ultimate political risk comes down to this: to the extent that virtual community takes over for face-to-face community, we get a mismatch between bonds of social affiliation, which are non-territorial, and political systems, which are territorial. How do political jurisdictions govern when the citizens within those boundaries have nothing to do with each other or with the realities of the place?

The answer: we do not govern. Transnational corporations, via the World Trade Organization, take care of that. We may love our computers for the way they assist us in our work and for certain pleasures they may also bring us, but, please, let's not call them *empowering*.

# MEGATECHNOLOGY

It is not only individual technologies which need systemic ideological consideration, but what they combine to achieve. For example, as recently as two decades ago it was possible to speak about two different parts of the planet as distinct places with distinct cultures, living habits, conceptual frameworks, behaviors, and power arrangements. It was also possible to speak of distinctly different geographies. And one could sensibly speak about individual technologies as if they were distinct from one another: television as opposed to computers; lasers as opposed to satellites.

However, technological evolution has brought us to the point where such distinctions among cultures, places, systems of organization, and technological forms are being wiped out under the homogenization drives of a much larger technical juggernaut. Telecommunications, high-speed computer technology, satellite systems, robotics, lasers, and other new technologies have made possible, practical, and inevitable an interlocked worldwide communication system that enables corporate actors to perform globally with unprecedented speed and efficiency. In such a system corporations themselves are an intrinsic part of the technical machine. In fact, they are technical forms, too, inventing the machines that operate on this global scale and in turn being spawned by them in an accelerating symbiotic cycle.

Finally, there is one more technical form to complete the picture: the recently restructured global economic system itself, which is specifically designed to overcome resistance to the megatechnological homogenization drive.

The big trade agreements are an intrinsic part of the global technical structure; in fact they are the "consciousness" of the megadevelopment, megatechnological, monocultural model that encircles the globe and permeates our lives.

In such a context, democracy has a difficult future. In fact, democracy is already suffering its greatest setback, as a direct result of this *de facto* conspiracy of technical structures, technologies themselves, and corporate purposes, all within the Western development paradigm. Understanding of that entire set of forces, *megatechnology*, must be grasped quickly.

Otherwise we will be led blind and powerless through a destruction of nature, culture, and diversity beyond anything that has preceded it.

Individual technologies have defined roles to play: Television serves as the worldwide agent of imagery for the new global corporate vision; computers are the nervous system that facilitate the setup of new global organizations; trade agreements wipe out resistance; telecommunications provide instant capital and resource transfer; genetics and space technologies expand the world market into the new wilderness areas — the internal cell structure of living creatures and the far reaches of untrammeled space. Together, these and other technologies combine to form the new technosphere that is anathema to democracy and diversity.

The answer to the trend is, of course, to work to reverse it, and to bring real power back to the local community, while supporting communities, cultures, and nations that attempt to stand in the way of the juggernaut.

31

# ELECTRONIC MONEY AND THE CASINO ECONOMY

Richard Barnet and John Cavanagh

*Deregulation of banking and financial markets, combined with the new rules of free trade and the new technologies that offer instantaneous worldwide money transfers, have combined to profoundly transform the modes of financial activity all over the planet. Incomprehensibly large amounts of money are shifting from market to market and then back again in the time it takes to make a keystroke. Governments are left nearly helpless to ensure the stability of markets or currency values in the face of the tremendous acceleration of speculation. The role of the global financial gamblers in creating many of the current money crises has been seriously underreported in the media. Richard Barnet and John Cavanagh present a condensed history of these enormous changes and their consequences.*

O N JANUARY 30, 1995, twenty-four hours before President Bill Clinton orchestrated a $50 billion bailout of the Mexican economy, the world financial system came perilously close to meltdown. As news spread around global financial markets that Mexico was on the verge of defaulting on government bond payments, capital fled stock markets from Brazil and Argentina and even from countries as far away as Poland and the Czech Republic. On that day, Asian markets were spared only because stock markets were closed in observance of Chinese New Year. This sort of crisis is more than likely to recur in the coming years, and next time it might have even more devastating effects worldwide.

The root causes of this crisis are twofold: (1) the total deregulation of the global financial systems that leaves banks and other financial institutions without controls, and (2) the corresponding revolution in communications technology that has brought radical change in the scale, speed, and manner of financial activity.

This combination of factors has enabled currency speculators to run wild, moving their immense resources electronically, instantaneously, from country to country, beyond the abilities of any government to control the process. In this cybertech globalized world, money has become free of its place and, as we will see, from most connections to its former sources of value: commodities and services. Money itself is the product that money buys and sells.

Because of the tremendous financial requirements for playing in this global money game, banks and finance houses are quickly diminishing in number but increasing in size, hence becoming still more difficult to control. The net effect is that the world financial system has become exquisitely vulnerable to technological breakdown, the high-risk consequences of short-term speculation, and freelance decision making. If anything goes wrong in this fragile arrangement, which is increasingly likely in the context of a wired-up economy based on free trade — when a crisis in one place directly affects financial flows everywhere else — speculators panic, speculative funds are moved without warning (as happened in Mexico), and we are quickly threatened by a rapid domino effect among the world's interdependent stock markets. Global economic collapse is possible.

The following are some elements in this larger story.

## THE NATURE OF ELECTRONIC MONEY

Most business and personal financial transactions still involve cash, that is, the exchange of coins and bank notes issued by treasuries and central banks. According to the Federal Reserve, about 85 percent of dollar transactions are in cash at banks, supermarkets, gas stations, restaurants, and the like. But the trillions sloshing back and forth between countries, within and between corporations, and between large investors and entrepreneurs are transferred from one account to another through an electronic network. Unlike withdrawals at automated teller machines (ATMs), these large transactions do not take place in public view. The number of electronic transfers amounts to only 2 percent of the total transfers; yet these transactions involve five out of every six dollars that move in the world economy.

Traders still shout at one another at exchanges around the world, buying and selling money in one form or another, but more and more dollars, yen, or lire move from one account to another hundreds or thousands of miles away because someone in a quiet room has hooked into a global electronic network and punched a key. Well over $2 trillion a day travels across the street or across the world at unimaginable speed as bits of electronic information. A treasury bill, as James Grant, the editor of *Grant's Interest Rate Observer*, puts it, "no longer exists except as an entry on a computer tape" (Passell 1992).

Information technology has transformed global banking more than any other economic activity. The software that guides electronic networks now permits twenty-four-hour trading in a wide variety of money products — securities, options, futures, and so on — all across the planet, and it has changed the human relations of banking. As Felix Rohatyn of Lazard Freres puts it: "People buy and sell blips on an electronic screen. They deal with people they never see, they talk to people on the phone in rooms that have no windows. They sit and look at screens. It's almost like modern warfare, where people sit in bunkers and look at screens and push buttons and things happen" (Sampson 1989).

The sheer size of global financial operations is reducing costs substantially. Any multimillion-dollar transfer across the globe can be accomplished for just 18 cents. By developing the most advanced foreign-exchange software, Bankers Trust was able to achieve a ten-second advantage over other traders — enough time, according to a 1987 Office of Technology Assessment study, to execute four or five trades. The opportunity to react to new information a few seconds ahead of the market can be worth billions (O'Brien 1992).

The introduction of state-of-the-art information technology has changed what banks are and what banks do. Computers and electronic communications networks have expanded the markets for money products and reduced the costs of making transfers, in large measure by eliminating thousands of jobs for clerks, tellers, messengers, and the like. But the installation of the automated systems has required huge capital investments. In 1990, commercial banks in the United States spent $15 billion on information technology. The need to amass large investment funds for such purposes has encouraged the consolidation of investment and banking corporations. Firms merge to save costs by sharing expensive data systems. These systems facilitate the speedy settlement of money trading; even a few seconds of exposure before a transfer is settled can spell disaster if millions of dollars are involved.

In other words, global banking has become highly dependent on a few centralized information operations to accomplish and monitor the transfers. CHIPS is the New York Clearing House Interbank Payment System. Inside a reinforced concrete-and-glass office building on a run-down block on Manhattan's West Side, two Unisys A-15 J mainframe computers about the size of refrigerators dispatch funds across the earth. Requests for payment stream in through 134 telephone lines, and, after the requests are screened for possible fraud by twenty-two electronic black boxes, the mainframes move the money, as *New York Times* writer Peter Passell (1992) puts it, in the form of "weightless photons through the electromagnetic ether."

As bankers contemplate this electronic money web, the nightmare — which most dismiss — is that a massive fraud, a flash of lightning, or a diabolical computer virus could trigger power failure, scrambled money messages, gridlock, and breakdown in the global banking system and lead to the world's first computer-driven worldwide financial panic. CHIPS takes all this seriously enough to adopt elaborate security arrangements, to put in auxiliary power and water systems, and to replicate the entire Manhattan operation just across the river in New Jersey, down to a maze of white-walled rooms, a network of telephone lines, a Halon fire-protection system, and water-resistant ceilings.

According to Peter Passell, a $20 million theft did occur in 1989, a fraudulent transfer from a Zurich bank to the State Bank of New South Wales via its New York branch. A Malaysian con man secured the cooperation of two employees of the Swiss Bank and conjured up a fictitious bank in Cameroon to work the scheme. The thieves were caught and convicted. The $20 million had been transferred in a fraction of a second, but recovering it took longer. Three years later, $12 million of it was still missing. Despite all the technological precautions and hurdles, even more imaginative inside jobs on an even larger scale are possible.

John Lee, president of the New York Clearing House Association, estimates that 99 percent of CHIPS transactions are legitimate. That may well be true, given the huge volume of daily transactions. Nevertheless, the speed and anonymity of the global money-transfer system presents an opportunity for large-scale criminal operations and tax fraud.

Electronic transfers are secret. Anyone with funds in the bank who prefers to hide them from regulators, creditors, wives, or husbands can communicate with the bank by fax or modem and order wire transfers across the globe without ever speaking to a bank officer. *Tax havens* are nesting grounds for criminal gains or untaxed profits. Indeed, most of the deposits sitting in these out-of-the-way places are there to avoid scrutiny by regulatory and taxing authorities. Typically, tax havens are tiny — Cayman Islands, Bahamas, Bermuda, Cape Verde, Hong Kong, Bahrain — mostly islands featuring warm weather, good flight connections, and plenty of faxes. Grand Cayman's financial district is reputed to have the highest concentration of fax machines in the world to serve its 548 banking outposts, which hold assets of about $400 billion.

The volume and reach afforded by instantaneous banking transactions across the world make global banking highly profitable, but some economists fear that these same characteristics could also be its undoing. On a typical day, well over a hundred banks are sending and receiving pay orders via CHIPS at the rate of $2 billion a minute. Unlike payments in currency, which are final, electronic orders to pay are not settled until the close of the business day, and then the accounts are cleared multilaterally. Passell (1992) likens the process to a poker game: "Each institution that is in arrears makes payments into the kitty much the way the 'bank' settles accounts for a half-dozen players" when the game breaks up. Should a bank lack the funds to settle accounts at the end of its business day, the electronic entries would be reversed — *unwound* in global-banking lingo — and every bank engaged in a transfer to or from the defaulting bank would feel its effects. The gridlock caused by the hundreds of corrections, especially if multiple bank defaults are involved or a stock market crash is also occurring, could trigger a chain reaction of bank failures. The system could be shut down for weeks, during which time corporations would be starved for working capital. Bankers profess great confidence that such scenarios are highly improbable, but they acknowledge that the complexity, speed, and dynamism of global banking arrangements expose the system to hazards we cannot even imagine. That, they say, is always the risk of technological advance. And as with other technological catastrophes — from Chernobyl to Bhopal — a financial markets computer breakdown would ultimately injure innocent workers and civilians just as it has in Mexico.

## GLOBALIZATION
## AND THE PRESSURE TO DEREGULATE

The technology of money lending and the explosion in money packaging have outpaced banking regulations designed for a simpler and slower age. The pressures of globalization have been used to remove regulations of all sorts from the financial services industry; U.S. banks are subject to more regulations than their German or Japanese competitors and therefore, it is argued, the global playing field is not level. Bigger German and Japanese banks with broader powers are outcompeting global banks that fly the U.S. flag.

Changes in Japanese banking regulations are also putting Tokyo-based banks in a stronger competitive position. On October 18, two weeks before the 1992 presidential election, Secretary of the Treasury Nicholas Brady gave a speech to the American Bankers Association in which he said that increasing the competitiveness of the U.S. financial services industry was critical to stimulating growth in the U.S. economy. The key, he said, was to eliminate "the old arbitrary legal framework that governs the banking system, especially outdated restrictions on products and geography." In other words, banks should be free to leave their original neighborhoods — where they may have helped local business and the public — and go to Asia or Europe, or wherever the action is, to serve themselves.

The argument that globalization requires deregulation is at least a quarter-century old. Deregulation of the U.S. financial services industry has actually been underway for years, as part of a global shift in the relationship between governments and banks all over the world. To a great extent the U.S. financial services industry deregulated itself. By resorting to creative corporation rearrangements such as holding companies and mergers, the banking, brokerage, and insurance industries slipped out of the legislative restraints intended to limit their geographical reach and their permissible activities long before Congress acted to loosen them. Through its parent corporation, Citicorp, which is not a bank under the law, Citibank could operate as a credit-card banker in all fifty states, rendering irrelevant and unenforceable the New Deal legislation that was supposed to keep banks serving their own communities. To get around legal requirements that banks lend only a certain percentage of their cash reserves, Citibank could sell its loans to Citicorp, which is not subject to these requirements.

Congress had not anticipated that the nation's largest bank would make such effective use of the one-bank holding company to escape regulation, and friends of the banking industry in the Senate effectively blocked efforts to plug the loophole. By the 1980s, banks were not only operating across state lines but had become sellers of insurance as well. Brokerage houses and automobile manufacturers were now deeply involved in the real estate market. All had, one way or another, jumped over the fences Congress had put up to separate investment banks from commercial banks and to keep brokerage firms, insurance companies, and thrifts concentrated on the businesses for which they were chartered. Thanks to information technology and the ingenuity of lawyers, money now traveled faster, farther, and in ways never envisioned by banking legislation and regulatory authorities. As Clive Crook in the *Economist* puts it, deregulation "is often no more than an acknowledgment that the rules are no longer working" (Crook 1992).

But deregulation, whether by circumvention of official policy or by law, had unanticipated and extremely unpleasant consequences. Like war plans, bank regulations are written with the catastrophes of the previous generation in mind.

After the Great Depression, when the national banking system collapsed because of risky loans, the Federal Reserve was given authority to set interest-rate ceilings on deposits. Regulation Q, as this grant of regulatory authority was known, was designed to stop banks from offering higher interest rates as a way of competing for deposits. The theory was that if banks were paying high interest, they would have to earn more on their loans and would be under pressure to take big risks with depositors' money. Since the deposits were now insured by the Federal Deposit Insurance Corporation (FDIC), the risk would eventually fall on the taxpayers if the economy turned sour. In normal times the fees all the member banks paid into the FDIC are sufficient to cover the deposits of banks in trouble, but if failures were to reach a certain point, FDIC reserves would be exhausted, and Congress would have to come up with the money to pay off depositors. This is, of course, exactly what happened in the late 1980s in the infamous Savings and Loan industry debacle. But the roots of the problem were planted decades earlier.

## EVOLUTION OF "HOMELESS" MONEY

All through the Cold War years, U.S. savers were sending more of their money abroad to take advantage of higher returns. In 1966, under pressure from lobbies representing elderly and retired persons, the Federal Reserve Board agreed to let financial institutions such as brokerage houses and insurance companies pay market rates on consumer savings accounts. These new accounts offering higher returns for consumers were known as *money market funds*. As nominal interest rates soared in the 1970s, money market funds accumulated hundreds of billions of dollars. By 1979, savings banks, savings and loan associations (S&Ls), and credit unions, which had their deposits tied up in long-term low-interest home mortgages arranged before inflation became rampant, tottered on the edge of bankruptcy.

Congress came to the rescue with two pieces of legislation: one known as the Deregulation and Monetary Control Act of 1980 and the other the Garn–St. Germain Act of 1982. Essentially, these laws phased out regulatory limits on interest rates for savings institutions, allowed them to offer interest-paying checking accounts, and granted authority to make all sorts of loans. Previously, thrifts had survived by lending most of the home-mortgage money in the nation, but now they were permitted to make consumer loans and commercial real estate loans. At the same time, companies such as Sears, GM, and Prudential, along with the commercial banks, could expand further into the commercial mortgage market. By tradition and by law, commercial banks were in business to supply working capital and investment funds to industry. But now they rushed into the real estate market. Citibank increased its mortgage portfolio from $100 million to $14.8 billion in just ten years. All this competitive zeal to finance unneeded office buildings spelled disaster for the S&Ls. Half of them disappeared. Our children and millions more taxpayers yet unborn will have to come up with something under $1 trillion to repair the damage.

All through the last three decades, U.S. banks pursued another strategy to escape the regulators. They shifted more and more of their activities beyond U.S. shores, well out of reach of the Treasury or the Fed. Here, too, regulators inadvertently spurred the process. As U.S. corporations, armies, military installations, and government aid programs spread around the world in the 1950s, all spending billions in U.S. currency in other countries, the glut of dollars in the hands of foreigners became a serious world problem. By this time, Germany, Japan, and the other industrial countries were recovering from the shocks of World War II and were producing a flood of goods. It was neither necessary nor advantageous to import so much from the United States. Non-Americans had accumulated hundreds of billions of dollars more than they could possibly use to buy goods and services from the United States. Except for the fact that the dollar was the world's reserve currency backed by gold, the overvalued offshore dollars were becoming risky holdings. If the holders of offshore dollars were to cash them in, the United States would face financial catastrophe, because the Treasury promised to redeem dollars with gold at $35 an ounce. The obvious alternatives for the federal government were either to scale back expensive military commitments or to devalue the dollar. Both were inconsistent with America's self-image in the 1960s as the world's number-one superpower.

For the first time, the nation experienced severe balance of payments problems. As foreigners piled up unwanted, overvalued dollars in banks in London, Paris, Geneva, and Hong Kong, the doors of the gold depository at Fort Knox kept swinging open to accommodate the heavy traffic in gold bars bound for Europe. To stem the flow of gold, the Kennedy and

Johnson administrations tried to limit the amount of dollars U.S. banks could lend to foreigners and taxed foreign bonds issued in the United States. But these measures only succeeded in accelerating the outflow of dollars. U.S. banks, led by Citibank, were now firmly established in Europe and Asia, and offshore lending exploded in reaction to the U.S. government's efforts to keep Wall Street banks from lending to foreigners.

By the 1970s, for every dollar U.S. banks were lending to non-Americans from their domestic bank offices, they were lending six or seven more from offshore facilities that collectively came to be called the Euromarket. This pooling of funds, mostly in dollars, started in Europe to accommodate the financial needs of Communist China, but it soon became a global money pool that could be used by borrowers anywhere. The distinguishing feature of the Euromarket is that the money is denominated in a currency different from the official currency where the deposits are located. All such money is largely beyond the reach of national regulators in the countries of origin. When U.S. companies in need of capital abroad resorted to the Euromarket, they were complying with the U.S. policy to restrict capital outflow from the United States. But the buildup of this huge pool of offshore dollars created a formidable alternative to the U.S. capital market. IBM was the pioneer among U.S.-based companies to make creative use of the Euromarket, but soon many U.S. companies operating outside the United States were financing their overseas operations without resorting to banks in their home country. The Euromarket expanded into bond issues and then began offering a menu of increasingly arcane money products. Soon it was serving as a "connecting rod" for financial markets around the world that once were entirely separate.

# EMERGENCE OF "CASINO ECONOMICS"

Money itself was becoming a truly global product. In 1973, the gross sum in Eurocurrency accounts all over the world was $315 billion; by 1987, the total was nearly $4 trillion. This fantastic expansion was hastened by the series of deregulations of international money transactions that began when the Nixon administration forced the end of fixed exchange rates in August 1971, and governments everywhere lost much of their power over money. The value of money was now set in increasingly integrated global marketplaces, as foreign exchange traders all around the world haggled over how many lire or drachmas an ever-fluctuating dollar could buy at any instant in time. In the 1970s, the eminent economist Milton Friedman had convinced the Chicago Mercantile Exchange, which had established a lively futures market in hog bellies and other agricultural products in order to protect farmers and food companies from the volatility of farm prices, that a futures market for money products would be a smart idea. The more exchange rates fluctuated, the more interested investors would become in hedging their bets with contracts to buy or sell at a set price on a set date. The betting possibilities were limitless. By 1989, 350 varieties of futures contracts, most of which were financial, were traded in Chicago and in the seventy-plus new exchanges that had sprouted up across the world.

U.S. officials played the key role in the transformation of world financial markets, most notably on two occasions. The first was in 1971, when Nixon closed the "gold window." No longer was it possible to redeem dollars for gold. This meant that non-Americans had to keep their dollars on deposit somewhere in the world or convert them into some other currency. The second event came eight years later when Paul Volcker, then chair of the Federal Reserve Board, tried to fight inflation in the United States by cutting the money supply. He used the standard tool — charging substantially higher interest rates to commercial banks to obtain dollars from the Federal Reserve. Since the dollar was the reserve currency for the world, however, the Fed had unwittingly raised interest rates everywhere, and both interest rates and exchange rates began fluctuating wildly. As Michael Lewis puts it in his book *Liar's Poker* (1989), "Overnight the bond market was transformed from a backwater into a casino." The buying, selling, and lending of monetary products worldwide became businesses in themselves. Most of it had little or nothing to do with investment in either production or commerce. (However, as exchange rates became more volatile, hedging became almost a necessity for some transnational businesses.) Foreign direct investment in the Third World fell as the leading commercial banks of the world saw that they could reap quicker profits in commissions, fees, and interest by "recycling" tens of billions of "petrodollars" from the coffers of Kuwait and Saudi Arabia to the governments and their business associates in poor countries.

As Richard O'Brien, chief economist of American Express Bank, notes (1992), "Deregulation and liberalization clearly encourage globalization and integration. Liberal markets and systems tend to be open, providing greater ease of access, greater transparency of pricing and information." The flow of accessible information offers a global environment that is hospitable to homeless money, promoting what O'Brien calls "the end of geography" in the finance and investment business.

The rise of global financial markets makes it increasingly difficult for national governments to formulate economic policy, much less to enforce it. In the increasingly anarchic world of high-speed money, the dilemma facing national political leaders is clear: Impose regulations, then sit back and watch how quickly financial institutions slip away by changing their looks, disappearing into other corporations, or otherwise rearranging their affairs to make life difficult for the regulators. At the same time, bankers argue that to the extent the regulations are observed, they pose a handicap in international competition. Yet the history of deregulation is littered with scandals and financial foolishness for which a handful of bankers, but mostly millions of taxpayers and depositors, have paid a heavy price.

Governments are periodically taught chilling lessons about how much control they have lost over the money they print. In September 1992, a frenzy of twenty-four-hour-a-day trading in European currencies forced the central banks of Finland, Italy, Spain, and Britain to devalue their currencies and to spend DM24 billion to prop up the lira and £10 billion to keep the British currency afloat. The British prime minister, who had made a public vow never to do what currency speculators around the world forced him to do, could not defend the pound even after the Bank of England raised interest rates 5 percentage points. The exchange of one currency for another, according to estimates of the Bank of International Settlements, is now about $640 billion a day. Not more than 10 percent of this huge volume of currency trading that causes governments to quake and some to fall has anything to do with normal commercial transactions, in which people or companies actually need to convert one currency to another to purchase foreign goods or services. No longer rooted in any community or nation, money was losing any relationship to the concrete world of goods and services. The value of money was now totally afloat and was based solely on how it was viewed by money traders and speculators.

## GLOBAL RACE TO DEREGULATE

On October 27, 1986, the "Big Bang," as the chair of the London Stock Exchange first called it, went off in the city of London, ending two hundred years of comfortable, stately, and expensive trading practices on the London Stock Exchange. Overnight, the market was deregulated and opened to foreign banks and securities firms of all sorts. An electronic marketing system modeled on the new U.S. computer-age stock exchange, NASDAQ, was installed to take the place of old-fashioned floor trading. Traders could now bypass London and deal directly with markets in New York and Tokyo at much less cost. Deregulation was a strategy for trying to get lost business back. As the New York Stock Exchange had done more than ten years earlier, the London Stock Exchange abolished fixed commissions for traders, and it now permitted firms to act as both wholesale dealers and brokers. Suddenly, U.S. commercial banks that were barred from the securities business at home could plunge into this market in London, neatly jumping over the wall of separation between investment and commercial banking provided under the Glass-Steagall Act of 1933, the cornerstone of modern U.S. banking regulation. (With the Great Crash and its consequences still fresh in mind, the act was intended to forbid banks to act as underwriters for corporate securities.)

The global expansion through large corporate mergers and acquisitions gathered steam in the 1970s, and this global restructuring of industry required the amassing of huge amounts of capital. At first, large banks dominated this market because they were the ones with the financial power and connections to syndicate large loans through networks of foreign banks. But in the 1980s, as capital needs mushroomed, corporations in need of funds found that it was much cheaper to raise the capital by issuing bonds and other sorts of commercial paper. Financial institutions of all sorts packaged a bunch of small loans and sold them as securities on world markets.

Borrowers all over the world, including the largest corporations, could now shop around the world for money, and they could borrow it in many different forms on a wide variety of terms. Investors could hedge against risks in one national economy or in one industry by buying foreign stocks. Global markets in securities offered opportunities for diversification. Laws and regulations that had previously put international investments out of bounds came tumbling down. Markets in securities were losing what few geographical ties were left. It was now possible to invest in the New York market by buying New York Stock Exchange index shares on the Chicago Board Options Exchange.

The Big Bang triggered an explosion of deregulation in other financial centers all over the world. Screen-based markets offering instantaneous flows of global information took over an ever larger share of business from traditional floor trading. In addition to the speed and convenience, there were fees and taxes to be saved. Stocks in foreign companies became internationally traded products. London, Amsterdam, Paris, Frankfurt, and Zurich competed in offering the most cosmopolitan menu of stocks, options, swaps, and futures in companies around the world. By 1990, the buying and selling of foreign equities on the London Exchange exceeded that of British equities. The New York Stock Exchange and the Tokyo Exchange still deal primarily in the stocks of companies based in their own countries, but to attract international business, according to New York Stock Exchange chairman William Donaldson, U.S. traders will have to put an end to parochialism and encourage more deregulation: "If this nation is to be the international market for securities, we must recognize the obvious, that not all the quality companies in the world are U.S. companies, nor are all U.S. accounting standards and practices necessarily the only way of approaching disclosure" (O'Brien 1992).

## THE FINAL BARRIER

With the juggernaut of deregulation having just about completed its sweep across the developed world, there remained one final barrier to ultimate freedom of movement for money and for the ability of the great financial conglomerates to control world markets. That barrier was among the poor countries of the Third World, who still stubbornly refused to open their commercial banking sector to outside domination. The Uruguay Round of the General Agreement on Tariffs and Trade took care of that.

In most of the world's poorest countries, foreign banks were traditionally welcomed for the services they performed, but only up to a certain point. The foreign banks were appreciated as sellers of retail credit and providers of capital under controlled, specific conditions. But foreign banks, with few exceptions, had been prohibited from buying into ownership positions in commercial banking. Third World governments argued that since finance is central to development, the financial services industry should remain firmly in domestic hands, serve domestic interests, and keep money within the economy.

The United States led the challenge against the Third World's control of its own financial markets during the Uruguay Round of GATT negotiations. The United States and other Western nations argued that "efficiency" and "fairness" required that all foreign banks be accorded national treatment in every country. *National treatment* essentially means that foreign banks must be treated just as if they were local banks, so, for example, U.S. banks must be permitted entry into Third World financial markets *even if they gain full control of the local institutions.* Local governments would have to give up all attempts to sustain control over local financing activity.

This was one of several important points that kept GATT negotiations stalled for seven years, but eventually the United States and the other

Western powers forced the poor nations to cave in, and a financial invasion is now underway.

While those negotiations proceeded, the United States pushed hard for deregulation of financial services with Mexico and secured an agreement that the U.S. negotiator said would give U.S. banks "dramatic new opportunities," a situation later solidified by NAFTA. As a result, one Treasury official bragged at an off-record briefing, "They [Mexico] gave us their financial system." Indeed they had, and in January 1995, the world was given a taste of the consequences. The Mexican economy will not recover for a long while. Ordinary Mexican citizens will ultimately pay the bills for the bailout by the United States of hundreds of its own speculators, notably Chase Manhattan and Goldman Sachs.

Clearly, this was just the first of many such debacles to come. In a globalized economy, wired together by technologies capable of moving unimaginable funds instantaneously around the globe at the behest of speculators and immune to any ability to regulate or control this movement, we are in for more frequent catastrophes. Yet this is a condition the world will not be able to tolerate for long. It makes banking services even more difficult and distant for local communities, small business, and ordinary people; worst of all, it puts the entire international economic apparatus into a most precarious situation. Global finance could tumble down quickly, like the house of cards it has become.

Ultimately, change must come in the form of a financial system not based on speculation, a system that uses funds with geographic roots and some connection to goods and services that cater, as they once did, to the interests of local and regional economies. The examples of the Grameen Bank in Bangladesh and the South Shore Bank in Chicago, running directly counter to the trend, are informative, optimistic models. Only by such a change in direction can the financial community be remotely in service to ecological and social sustainability.

# 32

# EXERCISING POWER OVER CORPORATIONS THROUGH STATE CHARTERS

Richard L. Grossman and Frank T. Adams

*Richard L. Grossman and Frank T. Adams are coauthors of a booklet that has circulated among hundreds of activist groups and generated considerable public controversy:* Taking Care of Business — Citizenship and the Charter of Incorporation *(1993). The booklet focuses on a little-noted but extremely significant point: A corporation's existence and the rules by which it operates are based on state charters of incorporation. These charters can be changed. Corporations can be forced to follow new rules or else be dismantled. The following chapter is adapted from the booklet.*

*Grossman is also the coauthor, with Richard Kazis, of* Fear at Work: Job Blackmail, Labor and the Environment *(1982). From 1976 to 1984, Grossman was director of Environmentalists for Full Employment. He now codirects the Program on Corporations, Law and Democracy, in Cambridge, Massachusetts.*

*Frank T. Adams began organizing interracial community–based groups in 1958. He is the author of five books on social change, including* Putting Democracy to Work: A Practical Guide for Starting and Managing Worker-Owned Businesses *(1992).*

CORPORATIONS CAUSE harm every day. Why do their harms go unchecked? How can they dictate what we produce, how we work, what we eat, drink, and breathe? How did a self-governing people let this come to pass?

Corporations were not supposed to reign in the United States.

When we look at the history of the United States, we learn that citizens intentionally defined corporations through *charters* — the certificates of incorporation.

In exchange for the charter, a corporation was obligated to obey all laws, to serve the common good, and to cause no harm. Early state legislators wrote corporation laws and actual charters to limit corporate authority and to ensure that when a corporation caused harm, they could revoke the corporation's charter.

During the late nineteenth century, however, corporations subverted state governments, and took over our power to put charters of incorporation to the uses originally intended.

Corporations may have taken our political power, but they have not taken our constitutional sovereignty. Citizens are guaranteed sovereign authority over government officeholders. Every state still has legal authority to grant and to revoke corporate charters. Corporations, large or small, still must obey all laws, serve the common good, and cause no harm.

Today, in our names, state legislators still give charters to individuals who want to organize businesses and still write corporation codes. Corporations cannot function — own property, borrow money, hire and fire, manufacture or trade, sign contracts, sell stock, sue and be sued, accumulate assets or debts — without the continued permission of state officeholders.

Our right to define corporations in charters and state laws is as crucial to self-government as our right to vote. Both are basic franchises, essential tools of liberty.

## A HOSTILE TAKEOVER

The U.S. Constitution makes no mention of corporations. Yet the history of constitutional law is, as former Supreme Court Justice Felix Frankfurter said, "the history of the impact of the modern corporation upon the American scene."

Today's business corporation is an artificial creation, shielding owners and managers while preserving corporate privilege and existence. Artificial or not, corporations have won more rights under law than people have — rights that government has frequently protected with armed force.

Investment and production decisions that shape our communities and rule our lives are made in boardrooms, regulatory agencies, and courtrooms. Judges and legislators have made it possible for corporate leaders to keep decisions about money, production, work, and ownership beyond the reach of democracy; they have created a corporate system under law.

This is not what many early Americans had in mind.

After the American Revolution, a struggle took place between those who sought popular self-governance with equal protection of the laws and those who sought minority rule, with some classes possessing special privileges. Minority rule won out: Native peoples, slaves, women and men without property were denied political rights. Formulating a definition of WE THE PEOPLE became a continuing political and organizing challenge — as it is to this day.

Notwithstanding, few people wanted corporations. When the first corporations were chartered, the people did not rely upon incorporators' promises. Instead, they wielded total authority over every aspect of corporate form and function. This was reflected in legal theory, laws and customs, and popular culture.

Earlier Americans were determined to keep investment and production decisions local and democratic. They believed corporations were neither inevitable nor always appropriate, and so created successful worker-owned enterprises, cooperatives and neighborhood shops, and efficient businesses owned by cities and towns. For a long time, even chartered corporations functioned well under sovereign citizen control.

But while they were weakening charter laws, corporate leaders also were manipulating the legal system to take away our property rights. "Corporations confronted the law at every point. They hired lawyers and created whole law firms," according to law professor Lawrence M. Friedman. "They bought and sold governments."

Under pressure from industrialists and bankers, a handful of nineteenth-century judges gave corporations more rights in property than human beings enjoyed in their persons.

Corporations persuaded courts to assume that huge, wealthy corporations competed on equal terms with neighborhood businesses or individuals. The courts declared that corporate contracts and the rate of return on investment were property that could not be meddled with by citizens or by elected representatives. Judges redefined *the common good* to mean maximum corporate production and profit.

• • •

Some citizens reacted to this hostile takeover by organizing to reclaim their authority over corporations. Mobilizing their cities and towns, citizens pressured legislators to protect states' economic rights for many decades.

Others turned to the federal government to guarantee worker and consumer justice, to standardize finance and stock issues, to prevent trusts and monopolies, and to protect public health and the environment.

The major laws that created regulatory and managing agencies actually give corporations great advantages over citizens. Some, like the National Labor Relations Act and the National Labor Relations Board, intended that the government aid citizens against the corporation. But these laws and agencies were shaped by corporate leaders, then diminished by judges. They neither prevent harms, nor correct wrongs, nor restore people and places. These regulatory laws were — and remain — reporting and permitting laws, laws to limit competition, to adjust market imperfections, and to manage destruction.

Regulatory agency administrators assume that corporations have prerogatives over labor, investment, and production. They regard land, air, and water as corporations' raw materials and as lawful places to dump corporate poisons. Like the courts, agencies give corporate leaders (and politicians) license to equate corporate goals with the public interest.

## A HIDDEN HISTORY

For one hundred years after the American Revolution, citizens and legislators fashioned the nation's economy by directing the chartering process.

They knew that English kings chartered the East India Company, the Hudson's Bay Company, and colonial settlements such as the Virginia Company, the Carolina Company, and the Massachusetts Bay Company, in order to control property and commerce. Kings appointed governors and judges, dispatched soldiers, and dictated taxes, investments, production, labor, and markets.

Having thrown off English rule and transformed corporate governments into constitutionalized states, the revolutionaries did not give governors, judges, or generals the authority to charter corporations. Citizens made certain that elected legislators issued charters, one at a time and for a limited number of years. They kept a tight hold on corporations by spelling out the rules each had to follow, by holding corporate managers, directors, and stockholders liable for harms or injuries, and by revoking charters.

Side by side with these legislative controls, legislators experimented with — and actively nurtured — various forms of enterprise and finance. Artisans and mechanics owned and managed diverse businesses. Farmers and millers organized profitable cooperatives; shoemakers created unincorporated business associations.

The idea of limited partnerships was imported from France. Land companies used various and complex arrangements and were not incorporated. None of these enterprises had the power of today's corporations.

Towns routinely promoted agriculture and manufacture. They subsidized farmers, public warehouses, and municipal markets; they protected watersheds and discouraged overplanting. State legislatures issued not-for-profit charters to establish universities, libraries, firehouses, churches, and charitable associations, along with new towns.

• • •

Because of widespread public involvement, early legislators granted very few charters and only after long, hard debate. Legislators usually denied charters to would-be incorporators when communities opposed the prospective business project.

Citizens shared the belief that granting charters was their exclusive right. Moreover, as the Supreme Court of Virginia reasoned in 1809, if the applicants' "object is merely private or selfish; if it is detrimental to, or not promotive of, the public good, they have no adequate claim upon the legislature for the privileges."

Citizens governed corporations by detailing rules and operating conditions not just in the charters but also in state constitutions and in state laws. Incorporated businesses were prohibited from taking any action that legislators did not specifically allow.

States limited corporate charters to a set number of years. Maryland legislators restricted manufacturing charters to forty years, mining charters to fifty, and most others to thirty years. Pennsylvania limited manufacturing charters to twenty years. Unless a legislature renewed an expiring charter, the corporation was dissolved, and its assets were divided among the shareholders.

Citizen-authority clauses dictated rules for issuing stock, for shareholder voting, for obtaining corporate information, and for paying dividends and keeping records. They limited capitalization, debts, land holdings, and sometimes profits. They required a company's accounting books to be turned over to a legislature upon request.

The power of large shareholders was limited by scaled voting, so that large and small investors had equal voting rights. Interlocking directorates were outlawed. Corporations were prohibited from owning other corporations. Shareholders had the right to remove directors at will.

Sometimes the rates that railroad, turnpike, and bridge corporations could charge were set by legislators. Some legislatures required incorporators to be state citizens. Other legislators directed their states to purchase corporate stocks in order to stay closely engaged in firms' operations.

Early in the nineteenth century, the New Jersey legislature declared its right to take over ownership and control of corporate properties. Pennsylvania established a fund from corporate profits that was used to buy private utilities and make them public. Many states followed suit.

Citizens kept banking corporations on particularly short leashes. Bank charters were limited from three to ten years. They had to get legislative approval to increase their capital stock or to merge. Some state laws required banks to make loans for local manufacturing, fishing, and agriculture enterprises, and to the states themselves. Banks were forbidden to engage in trade.

Private banking corporations were banned altogether by the Indiana Constitution in 1816 and by the Illinois Constitution in 1818.

People did not want business owners hidden behind legal shields but in clear sight. That is what they got. As the Pennsylvania legislature stated in 1834, *"A corporation in law is just what the incorporating act makes it. It is the creature of the law and may be molded to any shape or for any purpose that the Legislature may deem most conducive for the general good."*

• • •

In Europe, charters protected directors and stockholders from liability for debts and harms caused by their corporations. American legislators rejected this corporate shield. Led by Massachusetts, most states refused to grant such protection. Bay State law in 1822 read, "Every person who shall become a member of any manufacturing company . . . shall be liable, in his individual capacity, for all debts contracted during the time of his continuing a member of such corporation."

The first constitution in California made each shareholder "individually and personally liable for his proportion of all [corporate] debts and liabilities." Ohio, Missouri, and Arkansas made stockholders liable over and above the stock they actually owned. In 1861, Kansas made stockholders individually liable "to an additional amount equal to the stock owned by each stockholder."

Prior to the 1840s, courts generally supported the concept that incorporators were responsible for corporate debts. Through the 1870s, seven state constitutions made bank shareholders doubly liable. Shareholders in manufacturing and utility companies were often liable for employees' wages. Until the Civil War, most states held corporate investors and officials liable.

• • •

The penalty for abuse or misuse of the charter was revocation of the charter and dissolution of the corporation — not a minor punishment.

Revocation clauses were written into Pennsylvania charters as early as 1784. The first revocation clauses were added to insurance charters in 1809 and to banking charters in 1814. Even when corporations met charter requirements, legislatures sometimes decided not to renew those charters.

States often revoked charters by using *quo warranto* (by what authority) proceedings. In 1815, Massachusetts Justice Joseph Story ruled in *Terrett* v. *Taylor*, "A private corporation created by the legislature may lose its franchises by a misuser or nonuser of them. . . . This is the common law of the land, and is a tacit condition annexed to the creation of every such corporation."

Four years later, the U.S. Supreme Court tried to strip states of this sovereign right. Overruling a lower court, Chief Justice John Marshall wrote in *Dartmouth College* v. *Woodward* that the U.S. Constitution prohibited New Hampshire from revoking a charter granted to the college by King George III. That charter contained no reservation or revocation clauses, Marshall said.

The court's attack on state sovereignty outraged citizens. Protest pamphlets rolled off the presses. Thomas Earl wrote, "It is aristocracy and despotism, to have a body of officers, whose decisions are, for a long time, beyond the control of the people. The freemen of America ought not to rest contented, so long as their Supreme Court is a body of that character." Said Massachusetts legislator David Henshaw, "Sure I am that, if the American people acquiesce in the principles laid down in this case, the Supreme Court will have effected what the whole power of the British Empire, after eight years of bloody conflict, failed to achieve against our fathers."

Opponents of Marshall's decision believed the ruling cut the heart out of state sovereignty. They argued that a corporation's basic right to exist — and to wield property rights — came from a grant that only the state had the power to make. Therefore, the court had exceeded its authority by declaring the corporation beyond the reach of the legislature that created it in the first place.

People also challenged the Supreme Court's decision by distinguishing between a corporation and an individual's private property. The corporation existed at the pleasure of the legislature to serve the common good and was of a public nature. New Hampshire legislators and any other elected state legislators had the absolute legal right to dictate a corporation's property use by amending or repealing its charter.

State legislators were stung by citizen outrage. They were forced to write amending and revoking clauses into new charters, state laws, and constitutions, along with detailed procedures for revocation. In 1825, Pennsylvania legislators adopted broad powers to "revoke, alter or annul the charter" at any time they thought proper. New York state's 1828 corporation law specified that every charter was subject to alteration or repeal. Delaware voters passed a constitutional amendment in 1831 limiting all corporate charters to twenty years. Other states, including Louisiana and Michigan, passed constitutional amendments to place precise time limits on corporate charters.

President Andrew Jackson enjoyed wide popular support when he vetoed a law extending the charter of the Second Bank of the United States in 1832. That same year, Pennsylvania revoked the charters of ten banks.

During the 1840s, citizens of New York, Delaware, Michigan, and Florida required a two-thirds vote of their state legislatures to create, continue, alter, or renew charters. In 1849, the New York legislature instructed the attorney general to annul any charter whose applicants had concealed material facts and to sue to revoke a charter on behalf of the people whenever he believed necessary.

Over several decades starting in 1844, nineteen states amended their constitutions to make corporate charters subject to alteration or revocation by legislatures.

As late as 1855, citizens had support from the U.S. Supreme Court. In *Dodge* v. *Woolsey*, the court ruled the people of the states "[have not] released their powers over the artificial bodies which originate under the legislation of their representatives."

## STRUGGLES FOR CONTROL

Contests over charters and the chartering process were not abstractions. They were battles to control labor, resources, community rights, and political sovereignty. This was a major reason why members of the disbanded Working Men's Party formed the Equal Rights Party of New York State. The party's 1836 convention resolved that lawmakers "legislate for the whole people and not for favored portions of our fellow citizens."

This political agenda had widespread support in the press. A New Jersey newspaper wrote in an editorial typical of the 1830s, "The Legislature ought cautiously to refrain from increasing the irresponsible power of any existing corporations, or from chartering new ones, [else people would become] mere hewers of wood and drawers of water to jobbers, banks and stockbrokers."

With these and other prophetic warnings still ringing in their ears, citizens began to feel control over their futures slipping out of communities and out of their hands. Corporations were abusing their charters to become conglomerates and trusts. They were converting the nation's treasures into private fortunes, creating factory systems and company towns. Political power began flowing to absentee owners intent upon dominating people and nature.

As the nation moved closer to civil war, farmers were forced to become wage earners, increasingly separated from their neighbors, farms, and families. They became fearful of unemployment — a new fear that corporations quickly learned to exploit.

In factory towns, corporations set wages, hours, production processes and machine speeds. They kept blacklists of labor organizers and workers who spoke up for their rights. Corporate officials forced employees to accept humiliating conditions, while the corporations agreed to nothing.

• • •

Recognizing that workers were organizing to resist, industrialists and bankers pressed on, hiring private armies to keep workers in line. They bought newspapers and painted politicians as villains and businessmen as heroes. Bribing state legislators, they then announced that legislators were corrupt, that they used too much of the public's resources and time to scrutinize every charter application and corporate operation.

Flaunting new wealth and power accumulated during the Civil War, corporate executives paid *borers* to infest Congress and state capitals, bribing elected and appointed officials alike. They pried loose from the public trust more and more land, minerals, timber, and water. Railroad corporations alone obtained over 180 million free acres of public lands by the 1870s and extorted millions of dollars in direct subsidies.

Little by little, legislators gave corporations limited liability, decreased citizen authority over corporate structure, governance, production and labor, and granted ever longer terms for the charters themselves.

• • •

But even as businesses secured general incorporation laws for mining, agriculture, transportation, banking, and manufacturing businesses, citizens held on to the authority to charter. Specifying company size, shareholder terms, and corporate undertakings remained a major citizen strategy.

During the 1840s and 1850s, states revoked charters routinely. In Ohio, Pennsylvania, and Mississippi, banks lost charters for frequently "committing serious violations . . . which were likely to leave them in an insolvent or financially unsound condition." In Massachusetts and New York, turnpike corporations lost charters for "not keeping their roads in repair."

Rhode Island enacted a law requiring corporate dissolution for "fraud, negligence, misconduct." Language was added to the Virginia Constitution enabling "all charters and amendments of charters to be repealed at any time by special act."

New York, Ohio, Michigan, and Nebraska revoked the charters of oil, match, sugar, and whiskey trusts. Courts in each state declared these trusts illegal, because in creating the trusts, the corporations had exceeded the powers granted by their charters. "Roaming and piratical corporations" such as Standard Oil of Ohio, then the most powerful corporation in the world, refused to comply and started searching for "a Snug Harbor" in another state.

"No [state] constitutional convention met, between 1860–1900, without considering the problems of corporations," according to Friedman.

Farmers and rural communities, groaning in misery at the hands of railroad, grain, and banking corporations, ran candidates for office who supported states' authority "to reverse or annul at any time any chartered privilege."

The Farmers' Anti-Monopoly Convention, meeting in Des Moines in 1873, resolved that "all corporations are subject to legislative control; [such control] should be at all times so used as to prevent moneyed corporations from becoming engines of oppression."

Because all these and other powerful resistance movements directly challenged the harmful corporations of their times, and because they kept pressure on state representatives, revocation and amendment clauses can be found in state charter laws today.

## JUDGE-MADE LAW

However, maintaining strong charter laws and state corporation codes was ineffective once courts started aggressively applying legal doctrines that made protection of corporations and corporate property the center of constitutional law.

Following the Civil War and well into the twentieth century, appointed judges gave privilege after privilege to corporations. They freely reinterpreted the U.S. Constitution and transformed common law doctrines.

Judges gave certain corporations the power of "eminent domain." They eliminated jury trials to determine whether corporations caused harm and to assess damages.

Judges also took the right to oversee corporate rates of return and prices, a right that has been entrusted to elected legislators by the U.S. Constitution. They laid the legal foundation for regulatory agencies to be primarily answerable to the courts — not to Congress.

The courts even ruled that workers were responsible for causing their own injuries on the job. The Kentucky Court of Appeals had prefigured this doctrine in 1839: "Private injury and personal damage . . . must be expected" when one goes to work for a corporation bringing "progressive improvements." This judicial invention came to be called "the assumption of risk."

Traditionally, under common law courts had not permitted trespass or nuisance to be excused by the alleged good works a corporation might claim. Nor could a corporation's lack of intent to cause harm decrease its legal ability for injuries it caused to persons or the land.

Large corporations, especially railroad and steamship companies, pressured judges to reverse this tradition by creatively interpreting the commerce and due process clauses of the U.S. Constitution. Armed with a new concept that they called *substantive due process*, judges declared one state law after another as unconstitutional. Wages and hours laws (such as those banning payment in corporate scrip or those prohibiting child labor), along with rate laws for grain elevators and railroads, were tossed out.

Judges also established the managerial prerogative and business judgment doctrines, giving corporations legal justification to deny First Amendment rights of free speech and assembly on company property and to block democracy from passing through boardroom doors.

Another blow to citizen constitutional authority came in 1886. The Supreme Court ruled in *Santa Clara County* v. *Southern Pacific Railroad* that a private corporation was a "natural person" under the U.S. Constitution and thus sheltered by the Bill of Rights and the Fourteenth Amendment.

Using the Fourteenth Amendment, which had been added to the Constitution to protect freed slaves, the justices struck down hundreds more local, state, and federal laws enacted to enforce citizen sovereignty over corporations. The high court ruled that elected legislators, in enabling people to protect their communities and livelihoods from corporate domination, had been taking corporate property without due process.

Emboldened, some judges went further, declaring unions were civil and criminal conspiracies and enjoining workers from striking. Governors and presidents backed these judges with police and armies.

Judges had positioned the corporation to become "America's representative social institution," "an institutional expression of our way of life."

• • •

"Chartermongering" by state legislators unleashed state competition to attract as many corporations as possible. In exchange for taxes, fees, and whatever else they could get their hands on, some state officials happily provided new homes to Standard Oil and other corporations.

Led by New Jersey and Delaware, legislators watered down or removed citizen authority clauses. They limited the liability of corporate owners and managers then started handing out charters that literally lasted forever.

By the early 1900s, twenty-six corporate trusts ended up controlling 80 percent or more of production in their markets. There were trusts for almost everything: matches, whiskey, cotton, alcohol, corks, cement, stoves, ribbons, bread, beef.

During the so-called Progressive Era (around the turn of the twentieth century), corporations operated as ruthlessly as any colonial trading monopoly in the 1700s. Blood was often spilled resisting these legal fictions.

Corporations owned resources, production, commerce, trade, prices, jobs, politicians, judges, and the law. Over the next half-century, as a U.S. congressional committee concluded in 1941, "The principal instrument of the concentration of economic power and wealth has been the corporate charter with unlimited power."

Today, many U.S. corporations are transnational. Still, no matter how piratical they may be or how far they may roam, the corrupted charter and bastardized state corporation code remain the legal bases of their existence.

## TAKING BACK THE CHARTERS, TAKING BACK THE LAW

We are out of the habit of contesting the legitimacy of the corporation, or of challenging concocted legal doctrines, or of denying courts the final say over our economic lives.

For most of this century, citizens have organized valiantly to limit individual corporate harms but have not sought to end the ability of corporations to govern. We've forgotten how to use our state chartering process and corporation laws to dissolve corporations or to define corporations on our terms.

Today, too many organizing campaigns accept the corporation's rules and wrangle on corporate turf. We lobby a captive Congress for limited laws. We have no faith in regulatory agencies but turn to them for relief. We plead with corporations to be socially responsible then show them how to increase profits by being a bit less harmful.

How much more strength, time, and hope will we invest in such dead ends?

• • •

Today, corporate charters can be gotten easily by filling out a few forms and by paying modest fees.

State legislatures delegate authority to public officeholders to rubber-stamp the administration of charters and the chartering process. The secretary of state and the attorney general — sometimes elected, sometimes appointed — are the officials most often involved.

In all states, legislatures continue to have the historical and legal obligation to grant and rewrite charters and to write state corporation laws to end corporate assaults upon life, property, and democracy.

In Illinois, the law reads as follows:

12.50 Grounds for judicial dissolution. A Circuit Court may dissolve a corporation:

(a) in an action by the Attorney General, if it is established that:

1. the corporation obtained its certificates of incorporation through fraud; or

2. the corporation has continued to exceed or abuse the authority conferred upon it by law, or has continued to violate the law . . .

3. in an action by a shareholder, if it is established that . . . the directors or those in control of the corporation have acted, or are acting, or will act in a manner that is illegal, oppressive or fraudulent; . . . or if it is established that dissolution is reasonably necessary because the business of the corporation can no longer be conducted to the general advantage of its shareholders.

After entering an order of dissolution, "the Court shall direct the winding up and liquidation of the corporation's business and affairs."

In Delaware, Section 284 of the corporation law says that chancery courts can revoke the charter of any corporation for "abuse or misuse of its powers, privileges, or franchises."

New York requires dissolution when a corporation abuses its powers or acts "contrary to the public policy" of the state. The law calls for a jury trial in charter revocation cases.

The Model Business Corporation Act, first written in 1931 by the committee on corporate laws of the American Bar Association and revised twice since, is the basis for chartering laws in more than half the states and the District of Columbia. Although strongly protecting corporate property, this model law gives courts full power to liquidate the assets of a corporation if such assets are "misapplied or wasted."

It requires the secretary of state "from time to time" to list the names of all corporations that have violated their charters along with the facts behind the violations. Decrees of involuntary dissolution can be issued by the secretary of state and by courts.

Corporations chartered in other states are called foreign corporations. Corporations chartered in other nations are called alien corporations. Legislatures allow foreign or alien corporations to go into business in their states through this same chartering process. Either may establish factories or do business after obtaining a state's certificate of authority.

In Illinois, foreign corporations are "subject to the same duties, restrictions, penalties and liabilities now or hereafter imposed upon a domestic corporation of like character."

• • •

When we limit our thinking only to existing labor or environmental law, or to the courts, or to elections, we give up opportunities to force our elected officials to defend the Constitution of the United States from the powerful corporate fictions that undermine our republican form of government.

When we accept corporate definitions of property and judge-made laws granting corporations greater rights than humans, we reject the rich histories of struggle for the common good and of human authority over corporations.

When we accept today's corporation as inevitable, we shrink from demanding what we know is necessary and right. We throw away strategies and tactics we can use to end corporate rule.

Today, we need to get corporations out of our air and water; end corporate domination of investment and jobs; expel corporations from our elections, from our lawmakers' offices, from our judges' chambers, and from our schools; and begin investment transitions in areas ranging from energy to agriculture.

So we will have to educate ourselves and one another about corporations, about our rights, and about history and democracy and law. We will have to organize, educate, and agitate in political arenas where we are not accustomed to operating.

Stockholders have authority to seek injunctions and file corporation dissolution suits if they have reason to believe managers are acting illegally, oppressively, fraudulently, or are misusing or wasting corporate assets.

The majority of people (who do not own corporate stocks) will need to figure out how to pressure the few who do own stocks to change the ways that corporations are run.

We citizens of our states have the right to amend and revoke charters of harm-causing corporations. By initiating amendment and revocation actions, we can set in motion organizing efforts to freeze corporate assets, dissolve offending corporations, save jobs, and recharter new enterprises that do not have the vast privileges and immunities enjoyed by today's corporations.

We must begin getting corporations that are chartered in our states — that are chartered in our names — off the backs of people around the world.

As in the first half of the nineteenth century, we the people can require would-be incorporators to request *from us* the privilege of doing business in our states. We can write our rules into the charters and our state corporation codes.

For starters, workers must have free speech and other Bill of Rights protections; managers, directors, and shareholders must be liable for all corporate debts and harms; only natural persons may be permitted to own corporations (that is, one corporation may not own another corporation).

We can change judge-made law, such as doctrines that declare corporations to be legal persons and that give corporate managers sole authority over investment, production, and job decisions.

We can place ceilings on corporate salaries and require increasing levels of worker and community ownership. We can keep corporate size down by limiting capitalization. We can ban corporations from participating in our elections and our lawmaking and keep corporations from advertising on public policy and legal issues.

We can get corporations out of our schools.

We can use charters and state corporation codes to prevent corporations from manufacturing or selling destructive products (such as paper made from trees when many alternatives exist), from hiring scabs to replace striking workers, and from using deadly chemicals (such as chlorine) or disruptive industrial processes (such as rDNA).

We can end tax deductions for corporate salaries, legal fees, advertising, and fines. We can increase corporate tax rates.

We have the authority to redefine worker and community rights as constitutionally protected property rights and to bestow broad legal standing upon other species and the natural world.

We can direct public subsidies to cooperatives and other enterprises that remain subordinate to the sovereign people and that serve the public trust.

Our sovereign right to decide what is produced, to own and organize our work, and to respect the earth is as American as a self-governing people's right to vote.

In our democracy, we can shape the nation's economic life and define the nation's institutions of enterprise any way we want.

In fact, such efforts are getting underway. In communities dominated by giant corporations, people who had been organizing to stop corporate harms one at a time and who had been mired in long struggles with alphabet-soup regulatory agencies are shifting their focus to the legal fictions called corporations.

People are convening "Rethinking the Corporation, Rethinking Democracy" meetings, researching state corporation laws, studying our constitutions, examining corporate charters. They are helping one another break the grip of the global corporate culture and undo the corporate colonization from our minds. They are forging education and organizing strategies to shift rights and powers from corporations back to people, communities, and nature.

Out of such struggles can arise national and global movements powerful enough to dismantle the most tyrannical corporations and to transform those corporations that remain into dedicated servants of the common good.

# PART IV

# STEPS TOWARD
# RELOCALIZATION

*By now it should be clear that the expansion of the global economy directly leads to a corresponding contraction of the local economies that it largely replaces. This inevitably marginalizes and renders obsolete a large segment of the populations of both the industrial and the so-called developing countries. At the same time, it devastates the natural world, homogenizes cultures, and destroys communities, depriving their members of any semblance of control over their own lives. This process must be brought to a halt — moreover, it must be reversed — even if, from today's grim perspective, this may seem difficult to achieve.*

*Until recently, the vast bulk of humanity relied only upon the local economy for its livelihood. Today's problems will eventually be solved by recognizing that local production for local consumption — using local resources, under the guidance and control of local communities, and reflecting local and regional cultures and traditions within the limits of nature — is a far more successful direction than the currently promoted, clearly utopian, globally centralized, expansionist model. Local economies are far more likely to produce stable and satisfied communities and to protect nature than any system based on a theoretically constant expansion of production and consumption and the eternal movement of commodities across thousands of miles of land and sea.*

*This does not mean that all trade is undesirable; only that its role must be limited to providing those things that cannot be provided locally. Contrary to what global economics tell us,* import substitution, *that is, the process whereby nations choose to produce more products locally rather than increase imports and exports, must again become the order of the day.*

*A favorite charge by the defenders of globalism is that local economies can be harshly "provincial" and autocratic, yet there is considerable historical evidence that local and indigenous economic-political systems have usually been more stable and peaceful than the chaotic current display in the Balkans, usually warned about. And they are surely more democratic than centralized corporate globalism. Indeed, in many cases of conflict it has been external interventions that have set small societies against one another.*

*As for losing touch with the world beyond the region, it is obvious that not every technology of transport or communications is about to be abandoned. Hopefully it will only be those technologies that lead to the centralizing of economic power beyond the possibility of citizen control and to the declining health of the natural world.*

*The chapters in this part consider some of the ideas that provide the rationale for the local economy, and explore strategies required to assist a transition toward a more viable, more satisfying, and incomparably more sustainable world.*

# 33

## SHIFTING DIRECTION
### From Global Dependence to Local Interdependence

Helena Norberg-Hodge

*The arguments for changing directions — that is, for abandoning the emerging global economy in favor of community-based, localized, highly diversified economies — may be compelling, but such a change is clearly not in the interests of transnational corporations or the governments they put into power. New political alignments may eventually prove effective, but meanwhile, citizens can already undertake a host of local activities that contribute toward the creation of new community-based economies. Some are well underway. Helena Norberg-Hodge lists and describes some of those initiatives and suggests what their contributions might be.*

A ROUND THE world — from North to South, from far left to far right — recognition of the destructive effects of economic globalization is growing. However, the conviction that the solutions lie with localizing economic activity is far less widespread. Many people seem to find it difficult even to imagine a shift toward a more local economy. "Time has moved on," one hears. "We live in a globalized world."

On the surface, this is a perfectly reasonable point of view. How, after all, can we expect to tackle today's global ecosocial crises except on a global level? But it's not that simple. We need to distinguish between efforts merely to counter further globalization and efforts that can bring real solutions. The best way to halt the runaway global economy would undoubtedly be through multilateral treaties that would enable governments to protect people and the environment from the excesses of free trade. But such international steps would not in themselves restore health to economies and communities. Long-term solutions to today's social and environmental problems require a range of small, local initiatives that are as diverse as the cultures and environments in which they take place. When seen as going hand in hand with policy shifts away from globalization, these small-scale efforts take on a different significance. Most importantly, rather than thinking in terms of isolated, scattered efforts, it is helpful to think of institutions that will *promote small scale on a large scale.*

## CONCEPTUAL RESISTANCE TO LOCALIZATION

Moving toward the local can still seem impractical or utopian. One reason is the belief that an emphasis on the local economy means total self-reliance on a village level, without any trade at all. The most urgent issue today, however, isn't whether people have oranges in cold climates but whether their wheat, eggs, or milk should travel thousands of miles when they could all be produced within a 50-mile radius. In Mongolia, a country that has survived on local milk products for thousands of years and that today has twenty-five million milk-producing animals, one finds mainly German butter in the shops. In Kenya, butter from Holland is half the price of local butter; in England, butter from New Zealand costs far less than the local product; and in Spain, dairy products are mainly Danish. In this absurd situation, individuals are becoming dependent for their everyday needs on products that have been transported thousands of miles, often unnecessarily. The goal of localization would not be to eliminate all trade but to reduce unnecessary transport while encouraging changes that would strengthen and diversify economies at both the community and national levels. The degree of diversification, the goods produced, and the amount of trade would naturally vary from region to region.

Another stumbling block is the belief that a greater degree of self-reliance in the North would undermine the economies of the Third World, where people supposedly need northern markets to lift themselves out of poverty. The truth of the matter, however, is that a shift toward smaller scale and more localized production would benefit both North and South — and allow for more meaningful work and fuller employment all around. Today, a large portion of the South's natural resources is delivered to the North, on increasingly unfavorable terms, in the form of raw materials; the South's best agricultural land is devoted to growing food, fibers, even flowers for the North; and a good deal of the South's labor is used to manufacture goods for northern markets. Rather than further impoverishing the South, producing more ourselves would allow the South to keep more of its resources and labor for itself.

It is very important to understand the differences between the economies of the North and the South. A project that might work well in the North is not guaranteed to be beneficial in less industrialized economies. For instance, introducing microloans for small-scale enterprise may actually contribute to the destruction of local, nonmonetized economies and create dependence on a highly volatile and inequitable global economy, where factors such as currency devaluation can prove disastrous. By the same token, we should recognize that pulling a thousand people away from sure subsistence in a land-based economy into an urban context where they compete for a hundred new jobs is not a net gain in employment: Nine hundred people have, in effect, become *un*employed.

The idea of localization also runs counter to the belief that fast-paced urban areas are the locus of "real" culture and diversity, while small, local communities are invariably isolated backwaters where small-mindedness and prejudice are the norm. It isn't strange that this should seem so. The whole industrialization process has systematically removed political and economic power from rural areas and engendered a concomitant loss of self-respect in rural populations. In small communities today, people are often living on the periphery, while power — and even what we call *culture* — is centralized somewhere else.

Rural life in the West has been marginalized for many generations, and most Westerners thus have a highly distorted notion of what life in small communities can be. And even though much of the Third World is made up of villages, colonialism and development have left an indelible mark. In order to see what communities are like when people retain real economic power at the local level, we would have to look back — in some cases hundreds of years — to before these changes occurred. As I pointed out in an earlier chapter, I have seen with my own eyes how the largely self-reliant, community-based culture of Ladakh was transformed by economic development. Only a decade ago, the traditional culture was suffused with vibrancy, joy, and a tolerance of others that was clearly connected with people's sense of self-esteem and control over their own lives. Economic development, however, dismantled the local economy; decision-making power was shifted almost overnight from the household and village to bureaucracies in distant urban centers; the media educated children for a "glamorous" urban life-style completely unrelated to the local context and alien to that of their elders. If economic trends continue to

undermine cultural vibrancy and self-esteem, future impressions of village life in Ladakh may soon be little different from Western stereotypes
of small-town life.

An equally common myth that clouds thinking about more human-
scale rural economies is that "there are too many people to go back to the
land." It is noteworthy that a similar skepticism does not accompany the
notion of urbanizing the world's population. What is too easily forgotten
is that the majority of the world's people today — mostly in the Third
World — already *are* on the land. To ignore them and speak as if people
are urbanized as part of the human condition is a very dangerous misconception that helps to fuel the whole urbanization process. It is considered
"utopian" to suggest a ruralization of America's or Europe's population;
but China's plans to move 440 million people into the cities during the
next few decades hardly raises eyebrows. This "modernization" of
China's economy is part of the same process that has led to unmanageable
urban explosions all over the South — from Bangkok and Mexico City to
Bombay, Jakarta, and Lagos. In these cities, unemployment is rampant,
millions are homeless or live in slums, and the social fabric is unraveling.

Even in the North, urbanization continues. Rural communities are
being steadily dismantled, their populations pushed into spreading subur-
banized megacities. In the United States, where only 2 percent of the
population lives on the land, farms are still disappearing at the rate of
thirty-five thousand per year. It is impossible to offer that model to the rest
of the world, where the majority of people earn their living as farmers.
But where are the people saying, "We are too many to move to the city"?

Instead we hear that urbanization is necessary because of overpopulation. The implicit assumption is that centralization is somehow more efficient, that urbanized populations use fewer resources. When we take a
close look at the real costs of urbanization in the global economy, however, we can see how far this is from the truth. Urban centers around the
world are extremely resource-intensive. The large-scale, centralized systems they require are almost without exception more stressful to the environment than small-scale, diversified, locally adapted production. Food
and water, building materials, and energy must all be transported great
distances via vast energy-consuming infrastructures; their concentrated
wastes must be hauled away in trucks and barges or incinerated at great
cost to the environment. In their identical glass and steel towers with windows that never open, even air to breathe must be provided by fans,
pumps, and nonrenewable energy. From the most affluent sections of
Paris to the slums of Calcutta, urban populations depend on transport for
their food, so that every pound of food consumed is accompanied by sev-

eral pounds of petroleum consumption and significant amounts of pollution and waste.

What's more, these Westernized urban centers — whether in tropical Brazil, arid Egypt, or subarctic Scandinavia — all use the same narrow range of resources while displacing more locally adapted methods that made use of local resources, knowledge, and biological diversity. Children in Norwegian fishing villages enjoy eating cod, while people on the Tibetan plateau prefer their staple barley. Yet they are increasingly encouraged to eat the same food that is eaten in the industrial world. Around the world people are being pulled into a monoculture, which is leveling both cultural and biological diversity. The urbanizing global economy is thus creating artificial scarcity by ignoring local systems of knowledge and educating children to become dependent on a highly centralized economy. The end result is disastrously high levels of unemployment, increased competition, and heightened ethnic conflict.

It is precisely because there *are* so many people that we must abandon the globalized economic model, which can only feed, house, and clothe a small minority. It is becoming essential to support knowledge systems and economic models that are based on an intimate understanding of diverse regions and their unique climates, soils, and resources.

In the North, where we have for the most part long been separated from the land and from each other, we have large steps to take. But even in regions that are highly urbanized, we can nurture a new connection to place. By reweaving the fabric of smaller communities within large cities and by redirecting economic activity toward the natural resources around such communities, cities can regain their regional character, become more livable, and lighten their burden on the environment. Our task will be made easier if we support our remaining rural communities and small farmers: They are the key to rebuilding a healthy agricultural base for stronger, more diversified economies.

## SHIFTING DIRECTION

Many individuals and organizations are already working from the grass roots to strengthen their communities and local economies. Yet for these efforts to succeed, they need to be accompanied by policy changes at the national and international levels. How, for example, can grass-roots participatory democracy be strengthened unless limits are placed on the political power of huge corporations? How can local support alone enable small producers and locally owned shops to flourish if corporate welfare and free trade policies heavily promote the interests of large-scale producers and marketers? How can we return to a local context in education if monocultural media images continue to bombard children in every corner of the planet? How can local efforts to promote the use of locally available renewable energy sources compete against massive subsidies for huge dams and nuclear power plants?

The policy changes that would allow space for more community-based economies to flourish will certainly elicit objections. Some will claim that the promotion of decentralization is "social engineering" that would seriously dislocate the lives of many people. While it is true that some disruption would inevitably accompany a shift toward the local, it would be far *less* than that caused by the current rush toward globalization. It is in fact today's "jobless growth" society that entails social and environmental engineering on an unprecedented scale, as vast stretches of the planet and whole societies are reconfigured to conform to the needs of global growth — encouraged to abandon their languages, their foods, and their architectural styles for a standardized monoculture.

Others will interpret financial incentives for more localized production as "subsidies." However, these incentives should be seen as alternatives to current subsidies for globalization; that is, for transport, communications, energy infrastructures, education, and R&D in the technologies of large-scale centralized production. Moving in the direction of the local will actually cost *less* than we are now spending to move toward the global.

Rethinking our direction means looking at the entire range of public expenditures:

• The money currently spent on long-distance road transport alone offers an idea of how heavily subsidized the global economy is. In the United States, where there are already about 2.5 million miles of paved roads, another $80 billion has been earmarked for highways in the next few years, and plans are even being considered for a road link between Alaska and Siberia. The European Community, meanwhile, is planning to spend $120 billion ecus to add an additional 7,500 miles of superhighways across Western Europe by 2002 and is considering a tunnel to connect Europe with Africa. Throughout the South, scarce resources are similarly being spent. In New Guinea, for example, $48 million was spent on 23 miles of roads that allow timber interests to harvest and bring logs to the export market.

Shifting this support toward a range of transport options that favor smaller, more local enterprises would have enormous benefits, from the creation of jobs to a healthier environment to a more equitable distribution of resources. Depending on the local situation, transport money could be spent on building bike paths, foot paths, paths for animal transport, boat and shipping facilities, or rail service. Even in the highly industrialized world, where dependence on centralizing infrastructures is deeply entrenched, a move in this direction can be made. In Amsterdam, for example, steps are being taken to ban cars from the heart of the city, thus allowing sidewalks to be widened and more bicycle lanes to be built.

• Large-scale energy installations are today heavily subsidized. Phasing out these multibillion-dollar investments while offering real support for locally available renewable energy supplies would result in lower pollution levels, reduced pressure on wilderness areas and oceans, and less dependence on dwindling petroleum supplies and dangerous nuclear technologies. It would also help to keep money from leaking out of local economies.

• Agricultural subsidies now favor large-scale industrial agribusinesses. Subsidies include not only direct payments to farmers but funding for research and education in biotechnology and chemical- and energy-intensive monoculture. Shifting those expenditures toward those that encourage smaller-scale, diversified agriculture would help small family farmers and rural economies while promoting biodiversity, healthier soils, and fresher food. Urbanized consumers may not be aware that most agricultural subsidies benefit huge corporations such as Cargill and other middlemen, not small farmers.

• Government expenditures for highway building promote the growth of corporate "superstores" and sprawling malls. Spending money instead to build public markets — such as those that were once found in virtually every European town and village — would enable local merchants and artisans with limited capital to sell their wares. This would enliven town centers and cut down on fossil fuel use and pollution. Similarly, support for farmers' markets would help to revitalize both the cities and the agricultural economy of the surrounding region while reducing money spent to process, package, transport, and advertise food.

• Television and other mass telecommunications have been the recipients of massive subsidies in the form of R&D, infrastructure development, educational training, and other direct and indirect support. They are now rapidly homogenizing diverse traditions around the world. Shifting support toward building facilities for local entertainment — from music and drama to puppet shows and festivals — would offer a healthy alternative.

• At present, investments in health care favor huge, centralized hospitals meant to serve urban populations. Spending the same money instead on a greater number of smaller clinics that relied less on high technology and more on health practitioners would bring health care to more people and boost local economies.

• Creating and improving spaces for public meetings, from town halls to village squares, would encourage face-to-face exchanges between decision makers and the public, serving both to enliven communities and to strengthen participatory democracy. In Vermont, for example — where participatory democracy is still alive and well — people attend town meetings for lively debates and votes on local issues.

In addition to the direct and indirect subsidies given them, large-scale corporate businesses also benefit from a range of government regulations — and in many cases, a lack of regulations — at the expense of smaller, more localized enterprises. Although big business complains about red tape and inefficient bureaucracy, the fact is that much of it could be dispensed with if production were smaller in scale and based more locally. In today's climate of unfettered "free" trade, some government regulation is clearly necessary, and citizens need to insist that governments be allowed to protect their interests. This could best come about through international treaties in which governments agree to change the "rules of the game" to encourage real diversification and decentralization in the business world. There are many areas that need to be looked at in this regard:

• The *free flow of capital* has been a necessary ingredient in the growth of transnational corporations. Their ability to shift profits, operating costs, and investment capital to and from all of their far-flung operations enables them to operate anywhere in the world and to hold sovereign nations hostage by threatening to pack up, leave, and take their jobs with them. Governments are thus forced into competition with one another for the favors of these corporate vagabonds and try to lure them with low labor costs, lax environmental regulations, and substantial subsidies. Small local businesses, given no such subsidies, cannot hope to survive this unfair competition.

• Today, governments of every stripe are embracing *free trade policies* in the belief that opening themselves up to economic globalization will cure their ailing economies. Instead, a careful policy of using tariffs to regulate the import of goods that could be produced locally would be in the best interests of the majority. Such "protectionism" is not aimed at fellow citizens in other countries; rather it is a way of safeguarding the local culture, jobs, and resources against the excessive power of the transnationals.

• In almost every country, *tax regulations* discriminate against small businesses. Small-scale production is usually more labor-intensive, and heavy taxes are levied on labor through income taxes, social welfare taxes, value-added taxes, and so on. Meanwhile, tax breaks (such as accelerated depreciation and investment tax credits) are handed out on the capital- and energy-intensive technologies used by large corporate producers. Reversing this bias in the tax system would not only help local economies but would create more jobs by favoring people instead of machines. Similarly, taxes on the energy used in production would encourage businesses that are less dependent on high levels of technological input — which, again, means smaller, more labor-intensive enterprises. And if gasoline and diesel fuel were taxed so that prices reflected real costs — including some measure of the environmental damage their consumption causes — there would be a reduction in transport, an increase in regional production for local consumption, and a healthy diversification of the economy.

• Small businesses are discriminated against through the *lending policies of banks*, which charge them significantly higher interest rates for loans than they charge big firms. They also often require that small business owners personally guarantee their loans — a guarantee not sought from the directors of large businesses.

• An unfair burden often falls on small-scale enterprises through *regulations aimed at problems caused by large-scale production*. Battery-style chicken farms, for example, clearly need significant environmental and health regulations. Their millions of closely kept fowl are highly prone to disease; their tons of concentrated effluent need to be safely disposed of; and their long-distance transport entails the risk of spoilage. Yet a small producer, such as a farmer with a few hundred free-range chickens, is subject to essentially the same regulations, often raising costs to levels that can make it impossible to remain in business. Large-scale producers can spread the cost of compliance over a greater volume, making it appear that they enjoy economies of scale over smaller producers. Such discriminatory regulations are widespread. For example, a local entrepreneur wanting to bake cookies at home to sell at a local market would in most cases need to install an industrial kitchen to meet health regulations. Such a regulation makes it economically impossible to succeed.

• Local and regional *land use regulations* can be amended to protect wild areas, open space, and farmland from development. Political and financial support could be given to the various forms of land trusts that have been designed with this in mind. In the United States, there are now over nine hundred such trusts protecting more than 2.7 million acres of land. In some cases, local governments have used public money to buy the development rights to farmland, thereby simultaneously protecting the land from suburban sprawl while reducing the financial pressure on farmers. Studies have also shown that developed land costs local governments significantly more in services than the extra tax revenues generated — meaning that when land is developed, taxpayers not only lose the benefits of open space but also lose money.

• In urban areas, *zoning regulations* usually segregate residential, business, and manufacturing areas — a restriction necessitated by the needs and hazards of large-scale production and marketing. These could be changed to enable an integration of homes, small shops, and artisan or other small-scale production sites, as was traditional in the world's great cities. A rethinking of restrictions on community-based ways of living would also be beneficial. Zoning and other regulations aimed at limiting high-density developments often end up prohibiting environmentally sound living arrangements such as cohousing and ecovillages.

In the Third World, the majority are still living in small towns and rural communities and are largely dependent on a local economy. In this era of rapid globalization, the most urgent challenge is to stop the tide of urbanization and globalization by strengthening these local economies. A number of policy level changes could help to do so:

• Large dams, fossil-fuel plants, and other large-scale energy and transport infrastructures are geared toward the needs of urban areas and export-driven production. Shifting support toward a decentralized, renewable-energy infrastructure would help to stem the urban tide by strengthening villages and small towns. Since the energy infrastructure in the South is not yet very developed, this could be realistically implemented in the near future if there were sufficient pressure from activists lobbying northern banks and funding agencies.

• Colonialism, development, and now free trade and globalization have meant that the best land in the South is used to grow crops for northern markets. Shifting the emphasis to diversified production for local consumption would not only improve the economies of rural communities but also lessen the gap between rich and poor while eliminating much of the hunger that is now so endemic in the so-called developing parts of the world.

• Countries in the South are also being hit hard by free trade agreements such as GATT and NAFTA. They would be far better off if, contrary to the aim of such treaties, they were allowed to protect and conserve their natural resources, nurture national and local business enterprises, and limit the impact of foreign media and advertising on their culture. Since free trade can pull people away from a relatively secure local economy and put them on the bottom rung of the global economic ladder, even "fair trade" may not always be in the long-term interest of the majority in the South.

• The South would benefit enormously from an end to the promotion of Western-style monocultural education. Instead, efforts are needed that would give preeminence to the local language and values while promoting more location-specific knowledge adapted to the bioregion and the culture.

• Local economies and communities in the South would also benefit if support for capital- and energy-intensive, centralized, health care based on a Western model were shifted toward more localized and indigenous alternatives.

• It is also of critical importance to elevate the status of primary producers (especially farmers) and rural life in general. In the South today, the message being transmitted by the media, advertising, and tourism is that rural life is, in effect, a lower evolutionary stage. This message puts intense psychological pressure on people to become modern, urban consumers. This indoctrination process can be countered through the use of a variety of media, from comic books to theater and films, and through exchange programs that expose people in the South to the realities of life in the North. I have termed efforts of this sort *counterdevelopment*, since they are conscious attempts to counter the forces that are promoting an unsustainable, highly polluting, consumer life-style around the world.

In the South, the majority of people still get their spiritual, cultural, and economic strength from their connection to the place where they live. We need to keep in mind how our assumptions about human nature and about the "efficiency" and "superiority" of Western industrial culture are helping to destroy the existing fabric of local economy and community. Before the incursion of the West, people enjoyed singing their own songs, speaking their own language, eating the food from their own region. Even today, most adults would prefer to be able to maintain their culture and remain in their communities. Rather than pulling people into westernized urban centers where they are robbed of their cultural and personal identity and made dependent on a global economy, we need to allow people to stay where they are and be who they are.

# GRASS-ROOTS INITIATIVES

Economic localization should entail an adaptation to cultural and biological diversity; therefore no single blueprint would be appropriate everywhere. The range of possibilities for local grass-roots efforts is as diverse as the locales in which they would take place. The following survey is by no means exhaustive but illustrates the sorts of steps being taken today.

• In a number of places, community banks and loan funds have been established to increase the capital available to local residents and businesses and allow people to invest in their neighbors and their community, rather than in distant corporations.

• "Buy-local" campaigns help local businesses survive even when pitted against heavily subsidized corporate competitors. The campaigns not only help keep money from leaking out of the local economy but also help educate people about the hidden costs to the environment and to the community in purchasing less expensive but distantly produced products. Across the United States, Canada, and Europe, grass-roots organizations have sprung up in response to the intrusion of huge corporate marketing chains into rural and small-town economies. For example, the McDonald's corporation — which added nine hundred restaurants worldwide in 1993 and plans to add a new restaurant every nine hours in the coming years — has met with grass-roots resistance in at least two dozen countries. Polish activists, for instance, succeeded in blocking the construction of a McDonald's in an old section of Cracow, and activists in India are working to keep McDonald's from entering that market. In the United States and Canada, the rapid expansion of Wal-Mart, the world's largest retailer, has spawned a whole network of activists working to protect jobs and the fabric of their communities from these sprawling superstores.

• An effective way of guaranteeing that money stays within the local economy is through the creation of local currencies. Local Exchange Trading Systems (LETS) schemes have sprung up in the United Kingdom (where there are over 250 in operation), and in Ireland, Canada, France, Argentina, the United States, Australia, and New Zealand. These initiatives have psychological benefits that are just as important as the economic benefits: A large number of people who were once merely "unemployed" and therefore "useless" are becoming valued for their skills and knowledge. [See chapter by Susan Meeker-Lowry.]

• Another idea is the creation of local "tool lending libraries," whereby people can share tools on a community level. By reducing the need for everyone to have their own agricultural or forestry equipment, gardening implements, or home repair tools, people can keep money within the local economy while simultaneously fostering the sense of neighborly cooperation that is a central feature of real community.

• One of the most exciting grass-roots efforts is the Community Supported Agriculture (CSA) movement, in which consumers link up directly with a nearby farmer. Significantly, in a country where small farmers linked to the industrial system continue to fail every year at an alarming rate, not a single CSA in the United States has failed for economic reasons. [See chapter by Daniel Imhoff.]

• By connecting farmers directly with urban consumers, farmers' markets similarly benefit local economies and the environment. In New York City, there are now over two dozen farmers' markets, which add several million dollars annually to the incomes of farmers in nearby counties. Cornell University's "New Farmers New Markets" program aims to add to these numbers by recruiting and training a new generation of farmers to sell at the city's markets. The project is particularly interested in attracting unemployed immigrants who have extensive farming skills.

• The movement to create ecovillages is perhaps the most complete antidote to dependence on the global economy. Around the world, people are building communities that attempt to get away from the waste, pollution, competition, and violence of contemporary life. Many communities rely on renewable energy and are seeking to develop more cooperative local economies. The Global Ecovillage Network links several of these communities worldwide.

• Creating local economies means *rethinking education* — examining the connection between ever greater specialization and increasing dependence on an ever larger economic arena. Today, modern education is training children around the world for the centralized global economy. Essentially the same curriculum is taught in every environment, no matter what the cultural traditions or local resources. Promoting regional and local adaptation in the schools would be an essential part of the revitalization of local economies. Training in locally adapted agriculture, architecture, artisan production (pottery, weaving, and so on), and appropriate technologies suited to the specifics of climate and local resources would further a real decentralization of production for basic needs. Rather than educating the young for ever greater specialization in a competitive, "jobless growth" economy, children would be equipped for diverse economic systems, that depended primarily — but not exclusively — on local resources. This, of course, would not mean that information about the rest of the world would be excluded; on the contrary, knowledge about other cultures and cultural exchange programs would be an important part of the educational process.

# RECONNECTING
# TO COMMUNITY AND PLACE

The economic changes just described will inevitably require shifts at the personal level. In part, these involve rediscovering the deep psychological benefits — the joy — of being embedded in community. Children, mothers, and old people all know the importance of being able to feel they can depend on others. The values that are the hallmarks of today's fast-paced atomized industrial society, on the other hand, are those of a "teenage boy culture." It is a culture that demands mobility, flexibility, and independence. It induces a fear of growing old, of being vulnerable and dependent.

Another fundamental shift involves reinstilling a sense of connection with the place where we live. The globalization of culture and information has led to a way of life in which the nearby is treated with contempt. We get news from China but not next door, and at the touch of a television button we have access to all the wildlife of Africa. As a consequence, our immediate surroundings seem dull and uninteresting by comparison. A sense of place means helping ourselves and our children to see the *living environment around us*: reconnecting with the sources of our food (perhaps even growing some of our own) and learning to recognize the cycles of seasons, the characteristics of the flora and fauna.

Ultimately, we are talking about a spiritual awakening that comes from making a connection to others and to nature. This requires us to see the world within us, to experience more consciously the great interdependent web of life, of which we ourselves are among the strands.

# 34

# CONSERVING COMMUNITIES

## Wendell Berry

*Wendell Berry is a poet, a teacher (at the University of Kentucky), an ecologi-
cal thinker (with a huge following), and a prophet par excellence of traditional
rural society. He is also a small farmer in Port Royal, Kentucky, where his father farmed before him. This chapter is a passionate plea for a return to community, but also an argument that a new political opportunity now exists.
Berry foresees a novel political realignment that represents "the party of community" against the "parties of globalization."*

*Berry is the author of numerous books of poetry and fiction and ten books of
nonfiction, including the celebrated best-seller* The Unsettling of America
*(1977), described by the Los Angeles Times as "the missing link between the
crisis of the spirit and the crisis of the mass machine culture we live in." Berry's
most recent book is* Another Turn of the Crank *(1995).*

IN OCTOBER 1993, the *New York Times* announced that the United
States Census Bureau would "no longer count the number of Americans who live on farms." In explaining the decision, the *Times* provided
some figures as troubling as they were unsurprising. Between 1910 and
1920, we had 32 million farmers living on farms — about one-third of our
population. By 1950, the number had declined, but our farm population
was still 23 million. By 1991, the number was only 4.6 million, less than 2
percent of the national population. That is, our farm population had declined by an average of almost a half-million people a year for forty-one
years. In addition, by 1991, 32 percent of our farm managers and 86 percent of our farm workers did not live on the land they farmed.

These figures describe a catastrophe that is now virtually complete.
They announce that we no longer have an agricultural class that is or that

can require itself to be recognized by the government; we no longer have a "farm vote" that is going to be of much concern to politicians. U.S. farmers, who over the years have wondered whether or not they counted, may now put their minds at rest: They do not count. They have become statistically insignificant.

We must not hesitate to recognize and to say that this statistical insignificance of farmers is the successful outcome of a national purpose and a national program. It is the result of great effort and of principles vigorously applied. It has been achieved with the help of expensive advice from university and government experts, by the tireless agitation and exertion of the agribusiness corporations, and by the renowned advantages of competition — among our farmers themselves and with farmers of other countries. As a result, millions of country people have been liberated from farming, land ownership, self-employment, and the other alleged "idiocies" of rural life.

The disintegration of our agricultural communities is not exceptional any more than it is accidental. This is simply the way a large, exploitative, absentee economy works. For another example, here is a *New York Times* news service report on "rape and run" logging in Montana: "Throughout the 1980's, the Champion International Corp. went on a tree-cutting binge in Montana, leveling entire forests at a rate that had not been seen since the cut-and-run logging days of the last century. Now the hangover has arrived. After liquidating much of its valuable timber in the Big Sky country, Champion is quitting Montana, leaving behind hundreds of unemployed mill workers, towns staggered by despair and more than 1,000 square miles of heavily logged land."

The article goes on to speak of the revival of "a century-old complaint about large, distant corporations exploiting Montana for its natural resources and then leaving after the land is exhausted." It quotes a Champion spokesperson, Tucker Hill, who said, "We are very sympathetic to those people and very sad. But I don't think you can hold a company's feet to the fire for everything they did over the last twenty years."

If you doubt that exhaustion is the calculated result of such economic enterprise, you might consider the example of the mountain counties of eastern Kentucky from which, over the last three-quarters of a century, enormous wealth has been extracted by coal companies that have left the land wrecked and the people poor.

The same kind of thing is now happening in banking. In the county next to mine an independent local bank was recently taken over by a large out-of-state bank. Suddenly some of the local farmers and the small business people, who had been borrowing money from that bank for twenty years and whose credit records were good, were refused credit because they did not meet the requirements of a computer in a distant city. Old and valued customers now find that they are known by category rather than character. The directors and officers of the large bank clearly have reduced their economic thinking to one very simple question: "Would we rather make one big loan or many small ones?" Or to put it only a little differently: "Would we rather support one large enterprise or many small ones?" And they have chosen the large over the small.

This economic prejudice against the small has, of course, done immense damage for a long time to small or family-sized businesses in city and country alike. But that prejudice has often overlapped with an industrial prejudice against anything rural and against the land itself, and this prejudice has resulted in damages that are not only extensive but also long-lasting or permanent.

As we all know, we have much to answer for in our use of this continent from the beginning, but in the last half-century we have added to our desecrations of nature a virtually deliberate destruction of our rural communities. The statistics I cited at the beginning are incontrovertible evidence of this; but so is the condition of our farms and forests and rural towns. If you have eyes to see, you can see that there is a limit beyond which machines and chemicals cannot replace people; there is a limit beyond which mechanical or economic efficiency cannot replace care.

What I have been describing is not, I repeat, exceptional or anomalous. I am talking about the common experience, the common fate, of rural communities in our country for a long time. It has also been, and it will increasingly be, the common fate of rural communities in other countries. The message is plain enough, and we have ignored it for too long: The great, centralized economic entities of our time do not come into rural places in order to improve them by "creating jobs." They come to take as much of value as they can take, as cheaply and as quickly as they can take it. They are interested in "job creation" only so long as the jobs can be done more cheaply by humans than machines. They are not interested in the good health — economic, natural, or human — of any place on this earth. If you should undertake to appeal or complain to one of these great corporations on behalf of your community, you would discover something most remarkable: These organizations are organized expressly for the evasion of responsibility. They are structures in which, as my brother says, "the buck never stops." The buck is processed up the hierarchy until finally it is passed to "the shareholders," who characteristically are too widely dispersed, too poorly informed, and too unconcerned to be responsible for anything. The ideal of the modern corporation is to be anywhere (in terms of its own advantage) and nowhere (in terms of local account-ability). The message to country people, in other words, is, Don't expect favors from your enemies.

That message has a corollary that is just as plain and just as much ignored: The governmental and educational institutions, from which rural people should by right have received help, have not helped. Rather than striving to preserve the rural communities and economies and an adequate rural population, these institutions have consistently aided, abetted, and justified the destruction of every part of rural life. They have eagerly served the superstition that all technological innovation is good. They have said repeatedly that the failure of farm families, rural businesses, and rural communities is merely the result of progress, and such efficiency is good for everybody.

We now obviously face a world that supranational corporations and the governments and educational systems that serve them may well control entirely for their own convenience — and, inescapably, for the inconvenience of all the rest of us. This world will be a world in which the cultures that preserve nature and rural life will be simply disallowed. It will be, as our experience already suggests, a postagricultural world. But as we now begin to see, you cannot have a postagricultural world that is not also postdemocratic, postreligious, and postnatural — in other words it will be post-human, contrary to the best that we have meant by *humanity*.

In their dealings with the countryside and its people, the promoters of the so-called global economy are following a set of principles that can be stated as follows. They believe that a farm or a forest is or ought to be the same as a factory; that care is only minimally involved in the use of the land; that affection is not involved at all; that for all practical purposes a machine is as good as (or better than) a human; that the industrial standards of production, efficiency, and profitability are the only standards that are necessary; that the topsoil is lifeless and inert; that soil biology is safely replaceable by soil chemistry; that the nature of the ecology of any given place is irrelevant to the use of it; that there is no value in human community or neighborhood; and that technological innovation will produce only benign results.

These people see nothing odd or difficult in the idea of unlimited economic growth or unlimited consumption in a limited world. They believe that knowledge is and ought to be property and power. They believe that education is job-training. They think that the summit of human achievement is a high-paying job that involves no work. Their public claim is that they are making a society in which everybody will be a winner, but their private aim has been to reduce radically the number of people who, by the measure of our historical ideals, might be thought successful: the self-employed, the owners of small businesses or small usable properties, those who work at home.

The argument for joining the new international trade agreements has been that there is going to be a one-world economy, and we must participate or be left behind — though, obviously, the existence of a one-world economy depends on the willingness of all the world to join. The theory is that under the rule of international, supposedly free trade, products will naturally flow from the places where they can be best produced to the places where they are most needed. This theory assumes the long-term safety and sustainability of massive international transport, for which there are no guarantees — just as there are no guarantees that products will be produced in the best way or to the advantage of the workers who produce them or that they will reach or can be afforded by the people who need them.

There are other unanswered questions about the global economy, two of which are paramount: (1) How can any nation or region justify the destruction of a local productive capacity for the sake of foreign trade? (2) How can people who have demonstrated their inability to run national economies without inflation, usury, unemployment, and ecological devastation now claim that they can do a better job in running a global economy? U.S. agriculture has demonstrated by its own ruination that we cannot solve economic problems just by increasing scale, moreover, that increasing scale is almost certain to cause other problems — ecological, social, and cultural.

We can't go too much further, maybe, without considering the likelihood that humans are not intelligent enough to work on the scale that our technological abilities tempt us to. Some such recognition is undoubtedly implicit in U.S. conservatives' long-standing objection to a big central government; so it has been odd to see many of these same conservatives pushing for the establishment of a supranational economy that would inevitably function as a government far bigger and more centralized than any dreamed of before. Long experience has made it clear — as we might say to the liberals — that to be free we must limit the size of government and we must have some sort of home rule. But it is just as clear — as we might say to the conservatives — that it is foolish to complain about big government if we do not do everything we can to support strong local communities and strong community economies.

But in helping us to confront, understand, and oppose the principles of the global economy, the old political alignments have become virtually useless. Communists and capitalists are alike in their contempt for country people, country life, and country places. They have exploited the countryside with equal greed and disregard. They are alike even in their plea that damaging the present environment is justified in order to make "a better future."

The dialogue of Democrats and Republicans or of liberals and conservatives is likewise useless to us. Neither party is interested in farmers or farming, in the good care of the land, or in the quality of food. Nor are they interested in taking the best care of our forests. Leaders of both parties are equally subservient to the supranational corporations. NAFTA and the new GATT revisions are the proof.

Moreover, the old opposition of country and city, which was never useful, is now more useless than ever. It is, in fact, damaging to everybody involved, as is the opposition of producers and consumers. These are not differences but divisions that ought not to exist because they are to a considerable extent artificial. The so-called urban economy has been just as hard on urban communities as it has been on rural ones.

All these conventional affiliations are now meaningless, useful only to those in a position to profit from public bewilderment. A new political scheme of opposed parties, however, is beginning to take form. This is essentially a two-party system, and it divides over the fundamental issue of community. One of these parties holds that community has no value; the other holds that it does. One is the party of the global economy; the other I would call simply the party of local community. The global party is large, though not populous, immensely powerful and wealthy, self-aware, purposeful, and tightly organized. The community party is only now coming aware of itself; it is widely scattered, highly diverse, small though potentially numerous, weak though latently powerful, and poor though by no means without resources.

We know pretty well the makeup of the party of the global economy, but who are the members of the party of local community? They are people who take a generous and neighborly view of self-preservation; they do not believe that they can survive and flourish by the rule of dog-eat-dog; they do not believe that they can succeed by defeating or destroying or selling or using up everything but themselves. They want to preserve the precious things of nature and of human culture and pass them on to their children. They want the world's fields and forests to be productive; they do not want them to be destroyed for the sake of production. They know you cannot be a democrat (small *d*) or a conservationist and at the same time a proponent of the supranational corporate economy. They know from their experience that the neighborhood, the local community, is the proper place and frame of reference for responsible work. They see that no commonwealth or community of interest can be defined by greed. They know that things connect — that farming, for example, is connected to nature, and food to farming, and health to food — and they want to preserve the connections. They know that a healthy local community cannot be replaced by a market or an information highway. They know that, contrary to all the unmeaning and unmeant political talk about "job creation," work ought not to be merely a bone thrown to the otherwise unemployed. They know that work ought to be necessary; it ought to be good; it ought to be satisfying and dignifying to the people who do it and genuinely useful and pleasing to those for whom it is done.

The party of local community, then, is a real party with a real platform and an agenda of real and doable work. It has, I might add, a respectable history in the hundreds of efforts, over several decades, to preserve local nature and local health or to sell local products to local consumers. Such efforts now appear to be coming into their own, attracting interest and energy in a way they have not done before. People are seeing more clearly all the time the connections between conservation and economics. They are seeing that a community's health is largely determined by the way it makes its living.

The natural membership of the community party consists of small farmers, ranchers, and market gardeners; worried consumers; owners and employees of small businesses; self-employed people; religious people; and conservationists. The aims of this party really are only two: the preservation of ecological diversity and integrity and the renewal, on sound cultural and ecological principles, of local economies and local communities.

So now we must ask how a sustainable local community (which is to say a sustainable local economy) might function. I am going to suggest a set of rules that I think such a community would have to follow. I do not consider these rules to be predictions; I am not interested in foretelling the future. If these rules have any validity, that is because they apply now.

If the members of a local community wanted their community to cohere, to flourish, and to last, these are some of the things they would do:

1. Always ask of any proposed change or innovation: What will this do to our community? How will this affect our common wealth?

2. Always include local nature — the land, the water, the air, the native creatures — within the membership of the community.

3. Always ask how local needs might be supplied from local sources, including the mutual help of neighbors.

4. Always supply local needs first (and only then think of exporting products — first to nearby cities, then to others).

5. Understand the ultimate unsoundness of the industrial doctrine of "labor saving" if that implies poor work, unemployment, or any kind of pollution or contamination.

6. Develop properly scaled value-adding industries for local products to ensure that the community does not become merely a colony of the national or global economy.

7. Develop small-scale industries and businesses to support the local farm and/or forest economy.

8. Strive to produce as much of the community's own energy as possible.

9. Strive to increase earnings (in whatever form) within the community for as long as possible before they are paid out.

10. Make sure that money paid into the local economy circulates within the community and decrease expenditures outside the community.

11. Make the community able to invest in itself by maintaining its properties, keeping itself clean (without dirtying some other place), caring for its old people, and teaching its children.

12. See that the old and the young take care of one another. The young must learn from the old, not necessarily and not always in school. There must be no institutionalized childcare and no homes for the aged. The community knows and remembers itself by the association of old and young.

13. Account for costs now conventionally hidden or externalized. Whenever possible, these must be debited against monetary income.

14. Look into the possible uses of local currency, community-funded loan programs, systems of barter, and the like.

15. Always be aware of the economic value of neighborly acts. In our time, the costs of living are greatly increased by the loss of neighborhood, which leaves people to face their calamities alone.

16. A rural community should always be acquainted and interconnected with community-minded people in nearby towns and cities.

17. A sustainable rural economy will depend on urban consumers loyal

to local products. Therefore, we are talking about an economy that will always be more cooperative that competitive.

These rules are derived from Western political and religious traditions, from the prompting of ecologists and certain agriculturalists, and from common sense. They may seem radical, but only because the modern national and global economies have been formed in almost perfect disregard of community and ecological interests. A community economy is not an economy in which well-placed persons can make a "killing." It is an economy whose aim is generosity and a well-distributed and safe-guarded abundance. If it seems unusual to work for such an economy, then we must remember that putting the community ahead of profit is hardly unprecedented among community business people and local banks.

How might we begin to build a decentralized system of durable local economies? Gradually, I hope. We have had enough of violent or sudden changes imposed by predatory external interests. In many places, the obvious way to begin the work I am talking about is with the development of a local food economy. Such a start is attractive because it does not have to be big or costly; it requires nobody's permission; and it can ultimately involve everybody. It does not require us to beg for mercy from our exploiters or to look for help where consistently we have failed to find it. By *local food economy* I mean simply an economy in which local consumers buy as much of their food as possible from local producers and in which local producers produce as much as they can for the local market.

Several conditions now favor the growth of local food economies. On the one hand, the costs associated with our present highly centralized food system are going to increase. Growers in central California, for example, can no longer depend on an unlimited supply of cheap water for irrigation. Transportation costs can only go up. Biotechnology, variety patenting, and other agribusiness innovations, intended to extend corporate control of the food economy, will increase the cost of food, both economically and ecologically.

On the other hand, consumers are increasingly worried about the quality and purity of their food, and so they would like to buy from responsible growers close to home. They would like to know where their food comes from and how it is produced. They are increasingly aware that the larger and more centralized the food economy becomes, the more vulnerable it will be to natural or economic catastrophe, to political or military disruption, and to bad agricultural practices.

For all these reasons and others, we need urgently to develop local food economies wherever they are possible. Local food economies would improve the quality of the food. They would increase consumer influence over production and allow consumers to become participatory members in their own food economy. They would help to ensure a sustainable, dependable supply of food. By reducing some of the costs associated with long supply lines and large corporate suppliers (packaging, transportation, advertising, and so on), local food economies would reduce the cost of food at the same time that they would increase income to growers. They would tend to improve farming practices and increase employment in agriculture.

Of course, no food economy can or ought to be *only* local. But the orientation of agriculture to local needs, local possibilities, and local limits is simply indispensable to the health of both land and people and undoubtedly to the health of democratic liberties as well.

For many of the same reasons, we need also to develop local forest economies, of which the aim would be the survival and enduring good health of both our forests and their independent local communities. We need to preserve the native diversity of our forests as we use them. As in agriculture, we need local, small-scale, nonpolluting industries to add value to local forest products. We also need local supporting industries (saw mills, woodworking shops, and so on) for the local forest economy.

As support for sustainable agriculture should come most logically from consumers who consciously wish to keep eating, so support for sustainable forestry might logically come from loggers, mill workers, and other employees of the forest economy who consciously wish to keep working. But many people have a direct interest in the good use of our forests: farmers and ranchers with woodlots; all who depend for pure water on the good health of forested watersheds; the makers of wood products; conservationists; and so on.

What we have before us, if we want our communities to survive, is the building of an adversary internal economy to protect against the would-be global economy. To do this, we must somehow learn to reverse the flow of the siphon that has for so long drawn resources, money, talent, and people out of our countryside, often with a return only of pollution, impoverishment, and ruin. We must figure out new ways to affordably fund the development of healthy local economies. We must find ways to suggest economically — for no other suggestion will be ultimately effective — that the work, the talents, and the interest of our young people are needed at home.

Our whole society has much to gain from the development of local land-based economies. They would carry us far toward the ecological and cultural ideal of local adaptation. They would encourage the formation of adequate local cultures (and this would be authentic multiculturalism). They would introduce into agriculture and forestry a spontaneous and natural quality control, for neither consumers nor workers would want to see the local economy destroy itself by abusing or exhausting its resources. And they would complete at last the task of freedom from colonial economics begun by our ancestors more than two hundred years ago.

# 35

# GANDHI'S *Swadeshi*

## The Economics of Permanence

### Satish Kumar

*The teachings of Mahatma Gandhi were powerful enough to play a major role in the nonviolent revolution that overthrew British colonialism in India. They are clearly still of utmost relevance today. Central to Gandhi's philosophy was the principle of* swadeshi, *which, in effect, means local self-sufficiency. Satish Kumar elaborates on this important concept.*

*Kumar is a Gandhian scholar and also a thinker and activist in the tradition of E. F. Schumacher. Born in Bikaner, in Rajastan, India, Kumar was a Jain monk early in life, then joined the Gandhian movement and later, quite literally, walked around the world. He finally settled in England, where he is now the editor of* Resurgence *magazine and runs the Schumacher Society, the Schumacher Lecture Series, and Schumacher College. He is also the head of Green Books, an ecologically oriented publishing company.*

M AHATMA GANDHI was a champion of *swadeshi*, or home economy. People outside India know of Gandhi's campaigns to end British colonialism, but this was only a small part of his struggle. The greater part of Gandhi's work was to renew India's vitality and regenerate its culture. Gandhi was not interested simply in exchanging rule by white sahibs for rule by brown sahibs; he wanted the government to surrender much of its power to local villages.

For Gandhi, the spirit and the soul of India rested in the village communities. He said, "The true India is to be found not in its few cities but in its seven hundred thousand villages. If the villages perish, India will perish too." Swadeshi is a program for long-term survival.

## PRINCIPLES OF SWADESHI

Gandhi's vision of a free India was not of a nation-state but a confederation of self-governing, self-reliant, self-employed people living in village communities, deriving their right livelihood from the products of their homesteads. Maximum economic and political power — including the power to decide what could be imported into or exported from the village — would remain in the hands of the village assemblies.

In India, people have lived for thousands of years in relative harmony with their surroundings: living in their homesteads, weaving homespun clothes, eating homegrown food, using homemade goods; caring for their animals, forests, and lands; celebrating the fertility of the soil with feasts; performing the stories of great epics, and building temples. Every region of India has developed its own distinctive culture, to which traveling storytellers, wandering *saddhus,* and constantly flowing streams of pilgrims have traditionally made their contribution.

According to the principle of swadeshi, whatever is made or produced in the village must be used first and foremost by the members of the village. Trading among villages and between villages and towns should be minimal, like icing on the cake. Goods and services that cannot be generated within the community can be bought from elsewhere.

Swadeshi avoids economic dependence on external market forces that could make the village community vulnerable. It also avoids unnecessary, unhealthy, wasteful, and therefore environmentally destructive transportation. The village must build a strong economic base to satisfy most of its needs, and all members of the village community should give priority to local goods and services.

Every village community of free India should have its own carpenters, shoemakers, potters, builders, mechanics, farmers, engineers, weavers, teachers, bankers, merchants, traders, musicians, artists, and priests. In other words, each village should be a microcosm of India — a web of loosely interconnected communities. Gandhi considered these villages so important that he thought they should be given the status of "village republics."

The village community should embody the spirit of the home — an extension of the family rather than a collection of competing individuals. Gandhi's dream was not of personal self-sufficiency, not even family self-sufficiency, but the self-sufficiency of the village community.

The British believed in centralized, industrialized, and mechanized modes of production. Gandhi turned this principle on its head and envisioned a decentralized, homegrown, hand-crafted mode of production. In his words, "Not mass production, but production by the masses."

By adopting the principle of production by the masses, village communities would be able to restore dignity to the work done by human hands. There is an intrinsic value in anything we do with our hands, and in handing over work to machines we lose not only the material benefits but also the spiritual benefits, for work by hand brings with it a meditative mind and self-fulfillment. Gandhi wrote, "It is a tragedy of the first magnitude that millions of people have ceased to use their hands as hands. Nature has bestowed upon us this great gift which is our hands. If the craze for machinery methods continues, it is highly likely that a time will come when we shall be so incapacitated and weak that we shall begin to curse ourselves for having forgotten the use of the living machines given to us by God. Millions cannot keep fit by games and athletics and why should they exchange the useful productive hardy occupations for the useless, unproductive and expensive sports and games." Mass production is only concerned with the product, whereas production by the masses is concerned with the product, the producers, and the process.

The driving force behind mass production is a cult of the individual. What motive can there be for the expansion of the economy on a global scale, other than the desire for personal and corporate profit?

In contrast, a locally based economy enhances community spirit, community relationships, and community well-being. Such an economy encourages mutual aid. Members of the village take care of themselves, their families, their neighbors, their animals, lands, forestry, and all the natural resources for the benefit of present and future generations.

Mass production leads people to leave their villages, their land, their crafts, and their homesteads and go to work in the factories. Instead of dignified human beings and members of a self-respecting village community, people become cogs in the machine, standing at the conveyor belt, living in shanty towns, and depending on the mercy of the bosses. Then fewer and fewer people are needed to work, because the industrialists want greater productivity. The masters of the money economy want more and more efficient machines working faster and faster, and the result would be that men and women would be thrown on the scrap heap of unemployment. Such a society generates rootless and jobless millions living as dependents of the state or begging in the streets. In swadeshi, the machine would be subordinated to the worker; it would not be allowed to become the master, dictating the pace of human activity. Similarly, market forces would serve the community rather than forcing people to fit the market.

Gandhi knew that with the globalization of the economy, every nation would wish to export more and import less to keep the balance of payments in its favor. There would be perpetual economic crisis, perpetual unemployment, and perpetually discontented, disgruntled human beings.

In communities practicing swadeshi, economics would have a place but would not dominate society. Beyond a certain limit, economic growth becomes detrimental to human well-being. The modern worldview is that the more material goods you have, the better your life will be. But Gandhi said, "A certain degree of physical comfort is necessary but above a certain level it becomes a hindrance instead of a help; therefore the ideal of creating an unlimited number of wants and satisfying them, seems to be a delusion and a trap. The satisfaction of one's physical needs must come at a certain point to a dead stop before it degenerates into physical decadence. Europeans will have to remodel their outlook if they are not to perish under the weight of the comforts to which they are becoming slaves."

In order to protect their economic interests, countries go to war — military war as well as economic war. Gandhi said, "People have to live in village communities and simple homes rather than desire to live in palaces." Millions of people will never be able to live at peace with each other if they are constantly fighting for a higher living standard.

We cannot have real peace in the world if we look at each other's countries as sources for raw materials or as markets for finished industrial goods. The seeds of war are sown with economic greed. If we analyze the causes of war throughout history, we find that the pursuit of economic expansion consistently leads to military adventures. "There is enough for everybody's need, but not enough for anybody's greed," said Gandhi. Swadeshi is thus a prerequisite for peace.

The economists and industrialists of our time fail to see when enough is enough. Even when countries reach a very high material standard of living, they are still caught up with the idea of economic growth. Those who do not know when enough is enough will never have enough, but those who know when enough is enough already have enough.

Swadeshi is the way to comprehensive peace: peace with oneself, peace between peoples, and peace with nature. The global economy drives people toward high performance, high achievement, and high ambition for materialistic success. This results in stress, loss of meaning, loss of inner peace, loss of space for personal and family relationships, and loss of spiritual life. Gandhi realized that in the past, life in India was not only prosperous but also conducive to philosophical and spiritual development. Swadeshi for Gandhi was the spiritual imperative.

# THE RISE OF ENGLISH COLONIALISM

Historically, the Indian local economy was dependent upon the most productive and sustainable agriculture and horticulture and on pottery, furniture making, metal work, jewelry, leather work, and many other economic activities. But its basis had traditionally been in textiles. Each village had its spinners, carders, dyers, and weavers who were the heart of the village economy. However, when India was flooded with machine-made, inexpensive, mass-produced textiles from Lancashire, the local textile artists were rapidly put out of business, and the village economy suffered terribly. Gandhi thought it essential that the industry be restored, and started a campaign to stem the influx of British cloth. Due to his efforts, hundreds of thousands of untouchables and caste Hindus joined together to discard the mill-made clothes imported from England or from city factories and learned to spin their own yarn and weave their own cloth. The spinning wheel became the symbol of economic freedom, political independence, and cohesive and classless communities. The weaving and wearing of homespun cloth became marks of distinction for all social groups.

Also responsible for the destruction of India's home economy in the eighteenth century was the introduction of British education under colonial rule. Lord Macaulay, introducing the India Education Act in the British Parliament, said, "A single shelf of a good European library was worth the whole native literature of India. . . . Neither as a language of the law, nor as a language of religion has the Sanskrit any particular claim to our engagement. . . . We must do our best to form a class of persons, Indian in blood and color but English in taste, in opinions, in morals and in intellect."

This aim was pursued with the entire might of the British Raj. Traditional schools were replaced by colonial schools and universities. Wealthy Indians were sent to public schools such as Eton and Harrow and universities such as Oxford and Cambridge. Educated Indians increasingly learned English poetry, English law, and English customs to the neglect of their own culture. Reading Shakespeare and the *London Times* became much more fashionable than reading Indian classics such as the *Ramayana*, the *Mahabarata*, the *Vedas*, and the *Upanishads*. Educated Indians saw their own culture as backward, uncivilized, and old-fashioned. They wanted to become rulers of India, but they wanted to rule like the British.

If there was any one person who represented this type of Western-educated Indian it was Jawaharlal Nehru, who became the first prime minister after independence. Nehru sought to promote the industrialization of India not via the capitalist route but by centralized planning. His inspiration came from the intellectuals of the London School of Economics and the Fabian Society — the Labour Party's think tank.

Gandhi, on the other hand, believed that India's essential contribution to the world was simply her Indian-ness. He felt that Indians should recognize their own genius and not try to copy Western culture, which was simply a tool of colonization. Economics and politics should not simply be concerned with material things but should be the means to the fulfillment of cultural, spiritual, and religious ends. In fact, economics should not be separated from the deep spiritual foundations of life. This can be best achieved, according to Gandhi, when every individual is an integral part of the community; when the production of goods is on a small scale; when the economy is local; and when homemade handicrafts are given preference. These conditions are conducive to a holistic, spiritual, ecological, and communitarian pattern of society.

In Gandhi's view, spiritual values should not be separated from politics, economics, agriculture, education, and all the other activities of daily life. In this integral design, there is no conflict between spiritual and material. It is no good for some people to close themselves in a monastic order practicing religion and for other people to say that a spiritual life is only for saints and celibates. Such a separation of religion from society will breed corruption, greed, competition, power mania, and the exploitation of the weak and poor. Politics and economics without idealism will be a kind of prostitution, like sex without love.

Someone asked Gandhi, "What do you think of Western civilization?" He simply replied, "It would be a good idea." For Gandhi a machine civilization was no civilization. A society in which workers had to labor at a conveyor belt, in which animals were treated cruelly in factory farms, and in which economic activity necessarily lead to ecological devastation could not be conceived of as a civilization. Its citizens could only end up as neurotics, the natural world would inevitably be transformed into a desert, and its cities into concrete jungles. In other words, global industrial society, as opposed to society made up of largely autonomous communities committed to the principle of swadeshi, is unsustainable. Swadeshi for Gandhi was a sacred principle — as sacred for him as the principle of truth and nonviolence. Every morning and evening, Gandhi repeated his commitment to swadeshi in his prayers.

Unfortunately, within six months of independence, Gandhi was assassinated, and Nehru gained a free hand in shaping the economy of India. Nehru found Gandhian thinking too idealistic, too philosophical, too slow, and too spiritual. He gathered around him Western-educated bureaucrats, and the enterprise to which they were jointly committed made them the unwitting agents of economic colonization. They pressed ahead with the construction of large dams and big factories, which for them were the temples and cathedrals of the new India. The spirit of dedication, idealism, and self-sacrifice that had been paramount under the leadership of Gandhi was quickly replaced by a lust for power, privilege, comfort, and money. Nehru and his colleagues followed the opposite path to that of swadeshi, and since that time, the history of India has been the history of corruption and political intrigue at the highest level. The political colonization of India might have ended officially with independence in 1947, but her economic colonization continued unabated and at an even greater pace. She has been turned into a playground for global economic forces.

## COLONIALISM WITHOUT THE COLONIALISTS

Now, India continues to be ruled in the English way, but without English rulers. This is the tragedy of India, and there is no end in sight. The industrialists, the intellectuals, and the entrepreneurs in collusion with the government still see the salvation of India in her subordination to the policies of the World Bank and GATT. They see India as part of the global economy working hand in glove with the multinational corporations.

However, discontent among the Indian people is growing rapidly. The failures of the Congress Party under Nehru, his daughter, Indira Gandhi, and her son, Rajiv Gandhi, are fully evident to all. As Mahatma Gandhi predicted, the body politic is seething with corruption. The poor are poorer than ever, and the growing middle classes are turning away from the Congress Party and supporting either local parties or the Hindu Nationalist Party. The farmers are agitating against the patenting of their seeds by multinational companies. The global economy of GATT is built on sand. Even though it may appear that its grip is firm, it has no grassroots support, and as its true implications become apparent, the people of India, among whom the teachings of Gandhi are still very much alive, will react against it and will return to swadeshi for the re-enchantment of their local culture, their community, and their lives. In fact, the lessons of swadeshi may bring hope for an economics of permanence even among Westerners, once the fraudulent promise of economic growth and industrialism is exposed.

# 36

# COMMUNITY SUPPORTED AGRICULTURE
## *Farming with a Face on It*

### Daniel Imhoff

*If we are serious about unhooking ourselves from a system in which our aver-
age pound of food travels more than 1300 miles, often across oceans, then we
must encourage local food production for local consumption. In the global
economy, all the cards are stacked toward corporate agriculture for export, but
the vital new Community Supported Agriculture movement offers an alternative path toward environmentally sustainable agriculture.*

*Daniel Imhoff writes extensively on issues of agriculture, environment, and
design for* Communication Arts *magazine and* Farmer to Farmer.

*I*N JAPAN, it's referred to as "farming with a face on it." Europeans call
such arrangements *subscription farming*. "Linking Farmers with Consumers" (LFC) is yet another phrase used in the United Kingdom. The
term adopted by some four hundred farms in the United States is
*Community Supported Agriculture*, or CSA for short. All of these terms
translate into one of the most dynamic new developments in small-scale
farming. Community Supported Agriculture (the term I'll use in this
chapter), serves as an umbrella for farmers striving to achieve a number of
goals: mutually beneficial relationships with a community of consumers;
environmentally sustainable farming practices; and public education on
contemporary agricultural issues.

To understand the powerful concept behind the CSA, one first has to
examine the conventional food system that has been developing in industrialized countries over the past half-century. In the United States, for ex-

ample, the average food item journeys some 1,300 miles before becoming a part of a meal. Fruits and vegetables are refrigerated, waxed, colored, irradiated, fumigated, packaged, and shipped. None of these processes enhances food quality but merely enables distribution over great distances and helps increase shelf-life. Between production, processing, distribution, and preparation, 10 calories of energy are required to create just 1 calorie of food energy.

Despite tremendous opportunities to grow a wide range of fruits and vegetables in nearly every region of the country, produce is rapidly disappearing from the local economy. Food production has increasingly become dominated by faraway, monolithic machinery- and chemical-intensive operations specializing in single crops. Much of this long-distance specialization and distribution is done in the name of economic efficiency, but in fact, the farther food is transported, the more waste is created — in terms of fuel, packaging, refrigeration, and spoilage.

Furthermore, while millions of farmers have vanished from the local landscape since the 1940s, generations of consumers have completely lost touch with their food supply. Today's average consumers have little knowledge of how or by whom their food was grown. Armed with an "expect more, pay less" mentality, they have become accustomed to purchasing "cheap" produce from all over the world, regardless of season. To many people's minds, lettuce, tomatoes, and berries never go out of season, because they miraculously continue to appear in grocery produce sections. There is neither a farm nor a farmer's face associated with the food that sustains them.

As the move toward anonymous agrigiants and supermarket conglomerates continues to accelerate, Community Supported Agriculture has emerged as a viable model for local food production. The concept is simple. Farmers and consumers join together to create markets for reasonably priced, pesticide-free, seasonal foods. In a community-supported farm, the consumer pays a share in early spring to meet the farmer's operating expenses for the upcoming season. In return for their investment, shareholders receive a steady supply of edible dividends throughout the growing season. Most CSAs produce a wide variety of organically grown vegetables, herbs, and cut flowers. Others offer fruit, honey, or animal products such as meat, eggs, and milk. Some even provide firewood. Weekly distribution takes place at a prearranged time and location, but many CSAs also offer convenient door-to-door delivery for an additional cost. Although there is no standard, an average share supplies three people for approximately a week.

Consumers enrolling in a CSA do far more than purchase food from a known producer. By paying in advance, they allow the farmer to raise in-terest-free operating capital. Members also have the option to contribute to the work in many cases: harvesting, weeding, distributing, and so on. And because there are no guarantees that any or all crops will succeed, they share the financial risks along with the farmer. At the same time, the chance is high that the members' investment will pay off. The marketing is already taken care of in advance, and there is no middleman to mark up the products, so a CSA usually delivers high-quality products at below market prices.

One potential drawback for members is that they forego the freedom of choice that shopping offers. Instead, they receive whatever is in season from the farm. The nutritional benefit of eating freshly picked, organic food is obvious. But this arrangement can inspire new culinary challenges as well. To help customers make the most of their somewhat limited se-lections or to introduce an unusual food item, many CSAs include recipes in their shipments. As this direct marketing approach has taken root, other CSAs have begun to include foods from neighboring farmers, offer-ing members increased variety. Some CSAs have even established rela-tionships with other farms across the country to continue supplying food throughout the winter months.

• • •

In Trimble County, Kentucky, just a few miles from the home of Wendell Berry, Steve Smith started one of the four hundred CSAs operating in the United States since 1986. This is the heartland of tobacco country, and Smith farms the same land his grandfather cultivated, a rectangular sec-tion of bottom land surrounded by forest. But rather than depending solely on tobacco (he farms 3.5 acres of tobacco organically), Smith started a CSA in 1992. On just a 3-acre intensive garden, he supplies ninety-two families in Louisville, less than 60 miles away, with a bushel of produce thirty-three weeks per year. He also raises an acre of organic seeds.

Berry expresses great appreciation for his young neighbor's farm. "Our cities import food from California," he says, "but this is one of the best places in America for the revival of agriculture." What truly impresses Berry is how Smith tries to do everything as economically as possible. His house is clean and simple ("a box with a porch around it") and the young farmer's only machinery are a small tractor and a rototiller. He also owns a pair of horses, which Berry inspired him to learn to work. Smith's efforts demonstrate that running a successful small-scale farm doesn't re-quire an overwhelming amount of capital. In fact, he doesn't even have to take a bank loan to cover his operating expenses.

After experimenting with organic practices for nearly seven years, Smith decided to try Community Supported Agriculture. He did his marketing during the winter months. The local media picked up on his idea to create a subscription farm, and a few radio interviews and newspaper articles generated more than enough economic commitment for him to proceed with the project. Almost immediately he had a waiting list of willing subscribers — a common experience among many CSAs.

Modest and mild mannered, Smith attributes much of his success to good luck and to Eliot Coleman's book, *The New Organic Grower* (1989). But walking the rows of his large-scale garden, looking out over the woods surrounding his field, surveying the great variety of vegetables purposely timed for a series of weekly deliveries, one can readily see the hard work and vision of an extremely skillful farmer. The small scale and sense of land stewardship are so inspiring that this should be a necessary and fundamental part of our modern agricultural system.

## SUSTAINABLE FARM PRACTICES

While each CSA farm has its own values and unique organizational structure, most share a common commitment to more sustainable farm practices. Eliminating agrochemicals and minimizing off-farm inputs remains a consistent goal of Community Supported Agriculture. Three principal farming methods are employed to attain this. *Bio-intensive agriculture*, derived from the French intensive method, focuses on a highly efficient system of raised-bed gardening, in which farmers can produce extremely high yields in the smallest possible area. *Bio-dynamic farming* seeks to create a completely self-sufficient farm by maximizing plant and animal diversity and minimizing off-farm inputs, such as commercial fertilizers and fuel. On a bio-dynamic farm, animals supply the necessary muscle and manure to cultivate and fertilize the fields. Finally, *conventional organic farming* differs from both of the above, in that off-farm inputs (such as fertilizers, machinery, or fuel) may be employed more liberally, but not herbicides or pesticides.

Regardless of the method, the small-scale CSA approach is far more sustainable than our conventional system, in which three times as much energy is employed to grow 1 calorie of food energy (excluding processing, distribution, and preparation). First of all, the chemical-free methods just mentioned are labor-intensive rather than machinery-intensive. Instead of specializing in large monocrops, which leach soil nutrients and make crops highly susceptible to weed and pest pressures, CSAs grow a great variety of crops. Emphasis is also placed on creating healthy soil by manuring, composting, and other natural methods. Regular crop rotations prevent soil fungi or other pests from establishing themselves. Soil erosion and groundwater pollution — among the most severe problems in conventional agriculture — are all addressed through these three primary cultivation practices.

· · ·

According to one survey, the farthest distance food travels in a North American CSA is 200 miles, a tremendous improvement on conventional food's 1,300 mile average. This localized, direct marketing limits the need for packaging. Members receive weekly allotments in a bag, basket, or box, all of which can be reused or recycled.

In the industrial farm system, 25 percent of the food produced never makes it to the table due to spoilage during transportation or in the grocery bins. Small CSA farms carefully plan in advance how much to supply a specific market. Because the food is harvested immediately prior to delivery and is then shipped directly to the customer's door, spoilage is drastically reduced. Fruits and vegetables that do spoil never have to leave the farm. They can be fed to the animals or returned to the soil as compost. Rejecting perfectly edible food for cosmetic imperfections or nonuniform sizing — a common practice in conventional farm practices — is also eliminated. Finally, many CSAs that require their members to pick up their weekly shares at the farm also encourage them to bring their kitchen scraps to contribute to the compost.

The nutritional value of eating fresher, locally produced seasonal foods is more than enough reason for joining a CSA. But the growing concern about farm chemicals is even more compelling. In 1993, the United States National Research Council issued a report titled "Pesticides in the Diets of Infants and Children," advocating more stringent pesticide laws to protect children. The report stopped short of warning against particularly dangerous foods, but it did explain that pesticide tolerance levels for adults (which form the basis for fruit and vegetable regulation) do not apply to children, who are much more vulnerable. Because Washington has been very slow to enact tougher pesticide regulations based on these conclusions, many parents are seizing the initiative to ensure their families eat only pesticide-free foods by joining or helping to establish CSAs.

If there is a standard model or average CSA in the United States, it would probably serve sixty to seventy families using approximately 3 acres of farmland, excluding grazing land or feed crops for animals. Its annual budget would range somewhere between $50,000 and $75,000, with a share costing $400 per year.

The average customer is a little more identifiable. An overwhelming majority of shareholders are white professionals living in urban areas who want a deeper connection to their food source. They're also willing to support farmers who can guarantee a steady supply of "clean" food for their families. These households can afford to pay for their food months in advance, a privilege people living from paycheck to paycheck can't consider. A number of CSAs have tried to address this issue by accepting labor and food stamps in return for shares, in order to accommodate members from across the economic spectrum. Interestingly enough, in nearly all cases, members who invest in a CSA pay slightly less for what they receive than they would if they purchased organic produce on the commercial market. Such is the blessing of direct marketing.

## THE SHORT, AMAZING HISTORY OF CSAs

The movement toward CSAs is worldwide. In fact, Community Supported Agriculture's modern roots can be traced to the outskirts of Tokyo in the mid 1960s, where farmer-consumer associations known as *teiki* were formed to create reliable sources for safe, reasonably priced food. On the Ohira farm in the Setagaya ward of Tokyo, one farmer resumed his former organic cultivation practices in 1965 when his health was threatened by the petrochemicals he was using. This meant going back to the labor-intensive methods of bygone generations, efforts not compensated for when competing head-on with the conventional market. After some of his neighbors realized the uncompensated value of these clean farming practices, they decided to create a system that would guarantee consistent demand for Ohira's product so that he could focus on his specialty — raising organic crops. The Ohira farm, one of the most successful Community Supported Agriculture programs existing today, now includes fourteen farmers serving four hundred Tokyo families. Around that same time, a group of some two hundred housewives formed a *teikei* to purchase milk in bulk. In the past three decades, that association has grown to comprise nearly 190,000 members. One estimate indicates that as many as 200,000 Japanese families have entered into mutually supportive relationships with farmers.

Direct marketing caught on in Europe in 1968, when West Germany's first CSA was cofounded by Trauger Groh, who later helped introduce the idea in the United States. This CSA was unique because of the source of its financial support. While banks and lending institutions throughout the industrialized world have increasingly adopted policies favoring large-scale, chemical-intensive operations, this CSA was funded by a progressive bank dedicated to keeping small farmers on the land. Groh's farm also established the link between CSAs and the principles of bio-dynamic farming, often employed in Europe and North America.

In 1978, joining with a bio-dynamic farm outside Geneva, Switzerland, 550 people contributed $500 up front in return for weekly produce deliveries. The success of this association spawned others in the country, including a Zurich-based farm that supplied milk for six hundred families and vegetables for four hundred. American-born Jan Vandertuin was involved in the Zurich project, and he transplanted the model to the United States. Vandertuin helped establish the country's first CSA, the Apple Orchard Project, in South Egremont, Massachusetts, in 1985. From the Northeast, the idea rapidly spread to nearly every state in the country, with different versions appearing almost simultaneously by the early 1990s. In 1994, an estimated four hundred CSAs were providing food to some eighty thousand people, up from just two community supported farms in 1987.

The UK has also experienced growth in CSAs, concurrent with a slow but steady increase in local bartering systems known as LETS (Local Employment and Trading Systems). According to the UK Soil Association, there are now some eighty initiatives in their Linking Farmers with Consumers project (LFC). On many of these CSAs, members contribute their shares in labor rather than cash in return for food.

Today, *CSA* serves as an umbrella term for a great variety of small farm programs. In the Eastern United States, for example, many CSA organizations represent true partnerships between farmers and members, where work, successes, and failures are shared equally. Consumers often take on much of the risk by paying farmers before receiving anything in return. In the Western states, Community Supported Agriculture has emerged as a direct marketing concept, where subscription members are just one crucial part of the overall business strategy, which also includes farmer's markets and wholesale distribution centers.

## KEEPING FARMERS ON THE LAND

Since 1981, more than 620,000 productive farm families (20 percent of the total) have been put out of business in the United States. Community Supported Agriculture offers a way for family farmers to maintain themselves as dynamic players in the local economy. Yet the biggest hurdle in starting a CSA is the very same pressure that is forcing families off the land and contributing to short-term, nonsustainable farm practices: land values. Because farm land is often valued, appraised, and taxed at the same rate it would be for residential or commercial development, the prospect of buying land to start a CSA is nearly out of the question. Many CSAs already own their own land, or receive it as donations, or eventually have it officially established in a nonprofit land trust, so that it can be used in perpetuity to serve the community's needs for clean, safe food. Unfortunately, the problem of land value makes it improbable that CSAs will become the dominant model for food production. It does, however, highlight the desperate need for more progressive tax structures and conservation programs for agricultural lands. In the meantime, agribusiness, which manages arable land on the basis of profitability rather than long-term economic and ecological imperatives, is expected to own some 25 percent of all agricultural land in the United States by the year 2000.

Along with the obvious material, nutritional, economic, and environmental benefits of Community Supported Agriculture, there is another essential role that these farms can play in the community. A CSA connects consumers with the landscape in which their food is grown and the people (and animals) that produce it. Parents have reported that their children have even started to eat more vegetables after visiting the farm, having experienced for the first time the exciting process of gardening.

As was mentioned above, CSA members often participate in the duties of farming, performing tasks as simple as harvesting crops or as complex as plowing a field behind a draught-horse. Most farms have work days for members who want to get their hands dirty. Nearly every one has a harvest celebration, where families visit the farm to experience the operation.

This knowledge not only serves the intellect but also the spirit. For many people, having a farm is a dream that will never be realized in today's society. The high price of land is one obstacle; the lack of skills required to successfully operate a farm is another. But whatever the reason for which we've become so disconnected with the land, a CSA enables people to understand what is involved in raising their food and to participate in strengthening the community economic system.

In more than a few instances, Community Supported Agriculture has assumed the ambitious role of social worker as well as food provider. In 1989, a CSA garden was established in Great Barrington, Massachusetts, where farming has become virtually extinct. One of the many goals of that project was to encourage the participation, both as consumers and as workers, of the small population of mentally handicapped people living in the nearby town of Berkshire Village. In a similar vein, the Nattick Community Farm in Boston has been offering summer employment for 130 "youth at risk" each year. This farm is not only subsidized by CSA enrollment but receives a large share of its budget from the town's Department of Recreation and Human Services, which recognizes the value of educating and employing children on the farm. Other CSAs, such as the Homeless Garden Project in Santa Cruz, California, are dedicated to providing jobs and sustenance to the city's many homeless people.

## HOW FAR CAN CSA GO?

The dramatic increase in Community Supported Agriculture in the past decade reveals that there is a keen interest on the part of farmers and consumers to create social relationships in their communities. There is certainly a tremendous opportunity for more such farms all over the country. CSA pioneer Trauger Groh explains that "while some community farms do go out of business, many more are being born than are dying." The best evidence for this is that so many successful CSAs boast waiting lists of families anxious to become members.

While the economics of Community Supported Agriculture are impressive, author and organic farmer Eliot Coleman argues that the name should be changed to give it wider appeal among farmers if the movement is going to go any further. "I find the term Community Supported Agriculture denigrating to farmers," he says, "as if the farmer depended upon the charity of the community. This is a good deal for the consumer and for the farmer. It's really one of the most exciting economic movements in small-scale agriculture today. The name should reflect what it's all about. The best I've come up with is *mutual farms*." Coleman most admires the Japanese expression "farming with a face on it."

Whichever term ultimately emerges, one thing is certain: The impacts of these efforts will be felt increasingly in communities around the world as consumers recognize the value in establishing, in the places they call home, a direct relationship with the farmer who nurtures their food and with the natural growing cycles.

# 37

## COMMUNITIES
### *Building Authority, Responsibility, and Capacity*

David Morris

*There may be no better source for ideas on the nuts and bolts of retooling com-munities — including towns and cities — for greater economic sustainability and self-sufficiency than David Morris and the Institute for Local Self-Reliance. In this chapter Morris outlines the three pillars that facilitate a revitalization of the local: the need to regain local authority, responsibility, and capacity. He also surveys the current political scene and offers some practical programs for incremental improvement.*

PRESIDENT CLINTON urges Americans to ask not "What's in it for me?" but rather "What's in it for us?" He appeals to his audiences to develop "a new spirit of community, a sense that we're all in this together."

The president's words are compelling, but he is speaking to a nation taught for generations not to think in terms of "us." A nation of immigrants has little shared history or culture. Instead, the United States has emphasized the individual, not the group. We take it for granted that public is bad and private is good, that collective is bad and personal good, that cooperation is bad and competition good. We cherish slogans like "Don't tread on me." We are taught from the cradle that whenever the social becomes as important as the individual, we are heading down a slippery slope toward tyranny.

This harsh American emphasis on individualism has always been tempered by the historical presence of extended families, of ethnic neighborhoods, of family farms, and of small towns — places where people know when you're born and care when you die. But in the last generation, we have moved more frequently and increasingly farther from our places of birth. We are less rooted and less involved in our immediate communities. Neighborhood gathering places — cafés, grocery stores, even libraries and churches — are rapidly disappearing. Over 70 percent of us do not even know the people next door.

Little by little, we have lost our sense of mutual aid and cooperation. Two-thirds of us give no time to community activities. Fewer than half of all adult Americans now regard the idea of sacrifice for others as a positive moral virtue. Both inside and outside the workplace we are increasingly disconnected, looking out for number one, voting only for our narrow self-interest. "Virtual" communities and "virtual" corporations, where physical proximity is replaced by electronic "visits," are taking the place of tangible community involvement and contact. Meanwhile, the scale of public and private institutions continues to grow. Decisions are made in an unintelligible and inaccessible process remote from the people and places that will feel their impact.

Some view this decline in the importance of territorial communities as an inevitable consequence of modernity: In the global age, localism will naturally decline in importance. But this theory implies that public policy has been neutral on the issue. It has not.

Since the end of World War II, Democratic and Republican administrations have consistently pursued policies that have disabled rather than enabled close-knit, strong, and productive communities. Urban renewal programs literally bulldozed hundreds of inner-city neighborhoods. Federal housing programs subsidized suburban sprawl. Highway programs built roads at the expense of mass transit. In the 1980s, federal tax and regulatory policies encouraged leveraged buyouts and hostile takeovers that shuffled hundreds of billions of dollars in corporate assets and forced tens of thousands of workers to abandon their communities in search of jobs. The government has consistently supported centralizing rather that decentralizing technologies: nuclear power rather than solar energy; garbage incinerators rather than recycling; tomato harvesters rather than diversified crop farming.

## THE ARC OF COMMUNITY

Praise for community comes from both sides of the political spectrum. Conservatives such as Michael Novak have long applauded the virtues of family, voluntary associations, and a vibrant civil society. Likewise liberals such as Amitai Etzioni have emphasized the central role of kinship groups and tightly knit communities in fostering basic moral values such as mutual respect and nonviolence.

Communitarian liberals and social conservatives alike stress the equal importance of obligations and rights. The list of our responsibilities to one another is long and varied: voluntary blood and organ donation, regular voting, a willingness to pay taxes, and so forth. Such personal responsibility to the general welfare is an important component of strong communities.

But in and of itself, responsibility is not sufficient. Hundreds of communities that have exhibited the kinds of values that Novak and Etzioni embrace have been unable to defend themselves from powerful external forces. Middle-class neighborhoods in the Bronx were destroyed when the Port Authority of New York imposed the Cross-Bronx Expressway on them. In the 1970s, the close-knit Polish neighborhood of Poletown in Detroit was leveled to make way for a new automobile plant that never opened. As Alexis de Tocqueville wisely noted more than 150 years ago, "Without power and independence, a town may contain good subjects, but it can contain no active citizens."

Aside from responsibility, strong communities need sufficient authority to make the rules that can ensure their future. In the late 1970s, for instance, Vermont enacted a land use law that included, along with the ubiquitous environmental impact statement, an economic impact statement as well. On the basis of this economic assessment, the state denied a building permit for a regional mall because it would have destroyed the downtown business sector of nearby Burlington. The citizens of Vermont and Burlington properly exercised the right to defend their neighbors' businesses and jobs against absentee-owned regional superstores, whose workforce consists largely of temporary, part-time employees.

Governments often view communities as obstructionist, unwilling to accept even necessary development. Government officials have even invented an acronym — NIMBY (not in my backyard) — to describe this phenomenon. Yet in many cases, citizen opposition is not so much a knee-jerk, innate obstructionism than it is a reflection of their lack of inclusion in the project's conception and design.

For years, Georgia state officials had tried to impose large landfills on small rural communities. For five years, the siting process was paralyzed by local opposition. Finally, Georgia allowed its citizens to design their own policies. After nearly ninety public meetings over four months, the citizens of Atkinson County resolved to accept a landfill that could handle only their own wastes and not those of other communities. Significant local authority can beget personal responsibility.

Yet responsibility and authority are both inadequate without the power and self-confidence that comes from owning productive capacity. Today we have lost most of the skills of self-reliance and no longer own the productive capacity needed to balance central economic and political authority. Over 85 percent of us work for someone else, and for most of us that someone else does not live nearby.

Communities with widespread local ownership tend to be more vibrant and stable. Citizens participate more in local affairs. Local owners have a stake in the community. Their children go to local schools. The world's largest producer of automated mailing systems for wooden pallets — Viking Inc. of Fridley, Minnesota — is owned by its 120 workers. Vice President Dean Bodem acknowledges that the company would have left the state if it had not been employee-owned. "Because the employees own the company, it really ties us to Minnesota. If someone else would have bought this company, there's a high probability that they would have moved it." Viking's worker-owners know that their business generates the revenues used, in part, to educate their children (Beal 1993).

Contrast this with the situation in northwest Indiana. The Calumet Project for Industrial Jobs evaluated seventeen plant closings from the 1980s and concluded that eleven could probably have been stopped via early intervention. All of the plants were absentee-owned. Most had recently changed hands. Plant closings, job loss, social disruption — such are the hazards of giving external authorities control over a community's life and work.

Social conservatives and communitarian liberals alike are apt to recite the proverb "Give a man a fish, and he will be without hunger for a day. Teach a man to fish, and he will never be hungry." Yet the ability to fish will not keep someone from starving if he or she lacks the authority to prevent overfishing or to stop the pollution that can destroy the fishes' spawning grounds. And even these considerations are immaterial if the person fishing bears no greater responsibility to the community at large — for safeguarding the environment, providing social services, and enabling the individual to pursue his or her own livelihood.

Authority, responsibility, capacity — these are the cornerstones of sustainable communities. While both liberals and conservatives see the importance of personal responsibility, neither believes strongly in delegating that authority to communities or in administering public policies that promote locally owned productive capacity. In this respect, liberals and conservatives alike subscribe to the Darwinian model of economic evolution, in which large-scale institutions appear as an inevitable stage in economic history.

There is no label for those who believe in strong territorial communities. *Anarchist* would be historically appropriate. But the word has long since lost its original connotation as a belief in personal responsibility and humanly scaled institutions and has come to mean instead a lack of structure and discipline. Historically, the term *progressive* described a movement committed to public ownership and direct democracy. The challenge to modern-day progressives is to integrate concern for communities and support for humanly scaled technologies and organizations into their platforms.


# SCALE

"The real voyage of discovery," Marcel Proust observed, "lies not in seeking new lands but in seeing with new eyes." We need to see our communities not only as places of residence, recreation, and retail but also as places that nurture active citizens who make the rules that govern their lives and who have the skills and productive capacity to generate real wealth. Local economies must be more than branch plants of planetary corporations. Local government must be more than simply a body that reacts to higher levels of government.

Seeing with new eyes means challenging the conventional wisdom that bigger is better and that separating the producer from the consumer, the banker from the depositor, the worker from the owner is an inevitable outcome of modern economic development. Surprisingly little evidence supports this conventional wisdom. In every sector of the economy the evidence yields the same conclusion: Small is the scale of efficient, dynamic, democratic, and environmentally benign societies.

In education, for instance, one recent, exhaustive study on school size found that small schools have less absenteeism, lower dropout rates, fewer disciplinary problems, and higher teacher satisfaction than big schools. Commenting on this study by University of Chicago education professor Anthony Bryk, *New York Times* reporter Susan Chira (1993) notes that "now many researchers and educators alike see big urban high schools — those with 2,000 to 5,000 students — as Dickensian workhouses, breeding violence, dropouts, academic failure and alienation." By contrast, schools with 400 students or fewer have "fewer behavioral problems, better attendance and graduation rates, and sometimes higher grades and test scores. At a time when more children have less support from their families, students in small schools form close relationships with teachers." Acting on these insights, Chicago, Philadelphia, New York, and other cities have begun subdividing existing school buildings into several autonomous schools.

The same scale of institution that best cares for our children best cares for our money. "[O]nce a bank is larger than $400 million in deposits, economies of scale appear to be exhausted," acknowledges Robert Parry, president of the San Francisco Federal Reserve Bank. In 1990, 11,194 of the 12,165 banks in the United States had assets under $300 million. The Southern Finance Project compared banks that focused on their surrounding community to those lending all over the country. Banks that restricted lending to local borrowers were more than twice as profitable as those whose loans were geographically dispersed. Those that stayed close to home actually reduced overhead costs and suffered significantly fewer bad loans.

In manufacturing, too, small scale pertains. From 1979 to 1989, small and medium-sized businesses created more than twenty million new jobs, while the five hundred largest U.S. companies eliminated almost four million jobs. Small manufacturers constitute over 98 percent of the 360,000 U.S. manufacturing enterprises. Two-thirds of these have fewer than twenty employees.

## DEMOCRATIZING THE ECONOMY

How much authority is the federal government willing to delegate to local communities? Will local ownership or decentralized production technologies become central elements in its strategic plans?

The Clinton administration has said it believes in making workers partners with management. Yet it is unclear whether this empowerment means ownership and control. Secretary of Labor Robert Reich argued that jobs, not ownership, should be the key objective. It does not matter to him whether a factory is owned by Toyota or General Motors as long as that factory is located in the United States. Reich may be right when he compares two global corporations such as Toyota and GM, whose strategic plans are becoming increasingly similar. He is wrong, however to compare a locally owned company, which has a stake in the community, to a multinational corporation, whatever its country of origin.

The president's desire to build a partnership between management and labor is occurring at a time when corporations are increasingly breaking ties with their workers. The average blue-collar worker receives only seven days notice before losing his or her job and only two days when not backed by a union. The UCLA Institute for Industrial Relations reports that contract workers without benefits or security comprise 24 percent of current corporate payrolls, with a 40 percent share expected by the end of the decade. A temporary workforce does not bode well for community stability.

Making workers partners in business means, at the least, making them owners. About ten thousand companies now have Employee Stock Ownership Plans (ESOPs). In about 29 percent of these companies, the workers own the majority share. But ESOPs are not the only form of ownership available. As Gar Alperovitz of the Institute for Policy Studies has pointed out, there are many kinds of customer- or worker-owned institutions in this country: 13,000 credit unions, nearly one hundred cooperative banks, more than a hundred cooperative insurance companies, almost 2,000 municipal utilities, and about 115 telecommunications cooperatives.

In the financial sector, the government could build a nationwide network of community banks from the debris of the bankrupt savings and loan (S&L) institutions. Tom Schlesinger, director of the Southern Finance Project (SFP) calls this "making lemonade from S&L lemons." As of spring 1993, according to the SFP, the federal government owned eighty-one thrifts with more than a thousand branches. Over four hundred of these branches are located in low- and moderate-income communities in twenty-five states and 150 cities.

The Resolution Trust Corporation (RTC), formed in 1989 to oversee the closure and sale of bankrupt thrifts, has ignored the needs of communities and instead has curried favor with huge national banks. The RTC is closing dozens of branches in communities already suffering from a lack of access to capital, while the RTC's pattern of sales has sharply increased the concentration of capital in local banking markets previously characterized by healthy levels of competition.

The RTC should be required instead to favor community-based institutions when selling deposits. One billion dollars could be diverted from the several billion dollars proposed for expanding enterprise zones (now called empowerment zones). Given the current 6 percent equity capital requirement for banks, $1 billion could fully capitalize all 427 community banks with deposits of $12.9 billion. A targeted, aggressive network of neighborhood development banks arguably would galvanize far more beneficial community development than an equal number of enterprise zones.

Local government is the level of government about which the citizenry is the least cynical. A recent study from the Kettering Foundation concludes, "We have found that people's perception of having a diminished voice in national politics does not hold true on the local level."

Most local governments rely on property taxes as their primary source of income. Raising property taxes encourages middle-class homeowners and businesses to move to a neighboring jurisdiction with lower taxes. The effect is to encourage jurisdictions to compete against one another and to exacerbate the disparity of service levels between rich and poor communities. The federal government, on the other hand, relies primarily on income taxes and cannot be played off against other jurisdictions (except by big corporations that can move to offshore locations).

## TRAVEL AND TRANSPORT

Transportation systems that rely on private cars and trucks are the enemies of community. By their nature they invade and fragment. In *The Death and Life of Great American Cities* (1961), Jane Jacobs describes the process in central cities: "Traffic arteries, along with parking lots and filling stations, are powerful and insistent instruments of city destruction. To accommodate them, city streets are broken down into loose sprawls, incoherent and vacuous for anyone afoot. Downtowns and other neighborhoods that were marvels of close-grained intricacy and compact mutual support are casually disemboweled. Landmarks are crumbled or are so sundered from their contexts in city life as to become irrelevant trivialities. City character is blurred until every place becomes more like every other place, all adding up to Noplace."

Physical transportation now claims about one-third of the land mass of cities. If national statistics are translated to the community level, every neighborhood has two or three people killed each year by cars and dozens more who suffer serious injury.

Perhaps more than any of its predecessors, the Clinton administration is filled with people who understand the enormous social, economic, and environmental costs of our transportation systems. Whether they will ever aggressively confront the country with this reality is doubtful, especially after their bruising setback over the elegantly designed but quite modest BTU tax on carbon usage. One of their priority issues is to reduce vehicle-generated pollution. Although interested in the type of fuel that powers the vehicle, they have to date evidenced less interest in the burdens imposed by the vehicle itself.

Americans love cars and hate welfare. Presidents need to speak to that dichotomy from the bully pulpit and explain that our private vehicles are by far the nation's biggest "welfare cheats." The highway trust fund is a unique, self-perpetuating paving-and-construction fund financed by a dedicated tax. Yet even the tens of billions of dollars each year that swell the highway trust fund cover only about half the cost of roads and a tiny fraction of the overall medical, social, environmental, police, and fire costs generated by vehicular use. By some estimates, the subsidy to cars and trucks is well over $300 billion a year, thirty times more than the federal government gives in aid to cities. If U.S. citizens had to pay the true costs of personal vehicles, they would not be able to afford them.

If physical transportation is the enemy of a sound economy, a clean environment, and strong, cohesive territorial communities, electronic transportation can be their friend.

The Clinton administration is aggressively promoting a national high-speed telecommunications infrastructure. Yet as of 1995, the federal government's role appears limited to accelerating the construction process, not designing the infrastructure so that it revitalizes communities. The Clinton proposal, for example, excludes at least in its first phase the quintessential community-based information institution — the public library. More than 60 percent of all Americans visit a library at least once a year. The public library represents cooperation and community in the age of competition and globalism. An information policy that puts community first would place America's fifteen thousand public libraries at the head of the connection line.

Who will own the new information infrastructure? Who will be able to access it, and on what terms? Mitch Kapor, head of the Electronic Frontier Foundation, worries that the future information system could look more like the present cable television setup than the present telephone or Internet systems. His nightmare is that "we could have tremendous bandwidth into the home and individuals and groups not have any access to it but continue to be passive recipients for whatever the people who control access to that medium want to do with it."

## SUSTAINABLE DEVELOPMENT:
### LOCAL CAPACITY

Improving efficiency reduces our reliance on imported materials. Recycling further reduces that dependence and also generates a supply of valuable industrial materials close to the final customer. Manufacturers tend to locate near the sources of raw materials. Now many are locating near large suppliers of used materials. In the hierarchy of solid waste management, reuse is better than recycling. Because transportation costs are high for shipping whole recyclable products back to remote manufacturers, reuse further localizes the economy.

When we need new materials, an environmentally friendly approach recommends that we use renewable resources. This, too, favors a shortening of the distance between producer and consumer. Minnesota, for instance, has sufficient winds to generate many times more electricity than the state consumes. A rooftop in Phoenix, Arizona, covered with solar cells can generate sufficient electricity not only to heat and cool the home but to run the family's electric car. Neither Arizona nor Minnesota need to be reliant on Saudi oil or Wyoming coal.

Wind and direct sunlight can provide significant quantities of energy, but they cannot supply molecules to make a physical product. For that, we need to use another renewable resource: the stored solar energy in plant matter. Anything that can be made out of hydrocarbon — chemicals, fibers, plastics, paints — can be made, and probably once was made, out of a carbohydrate. The first plastic, invented in the 1880s, was made not from petroleum but from cotton. The first synthetic fiber was not nylon but rayon made from wood pulp.

The low cost of transporting oil encourages large plants to locate far away from their raw material supplies. Plant matter, on the other hand, is bulky and expensive to transport and encourages modestly scaled biorefineries located near their raw material providers. In the future, cooperative biorefineries could use fast-growing trees or grasses and even single-cell algae as their raw material.

Consider the two futures implied by two Minnesota refineries. Just south of Saint Paul stands the Koch Petroleum refinery. It produces about 40 percent of Minnesota's transportation fuels, or 800 million gallons a year. Koch is an out-of-state corporation. Its raw materials are imported. Its facility is harmful to both its workers and its neighbors.

Compare this ecological eyesore with a biorefinery located three hours southwest of Saint Paul in Marshall, Minnesota. Minnesota Corn Processors (MCP) is owned by twenty-seven hundred corn farmers. Its plant produces corn meal, corn oil, carbon dioxide, corn syrup, ethanol, and industrial starch. Virtually all its raw materials are purchased locally. Virtually all its sales are in the region in which it is located. MCP is highly profitable, yet it satisfies only 2 percent of Minnesota's transportation needs and produces about 35 million gallons of ethanol a year.

Which raw material and organizational structure is best suited to a strong Minnesota economy: two absentee-owned Koch-type refineries or fifty cooperatively owned MCP-type refineries?

Twenty years ago, recycling, solar energy, and biochemicals were futurist dreams. Today, they have become increasingly cost-effective. In
1980, it was cheaper to throw away a ton of garbage than to recycle it. In
1993, in most parts of the country, the opposite is true. In 1980, the cost of
electricity generated from wind turbines was about seven times the price
of conventional electricity. Today, in some parts of the country, wind-elec-
tric generators are the least expensive of all new power plants. In 1985,
few consumer products were primarily derived from plants. Today, such
goods compete in almost every major category. Biopaints have captured 3
percent of the paint market. Vegetable oil–based inks have at least 8 percent of the ink market.

Today recycling, solar energy, and biological products are significant
businesses, even major industries. But they are still at the margins of the
economy. The task of any government should be to make these industries
central to the economy and to do so in a way that fosters community.

The federal government can facilitate this process by, for example,
mandating that products contain minimum amounts of recycled content.
A dozen states already have such legislation applied to newspapers, telephone books, fiberglass insulation and glass, and plastic containers. A federal law would overnight create huge markets for recycled materials and
make manufacturers responsible for their products even after disposal.

Federal procurement could also accelerate the introduction of decentralized devices such as solar cells and fuel cells. On the spending side of
the equation, the federal government should put R&D funds for renewable resource–based technologies at the top of the agenda.

## LOCAL AND GLOBAL

It is not enough for the federal government to promote strong communities with national programs. In an increasingly planetary economy, strong
communities must be nurtured and protected by international policies
too. As Robert Kuttner has noted, "[I]n the newly turbulent global economy, a social contract in one company is as elusive as 'socialism in one
country.' Even a manager with the best will in the world — and the best
union — cannot guarantee that the company will be in business next
decade, or even next year, to reciprocate the workers' loyalty. The larger
social contract is the responsibility of the government."

Free trade agreements, our courts have ruled, supersede state and
federal laws. What is the potential impact and reach of existing trade
agreements? Consider a recent European Commission (EC) report. Responding to a barrage of U.S. criticism concerning European trade barri-

ers, the EC listed the kinds of U.S. laws it considered protectionist: California legislation requiring a minimum amount of recycled content in glass containers sold within that state; restrictions in twenty-nine states on foreign ownership of land; labels that tell the customers where a car was assembled.

All the laws the EC criticizes were democratically enacted by communities to reduce pollution, create jobs, or retain a measure of influence over their own futures. All of these laws are threatened by misguided free trade policies. In the nineteenth century, the U.S. Supreme Court used the interstate commerce clause of the U.S. Constitution to severely limit the authority of the states and cities to enact rules that would protect their small farms, small businesses, and neighborhoods. In the late twentieth century, international trade panels are doing the same.

Those who oppose and those who support new trade agreements agree on one thing: The world economy is broken and needs new rules. The debate is about what those rules should be. Those who favor strong communities do not accept that trade agreements should have as their only objective the elimination of all obstacles to the flow of resources.

Trade agreements should establish minimum, not maximum, global environmental and social standards, as the United States did in 1938. That year, Congress enacted the Fair Labor Standards Act (FLSA) to discourage states from competing for business investment by lowering the quality of life of their residents. The FLSA created national minimum wage and maximum hour standards but allowed individual states to exceed these standards. In the 1970s and 1980s, federal environmental legislation usually embraced the same principle by establishing minimum, not maximum, pollution standards.

Delegating authority to communities, some argue, is an invitation to oppress minorities. Sociologists and political scientists worry about cultural insularity and isolation that could lead to Yugoslav-type ethnic violence. This fear of balkanization is a formidable concern and not easily deflected. Cohesive, self-conscious communities will undoubtedly view themselves as different and perhaps superior to their neighbors. But this does not mean they will instigate violence or wars. History shows that most wars result from unsustainability, territorial ambitions, a lack of material resources, or a desire to conquer new markets.

Authority, responsibility, capacity: the ARC of community. Without authority, democracy is meaningless. Without responsibility, chaos ensues. Without a productive capacity, we are helpless to manage our affairs and determine our economic future. Policy should be evaluated on the basis of how it strengthens all three cornerstones of strong communities.

# 38

# COMMUNITY MONEY
## *The Potential of* Local *Currency*

### Susan Meeker-Lowry

*If the formal economy no longer provides people with the goods and services they require, then people will provide them for each other by re-establishing informal local economies based on mutually beneficial exchange. Among the most promising experiments are the new local currency schemes now underway in the United States, Canada, Europe, and Australia. Legal and easily manageable, alternative currencies enable people to step outside a system that in any case is abandoning them. Susan Meeker-Lowry is a Vermont journalist who writes extensively about these matters for such publications as* Z Magazine, Earth Island Journal, *and* Woman of Power. *She is presently editor of* Food and Water Journal. *Her books include* Invested in the Common Good *(1995), and* Economics as if the Earth Really Mattered *(1988).*

THROUGHOUT HISTORY and around the globe, people have always traded and bartered with each other. As economies became more complex, money was created as a more convenient means of exchange. In those early days, money was generally a *commodity* — something highly valued by the people who agreed to use it. Iron nails were used as money in Scotland; dried cod in Newfoundland; sugar in some West Indies islands; salt in ancient Rome; wampum by Native Americans; and corn in Massachusetts in the 1600s. Sometimes money was backed by a commodity. The first Latin coins were stamped with the image of a cow and could be redeemed for cattle.

Paper money was created in the 1700s. It was basically an IOU backed by gold and silver, but these standards were abandoned (first in 1933 by President Roosevelt for U.S. citizens, then in 1971 by President Nixon for everyone else), so today our money is backed by nothing but promises (and debt). Thomas Greco, Jr., author of *New Money for Healthy Communities* (1994), states that "the proper kind of money used in the right circumstances is a liberating tool that can allow the fuller expression of human creativity. . . . Money has not lived up to its potential as a liberator because it has been perverted by the monopolization of its creation and by politically manipulating its distribution — which makes it available to the favored few and scarce for everyone else."

Greco outlines three basic ways in which conventional money malfunctions: (1) there is never enough of it; (2) it is misallocated at its source so that it goes to those who already have lots of it; and (3) it systematically pumps wealth from the poor to the rich. The symptoms of a "polluted" money supply are too familiar: inflation, unemployment, bankruptcies, foreclosures, increasing indebtedness, homelessness, and a widening gap between rich and poor. In the United States, the wealthiest 1 percent of households owns nearly 40 percent of the nation's wealth, and the top 20 percent (households worth $180,000 or more) have more than 80 percent of the country's wealth. Edward N. Wolff, an economics professor at New York University, says, "We are the most unequal industrialized country in terms of income and wealth, and we're growing more unequal faster than the other industrialized countries."

Poverty and unemployment levels are fast approaching those of the Depression years. The most obvious contribution that local currency schemes can make is to give people access to money — not in the form of the *national* currency but in that of local currency with which to acquire the goods, services, and care that they require.

In many communities around the country, people are taking control by creating their own currency. This is completely legal and, as organizers are finding, often very empowering. The move toward local currency is not only motivated by the desire to bridge the gap between what we earn and what we need to survive financially (although this plays a role, of course). It is also seen as a community-building tool. Community currency isn't new. In fact, it wasn't until 1913 that the Federal Reserve Act mandated a central banking system. Before that act, currency in the United States was based on everything from lumber to land. Then, during the Great Depression of the 1930s, scrip was often issued and exchanged for goods and services when federal dollars were scarce. Examples include wooden money in Tenino, Washington; cardboard money issued in Raymond, Washington, with a picture of a big oyster on the back; and corn-backed money in Clear Lake, Iowa. Scrip was even issued by Vassar seniors that consisted of pea green, blue, and yellow cards. Scrip was used to pay teachers in Wildwood, New Jersey, and to make the payroll in Philadelphia and numerous other cities and towns across the country. Scrip was issued by state governments, school districts, merchants, business associations, various agencies, even individuals.

Community currency is a tool that can help revitalize local economies by encouraging wealth to stay within a community rather than flowing out. It provides valuable information about the community's balance of trade. For example, if a currency is valued only in a certain region, then it cannot be used for goods or services from outside that region (unless the recipient agrees to spend it in the region of origin).

Today's community currencies, like those of the Depression, are varied and diverse. Some are *true currencies*; that is, they physically exist and are traded for goods and services such as federal dollars. Other systems are actually barter or work exchange networks with no physical currency exchanged. Still others resemble the scrip common during the Depression. The "rules" for these currencies also vary, depending on the needs and desires of community members. What they have in common is a commitment to community building, to supporting what's local, and to gaining a greater understanding of the role of economics and money in our daily lives. Local currencies are backed by something tangible that the community agrees has value, as the examples that follow illustrate.

# LOCAL EXCHANGE TRADING SYSTEMS (LETS)

LETS was created by Michael Linton in the Comox Valley of British Columbia in 1983. As an unemployed computer programmer with an interest in community economics, Linton saw that many people were in a similar position: They had valuable skills they could offer each other but had no money. He also saw the limitations of a one-on-one barter system: If a plumber wanted the services of an electrician, but the electrician didn't need plumbing help, the transaction couldn't take place. LETS solves the problem by opening the exchange to a whole community of members.

Here's how it works: Joe cuts firewood for Mary, who is a welder. Mary is now in debt to the system for the amount of the transaction ($75, let's say), and Joe's account is credited for that amount. A few day's later, Joe calls Mark for help fixing his car. Joe's credit is reduced by the $50 Mark charged, and Mark's account is credited with that amount. Then Mark wants some welding, calls Mary, and so it goes. The unit of exchange, what Linton calls *the green dollar,* remains where it is generated and provides a continually available source of liquidity. The ultimate resource of the community, the productivity, skills, and creativity of its members is not limited by a lack of money. These resources are the "backing" behind green dollars.

Several years ago, Linton wrote, "Money is really just an immaterial measure, like an inch, or a gallon, a pound, or degree. While there is certainly a limit on real resources — only so many hours in the day — there need never be a shortage of measure. . . . Yet this is precisely the situation in which we persist regarding money. Money is, for the most part, merely a symbol, accepted to be valuable generally throughout the society that uses it. Why should we ever be short of symbols to keep account of how we serve one another?"

In LETS, green dollars exist only as records kept on paper or on a computer data base. Transactions are reported by phone to a central coordinator, and members receive monthly statements and regular listings of members and their services. The original system in the Comox Valley started with just six people, and four years later had as many as five hundred members, including several businesses.

Today there are nearly two hundred LETS in Britain, and variations on the theme exist in the United States, Canada, the United Kingdom, and Australia.

Activist Nick England says that in Britain, "LETSystems are part of a wider movement toward permaculture and sustainability. They are inherently ecological, since they are needs-oriented and local. At first they work alongside the conventional economy but, as more networks form, they could bring about a network of sustainable communities. The one we started in our city now has nearly 100 members offering bicycle and car maintenance, music and language lessons, gardening, childcare, food and food processing, craftwork, manual labor, massage, and many other resources."

Joel Russ is the cofounder of a LETS group in the Slocan Valley of British Columbia that has been around since 1992. Joel writes,

> [A] problem with conventional money is that (as part of the vast international market system) it tends to flow to where it makes the most money — usually to the biggest cities, the trade and industrial centers, a good share of it finally coursing into and through the bank accounts of very wealthy weapons and oil peddlers.
>
> Such, after all, is the immense scope of The System. But most of us live closer to the other end of the scale, and we voluntary simplicists can often feel we have too little money for our needs. . . . A LETSystem keeps local energy local, rather than pouring it (in dollar-bill form) out of the community. LETS thus supports a truly

local economy. Those who believe in reducing their participation in the standard currency system, thereby contributing to reducing The System's pressure on natural systems, find LETS participation a meaningful ecological gesture.

Australia offers a major LETS success story. When Britain joined the European Union's Common Market, Australia lost its main export market. Food stocks destined for Britain had to be destroyed, and unemployment and bankruptcy became common. But LETS had found its way to Australia, providing welcome relief to people who became involved in these nonmonetary economies that developed in scattered communities around the country. In 1992, the Australian government invited Linton to set up LETS throughout the country, with the government providing funds for education, publicity, computer equipment, and other expenses. Businesses that joined, typically accepting 25 percent payment in LETS, found that their business increased. In Western Australia, it is estimated that LETSystems pumped the equivalent of A$3 million into the economy, which grew to include fifteen hundred businesses the first year. The same "rule" applies to these systems: Businesses can only spend LETS units locally. As a result, some give their LETS earnings to charity and qualify for a tax rebate. LETS earnings donated to charity have enabled churches to help unemployed youth and provide other necessary services. Patricia Knox, writing in the Winter 1995 *Earth Island Journal*, observes, "If the global economy crashes, Australia would be the country most likely to survive, having developed a thriving alternative economy."

LETS is not without its problems, of course. One of the most commonly asked questions is, "What about a person who spends heavily and then is unable or unwilling to repay?" In the early days, Linton said this did not happen often enough to be an issue:

> The simple willingness to undertake a commitment to provide fair value to another member of the community at some later date ensures that anyone who acts in good faith can spend as they need. Of course, a person who consistently fails to redeem their promises will thereby lose this opportunity, but at least the situation is of their own making. Most people who have no money are poor through no fault of their own. People suffer because they are so dependent on things beyond their control, like the export market, the bank rate, general consumer demand, commodity speculation, etc. Every transaction in a LETSystem is a matter of mutual consent.

But as the years passed, some systems, including the one in the Comox Valley, experienced high levels of debt. The group in Slocan Valley decided to impose a 300-clam (the name of their currency) limit for the first year of membership, and 500 thereafter in response to the problems posed by transiency within the community.

Another issue is how to determine the value of a green dollar (or a clam, acorn, or whatever name a currency is given). Most systems start out with one unit of their currency equaling one federal dollar. Yet many, especially people who feel the inequities of the paid wage system, want to move away from the conventional value system. Why, they ask, should one person's labor be worth three or four times what someone else earns? Alternative systems, they argue, should address these inequities directly.

There are many reasons given to justify keeping a LETS unit relatively equal to a dollar, especially at first. For one thing, it's what most of us are accustomed to. If a community desires business participation, as most do, a federal dollar equivalent seems almost essential. Yet, even without consciously attempting to de-link the value of LETS from the federal dollar, LETS members come to value each other as people rather than as the dentist, plumber, lawyer, babysitter, or gardener, and they begin to trade more on an hour-for-hour basis. After a while, people get creative. Too often we value ourselves only for what we are paid to do. We forget that our hobbies and other skills and interests are also gifts we can offer to community members. The simplistic new age slogan "do what you love and the money will follow" actually has a chance of success in a system that values people over profit and isn't ruled by scarcity.

LETSystems have a tendency to flourish during hard financial times and shrink when the economy turns around, probably because it's easier (read more expedient) to pay cash for something than to arrange to work at a later date in exchange for it. Plus, if we have more money, it's probably because we are working more hours for it, leaving fewer hours for LETS commitments. So, for LETS to play a major role in transforming our economy into one that is locally/regionally based and community controlled, members must make a commitment to it in both good times and bad. Without this commitment, LETS's real potential to contribute to systemic change (rather than just creating more purchasing power) is undermined.

## SCRIP

The E. F. Schumacher Society, based in Great Barrington, Massachusetts, has been at the forefront of community-based economics since it was founded in 1980 to promote the work of E. F. Schumacher (author of *Small Is Beautiful* [1973]). Robert Swann, the society's president, was involved in economic alternatives for years before the society was founded. Along with Ralph Borsodi, Swann pioneered the community land trust model in the 1960s and in the 1970s developed the revolving loan fund model with the Institute for Community Economics. In addition to questioning conventional private land ownership and project financing (both of which are skewed to benefit monied interests over the rest of us), Swann has tirelessly sought alternatives to the federal currency system.

In 1989, a deli in Great Barrington had to relocate because its lease was running out; a new lease would double the rent. Frank, the owner of the deli, went to several banks to borrow money to move to another location and was turned down. Finally, he approached SHARE (Self-Help Association for a Regional Economy), the Schumacher Society's loan-collateralization program. Susan Witt, SHARE's administrator, suggested that he issue his own currency and sell it to his customers to raise the money he needed. Each note sold for $9 and could be redeemed for $10 worth of food, and was dated so that redemption was staggered over time.

"I put 500 notes on sale and they went in a flash. It was astonishing," Frank said. Before long, Deli-Dollars were turning up all over town as people exchanged them instead of U.S. dollars for goods, services, or debts. In effect, these paper notes, which were essentially nothing more than small, short-term loans from customers, became a form of community currency. They so excited the people of Great Barrington that they were followed by Farm Preserve Notes issued cooperatively by Taft Farms and the Corn Crib. Each farm raised about $3,500 the first year and issued new notes in succeeding years. Five other businesses also issued scrip, including the Monterey General Store and Kintaro (a Japanese restaurant and sushi bar). Together, these businesses raised thousands of dollars to finance their operations that they couldn't have obtained through conventional sources. These success stories drew the attention of the *New York Times*, the *Washington Post*, ABC, NBC, CNN, and Tokyo television and have inspired projects around the country.

Susan Witt sees these programs as part of a larger strategy to strengthen regional economies:

> Basically, we're looking to find the way in which wealth generated in the region can be kept in the region. Our local banks, which did a very good job of that in the past, have now been bought up by larger and larger holding companies. So the deposits, the earnings, of rural regions and inner cities become like the wealth generated in Third World areas: It tends to all flow out into a few central, international, urban centers.

A regional currency is ultimately the way that communities can regain independence and begin to unplug from the federal system: to take back their rights to generate their own regional currencies. As our area of Great Barrington gets used to exchanging Berkshire Farm Preserve Notes and Deli-Dollars, we hope it will be the beginning of a true, independent, regional currency that's broadly circulated.

## ITHACA HOURS

In the United States, the community currency receiving the most attention these days is the Ithaca Hours in Ithaca, New York. The system was created in 1991 by Paul Glover, a community economist, ecological designer, and author of *Los Angeles: A History of the Future* (1984). Since then, close to $50,000 in local currency has been issued to over nine hundred participants and has been used by hundreds more. While this may not sound like much, these Ithaca Hours have circulated within the community many times, generating hundreds of thousands of dollars of local trading and adding substantially to what Glover calls "our Grassroots National Product."

Each Ithaca Hour is equivalent to $10 because that's the approximate average hourly wage in Tompkins County. The notes come in five denominations from a two-Hour note down to a one-eighth-Hour note, and the currency design features native flowers, waterfalls, crafts, farms, and people respected by the community. Since the currency must be easily distinguishable from federal currency, they are a slightly different size from federal bills and are multicolored, some are even printed on locally made watermarked cattail paper. Participants are able to use Hours for rent, plumbing, carpentry, car repair, chiropractic, food (two large locally owned grocery stores and various farmers' market vendors accept them), firewood, childcare, and numerous other goods and services. Some movie theaters accept Hours, as do bowling alleys and the local Ben & Jerry's.

Participants pay one U.S. dollar to join and receive four Hours when agreeing to be listed as backers of the money. A free newsletter, *Ithaca Money*, is published six times a year and lists a directory of members' services and phone numbers along with related articles, ads, and announcements. Every eight months, those listed in the newsletter may apply to be paid an additional two Hours for their continuing participation. This is how the supply of currency in the community is carefully and gradually increased.

While ostensibly everyone's work is valued equally, some negotiation does take place for certain services such as dentistry, legal counsel, massage therapy, and others that typically cost more than $10 an hour. Glover explains, "With Ithaca Hours, everyone's honest hour of labor has the same dignity. Still, there are situations where an Hour for an hour doesn't work. For example, a dentist must collect several Hours for each work hour because the dentist and receptionist and assistant are working together, using equipment and materials that they must pay for with dollars. So, a lot of negotiating must take place."

Potluck dinners are held monthly, and it is at these gatherings that members get together and discuss Hour-related business. Occasionally members decide to grant Hours to a well-deserving community organization. So far, more than $4,000 has been donated to twenty community organizations. Members have plans to develop a community cannery, to start a recycling warehouse, and to buy land to be held in trust. "We regard Hours as real money, backed by real people, time, skills, and tools," Glover states. Loans of Hours are made without interest charges.

What about the federal government? Glover says their main concerns are that Ithaca Hours have a design different from federal dollars and that they may be counted as taxable income when accepted for trades or services of a taxable nature.

To make it easier for other communities to start similar systems, Glover has created a Hometown Money Starter Kit (for US$25 or 2.5 Ithaca Hours) that explains step-by-step the start-up and maintenance of an Hour system. The kit also includes sample forms, articles, insights, samples of Hours, and back issues of *Ithaca Money*. Glover is also more than willing to answer questions by e-mail. The kit has been requested by four hundred communities in forty-eight states, and printed local currencies are in use in twenty-one communities, including Eugene, Oregon; Syracuse, New York; Butte County, California; Santa Fe, New Mexico; and Kansas City, Missouri. Several more communities are in the planning stages.

While local currency can be a lot of fun, it is also lots of hard work and responsibility. The group initiating the currency must be clear about what they are doing and why. In regions consisting of several smaller communities (as opposed to cities such as Ithaca), organizing can be more difficult, too. Some federal dollars will be needed to print money, informational flyers, and member directories, and those dollars may need to be raised by fundraising or grant writing.

Most people who start community currency systems believe it is important to sign up several businesses in addition to individuals. Yet it's important that trading not be confined to these establishments. The point is to enhance community members' ability to trade amongst themselves. Glover suggests restraining prominent businesses' per-purchase acceptance of local currency so that their capacity to spend local money expands gradually. He also encourages active outreach to bring in smaller businesses and individuals with diverse skills. However, logistics and technicalities aside, the most important thing before launching any currency system is to know your community. Lacking this, the first organizing task is to get out there and talk with folks to find out where they're coming from and what they want. A system can begin with a few pioneers and expand as the community gradually understands it.

## TIME DOLLARS

"Time is a resource that we don't use too well," says Edgar Cahn, creator of the Time Dollars. "The ideal here is to convert our time into social purpose and civic empowerment." Cahn initiated the Time Dollar Network in 1983 as a way to link various exchange programs and strengthen community relationships. Unlike LETS and Hours, each hour of service earns the same credit as any other hour regardless of level of skill. Time Dollars combines aspects of barter and volunteering and, like the other models described, works best when community members fine-tune it to suit their unique needs. Today, there are Time Dollar programs in 150 communities in thirty-eight states involving thousands of people. Members offer a wide range of services to each other such as childcare, tutoring, hospital visits, home repairs, shopping, and legal services. Computerized savings accounts keep track of members' credits, which can be used by oneself or given away. In fact, credits are often donated to congregations, tenant associations, and other organizations that can use them.

Cahn and Jonathan Rowe, coauthors of *Time Dollars* (1992), like to point out the benefits formerly provided by "the kitchen table world" — the world of the family and close friends, where everybody helped each other and cared for each other without thoughts of remuneration. This was particularly so for childcare, information sharing, transportation, care for the elderly, mutual help in carpentry, painting, and remodeling projects, and the like. For most people in the industrial world, increasingly isolated and fragmented, the kitchen table world no longer exists. The things it represented, say Cahn and Rowe, "companionship, entertainment, security, intimacy, even gossip, must now be bought for money." Increasingly it is the television and the computer, and soon it will be the information superhighway, that will replace the kitchen table world.

People have become purchasers of community and care rather than participants in providing them, say Cahn and Rowe, and inevitably they are rapidly losing the capacity to do these things, and the result is an ever enlarging circle of dependency and need.

Cahn started the first Time Dollar program in Miami, called Friend to Friend. It is one of the most successful programs, with more than sixteen hundred volunteers who put in nearly twelve thousand hours of service each month. In Wisconsin, every person who receives welfare can provide a needed service that accrues in nontaxable Time Dollars. In Brooklyn, Time Dollars supplements the health care benefits of Elderplan members. In New York City, Womanshare was created by Diana McCourt and Jane Wilson as a variation of Time Dollars to establish an economy that encourages friendship while valuing women's work. McCourt explains, "People have a lot of life skills that can be used to help each other. In Womanshare we have people who are homeless, and we have high-powered professionals. What's amazing is that everybody's time is worth the same."

Time Dollar programs have been set up in Boston, St. Louis, San Francisco, and El Paso. In Michigan and Missouri, programs have been launched with the help of local and state authorities. Several are already evolving into mini-economies, linking people from different generations. Young people are mowing lawns and painting houses for elderly neighbors, in some cases contributing their credits to other elderly people in need. Time Dollars can be seen as one means of demonetizing welfare, and in some programs (as in Brooklyn), Time Dollars have been incorporated into conventional medical care systems that provide services that dollars alone cannot buy. In this way the elderly become providers rather than simply consumers of care.

As Cahn states, "We've discovered that the range of the possible doesn't have to be limited by the availability of dollars, if you can convert people's time into purchasing power. When neighbors connect with each other, suddenly there's room for more connection."

## TOOL FOR CHANGE

When people first discover community currency and understand a bit about how it works, they are usually not inclined to be overly critical. It sounds so good, so freeing — just what the doctor ordered to address the sicknesses and diseases caused by our current economy and dependence on federal dollars. Plus, the idea of printing your own money is exciting and powerful. But to activists seeking strategies that not only challenge the current system but transform it, it's important to look at currency systems with a critical eye.

What's to prevent community currency from becoming just like federal money? Once people become used to it, won't it feel like just another commodity to earn and spend? While the principle of "everybody's work is equal" sounds good, the fact is that this is true for some but not all members. Where's the equity in this? Another concern is the role of businesses. Will businesses' participation limit the relationships between individuals in the system in favor of conventional consumer roles? How to value goods and services is also an issue. Should participants put a price on their services just like in the conventional money system, or should they be more creative? Should an Hour, for instance, have any dollar value at all? Could it represent just an hour of time? Finally, if we really want to get away from the feelings of greed, competition, scarcity, powerlessness, and inequity engendered by our conventional money system, why create another form of money? Why not just do away with currency totally and move toward a system that provides everyone with what they need in exchange for their labor?

The issue of scale is never easy, either. Some favor large state- or province-wide systems, others think the ideal size is at the neighborhood level. Most systems fall somewhere in between.

The problem (and the beauty) of models such as LETS or Hours is the specifics. Therefore, the answers to these questions really depend on the community implementing them. Whether a system is designed merely to increase buying power or to put a monkey wrench into business-as-usual depends on the values and politics of those who create it. Today, most (if not all) groups currently involved in some kind of community currency system, whether the barter model or the Hour or Time Dollar model, have stated that community building is a major goal, if not *the* major goal, of their project.

People also see community currencies as a means to help create more self-reliant local and regional economies. Since community currencies can be spent only in the community or the region where they are issued, goods and services that are dependent on resources from outside the region will have to be paid for in federal dollars. This can help people assess the resources available locally versus those imported from other places.

The Rocky Mountain Institute's Economic Renewal Program, designed to help people take charge of their community's economy, recommends that people take an inventory of all community resources as a first step. Part of this inventory process is knowing which goods and services the community provides for itself and which it imports from elsewhere. This helps identify areas for potential development. For example, if a community imports 80 percent of its food and yet has agricultural land sitting fallow, an obvious tactic would be to put land back into food production. Community currencies can provide similar information. A mechanic who has to import parts won't be able to accept LETS "green dollars" or Hours for those parts, but he or she can accept them for his or her time. The goal of community currency should not necessarily be to produce everything a community or a region needs. This is neither practical nor, in some cases, desirable. But community currencies are very helpful as a means of creating and sustaining self-reliance. "Rather than isolating communities," Glover explains, "local self-reliance gives them the strength to reach out to each other, to import and export more than before." Still, it makes sense to substitute local production and labor for imports when the resources and skills are available locally. In these days of global free trade, when jobs are exported to countries with cheap labor and lax environmental regulations, it's smart to create locally owned enterprises that hire local people to provide for local needs.

Unlike conventional money, which is based on scarcity and fosters competition, community currencies are designed to include everyone who wants to participate. By doing so, they take advantage of a wide range of skills and resources, unlike the conventional economy, which values certain skills and devalues or ignores others. As mentioned earlier, federal dollars tend to flow out of local communities, where they are needed the most, to those who already control large pools of wealth, such as banks and corporations. The very nature of community currency prevents this outflow.

Further, there is no benefit to hoarding huge numbers of Hours since their only worth is in local trade. You can't invest Hours in the stock market, they are worth nothing on international currency markets, and you probably wouldn't want to will a bunch of them to your grandchildren (except as a matter of curiosity). "Hour money has a boundary to it," Glover explains, "so Hour labor cannot enrich people who then take our jobs away to exploit cheap labor elsewhere. It must be respent back into the community from which it comes. It does not earn bank interest so it is not designed for hoarding. It benefits us only as a tool for spreading wealth."

But what's to prevent Hours from becoming like any other currency? The values and consciousness of its members. According to Glover, "Local currency activists generally seek to fundamentally transform society, rather than merely make it endurable." People starting currency systems must be very clear about what they are doing and why. If the goal is to move away from valuing people's time and labor only in federal dollars and to build community relationships within a system based on mutual respect and reciprocity, then members must ensure that the goals are being achieved and not left behind in the excitement of printing money and expanding individual spending power.

For any project to realistically work for systemic change, those implementing the project must have an understanding of the larger picture of which their project is a part. In the case of currency, we need to understand the history of money and trade relationships. We need to understand the role markets play in creating communities and interpersonal relationships, not to mention the hidden and not-so-hidden agendas of national and international markets. To intentionally remove ourselves from these larger markets in favor of creating stronger local ones is a political statement with repercussions that extend beyond our local communities. Currency activists say, "Of course. That's why we're doing it." But this may not be so obvious to people who join in after a system is set up and who view it mostly as a way of obtaining more buying power. The originators of currency systems have a responsibility to educate members regarding these larger issues. Not everyone has to agree, but there should be an overarching vision that doesn't get lost in the day-to-day practicalities.

Regarding the value of one person's labor in relation to another and the inequities in our current system that seem to be carried into alternatives (such as the dentist getting paid several Hours for one hour of work), the experience in many communities is that over time, as people get to know each other better, those higher paid professionals often lower their prices to system members. This happened in the original LETS in the Comox Valley, and it's happening in Ithaca today.

Glover reports that some professionals charge one Hour per hour voluntarily, in the spirit of the system. And a participant in Kansas City's Barter Bucks project states, "I can make $40 per hour on the outside, but I accept $10 an hour in Barter Bucks because I believe in the idea of equal pay." The fact that these changes of heart are happening in some places doesn't guarantee that they'll happen wherever a community currency is implemented. But they are an indication that people's good will and innate sense of cooperation are brought to life by a system that encourages them.

# 39

# "SHARING ONE SKIN"
## Okanagan Community

### Jeannette Armstrong

*Jeannette Armstrong is Okanagan, a member of the traditional council of the Penticton Indian Band in British Columbia, and is director of the En'owkin Centre, a school that teaches traditional Okanagan philosophy and practice. She is also a well-known activist on indigenous sovereignty issues and has been especially engaged in the international resistance to the Genome Diversity Project, which gathers Native genetic materials for eventual commercial exploitation.*

*In this chapter, Armstrong observes some key differences between the Okanagan views and practices of community — practices that have proven successful for thousands of years — and the views and practices of the dominant society, particularly focusing on psychological variations.*

*Armstrong's books include two works for children, as well as* Native Creative Process *(1991, with renowned Native architect Douglas Cardinal), a very popular novel,* Slash *(1985), and a collection of poetry.*

## IDENTITY AND RESPONSIBILITY

*I* AM FROM the Okanagan, a part of British Columbia that is much like most of California in climate — very dry and hot. Around my birthplace are two rock mountain ranges: the Cascades on one side and the Selkirks on the other. The river is the Columbia. It is the main river that flows through our lands, and there are four tributaries: the Kettle, the Okanagan/Smikamean, the San Poil, and the Methow.

My mother is a river Indian. She is from Kettle Falls, which is the main confluence of the Columbia River near Inchelieum. The Kettle River people are in charge of the fisheries in all of the northern parts of the Columbia River system in our territories. The Arrow Lakes and the tributaries from the Kettle flow south through the Columbia Basin. My great-grandmother's husband was a salmon chief and caretaker of the river in the north.

My father's people are mountain people. They occupied the northern part of British Columbia, known as the Okanagan Valley. My father's people were hunters — the people in the Okanagan who don't live in the river basin. They were always a separate culture from the river people. My name is passed on from my father's side of the family and is my great-grandmother's name. I am associated with my father's side, but I have a right and a responsibility to the river through my mother's birth and my family education.

So that is who I am and where I take my identity from. I know the mountains, and, by birth, the river is my responsibility: They are part of me. I cannot be separated from my place or my land.

When I introduce myself to my own people in my own language, I describe these things because it tells them what my responsibilities are and what my goal is. It tells them what my connection is, how I need to conduct myself, what I need to carry with me, what I project, what I teach and what I think about, what I must do and what I can't do. The way we talk about ourselves as Okanagan people is difficult to replicate in English. Our word for *people*, for *humanity*, for *human beings*, is difficult to say without talking about connection to the land. When we say the Okanagan word for ourselves, we are actually saying "the ones who are dream and land together." That is our original identity. Before anything else, we are the living, dreaming Earth pieces. It's a second identification that means human; we identify ourselves as separate from other things on the land.

The word *Okanagan* comes from a whole understanding of what we are as human beings. We can identify ourselves through that word. In our interaction, in our prayer, we identify ourselves as human as well, different from birds and trees and animals. When we say that, there is a first part of the word and an *s;* whenever you put an *s* in front of any word, you turn it into a physical thing, a noun. The first part of a word refers to a physical realm.

The second part of the word refers to the dream or to the dream state. *Dream* is the closest word that approximates the Okanagan. But our word doesn't precisely mean *dream*. It actually means "the unseen part of our existence as human beings." It may be the mind or the spirit or the intellect. So that second part of the word adds the perspective that we are mind as well as matter. We are dream, memory, and imagination.

The third part of the word means that if you take a number of strands, hair, or twine, place them together, and then rub your hands and bind them together, they become one strand. You use this thought symbolically when you make a rope and when you make twine, thread, and homemade baskets, and when you weave the threads to make the coiled basket. That third part of the word refers to us being tied into and part of everything else. It refers to the dream parts of ourselves forming our community, and it implies what our relationships are. We say, "This is my clan," or, "This is my people. These are the families that I came from. These are my great-grandparents," and so on. In this way I know my position and my responsibility for that specific location and geographic area. That is how I introduce myself. That is how I like to remember who I am and what my role is.

One of the reasons I explain this is to try to bring our whole society closer to that kind of understanding, because without that deep connection to the environment, to the earth, to what we actually are, to what humanity is, we lose our place, and confusion and chaos enter. We then spend a lot of time dealing with that confusion.

## SANITY, SELF, PLACE

As a child of ten, I once sat on a hillside on the reservation with my father and his mother as they looked down into the town on the valley floor. It was blackcap berry season, and the sun was very warm, but there in the high country, a cool breeze moved through the overshading pines. Bluebirds and wild canaries darted and chirped in nearby bushes, while a meadowlark sang for rain from the hillside above. Sage and wild roses sent their messages out to the humming bees and pale yellow butterflies.

Down in the valley, the heat waves danced, and dry dust rose in clouds from the dirt roads near town. Shafts of searing glitter reflected off hundreds of windows, while smoke and grayish haze hung over the town itself. The angry sounds of cars honking in a slow crawl along the black highway and the grind of large machinery from the sawmill next to the town rose in a steady buzzing overtone to the quiet of our hillside.

Looking down to the valley, my grandmother said (translated from Okanagan), "The people down there are dangerous, they are all insane."

My father agreed, commenting, "It's because they are wild and scatter anywhere."

I would like to explain what they meant when they said this. I do not wish to draw conclusions about the newcomers' culture or psychology. However, I do wish to highlight some differences between the mainstream view and the Okanagan view of self, community, surroundings, and time and to explain something of the Okanagan view of a healthy, whole person. I comment on these things only as I personally perceive them. I do not speak for the Okanagan people, but my knowledge comes from my Okanagan heritage.

## The Four Capacities of Self

The first difference I want to explore is our ideas of what we are as human beings, as individual life forces within our skins. I'd also like to explore how we might think of ourselves in relation to the unseen terrain we traverse as we walk the land and in consequence how we perceive the effect on the world around us.

When we Okanagans speak of ourselves as individual beings within our bodies, we identify the whole person as having four main capacities that operate together: the physical self, the emotional self, the thinking-intellectual self, and the spiritual self. The four selves have equal importance in the way we function within and experience all things. They join us to the rest of creation in a healthy way.

The physical self is one part of the whole self that depends entirely on the parts of us that exist beyond the skin. We survive within our skin and inside the rest of our vast "external" selves. We survive by the continuous interaction between our bodies and everything around us. We are only partly aware of that interaction in our intellect, through our senses. Okanagans teach that the body is Earth itself. Our flesh, blood, and bones are Earth-body; in all cycles in which Earth moves, so does our body. We are everything that surrounds us, including the vast forces we only glimpse. If we cannot continue as an individual life form, we dissipate back into the larger self. Our body-mind is extremely knowledgable in that way. As Okanagans we say the body is sacred. It is the core of our being, which permits the rest of the self to be. It is the great gift of our existence. Our word for *body* literally means "the land-dreaming capacity."

The emotional self is differentiated from the physical self, the thinking-intellectual self, and the spiritual self. In our language, the emotional self is that which connects to other parts of our larger selves around us.

We use a word that translates as *heart*. It is a capacity to form bonds with particular aspects of our surroundings. We say that we as people stay connected to each other, our land, and all things by our hearts.

As Okanagans we teach that the emotional self is an essential element of being whole, human, and Okanagan. We never ask a person, "What do you think?" Instead we ask, "What is your heart on this matter?" The Okanagan teaches that emotion or feeling is the capacity whereby community and land intersect in our beings and become part of us. By this capacity, we are one with others and all our surroundings. This bond is a priority for our individual wholeness and well-being. The strength with which we bond in the widest of circles gives us our criterion for leadership. It is the source from which the arts spring in celebration and affirmation of our connectedness.

The thinking-intellectual self has another name in Okanagan. Our word for *thinking/logic* and *storage of information* (*memory*) is difficult to translate into English because it does not have an exact correlation. The words that come closest in my interpretation mean "the spark that ignites." We use the term that translates as "directed by the ignited spark" to refer to analytical thought. In the Okanagan language this means that the other capacities we engage in when we take action are directed by the spark of memory once it is ignited. We know in our traditional Okanagan methods of education we must be disciplined to work in concert with the other selves to engage ourselves beyond our automatic-response capacity. We know too that unless we always join this thinking capacity to the heart-self, its power can be a destructive force both to ourselves and to the larger selves that surround us. A fire that is not controlled can destroy.

The spirit self is hardest to translate. It is referred to by the Okanagan as a part both of the individual being and of the larger self of which all things are part. We translate the word used for our spirit self as "without substance while moving continuously outward." The Okanagan language teaches us that this self requires a great quietness before our other parts can become conscious of it and that the other capacities fuse together and subside in order to activate it. Okanagans describe this capacity as the place where all things are. It teaches that this old part of us can "hear/interpret" all knowledge being spoken by all things that surround us, including our own bodies, in order to bring new knowledge into existence. The Okanagan says that this is the true self, and it has great power. It is a source for all things and affects all things if we engage it within the rest of our life-force activity. The Okanagan refer to it as the living source of our life.

## Community: Our One Skin

The second difference I want to explore has to do with community and family. The Okanagan teach that each person is born into a family and a community. No person is born isolated from those two things. You are born into a way of interacting with one another. As an Okanagan you are automatically a part of the rest of the community. You belong. You are them. You are within a family and community. You are that which is family and community; within that you cannot be separate.

All within family and community are affected by the actions of any one individual, and so all must know this in their individual selves. The capacity to bond is absolutely critical to individual wellness. Without it the person is said to be "crippled/incapacitated" and "lifeless." Not to have community or family is to be scattered or falling apart, which is how my father put it that day on the hillside.

The Okanagan refer to relationship to others by a word that means "our one skin." This means that we share more than a place; we share a physical tie that is uniquely human. It also means that the bond of community and family includes the history of the many who came before us and the many ahead of us who share our flesh. We are tied together by those who brought us here and gave us blood and gave us place. Our most serious teaching is that community comes first in our choices, then family, and then ourselves as individuals, because without community and family we are truly not human.

## The Language of the Land

The third difference between the Okanagan perception of the self and that of the dominant culture has to do with the "us" that is place: the capacity to know we are everything that surrounds us; to experience our humanness in relation to all else and in consequence to know how we affect the world around us.

The Okanagan word for "our place on the land" and "our language" is the same. We think of our language as the language of the land. This means that the land has taught us our language. The way we survived is to speak the language that the land offered us as its teachings. To know all the plants, animals, seasons, and geography is to construct language for them.

We also refer to the land and our bodies with the same root syllable. This means that the flesh that is our body is pieces of the land come to us through the things that the land is. The soil, the water, the air, and all the other life forms contributed parts to be our flesh. We are our land/place. Not to know and to celebrate this is to be without language and without land. It is to be dis-placed.

The Okanagan teach that anything displaced from all that it requires to survive in health will eventually perish. Unless place can be relearned, all other life forms will face displacement and then ruin.

As Okanagan, our most essential responsibility is to bond our whole individual and communal selves to the land. Many of our ceremonies have been constructed for this. We join with the larger self and with the land, and rejoice in all that we are. We are this one part of the Earth. Without this self and this bond, we are not human.

### Hands of the Spirit

The fourth difference has to do with the idea that, as Earth pieces, we are an old life form. As old life forms, we each travel a short journey through time, in which we briefly occupy a space as part of an old human presence on the land.

The Okanagan word for *Earth* uses the same root syllable as the word for our spirit self. It is also the word that refers to all life forces as one spirit. Everything we see is a spirit. Spirit is not something that is invisible, subjective, or in the mind. It exists. We are a microscopic part of that existence. The Okanagan teach that we are tiny and unknowledgable in our individual selves, but the whole-Earth part of us contains immense knowledge. Over the generations of human life, we have come to discern small parts of that knowledge, and humans house this internally. The way we act has significant effects on Earth because it is said that we are the hands of the spirit, and as such we can fashion Earth pieces with our knowledge and therefore transform the Earth. We are keepers of Earth because we are Earth. We are old Earth.

## CREATING COMMUNITIES OF HEART

The discord that we see around us, to my view from inside my Okanagan community, is at a level that is not endurable without consequences to the human and therefore to everything that the human influences. A suicidal coldness is seeping into and permeating all levels of interaction; there is a dispassion of energy that has become a way of life in illness and other forms of human pain. I am not implying that we no longer suffer for each other as humans but rather that such suffering is felt deeply and continuously and cannot be withstood, so feeling must be shut off.

I think of the Okanagan word used by my father to describe this condition, and I understand it better. Translation is difficult, but an interpretation in English might be "people without hearts."

As I mentioned earlier, the Okanagan self is defined as having four capacities, each separate though fully cooperating when we achieve whole human capacity and wellness.

The emotional self, the part that forms bonds to the larger selves of family, community, and land, is described by a term that translates as "the heart's rhythmical beat," signifying a living being. We say that we are connected to each other, to our land, and to all things by our heartbeats; it is a pattern that is in rhythm with others rather than creating dissonance and adversity.

Okanagans say that heart is where community and land come into our beings and become part of us because they are as essential to our survival as our own skin. By this bond, we subvert destruction to other humans and to our surroundings and ensure our own survival.

When the phrase *people without hearts* is used, it means people who have lost the capacity to experience the deep generational bond to other humans and to their surroundings. It refers to collective disharmony and alienation from land. It refers to those who are blind to self-destruction, whose emotion is narrowly focused on their individual sense of well-being without regard to the well-being of others in the collective.

The results of this dispassion are now being displayed as large nation-states continuously reconfiguring economic boundaries into a world economic disorder to cater to big business. This is causing a tidal flow of refugees from environmental and social disasters, compounded by disease and famine as people are displaced in the rapidly expanding worldwide chaos. War itself becomes continuous as dispossession, privatization of lands, and exploitation of resources and a cheap labor force become the mission of "peacekeeping." The goal of finding new markets is the justification for the westernization of "undeveloped" cultures.

Indigenous people, not long removed from our cooperative self-sustaining life-styles on our lands, do not survive well in this atmosphere of aggression and dispassion. I know that we experience it as a destructive force, because I personally experience it so. Without being whole in our community, on our land, with the protection it has as a reservation, I could not survive. In knowing that, I know the depth of the despair and hopelessness of those who are not whole in a community or still on their own land. I know the depth of the void. I fear for us all, as the indigenous peoples remaining connected to the land begin to succumb or surrender. I fear this as the greatest fear for all humanity. I fear this because I know that without my land and my people I am not alive. I am simply flesh waiting to die.

Could it be that all people experience some form of this today? If this is so, it seems to me that it is in the matter of the heart where we must reconstruct. Perhaps it is most important to create communities with those who have the insight to fear, because they share strong convictions. Perhaps together they might create working models for re-establishing what is human in community. However, fear is not enough to bind together community, and I cannot help but be filled with pessimism, for what I continue to see is the breakdown of emotional ties between people. I see a determined resistance to emotional ties of any kind to anything.

I see the thrust of technology into our daily lives, and I see the ways we subvert emotional ties to people by the use of communications that serve to depersonalize. I see how television, radio, telephone, and now computer networks create ways to promote depersonalized communication. We can sit in our living rooms and be entertained by extreme violence and destruction and be detached from the suffering of the people. We can call on the phone or send e-mail to someone we may never speak to in person.

Through technology there is a constant deluge of people who surround us but with whom we have no real physical or personal link, so we feel nothing toward them. We get to the condition where we can walk over a person starving or dying on the street and feel nothing, except perhaps curiosity. We can see land being destroyed and polluted and not worry as long as it's not on our doorstep. But when someone is linked to us personally, we make decisions differently. We try harder to assist that person because we (or someone we know) care deeply for the person.

Community is formed by people who are acting in cooperation with each other. Each person is cared for because each is bound to someone else through emotional ties, and all in the community are bound by generations of interactions with one another. Extended family is a healthy, essential part of this. Healthy extended families in community interact with each other over generations through intermarriage and the shared experience of mutual crisis conditions to create customs that sustain them and their offspring and ensure survival.

The customs of extended families in community are carried out through communing rather than communicating. I want to illuminate the significance of communing and point out that through its loss we have become dehumanized. To me, *communing* signifies sharing and bonding. *Communicating* signifies the transfer and exchange of information. The Okanagan word close in meaning to communing is "the way of creating compassion for." We use it to mean the physical acts we perform to create the internal capacity to bond.

One of the critical losses in our homes in this society originates in the disassociation we experience as a result of modern "communications" technology. People emotionally associate more with characters on television than with people in their lives. They become emotional strangers to each other and emotional cripples in the family and community.

In a healthy whole community, the people interact with each other in shared emotional response. They move together emotionally to respond to crisis or celebration. They "commune" in the everyday act of living. Being a part of such a communing is to be fully alive, fully human. To be without community in this way is to be alive only in the flesh, to be alone, to be lost to being human. It is then possible to violate and destroy others and their property without remorse.

With these things in mind, I see how a market economy subverts community to where whole cities are made up of total strangers on the move from one job to another. This is unimaginable to us. How can a person be a human while continuously living in isolation, fear, and adversity? How can people twenty yards away from each other be total strangers? I do see that having to move continuously just to live is painful and that close emotional ties are best avoided in such an economy. I do not see how one remains human, for community to me is feeling the warm security of familiar people like a blanket wrapped around you, keeping out the frost. The word we use to mean community loosely translates to "having one covering," as in a blanket. I see how family is subverted by the scattering of members over the face of the globe. I cannot imagine how this could be family, and I ask what replaces it if the generations do not anchor to each other. I see that my being is present in this generation and in our future ones, just as the generations of the past speak to me through stories. I know that community is made up of extended families moving together over the landscape of time, through generations converging and dividing like a cell while remaining essentially the same as community. I see that in sustainable societies, extended family and community are inseparable.

The Okanagan word we have for *extended family* is translated as "sharing one skin." The concept refers to blood ties within community and the instinct to protect our individual selves extended to all who share the same skin. I know how powerful the solidarity is of peoples bound together by land, blood, and love. This is the largest threat to those interests wanting to secure control of lands and resources that have been passed on in a healthy condition from generation to generation of families.

Land bonding is not possible in the kind of economy surrounding us, because land must be seen as real estate to be "used" and parted with if necessary. I see the separation is accelerated by the concept that "wilderness" needs to be tamed by "development" and that this is used to justify displacement of peoples and unwanted species. I know what it feels like to be an endangered species on my land, to see the land dying with us. It is my body that is being torn, deforested, and poisoned by "development." Every fish, plant, insect, bird, and animal that disappears is part of me dying. I know all their names, and I touch them with my spirit. I feel it every day, as my grandmother and my father did.

I am pessimistic about changes happening: the increase of crimes, worldwide disasters, total anarchy, and the possible increase of stateless oligarchies; borders are disappearing, and true sustainable economies are crumbling. However, I have learned that crisis can help build community so that it can face the crisis itself.

I do know that people must come to community on the land. The transiency of peoples crisscrossing the land must halt, and people must commune together on the land to protect it and all our future generations. Self-sustaining indigenous peoples still on the land are already doing this and are the only ones now standing between society and total self-destruction. They present an opportunity to relearn and reinstitute the rights we all have as humans. Indigenous rights must be protected, for we are the protectors of Earth.

I know that being Okanagan helps me have the capacity to bond with everything and every person I encounter. I try always to personalize everything. I try not to be "objective" about anything. Everything becomes valuable to me in that way. I try where I can to engage others in the same way. I fear those who are unemotional, and I solicit emotional response whenever I can. My community and my family and therefore my land has increased greatly. I do not stand silently by. I stand with you against the disorder.

# 40

# PRINCIPLES OF
# BIOREGIONALISM

## Kirkpatrick Sale

*Sometimes called "watershed economics," bioregionalism is a growing movement in the United States that advocates economies of self-sufficiency within naturally articulated "bioregional" boundaries. Finding many of its roots in Native practice, bioregionalism emphasizes that culture, community, and economics are rooted in a geographic place that needs constant observation and protection. Trade with other places is possible and sometimes desirable, but submission to a globalized economy of nation-states is anomalous to bioregionalists.*

*Since bioregionalism focuses on the local, we rarely learn of it in mass media; but in this chapter, Kirkpatrick Sale presents an overview of the principles by which bioregionalism operates, and advocates its viability. Sale is codirector of the E. F. Schumacher Society and a founder of the Green Party of New York. His many best-selling books include* SDS *(1974),* Human Scale *(1980),* Dwellers in the Land *(1985),* The Conquest of Paradise *(1990), and most recently,* Rebels Against the Future *(1995), in which he argues that the much-maligned Luddite movement of nineteenth-century England was absolutely correct in its observations that mass-production technologies would destroy livelihood and community. Sale's articles appear frequently in the* New York Times *and the* New York Review of Books, *and he is a contributing editor of* The Nation.

$I$T IS NOT so difficult to imagine the alternative to the peril the industrio-scientific paradigm has placed us in. It is simply to become "dwellers in the land." We must try to understand ourselves as participants in and not masters over the biotic community — a "reinvention of the human at the species level," in the philosopher Thomas Berry's telling phrase.

But to become dwellers in the land, to come to know the earth fully and honestly, the crucial and perhaps only and all-encompassing task is to understand *place*, the immediate, specific place where we live. The kinds of soil and rocks under our feet; the source of the waters we drink; the meaning of the different kinds of winds; the common insects, birds, mammals, plants, and trees; the particular cycles of seasons; the times to plant and harvest and forage — these are the things that are necessary to know. The limits of its resources; the carrying capacities of its lands and waters; the places where it must not be stressed; the places where its bounties can best be developed; the treasures it holds and the treasures it withholds — these are the things that must be understood. And the cultures of the people, of the populations native to the land and those who have grown up with it, the human, social, and economic arrangements shaped by and adapted to the geomorphic ones, in both urban and rural settings — these are the things that must be appreciated.

That, in essence, is *bioregionalism*.

•  •  •

Bioregionalism is at once very simple and very complicated.

Very simple, because all of its components are *here*, unhidden, right around us, right where we live; because we know that other people, ancient and, in our terms, perhaps unsophisticated, understood these things and lived for uncomplicated centuries by them. To discover and present the kind of information basic to a bioregional society is not difficult. There are still many older people among us today who know some of the wisdom of our forebears, and the discipline of modern ecology uses contemporary scientific procedures that can help us construct the rest of the bioregional body of knowledge.

Very complicated, because bioregionalism is so at odds with the conventional way of looking at the world nowadays that it must strike most people at first as too limiting and provincial, or quaintly nostalgic, or wide-eyed and utopian, or simply irrelevant — or all of those.

Obviously, it will take a considerable change in attitude before our industrial society begins first to abandon the notion of controlling and remaking the world in the name of a global monoculture and then to realize that maybe what it calls *provincial* is merely the kind of minding-your-own-business attention to local reforms that might just save the world.

# BECOMING BIOREGIONAL

It is possible to get a sense of the bioregional concept by following some of its natural practices.

## Knowing the Land

We may not become as sophisticated about the land we live upon and its resources as the original inhabitants. But any one of us can walk the territory and see what inhabits it, become conscious of the birdsongs and waterfalls and animal droppings, follow a brooklet to a stream and down to a river, and learn when to set out tomatoes, which kind of soil is best for celery, and where blueberries thrive. On a more sophisticated level, we can develop a resource inventory for the region, using information from the local Forest Service to map and count the area's trees; we can check hydrological surveys to determine waterflows, runoffs, and hydropower sites; collect biological profiles of the native annual and perennial food plants; learn annual climatic conditions and the full potentials of solar, wind, and water power; and study human land-use patterns and optimal settlement areas. Out of all that information — much of it already available though not broken down on a bioregional basis — we could ultimately determine with some grandeur the carrying capacity of the region.

Now that does sound a bit bucolic, I realize, and it may be hard to see immediately how it translates into urban terms. But every city is part of a region, after all, and depends on the surrounding countryside for many of its resources and much of its market, and every city is built upon a natural foundation. Knowing the land for the urban dweller, then, means learning the details of the trade and resource dependency between city and country and the population limits appropriate to the region's carrying capacity. It also suggests exploring the natural potential of the land on which the city rests — for though our huge conurbations have largely displaced natural life by diverting rivers, cutting down forests, paving over soils, and confining most animal life to zoos and parks, it is also true that we can discover and measure the possibilities for rooftop gardens, solar energy, recycling, urban silviculture, and the like.

## Learning the Lore

Every place has a history, a record of how both the human and natural possibilities of the region have been explored, and this must be studied with new eyes: There is more to discover, as farmer-philosopher Wes

Jackson puts it, than to invent. And though not every place has kept its history properly alive, a fountain of information still exists if we will but tap it.

Obviously we will not want or be able to live exactly as the ancients did. But every serious historical and anthropological exploration of their ways and wisdom shows that earlier cultures, particularly those well-rooted in the earth, knew a number of important things that we are only now learning about: the value of herbal medicines, for example, or methods and times of burning prairie grassland, or siting and building houses for maximum passive-solar effect, or the regular and central role of women in tribal decision making. If nothing else, such history helps us realize that the past was not as bleak and laborious and unhealthy as the high-energy high-tech proponents try to portray it. It was E. F. Schumacher who reminded us that when the modern world organized its thinking "by some extraordinary structure we call objective science," it discarded the "two great teachers" of humanity: "the marvelous system of living nature" and "the traditional wisdom of mankind" by which we know about it.

## Realizing the Potential

Once the place and its possibilities are known, the bioregional task is to see how this potential can best be realized *within* the boundaries of the region, using all the biotic and geological resources to their fullest, constrained only by the logic of necessity and the principles of ecology.

Self-reliance, not so much at the individual as at the regional level, is thus inherent in the bioregional concept. We might begin to think of how much of any region's human and material resources are ignored or squandered because the region looks to faraway sources and depends on extrinsic goods and services. We might look at how much of a region's wealth is exported to distant banks or home offices or absentee owners instead of being used to "water the garden" at home.

Finally, we recognize that bioregionalism of course stands in sharp contrast to the industrio-scientific paradigm in almost every aspect. It might be useful to compare the basic tenets of each to see their differences starkly:

|          | Bioregional Paradigm | Industrio-Scientific Paradigm |
|----------|----------------------|-------------------------------|
| *Scale*   | Region               | State                         |
|          | Community            | Nation/World                  |
| *Economy* | Conservation         | Exploitation                  |
|          | Stability            | Change/Progress               |
|          | Self-Sufficiency     | Global Economy                |
|          | Cooperation          | Competition                   |
| *Polity*  | Decentralization     | Centralization                |
|          | Complementarity      | Hierarchy                     |
|          | Diversity            | Uniformity                    |
| *Society* | Symbiosis            | Polarization                  |
|          | Evolution            | Growth/Violence               |
|          | Division             | Monoculture                   |

## ESTABLISHING BIOREGIONAL BOUNDARIES

The face of the earth is organized not into artificial states but natural regions, and those regions, while varying greatly in size, are generally much more limited than those defined by national boundaries.

The natural region is the bioregion, defined by the qualities Gaia has established there, the "givens" of nature. It is any part of the earth's surface whose rough boundaries are determined by natural characteristics rather than human dictates, distinguishable from other areas by particular attributes of flora, fauna, water, climate, soils, and land forms, and by the human settlements and cultures those attributes have given rise to. The borders between such areas are usually not rigid — nature works of course with flexibility and fluidity — but the general contours of the regions themselves are not hard to identify by using a little ecological knowledge. Indeed, those contours are generally felt, understood, or in some way sensed by many of the inhabitants of the area, particularly those closest to the land — farmers, ranchers, hunters, hikers, fishers, foresters, ecologists, botanists, and most especially (for America) the tribal Indians still in touch with their ancient traditions that for centuries have known the earth as sacred and its well-being as imperative.

## Ecoregion

The widest natural region, taking its character from the broadest distribution of native vegetation and soil types, might be called the *ecoregion*. It is a huge area of perhaps several hundred thousand square miles, normally (in the American setting) covering several states, its outlines determined largely by the spread of its trees or grasses at the time when its natural development was at its climax phase of maturity and stability. The boundaries are likely to be most imprecise at this stage, but one can identify about forty such ecoregions across the North American continent.

The Ozark Plateau is a good example. It covers some 55,000 square miles clearly demarcated by the Missouri, Mississippi, and Arkansas rivers, uplifted in a dome some 2,000 feet above the surrounding terrain. Its natural forest of predominantly oak and hickory is distinguishable from the pine forests to the south and the tall-grass prairie to the west, and its calcareous and chert soils are distinct from the non-calcareous deposits to the east and the sandstones and shales to the south and west. Or take the Sonoran Desert — that arid, scrub-brush area of perhaps 100,000 square miles that stretches from the southern foothills of the Sierra Nevada and the Mojave Desert down along the Gulf of California to the Sonora River and the northern edges of the Sinaloan forest. It is distinct in vegetation as the province of the creosote bush, saguaro and cardon cacti, jojoba, ironwood, and white bursage; in native animal life as the territory of bighorn sheep, pronghorns, and Gambel's quail; in climate as a hot, dry land of double cycles of rain and drought each year.

## Georegion

Within the large ecoregion it is possible to distinguish smaller bioregions with their own coherent characteristics, identified most often by clear physiographic features such as river basins, valleys, and mountain ranges, and often some special floral and faunal traits. A *watershed* — the flows and valleys of a major river system — is a particularly distinctive kind of georegion, more easily mapped than most, with aquatic and riverine life usually quite special to that area and with human settlements and economies peculiar to that river.

Within the Ozark ecoregion, for example, the White River watershed forms a discrete georegion easily visible from the air, and much of the biota around its major lakes — beaver, table rock, bull shoals, norfolk — can be differentiated, though sometimes in only marginal ways, from the rest of the ecoregion. The Central Valley of California forms another readily visible georegion within a Northern California ecoregion. It is a lush stretch of 20,000 square miles or so along the Sacramento and San Joaquin rivers, whose native wildlife before the dominance of agribusiness included ducks, geese, swans, tule elk, condors, coyote, grizzly bears, and antelope — a mix celebrated by the Indian tribes of the region exactly because of its distinctiveness. Its vegetation and climate make it quite different from the coastal forests, Sierra foothills, and Klamath mountains, which share the ecoregion with the Central Valley.

## Morphoregion

Finally, in some places, the georegions break down into a series of smaller territories of perhaps several thousand square miles, identifiable by distinctive life forms on the surface — towns and cities, mines and factories, fields and farms — and the special land forms that gave rise to those particular features in the first place. A watershed, for example, will often change its character perceptibly as it flows from its headwaters to its mouth.

The Connecticut River Basin, to take an obvious example, is a long and fertile georegion running from Canada down to the Long Island Sound. Although it is obviously a coherent watershed, it undergoes several evident changes: In the north, cutting through the hilly country of Vermont and New Hampshire, it is mostly pinched and narrow, with the forest vegetation very near the water's edge and the human settlements small and far between; when the valley broadens out below the Deerfield River, in Massachusetts, the hills and forests recede and dairy, tobacco, and vegetable farms spread out on both sides of the river, with several sizeable cities along the way; finally, as it reaches the solid and resistant Meshomiac foothills around Middletown, the river takes on a sylvan look again, with steeper slopes, so there are few human settlements until the saltwater towns around Seabrook Harbor.

Ultimately, the task of determining the appropriate bioregional boundaries — and how seriously to take them — will always be left up to the inhabitants of the area. One can see this fairly clearly in the case of the Indian peoples who first settled the North American continent. Because they lived off the land, they distributed themselves to a remarkable degree along the lines of what we now recognize as bioregions.

Take, for example, the tribal conglomeration of Algonkian-speaking peoples along the eastern seaboard. Before the arrival of European invaders, they settled over a territory stretching from somewhere near the Gulf of St. Lawrence down to Chesapeake Bay — very nearly what a bioregionalist would recognize as the ecoregion of the Northeast hardwoods, characterized by birch and beech in addition to conifers, with largely podzol and blue podzolic soils, and an annual rainfall of 45 to 47 inches, highest in July and lowest in January. Within this broad language group were more than a dozen tribes, which settled and for centuries maintained separate and successful homelands in areas roughly coincident with what we could recognize as georegions. The Pennacook, for example, lived along the Merrimack River watershed; the Massachuset lived around Massachusetts Bay; the Montauk confederacy settled throughout most of Long Island; and the Mahican occupied an extended Hudson River watershed from Lake Champlain down to the Catskills. The pattern continues: Subtribes or language subgroups were distributed in areas roughly similar to morphoregions, smaller territories still matching geographical forms.

Nothing demonstrates better how well-grounded bioregionalism is than this kind of accordance; nothing shows better how, far from being either an esoteric or exotic idea, or some made-up contrivance of contemporary do-gooders, it is a concept inherent in the cultures of age-old peoples who knew the ways of nature best. That is why I think the final distinctions about bioregional boundaries and the various scales at which to create human institutions can be safely left to people who live there, providing only that they have undertaken the job of honing their bioregional sensibilities and making acute their bioregional consciousnesses.

## SCALE AND COMMUNITY

Now we come to the the issues of scale, and these have to do with the smaller sets of living webs, the natural human settlements within regions: *communities*. All biotic life is divided into communities, which, though differing in size, complexity, development, and stability, exist everywhere, throughout every econiche. If one were to look for the single basic building block of the ecological world, it would be the community.

For the ecologist, a community is essentially a self-sufficient and self-perpetuating collection of different species that have adapted as a whole to the conditions of their habitat. There may be only a comparatively few species, as in barren arctic regions where simple microorganisms predominate; or there may be thousands, as in a warm temperate forest where in a single acre (according to one estimate) there may be something like 50,000 vertebrates, 662,000 ants, 372,000 spiders, 90,000 earthworms, 45,000 termites, 19,000 snails, 89 million mites, 28 million collembola, and some 5,000 pounds of plant life divided into at least 2,000 species.

There are no exact limits on the geographical extent or number of organisms or total population of a biotic community, but there are general constraints that inevitably affect its structure and size. They have to do, more than anything else, with energy in its broadest sense: There are producers of energy (plants), consumers (from fungi to carnivores), and decomposers (from microorganisms to termites); and there must be some sort of circular balance among all of them for the successful life of the system. When one or another species uses an unusual amount of energy, the change will eventually affect all other species and may in time lead to a new configuration of the community. For example, when tall shade plants begin to dominate a grove, using extra energy from sun and soils, they squeeze out certain other mid-sized species no longer able to get sufficient photosynthetic energy, but at the same time they allow many other shade-tolerant species to take root and thrive beneath them.

The community, the bounded community, is not merely an abstract elaboration concocted by biologists or imposed by ecologists. It is the observable reality of a place, as real as the functions — as I see it in the summer outside my window — of the bumblebees pollinating the zucchini, the termites eating away the dead logs, the frogs in the stream catching insects, and the copperheads catching frogs. The animals and plants of course aren't conscious of being a part of a niche of related organisms; it is simply how they live, no more, no less.

Humans, too, have always lived by community — both the community joined to the surrounding species with which they interact for the necessities of life and the purely human community with which they have evolved their unique social forms. Of the more than tens of billions of people who have lived since the time of the Cro-Magnons, microbiologist René Dubos has noted, "the immense majority of them have spent their entire life as members of very small groups . . . rarely of more than a few hundred persons. The genetic determinants of behavior, and especially of social relationships, have thus evolved in small groups during several thousand generations." Nor, despite appearances in some places, has the community vanished, even now. The eminent anthropologist George Peter Murdoch reported after an exhaustive ten-year cross-cultural survey that the institution of the community occurs "in every known human society," and there is no part of the world where people live alone or in isolated families.

The bioregional mosaic, then, would seem logically to be made up basically of communities as textured, developed, and complex as we could imagine, each having its own identity and spirit, but each of course having something in common with its neighbors in a shared bioregion.

# ECONOMY

A bioregional economy would seek first to maintain rather than use up the natural world, to adapt to the environment rather than exploit it or manipulate it, and to conserve not only the resources but also the relationships and systems of the natural world. Second, it would seek to establish a stable means of production and exchange rather than one always in flux and dependent upon continual growth and constant consumption.

So, at its base, a bioregional economy would depend upon a minimum number of goods and the maximum use of human labor and ingenuity. For energy, it would obviously depend on the various forms of solar power appropriate to the region; for transportation, on human-powered machines and electric vehicles and trains, along with settlement patterns that encourage walking and biking; for agriculture, on organic and pest-management farming, perennial polyculture, aquaculture, and permaculture, with markets geared to seasonal and regional foods supplemented by extensive greenhouse use; for industry, on local crafters and artisans rather than factory production, on natural materials and nonpolluting processes, emphasizing durability and quality. At all points, in all processes, the system's goals would be to cut down on energy and resource use, minimize production and "throughput," reward conservation and recycling, and hold population and commodity stocks at a roughly constant and balanced level. Sustainability, not growth, would be its goal.

Such an economy, in spite of its divergence from the present one, is really not all that difficult to imagine. Indeed, many of its workings have been written about quite extensively in recent years by scholars who have advocated a system of "soft-energy paths" and "conservancy" and "eco-consciousness" — or what has generally come to be called the *steady-state economy*. One of the earliest and most insightful of these scholars, Herman E. Daly, speaks of the connection this way: "A steady-state economy fits easily into the paradigm of physical science and biology — the earth approximates a steady-state open system, as do organisms. Why not our economy also, at least in its physical dimensions of bodies and artifacts? Economists may continue to maximize value, and value could conceivably grow forever, but the physical mass in which value inheres must conform to a steady state, and the constraints of physical constancy on value growth will be severe and must be respected."

We will have to measure our lives in terms of clean air rather than large cars; of healthy, chemical-free food rather than supermarket frozen convenience; of autonomous workplaces rather than fat paychecks; of days without rush hours and television commercials and junk mail. Such things, though not measured by the traditional GNP (aptly called *gross*), are not without value — indeed, for many they are of primary value — and in any sensible reckoning ought to be considered part of one's living standard. The bioregional economy must be labor-intensive rather than energy-intensive. It must produce more durable goods in order to reduce waste, so it will emphasize quality rather than quantity. It must reduce pollution of air, water, and food, so it will improve public health. It must eliminate the inflation inherent in a growth economy, so it will make income, expenditures, and whole currencies more stable.

## SELF-SUFFICIENCY

Successful early societies were of course self-sufficient by necessity, almost by definition — because if they weren't, they simply wouldn't have existed.

In the natural realm, self-sufficiency is not normally found at the level of one species or small community, because interdependency is the rule: The beehive, however self-contained and self-regulated it may be, absolutely depends upon nearby trees and flowers and natural materials for its existence. But at the level of the ecosystem, self-sufficiency is the norm, for at that level there is a sufficiently abundant population for successful interaction among the species and a sufficiently wide territory for resources to sustain them all.

The same rule seems appropriate for human self-sufficiency as well. It is no doubt possible for a community of a thousand people to carve out a living for itself, dependent on a wide range of plant and animal species but totally isolated from other human communities; but then it is also possible for a single individual to live a hermetic life of perpetual isolation deep in the backwoods that might have to be called self-sufficient. For a fully enriched and developed life, however, that includes not only material enrichment and convivial association but also cultural enlargement, surely a wider circle than that is desirable. And for anything approaching the standard where we might have a wide range of food, some choice in necessities, and some sophistication in luxuries — the population to sustain a university and a hospital and a symphony orchestra — a full-scale morphoregion would seem to be necessary.

Within almost any imaginable bioregion in North America or elsewhere (with significant exceptions in certain brutally ravaged parts of Africa and Asia), there are sufficient resources to provide a stable and satisfying life, though indeed their abundance and splendor might vary greatly. Certainly, there is not a single bioregion in this country, even at the geographical level, that would not, if it looked to all its natural endowments, be able to provide its residents with sufficient food, energy, shelter, and clothing, their own health care and education and arts, their own manufactures and crafts. Each region would need to learn to adapt to its natural circumstances, developing energy based on available resources (wind in the Great Plains; water in New England; wood in the Northwest), growing food appropriate to the climate and soils, creating crafts and industries according to the given ores and minerals, woods and leathers, cloths and yarns.

• • •

Far from being deprived, even the most unendowed bioregion can in the long run gain in economic health with a careful, deliberate policy of self-sufficiency. The reasons are various:

• A self-sufficient bioregion would be more economically stable, more in control of investment, production, and sales, and hence more insulated from the boom-and-bust cycles engendered by distant market forces or remote political crises. And its people, with a full close-up knowledge of both markets and resources, would be able to allocate their products and labor in the most efficient way, to build and develop what and where they want to at the safest place, to control their own money supply and currency value without extreme fluctuations — and to adjust all those procedures with comparative ease when necessary.

• A self-sufficient bioregion would not be in vassalage to far-off and uncontrollable bureaucracies or transnational corporations. Not caught up in the vortex of worldwide trade, it would be free from the vulnerability that *always* accompanies dependence in some degree or another, as the Western world discovered with considerable pain when OPEC countries quadrupled the prices of oil.

• A self-sufficient bioregion would be, plainly put, richer than one enmeshed in extensive trade, even when trade balance is favorable. Partly this is because no part of the economy need be devoted to paying for imports, a burden that severely taxes even an industrial country such as the United States and that simply drains nations heavily dependent on imports, such as Britain, Brazil, Mexico, and most of the nonindustrial Third World. Partly this is because enterprises could devote themselves to their own markets and undertake what Jane Jacobs calls *import replacement*, a process with economic and creative multiplier effects that enrich all segments of the economy. And partly this is because the region would not have to spend its money on transportation.

- A self-sufficient bioregion would be in control of its own currency, so it could receive immediate feedback on the workings of the economy and avoid the structural flaws that beset most regions whose money is largely controlled from outside. Local currencies, moreover, can be kept steady and basically free from inflation, and can usually be confined to the region to encourage reinvestment and prevent the flight of capital.

- A self-sufficient bioregion, finally, would be healthier and able to enjoy a more productive economy on the one hand while escaping the massive expenditures of medical treatment on the other. Not only could it be free of the chronic diseases of industrialization that are known to increase in perfect synchronization with the GNP (cancer, ischemic heart disease, diabetes, diverticulosis, tooth caries) but it can spare itself the applied toxicity we now take for granted. Locally grown and marketed foods, for example, do not need to be sprayed with chemicals to make them appealing or increase their shelf life, nor must they be stored with insecticides and rodenticides, nor be processed and packaged with polymers and plastics.

- A self-sufficient bioregion would foster a more cohesive, more self-regarding, more self-concerned populace, with a developed sense of community and comradeship and the pride and resilience that come with the exercise of competence, control, stability, and independence.

• • •

Self-sufficiency, I must add, before I am badly misunderstood, is not the same thing as isolation, nor does it preclude all kinds of trade at all times. It does not require connections with the outside, but within strict limits — the connections must be nondependent, nonmonetary, and noninjurious — it allows them. And, in one area, it encourages them.

There are no barriers to knowledge, and it would be foolish to imagine constructing them. Indeed, it may be the self-sufficient society that most needs information from without — about new techniques and inventions, new materials and designs, and innovations scientific, cultural, technical, political, and otherwise. The society secure in its competence and satisfied in its needs would do best to keep itself open to ideas from beyond its edges, its antennae ever alert.

Thus we come, organically almost, to the principle of cooperation.

As the workings of self-regulation tend to direct toward conservation and stability, the Gaian premium is obviously upon the associations that create harmony rather than discord, equilibrium rather than turbulence. The successful ecosystem requires its many parts to operate smoothly together, regularized and interdependent over time.

There's no question that cooperation is the underlying principle of non-human life forms. Lynn Margulis's work, for one, shows conclusively that stromatolitic bacteria — about the most ancient form of life that we have been able to discover — have structures and functions quite similar to those found in all higher plants and animals. This indicates that life forms over these countless millennia have been based on "an interlinking, highly cooperating, and organized set of bacterial components." There's also not very much question about cooperation having been the underlying principle of all early human societies. The killer-ape human of pseudo-anthropology once popular in the West has been discredited now, and the theories of people such as the Leakeys in Kenya and C. K. Brain and Elizabeth Vrba have pretty well established that a basic sense of mutual aid was instrumental in the success of hominid communities as recently as 3.5 million years ago.

In fact, the Darwinian notion that ceaseless competition promoted the survival of the fittest individual has by now generally given way to the understanding that evolutionary success was due to the survival of the fittest *community* through interlocking cooperation. Those families and bands that united and learned to cooperate for the tending of fire, the sharing of food, the hunting of large animals, the securing of campsites (or, in current anthropological parlance, *home bases*), were more likely to survive than any others. That kind of cooperation, then, over several *hundred thousand* years, is actually inbred in the human species; Dubos and other biologists argue that those qualities — collaboration, teamwork, sodality, and federation — are genetically encoded in our beings.

The argument for the bioregional economy is obvious enough: The marketplace of our traditional capitalist economy, with its emphasis on competition, exploitation, and individual profit, needs to be phased out. E. F. Schumacher, for twenty years the chief economist of Britain's National Coal Board, came to see this clearly: "The market represents only the surface of society," he wrote, "and its significance relates to the momentary situation as it exists there and then. There is no probing into the depths of things, into the natural or social facts that lie behind them." Market economics simply does not reflect the real — the ecological — world.

# 41

# IN FAVOR OF A NEW
# PROTECTIONISM

## Colin Hines and Tim Lang

*Protectionism has received a bad name, due to the constant charge by promoters of globalism that any attempt to preserve regional or community values, traditional economies, or local jobs is an assault against the higher cause of the global economy. As we have seen, however, the global economy is little more than a protectionist tactic used by TNCs and banks against any ability of communities to preserve their own sustainability or that of nature.*

*In this chapter, the authors turn the tables on critics of protectionism. They argue that the preservation of livelihoods and community is itself the higher goal, far more urgent than preserving the globalism that is already failing.*

*Colin Hines is the former coordinator of Greenpeace International's Economics Unit, and is codirector of the International Forum on Globalization–Europe. Tim Lang is professor of food policy at Thames Valley University and an activist in the cause of local food production. Lang and Hines are coauthors of a book on these themes,* The New Protectionism *(1994).*

SARAH PARKIN, former chair of the British Green Party, once said of free market ideologues that "they believe in a happy ending, unparalleled outside Disneyland." This happy ending accompanies the belief that jobs are not lost by international free trade but are merely shifted around, and that wages of billions of low-paid Third World workers will rise enough for them to purchase all the high-tech goods and services that First Worlders expect to export.

As with other corporate utopia schemes, there is now enough evidence to be sure that this one is indeed a fantasy and that now is a good time to take another route entirely. We strongly believe in regenerating interest in a realistic system for the preservation of communities, economies, and livelihoods; a return to the security provided by a local self-sufficiency that emphasizes local economic control and local production for local consumption, *protected* by a modernized trade philosophy that restricts unnecessary aspects of international trade. We call such practical measures *the new protectionism*.

## ORTHODOX ECONOMISTS:
## LIVING IN DENIAL

The economic orthodoxy's stalwart belief that globalization will be the panacea to solve all problems leads its economists to deny the facts as they are now emerging. Symptomatic of this denial was the OECD's failure, in its 1994 *Jobs Study*, even to address the issue of the sudden loss of consumer demand (purchasing power) resulting from lower wages and fewer jobs. The rapid replacement of secure jobs by short-term contracts, part-time or lower-paid work, or unemployment sharply reduces overall effective purchasing power and is introducing a spreading culture of insecurity that is replacing John K. Galbraith's culture of contentment nearly as quickly as he had named it (Galbraith 1992). Economic journalists are commenting that a new and desperate situation has already arrived in the markets for housing, household goods, and private cars in both the United Kingdom and the United States.

In the United Kingdom, the situation is most obvious in housing. In the 1980s, under the Thatcher government, male jobs declined with the destruction of British manufacturing, but much of the anxiety was held in check by an explosion of property values, which temporarily masked the real situation. Today, however, the unemployment trends are worsening effective demand in housing and all the sectors allied to it (Bassett 1995). The housing market is now resolutely flat. And it recently became headline news when a professor of finance suggested that in real terms housing prices could fall by 20 percent over the next twenty years.

Still, it was not until the start of the 1990s recession that British politicians finally began actually to criticize consumers for not consuming enough. This echoed remarks about the same time in the United States by President Bush, who urged the purchase of refrigerators and cars as a patriotic act. But such rhetoric was skirting dangerous political ground, because consumers were absolutely correct to be feeling insecure. In 1995, the International Labor Organization announced that one-third of the world's willing-to-work population was either unemployed or underemployed, the worst situation since the 1930s (ILO 1995).

This sober reality still failed to dent the breezy optimism of the institutions of the dominant political economy. The World Bank asserted that "wage incomes will rise in labor-intensive ASEAN countries, China, and South Asia and fall in other countries, because of the increased competition in the goods in which they now specialize." The Bank anticipates few problems in this because, they say, "this fall in [Western] incomes will be more than compensated for by price reductions" (World Bank 1995).

As Jeff Faux (1993) of the U.S. Economic Policy Institute has argued, "One does not have to be an expert in economics to see that the world economy cannot continue with all nations expanding exports and constricting the ability of their workers to buy imports."

Eighty years earlier, Henry Ford, no softie toward his workers, put it more succinctly: "If you cut wages, you just cut the number of your customers." Orthodox political economists of today seem to have forgotten this vital connection.

## GLOBALIZATION AND JOB LOSS

Recently there has been a creeping acceptance that globalization does lead to lower wage economies. Professor Adrian Wood (1994) has calculated a loss of 9 million jobs from North to South in recent years. The pressure to respond in the United Kingdom by reducing real wages and "downsizing" labor forces has been a hallmark of U.K. government policy since the late 1970s in an effort to prevent such U.K. industries from relocating to lower-wage countries with less regulated economies. England now advertises its remarkably low wages as *inducements* to new industry.

In 1993, manufacturing labor costs in West Germany were U.S.$24.9 per hour. In Japan, they were $16.9; in the United States, $16.4; in France, $16.3; and in the United Kingdom, $12.4. But compare those with South Korea's manufacturing labor costs at $4.90 per hour; Hungary's at $1.80; and China's at 50 cents! This is why companies such as the Italian sportswear and shoemaker Fila have, in the words of one commentator, "found one way of coping with a fundamental problem of European manufacturing. It is trying not to have any" ("Can Europe Compete?" 1994).

While the economists try to persuade us that significant corporate relocation does not occur, the French Senate's finance committee has already argued that much of the present unemployment in France is the direct result of the siting of factories where wages are a fraction of those in France.

And a 1993 survey of ten thousand large and medium-sized West German companies found that one in three intend to transfer part of their production to Eastern Europe or Asia, because of lower wages and more lenient environmental standards (Gepillard 1994). Such reports add to the corporate ability to blackmail labor.

In the United Kingdom's high-tech service sectors, companies such as the National Westminster Bank, Abbey National, British Telecom, Procter and Gamble, London Transport, Citicorp, and Singapore Airlines are reported as directly or indirectly using Indian computer programmers, most of whom earn less than $3,000 a year. New Electronic Export Zones are being set up near New Delhi, Bombay, Calcutta, Cochin, Kandia, and Madras that offer high-quality and high-tech services on vastly lower wages than Europe can offer.

The orthodoxy's usual response to such concerns is that such relocations are restricted to a few industries, and that most of the trade happens between OECD countries anyway.

This overlooks two points. Firstly, national governments have had their powers to control economic processes seriously diminished. The 1994 GATT agreement now gives extraordinary powers to the WTO over trade matters. Secondly, nearly 40 percent of OECD trade is with non-OECD countries; trade with China is "now the most dynamic element of OECD trade." In other words, when world trade occurs less and less in zones — and when free trade deals such as the European Economic Area (the EU plus EFTA), NAFTA and, in the South, MercoSur, are increasingly "leaky" — there is little chance of national action.

## THE ROLE OF NEW TECHNOLOGY

Automation trends are now occurring in every sector as corporations use the full benefits of new technologies to restructure. But new technologies are not just hardware. "Management by stress," where production is deliberately accelerated to reveal areas of weakness, involves workers themselves in identifying the weak points and then introduces design and procedure changes to increase perpetually the pace of production, often resulting in increased injuries. Worker stress under these conditions has reached near epidemic proportions in Japan (Rifkin 1995). Where is the progress here?

It is not only the assembly line worker who suffers stress. As Jeremy Rifkin points out, management is also subject to the new combination of management systems and new technology. Layers of middle management are eliminated to make structures more "computer-friendly"; organizational pyramids are flattened; and work teams are created. Such "re-engineering" typically results in a greater than 40 percent loss of jobs, many of them middle management jobs (Rifkin 1995).

When employment in manufacturing sectors was hit by restructuring in which new technology was a key factor, the political response was that the decline of employment in the "old" industries would be compensated by a growth of the service sector. But now, new technology is taking out the service jobs, too. Most of the recent cutbacks in the United States have been in the service industries, such as banking, insurance, accounting, law, communications, airlines, retailing, and hotels. According to Andersen Consulting in 1993, U.S. banking and savings institutions were anticipated to lose seven hundred thousand jobs over the next seven years. In the United Kingdom, the current wave of bank and other mergers suggests a similar pattern.

Meanwhile, the global economy is undergoing a phenomenal concentration of power into the hands of transnational corporations (TNCs). The combined sales of just the world's largest 350 TNCs total one-third of the GNPs of all industrialized countries. The largest 100 of the 37,000 TNCs account for over $4 trillion of world assets, of which $2 trillion is outside of the country of origin (Breverton 1994). Although the top 350 TNCs control 40 percent of world merchandise trade, the largest 15 have a gross income larger than the GDP of 120 countries (Lang 1993). These were the companies who pushed for the GATT Uruguay Round and who have sufficient capital to exploit fully the new technologies; they are often in the forefront of automation.

In sum, this formidable (and rising) concentrated control over world output is not hopeful news for employment. The world's total of one hundred thousand TNCs, large and small, employs only 65 million people, just 3 percent of the world's estimated workforce. TNCs have shed labor heavily. In just one year, March 1992 to 1993, according to the Institute of Directors, the top one thousand British companies shed 1.5 million jobs and reduced their total workforce from 8.6 million to just over 7 million. Small enterprises will not be able to take up the slack.

## THE NEW PROTECTIONISM

Transnational corporations and international capital have become the de facto new world government, and their increasing control over the global economy is underpinned by the free trade orthodoxy. Existing world bodies, under the United Nations umbrella, already suffer a democratic deficit and are unable or unwilling to act before this new world order. In addition, the globalization process is also reducing the power of national governments to provide what their populations require.

We believe it is time to rethink the future direction of global economics. The key issue is to put governments at local, regional, and national levels back in control of their economies and to relocalize and rediversify these economies. The way to do this lies in applying what we call the New Protectionism.

First, two points of clarification. The New Protectionism, as we have formulated it, is neither antitrade nor autocratic. Its goal is maximum local trade within diversified, sustainable local economies and minimum long-distance trade. We use *local* here to refer to part of a country and *regional* to signify a geographical grouping of countries (Lang 1993).

The ultimate goal is to build up truly sustainable economies and to shift away from economies that subjugate local jobs to global pressures. Here are some steps to that end:

• *Import and export controls.* These should be introduced on the national and regional bloc levels, with the aim of allowing localities and countries to produce as much of their own food, goods, and services as they possibly can. Only goods that cannot be provided nationally should be obtained regionally, with long-distance trade the very last resort. Goals should be set for each economic sector.

• *Local control of capital.* Currently, with barriers to trade being dismantled and international capital flow virtually unfettered, national treasuries have lost control over their economic destiny. There should be controls on banks and pensions, insurance and investment funds to ensure the investment of the majority of funds within the locality where they are generated and/or needed; in other words, an "invest-here-to-prosper-here" policy.

• *Controls on TNCs.* TNC activities need to be brought back under national government control, even at the risk of abjugating the GATT and WTO agreements. Access to a country's economy would depend upon compliance with a "site-here-to-sell-here" policy. TNCs need to be subjected to greater transparency and shareholder power or else be broken up. Controls need to be placed on the siphoning of company profit and individual earnings using off-shore accounts.

• *New competition policy.* The domination by big companies is a feature of economic life that requires urgent debate. Many should be broken up, thus guaranteeing the local competition needed to maintain the impetus for improved products, more efficient resource use and the provision of choice.

• *Trade and aid for self-reliance.* GATT should be transformed into a General Agreement for Sustainable Trade. Aid, technological transfer, and the residual international trade should be geared to the cultivation of sustainable local economies, with the goal of fostering maximum employment through sustainable regional self-reliance.

• *Introduction of resource taxes.* These would help fund the needed radical economic transition and would be environmentally advantageous. Competition from regions without such taxes could be held at bay by the reintroduction of tariffs and controls. Relocalization would mean that adverse environmental effects would be experienced locally, thus increasing the impetus and potential for control and improved standards.

• *Re-empowerment of government.* In the name of globalization, government is inexorably shifting away from the local to the international levels (and to the TNCs). This needs to be reversed. Global institutions need to be reoriented with the focus redirected to the local. Local, state, and regional governments need to have control over access to markets and to foster more local savings and banking systems.

## DIFFERENCES BETWEEN
## THE OLD AND THE NEW PROTECTIONISM

Within the United Kingdom, a number of arguments are given against a New Protectionism. We address these in turn.

• *The United Kingdom lives by trade and dies without it.* This argument fudges the greater question, What sort of trade? When the United Kingdom was the dominant world power, the wealthy did indeed benefit by trade. Today, trade pressures are costing jobs, driving the deregulation of wages and social and environmental conditions, reducing elected governments' control over their economies, and thus undermining the value of democracy. British society is dying *with* globalization, not without it.

• *Lack of competition is inefficient.* This argues that consumers lose if local companies and jobs are protected. However, giant corporations compete for purchasers' favors by cutting costs through shedding workers. This, in turn, cuts consumers and economic problems result. Under the New Protectionism, the emphasis on local markets and limited company size would encourage the positive aspects of competition: the impetus to be cost competitive, to utilize better designs, and to make more efficient use of resources. Eliminating competition from countries where wages, working conditions, and environmental laws are more lax than in the United Kingdom will allow these standards to increase.

- *Even if such change were desirable, no one country can go it alone.* Both Labour and Conservative governments know the power of the global financial markets. The New Protectionism cannot be achieved through autarky or go-it-alone policies. One argument currently being voiced is that the New Protectionism will emerge in affluent areas of the world, such as the European Union or North America, on the grounds that those markets are big and powerful enough to dictate conditions to international capital and TNCs. Other regions would follow suit very quickly. Another argument is that the case for self-reliance emerges strongest at the periphery of an economy, just as we already see arguments for and experience of community self-reliance movements emerging in the battered post-industrial cities or in the marginalized Third World. In either case, the future shape of the rapidly emerging regional trading blocks (EU, NAFTA, ASEAN, MercoSur, and so on) will both facilitate transition and serve as foci for debate about the future.

- *A fortress economy in Europe would be unfair to the poor of the Third World, who depend on trade to escape poverty.* A handful of Third World countries, mostly in Asia, dominate trade with and receive most of the foreign direct investment from the OECD. During the transition period to the New Protectionism, they could substitute this trade with interregional trade. For the rest of the developing countries, and indeed for most of Eastern Europe, the present system forces such countries to distort their economies to produce the cheapest exports, usually in competition with poor countries. Competition is not just setting poor against rich workers but poor against poor; it prevents resources from meeting the basic needs of the poor majority. The key challenge is not to encourage further spirals of ruthless competition but to rewrite aid and trade rules such that they facilitate the cultivation and diversification of local economies everywhere on Earth. Only then will the needs of the poor be met.

- *The New Protectionism will pander to and play into the hands of right-wing nationalism.* We fear just the opposite. The adverse effects of the present globalization process include the spread of what could be termed "free market fascism." Only the hope and deeper security offered by the New Protectionism can help reverse the very conditions and anxieties that foster the rise of the ugly nationalist Right.

• *Protectionism failed in the 1930s, and it failed in Communist countries everywhere.* In the 1930s, protectionism was nationalist and designed to protect the powerful. The goal was for each protected industry or country to increase its economic strength and then compete at the expense of others. The more countries did this, the less trade occurred between them. Closed economies attempted by Communist regimes are different from the New Protectionism in that the latter's internal competition and the international flow of ideas and technology will ensure that the stagnation and environmental degradation so often found in the Communist regimes will not be repeated. The New Protectionism sets different goals, such as the minimization of the need to trade with other countries if the traded goods and services can be produced domestically. Why encourage a downward spiral toward less diversity in economic activity within each country, which only pits worker against worker and living standards against living standards?

● ● ●

Unless people have work, hope, and the promise of a decent quality of life, society is destabilized.

The globalization orthodoxy is caught in a double bind. On the one hand, it is pushed to restructure and to shed labor. On the other hand, it is pulled by the need to have consumers. Already there is a rising chorus of voices against the current orthodoxy. Even from within the supposedly successful Asian Tigers, there are critiques of the damage: rampant injustice, social dislocation, inequality, and insecure work. The message of the globalization orthodoxy tells people, "You might not be needed."

We have not argued that the clock be turned back. Our case is that with barriers to trade now tumbling down, to the advantage of the global giants — companies and trading countries — the structural basis of the new culture of insecurity is laid bare. Insecurity on a scale not seen since the 1930s must be dealt with effectively; if not, history could repeat itself. One only needs to remember Mussolini's chilling pragmatism: "Fascism was . . . not a doctrine worked out beforehand in detailed elaboration; it was born of the need for action."

# 42

# CROSS-BORDER ORGANIZING

## Mark Ritchie

*Earlier, Wendell Berry noted that an entirely new political alignment is now underway, and he set out to articulate some of its characteristics. Few of these characteristics had anything to do with the old left-right categories. Mark Ritchie follows that line of thought with his observations on prior experiences and new opportunities in cross-border and cross-constituency organizing.*

*Ritchie was among the very first vocal critics and organizers in what became an international movement against NAFTA and GATT. He has been at the forefront on many major issues over the past three decades, most notably as a leader of the Nestlé Infant Formula boycott campaign of the 1970s and 1980s. He is now president of the Institute for Agriculture and Trade Policy (IATP) in Minneapolis, advocating in behalf of small farmers.*

ONE OF the most important political developments in the age of globalization has been the emergence of new and surprising alliances within countries and, significantly, across national boundaries. The GATT debate in particular prompted cross-border organizing at an unprecedented level, producing an array of strange bedfellows. Traditional antagonists as politically far apart as Ralph Nader and Pat Buchanan are finding some common ground on trade issues. And other successful recent organizing efforts in the United States have been distinctively right/left combinations.

For example, the campaign to stop the patenting of life forms by the biotechnology industry has the support of every major church leader in the country, from conservative Southern Baptist to Reformed Jew and Muslim. Each tradition argues that it is a sacrilege to redesign and patent life, which is more properly the province of God. Similarly, the campaigns to influence parents and young people to turn off their television for a week sponsored by TV-Free America, a Washington, D.C.–based group, garnered unprecedented national attention and support in its first year, including the support of a coalition that ranged from the Christian Right to the National Education Association.

Aside from Nader and Buchanan, the anti-GATT and NAFTA trade alliance included a wide spectrum of what would have previously been called right and left elements. This diversity of views and constituencies gave the campaigns much of their strength. For example, it was James Goldsmith, a former industrialist and now a French Euro-MP and president of the group *Europe des Nations,* who wrote one of the most influential books of the entire GATT debate, *The Trap* (1993), in which he clearly spelled out the dangers he saw for farmers, peasants, workers, and small companies. As a result, Goldsmith was invited to the United States by the national grass-roots Citizens Trade Campaign to help reach out to major business leaders and members of Congress who shared our concerns about the threat of the GATT text as proposed. At the same time, such new formations and relationships are still very unsure and unstable.

## BREAKING NEW GROUND TOGETHER

Although global organizing goes as far back as the worldwide antislavery movement of the 1800s, the emergence of widespread cross-border organizing, networking, and coalition building has developed in the last twenty years in direct response to the globalized economy.

In the 1970s, for example, the United Farmworkers Union was able to successfully extend abroad its boycott of nonunion grapes with the help of solid trade union support in Europe. A few years later, the boycott against the Nestlè company to get them to stop their deadly promotion of artificial infant formula was successfully organized in over fifty countries. Around the same time, workers in a number of industries, including autos, chemicals, and food processing, began to form international joint councils to pursue organizing on a global scale.

In the 1980s, some of the most important cross-border organizing happened in the agriculture and family-farm sector. For example, in October 1983, the First International Farm Crisis Summit was held in Ottawa, Canada with peasant, farmworker, landless, and family-farm organization leaders from nearly fifty countries. Perhaps the most important outcome of this meeting was the recognition of the similarities between the situations being faced by all of the delegates in their home countries. In each case, multinational agribusiness firms had gained support of national governments to drive down the prices paid to food producers and to push smaller producers off of their land.

As each representative spoke about the situation at home, it became clear that all family farmers faced the exact same struggles and that they needed to work together if they were going to have any hope of surviving. The arguments made by the agribusiness corporations to their own governments concerned their need for special favors to "compete" in the international market against other countries. This strategy — underpaying small farmers under the guise of boosting the international competitiveness of agribusiness exports — remains today the driving logic behind the worldwide crisis in agriculture.

Another good example of cross-border organizing during this time was the decision by Baldemar Velasquez, president of the Farm Labor Organizing Committee based in Ohio, to begin organizing farm labor on both sides of the U.S. and Mexican borders. Workers on both sides were working in the same companies and harvesting the same crops, such as tomatoes or pickle cucumbers. Formerly set against each other, the workers found they shared many concerns and could take joint actions.

Another example of a profoundly successful international strategy was the global dis-investment campaign of the 1980s waged by the African National Congress that helped end apartheid in South Africa.

Also in the 1980s, indigenous peoples who faced the global threat from the development juggernaut of global corporations began to meet together regularly in organized bodies, such as the International Indian Treaty Council. A number of specific conflicts over a wide range of issues, such as the case of Conoco Oil in the Amazon region of Ecuador, were the subjects of global campaigns by Native peoples and their supporters. Now, recognizing the immense threat to national sovereignty of Native nations posed by NAFTA and GATT, new alliances have developed among Native Nations, particularly in the United States, Canada, and Mexico. Similar cross-border work is being done in resistance to the Human Genome Diversity project, uniting the efforts of North American Indians with those in Panama, the Amazon, and elsewhere.

International organizing exploded in the 1990s, especially with the huge cross-border campaigns that developed in response to the Canada-U.S. Free Trade Agreement and the North American Free Trade Agreement, and with the global campaign centered around the renegotiation of GATT. Building upon the experiences, relationships, and networks of previous efforts while making use of new communications technologies, these new campaigns began to find the synergies needed to mount serious challenges to global monopolies.

One of the most widespread and successful recent efforts was the global "50 Years Is Enough" campaign aimed at defunding the World Bank and the International Monetary Fund. Launched on the fiftieth anniversary of the founding of these institutions, well-organized efforts sprouted in over forty countries and reached their culmination at the World Bank meeting in Madrid in 1994. There is little doubt that this campaign deserves substantial credit for the significant reforms that seem to be emerging at the bank, though the struggle is far from done.

## STRATEGIC LESSONS

Undoubtedly, global campaigning and cross-border organizing will continue to grow in importance into the next century. In order for these efforts to have the greatest possible impact, it is necessary to identify their strengths and weaknesses and to draw lessons that can inform future struggles. While this chapter is not a comprehensive analysis, it outlines some areas that need careful and thorough examination.

### Self-Interest and Solidarity

First, many successful efforts are those based more on perceived self-interest on the part of all partners as opposed to simple shows of solidarity. I do not mean to denigrate the importance of solidarity in ethical, social, and political questions but merely to recognize that the strongest organizing impetus is often self-interest. For example, the GATT agricultural agreement proposed by President Reagan in 1987 threatened family farmers in the United States, Europe, India, Mexico, Japan, Korea, Guatemala, Nigeria, and Norway, while providing a boon for agribusiness corporations everywhere. On the basis of perceived self-interest, family farmers from all over the planet were able to work together to support each other's efforts in their home countries and to work collectively on special occasions, such as joining in huge demonstrations against the proposed GATT agricultural agreement in Brussels and in Geneva.

The leadership among all the farm groups was shown by the farmers of India, who first called attention to the dangers of the proposed intellectual property provisions of the new GATT for farmers, peasants, and indigenous people everywhere. They organized giant protests in India — up to one million farmers — which captured the imagination of farmers in other places and alerted them to the potential problems. Soon delegations were traveling to joint meetings where mutual help was developed. As a result, changes were made in the final GATT agreement, though they were not sufficient to address all of the problems. The Indian farmers have continued their protests to this day and have gained strength through the international solidarity that they spawned. They have generated enough pressure so that their parliament rejected the WTO provisions in intellectual property, even after the administrative branch had already caved in to the WTO. [See chapter by Vandana Shiva and Radha Holla-Bhar.]

As part of their international efforts, leaders from Indian farm movements continue to travel to dozens of countries on every continent. They speak to rallies of farmers, produce videotapes and radio shows, and develop ingenious means to protect and preserve biodiversity in the face of the corporate onslaught. They spawned international relations among farmers and indigenous people that today form the basis of an international campaign aimed at overturning many aspects of the WTO's intellectual property provisions when they come up for review.

Organizing on the basis of self-interest also requires a very careful construction of the demands so that they are win-win for all sides. While the media and the politicians often frame global issues as win-lose between nations, that way of thinking simply doesn't work in cross-border organizing. What is necessary is that U.S. farmers not see Brazilian farmers as their enemies but that farmers in both countries, under attack from agribusiness via GATT, join efforts to resist the root cause of their problems.

## Local-Local Relations

A second lesson is that connections made directly between local or state-level organizations can often be more durable and productive than those made between national organizations. Often, national groups and their leaders develop close ties to governments and are therefore more reluctant or resistant to work closely with counterparts in other countries. This is not always the case, but it can be a serious problem. At the level of a state or provincial farm or environmental organization, however, local leadership is often much more motivated, appreciative, and creative in building work relations with sister groups at the local and state levels in other countries.

Perhaps the best example of this kind of networking has been the development of closer ties between U.S. and Mexican farmers. The links at the national level are constrained by the grip that the PRI ruling party, often called the world's most perfect dictatorship, has on the "official" national farm group in Mexico. However, farmers in many independent state-level organizations in Mexico have built strong ties with state-level Farmers Union chapters in the United States that lobby on NAFTA and a range of other issues of mutual interest.

One concrete result of this alliance was the request by the farmers of northern Mexico to the Farmers Union of Kansas for assistance in purchasing high-quality used farm machinery, which was not available at a reasonable price in Mexico. The farmers in Kansas bought the machinery from neighbors and then drove it down to the Mexican border. There the U.S. farmers turned the machinery over to their colleagues from Mexico, and the president of the Kansas Farmers Union had this to say: "I find little difference between the American farmer and the Mexican farmer other than the size of our operations. The problems are similar. Both of us are being exploited by non-competitive, monopolistic TNCs in the marketplace and we both suffer from corrupt governments."

## Personal Relationships

A third lesson is the importance of personal relationships. As in all aspects of life and politics, it is the people that matter. The success of all previous efforts has been built upon a slow and careful process of building trust and then transferring this trust to others. Individuals from all over the planet became friends as a result of the Nestlè boycott; these same people laid the groundwork for global organizing on trade issues. Individuals from the United States, Mexico, and Canada who had worked together over a long period of time on many issues were able to quickly pull together a tri-national campaign around NAFTA.

As a result, it was possible to rapidly organize an international farmers protest at the GATT ministerial session held in Brussels, Belgium, in December 1980. This session, which was planned to complete the re-negotiations of GATT, became the focus of intense active pressure from farm groups all over the planet. In addition to protests and lobbying back in home countries, thousands of farmers from nearly fifty countries came to Brussels to march, lobby, and demonstrate and to try to hammer out the framework of a good international trade agreement from the perspective of family farmers and peasants.

The Farmers Union of the United States developed a comprehensive proposal called the General Agreement on Prices and Production. On the basis of personal relationships that had developed over several years of conferences, protests, and meetings, it was possible to gain widespread support for the proposal and to use it as the basis for discussion at an international assembly hosted in Brussels by the Association of European Farmers Unions. Immediately following this assembly, over forty thousand farmers and their supporters from environmental, consumer, labor, and citizen groups marched in solidarity with the proposal. The event brought so much pressure to bear that the talks broke down over agriculture and eventually caused a five-year delay in finalizing this agreement.

Then in 1994, in the runup to the vote on the Uruguay Round of GATT, a similar mass demonstration of farmers from Germany, France, Holland, Belgium, Norway, Japan, and the United States among others again came to Brussels to once again protest GATT's devastating effects on small farmers everywhere.

## Long-Term Perspective

A fourth lesson is that we need to think in terms of very long-term campaigns. Of those mentioned previously, each had at least ten years of major campaigning, and some have continued another decade or longer. The Nestlè Boycott, for example, started in 1977, reached a settlement with Nestlè in 1984, and then had to be restarted in 1988 because Nestlè reneged on the agreement. The campaign is still going strong today, especially in Europe. In 1989 there was a ten-year anniversary gathering in Manila that brought together infant formula activists from sixty countries to celebrate victories and to plan for the next decade of this struggle.

Once it becomes clear that a campaign may take twenty years or more to succeed, consideration must be given to planning the development of new leadership among younger people who will need to take over full control as time passes. This is at once the easiest and hardest lesson to learn. It is easy in the sense that there are, without doubt, many talented and dedicated activists and visionaries in each generation who are committed to working for social justice — forgoing high-paying jobs and the perks of the corporate society. Finding new leaders is the easy part. Getting older leaders to step aside is much harder.

We cannot win at the international level without maximum cooperation and solidarity. The lessons we are learning in our cross-border work have the same meaning here at home. Careful attention to relationships, work with strange bedfellows, and new ways of thinking will help us break out of the negative spiral we are in and onto the path toward a sustainable future.

# 43

# THE LAST WORD
## *Family, Community, Democracy*

### Edward Goldsmith

*Finally, the point must be literally brought home, into our houses and communities, that the process of globalization and development has also been the process of removing from the local economy, the community, and the family the abilities to sustain themselves free of state and corporate domination. Cooperative interactions and services, once performed freely and successfully within communities, have been monetized and removed from any semblance of local control, thus making all people vulnerable to distant interests. The same can be said of the natural world's abilities to sustain itself without human transformation and management as the functions it once fulfilled for free have been taken over and commodified by the state and the corporations. To reverse this grim process, which is leading to nothing but social and environmental devastation, we need to identify the ways that corporations and the state have usurped all aspects of our lives and reestablish viable local communities and participatory democracy.*

T HE DEVELOPMENT of the global economy, which has been institutionalized with GATT and the WTO, is supposed to usher in an era of unprecedented prosperity for all. However, as the contributors to this book have shown, this assertion is false.

Since the end of World War II, trillions of dollars have been poured into development schemes by multinational development banks, bilateral aid agencies, and private enterprises. Revolutionary new technologies have transformed the agriculture, industry, and service sectors alike. Tariffs have been drastically reduced, and small companies that catered to the domestic economy have been systematically replaced by vast transnational corporations. World GNP has increased by five times, and world trade by twelve times. If the conventional wisdom held true, then the world should have been transformed into a veritable paradise. Poverty, unemployment, malnutrition, homelessness, disease, and environmental disruption should be but vague memories of our barbaric and underdeveloped past. Needless to say, the opposite has proven true. Never have these problems been more serious and more widespread.

By signing the Uruguay Round of GATT, governments have further accelerated global economic growth and development by removing all constraints on trade, regardless of social, ecological, and moral implications. Instead of accepting the incontrovertible empirical evidence that economic globalization can only increase the problems we face today, governments, under pressure from the TNCs, insist in pursuing it still further.

To solve these problems, society must follow the very opposite path. Instead of seeking to create a single global economy, controlled by vast and ever less controllable transnational corporations, we should instead seek to create a diversity of loosely linked, community-based economies managed by much smaller companies and catering above all (though not exclusively) to local or regional markets. It is not economic globalization that we should aim for but the reverse: *economic localization*.

This does *not* mean reconstituting the past. We have been indelibly marked by the experience of the last decades, and the local economies that we now seek to create cannot be slavish imitations of those that previously prevailed. However, since until recently, economies have always been largely localized, their experience from the past must seriously be considered.

## REPLACEMENT OF THE SOCIAL ECONOMY

For perhaps as much as 95 percent of our tenancy of this planet, all those functions that today are fulfilled by the state and the corporations were fulfilled by the family or, more precisely, the household as part of the larger community. The household produced most of its own food, though the more demanding tasks involved cooperation between households and the community as a whole. The household made most of its own clothes and other artifacts and acquired those that it did not make from within the community. The household brought up the young and looked after the old and the sick. The community itself administered justice, maintained social order, and ensured that the traditional religious ceremonies were properly performed. It was thus to a large extent self-sufficient and self-governing. What is more, as David Korten notes, the fulfillment of these functions at the local level also "served to maintain the social bonds of trust and obligation, the 'social capital' of the community." (1994)

In *Biosphere Politics* (1991), Jeremy Rifkin quotes labor historian Harry Braverman, who tells us that in the United States as recently as 1890 even those families living in highly industrialized regions, such as the coal and steel communities of Pennsylvania, "were still producing virtually all of their food at home — over half the families raised their own poultry, live-stock and vegetables, purchasing only potatoes at the market." On the basis of the criteria applied today by economists, governments, and international agencies, those communities, mainly in the Third World, that have succeeded in remaining largely self-sufficient and self-reliant are taken to be underdeveloped and poverty-stricken and are targeted for immediate and accelerated development.

David Korten (1994) refers to the nonmonetized economy of the household and the community as "the social economy." For him, "social economies are by nature local, non-waged, non-monetized, and non-market. Therefore, they are not counted in national income statistics, do not contribute to measured economic growth, and are undervalued by policy makers, who count only activities in the market economy as productive contributions to national output."

If, until very recently, human families and communities were quite capable of looking after themselves without the intervention of any state institutions or corporations, so were the highly diverse ecosystems that make up the natural world. Indeed, human life and that of all other living things have always depended upon the inestimable benefits provided by the normal functioning of the geosphere as a whole.

As development proceeds, however, even nature's critical functions are systematically taken over by the state and by corporations. Thus the nitrogen used to fertilize our land is increasingly produced at great cost in factories rather than fixed by nitrogen-fixing bacteria on the roots of leguminous plants. The water we use, instead of being stored for free in the aquifers beneath the forest floor, is increasingly stored in large, human-made reservoirs. The process of paying for what was freely available already applies to our drinking water, as more and more of those who can afford it now buy bottled water rather than drink polluted tap water. This may soon apply to fresh air, as already it is often only the wealthy who can best afford to live in areas relatively free of air pollution. With regard to

the formerly nonmonetized functions of health care, child rearing, education, and care of the infirm and the elderly, these have already been com-
mercialized; that is, they are disembedded from the normal social process.

Furthermore, certain economists (and some scientists) now propose
that, rather than reduce emissions of greenhouse gases, which are now
overwhelming the Gaian processes that have so far ensured the stability of
world climate, vast geo-engineering schemes should be devised to make
up for the loss. (Foremost is a plan to site fifty thousand 100-square-kilo-
meter mirrors in space in order to reflect away the heat of the sun and
keep the planet cool.) In other words, economic development is above all
the systematic takeover by the formal monetized economy of the functions that were previously fulfilled for free not only by "the social economy" but also by "the great economy," as Wendell Berry calls the
economy of the natural world.

The consequences of such an enterprise are of course dramatic. It can
only cause the demise of the social economy, as the household and the
community — its basic building blocks — are condemned to atrophy from
want of use and become incapable of fulfilling their natural functions.


## COMMUNITY DISINTEGRATION

Until recently, the family has always been the basic unit of social life.
More precisely, it has been the *extended family* rather than the truncated
*nuclear family* of the type we have today; an extended family that includes
grandparents, brothers and sisters, their spouses and children, and even
people who live in the same household, though they are not necessarily related. The extended family also formed an integral part of the community
within which all its members lived and worked and into which it practically merged. It did not exist as a little island of solidarity in a vast, indifferent nonsociety, as it does today in the Western world. [See chapter by
Jeannette Armstrong.] Still less had it disintegrated into its constituent
parts, in which the helpless and alienated individual has become the basic
unit of social (or rather asocial) behavior. For this and similar reasons we
must overcome our present prejudice against this irreplaceable institution, which we now tend to see as tyrannical, fundamentalist, and claus-
trophobic and whose virtues are being vaunted only by heartless right-
wing politicians of the Quayle-Gingrich-Thatcher types.

Much the same can be said for the word *community*, which also has
been captured by the right wing. Yet, like the family, it too is a basic and,

one might even say, natural unit of social organization. This it clearly must be, since we have lived in extended families and communities during the whole course of our biological, psychological, and cognitive evolution. In fact, we evolved as integral members of these key social units. Alexis de Tocqueville, that great student of town democracy in New England, saw the community as natural, indeed as God-given. "Man may create kingdoms," he wrote, "but the community seems to have sprung from the hand of God" (1839).

Not surprisingly, it seems to be only at the levels of the household and the community that most key social and economic functions can be effectively fulfilled, though to do so the household and the community must be sufficiently cohesive, imbued with the appropriate worldview, and in possession of the necessary resources.

Let us take an obvious example. One of the most serious problems our society faces today is a massive increase in social aberrations, such as crime, delinquency, drug addiction, alcoholism, and general violence. These problems are conspicuous by their absence in societies that have not yet been fully atomized; that is, where individuals have not been cut adrift from their family and community. Even today, for instance, one can walk in total safety through the poorest slums of Calcutta, where large numbers of people are homeless and sleep on the pavement. This is so because such people do not suffer the terrible social deprivation of an atomized society. They may be very poor and hungry, but the life they lead is still within their family groups, and it has meaning to them — which is ever less the case of the lives led by most people in the industrial world.

In a traditional community, social order is effectively maintained by an extremely powerful force: that of public opinion, which reflects traditional values and is fed by local gossip — a key instrument for ensuring adherence to community values and hence for preventing crime and other social problems. We have been taught to regard the pressure of public opinion as an intolerable intrusion into our lives. One of the great advantages of becoming an anonymous inhabitant of a big modern city is actually said to be that it liberates us from the tyranny of public opinion. Such "liberation" has also been one of the main attractions of economic development, progress, and atomization, which "liberate" people from the authority of parents or of traditional obligations to members of the community. But such "liberation" is only considered a blessing by those who do not distinguish between such constraints and the kind of constraints imposed on individuals by external organizations, such as the state and corporations. The latter constraints mainly serve the interests of the organizations themselves, which are usually in conflict with society and the natural world. The former are required for the community to be capable of existing as such and of fulfilling its essential functions.

In any case, no one has yet devised any alternative effective strategy for controlling crime and maintaining social order. The state may hire more police officers, spend billions on an ever more elaborate judicial system, and build more prisons, but all this has little effect. Such policies merely mask the symptoms of a social disease that, by rendering it more tolerable, they only serve to perpetuate. As the global economy marginalizes more people, this disease can only worsen and spread to those areas of the world that have succeeded in remaining relatively unaffected.

De Tocqueville "identified freedom with self-determination, and saw democracy as fostering freedom, precisely because it enabled people to participate in municipal government" (Boesche 1987). This could not be achieved if everyone were "free" to do his or her own thing without regard for social and ecological consequences, as we are in a modern atomized society.

## COMMUNITY AND DEMOCRACY

This brings us to the important notion of democratic government. If crime and other social aberrations can only be dealt with at a communal level, the same must be true of democratic government. If democracy is "government by the people for the people," it is difficult to regard as truly democratic the sort of political system under which we live, in which individuals limit their contribution to governing themselves to voting every four or five years for a candidate over whose political conduct, until the next election, they have absolutely no control. This is particularly the case today, as the corporate world has mastered the art of influencing election outcomes by massive and increasingly sophisticated public relations campaigns and has subordinated national interests everywhere to its own agenda. [See chapter by William Greider.]

If government is really to be by the people, then we must ourselves participate in the daily business of government, and it is clearly not at the national level, let alone the global level, that we can possibly do so. Our participation can only occur at the local level, among those of us who know each other, see each other regularly, and share the same interests and worldview.

Thomas Jefferson always insisted that only face-to-face participation in municipal government enables citizens to subordinate their immediate personal interests to the public good. (Though, as Helena Norberg-Hodge points out, in most traditional societies people see their own interests as inseparable from the public good.) Jefferson advocated that states should be broken up into local wards of such a size as to enable the full interaction and participation of citizens in their own government (Coleman 1994). De Tocqueville also noted how, in the New England town democracies where such conditions were largely met, "each person's cooperation in its affairs assures his attachment to its interests; the well-being it affords him secures his affection; and its welfare is the aim of his ambitions and his future exertions" (Herith 1986).

Jeffersonian democracy, according to some scholars, really owes much of its localist form to the example provided to the United States' Founding Fathers by the Iroquois people, who surrounded the American colonists in the eastern forests, and with whom they regularly traded. Hundreds of years before the arrival of the Europeans, the Iroquois had established an elaborate and highly participatory democracy. Indeed, in the Iroquois confederacy, power resided with the local villages, and decisions were taken by community consensus. Occasionally, the village would agree to delegate its authority on specific functions to a central council of all the communities, but ultimate power could be and was reclaimed by the local community when judged necessary. Real power, therefore, always resided at the local level, a fact that was acknowledged by many American colonists such as Benjamin Franklin, James Madison, and Jefferson himself, each of whose writings have made reference to the Iroquois (Grinde 1977; Johnson 1988).

The Swiss system of government may also provide a model. It has always been based on the commune, or *gemeinde*, which is largely self-governing. Traditionally, the *gemeinde* decides which taxes should be paid and how the community should spend money. It also actively oversees the communal administration, whose proposals and expenditures it can reject, and deals with such issues as public service, primary education, local police, and welfare for the poor and the sick. Really important decisions are made by a free assembly of the citizens.

Significantly, the commune existed long before the cantons into which the confederation is now divided. Communes located in a particular valley did occasionally join together to form loose organizations or alliances. However, it was only with the Napoleonic conquests at the beginning of the nineteenth century that they were raised to the rank of cantons, and even later that they were linked together to form the Swiss Confederation. Even then, the central government traditionally had relatively little power, partly because it is only elected for a year and partly because its political composition must reflect that of the parliament, which seriously limits the changes the central government can bring about.

Unfortunately, economic development, and in particular its globalization, spells the demise of the Swiss local economy. Among other things, development can only turn what were once self-governing communities into dormitory towns no longer capable of running themselves. Indeed, in recent times there has been a steady fall in the number of people who now take part in the local assemblies, and whereas the power once resided with the communes, it is increasingly the confederate government and the large corporations that now control the country's economic and social life. Of course, in the United States today, it is only a minority of the electorate that even bothers to vote in presidential elections.

By signing the GATT Uruguay Round and setting up the World Trade Organization, governments have effectively delegated the task of running their economic affairs to an international bureaucracy that is still more distant from people's lives, indifferent to local concerns, and subservient to the TNCs that the global economy has truly been designed to serve. [See chapter by Ralph Nader and Lori Wallach.] In other words, we have moved still further away from true democracy.

Real democracy, in the form of government by a loose association of substantially self-governing communities, is only possible if the economy is organized to serve democratic structures, and is not possible if you have corporate economic domination. Political localization requires economic localization, and the conduct of the economy is yet another function that has to be fulfilled primarily at the community level.


## SELF-SUFFICIENCY

Jefferson also considered that self-governing communities should be self-sufficient, or at least that they should produce their own food, shelter, and clothes. This was essential in order to foster the honesty, industry, and perseverance on which democracy must be built (Kemmis 1990). Mahatma Gandhi fully agreed. The principle of *swadeshi*, which was critical to his philosophy, meant deriving one's resources from one's own area rather than importing them from elsewhere. [See chapter by Satish Kumar.] Professor Ray Dasmann of the University of California at Santa Cruz says the same thing in a different way. He contrasts "ecosystem man," who lives off his local ecosystem, with "biosphere man," who lives off the whole biosphere. For Dasmann, it is only when we learn once more to become ecosystem people that our society will become truly sustainable.

Traditional communities are well capable of living off the resources of their ecosystems in a highly sustainable manner, firstly because, unlike export-oriented corporations that overtax the land and then move elsewhere, traditional communities have no other land available to them. It is also because they have developed cultural patterns that enable them to do so. It should be obvious that people who have lived in the same place for hundreds of years must have developed the food-producing practices that enable them to make the optimum use of their resources and also to make sure that such practices are rigorously applied. In other words, traditional communities alone are in possession of the requisite knowledge and capacities for living in their place.

Open-minded people who have studied agriculture as practiced by local communities in traditional societies have confirmed this. It was certainly true of agricultural experts sent by the British government at the end of the nineteenth century to see how Indian farming methods could be improved. Both A.O. Hume (1878) and John Augustus Voelcker (1893) wrote that traditional Indian agriculture was perfectly adapted to local conditions and could not be improved. To the dismay of British authorities, Voelcker alleged that it would be easier for him to suggest improvements to British than to Indian agriculture.

Even the World Bank, which has spearheaded the modernization of agriculture in the Third World, admitted in one of its more notorious reports that "smallholders in Africa are outstanding managers of their own resources — their land and capital, fertilizer and water" (World Bank 1981). Why then modernize agriculture and push the smallholders into the slums? The answer, as the report fully admits, is that subsistence farming is incompatible with the development of the market.

For this reason, the community is best seen — as it always has been among traditional societies — as made up not only of its human members but of all the living and nonliving things that make up an ecosystem. Wendell Berry sees the community in just this way. "If we speak of a healthy community" he writes, "we cannot be speaking of a community that is only human. We are talking about a neighborhood of humans in a place, plus a place itself: the soil, the water, its air, and all the families and tribes of the non-human creatures that belong to it. What is more, it is only if this whole community is healthy that its members can remain healthy and be healthy in body and mind and live in a sustainable manner" (Berry 1992). It follows that a human community that has learned to maintain the health of the larger ecological community should be the one to have primary access to its natural wealth.

Once communities have been deprived of the exclusive use of their wealth; once it has been privatized or made available to all comers — a situation that superficially sounds desirable and "democratic" — then its exploitation and rapid destruction becomes inevitable. This is precisely what happens when we set up the global economy; a system of absentee owners.

This brings us to what may be the most important argument of all for returning to the local community–based economy. If the world's environment is being degraded so rapidly, with a corresponding reduction in its capacity to sustain complex forms of life such as the human species, it is because it cannot sustain the present impact of our economic activities. To increase this impact still further, as we are doing by creating a global economy based on free trade, is both irresponsible and cynical. The only responsible policy must, on the contrary, be to *drastically reduce this impact,* and it is only in the sort of economy in which economic activities are carried out on a far smaller scale and cater primarily to a local or regional market that we can hope to do so.


# THE INEVITABLE BREAKDOWN
# OF THE GLOBAL ECONOMY

The great takeover that I have described cannot proceed indefinitely. It has already proceeded to where the state and the corporations are rapidly becoming incapable of fulfilling the functions they have taken over from the family, the community, and the ecosystem, except on an increasingly insignificant scale. This is also true of the takeover of the functions previously fulfilled by ecosystems and the biosphere: that of maintaining the necessary conditions for life on this planet.

For instance, if world climate is to be stabilized it will not be by the absurd geo-engineering works proposed today but by increasing the biosphere's capacity to absorb carbon dioxide, the main greenhouse gas. This means allowing the world's badly depleted forests to recover and drastically reducing emissions of greenhouse gases. This is only feasible if the global economy is replaced by a localized economy with its vastly reduced energy and resource requirements.

Another key function that the state is no longer capable of assuming is the provision of welfare to those in need. Even before the global economy was formally institutionalized, the cost of monetized welfare was in many industrial countries growing faster than GNP and quite clearly could not be sustained for long. Today, however, in order to maximize competitiveness, welfare provisions are being systematically dismantled at breakneck speed, even though, ironically, the need for them is simultaneously being dramatically increased by economic globalization.

Both in the United Kingdom and the United States, one of the first sectors of the welfare state to be dismantled is that providing care for the mentally ill. The excuse is that community care for such people is more effective than what the state can provide. It is very encouraging that the state should admit this, but unfortunately there are now few family-based, cohesive communities left that are willing or indeed capable of re-assuming this task. As a result, the mentally ill have been left to their own devices. Many of them now sleep on park benches or under bridges, and in London alone they make up more than 40 percent of the homeless. On current trends, it is more than likely that orphans, abandoned children, the physically handicapped, the aged, and the infirm will soon suffer a similar fate.

Another key function that the state and corporations are ever less capable of fulfilling is the basic provision of food and material goods, which in the modern world is usually met through jobs. But the global economy will be able to function with only a small fraction of the present work force, as has been pointed out throughout this book. According to a recent article in *Le Monde Diplomatique*, Paris, the formal economy in the Ivory Coast will within a few years provide less than 6 percent of the jobs required, and that country's lot is probably already not unique (Sanches 1993).

What is more, successive World Bank structural adjustment programs among Third World nations have drastically reduced the purchasing power of even those who still have jobs. This is also increasingly the case in the industrial world, which is now being subjected to its own form of structural adjustment, with salaries slashed, long-term contracts replaced by short-term contracts, full-time work replaced by part-time work, and men replaced by women at lower salaries. Obviously, people who have no jobs or who are paid slave wages and who no longer have access to welfare benefits cannot buy many goods and services, while the computers, with which many of them will have been replaced, can buy none at all. As consumption falls, the formal economy will provide still fewer jobs, further reducing consumption and, in turn, further reducing the number of jobs it can provide. We will thus be caught up in a veritable chain reaction that must continue until the formal economy ceases to be a significant source of jobs, food, and other goods and services for the bulk of humanity on this planet. By marginalizing so many people, the formal economy will *have marginalized itself.*

As the formal economy continues to disintegrate, most people will be forced by necessity to learn to live outside it. In such a situation, the LETS, Time Dollar, and Community-Supported Agriculture arrangements described in this book are not mere curiosities — initiatives that are too small in scale to make any significant contribution to today's ever more daunting problems. On the contrary, they may provide the very foundations for resurgent local economies that alone can fill the void created by marginalization of the formal economy.

As the corporations and the state become ever less capable of fulfilling the key functions that they took over from local economies, there will be no alternative but to allow the local economies with their nonmonetized social economies to reassume many of these functions.

We must in fact do the reverse of what a country like Japan is now being forced to do. By its adherence to GATT, Japan must industrialize both its traditional agricultural system of small family farmers and its vibrant traditional retail sector that is still made up of small neighborhood shops. The path is now open for these key sectors of the Japanese economy to be taken over by the Cargills, Monsantos, and Wal-Marts, with the inevitable rise in unemployment and social disintegration that this must bring about. Until recently in Japan, unemployment had been kept down to about 2 percent of the work force (by 1996, it rose up to 3.4 percent); families had remained largely intact; and crime and delinquency had been very low. All this will now change.

• • •

As we have seen, our social economy is at present ill-equipped to take on any new functions, as the viable households and communities and ecosystems that previously fulfilled these functions have been seriously degraded under the impact of past economic development.

Our only hope is that these institutions should reconstitute themselves. This is not as vain a hope as it might seem. Indeed, if most people are to be marginalized and many of them rendered destitute by the global economy, they will not simply sit down quietly and starve. Many will undoubtedly revolt against the big corporations that use up their resources, pollute their land and rivers, produce food and consumer goods that only the elite can afford, and provide only a few high-technology jobs that are filled by specialists from abroad. Significantly, in India, the corporations are already under assault, especially in Karnataka, where in 1995 the headquarters of the Cargill Corporation was burnt down and where in January 1996 the main Kentucky Fried Chicken (KFC) outlet in Bangalore, the state capital, was completely destroyed by members of the Karnataka State Farmers Association, which vowed to drive the company out of their state, and which it will almost certainly succeed in doing.

There is also likely to be more popular resistance to the state itself. This constantly occurred during the colonial era, when people were dispossessed of their lands and deprived of their livelihoods. Revolts are likely to occur even in the industrial world. In France, for instance, Mr. Chirac has apparently understood that if he slashes wages, dismantles the welfare state, and puts large numbers of people out of work, in order to satisfy the criteria for a single European currency, there will be many repetitions of the huge 1996 strike. The same could happen elsewhere.

We have seen similar signs of revolt in Mexico, where the Zapatistas have clearly articulated their opposition to NAFTA and the World Bank as destructive to their local economy and where, with the fall of the peso, even the middle class may soon find itself in alliance with Native groups.

Of course, most people will prefer a form of resistance that is not so extreme. And people's movements of all kinds and in all geographical areas seem to be emerging; organizations of dispossessed farmers and small holders, small businesspeople who cannot possibly survive globalization, environmentalists who only now are grasping the full environmental implications of the global economy, and trade unionists who have begun to appreciate that the working people in a world of globally centralized TNC power can have no control over their own futures. And there are those who believe, as I do, that communities should be allowed that measure of autonomy that is compatible with the fulfillment of their essential social, ecological, and economic functions. Even in such powerful countries as the United States, the signs of discontent are clearly visible. Organizations such as the International Forum on Globalization are finding that public events planned for three hundred people are producing crowds in the many thousands, as growing insecurity and anxiety are leading people to question and increasingly to reject present economic policies. A new protectionism is also being seriously discussed.

Meanwhile, people are beginning to reassume the functions that households and communities have always fulfilled and that provide their very raison d'être. LETS and CSA programs are being set up in more and more localities and increasing numbers of citizens are becoming involved. This trend is likely to become generalized as people become further marginalized and thus forced to recreate local, community-based economies. These are at least a few bright lights on an otherwise dismal horizon, and

Wendell Berry sees yet another. For him, the issue of the global economy versus the local community-based economy is likely to be the big issue of the next decade. It should provide the basis of a new political realignment. As Berry wrote in his chapter, the party of community, as he refers to it, will have little money and hence little power, but its adherents can only increase, and it may well become the party of the majority. If such a party were really to come to power, it could be in a position to develop and implement a coordinated strategy for ensuring a more painless transition to the sort of society and the sort of economy that alone can offer our children any future on this beleaguered planet.

# REFERENCES

*The following are references from chapters in this book:*

Baker, Randall. 1984. "Protecting the Environment Against the Poor." *Ecologist,* 14(2).

Barnet, Richard, and John Cavanagh. 1994. *Global Dreams: Imperial Corporations and the New World Order.* New York: Simon and Schuster.

Barnet, Richard, and Ronald E. Mueller. 1974. *Global Reach: The Power of the Multinational Corporations.* New York: Simon and Schuster.

Bassett, P. 1995. "Insecurity of Part-Time Jobs and Full-Time Mortgages." *Times* (11 April).

Beal, Dave. 1993. "A Piece of the Action." *St. Paul Pioneer Press* (14 June).

Beijing Ministerial Declaration on Environment and Development. June 19, 1991.

Bello, Walden, with David Kinley and Elaine Elison. 1982. *Development Debacle: The World Bank in the Philippines.* San Francisco: Institute for Food and Development Policy.

Bello, Walden, and Stephanie Rosenfeld. 1990. *Dragons in Distress: Asia's Miracle Economies in Crisis.* San Francisco: Institute for Food and Development Policy.

"Benefits of Big Mergers Said to Vanish Quickly." 1991. *American Banker,* (11 December).

Berry, Wendell. 1987. *Sex, Economy, Freedom and Community.* New York: Pantheon Books.

Boesche, Roger. 1987. "The Strange Liberalism of Alexis de Tocqueville." Ithaca, N.Y.: Cornell University Press. As quoted by Hultgren, John. 1994, "Democracy and Sustainability." Unpublished.

Bowers, C. A. 1993. *Education, Cultural Myths, and the Ecological Crisis: Toward Deep Changes.* Albany, N.Y.: State University of New York Press.

Borgstrom, Georg. 1967. *The Hungry Planet.* New York: Collier.

Breverton, T. D. 1994. "Rules Under Different Visions of Economy and Society: The Economic Vision." Paper presented at conference, The Evolution of Rules for a Single European Market, 8–11 September, at Exeter University.

Brown, Lester R. 1988. *State of the World*. Washington, D.C.: Worldwatch Institute.

Brundtland, Gro Harlem. 1987. "Our Common Future." United Nations Commission on Environment and Development (April).

Cahn, Edgar, and Jonathan Rowe. 1992. *Time Dollars*. Emmaus, Penn.: Rodale Press.

Cairns, J. 1975. *Cancer: Science and Society*. San Francisco: W. H. Freeman.

Calvert, John, and Larry Kuehn. 1993. *Pandora's Box*. Toronto: Our Schools/Ourselves Education Foundation.

"Can Europe Compete?" 1994. *Financial Times* (7 March).

Carson, Rachel. 1987. *Silent Spring*. Boston: Houghton Mifflin.

Chira, Susan. 1993. "Is Smaller Better? Educators Now Say Yes for High School." *New York Times* (14 July).

Clark, William C. 1989. "Managing Planet Earth." *Scientific American*. 261, (September).

Coleman, Dan. 1994. "Ecopolitics: Building a Green Society." New Brunswick, N.J.: Rutgers University Press. As quoted by Hultgren, John. 1994, "Democracy and Sustainability." Unpublished.

Coleman, Eliot. 1989. *The New Organic Grower: A Master's Manual of Tools and Techniques for the Home and Market Gardener*. Chelsea, Vt.: Chelsea Green.

Colchester, Marcus. 1993. "Slave and Enclave: Towards a Political Ecology of Equatorial Africa." *Ecologist,* 23(5).

Congressional Research Service. 1993. *Biotechnology, Indigenous Peoples, and Intellectual Property Rights*. Washington, D.C., Library of Congress.

Cornia, Giovanni Andrea, et. al., eds. 1992. *Africa's Recovery in the 1990s: From Stagnation and Adjustment to Human Development*. Mkandawire, Thandika: LC 92-18007.

Cringely, Robert. 1992. "Hollywood Goes Digital." *Forbes* (7 December).

Crook, Clive. 1992. "Fear of Finance." *The Economist* (September 19).

Daly, Herman. 1994. "Farewell Lecture to the World Bank." College Park: University of Maryland, School of Public Affairs (14 January).

Daly, Herman E., and John B. Cobb, Jr. 1989. *For the Common Good: Redirecting the Economy Toward Community, the Environment, and a Sustainable Future*. Boston: Beacon Press.

Daly, Herman E., and Robert Goodland. 1992. "An Ecological-Economic Assessment of Deregulation of International Commerce under GATT." Washington, D.C.: World Bank (September).

Danaher, Kevin, with Frances Moore Lappé and Rachel Schurman. 1988. *Betraying the National Interest*. San Francisco: Institute for Food and Development Policy.

Dauncey, Guy. 1988. *After the Crash: The Emergence of the Rainbow Economy.* London: Green Print Books.

Dembo, David, et. al. 1990. *The Abuse of Power: Social Performance of Multinational Corporations. The Case of Union Carbide.* New York: New Horizons Press.

de Tocqueville, Alexis. 1839. *Democracy in America.* New York: Random House.

————. "Threat to Freedom and Democracy." Durham: Duke University. As quoted in Hultgren, John. 1994. "Democracy and Sustainability." Unpublished.

Dumont, R., and N. Cohen. 1980. *The Growth of Hunger: A New Politics of Agriculture.* London: Marion Boyars.

Durning, Alan B. 1992. *How Much Is Enough?* New York: W. W. Norton.

Ekins, Paul. 1989. "Trade and Self-Reliance." *Ecologist.* 19(5).

Fanelli, José María, with Roberto Frenkel and Lance Taylor. 1992. "The World Development Report 1991: A Critical Assessment," *International Monetary and Financial Issues for the 1990's.* New York: U.N. Conference on Trade and Development.

Faux, Jeff. As quoted in Rothstein, R. 1993. "As the Good Jobs Go Rolling Away. . . Who Will Buy?" CEO/International Strategies (December).

Feder, Barnaby J. 1995. "Some Producers are Scowling at Meatpackers' Process." *New York Times* (17 October).

Fieldhouse, D. K. 1984. *Economics and Empire, 1830 to 1914.* London: Macmillan.

Ffrench-Davis, Ricardo, and Carlos Muñoz. 1992. "Economic and Political Instability in Chile." In Simon Teitel, ed. *Towards a New Development Strategy for Latin America.* Washington, D.C.: Inter-American Development Bank.

Ford, Henry. As quoted in Barnet, Richard, and John Cavanagh. 1994. *Global Dreams.* New York: Simon and Schuster.

Franke, R., and B. Chasin. 1981. "Peasants, Peanuts, Profits and Pastoralists." *Ecologist* 11(4).

French, Hilary. 1993. "Costly Tradeoffs Reconciling Trade and the Environment." Washington, D.C.: WorldWatch Institute.

Friedman, Lawrence M. 1973. *A History of American Law.* New York: Simon and Schuster.

Galbraith, John Kenneth. 1992. *The Culture of Contentment.* Boston: Houghton Mifflin.

Gepillard, A. 1994. "Germans Plan to Shift Production Abroad." *Financial Times* (31 May).

George, Susan, and Fabrizio Sabelli. 1994. *Faith and Credit: The World Bank's Secular Empire.* London: Penguin.

Gibbons, Ann. 1993. "Where are 'New' Diseases Born?" *Science* (6 August).

Glover, Paul. 1984. *Los Angeles: A History of the Future.* Los Angeles: Citizen Planners of Los Angeles.

Goldsmith, Edward, and Nicholas Hildyard. 1990. "The Earth Report No. 2." London: Mitchell Beazley.

Goodland, Robert. 1984. "Environmental Management in Tropical Agriculture." Boulder, Colo.: Westview Press.

Greco, Thomas, Jr. 1994. *New Money for Healthy Communities.* Tucson, Ariz.: T. H. Greco.

Grinde, Donald A., Jr. 1977. *The Iroquois and the Founding of the American Nation.* San Francisco: The Indian Historian Press.

Haavelmo, T. 1991. *The Big Dilemma: International Trade and the North-South Cooperation.* In *Economic Policies for Sustainable Development.* Manila: Asian Development Bank.

Harris, John. 1991. "Universities for Sale." *This Magazine* (September).

Hawken, Paul. 1993. *The Ecology of Commerce: A Declaration of Sustainability.* New York: HarperBusiness.

Hobsbawm, Eric. 1986. *Industry and Empire.* Harmondsworth: Pelican.

Hueting, R. "The Brundtland Report: A Matter of Conflicting Goals." *Ecological Economics* 2(2).

Hultgren, John. 1994. "Democracy and Sustainability." Unpublished.

———. 1995. "International Political Economy and Sustainability." Oberlin College, Unpublished.

Hume, A. O. 1878. "Agriculture Reform in India." London: W.H.Allen and Co.

"IBM Is Overhauling Disk Drive Business, Cutting Jobs, Shifting Production to Asia." 1993. *Wall Street Journal* (August).

Iglesias, Enrique. 1992. *Reflections on Economic Development: Toward a New Latin American Consensus.* Washington, D.C.: Inter-American Development Bank.

Inter-American Development Bank. 1992. *Economic and Social Progress in Latin America, 1992.* Washington D.C.: International Development Bank.

International Labor Organization. 1995. *World Employment,* Geneva: ILO.

Jacobs, Jane. 1961. *The Death and Life of Great American Cities.* Harmondsworth, Middlesex: Penguin.

Jacoby, E. H. 1961. "Agrarian Unrest in Southeast Asia." As quoted in G. L. Beckford. 1983. "Persistent Poverty." London: Zed Books.

Johansen, Bruce. 1988. "Indian Thought Was Often in Their Minds." In *Indian Roots of American Democracy*. Ithaca, N.Y.: Northeast Indian Quarterly, Cornell University.

Kelly, Kevin. 1994. *Out of Control: The Rise of Neo-Biological Civilizations*. New York: Addison-Wesley.

Kemmis, Daniel. 1990. "Community and the Politics of Place." Norman OK: University of Oklahoma Press. As quoted by Hultgren, John. 1994. "Democracy and Sustainability." Unpublished.

Knox, Patricia. 1995. "A New Green Economy? LETS Do It." *Earth Island Journal* (Summer).

Korten, David C. 1994. "Sustainable Livelihoods: Redefining the Global Social Crisis." (10 May).

————. 1995. *When Corporations Rule the World*. New York: Kumarian Press.

Lang, Tim, and Colin Hines. 1993. *The New Protectionism: Protecting the Future Against Free Trade*. New York: New Press.

Layton, Robert. 1995. "Functional.and Historical Explanations of Village Social Organization in Northern Europe." *Journal of the Royal Anthropological Institute* (December).

Leontif, Wassily. 1983. "National Perspective: The Definition of Problems and Opportunities." Paper presented at the National Academy of Engineering Symposium, 30 June.

Leontif, Wassily, and Faye Duchin. 1983. *The Future Impact of Automation on Workers*. New York: Oxford University Press.

Lewis, Michael. 1989. *Liar's Poker: Rising Through the Wreckage on Wall Street*. New York: Norton.

Lichteim, George. 1971. *Imperialism*. London: Penguin.

Linton, Michael. 1988. "Money and Community Economics." *Creation*, (July/August).

Lohr, Steve. 1993. "Potboiler Springs from Computer's Loins." New York Times (2 July).

Lucas, Brian. As quoted in Connor, Steve. 1992. "Breasts Provoke Patent Conflict." *The Independent* ( 19 February).

MacNeill, J. 1989. "Strategies for Sustainable Economic Development." *Scientific American* 261(3).

Magdoff, Harry. 1978. *Imperialism: From the Colonial Age to the Present*. New York: Monthly Review Press.

Marshall, George. 1990. "The Political Economy of Logging: The Barnett Inquiry into Corruption in the Papua New Guinea Timber Industry." *Ecologist* 20(5).

McNamara, Robert. 1995. *In Retrospect: The Tragedy and Lessons of Vietnam*. New York: Times Books.

Meller, Patricio. 1992. *Adjustment and Equity in Chile.* Paris: OECD.

Menotti, Victor. 1995. "Free Trade and the Environment." Unpublished.

Miller, Morris. 1991. *Debt and the Environment: Converging Crises.* New York: United Nations Publications.

Morgenson, Gretchen. 1993. "The Fall of the Mall." *Forbes* (24 May).

Morris, David. 1990. "Free Trade: The Great Destroyer." *Ecologist* 20(5).

Mussolini, Benito. As quoted in Palmer, R., and J. Calton. 1971. *History of the Modern World Since 1815.* New York: Knopf.

Nijar, G. S., and Yoke Ling Chee. 1992. "Briefing Papers for CSD. Intellectual Property Rights: The Threat to Farmers and Biodiversity." *Third World Resurgence,* No. 39.

O'Brien, Richard. 1992. *Global Financial Integration: The End of Geography.* New York: Council on Foreign Relations Press.

Office of Technology Assessment. 1991. *Energy in Developing Countries.* Washington, D.C.: U.S. Congress, Office of Technology Assessment.

Oswald, Ursula. 1991. *Estrategias de Supervivencia en la Ciudad de México.* Cuernavaca, Mexico: Centro Regional de Investigaciones Multidisciplinarias.

Owen, Roger, and Bob Sutcliffe. 1976. *Studies in the Theory of Imperialism.* London: Longman.

Partant, François. 1982. *La Fin du Développement.* Paris: François Maspero.

Passell, Peter. 1992. "Fast Money." *New York Times Magazine* (18 October).

Payer, Cheryl. 1991. *Lent and Lost: Foreign Credit and Third World Development.* London: Zed Books.

Pender, Kathleeen. 1995. "Greenspan Boosts Use of Technology: Fed Chief Says Software Aids Economy." *San Francisco Chronicle.*

Peterson, R. Neal, and Nora L. Brooks. 1993. "The Changing Concentration of U.S. Agricultural Production During the Twentieth Century." Fourteenth Annual Report to Congress on the status of the family farm, AIB-671, U.S. Economic Research Service, USDA No. 27, July.

Pimentel, D. et. al. 1987. "World Agriculture and Soil Erosion." BioScience, 37(4).

Reich, Robert. 1991. *The Work of Nations: Preparing Ourselves for 21st Century Capitalism.* New York: Random House.

"Retrospective Technology Assessment" Studies. 1977. National Science Foundation and Massachusetts Institute of Technology. (Available from National Technical Information Service, Research Services Branch, 5285 Port Royal Road, Springfield, Virginia 22161).

Richman, Louis. 1992. "When Will the Layoffs End?" *Fortune* (20 September).

Rifkin, Jeremy. 1995. *The End of Work: The Decline of the Global Labor Force and the Dawn of the Post-Market Era.* New York: G. P. Putnam's Sons.

Rigdon, Joan E. 1991. "Retooling Lives: Technological Gains are Cutting Costs and Jobs in Services." *Wall Street Journal* (24 February).

"Robot Farming." 1993. *The Futurist* (July–August).

Roy, J. 1990. "GE Is Assailed by U.S. Judge in WPPSS Case." *Wall Street Journal,* (27 September).

Russ, Joel. 1995. "Local Energy, Electric Currency" in Susan Meeker-Lowry, *Invested in the Common Good.* (New Society.)

Sampson, Anthony. 1989. *The Midas Touch: Money, People and Power from West to East.* London: BBC Books, Hedder and Staughton, 1989.

Sanches, Adérito Alain. 1993. "Explosif Mélange de la Croissance Urbaine et da la Régression des Services Publicques." *Le Monde Diplomatique* (May).

Schumacher, E. F. 1989. *Small Is Beautiful: Economics as if the Earth Really Mattered.* New York: Harper and Row.

Sclove, Richard. 1994. From a workshop at the International Forum on Globalization, San Francisco. Publication forthcoming.

———. 1995. *Democracy and Technology.* New York. The Guilford Press.

Seabrook, Jeremy. 1990. *The Myth of the Market: Promises and Illusions.* Harland Bideford, Devon: Green Books.

Sheahan, John. 1992. "Development Dichotomies and Economic Strategy." In Simon Teitel, ed. 1992. *Towards a New Development Strategy for Latin America.* Washington, D.C.: Inter-American Development Bank.

Shrybman, Steven. 1990. "International Trade and the Environment: An Environmental Assessment of the General Agreement on Tariffs and Trade." *Ecologist* 20(1).

Shultz, Eugene, ed. 1992. "The Wonders of the Neem Tree—Revealed" *Science* (17 January).

Sklar, Holly, ed. 1980. *Trilateralism: The Trilateral Commission and Elite Planning for World Management.* Boston: South End Press.

Smith, Adam. [1776] 1978. *The Wealth of Nations: Books I–III.* Harmondsworth, Middlesex: Penguin.

*Technological Change and Its Impact on Labor in Four Industries.* 1992. U.S. Department of Labor Bulletin Z409, October.

*Technology and Labor in Five Industries.* 1979. Washington, D.C.: U.S. Department of Labor, Bureau of Labor Statistics Bulletin 2033.

Tinbergen, J., and R. Hueting. 1991. "GNP and Market Prices: Wrong Signals for Sustainable Economic Development That Disguise Environmental Destruction." *Population and Environment.*

United Nations Conference on Trade and Development. 1992. "International Monetary and Financial Issues of the Nineties."

U.S. Department of Labor Bureau of Labor Statistics. 1994. "Business Establishment Survey." Provided from on-line search, 12 August.

van Liemt, Gijsbert. 1992. *Industry on the Move: Causes and Consequences of International Relocation in the Manufacturing Industry.* Geneva: International Labor Office.

————. 1993. "Labor-Management Bargaining in 1992." *Monthly Labor Review* (January).

Vitousek, P. M. et. al. 1986. "Human Appropriation of the Products of Photosynthesis." *BioScience* 37(4).

Voelcker, Augustus. 1893. "Report on The Improvement of Indian Agriculture." London: Eyre and Spottiswoode.

Walton, Sam, with John Huey. 1992. *Sam Walton, Made in America: My Story.* New York: Doubleday.

"Whose Common Future?" 1993. Special issue of the *Ecologist* 23(6).

Wilkerson, Isabel. 1995. "Paradox of '94: Gloomy Voters in Good Times." *New York Times* (31 October).

Wilkes, Alex. 1995. "Prawns, Profits and Protein: Aquaculture and Food Production." *Ecologist* 25(2–3).

Wood, A. 1994. *North-South Trade, Employment and Inequality: Changing Fortunes in a Skill-Driven World.* Oxford: Oxford University Press.

World Bank. 1981. *Accelerated Development in Sub-Saharan Africa.* Washington, D.C.: World Bank.

————. 1993. *Global Economic Prospects and the Developing Countries* 1993. Washington, D.C.: World Bank.

————. 1990. "Mexico: Basic Health Care Project." Staff Appraisal Report (8 November).

————. 1995. *Workers in an Integrating World.* Washington, D.C.: World Bank.

*World Development Report* 1992. New York: Oxford University Press.

World Health Organization. 1980. *The Global Eradication of Small Pox, Final Report of the Global Commission for the Certification of Small Pox Eradication.* Geneva: WHO.

Ziegler, Bart. 1994. "IBM Is Overhauling Disk Drive Business, Cutting Jobs, Shifting Production to Asia." *Wall Street Journal* (5 August).

# AUTHORS' BIBLIOGRAPHY

*The following is a selected list of relevant books and articles written by the authors represented in this book:*

Adams, Frank T., and Gary B. Hansen. *Putting Democracy to Work: A Practical Guide for Starting and Managing Worker-Owned Business.* San Francisco: Berrett-Koehler, 1992.

Armstrong, Jeannette. *The Native Creative Process: A Collaborative Discourse Between Douglas Cardinal and Jeannette Armstrong.* Pentincton, British Columbia: Theytus Books, 1991.

Barlow, Maude. "Campaign to Make Wal-Mart Responsible to Canadians and Our Communities." Council of Canadians, 1993.

———. *Parcel of Rogues: How Free Trade Is Failing Canada.* Toronto: Key Porter Books, 1991.

Barlow, Maude, and Bruce Campbell. *Take Back the Nation.* Toronto: Key Porter Books, 1991.

Barlow, Maude, and Heather-jane Robertson. *Class Warfare: The Assault on Canada's Schools.* Toronto: Key Porter Books, 1994.

Barnet, Richard. *The Economy of Death.* New York: Atheneum, 1969.

———. *The Lean Years: Politics in the Age of Scarcity.* New York: Simon and Schuster, 1980.

Barnet, Richard, and John Cavanagh. *Global Dreams: Imperial Corporations and the New World Order.* New York: Simon and Schuster, 1994.

Barnet, Richard, and Ronald E. Müeller. "Creating a Level Playing Field." *Technology Review,* May/June 1994.

———. *Global Reach: The Power of Multinational Corporations.* New York: Simon and Schuster, 1974.

———. "Just Undo It: Nike's Exploited Workers." *New York Times,* February 13, 1994.

Bello, Walden. *Brave New Third World: Strategies for Survival in the Global Economy.* London: Earthscan, 1990.

———. "High Speed Industrialization and Environmental Devastation in Taiwan." *Ecologist,* July–August 1990.

———. *People and Power in the Pacific: The Struggle for the Post–Cold War Order.* London/San Francisco: Pluto Press, with Food First and Transnational Institute (TNI), 1992.

———. "The World Bank and the IMF." *Z Magazine,* July–August 1994.

Bello, Walden, with Shae Cunningham and Bill Rau. *Dark Victory: The United States, Structural Adjustment and Global Poverty.* London: Pluto Press, 1994.

Bello, Walden, and Stephanie Rosenfeld. *Dragons in Distress: Asia's Miracle Economies in Crisis.* San Francisco: Institute for Food and Development Policy, 1990.

Berry, Wendell. *Home Economics: Fourteen Essays.* San Francisco: North Point Press, 1987.

———. *Sex, Economy, Freedom and Community.* New York: Pantheon Books, 1992.

———. *The Unsettling of America: Culture and Agriculture.* San Francisco: Sierra Club Books, 1977.

Berry, Wendell, with Wes Jackson and Bruce Colman. *Meeting the Expectations of the Land: Essays in Sustainable Agriculture and Stewardship.* San Francisco: North Point Press, 1984.

*The Case Against "Free Trade": GATT, NAFTA, and the Globalization of Corporate Power.* San Francisco/Berkeley: Earth Island Press and North Atlantic Books, 1993.

Cavanagh, John, ed. *Trading Freedom: How Free Trade Affects Our Lives, Work, and Environment,* San Francisco: Institute for Food and Development Policy, in association with Institute for Policy Studies and Between the Lines Press, 1992.

Cavanagh, John, with Sarah Anderson and Jill Pike. "World Bank and IMF Policies Hurt Workers at Home and Abroad." Washington, D.C.: Institute for Policy Studies, 1994.

Cavanagh, John, and Robin Broad. NAFTA's *Corporate Cadre: An Analysis of the U.S.-NAFTA State Captains.* Washington, D.C.: Institute for Policy Studies, 1993.

———. *Plundering Paradise: The Struggle for the Environment in the Philippines.* Berkeley: University of California Press, 1993.

Clarke, Tony. *Behind the Mitre: The Moral Leadership Crisis in the Canadian Catholic Church.* Toronto: HarperCollins, 1995.

Clarke, Tony, and Theresa Clarke. *Witness to Justice: A Society to be Transformed.* Ottawa: Concacan, 1979.

Cobb, Clifford. *Responsive Schools, Renewed Communities.* San Francisco: S.F.I.C.S. Press, 1992.

Cobb, Clifford, with John Cobb, Jr. *The Green National Product.* Lanham, Md.: University Press of America, 1994.

Daly, Herman, "The Perils of Free Trade." *Scientific American* Vol. 269, November 1993.

———. *Steady-State Economics: The Economics of Biophysical Equilibrium and Moral Growth.* San Francisco: W. H. Freeman, 1977.

———. "Sustainable Growth? No Thank You." *Resurgence,* No. 153.

Daly, Herman E., and John B. Cobb Jr. *For The Common Good: Redirecting the Economy Toward Community, the Environment, and a Sustainable Future.* Boston: Beacon Press, 1994.

Daly, Herman, Robert Goodland, and Mohammed El-Sarafy. *Population, Technology, and Lifestyle: The Transition to Sustainability.* Washington, D.C.: Island Press, 1994.

Daly, Herman E., and Kenneth N. Townsend, eds. *Valuing the Earth: Economy, Ecology and Ethics.* Cambridge, Mass: MIT Press, 1993.

Goldsmith, Edward. *The Great U Turn.* Harland Bideford, Devon: Green Books, 1988.

———. *The Way: An Ecological World-View.* Boston: Shambhala, 1993.

Goldsmith, Edward, and Nicholas Hildyard. *The Social and Environmental Effects of Large Dams.* San Francisco: Sierra Club Books, 1984.

Goldsmith, Edward, and Robert Prescott Allen. *A Blueprint for Survival.* Boston: Houghton Mifflin, 1972.

Goldsmith, James. *The Response: GATT and Global Free Trade.* New York: Carroll and Graff, 1994.

———. *The Trap.* New York: Carroll and Graff, 1993.

Goodland, Robert. "The Case That the World Has Reached Limits: More Precisely That Current Throughput Growth in the Global Economy Cannot Be Sustained." *Population and Environment: A Journal of Interdisciplinary Studies,* 13(3), Spring 1992.

Goodland, Robert, with Catherine Watson and George Ledec. *Environmental Management of Tropical Agriculture.* Boulder, Colo.: Westview Press, 1984.

Goodland, Robert, ed. *Race to Save the Tropics: Ecology and Economics for a Sustainable Future.* Washington, D.C.: Island Press, 1990.

Greider, William. *Secrets of the Temple: How the Federal Reserve Runs the Country.* New York: Simon and Schuster, 1987.

———. *Who Will Tell the People?* New York: Touchstone, 1992.

Grossman, Richard, and Frank T. Adams. "Taking Care of Business: Citizenship and the Charter of Incorporation." Charter Ink, P.O. Box 806, Cambridge, Mass., 02140, 1993.

Grossman, Richard, and Richard Kazis. *Fear at Work: Job Blackmail, Labor and the Environment.* New York: Pilgrim Press, 1982.

Halstead, Ted, with Clifford Cobb and Jonathan Rowe. "If the Economy Is Up, Why Is America Down?" *Atlantic Monthly Journal,* October 1995.

Harvard Working Group on New and Resurgent Diseases. "New and Resurgent Diseases: The Failure of Attempted Eradication." *Ecologist* 25(1).

Heredia, Carlos, and Mary Purcell. *The Polarization of Mexican Society: A Grassroots View of World Bank Economic Adjustment Policies.* Washington, D.C.: The Development GAP, 1994.

Khor, Martin. *The Future of North-South Relations: Conflict or Cooperation?* Penang, Malaysia: Third World Network, 1992.

———. *The Malaysian Economy: Structures and Dependence.* Kuala Lumpur, Malaysia: Institut Masyarakat, 1983.

———. *South-North Resource Flows and Their Implications for Sustainable Development.* A Third World Environment and Development Report. Penang, Malaysia: Third World Network, 1994.

———. "The Uruguay Round and the Third World." *Ecologist* 20(6).

Kimbrell, Andrew. *The Human Body Shop: The Engineering and Marketing of Life.* San Francisco: HarperCollins, 1993.

———. *The Masculine Mystique: The Politics of Masculinity.* New York: Ballantine Books, 1995.

Korten, David. *Community Organization and Rural Development: A Learning Process Approach.* New York: Ford Foundation, 1980.

———. *Getting to the 21st Century: Voluntary Action and the Global Agenda.* New York: Kumarian Press, 1990.

———. Sustainability and the Global Economy: Beyond Bretton Woods. Opening plenary presentation to the Environmental Grantmakers Association, Bretton Woods Hotel, N.J. October 1994.

———. "Sustainable Development." *World Policy Journal,* Winter 1991/1992.

———. "Sustainable Livelihood and the Global Social Crisis." *Why?* magazine, Fall/Winter 1994.

———. *When Corporations Rule the World.* New York: Kumarian Press, 1995.

Krebs, Al. *The Corporate Reapers: The Book of Agribusiness.* Washington, D.C.: Essential Books, 1992.

Mander, Jerry. *Four Arguments for the Elimination of Television.* New York: Morrow, 1977.

———. *In the Absence of the Sacred: The Failure of Technology and the Survival of the Indian Nations.* San Francisco: Sierra Club Books, 1991.

Meeker-Lowry, Susan. *Economics As if the Earth Really Mattered: A Catalyst Guide to Socially Conscious Investing.* Philadelphia: New Society Publishers, 1988.

―――. "The Potential for Local Currency." *Z Magazine,* July–August, 1995.

Morris, David. *The Carbohydrate Economy: Making Chemicals and Industrial Materials from Plant Matter.* Minneapolis, Minn: Institute for Local Self-Reliance, 1992.

―――. "Free Trade: The Great Destroyer." *Ecologist* 20(5).

―――. *Replacing Petrochemicals with Biochemicals: A Pollution-Prevention Strategy for the Great Lakes Region.* Minneapolis, Minn.: Institute for Local Self-Reliance, 1994.

―――. *Self-Reliant Cities: Energy and the Transformation of Urban America.* San Francisco: Sierra Club Books, 1982.

Morris, David, and Karl Hess. *Neighborhood Power: The New Localism.* Boston: Beacon Press, 1975.

Nader, Ralph. "NAFTA vs. Democracy." *Multinational Monitor,* October 1993.

―――. "Statement of Ralph Nader Before the Senate Finance Committee on the Uruguay Round Agreements of GATT." Public Citizen, March 16, 1994.

―――. *Testimony of Ralph Nader on the Uruguay Round of GATT Before the Trade Subcommittee of the House Ways and Means Committee.* Public Citizen, February 2, 1994.

Nader, Ralph, with Mark Green and Joel Seligman. *Taming the Giant Corporation.* New York: W. W. Norton, 1976.

Nader, Ralph, and William Taylor. *The Big Boys: Power and Position in American Business.* New York: Pantheon Books, 1986.

Norberg-Hodge, Helena. *Ancient Futures: Learning from Ladakh.* San Francisco: Sierra Club Books, 1991.

Norberg-Hodge, Helena, and Peter Goering. *From the Ground Up: Rethinking Industrial Agriculture.* London: Zed Books, 1993.

Rifkin, Jeremy. *Biosphere Politics: A New Consciousness for a New Century.* New York: Crown, 1991.

―――. *Declaration of a Heretic.* Boston: Routledge and Kegan Paul, 1985.

―――. *The End of Work: The Decline of the Global Labor Force and the Dawn of the Post-Market Era.* New York: G. P. Putnam's Sons, 1995.

Rifkin, Jeremy, and Ted Howard. *Entropy: A New World View.* New York: Viking, 1980.

Rifkin, Jeremy, and Nicanor Perlas. *Algeny.* New York: Viking, 1983.

Ritchie, Mark. "The General Agreement on Tariffs and Trade and Its Impact on Indigenous Peoples." *Workbook* 19(3).

Sachs, Wolfgang. *For Love of the Automobile: Looking Back Into the History of Our Desires.* Translated by Don Renault. Berkeley: University of California Press, 1992.

Sachs, Wolfgang, ed. *The Development Dictionary: A Guide to Knowledge as Power.* London: Zed Books, 1992.

———. ed. *Global Ecology: A New Arena of Political Conflict.* London: Zed Books, 1993.

Sale, Kirkpatrick. *Dwellers in the Land: The Bioregional Vision.* San Francisco: Sierra Club Books, 1985.

———. *Human Scale.* New York: Coward, McCann and Geoghagen, 1980.

———. *Rebels Against the Future: The Luddites and Their War on the Industrial Revolution. Lessons for the Computer Age.* Reading, Mass.: Addison-Wesley, 1995.

———. *Students for a Democratic Society (SDS).* New York: Vintage Books, 1974.

Shiva, Vandana. *Biotechnology and the Environment.* Penang, Malaysia: Third World Network, 1993.

———. *Close to Home: Women Reconnect Ecology.* Health and Development Worldwide. London: Earthscan, 1994.

———. "The Failure of the Green Revolution: A Case Study of the Punjab." *Ecologist* 21(2).

———. "Intellectual Piracy and the Neem Tree." *Ecologist* 23(6).

———. *Monocultures of the Mind: Biodiversity, Biotechnology, and the Third World.* Penang, Malaysia: Third World Network, 1993.

———. *Staying Alive: Women, Ecology, and Development.* London: Zed Books, 1989.

———. *The Violence of the Green Revolution: Third World Agriculture, Ecology, and Politics.* London: Zed Books, 1991.

Wallach, Lori. "Agreement Establishing WTO Should Be Summitted to the Senate for Treaty Ratification." Public Citizen, March 3, 1994.

———. "GATT Expansion Could Gut U.S. Food Safety Laws, Increase Potential Food Cancer Risk." Public Citizen, April 13, 1994.

———. "The Terms of the Uruguay Round of GATT Would Undermine Congressional Prerogatives." Public Citizen, March 7, 1994.

Wilson, Mary E., Richard Levins, and Andrew Spielman. *Disease in Evolution: Global Changes and the Emergence of Infectious Diseases.* New York: New York Academy of Sciences, 1994.

# BACKGROUND BIBLIOGRAPHY

*The following are additional books on themes raised in this book:*

Barry, Tom. *Zapata's Revenge: Free Trade and the Farm Crisis in Mexico.* Boston: South End Press, 1995.

Berry, Thomas. *The Dream of the Earth.* San Francisco: Sierra Club Books, 1988.

Bowers, C. A. *Educating for an Ecologically Sustainable Culture: Rethinking Moral Education, Creativity, Intelligence, and other Modern Orthodoxies.* Albany, N.Y.: State University of New York Press, 1994.

—————. *Education, Cultural Myths, and the Ecological Crisis: Toward Deep Changes.* Albany, N.Y.: State University of New York Press, 1993.

Brecher, Jeremy, with John Brown Childs and Jill Cutler, eds. *Global Visions: Beyond the New World Order.* Boston: South End Press, 1993.

Brecher, Jeremy, and Tim Costello. *Global Village or Global Pillage: Economic Reconstruction from the Bottom Up.* Boston: South End Press, 1995.

Cahn, Edgar, and Jonathan Rowe. *Time Dollars.* Emmaus, Penn.: Rodale Press, 1992.

*The Case Against "Free Trade": GATT, NAFTA, and the Globalization of Corporate Power.* San Francisco/Berkeley: Earth Island Press and North Atlantic Books, 1993.

Chomsky, Noam. *World Orders Old and New.* New York: Columbia University Press, 1994.

Clark, John. *Democratizing Development: The Role of Voluntary Organizations.* New York: Kumarian Press, 1991.

Collier, George. *Basta! Land and the Zapatista Rebellion in Chiapas.* Oakland, Calif.: Institute for Food and Development Policy, 1994.

Collins, Joseph, and John Lear. *Chile's Free-Market Miracle: A Second Look.* Oakland, Calif.: Institute for Food and Development Policy, 1995.

Critchfield, Richard. *Villages.* Garden City, N.J.: Anchor Press/Doubleday, 1983.

Danaher, Kevin, ed. *Fifty Years Is Enough: The Case Against the World Bank and the International Monetary Fund.* Boston: South End Press, 1994.

Dawkins, Kristin. *NAFTA, GATT and the World Trade Organization: The Emerging New World Order.* Westfield, N.J.: Open Media, 1994.

Garrett, Laurie. *The Coming Plague: Newly Emerging Diseases in a World Out of Balance.* New York: Farrar, Straus and Giroux, 1994.

George, Susan. *The Debt Boomerang: How Third World Debt Harms Us All.* London: Pluto Press, 1992.

George, Susan, and Fabrizio Sabelli. *Faith and Credit: The World Bank's Secular Empire.* London: Penguin, 1994.

Glendinning, Chellis. *"My Name Is Chellis and I'm in Recovery from Western Civilization."* Boston: Shambhala, 1994.

Hancock, Graham. *Lords of Poverty: The Power, Prestige, and Corruption of the International Aid Business.* New York: Atlantic Monthly Press, 1989.

Hawken, Paul. *The Ecology of Commerce: A Declaration of Sustainability.* New York: HarperBusiness, 1993.

Henderson, Hazel. *Paradigms in Progress: Life Beyond Economics.* Indianapolis, Ind.: Knowledge Systems, 1991.

Meadows, Donellah, Dennis L. Meadows, and Jorgen Randers. *Beyond the Limits.* Post Mills, Vt.: Chelsea Green, 1992.

Norgaard, Richard B. *Development Betrayed: The End of Progress and a Coevolutionary Revisioning of the Future.* London: Routledge and Kegan Paul, 1994.

Postman, Neil. *Technopoly: The Surrender of Culture to Technology.* New York: Knopf, 1992.

Raghavan, Chakravarthi. *Recolonization: GATT, the Uruguay Round and the Third World.* Penang, Malaysia: Third World Network, 1990.

Rich, Bruce. *Mortgaging the Earth: The World Bank, Environmental Impoverishment, and the Crisis of Development.* Boston: Beacon Press, 1994.

Roszak, Theodore. *The Cult of Information: The Folklore of Computers and the True Art of Thinking.* New York: Pantheon Books, 1986.

Sclove, Richard. *Democracy and Technology.* New York: The Guiford Press, 1995.

Seabrook, Jeremy. *The Myth of the Market: Promises and Illusions.* Harland Bideford, Devon: Green Books, 1990.

Sessions, George, ed. *Deep Ecology for the 21st Century: Readings on the Philosophy and Practice of the New Environmentalism.* Boston: Shambhala, 1995.

Shuman, Michael. *Towards a Global Village: International Community Development Initiatives.* London: Pluto Press, 1994.

Sklar, Holly. *Chaos or Community: Seeking Solutions, Not Scapegoats, for Bad Economics.* Boston: South End Press, 1995.

———. ed. 1980. *Trilateralism: The Trilateral Commission and Elite Planning for World Management.* Boston: South End Press.

Vandermeer, John, and Ivette Perfecto. *Breakfast of Biodiversity: The Truth About Rainforest Destruction.* Oakland, Calif.: Institute for Food and Development Policy, 1995.

# ORGANIZATIONS

*These are some of the organizations active on trade and globalization issues.*

ACTION CANADA NETWORK
4 Jeffrey Ave.
Ottawa, Ontario
K1K 0E2 Canada
Phone: 613-746-5256
Fax: 613-233-6776

BANK INFORMATION CENTER
2025 I St. NW, Suite 522
Washington, DC 20006
Phone: 202-466-8191
Fax: 202-466-8189

BORDER ECOLOGY PROJECT
Box 5
Naco, AZ 85620
Phone: 602-432-7456

CANADIAN CENTER FOR POLICY
  ALTERNATIVES
904-251 Laurier Ave. West
Ottawa, Ontario
K1P 5J6 Canada
Phone: 613-563-1341
Fax: 613-233-1458

CENTER FOR INTERNATIONAL
  ENVIRONMENTAL LAW
1621 Connecticut Ave. NW,
Suite 300
Washington, DC 20009-1076
Phone: 202-332-4840

CENTER FOR STUDY OF RESPONSIVE
  LAW
PO Box 19367
Washington, DC 20036
Phone: 202-387-8030
Fax: 202-234-5176

COMMUNITY NUTRITION INSTITUTE
2001 S St. NW, Suite 530
Washington, DC 20009
Phone: 202-462-4700
Fax: 202-462-5241

CORDILLERA WOMEN'S EDUCATION
  AND RESOURCE CENTER
PO Box 7691
GARCOM Baguio (752)
DAPO 1300 Domestic Road
Pasay City, Philippines
Phone: 63-74-442-5347
Fax: 63-74-442-5347

COUNCIL OF CANADIANS
904-251 Laurier Ave. W.
Ottawa, Ontario
K1P 5J6 Canada
Phone: 613-233-2773
Fax: 613-233-6776

DEVELOPMENT GROUP FOR
  ALTERNATIVE POLICIES
C927 15th St. NW, fourth floor
Washington, DC 20005
Phone: 202-898-1566
Fax: 202-898-1612

E. F. Schumacher Society
Box 76A, RD 3
Great Barrington, MA 01230
Phone: 413-528-1737

ECOROPA
24, rue de l'Ermitage
75020 Paris, France
Phone: 33-1-4636-4525
Fax: 33-1-4349-6970

Earth Island Institute
300 Broadway
San Francisco, CA 94133
Phone: 415-788-3666
Fax: 415-788-7324

En'owchin Center
257 Brunswick St.
Penticton, B.C.
V2A 5P9 Canada
Phone: 604.493.7181
Fax: 604.493.5302

Equipo Pueblo
Francisco Field Jurado 51
Colonia Independencia
03630 México, D.F., México
Phone: 011-525-539-0015
Fax: 011-525-672-7453

Focus on the Global South
c/o CUSRI
Chulalongkore University
Prachuabmoh, Phyathai Road
Bangkok, 10330 Thailand
Fax: 662-255-9976

Foundation on Economic Trends
1130 17th St. NW, Suite 630
Washington, DC 20036
Phone: 202-466-2823
Fax: 202-429-9602

Friends of the Earth
1025 Vermont Ave. NW
Washington, DC 20005
Phone: 202-783-7400 ext.284
Fax: 202-783-0444

Global Exchange
2017 Mission St., Suite 303
San Francisco, CA 94110
Phone: 415-255-7296
Fax: 415-255-7698

Greenpeace U.S.
1436 U Street NW
Washington, DC 20009
Phone: 202-462-1177
Fax: 202-462-4507

The Humane Society of the US
3445 Oakwood Terrace
Washington, DC 20010
Phone: 202-265-6231
Fax: 202-265-6237

Institute for Agriculture and
   Trade Policy
1313 5th St., Suite 303
Minneapolis, MN 55414
Phone: 612-379-5980
Fax: 612-379-5982

Institut d'Etude sur la
   Globalisation Economique
42 rue de Sorbier
75020 Paris, France
Phone: 33-1-46-36-45-25
Fax: 33-1-43-49-69-70

Institute for Food and Develop-
   ment Policy (Food First)
398 60th St.
Oakland, CA 94618
Phone: 510-654-4400
Fax: 510-654-4551

Institute for Local Self-
   Reliance
1313 5th St.
Minneapolis, MN 55414
Phone: 612-379-3815
Fax: 612-379-3920

INSTITUTE FOR POLICY STUDIES:
WORKING GROUP ON THE WORLD
ECONOMY
1601 Connecticut Ave.
Washington, DC 20009
Phone: 202-234-9382
Fax: 202-387-7915

INTERNATIONAL CENTER FOR
TECHNOLOGY ASSESSMENT
310 D St. NE
Washington DC 20002
Phone: 202-547-9359
Fax: 202-547-9429

INTERNATIONAL FORUM ON
GLOBALIZATION
P.O. Box 12218
San Francisco, CA 94112
Phone: 415-771-3394
Fax: 415-771-1121

INTERNATIONAL LABOR RIGHTS
EDUCATION AND RESEARCH FUND
(ILRERF)
100 Maryland Av. NE Box 74
Washington, DC 20009
Phone: 202-265-4440
Fax: 202-543-5999

INTERNATIONAL RIVERS NETWORK
1847 Berkeley Way
Berkeley, CA 94703
Phone: 510-848-1155
Fax: 510-848-1008

INTERNATIONAL SOCIETY FOR
ECOLOGY AND CULTURE
*U.S.:* PO Box 9475
Berkeley, CA 94709
Phone: 510-527-3873
Fax: 510-527-3873
*U.K.:* 21 Victoria Square
Clifton, Bristol BS8 4ES
United Kingdom
Phone: 44-1179-731-575
Fax: 44-1179-744-853

ITHACA HOURS
Box 6578
Ithaca, NY 14581

LETS
Landsman Community Services, Ltd.
1660 Embelton Crescent
Courtenay, BC V9N 6N8
Phone: 604-338-0213/0234

MEXICAN ACTION NETWORK ON
FREE TRADE
Explanada 705
México D.F., 11000, México
Phone: 011-525-540-2858
Fax: 011-525-556-9316

PROGRAM ON CORPORATIONS, LAW,
AND DEMOCRACY
211.5 Bradford St.
Provincetown, MA 02657
Phone: 508-487-3151
Fax: 508-487-3151

PEOPLE-CENTERED DEVELOPMENT
FORUM
14 E. Seventeenth St., Suite 5
New York, NY 10003
Phone: 212-620-7137
Fax: 212-242-1901

PROBE INTERNATIONAL
225 Brunswick Ave.
Toronto, Ontario
M5S 2M6 Canada
Phone: 416-964-9223
Fax: 416-904-9230

PUBLIC CITIZEN
Global Trade Watch
215 Pennsylvania Ave. SE
Washington, DC 20003
Phone: 202-546-4996
Fax: 202-547-7392

PUBLIC MEDIA CENTER
466 Green St.
San Francisco, CA 94133
Phone: 415-434-1403
Fax: 415-986-6779

RENACE(Chilean Ecological
Action Network)
Seminario 774 Nunoa
Santiago, Chile
Phone: 56-2-223-4483
Fax: 56-2-223-4522

Rainforest Action Network
450 Sansome St., Suite 700
San Francisco, CA 94105
Phone: 415-398-4404
Fax: 415-398-2732

Redefining Progress
One Kearny St., Fourth floor
San Francisco, CA 94108
Phone: 415-781-1191
Fax: 415-781-1198

Research Foundation for
Science, Technology and
Natural Resource Policy
A-60 Haus Khas
New Delhi, India 110016
Phone: 91-11-665-003
Fax: 91-11-685-6795

Sierra Club
85 Second Street
San Francisco, CA 94105
Phone: 415-977-5500
Fax: 415-977-5799

South and Meso American
Indian Information Center
PO Box 28703
Oakland, CA 94604
Phone: 510-834-4263
Fax: 510-834-4264

Southeast Regional Economic
Justice Network
413 East Chapel Hill St., Suite 110
Durham, NC 27701
Phone: 919-683-4310
Fax: 919-683-3428

Southwest Network for Environ-
mental and Economic Justice
211 Tenth St.
Albuquerque, NM 87102
Phone: 505-527-3873
Fax: 505-527-3873

Student Environmental Action
Coalition (SEAC)
815 16th St. NW
Washington, DC 20006
Phone: 202-783-3993
Fax: 202-783-3591

Sustainable Agriculture, Food
and Environmental Alliance
38 Ebury St.
London SW1 W0LU, UK
Phone: 44-81-579-5000
Fax: 44-81-566-1353

Texas Center for Policy Studies
PO Box 2618
Austin, TX 78768
Phone: 512-474-0811

The Other Economic Summit/
Americas (TOES/Americas)
PO Box 12003
Austin, TX 78711
Phone: 512-476-4130
Fax: 512-476-4759

Third World Network
228 Macalister Road
Penang, Malaysia
Phone: 60-4-226-6728
Fax: 60-4-226-4505

The Transnational Institute
Paulus Potterstraat 20
1071 DA Amsterdam
The Netherlands
Phone: 011-31-20-662-6608

Wuppertal Institute for
Climate, Energy and the
Environment
Doppersberg 19
D-42103 Wuppertal, Germany
Phone: 011-49-202-24920
Fax: 011-49-202-2492138

The editors gratefully acknowledge permission to reprint portions of the following copyrighted materials:

From *The End of Work* by Jeremy Rifkin, published by G. P. Putnam's Sons, © 1995 by Jeremy Rifkin. Reprinted by permission of the author; from "New and Resurgent Diseases," article by the Harvard Working Group on New and Resurgent Diseases in *The Ecologist*, 25 (1). Reprinted by permission of the authors; from *The Trap* by James Goldsmith, published by Carroll and Graff: N.Y., © 1993 by James Goldsmith. Reprinted by permission of the author; from *When Corporations Rule the World* by David Korten, published by Kumarian Press: New York, © 1995. Reprinted by permission of the author; from "The Perils of Free Trade," article by Herman E. Daly in *Scientific American*, November 1993. Reprinted with permission. © 1993 by Scientific American, Inc. All rights reserved; "Structural Adjustment and the Polarization of Mexican Society" by Carlos Heredia and Mary Purcell, excerpted from *The Polarization of Mexican Society: A Grassroots View of World Bank Economic Adjustment Policies,* published by Equipo Pueblo: Mexico City, and The Development GAP: Washington, D.C., © 1994. Reprinted with permission of the publisher; from *Who Will Tell the People* by William Greider, published by Simon and Schuster: New York, © 1987. Reprinted by permission of the author; from *Global Ecology: A New Arena of Political Conflict,* edited by Wolfgang Sachs, published by Zed Books: London, © 1992. Reprinted by permission of the publisher; from *Global Dreams: Imperial Corporations and the New World Order* by Richard Barnet and John Cavanagh, published by Simon and Schuster: New York, © 1994. Reprinted by permission of the authors; from "Taking Care of Business: Citizenship and the Charter of Incorporation" by Richard Grossman and Frank T. Adams, published by Charter Ink: Cambridge, © 1993. Reprinted by permission of the authors.

# INDEX

# THE EDITORS

JERRY MANDER was president of the San Francisco advertising company Freeman, Mander & Gossage in the 1960s, but then turned his talents to environmental campaigns. He authored the successful 1960s Sierra Club campaigns that kept dams out of the Grand Canyon, established Redwood National Park and others, and successfully opposed production of the Supersonic Transport (SST). For these and other campaigns the *Wall Street Journal* called Mander "the Ralph Nader of advertising." In 1971, Mander cofounded the country's first nonprofit advertising agency, Public Interest Communications, which served only nonprofit environmental, community, and social action groups. Since 1980, Mander has been a senior fellow at Public Media Center, which has campaigned for Sierra Club, Friends of the Earth, Greenpeace, Planned Parenthood, Public Citizen, the James Bay Coalition, and hundreds of other organizations. Mander is also currently program director of the Foundation for Deep Ecology and is one of the cofounders (with Goldsmith and others) of the International Forum on Globalization, a new international alliance of activists, writers, philosophers, and economists, many of whom are represented in these pages. Mander's best selling books include *Four Arguments for the Elimination of Television* (1977) and *In the Absence of the Sacred* (1991).

• • •

EDWARD GOLDSMITH studied philosophy and economics at Oxford but sees himself as largely self-taught. He is one of the pioneers of the ecological movement in the United Kingdom and for over thirty years has been involved in campaigns against the nuclear industry, large dams, the World Bank, the FAO, and others. He has also run as a Green Party candidate in three regional elections. Goldsmith has lectured at universities in many countries and taught courses at Michigan University and Sangamon State University. He helped set up an International Honors Program Global Ecology Course (in association with Bard College) and is a member of its staff. Goldsmith is the founding editor of the *Ecologist,* the lead-ing European environmental journal, and is the author of hundreds of ar-ticles and many books, including *The Way: An Ecological World View* (1991), *The Great U-Turn* (1988), *The Social and Environmental Effects of Large Dams* (1984, with Nicholas Hildyard), and *A Blueprint for Survival* (1972, with Robert Prescott Allen), which triggered the foundation of the British Green Party. He was awarded the Right Livelihood Award (also referred to as the alternative Nobel Prize) in Stockholm in 1991 and the same year was made a Chevalier of the Légion d'Honneur in France.